Cambridge Tracts in Theoretical Computer Science 50

Process Algebra: Equational Theories of Communicating Processes

Process algebra is a widely accepted and much used technique in the specification and verification of parallel and distributed software systems. This book sets the standard for the field. It assembles the relevant results of most process algebras currently in use, and presents them in a unified framework and notation.

The authors describe the theory underlying the development, realization and maintenance of software that occurs in parallel or distributed systems. A system can be specified in the syntax provided, and the axioms can be used to verify that a composed system has the required external behavior. As examples, two protocols are completely specified and verified in the text: the Alternating-Bit communication Protocol, and Fischer's Protocol of mutual exclusion.

The book serves as a reference text for researchers and graduate students in computer science, offering a complete overview of the field and referring to further literature where appropriate.

J. C. M. BAETEN is Professor of formal methods in the Division of Computer Science at Eindhoven University of Technology, Netherlands.

T. BASTEN is Professor of computational models in the Faculty of Electrical Engineering at Eindhoven University of Technology, Netherlands, and Research Fellow at the Embedded Systems Institute, Eindhoven.

M. A. RENIERS is Assistant Professor in the Division of Computer Science at Eindhoven University of Technology, Netherlands.

Cambridge Tracts in Theoretical Computer Science 50

Titles in the series

A complete list of books in the series can be found at
http://www.cambridge.org/uk/series/sSeries.asp?code=CTTC.
Recent titles include the following:

21. D. A. Wolfram *The Clausal Theory of Types*
22. V. Stoltenberg-Hansen, Lindström & E. R. Griffor *Mathematical Theory of Domains*
23. E.-R. Olderog *Nets, Terms and Formulas*
26. P. D. Mosses *Action Semantics*
27. W. H. Hesselink *Programs, Recursion and Unbounded Choice*
28. P. Padawitz *Deductive and Declarative Programming*
29. P. Gärdenfors (ed.) *Belief Revision*
30. M. Anthony & N. Biggs *Computational Learning Theory*
31. T. F. Melham *Higher Order Logic and Hardware Verification*
32. R. L. Carpenter *The Logic of Typed Feature Structures*
33. E. G. Manes *Predicate Transformer Semantics*
34. F. Nielson & H. R. Nielson *Two-Level Functional Languages*
35. L. M. G. Feijs & H. B. M. Jonkers *Formal Specification and Design*
36. S. Mauw & G. J. Veltink (eds.) *Algebraic Specification of Communication Protocols*
37. V. Stavridou *Formal Methods in Circuit Design*
38. N. Shankar *Metamathematics, Machines and Gödel's Proof*
39. J. B. Paris *The Uncertain Reasoner's Companion*
40. J. Desel & J. Esparza *Free Choice Petri Nets*
41. J.-J. Ch. Meyer & W. van der Hoek *Epistemic Logic for AI and Computer Science*
42. J. R. Hindley *Basic Simple Type Theory*
43. A. S. Troelstra & H. Schwichtenberg *Basic Proof Theory*
44. J. Barwise & J. Seligman *Information Flow*
45. A. Asperti & S. Guerrini *The Optimal Implementation of Functional Programming Languages*
46. R. M. Amadio & P.-L. Curien *Domains and Lambda-Calculi*
47. W.-P. de Roever & K. Engelhardt *Data Refinement*
48. H. Kleine Büning & T. Lettman *Propositional Logic*
49. L. Novak & A. Gibbons *Hybrid Graph Theory and Network Analysis*
51. H. Simmons *Derivation and Computation*
52. P. Blackburn, M. de Rijke & Y. Venema *Modal Logic*
53. W.-P. de Roever et al *Concurrency Verification*
54. Terese *Term Rewriting Systems*
55. A. Bundy et al *Rippling: Meta-Level Guidance for Mathematical Reasoning*

Process Algebra: Equational Theories of Communicating Processes

J. C. M. BAETEN
T. BASTEN
M. A. RENIERS
Eindhoven University of Technology, Netherlands

CAMBRIDGE UNIVERSITY PRESS
Cambridge, New York, Melbourne, Madrid, Cape Town, Singapore, São Paulo, Delhi

Cambridge University Press
The Edinburgh Building, Cambridge CB2 8RU, UK

Published in the United States of America by Cambridge University Press, New York

www.cambridge.org
Information on this title: www.cambridge.org/9780521820493

First published 2010

Printed in the United Kingdom at the University Press, Cambridge

A catalogue record for this publication is available from the British Library

ISBN 978-0-521-82049-3 Hardback

Additional resources for this publication at www.processalgebra.org

---

Contents

Forewords

Tony Hoare
Cambridge, United Kingdom, February 2009

Algebra is the simplest of all branches of mathematics. After the study of numerical calculation and arithmetic, algebra is the first school subject which gives the student an introduction to the generality and power of mathematical abstraction, and a taste of mathematical proof by symbolic reasoning. Only the simplest reasoning principle is required: the substitution of equals for equals. (Even computers are now quite good at it.) Nevertheless, the search for algebraic proof still presents a fascinating puzzle for the human mathematician, and yields results of surprising brevity and pleasing elegance.

A more systematic study of algebra provides a family tree that unifies the study of many of the other branches of mathematics. It identifies the basic mathematical axioms that are common to a whole sub-family of branches. The basic theorems that are proved from these axioms will be true in every branch of mathematics which shares them. At each branching point in the tree, the differences between the branches are succinctly highlighted by their choice between a pair of mutually contradictory axioms. In this way, algebra is both cumulative in its progress along the branches, and modular at its branching points.

It is a surprise to many computer programmers that computer programs, with all their astronomical complexity of structure and behavior, are as amenable to the axioms of algebra as simple numbers were at school. Indeed, algebra scales well from the small to the large. It applies to the large-scale behavior of systems evolving concurrently in parallel; and it underlies the manipulation of the minute detail of the individual instructions of code. At the highest level, algebraic reasoning provides the essential basis for program transformations that match the structure of a complete system to that of the available hardware configuration; and at the lowest level, it provides the justification for optimization of the code of a program so as to achieve the full potential of the processor instruction set.

This book exploits the power of algebra to explore the properties of concurrent programs, particularly those that control the behavior of distributed systems, communicating with neighbors on identified channels. It starts with the simplest theories at the base of the tree, and gradually extends them in a modular way by additional axioms to deal with sequential programming as well as concurrent, and with communication as well as assignment. In the later chapters, it exploits the modularity of algebra to describe priorities, probabilities, and mobility.

The technical approach of the book is grounded in Computer Science. It emphasizes term models based on the syntax of the operators used in the algebra, and it justifies the axioms by appeal to the execution of the terms as programs. Its crowning achievement is to exploit the unifying power of algebra to cover a range of historic theories, developed for various purposes up to 20 years ago. Earlier these theories were thought to be irreconcilable rivals; but as a result of research by the authors of this book and others, the rivals are now seen to be close family members, each superbly adapted to the particular range of problems that it was designed to tackle.

Robin Milner
Cambridge, United Kingdom, February 2009

Nowadays, much of what is still called 'computing' involves the behavior of composite systems whose members interact continually with their environment. A better word is 'informatics', because we are concerned not just with calculation, but rather with autonomous agents that interact with – or inform – one another. This interactivity bursts the bounds of the sequential calculation that still dominates many programming languages. Does it enjoy a theory as firm and complete as the theory of sequential computation? Not yet, but we are getting there.

What is an informatic process? The answer must involve phenomena foreign to sequential calculation. For example can an informatic system, with many interacting components, achieve deterministic behavior? If it can, that is a special case; non-determinism is the norm, not the exception. Does a probability distribution, perhaps based upon the uncertainty of timing, replace determinism? Again, how exactly do these components interact; do they send each other messages, like email, to be picked up when convenient? – or is each interaction a kind of synchronized handshake?

Over the last few decades many models for interactive behavior have been proposed. This book is the fruit of 25 years of experience with an algebraic approach, in which the constructors by which an informatic system is assembled are characterized by their algebraic properties. The characteristics are temporal, in the same way that sequential processes are temporal; they are also spatial, describing how agents are interconnected. And their marriage is complex.

The authors have teased out primitive elements of this structure. In doing so they have applied strict mathematical criteria. For example, to what extent can the dynamic characteristics of a set of process constructors be reflected, soundly or completely, by a collection of algebraic axioms? And to what extent can the authors' calculus ACP (Algebra of Communicating Processes) be harmonized with other leading calculi, especially Hoare's CSP (Communicating Sequential Processes) and Milner's CCS (Calculus of Communicating Systems)? Consideration of these questions gives the book a firm and appreciable structure. In particular, it shows up a shortcoming of what (for some 50 years) has been called automata theory: that theory never seriously attempted to model the ways in which two automata might interact.

So it may seem that the book is mainly an account of the frontiers of research into process theory. It is much more, and I hope that syllabus designers will take note: the presentation is lucid and careful, enriched with exercises, to the extent that many parts of it can be used as a basis for university courses, both undergraduate and postgraduate. If in such courses we expose students to theories that are still advancing, then they share the excitement of that progress.

Jan Bergstra
Amsterdam, the Netherlands, February 2009

This book about process algebra improves on its predecessor, written by Jos Baeten and Peter Weijland almost 20 years ago, by being more comprehensive and by providing far more mathematical detail. In addition the syntax of ACP has been extended by a constant 1 for termination. This modification not only makes the syntax more expressive, it also facilitates a uniform reconstruction of key aspects of CCS, CSP as well as ACP, within a single framework.

After renaming the empty process (ϵ) into 1 and the inactive process (δ) into 0, the axiom system ACP is redesigned as BCP. This change is both pragmatically justified and conceptually convincing. By using a different acronym instead of ACP, the latter can still be used as a reference to its original meaning, which is both useful and consistent.

Curiously these notational changes may be considered marginal and significant at the same time. In terms of theorems and proofs, or in terms of case studies, protocol formalizations and the design of verification tools, the specific details of notation make no real difference at all. But by providing a fairly definitive and uncompromising typescript a major impact is obtained on what might be called 'nonfunctional qualities' of the notational framework. I have no doubt that these nonfunctional qualities are positive and merit being exploited in full detail as has been done by Baeten and his co-authors. Unavoidably, the notational evolution produces a change of perspective. While, for instance, the empty process is merely an add on feature for ACP, it constitutes a conceptual cornerstone for BCP.

Group theory provides different notational conventions (additive and multiplicative) for the same underlying structure, and in a similar fashion, the format of this book might be viewed as a comprehensive and consistent notational convention for a theory of process algebra. But the same theory might instead be captured, when used in another context, with a different preferred notation.

Process algebra as presented here is equational logic of processes viewed as a family of first order theories. Each theory is provided with its Tarski semantics, making use of many-sorted algebras with total operations and nonempty sorts. Although this may sound already quite technical and may be even prohibitive for a dedicated computer scientist, these are the most stable and clear-cut semantic principles that mathematical logic has developed thus far. When developing axioms for process algebras the authors do not deviate from that path for ad hoc reasons of any kind. Thus there is a very clear separation between the logical metatheory, consisting of first order equational logic and its model-theory on the one hand and the many design decisions concerning the subject matter that is process theory on the other hand. A prominent methodological principle underlying the work is that the significant ramification of design decisions concerning various process formalisms can be made systematic in a way comparable to the development of say ring theory in mathematics.

In addition to making use of first order logic, the equational form of most axioms allows a systematic exploitation of technical results from term rewriting. This is not a matter of process theory per se but it is proving helpful throughout the book.

One may ask why process algebra should be considered a topic in computer science and not just in applied mathematics. While some parts of process theory are now moving in the direction of systems biology, the process algebras covered in this book may sooner or later show up in physics. Quantum process algebras have not been covered here but various forms already exist and that kind of development is likely to continue for many more years.

Just like its predecessor has been for many years, this book will definitely be useful as a reference work for research in process theory.

Preface

What is this book about?

This book sets the standard for process algebra. It assembles the relevant results of most process algebras currently in use, and presents them in a unified framework and notation. It addresses important extensions of the basic theories, like timing, data parameters, probabilities, priorities, and mobility. It systematically presents a hierarchy of algebras that are increasingly expressive, proving the major properties each time.

For researchers and graduate students in computer science, the book will serve as a reference, offering a complete overview of what is known to date, and referring to further literature where appropriate.

Someone familiar with CCS, the Calculus of Communicating Systems, will recognize the minimal process theory MPT as basic CCS, to which a constant expressing successful termination is added, enabling sequential composition as a basic operator, and will then find a more general parallel-composition operator. Someone familiar with ACP, the Algebra of Communicating Processes, will see that termination is made explicit, leading to a replacement of action constants by action prefixing, but will recognize many other things. The approaches to recursion of CCS and ACP are both explained and integrated. Someone familiar with CSP, Communicating Sequential Processes, will have to cope with more changes, but will see the familiar operators of internal and external choice and parallel composition explained in the present setting.

The book is a complete revision of another (Baeten & Weijland, 1990). Moreover, as the unification theme has become more important, it can also be seen as a successor to (Milner, 1989) and (Hoare, 1985).

Process algebra has become a widely accepted and used technique in the specification and verification of parallel and distributed software systems. A system can be specified in the syntax provided, and the axioms can be used to verify that a composed system has the required external behavior. As examples, a couple of protocols are completely specified and verified in the text: the Alternating-Bit communication Protocol, and Fischer's protocol of mutual exclusion. The book explains how such a task can be undertaken for any given parallel or distributed system. As the system gets bigger though, tool support in this endeavor, using for example the mCRL2 tool set, will become necessary.

Despite the breadth of the book, some aspects of process algebra are not covered. Foremost, relationships with logic, important when discussing satisfaction of requirements, are not addressed (except briefly in Chapter 10). This was left out as it does not pertain directly to the algebraic treatment and would make the book too voluminous. Readers interested in this subject may refer to (Bradfield & Stirling, 2001). Some of the extensions (probabilities, priorities, and mobility) are only briefly touched upon; references are given to literature that provides a more in-depth treatment.

How to use this book?

The book can be used in teaching a course to students at advanced undergraduate or graduate level in computer science or a related field. It contains numerous exercises varying in difficulty. Such a course should cover at least Chapters 1 through 8, together comprising a complete theory usable in applications. From the remaining chapters, different choices can be made, since the chapters can be read independently. The text is also suitable for self-study.

Chapter 1 presents an introduction that delineates more precisely the field of process algebra. It also gives a historic overview of the development of the field. In Chapter 2, some notions are explained that are used in the remainder of the book. The material concerns equational theories, algebras, and term rewriting systems. Chapter 3 covers the semantic domain of transition systems. The notion of bisimilarity is explained, and the concept of a structural operational semantics, a standard way to assign transition systems to terms in a language, is introduced. Some relevant theorems about structural operational semantics are presented and are used in the remainder of the book when providing semantics to equational theories.

Chapter 4 starts with process algebra. A minimal process theory is presented, that illustrates the basic steps involved in establishing a set of laws and a model for an equational theory. Then, two basic extensions are considered: first, the extension with the successful-termination constant 1, and second, the extension with projection operators. Differences between the two types of extensions are explained. As a prequel to the succeeding chapter, the extension with the iteration operator is considered. By means of this operator, some infinite processes can be defined.

Chapter 5 is devoted to recursion, which is the main means of specifying non-terminating processes. It is shown how to define such processes, and how to reason with them. The unbounded stack is considered as a first example.

Chapter 6 adds sequential composition. Furthermore, it looks at renaming operators, and operators that can block or skip part of a process. Chapter 7 adds parallel composition and communication. Buffers and bags are considered as examples. As a larger example, the specification of the Alternating-Bit Protocol is presented.

Chapter 8 considers abstraction, which enables one to hide some of the behavior of a system in order to focus on the rest. It is the central ingredient for verification. As an example, a verification is presented of the Alternating-Bit Protocol. The notions of divergence and fairness are explained and treated.

Chapter 9 gives a short introduction to the extension with explicit timing. Fischer's protocol is presented as an example. Chapter 10 considers the interplay between data and processes, and at the same time takes a closer look at the notion of a state, and what can be observed from it. Chapter 11 briefly covers some extensions to and variants of the basic theories, namely priorities, probabilities, mobility, and different forms of parallel composition. The book concludes with Chapter 12, which considers other semantics, besides bisimulation semantics, and their interrelations.

The book is supported through the website **www.processalgebra.org**. This website contains supplementary material, such as solutions to selected exercises, slides presenting the book content, additional exercises and exam problems, a tool to support algebraic reasoning, an up-to-date process algebra bibliography, and much more. Lecturers, students, and researchers are invited to have a look at the website, to get the most out of using the book.

Acknowledgements

A book like this can only be written thanks to the contributions and support of many individuals. The authors wish to acknowledge Luca Aceto, Suzana Andova, Jan Bergstra, Maarten Boote, Victor Bos, Beverley Clarke, Clare Dennison, Henk Goeman, Jan Friso Groote, Evelien van der Heiden, Leszek Holenderski, Abigail Jones, Hugo Jonker, Gerben de Keijzer, Uzma Khadim, Fabian Kratz, Kim Larsen, Bas Luttik, Jasen Markovski, Sjouke Mauw, Kees Middelburg, Mohammad Mousavi, Dennis van Opzeeland, Ralph Otten, Alban Ponse, Isabelle Reymen, Maria van Rooijen, Eugen Schindler, Natalia

Sidorova, David Tranah, Pieter Verduin, Jeroen Voeten, Marc Voorhoeve, Peter Weijland, and Tim Willemse.

1

Process algebra

1.1 Definition

This book is about *process algebra.* The term ‘process algebra’ refers to a loosely defined field of study, but it also has a more precise, technical meaning. The latter is considered first, as a basis to delineate the field of process algebra.

Consider the word ‘process’. It refers to *behavior* of a *system.* A system is anything showing behavior, in particular the execution of a software system, the actions of a machine, or even the actions of a human being. Behavior is the total of events or actions that a system can perform, the order in which they can be executed and maybe other aspects of this execution such as timing or probabilities. Always, the focus is on certain aspects of behavior, disregarding other aspects, so an abstraction or idealization of the ‘real’ behavior is considered. Rather, it can be said that there is an *observation* of behavior, and an action is the chosen unit of observation. Usually, the actions are thought to be discrete: occurrence is at some moment in time, and different actions can be distinguished in time. This is why a process is sometimes also called a *discrete event system.*

The term ‘algebra’ refers to the fact that the approach taken to reason about behavior is algebraic and axiomatic. That is, operations on processes are defined, and their equational laws are investigated. In other words, methods and techniques of universal algebra are used (see e.g., (MacLane & Birkhoff, 1967)). To allow for a comparison, consider the definition of a *group* in universal algebra.

Definition 1.1.1 (Group) A *group* is a structure $(G, *, ^{-1}, u)$, with G the universe of elements, binary operator $*$ on G, unary operator $^{-1}$, and constant $u \in G$. For any $a, b, c \in G$, the following laws, or axioms, hold:

- $a * (b * c) = (a * b) * c$;

- $u * a = a = a * u$;
- $a * a^{-1} = a^{-1} * a = u$.

So, a group is any mathematical structure consisting of a single universe of elements, with operators on this universe of elements that satisfy the group axioms. Stated differently, a group is any *model* of the *equational theory of groups*. Likewise, it is possible to define operations on the universe of processes. A *process algebra* is then any mathematical structure satisfying the axioms given for the defined operators, and a process is then an element of the universe of this process algebra. The axioms allow *calculations* with processes, often referred to as *equational reasoning*.

Process algebra thus has its roots in universal algebra. The field of study nowadays referred to as process algebra, however, often, goes beyond the strict bounds of universal algebra. Sometimes the restriction to a single universe of elements is relaxed and different types of elements, different sorts, are used, and sometimes binding operators are considered. Also this book goes sometimes beyond the bounds of universal algebra.

The simplest model of system behavior is to see behavior as an input/output function. A value or input is given at the beginning of a process, and at some moment there is a(nother) value as outcome or output. This behavioral model was used to advantage as the simplest model of the behavior of a computer program in computer science, from the start of the subject in the middle of the twentieth century. It was instrumental in the development of (finite-state) *automata theory*. In automata theory, a process is modeled as an automaton. An automaton has a number of *states* and a number of *transitions*, going from state to state. A transition denotes the execution of an (elementary) action, the basic unit of behavior. Besides, an automaton has an initial state (sometimes, more than one) and a number of final states. A behavior is a run, i.e., an execution path of actions that lead from the initial state to a final state. Given this basic behavioral abstraction, an important aspect is when to consider two automata equal, expressed by a notion of equivalence, the *semantic equivalence*. On automata, the basic notion of semantic equivalence is language equivalence: an automaton is characterized by the set of runs, and two automata are equal when they have the same set of runs. An algebra that allows equational reasoning about automata is the algebra of regular expressions (see e.g., (Linz, 2001)).

Later on, the automata model was found to be lacking in certain situations. Basically, what is missing is the notion of *interaction*: during the execution from initial state to final state, a system may interact with another system. This is needed in order to describe parallel or distributed systems, or so-called *reactive* systems. When dealing with models of and reasoning about interacting systems, the phrase *concurrency theory* is used. Concurrency theory is the theory of interacting, parallel and/or distributed systems. Process algebra is usually considered to be an approach to concurrency theory, so a process algebra will usually (but not necessarily) have *parallel composition* as a basic operator. In this context, automata are mostly called *transition systems*. The notion of equivalence studied is usually not language equivalence. Prominent among the equivalences studied is the notion of *bisimilarity*, which considers two transition systems equal if and only if they can mimic each other's behavior in any state they may reach.

Thus, a usable definition of *the field of process algebra* is the field that studies the behavior of parallel or distributed systems by algebraic means. It offers means to describe or *specify* such systems, and thus it has means to talk about parallel composition. Besides this, it can usually also talk about alternative composition (choice between alternatives) and sequential composition (sequencing). Moreover, it is possible to reason about such systems using algebra, i.e., equational reasoning. By means of this equational reasoning, *verification* becomes possible, i.e., it can be established that a system satisfies a certain property. Often, the study of transition systems, ways to define them, and equivalences on them are also considered part of process algebra, even when no equational theory is present.

1.2 Calculation

Systems with distributed or parallel, interacting components abound in modern life: mobile phones, personal computers interacting across networks (like the web), and machines with embedded software interacting with the environment or users are but a few examples. In our mind, or with the use of natural language, it is very difficult to describe these systems exactly, and to keep track of all possible executions. A formalism to describe such systems precisely, allowing reasoning about such systems, is very useful. Process algebra is such a formalism.

It is already very useful to have a formalism to describe, to specify interacting systems, e.g., to have a compact term specifying a communication protocol. It is even more useful to be able to reason about interacting systems, to verify properties of such systems. Such verification is possible on transition systems: there are automated methods, called *model checking* (see e.g., (Clarke *et al.*, 2000)), that traverse all states of a transition system and check that a certain property is true in each state. The drawback is that transition systems grow very large very quickly, often even becoming infinite. For instance, a system having 10 interacting components, each of which has 10 states, has a total number of 10 000 000 000 states. It is said that model-checking techniques suffer from the *state-explosion problem*. At the other end, reasoning can take place in logic, using a form of deduction. Also here, progress is made, and many *theorem-proving tools* exist (see e.g., (Bundy, 1999)). The drawback here is that finding a proof needs user assistance, as the general problem is undecidable, and this necessitates a lot of knowledge about the system.

Equational reasoning on the basis of an algebraic theory takes the middle ground, in an attempt to combine the strengths of both model checking and theorem proving. Usually, the next step in the procedure is clear. In that sense, it is more rewriting than equational reasoning. Consequently, automation, which is the main strength of model checking, can be done straightforwardly. On the other hand, representations are compact and allow the presence of parameters, so that an infinite set of instances can be verified at the same time, which are strong points of theorem proving.

As an example, Chapter 8 presents a complete verification of a simple communication protocol: it is verified that the external behavior of the protocol coincides with the behavior of a one-place buffer. This is the desired result, because it proves that every message sent arrives at the receiving end.

1.3 History

Process algebra started in the 1970s. At that point, the only part of concurrency theory that existed was the theory of Petri nets, conceived by Petri starting from his thesis in 1962 (Petri, 1962). In 1970, three main styles of formal reasoning about computer programs could be distinguished, focusing on giving semantics (meaning) to programming languages.

(i) *Operational semantics*: A computer program is modeled as an execution of an abstract machine. A state of such a machine is a valuation of variables; a transition between states is an elementary program instruction. The pioneer of this field is McCarthy (McCarthy, 1963).

(ii) *Denotational semantics*: In a denotational semantics, which is typically more abstract than an operational semantics, computer programs are usually modeled by a function transforming input into output. The most well-known pioneers are Scott and Strachey (Scott & Strachey, 1971).

(iii) *Axiomatic semantics*: An axiomatic semantics emphasizes proof methods proving programs correct. Central notions are program assertions, proof triples consisting of precondition, program statement, and postcondition, and invariants. Pioneers are Floyd (Floyd, 1967) and Hoare (Hoare, 1969).

Then, the question was raised how to give semantics to programs containing a parallel-composition operator. It was found that this is difficult using the methods of denotational, operational, or axiomatic semantics as they existed at that time, although several attempts were made. (Later on, it became clear how to extend the different types of semantics to parallel programming, see e.g., (Owicki & Gries, 1976) or (Plotkin, 1976).) Process algebra developed as an answer to this question.

There are two paradigm shifts that need to be made before a theory of parallel programs in terms of a process algebra can be developed. First of all, the idea of a behavior as an input/output function needs to be abandoned. The relation between input and output is more complicated and may involve *non-determinism*. This is because the interactions a process has between input and output may influence the outcome, disrupting functional behavior. A program can still be modeled as an automaton, but the notion of language equivalence is no longer appropriate. Secondly, the notion of *global* variables needs to be overcome. Using global variables, a state of a modeling automaton is given as a valuation of the program variables, that is, a state is determined by the values of the variables. The independent execution of parallel processes makes it difficult or impossible to determine the values of global variables at any given moment. It turns out to be simpler to let each process have its own local variables, and to denote exchange of information explicitly via *message passing*.

Bekič

One of the first people studying the semantics of parallel programs was Hans Bekič. He was born in 1936, and died due to a mountain accident in 1982. In the early seventies, he worked at the IBM lab in Vienna, Austria. The lab was well-known in the sixties and seventies for its work on the definition and semantics of programming languages, and Bekič played a part in this, working on the denotational semantics of ALGOL and PL/I. Growing out of his work on PL/I, the problem arose how to give a denotational semantics for parallel composition. Bekič tackled this problem in (Bekič, 1971). This internal report, and indeed all the work of Bekič, is made accessible through the book edited by Cliff Jones (Bekič, 1984). The following remarks are based on this book.

In (Bekič, 1971), Bekič addresses the semantics of what he calls 'quasi-parallel execution of processes'. From the introduction:

> Our plan to develop an *algebra of processes* may be viewed as a *high-level* approach: we are interested in how to compose complex processes from simpler (still arbitrarily complex) ones.

Bekič uses global variables, so a state is a valuation of variables, and a program determines an action, which gives in a state (non-deterministically) either *null* if and only if it is an end-state, or an elementary step, giving a new state and rest-action. Further, Bekič has operators for alternative composition, sequential composition, and (quasi-)parallel composition. He gives a law for quasi-parallel composition, called the 'unspecified merging' of the elementary steps of two processes. That law is definitely a precursor of what later would be called the expansion law of process algebra. It also makes explicit that Bekič has made the first paradigm shift: the next step in a merge is not determined, so the idea of a program as a function has been abandoned.

Concluding, Bekič contributed a number of basic ingredients to the emergence of process algebra, but he does not yet provide a coherent comprehensive theory.

CCS

The central person in the history of process algebra without a doubt is Robin Milner. A.J.R.G. Milner, born in 1934, developed his process theory CCS, the *Calculus of Communicating Systems*, over the years 1973 to 1980, culminating in the publication of the book (Milner, 1980) in 1980.

Milner's oldest publications concerning the semantics of parallel composition are (Milner, 1973; Milner, 1975), formulated within the framework of denotational semantics, using so-called transducers. He considers the problems caused by non-terminating programs, with side effects, and non-determinism. He uses operators for sequential composition, for alternative composition, and for parallel composition. He refers to (Bekič, 1971) as related work.

Next, in terms of the development of CCS, are the articles (Milner, 1979) and (Milne & Milner, 1979). In that work, Milner introduces *flow graphs*, with ports, where a named port synchronizes with the port with its co-name. Operators are parallel composition, restriction (to prevent certain specified actions), and relabeling (for renaming ports). Some laws are stated for these operators.

The two papers that put in place most of CCS as it is known to date, (Milner, 1978a) and (Milner, 1978b), conceptually built upon this work, but appeared in 1978. The operators prefixing and alternative composition are added and provided with laws. Synchronization trees are used as a model. The prefix τ occurs as a *communication trace*, i.e., what remains of a synchronization of a name and a co-name. Such a remains is typically unobservable, and later,

τ developed into what is now usually called the silent step. The paradigm of message passing, the second paradigm shift, is taken over from (Hoare, 1978). Interleaving is introduced as the observation of a single observer of a communicating system, and the expansion law is stated. Sequential composition is not a basic operator, but a derived one, using communication, abstraction, and restriction.

The paper (Hennessy & Milner, 1980), with Matthew Hennessy, formulates basic CCS, with two important semantic equivalence relations, observational equivalence and strong equivalence, defined inductively. Also, so-called Hennessy-Milner logic is introduced, which provides a logical characterization of process equivalence. Next, the book (Milner, 1980) was published, which is by now a standard process algebra reference. For the first time in history, the book presents a complete process algebra, with a set of equations and a semantic model. In fact, Milner talks about *process calculus* everywhere in his work, emphasizing the calculational aspect. He presents the equational laws as truths about his chosen semantic domain, transition systems, rather than considering the laws as primary, and investigating the range of models that they have. The book (Milner, 1980) was later updated in (Milner, 1989).

CSP

A very important contributor to the development of process algebra is Tony Hoare. C.A.R. Hoare, born in 1934, published his influential paper (Hoare, 1978) as a technical report in 1976. The important step is that he does away completely with global variables, and adopts the message-passing paradigm of communication, thus realizing the second paradigm shift. The language CSP, *Communicating Sequential Processes*, described in (Hoare, 1978) has synchronous communication and is a guarded-command language (based on (Dijkstra, 1975)). No model or semantics is provided. This paper inspired Milner to treat message passing in CCS in the same way.

A model for CSP was elaborated in (Hoare, 1980). This is a model based on trace theory, i.e., on the sequences of actions a process can perform. Later on, it was found that this model was lacking, for instance because deadlock behavior is not preserved. For this reason, a new model based on so-called failure pairs was presented in (Brookes *et al.*, 1984), for the language that was then called TCSP, *Theoretical* CSP. Later, TCSP was called CSP again. In the language, due to the less discriminating semantics when compared to the equivalence adopted by Milner and the presence of two alternative composition operators, it is possible to do without a silent step like τ altogether. The book (Hoare, 1985) gives a good overview of CSP.

Between CCS and CSP, there is some debate concerning the nature of alternative composition. Some say the + of CCS is difficult to understand (exemplified by the philosophical discussion on 'the weather of Milner'), and CSP proposes to distinguish between internal and external non-determinism, using two separate operators; see also (Hennessy, 1988a).

Some other process theories

Around 1980, concurrency theory and in particular process theory is a vibrant field with a lot of activity world wide. There is research on Petri nets, partially ordered traces, and temporal logic, among others. Other process theories are trace theory and the invariants calculus. In particular, there is the metric approach by De Bakker and Zucker (De Bakker & Zucker, 1982a; De Bakker & Zucker, 1982b). It has a notion of distance between processes: processes that do not differ in behavior before the n-th step have a distance of at most 2^{-n}. This turns the domain of processes into a metric space, that can be completed. Recursive equations allow to specify unbounded process behavior. In the metric approach by De Bakker and Zucker, solutions to an important class of recursive equations, so-called *guarded* recursive equations, exist by application of Banach's fixed point theorem. This result later influenced the development of process algebra, in particular the development of ACP.

ACP

Jan Bergstra and Jan Willem Klop started to work in 1982 on a question of De Bakker's as to what can be said about solutions of *unguarded* recursive equations. As a result, they wrote the paper (Bergstra & Klop, 1982). In this paper, the phrase 'process algebra' is used for the first time, with exactly the two meanings given in the first part of this chapter. The paper defines a process algebra with alternative, sequential, and parallel composition, but without communication. A model was established based on projective sequences, meaning that a process is given by a sequence of approximations by finite terms, and in this model, it is established that all recursive equations, both guarded and unguarded, have a solution. In adapted form, this paper was later published as (Bergstra & Klop, 1992). In (Bergstra & Klop, 1984a), this process algebra, called PA, for Process Algebra, was extended with communication to yield the theory ACP, the *Algebra of Communicating Processes*. Textbooks on ACP are (Baeten & Weijland, 1990; Fokkink, 2000).

Comparing the three most well-known process algebras to date, CCS, CSP, and ACP, it can be concluded that there is a considerable amount of work and applications realized in all three of them. In that sense, there seem to be no fundamental differences between the theories with respect to the range of applications. Historically, CCS was the first with a complete theory. Compared to the other two, CSP has the least distinguishing equational theory. More than the other two, ACP emphasizes the algebraic aspect: there is an equational theory with a range of semantic models. Also, ACP has the most general communication scheme: in CCS, communication is combined with abstraction, and also CSP has a restricted communication scheme.

Further developments

The development of CCS, CSP, and ACP was followed by the development of other process algebras, such as SCCS (Milner, 1983), CIRCAL (Milne, 1983), MEIJE (Austry & Boudol, 1984), and the process algebra of Hennessy (Hennessy, 1988a). Moreover, many process algebras were extended with extra features, such as timing or probabilities. A number of these extensions are also addressed in this book.

Over the years, many process algebras have been developed, each making its own set of choices in the different possibilities. The reader may wonder whether this is something to be lamented. In (Baeten *et al.*, 1991), it is argued that this is actually a good thing, as long as there is a good exchange of information between the different research groups, as each different process algebra has its own set of advantages and disadvantages. The theoretical framework developed in this book is generic, in the sense that most features found in other process algebras can be defined in it. Throughout the book, it is indicated how this can be achieved.

This book

This book follows the ACP approach in its emphasis on algebra. The main difference with the theory set out in (Bergstra & Klop, 1984a; Baeten & Weijland, 1990) is that successful termination is integrated in the theory almost from the beginning. As set out in (Baeten, 2003), this leads to some other changes in the theory. The basic theory starts with a prefixing operator as in CCS and CSP, and adds the sequential-composition operator, which is a basic operator in ACP, in a later chapter.

This book arose as a complete and thorough revision of the book (Baeten & Weijland, 1990). Although many changes have occurred, the approach and methodology remain the same. Also some parts of the text have remained almost unchanged. The book has been updated in many places to reflect the latest developments, making it the most complete and in-depth account of the state-of-the-art in process algebra at the time of writing.

Bibliographical remark

The historic overview of this section first appeared in (Baeten, 2005).

2

Preliminaries

2.1 Introduction

This second chapter introduces the basic concepts and notations related to equational theories, algebras, and term rewriting systems that are needed for the remainder of the book. Throughout the book, standard mathematical notations are used, in particular from set theory. Notation $\mathbf{N} = \{0, 1, 2, \ldots\}$ denotes the natural numbers.

2.2 Equational theories

A central notion of this book is the notion of an equational theory. An equational theory is a signature (defining a 'language') together with a set of equations over this signature (the basic laws). Every process algebra in this book is presented as a model of an equational theory, as outlined in the previous chapter.

Definition 2.2.1 (Signature) A *signature* Σ is a set of constant and function symbols with their arities.

The objects in a signature are called constant and function *symbols*. The reason for doing so is to distinguish between these purely formal objects and the 'real' constants and functions they are meant to represent. In Section 2.3, where interpretations of equational theories are discussed, this point is elaborated further. Note that a constant symbol can also be seen as a function symbol of arity zero.

Example 2.2.2 (Signature) As an example, consider the signature Σ_1 consisting of the constant symbol $\mathbf{0}$, the unary function symbol $\mathbf{s}$, and the binary function symbols $\mathbf{a}$ and $\mathbf{m}$.

Definition 2.2.3 (Terms) The set of all terms over a signature Σ and a set of variables V, notation $\mathcal{T}(\Sigma, V)$, is the smallest set that satisfies the following:

(i) each variable in V is a term in $\mathcal{T}(\Sigma, V)$;
(ii) each constant in Σ is a term in $\mathcal{T}(\Sigma, V)$;
(iii) if f is an n-ary function symbol ($n \geq 1$) and $t_1, \ldots, t_n$ are terms in $\mathcal{T}(\Sigma, V)$, then $f(t_1, \ldots, t_n)$ is a term in $\mathcal{T}(\Sigma, V)$.

In this book, it is always assumed that there are as many variables as needed. Therefore, often, the set of variables is omitted from the notation $\mathcal{T}(\Sigma, V)$, yielding the notation $\mathcal{T}(\Sigma)$ for all the terms over signature Σ. As a shorthand, terms over some signature Σ are also referred to as Σ-terms. A term that does not contain variables is called a *closed* or *ground* term. The set of all closed terms over signature Σ is denoted $\mathcal{C}(\Sigma)$. To emphasize that arbitrary terms in $\mathcal{T}(\Sigma)$ may contain variables, they are often referred to as *open* terms. Syntactical identity of terms is denoted by $\equiv$.

Definition 2.2.4 (Equational theory) An *equational theory* is a tuple (Σ, E), where Σ is a signature and E is a set of equations of the form $s = t$ where s and t are terms over this signature ($s, t \in \mathcal{T}(\Sigma)$). The equations of an equational theory are often referred to as *axioms*.

Example 2.2.5 (Equational theory) Table 2.1 gives equational theory $T_1 = (\Sigma_1, E_1)$, where Σ_1 is the signature of Example 2.2.2. The first entry of Table 2.1 lists the constant and function symbols in signature Σ_1. The second entry of the table introduces a number of variables and lists the equations in E_1. In this case, the equations of the equational theory contain variables x and y. It is assumed that variables can always be distinguished from the symbols of the signature. The equations have been given names to facilitate future reference. The attentive reader might recognize that the equations conform to the well-known axioms of *Peano arithmetic*, see e.g. (Van Heijenoort, 1967); however, strictly speaking, the symbols in the signature and the equations are still meaningless.

The objective of an equational theory is to describe which terms over the signature of this equational theory are to be considered equal. As the example equational theory shows, the equations of an equational theory often contain variables. When trying to derive equalities from a theory, it is allowed to substitute arbitrary terms for these variables.

Definition 2.2.6 (Substitution) Let Σ be a signature and V a set of variables. A *substitution* σ is a mapping from V to $\mathcal{T}(\Sigma, V)$. For any term t in $\mathcal{T}(\Sigma, V)$,

— T_1		
constant: $\mathbf{0}$;	unary: $\mathbf{s}$;	binary: $\mathbf{a}, \mathbf{m}$;
x, y;		
$\mathbf{a}(x, \mathbf{0}) = x$		PA1
$\mathbf{a}(x, \mathbf{s}(y)) = \mathbf{s}(\mathbf{a}(x, y))$		PA2
$\mathbf{m}(x, \mathbf{0}) = \mathbf{0}$		PA3
$\mathbf{m}(x, \mathbf{s}(y)) = \mathbf{a}(\mathbf{m}(x, y), x)$		PA4

Table 2.1. The equational theory $T_1 = (\Sigma_1, E_1)$.

$t[\sigma]$ denotes the term obtained by the simultaneous substitution of all variables in t according to σ. That is,

(i) for each variable x in V, $x[\sigma] = \sigma(x)$,
(ii) for each constant c in Σ, $c[\sigma] = c$, and
(iii) for any n-ary function symbol f ($n \geq 1$) and terms $t_1, \ldots, t_n$ in $\mathcal{T}(\Sigma, V)$, $f(t_1, \ldots, t_n)[\sigma]$ is the term $f(t_1[\sigma], \ldots, t_n[\sigma])$.

Example 2.2.7 (Substitution) Consider the term $t \equiv \mathbf{a}(\mathbf{m}(x, y), x)$ over the signature Σ_1 of Example 2.2.2. Let σ_1 be the substitution mapping x to $\mathbf{s}(\mathbf{s}(\mathbf{0}))$ and y to $\mathbf{0}$. Then, $t[\sigma_1]$ is the term $\mathbf{a}(\mathbf{m}(\mathbf{s}(\mathbf{s}(\mathbf{0})), \mathbf{0}), \mathbf{s}(\mathbf{s}(\mathbf{0})))$. Let σ_2 be the substitution mapping x to $\mathbf{s}(\mathbf{s}(y))$ and y to x; $t[\sigma_2]$ is the term $\mathbf{a}(\mathbf{m}(\mathbf{s}(\mathbf{s}(y)), x)$, $\mathbf{s}(\mathbf{s}(y)))$.

There is a standard collection of proof rules for deriving equalities from an equational theory. Together, these rules define the notion of *derivability* and they are referred to as the rules of *equational logic*.

Definition 2.2.8 (Derivability) Let $T = (\Sigma, E)$ be an equational theory; let V be a set of variables and let s and t be terms in $\mathcal{T}(\Sigma, V)$. The equation $s = t$ is derivable from theory T, denoted $T \vdash s = t$, if and only if it follows from the following rules:

(Axiom rule) for any equation $s = t \in E$,
$T \vdash s = t$;
(Substitution) for any terms $s, t \in \mathcal{T}(\Sigma, V)$ and any substitution $\sigma : V \to \mathcal{T}(\Sigma, V)$,
$T \vdash s = t$ implies that $T \vdash s[\sigma] = t[\sigma]$;
(Reflexivity) for any term $t \in \mathcal{T}(\Sigma, V)$,
$T \vdash t = t$;
(Symmetry) for any terms $s, t \in \mathcal{T}(\Sigma, V)$,
$T \vdash s = t$ implies that $T \vdash t = s$;

(Transitivity) for any terms $s, t, u \in \mathcal{T}(\Sigma, V)$,

$T \vdash s = t$ and $T \vdash t = u$ implies that $T \vdash s = u$;

(Context rule) for any n-ary function symbol $f \in \Sigma$ $(n \geq 1)$, any terms $s, t_1, \ldots, t_n \in \mathcal{T}(\Sigma, V)$, and any natural number i with $1 \leq i \leq n$,

$T \vdash t_i = s$ implies that

$T \vdash f(t_1, \ldots, t_n) = f(t_1, \ldots, t_{i-1}, s, t_{i+1}, \ldots, t_n)$.

Example 2.2.9 (Derivability) Consider equational theory $T_1 = (\Sigma_1, E_1)$ of Example 2.2.5. The following derivation shows that $T_1 \vdash \mathbf{a}(\mathbf{s}(\mathbf{0}), \mathbf{s}(\mathbf{0})) = \mathbf{s}(\mathbf{s}(\mathbf{0}))$. Let σ be the substitution that maps x to $\mathbf{s}(\mathbf{0})$ and y to $\mathbf{0}$.

1. $T_1 \vdash \mathbf{a}(x, \mathbf{s}(y)) = \mathbf{s}(\mathbf{a}(x, y))$ (Axiom PA2)
2. $T_1 \vdash \mathbf{a}(\mathbf{s}(\mathbf{0}), \mathbf{s}(\mathbf{0})) = \mathbf{s}(\mathbf{a}(\mathbf{s}(\mathbf{0}), \mathbf{0}))$ (line 1: substitution σ)
3. $T_1 \vdash \mathbf{a}(x, \mathbf{0}) = x$ (Axiom PA1)
4. $T_1 \vdash \mathbf{a}(\mathbf{s}(\mathbf{0}), \mathbf{0}) = \mathbf{s}(\mathbf{0})$ (line 3: substitution σ)
5. $T_1 \vdash \mathbf{s}(\mathbf{a}(\mathbf{s}(\mathbf{0}), \mathbf{0})) = \mathbf{s}(\mathbf{s}(\mathbf{0}))$ (line 4: context rule)
6. $T_1 \vdash \mathbf{a}(\mathbf{s}(\mathbf{0}), \mathbf{s}(\mathbf{0})) = \mathbf{s}(\mathbf{s}(\mathbf{0}))$ (lines 2 and 5: transitivity)

The derivation above is presented in a linear, line-based way. However, derivations are often easier to read if presented as a tree. Figure 2.1 visualizes the above tree as a so-called proof tree. In this case, the proof tree makes it explicit that the end result depends on two independent initial applications of basic axioms.

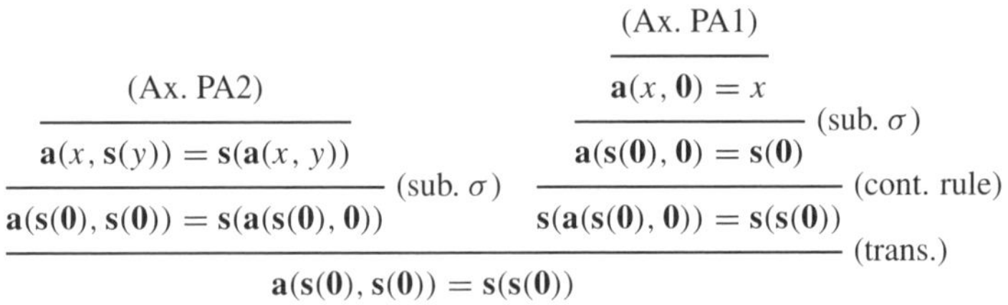

$$\dfrac{\dfrac{\dfrac{\text{(Ax. PA2)}}{\mathbf{a}(x, \mathbf{s}(y)) = \mathbf{s}(\mathbf{a}(x, y))}}{\mathbf{a}(\mathbf{s}(\mathbf{0}), \mathbf{s}(\mathbf{0})) = \mathbf{s}(\mathbf{a}(\mathbf{s}(\mathbf{0}), \mathbf{0}))}\ (\text{sub. } \sigma) \qquad \dfrac{\dfrac{\dfrac{\text{(Ax. PA1)}}{\mathbf{a}(x, \mathbf{0}) = x}}{\mathbf{a}(\mathbf{s}(\mathbf{0}), \mathbf{0}) = \mathbf{s}(\mathbf{0})}\ (\text{sub. } \sigma)}{\mathbf{s}(\mathbf{a}(\mathbf{s}(\mathbf{0}), \mathbf{0})) = \mathbf{s}(\mathbf{s}(\mathbf{0}))}\ (\text{cont. rule})}{\mathbf{a}(\mathbf{s}(\mathbf{0}), \mathbf{s}(\mathbf{0})) = \mathbf{s}(\mathbf{s}(\mathbf{0}))}\ (\text{trans.})$$

Fig. 2.1. A proof tree.

Of course, independent of the precise representation, it is not always very practical to give derivations with the level of detail as above. In the remainder, derivations are given in a more compact form. The above derivation, for example, can be reduced as follows:

$$T_1 \vdash \mathbf{a}(\mathbf{s}(\mathbf{0}), \mathbf{s}(\mathbf{0})) = \mathbf{s}(\mathbf{a}(\mathbf{s}(\mathbf{0}), \mathbf{0})) \doteq \mathbf{s}(\mathbf{s}(\mathbf{0})).$$

Note the difference between syntactical identity, as introduced in Definition 2.2.3, and derivability. Based on the reflexivity of derivability, syntactical identity implies derivability. For example, $\mathbf{s}(\mathbf{0}) \equiv \mathbf{s}(\mathbf{0})$ and $T_1 \vdash \mathbf{s}(\mathbf{0}) = \mathbf{s}(\mathbf{0})$. The converse is not true: $T_1 \vdash \mathbf{a}(\mathbf{0}, \mathbf{0}) = \mathbf{0}$ but not $\mathbf{a}(\mathbf{0}, \mathbf{0}) \equiv \mathbf{0}$.

Inductive proof techniques play an important role in the context of equational theories. They are often applicable for proving properties of (closed) terms over the signature of a theory. The example equational theory $T_1 = (\Sigma_1, E_1)$ of Table 2.1 can be used for demonstrating inductive proof techniques. The notion of so-called basic terms plays an important role in the examples that are given below. The reason why the terms are called *basic* terms becomes clear further on.

Definition 2.2.10 (Basic Σ_1-terms) Consider signature Σ_1 of Example 2.2.2. The set of *basic* Σ_1-terms is the smallest set $\mathcal{B}(\Sigma_1)$ such that (i) $\mathbf{0} \in \mathcal{B}(\Sigma_1)$ and (ii) $p \in \mathcal{B}(\Sigma_1)$ implies $\mathbf{s}(p) \in \mathcal{B}(\Sigma_1)$.

Note that this definition implies that the set of basic Σ_1-terms contains precisely all closed Σ_1-terms that can be written as $\mathbf{s}^n(\mathbf{0})$ for some $n \in \mathbf{N}$ where

$$\begin{aligned} \mathbf{s}^0(\mathbf{0}) &= \mathbf{0} \quad \text{and} \\ \mathbf{s}^{n+1}(\mathbf{0}) &= \mathbf{s}(\mathbf{s}^n(\mathbf{0})) \quad (\text{for } n \in \mathbf{N}). \end{aligned} \tag{2.2.1}$$

The first inductive proof technique that is commonly used in the context of equational theories is standard natural induction.

Example 2.2.11 (Natural induction) Consider the following property of *basic* Σ_1-terms in the context of equational theory $T_1 = (\Sigma_1, E_1)$ of Table 2.1. It uses the notation for basic terms introduced in (2.2.1).

$$\begin{aligned} &\text{For any } p, q \in \mathcal{B}(\Sigma_1) \text{ with } p = \mathbf{s}^m(\mathbf{0}) \text{ and } q = \mathbf{s}^n(\mathbf{0}), \\ &\quad T_1 \vdash \mathbf{a}(p, q) = \mathbf{s}^{m+n}(\mathbf{0}). \end{aligned} \tag{2.2.2}$$

The proof of (2.2.2) goes via *natural* induction on the *number of function symbols* in basic term q. In other words, the proof uses induction on n.

(Base case) Assume that $n = 0$, which means that $q \equiv \mathbf{0}$. From (2.2.1) and Axiom PA1, it easily follows that for all $m \in \mathbf{N}$

$$\begin{aligned} T_1 \vdash \mathbf{a}(p, q) &= \mathbf{a}(\mathbf{s}^m(\mathbf{0}), \mathbf{s}^0(\mathbf{0})) = \mathbf{a}(\mathbf{s}^m(\mathbf{0}), \mathbf{0}) = \mathbf{s}^m(\mathbf{0}) \\ &= \mathbf{s}^{m+n}(\mathbf{0}). \end{aligned}$$

(Inductive step) Assume that (2.2.2) holds for all n at most k (with $k \in \mathbf{N}$). It follows from (2.2.1) and Axiom PA2 that for all $m \in \mathbf{N}$

$$\begin{aligned} T_1 \vdash \mathbf{a}(p, q) &= \mathbf{a}(\mathbf{s}^m(\mathbf{0}), \mathbf{s}^{k+1}(\mathbf{0})) = \mathbf{s}(\mathbf{a}(\mathbf{s}^m(\mathbf{0}), \mathbf{s}^k(\mathbf{0}))) \\ &= \mathbf{s}(\mathbf{s}^{m+k}(\mathbf{0})) = \mathbf{s}^{m+k+1}(\mathbf{0}). \end{aligned}$$

By induction, it may be concluded that (2.2.2) is true for all (m and) n in $\mathbf{N}$.

It is possible to formulate a property for the $\mathbf{m}$ function symbol in signature Σ_1 that is very similar to property (2.2.2):

$$\begin{aligned} &\text{For any } p, q \in \mathcal{B}(\Sigma_1) \text{ with } p = \mathbf{s}^m(\mathbf{0}) \text{ and } q = \mathbf{s}^n(\mathbf{0}), \\ &\quad T_1 \vdash \mathbf{m}(p, q) = \mathbf{s}^{mn}(\mathbf{0}). \end{aligned} \tag{2.2.3}$$

The proof of property (2.2.3) also goes via induction on the number of function symbols of term q; it is left as Exercise 2.2.4.

Another important inductive proof technique is *structural* induction. Structural induction is a variant of natural induction that is particularly well suited for proving properties of closed terms over some signature.

Definition 2.2.12 (Structural induction) Let Σ be a signature. Let $P(t)$ be some property on terms over Σ. If,

(Base cases) for any constant symbol c in Σ,

$P(c)$

and

(Inductive steps) for any n-ary ($n \geq 1$) function symbol f in Σ and closed terms $p_1, \ldots, p_n$ in $\mathcal{C}(\Sigma)$,

the assumption that for all natural numbers i, with $1 \leq i \leq n$, $P(p_i)$ holds implies that $P(f(p_1, \ldots, p_n))$,

then $P(p)$ for any closed Σ-term p.

The following example illustrates structural induction in the context of equational theories.

Example 2.2.13 (Structural induction and elimination) Consider again the equational theory $T_1 = (\Sigma_1, E_1)$ of Example 2.2.5. An interesting property is the following so-called *elimination* property: any closed Σ_1-term can be written as a *basic* Σ_1-term as introduced in Definition 2.2.10. Since any basic term is a composition of **s** function symbols applied to the **0** constant symbol, this implies that the **a** and **m** function symbols can be eliminated from any closed term. At this point, it should be clear why the terms introduced in Definition 2.2.10 are called *basic* terms.

For any p in $\mathcal{C}(\Sigma_1)$, there is some $p_1 \in \mathcal{B}(\Sigma_1)$ such that $T_1 \vdash p = p_1$. (2.2.4)

The proof uses structural induction on the structure of closed term p.

(Base case) Assume that $p \equiv \mathbf{0}$. Since $\mathbf{0}$ is a basic Σ_1-term, the base case is trivially satisfied.

(Inductive steps)

(i) Assume $p \equiv \mathbf{s}(q)$, for some closed term $q \in \mathcal{C}(\Sigma_1)$. By induction, it may be assumed that there is some basic term $q_1 \in \mathcal{B}(\Sigma_1)$ such that $T_1 \vdash q = q_1$. Thus,

$$T_1 \vdash p = \mathbf{s}(q) = \mathbf{s}(q_1).$$

Clearly, because q_1 is a basic Σ_1-term, also $\mathbf{s}(q_1)$ is a basic term.

(ii) Assume $p \equiv \mathbf{a}(q, r)$, for some $q, r \in \mathcal{C}(\Sigma_1)$. Let $q_1, r_1 \in \mathcal{B}(\Sigma_1)$ be basic terms such that $T_1 \vdash q = q_1$ and $T_1 \vdash r = r_1$; furthermore, based on (2.2.1), assume that $m, n \in \mathbf{N}$ are natural numbers such that $q_1 = \mathbf{s}^m(\mathbf{0})$ and $r_1 = \mathbf{s}^n(\mathbf{0})$. Using (2.2.2) of Example 2.2.11, it follows that

$$T_1 \vdash p = \mathbf{a}(q, r) = \mathbf{a}(\mathbf{s}^m(\mathbf{0}), \mathbf{s}^n(\mathbf{0})) = \mathbf{s}^{m+n}(\mathbf{0}),$$

which is a basic Σ_1-term.

(iii) Assume $p \equiv \mathbf{m}(q, r)$, for some $q, r \in \mathcal{C}(\Sigma_1)$. Let $q_1, r_1 \in \mathcal{B}(\Sigma_1)$ be basic terms such that $T_1 \vdash q = q_1$ and $T_1 \vdash r = r_1$; assume that $m, n \in \mathbf{N}$ are natural numbers such that $q_1 = \mathbf{s}^m(\mathbf{0})$ and $r_1 = \mathbf{s}^n(\mathbf{0})$. Using (2.2.3), it follows that

$$T_1 \vdash p = \mathbf{m}(q, r) = \mathbf{m}(\mathbf{s}^m(\mathbf{0}), \mathbf{s}^n(\mathbf{0})) = \mathbf{s}^{mn}(\mathbf{0}).$$

Based on Definition 2.2.12, it is now valid to conclude that property (2.2.4) is true for all closed Σ_1-terms.

It is often necessary or useful to extend an equational theory with additional constant and/or function symbols and/or axioms.

Definition 2.2.14 (Extension of an equational theory) Consider two equational theories $T_1 = (\Sigma_1, E_1)$ and $T_2 = (\Sigma_2, E_2)$. Theory T_2 is an *extension* of theory T_1 if and only if Σ_2 contains Σ_1 and E_2 contains E_1.

Example 2.2.15 (Extension of an equational theory) Table 2.2 describes the extension of equational theory T_1 of Example 2.2.5 with an extra binary function symbol **e**. The first entry of Table 2.2 simply says that theory T_2 extends theory T_1. The other two entries of Table 2.2 list the *new* constant and function symbols in the signature of the extended theory, one symbol in this particular example, and the new axioms.

T_2			
T_1;			
binary: **e**;			
x, y;			
$\mathbf{e}(x, \mathbf{0})$	$=$	$\mathbf{s}(\mathbf{0})$	PA5
$\mathbf{e}(x, \mathbf{s}(y))$	$=$	$\mathbf{m}(\mathbf{e}(x, y), x)$	PA6

Table 2.2. The equational theory $T_2 = (\Sigma_2, E_2)$.

It is often desirable that an extension of an equational theory such as the one of Example 2.2.15 satisfies the property that it does not influence what equalities can be derived from the original theory. Observe that the requirement on the axioms in Definition 2.2.14 (Extension) already guarantees that any equalities that are derivable in the original theory are also derivable in the extended theory. However, the addition of new axioms may result in new equalities between terms of the original syntax that could not be derived from the original axioms. An extension that does not introduce any new equalities between terms in the original syntax is said to be *conservative*.

Definition 2.2.16 (Conservative extension) Let $T_1 = (\Sigma_1, E_1)$ and $T_2 = (\Sigma_2, E_2)$ be equational theories. Theory T_2 is a *conservative extension* of theory T_1 if and only if

(i) T_2 is an extension of T_1 and,
(ii) for all Σ_1-terms s and t, $T_2 \vdash s = t$ implies $T_1 \vdash s = t$.

Proposition 2.2.17 (Conservative extension) Equational theory T_2 of Table 2.2 is a conservative extension of theory T_1 of Table 2.1.

The proof of Proposition 2.2.17 is deferred to Section 3.2, where it follows naturally from the results introduced in Chapter 3. An alternative proof technique would be to use term rewriting, as introduced in Section 2.4.

Definition 2.2.16 requires that equalities between arbitrary open terms are preserved. It is not always possible to achieve this. Sometimes, only a weaker property can be established: only equalities between closed (or ground) terms can be preserved. The following definitions adapt the notions of extension and conservative extension.

Definition 2.2.18 (Ground-extension) Consider two equational theories $T_1 = (\Sigma_1, E_1)$ and $T_2 = (\Sigma_2, E_2)$. Theory T_2 is a *ground*-extension of theory T_1 if and only if Σ_2 contains Σ_1 and for all closed Σ_1-terms p and q, $T_1 \vdash p = q$ implies $T_2 \vdash p = q$.

Definition 2.2.19 (Conservative ground-extension) Let $T_1 = (\Sigma_1, E_1)$ and $T_2 = (\Sigma_2, E_2)$ be equational theories. Theory T_2 is a *conservative ground-extension* of theory T_1 if and only if

(i) T_2 is a ground-extension of T_1 and,
(ii) for all closed Σ_1-terms p and q, $T_2 \vdash p = q$ implies $T_1 \vdash p = q$.

An interesting property of equational theory T_2 is that any closed Σ_2-term can be written as a basic Σ_1-term, as defined in Definition 2.2.10.

Proposition 2.2.20 (Elimination) Consider equational theory T_2 of Table 2.2. For any $p \in \mathcal{C}(\Sigma_2)$, there is a basic Σ_1-term $p_1 \in \mathcal{B}(\Sigma_1)$ such that

$$T_2 \vdash p = p_1.$$

Proof Exercise 2.2.5. □

Elimination properties such as (2.2.4) in Example 2.2.13 and Proposition 2.2.20 often substantially simplify structural-induction proofs. To prove properties for closed terms over the signatures of the example equational theories T_1 and T_2, it now suffices to prove these properties for basic Σ_1-terms.

Example 2.2.21 (Structural induction and elimination) Consider the equational theory $T_2 = (\Sigma_2, E_2)$ of Example 2.2.15. An interesting property of closed Σ_2-terms is the following *commutativity* property for the **a** symbol.

For any closed terms $p, q \in \mathcal{C}(\Sigma_2)$, (2.2.5)

$$T_2 \vdash \mathbf{a}(p, q) = \mathbf{a}(q, p).$$

Consider (2.2.5) formulated in terms of basic Σ_1-terms:

For any *basic* terms $p_1, q_1 \in \mathcal{B}(\Sigma_1)$, (2.2.6)

$$T_2 \vdash \mathbf{a}(p_1, q_1) = \mathbf{a}(q_1, p_1).$$

Let p and q be some closed terms in $\mathcal{C}(\Sigma_2)$. Proposition 2.2.20 (Elimination) yields that there are basic terms $p_1, q_1 \in \mathcal{B}(\Sigma_1)$ such that

$$T_2 \vdash p = p_1 \text{ and } T_2 \vdash q = q_1.$$

Assuming that it is possible to prove (2.2.6), it follows that

$$T_2 \vdash \mathbf{a}(p, q) = \mathbf{a}(p_1, q_1) = \mathbf{a}(q_1, p_1) = \mathbf{a}(q, p),$$

which proves (2.2.5).

It remains to prove (2.2.6). It is straightforward to prove (2.2.6) using property (2.2.2). However, the purpose of this example is to show a proof that goes solely via induction on the structure of basic terms and does not use property (2.2.2) which is proven via natural induction. Note that basic terms are (closed) terms over a signature that is (usually) strictly smaller than the signature of the equational theory under consideration. In the case of basic Σ_1-terms, the reduced signature consists of the constant symbol **0** and the function symbol **s**, whereas the signature of Σ_2 contains the additional symbols **a**, **m**, and **e**. It is clear that the fewer symbols a signature contains, the fewer cases need to be considered in an induction proof.

The following auxiliary properties are needed.

For any closed term $p \in \mathcal{C}(\Sigma_2)$, (2.2.7)

$$T_2 \vdash \mathbf{a}(\mathbf{0}, p) = p$$

and

For any closed terms $p, q \in \mathcal{C}(\Sigma_2)$, (2.2.8)

$$T_2 \vdash \mathbf{a}(p, \mathbf{s}(q)) = \mathbf{a}(\mathbf{s}(p), q).$$

Both these properties can be proven using Proposition 2.2.20 and structural induction on *basic* terms (or (2.2.2)). Since the proofs are straightforward, they are deferred to the exercises. The proof of the commutativity property for basic terms is now as follows. Let $p_1, q_1 \in \mathcal{B}(\Sigma_1)$. The proof goes via induction on the structure of basic term q_1.

(Base case) Assume that $q_1 \equiv \mathbf{0}$. Using (2.2.7), it follows that

$$T_2 \vdash \mathbf{a}(p_1, \mathbf{0}) = p_1 = \mathbf{a}(\mathbf{0}, p_1).$$

(Inductive step) Assume that $q_1 \equiv \mathbf{s}(q_2)$ for some $q_2 \in \mathcal{B}(\Sigma_1)$. Assume that the desired commutativity property holds for term q_2, i.e., assume that $\mathbf{a}(p_1, q_2) = \mathbf{a}(q_2, p_1)$. Using (2.2.8), it follows that

$$\begin{aligned} T_2 \vdash \mathbf{a}(p_1, q_1) &= \mathbf{a}(p_1, \mathbf{s}(q_2)) = \mathbf{s}(\mathbf{a}(p_1, q_2)) = \mathbf{s}(\mathbf{a}(q_2, p_1)) \\ &= \mathbf{a}(q_2, \mathbf{s}(p_1)) = \mathbf{a}(\mathbf{s}(q_2), p_1) = \mathbf{a}(q_1, p_1). \end{aligned}$$

By induction, it may be concluded that (2.2.6) is true for all basic Σ_1-terms.

In the remainder, to improve readability, the distinction between base cases and inductive steps in structural-induction proofs is not always made explicit.

Exercises

2.2.1 Consider the equational theory $T_1 = (\Sigma_1, E_1)$ of Example 2.2.5. Give a proof tree for the fact $T_1 \vdash \mathbf{m}(\mathbf{s}(\mathbf{0}), \mathbf{s}(\mathbf{0})) = \mathbf{s}(\mathbf{0})$.

2.2.2 Consider again equational theory T_1 of Example 2.2.5. Is it true that $T_1 \vdash \mathbf{a}(\mathbf{s}(\mathbf{0}), \mathbf{s}(\mathbf{0})) = \mathbf{s}(\mathbf{0})$? Can you *prove* your answer via equational logic (see Definition 2.2.8 (Derivability))? Motivate your answer.

2.2.3 Consider the following equational theory:

Fun

unary: F;

x;

$F(F(F(x)))$	$= x$	E1
$F(F(F(F(F(x)))))$	$= x$	E2

Show that for all (open) terms t, $Fun \vdash F(t) = t$.

2.2.4 Prove property (2.2.3) in Example 2.2.11.
(Hint: use natural induction and property (2.2.2) in Example 2.2.11.)

2.2.5 Prove Proposition 2.2.20.
(Hint: see Examples 2.2.11 and 2.2.13, and Exercise 2.2.4.)

2.2.6 Prove (2.2.7) and (2.2.8) using Proposition 2.2.20 and structural induction on basic terms.
(Hint: see Example 2.2.21.)

2.2.7 Consider equational theory T_2 of Table 2.2. Prove that, for any open terms $s, t \in \mathcal{T}(\Sigma_2)$ and closed term $p \in \mathcal{C}(\Sigma_2)$,

$$T_2 \vdash \mathbf{a}(s, \mathbf{a}(t, p)) = \mathbf{a}(\mathbf{a}(s, t), p). \quad \text{(associativity)}$$

(Hint: use Proposition 2.2.20 and structural induction on basic terms.)

2.2.8 Consider equational theory T_2 of Table 2.2. Prove that, for any closed terms p and q in $\mathcal{C}(\Sigma_2)$,

$$T_2 \vdash \mathbf{m}(p, q) = \mathbf{m}(q, p). \quad \text{(commutativity)}$$

(Hint: see Example 2.2.21.)

2.2.9 Consider again equational theory T_2 of Table 2.2. Prove that, for any p, q, and r in $\mathcal{C}(\Sigma_2)$,

$$T_2 \vdash \mathbf{m}(\mathbf{a}(p, q), r) = \mathbf{a}(\mathbf{m}(p, r), \mathbf{m}(q, r)). \quad \text{(right distributivity)}$$

(Hint: use Proposition 2.2.20, property (2.2.5) of Example 2.2.21, and Exercise 2.2.7.)

2.3 Algebras

So far, equational theories were meaningless. In this section, the meaning or *semantics* of equational theories is considered. The meaning of an equational theory is given by an *algebra*.

Definition 2.3.1 (Algebra) An algebra $\mathbb{A}$ consists of a set of elements $\mathbf{A}$ together with constants in $\mathbf{A}$ and functions on $\mathbf{A}$. The set of elements $\mathbf{A}$ of an algebra $\mathbb{A}$ is called the *universe*, *domain*, or *carrier set* of $\mathbb{A}$.

Example 2.3.2 (Algebra $\mathbb{B}$) The structure $\mathbb{B} = (\mathbf{B}, \wedge, \neg, \mathit{true})$ is the algebra of the Booleans $\mathbf{B} = \{\mathit{true}, \mathit{false}\}$, where *true* is a constant, $\neg$ is the unary negation function on Booleans and $\wedge$ is the binary conjunction function on Booleans. Usually, these functions are defined by truth tables.

Example 2.3.3 (Algebra $\mathbb{N}$) Structure $\mathbb{N} = (\mathbf{N}, +, \times, \mathit{succ}, 0)$ is the algebra of the natural numbers $\mathbf{N} = \{0, 1, 2, \ldots\}$ with the unary successor function *succ*, the well-known binary functions $+$ and $\times$, and constant 0.

Note that the notation for natural numbers introduced in this example is consistent with the notation for natural numbers throughout this book, except that the $\times$ function is usually not explicitly written.

Definition 2.3.4 (Σ-algebra) Let Σ be a signature as defined in Definition 2.2.1. An algebra $\mathbb{A}$ is called a Σ-algebra when there is a mapping from the symbols of the signature Σ into the constants and functions of the algebra that respects arities. Such a mapping is called an *interpretation*.

Example 2.3.5 (Σ-algebra) Recall from Example 2.2.2 that Σ_1 is the signature containing constant **0**, unary function **s**, and binary functions **a** and **m**. The algebra $\mathbb{N}$ of Example 2.3.3 is a Σ_1-algebra with the interpretation ι_1 defined by

$$\begin{array}{ll} \mathbf{0} & \mapsto 0, \\ \mathbf{s} & \mapsto \mathit{succ}, \\ \mathbf{a} & \mapsto +, \text{ and} \\ \mathbf{m} & \mapsto \times. \end{array}$$

Observe that also ι_2 defined by

$$\begin{array}{ll} \mathbf{0} & \mapsto 0, \\ \mathbf{s} & \mapsto \mathit{succ}, \\ \mathbf{a} & \mapsto \times, \text{ and} \\ \mathbf{m} & \mapsto + \end{array}$$

is an interpretation that satisfies the requirement that arities are respected.

At this point, the emphasis on the distinction between constant and function *symbols*, on the one hand, and real constants and functions, on the other hand, becomes clear. A signature contains merely symbols without meaning; an algebra contains real constants and functions. The symbols in a signature are given a meaning by mapping them onto constants and functions in an algebra. The above example shows that more than one mapping is often possible.

Recall that an equational theory consists of a signature plus a set of equations (see Definition 2.2.4). The idea is to give meaning to an equational theory by interpreting the terms over the signature of the theory in an algebra, as defined above. The question arises whether an arbitrary interpretation preserving arities is suitable. The answer is, hopefully not very surprisingly, negative. An extra requirement is that the equations of the theory are in some sense true in the algebra. The following definition captures the notion of truth precisely.

Definition 2.3.6 (Validity) Let Σ be a signature, V a set of variables, and $\mathbb{A}$ a Σ-algebra with domain **A**. Let ι be an interpretation of Σ into $\mathbb{A}$.

A valuation $\alpha : V \to \mathbf{A}$ is a function that maps variables in V to elements of the domain of the algebra $\mathbb{A}$. For any open term t in $\mathcal{T}(\Sigma, V)$, $\iota_\alpha(t)$ is the element of **A** obtained by replacing all constant and function symbols in t by the corresponding constants and functions in $\mathbb{A}$ according to ι and by replacing all variables in t by elements of **A** according to α. That is,

(i) for each variable x in V, $\iota_\alpha(x) = \alpha(x)$,
(ii) for each constant c in Σ, $\iota_\alpha(c) = \iota(c)$, and
(iii) for any n-ary function symbol f ($n \geq 1$) and terms $t_1, \ldots, t_n$ in $\mathcal{T}(\Sigma, V)$, $\iota_\alpha(f(t_1, \ldots, t_n))$ is the term $\iota(f)(\iota_\alpha(t_1), \ldots, \iota_\alpha(t_n))$.

Let s and t be terms in $\mathcal{T}(\Sigma, V)$. Equation $s = t$ is *valid* in the algebra $\mathbb{A}$ under interpretation ι, notation $\mathbb{A}, \iota \models s = t$, if and only if, for all valuations $\alpha : V \to \mathbf{A}$, $\iota_\alpha(s) =_\mathbf{A} \iota_\alpha(t)$, where $=_\mathbf{A}$ is the identity on domain $\mathbf{A}$.

It is often clear from the context what interpretation from some given signature into some given algebra is meant; in such cases, the interpretation in the above notation for validity is usually omitted.

Example 2.3.7 (Validity) Consider equational theory T_1 of Example 2.2.5, the algebra $\mathbb{N} = (\mathbf{N}, +, \times, succ, 0)$ of natural numbers, and the interpretations ι_1 and ι_2 given in Example 2.3.5.

The equation $\mathbf{a}(x, y) = \mathbf{a}(y, x)$ is valid in the algebra $\mathbb{N}$ under both interpretations: $\mathbb{N}, \iota_1 \models \mathbf{a}(x, y) = \mathbf{a}(y, x)$ and $\mathbb{N}, \iota_2 \models \mathbf{a}(x, y) = \mathbf{a}(y, x)$ because both $m + n =_\mathbf{N} n + m$ and $m \times n =_\mathbf{N} n \times m$ are true for all natural numbers $m, n \in \mathbf{N}$.

On the other hand, the equation $\mathbf{a}(x, \mathbf{0}) = x$ (Axiom PA1 of the theory) is valid under interpretation ι_1, because $n + 0 =_\mathbf{N} n$ for all natural numbers $n \in \mathbf{N}$, but not valid under interpretation ι_2, since $n \times 0 =_\mathbf{N} n$ is not true in $\mathbb{N}$.

An algebra is said to be a *model* of an equational theory under some interpretation if and only if all axioms of the theory are valid in the algebra under that interpretation.

Definition 2.3.8 (Model) Let $T = (\Sigma, E)$ be an equational theory, $\mathbb{A}$ a Σ-algebra, and ι an interpretation of Σ into $\mathbb{A}$. Algebra $\mathbb{A}$ is a *model* of T with respect to interpretation ι, notation $\mathbb{A}, \iota \models T$ or $\mathbb{A}, \iota \models E$ (depending on what is most convenient), if and only if, for all equations $s = t \in E$, $\mathbb{A}, \iota \models s = t$. If $\mathbb{A}$ is a model of T it is also said that T is a *sound axiomatization* of $\mathbb{A}$.

Proposition 2.3.9 (Soundness) Let $T = (\Sigma, E)$ be an equational theory with model $\mathbb{A}$ under some interpretation ι. For all Σ-terms s and t,

$T \vdash s = t$ implies $\mathbb{A}, \iota \models s = t$.

Proof The property can be proven for derivations of arbitrary length via natural induction on the number of steps in a derivation. The details follow straightforwardly from Definitions 2.2.8 (Derivability) and 2.3.6 (Validity), and are therefore omitted. □

Example 2.3.10 (Models) Consider again the equational theory T_1 of Example 2.2.5, the algebra $\mathbb{N} = (\mathbf{N}, +, \times, succ, 0)$ of natural numbers, and the interpretations ι_1 and ι_2 given in Example 2.3.5. It is not difficult to verify that $\mathbb{N}$ is a model of T_1 under interpretation ι_1. However, it is not a model of T_1 under interpretation ι_2. Example 2.3.7 shows that Axiom PA1 is not valid under ι_2.

An equational theory usually has many models.

Example 2.3.11 (Models) Consider the following variant of the algebra of the Booleans of Example 2.3.2: $\mathbb{B}_1 = (\mathbf{B}, \wedge, \oplus, \neg, \mathit{false})$ where $\mathbf{B}$, *false*, $\neg$, and $\wedge$ are as in Example 2.3.2 and $\oplus$ is the binary *exclusive or* on Booleans. The exclusive or of two Boolean values evaluates to *true* if and only if precisely one of the two values equals *true*; that is, for $b_1, b_2 \in \mathbf{B}$, $b_1 \oplus b_2 =_{\mathbf{B}} \neg(b_1 \wedge b_2) \wedge \neg(\neg b_1 \wedge \neg b_2)$. Algebra $\mathbb{B}_1$ is a model of equational theory T_1 of Example 2.2.5 under the following interpretation:

$$\begin{aligned}
\mathbf{0} &\mapsto \mathit{false}\,, \\
\mathbf{s} &\mapsto \neg\,, \\
\mathbf{a} &\mapsto \oplus\,, \text{ and} \\
\mathbf{m} &\mapsto \wedge\,.
\end{aligned}$$

In order to prove that $\mathbb{B}_1$ is a model of T_1, it is necessary to show that Axioms PA1 through PA4 are valid in $\mathbb{B}_1$ under the above interpretation. Possible techniques are truth tables or Boolean algebra. The proof is left as Exercise 2.3.1.

It is also possible to obtain models of a theory by extending existing models. Adding elements to the domain of a model of a theory results in another model of the theory. This occurs, for example, in the context of extensions of an equational theory, as introduced in Definition 2.2.14 (Extension). The following corollary follows immediately from Definitions 2.2.14 and 2.3.8 (Model).

Corollary 2.3.12 (Extension) Let T_1 and T_2 be two equational theories such that T_2 is an extension of T_1. Any model $\mathbb{A}$ of T_2 is also a model of T_1, i.e., $\mathbb{A} \models T_2$ implies $\mathbb{A} \models T_1$.

Among all the models of an equational theory $T = (\Sigma, E)$, there is one special model, called the *initial algebra*, that validates precisely all equations of closed terms that are derivable from E. The initial algebra of an equational theory is an example of a so-called *quotient algebra*. To define the notion of a quotient algebra, some auxiliary definitions are needed.

Definition 2.3.13 (Equivalence) An equivalence relation on some universe of elements is a binary relation that is reflexive, symmetric, and transitive.

Example 2.3.14 (Equivalence) Let $T = (\Sigma, E)$ be some equational theory. Derivability as defined in Definition 2.2.8 is an equivalence on terms over signature Σ.

Definition 2.3.15 (Equivalence classes) Let U be some universe of elements and $\sim$ an equivalence relation on U. An *equivalence class* of an element is the set of all elements equivalent to that element: that is, for any element $u \in U$, the equivalence class of u, denoted $[u]_\sim$ is the set $\{v \in U \mid u \sim v\}$. Element u is said to be a *representative* of the equivalence class.

Definition 2.3.16 (Congruence) Let $\mathbb{A}$ be an algebra with universe of elements $\mathbf{A}$. A binary relation $\sim$ on $\mathbf{A}$ is a *congruence on* $\mathbb{A}$ if and only if it satisfies the following requirements:

(i) $\sim$ is an equivalence relation on $\mathbf{A}$ and,
(ii) for every n-ary ($n \geq 1$) function f of $\mathbb{A}$ and any elements $a_1, \ldots, a_n, b_1, \ldots, b_n \in \mathbf{A}$, $a_1 \sim b_1, \ldots, a_n \sim b_n$ implies that $f(a_1, \ldots, a_n) \sim f(b_1, \ldots, b_n)$.

Example 2.3.17 (Congruence) Let $T = (\Sigma, E)$ be some equational theory. The set of all Σ-terms $\mathcal{T}(\Sigma)$ forms an algebra with the constant and function symbols of Σ as its constants and functions (and the syntactical-identity relation $\equiv$ as the identity). It follows from the context rule in Definition 2.2.8 that derivability is a congruence on this term algebra.

Informally, Definition 2.3.16 states that, given some congruence on some algebra, equivalence classes of elements of the universe of the algebra can be constructed via the functions of the algebra independently of the representatives of the equivalence classes. This observation forms the basis of the following definition.

Definition 2.3.18 (Quotient algebra) Let $\mathbb{A}$ be an algebra and let $\sim$ be a congruence on $\mathbb{A}$. The *quotient* algebra $\mathbb{A}$ *modulo* $\sim$, notation $\mathbb{A}_{/\sim}$, has a universe consisting of the equivalence classes of $\mathbb{A}$ under $\sim$ and it has the following constants and functions:

(i) for each constant c of $\mathbb{A}$, $[c]_\sim$ is a constant of $\mathbb{A}_{/\sim}$;
(ii) for each n-ary function f of $\mathbb{A}$, $f_\sim$ is an n-ary function of $\mathbb{A}_{/\sim}$, where, for all $a_1, \ldots, a_n \in \mathbf{A}$,
$$f_\sim([a_1]_\sim, \ldots, [a_n]_\sim) = [f(a_1, \ldots, a_n)]_\sim.$$

An important example of a quotient algebra is the initial algebra of some given equational theory.

Definition 2.3.19 (Initial algebra) Let $T = (\Sigma, E)$ be an equational theory. Consider the algebra $\mathbb{C}(\Sigma)$ with the set $\mathcal{C}(\Sigma)$ of closed Σ-terms as its domain and the constant and function symbols of Σ as its functions and constants. Derivability is a congruence on the algebra $\mathbb{C}(\Sigma)$. The initial algebra of T, denoted $\mathbb{I}(\Sigma, E)$ is the quotient algebra $\mathbb{C}(\Sigma)$ modulo derivability.

Example 2.3.20 (Quotient/initial algebra) The elements in the domain of an initial algebra of an equational theory are sets of closed terms that are derivably equal. Consider, for example, equational theory $T_1 = (\Sigma_1, E_1)$ of Example 2.2.5. Examples of elements of the domain of $\mathbb{I}(\Sigma_1, E_1)$ are

$[\mathbf{0}]_\vdash = \{\mathbf{0}, \mathbf{a}(\mathbf{0}, \mathbf{0}), \mathbf{m}(\mathbf{0}, \mathbf{0}), \mathbf{m}(\mathbf{s}(\mathbf{0}), \mathbf{0}), \ldots\}$,
$[\mathbf{s}(\mathbf{0})]_\vdash = \{\mathbf{s}(\mathbf{0}), \mathbf{a}(\mathbf{s}(\mathbf{0}), \mathbf{0}), \mathbf{m}(\mathbf{s}(\mathbf{0}), \mathbf{s}(\mathbf{0})), \ldots\}$,
$[\mathbf{s}(\mathbf{s}(\mathbf{0}))]_\vdash = \{\mathbf{s}(\mathbf{s}(\mathbf{0})), \mathbf{a}(\mathbf{s}(\mathbf{0}), \mathbf{s}(\mathbf{0})), \mathbf{m}(\mathbf{s}(\mathbf{s}(\mathbf{0})), \mathbf{s}(\mathbf{0})), \ldots\}$,
et cetera.

Figure 2.2 visualizes the domain of $\mathbb{I}(\Sigma_1, E_1)$.

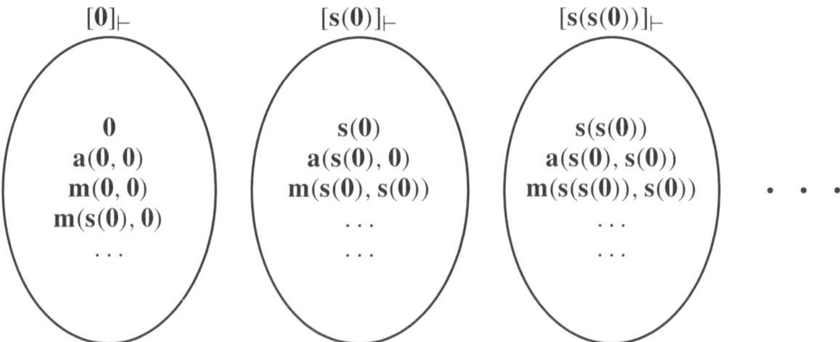

Fig. 2.2. The domain of the initial algebra of Example 2.3.20.

The constants in an initial algebra of an equational theory are the equivalence classes containing the constant symbols of the signature of the equational theory. The initial algebra $\mathbb{I}(\Sigma_1, E_1)$, for example, has one constant, namely $[\mathbf{0}]_\vdash$.

The functions in an initial algebra are obtained by lifting the function symbols in the signature of the equational theory to equivalence classes of derivably equal closed terms. Initial algebra $\mathbb{I}(\Sigma_1, E_1)$ has three functions, one unary function $\mathbf{s}_\vdash$ and two binary functions $\mathbf{a}_\vdash$ and $\mathbf{m}_\vdash$, that are defined as follows: for any closed Σ_1-terms p and q, $\mathbf{s}_\vdash([p]_\vdash) = [\mathbf{s}(p)]_\vdash$, $\mathbf{a}_\vdash([p]_\vdash, [q]_\vdash) = [\mathbf{a}(p, q)]_\vdash$, and $\mathbf{m}_\vdash([p]_\vdash, [q]_\vdash) = [\mathbf{m}(p, q)]_\vdash$.

Proposition 2.3.21 (Soundness) Let $T = (\Sigma, E)$ be an equational theory. The initial algebra $\mathbb{I}(\Sigma, E)$ is a model of T under the interpretation that maps any constant symbol c of Σ onto the equivalence class $[c]_\vdash$ and any function symbol f of Σ onto the corresponding function $f_\vdash$ as defined in Definition 2.3.18 (Quotient algebra).

Proof The property follows in a straightforward way from Definitions 2.2.8 (Derivability), 2.3.8 (Model), and 2.3.19 (Initial algebra). The details are illustrated by means of a concrete example.

Consider the equational theory $T_1 = (\Sigma_1, E_1)$. According to Definition 2.3.8 (Model), it must be shown that all axioms in E_1 are valid in the initial algebra $\mathbb{I}(\Sigma_1, E_1)$ under the interpretation ι defined above. Consider Axiom PA1: $\mathbf{a}(x, \mathbf{0}) = x$. To prove that PA1 is valid (see Definition 2.3.6 (Validity)), consider the valuation α that maps x to equivalence class $[p]_\vdash$ for some arbitrary closed Σ_1-term p. It must be shown that $\iota_\alpha(\mathbf{a}(x, \mathbf{0})) = \iota_\alpha(x)$.

The various definitions given so far imply that $\iota_\alpha(\mathbf{a}(x, \mathbf{0})) = \mathbf{a}_\vdash([p]_\vdash, [\mathbf{0}]_\vdash)$ $= [\mathbf{a}(p, \mathbf{0})]_\vdash$ and $\iota_\alpha(x) = [p]_\vdash$. It follows from the axiom rule and the substitution rule in Definition 2.2.8 (Derivability) that $T_1 \vdash \mathbf{a}(p, \mathbf{0}) = p$. Thus, Definition 2.3.19 (Initial algebra) yields that $[\mathbf{a}(p, \mathbf{0})]_\vdash = [p]_\vdash$, proving the desired property. □

As already mentioned, the initial algebra of an equational theory is a particularly interesting model of the theory because it precisely validates all the equations of closed terms that are derivable from the axioms of the theory. This property is called ground-completeness. Since an equational theory has a standard interpretation into its initial algebra (see Proposition 2.3.21), for convenience, this interpretation is often not explicitly mentioned and it is omitted in the notations for validity and soundness.

Proposition 2.3.22 (Ground-completeness) Let $T = (\Sigma, E)$ be an equational theory. For all *closed* Σ-terms p and q,

$\mathbb{I}(\Sigma, E) \models p = q$ implies $T \vdash p = q$.

Proof The property follows from Definitions 2.3.6 (Validity) and 2.3.19 (Initial algebra). Assume that $\mathbb{I}(\Sigma, E) \models p = q$, for closed Σ-terms p and q. It follows that $[p]_\vdash = [q]_\vdash$, which implies that $T \vdash p = q$. □

Ground-completeness of a model of some theory is an interesting property because it implies that the model does not validate any equations *of closed terms* that are not also derivable from the theory. The initial algebra of an equational theory is ground-complete for that theory by definition. However, ground-completeness is not necessarily restricted to the initial algebra of an equational theory; other models of the theory may also satisfy this property.

Definition 2.3.23 (Ground-completeness) Let $T = (\Sigma, E)$ be an equational theory with model $\mathbb{A}$ under some interpretation ι. Theory T is said to be a *ground-complete axiomatization* of model $\mathbb{A}$ if and only if, for all *closed* Σ-terms p and q,

$\mathbb{A}, \iota \models p = q$ implies $T \vdash p = q$.

Alternatively, it is said that model $\mathbb{A}$ is ground-complete for theory T.

The definition of ground-completeness is restricted to equations of *closed* terms. Of course, the property may also hold for equations of arbitrary open terms, in which case it is simply referred to as completeness.

Definition 2.3.24 (Completeness) Let $T = (\Sigma, E)$ be an equational theory with model $\mathbb{A}$ under some interpretation ι. Theory T is said to be a *complete axiomatization* of model $\mathbb{A}$ if and only if, for all *open* Σ-terms s and t,

$\mathbb{A}, \iota \models s = t$ implies $T \vdash s = t$.

It is also said that model $\mathbb{A}$ is complete for theory T.

Unfortunately, general completeness often turns out to be much more difficult to achieve than ground-completeness. Therefore, this book focuses on ground-completeness.

Example 2.3.25 (Completeness) Consider equational theory $T_1 = (\Sigma_1, E_1)$ of Example 2.2.5 and its initial algebra $\mathbb{I}(\Sigma_1, E_1)$. It has already been shown that the initial algebra is ground-complete. However, it is not complete for open terms. Consider, for example, the equation $\mathbf{a}(x, y) = \mathbf{a}(y, x)$ for variables x and y. This equation is valid in the initial algebra, $\mathbb{I}(\Sigma_1, E_1) \models \mathbf{a}(x, y) = \mathbf{a}(y, x)$, but it is not derivable; that is $T_1 \vdash \mathbf{a}(x, y) = \mathbf{a}(y, x)$ is not true. The proof of the former is left as Exercise 2.3.4. The latter can be shown by giving a model that does not validate $\mathbf{a}(x, y) = \mathbf{a}(y, x)$; if such a model exists, it follows from Proposition 2.3.9 (Soundness) that the equation cannot be derivable. Exercise 2.3.5 asks for a model of T_1 that does not validate $\mathbf{a}(x, y) = \mathbf{a}(y, x)$.

The notions of ground-completeness and completeness refer to a specific model of the theory under consideration. As a final remark concerning notions of completeness, it is interesting to observe that it is also possible to define a model-independent notion of completeness for equational theories. A theory is said to be ω-complete if and only if it is a complete axiomatization of its initial algebra. Although this definition refers to a model, namely the initial algebra, it can be considered model-independent because the initial algebra of an equational theory is constructed in a standard way from the theory. An equivalent formulation of ω-completeness is the following: an equational theory is ω-complete if and only if an equation of arbitrary open terms is derivable when all closed-term equations obtainable from it through substitutions are derivable.

The property of ω-completeness implies that all relevant equations are fully captured by derivability. Our example theory T_1 is not ω-complete. This follows immediately from Example 2.3.25 that shows that it is not complete with respect to its initial algebra. Despite the elegance implied by the property of ω-completeness, it is not considered in the remainder of this book, and therefore the definition is not stated formally. It is often not straightforward to obtain ω-completeness.

So far, three models have been given for the example theory $T_1 = (\Sigma_1, E_1)$ of Example 2.2.5, namely the algebra of the naturals of Example 2.3.10, the algebra of the Booleans of Example 2.3.11, and the initial algebra of Example 2.3.20. This raises the question whether these models are really different.

Definition 2.3.26 (Isomorphism of algebras) Let $\mathbb{A}_1$ and $\mathbb{A}_2$ be two algebras with domains $\mathbf{A}_1$ and $\mathbf{A}_2$, respectively. Algebras $\mathbb{A}_1$ and $\mathbb{A}_2$ are *isomorphic* if and only if there exists a bijective function $\phi : \mathbf{A}_1 \to \mathbf{A}_2$ and another bijective function ψ that maps the constants and functions of $\mathbb{A}_1$ onto those of $\mathbb{A}_2$ such that

(i) for any constant c of $\mathbb{A}_1$, $\phi(c) = \psi(c)$, and
(ii) for any n-ary ($n \geq 1$) function f of $\mathbb{A}_1$ and any elements $a_1, \ldots, a_n \in \mathbf{A}_1$, $\phi(f(a_1, \ldots, a_n)) = \psi(f)(\phi(a_1), \ldots, \phi(a_n))$.

Example 2.3.27 (Isomorphism) Consider again theory $T_1 = (\Sigma_1, E_1)$ of Example 2.2.5 and its models, namely the algebra $\mathbb{N}$ of Example 2.3.10, the algebra $\mathbb{B}_1$ of Example 2.3.11, and the initial algebra $\mathbb{I}(\Sigma_1, E_1)$ of Example 2.3.20. The algebras $\mathbb{N}$ and $\mathbb{I}(\Sigma_1, E_1)$ are isomorphic (see Exercise 2.3.6). Clearly, the algebra $\mathbb{B}_1$ is not isomorphic to the other two, because its domain has only two elements whereas the domains of the other two algebras have infinitely many elements.

Usually, algebras, and in particular models of equational theories, that are isomorphic are not distinguished. Thus, the algebra of the naturals $\mathbb{N}$ of Example 2.3.10 may be referred to as the initial algebra of the equational theory $T_1 = (\Sigma_1, E_1)$ of Example 2.2.5.

Exercises

2.3.1 Consider Example 2.3.11 (Models). Show that algebra $\mathbb{B}_1$ is a model of theory T_1.

2.3.2 Verify that $\mathbb{B}_1 \models \mathbf{s}(\mathbf{m}(x, y)) = \mathbf{a}(\mathbf{a}(\mathbf{s}(x), \mathbf{s}(y)), \mathbf{m}(\mathbf{s}(x), \mathbf{s}(y)))$ for algebra $\mathbb{B}_1$ of Example 2.3.11. Does this formula also hold in algebra $\mathbb{N}$ of Example 2.3.10?

2.3.3 Consider the algebra of natural numbers $(\mathbf{N}, +, \times, exp, succ, 0)$ that extends the algebra of Example 2.3.3 with the exponentiation function *exp*. Show that this algebra is a model of theory T_2 of Example 2.2.15.

2.3.4 Consider equational theory $T_1 = (\Sigma_1, E_1)$ of Example 2.2.5 and its initial algebra $\mathbb{I}(\Sigma_1, E_1)$ of Example 2.3.20. Show that $\mathbb{I}(\Sigma_1, E_1) \models \mathbf{a}(x, y) = \mathbf{a}(y, x)$, for variables x and y.
(Hint: use property (2.2.5) and Proposition 2.2.17 (Conservative extension).)

2.3.5 Consider again equational theory $T_1 = (\Sigma_1, E_1)$ of Example 2.2.5. Give a model that does not validate the equation $\mathbf{a}(x, y) = \mathbf{a}(y, x)$, for variables x and y.
(Hint: consider an algebra where the domain consists of two elements and map the **a** function symbol onto a projection function that gives for each pair of elements the first element of the pair.)

2.3.6 Consider the algebras $\mathbb{N}$ of Example 2.3.10 and $\mathbb{I}(\Sigma_1, E_1)$ of Example 2.3.20 (the initial algebra of theory $T_1 = (\Sigma_1, E_1)$ of Example 2.2.5). Show that the two algebras are isomorphic.

2.3.7 Show that the intersection of any number of congruences is again a congruence.

2.3.8 Let $T = (\Sigma, E)$ be an equational theory. Consider the algebra of closed terms $\mathbb{C}(\Sigma)$ as introduced in Definition 2.3.19 (Initial algebra). Let $\sim$ be the intersection of all congruence relations R on $\mathbb{C}(\Sigma)$ such that $\mathbb{C}(\Sigma)_{/R} \models E$. Show that $\sim$ coincides with derivability (which implies that $\mathbb{C}(\Sigma)_{/\sim}$ is isomorphic to the initial algebra $\mathbb{I}(\Sigma, E)$).

2.4 Term rewriting systems

Although equality in an equational theory is a symmetric relation, often the equations have an implied direction. This is already the case in primary school, where $2 + 2$ is to be replaced by 4, and not the other way around. Direction in an equational theory is formalized by the notion of a term rewriting system. Term rewriting systems can also be useful in proofs, as a proof technique.

Definition 2.4.1 (Term rewriting system) A *term rewriting system* is a tuple (Σ, R), where Σ is a signature and R is a set of rewrite rules. Let V be some set of variables. A rewrite rule is a pair (t_1, t_2) of terms over the signature Σ $(t_1, t_2 \in \mathcal{T}(\Sigma, V))$ such that t_1 is not just a variable in V and such that every variable that occurs in t_2 also occurs in t_1. Usually, a rewrite rule (t_1, t_2) is written $t_1 \to t_2$.

Example 2.4.2 (Term rewriting system) Consider again Example 2.2.5 and equational theory T_1 of Table 2.1. Consider the following derivation (showing that '2+2 = 4'):

$$\begin{aligned}&\mathbf{a}(\mathbf{s}(\mathbf{s}(\mathbf{0})), \mathbf{s}(\mathbf{s}(\mathbf{0}))) = \\ &\mathbf{s}(\mathbf{a}(\mathbf{s}(\mathbf{s}(\mathbf{0})), \mathbf{s}(\mathbf{0}))) = \\ &\mathbf{s}(\mathbf{s}(\mathbf{a}(\mathbf{s}(\mathbf{s}(\mathbf{0})), \mathbf{0}))) = \\ &\mathbf{s}(\mathbf{s}(\mathbf{s}(\mathbf{s}(\mathbf{0})))).\end{aligned}$$

As already mentioned, the equations of the equational theory in Table 2.1 appear to have a certain *direction* when applied in this derivation: when read from left to right they simplify terms; they *reduce* them. Writing $\to$ instead of $=$, the term rewriting system of Table 2.3 is obtained.

TRS_1		
constant: **0**;	unary: **s**;	binary: **a**, **m**;
x, y;		
$\mathbf{a}(x, \mathbf{0})$	$\to$	x
$\mathbf{a}(x, \mathbf{s}(y))$	$\to$	$\mathbf{s}(\mathbf{a}(x, y))$
$\mathbf{m}(x, \mathbf{0})$	$\to$	$\mathbf{0}$
$\mathbf{m}(x, \mathbf{s}(y))$	$\to$	$\mathbf{a}(\mathbf{m}(x, y), x)$

Table 2.3. The term rewriting system $TRS_1 = (\Sigma_1, R_1)$.

Definition 2.4.3 (One-step reduction relation) Let (Σ, R) be a term rewriting system and V some set of variables. The *one-step reduction* relation $\mapsto$ on terms in $\mathcal{T}(\Sigma, V)$ is the smallest relation that satisfies the following:

(i) $R \subseteq \mapsto$,
(ii) for any terms $s, t \in \mathcal{T}(\Sigma, V)$ and substitution $\sigma : V \to \mathcal{T}(\Sigma, V)$, $s \mapsto t$ implies $s[\sigma] \mapsto t[\sigma]$, and
(iii) for any n-ary function symbol $f \in \Sigma$, terms $s, t_1, \ldots, t_n \in \mathcal{T}(\Sigma, V)$, and natural number i such that $1 \leq i \leq n$, $t_i \mapsto s$ implies $f(t_1, \ldots, t_{i-1}, t_i, t_{i+1}, \ldots, t_n) \mapsto f(t_1, \ldots, t_{i-1}, s, t_{i+1}, \ldots, t_n)$.

Definition 2.4.4 (Reduction relation) Let (Σ, R) be a term rewriting system. The *reduction relation* $\mapsto\!\!\!\rightarrow$ on Σ-terms is the reflexive and transitive closure of the one-step reduction relation; that is, $\mapsto\!\!\!\rightarrow$ is the smallest relation that satisfies:

(i) $\mapsto \subseteq \mapsto\!\!\!\rightarrow$,
(ii) $\mapsto\!\!\!\rightarrow$ is reflexive, and
(iii) $\mapsto\!\!\!\rightarrow$ is transitive.

Note that the reduction relation of Definition 2.4.4 is very similar to derivability as defined in Definition 2.2.8. The only difference is that derivability is symmetric whereas reduction is not. This means that an equational theory can be interpreted as a term rewriting system by giving direction to the essentially undirected equations of the theory.

Definition 2.4.5 (Normal form) Let Σ be a signature and let t be a Σ-term. Term t is a *normal form* with respect to a term rewriting system (Σ, R) if and only if there is no Σ-term s such that $t \mapsto s$. Alternatively, such a term is said to be *in normal form*.

Term t *has a normal form* if and only if there is a normal form s such that $t \mapsto\!\!\!\rightarrow s$.

The goal of a term rewriting system is often to rewrite some term to obtain a result that is as simple as possible. Thus, it is a desirable property of such a term rewriting system that every term has a, preferably unique, normal form. The term rewriting system TRS_1 just presented has this property.

Definition 2.4.6 (Strong normalization) A term rewriting system (Σ, R) is *strongly normalizing* if and only if no Σ-term t allows an infinite sequence of reductions $t \mapsto t_1 \mapsto t_2 \mapsto \cdots$ (with $t_1, t_2, \ldots \in \mathcal{T}(\Sigma)$).

Definition 2.4.7 (Confluence) A term rewriting system (Σ, R) is *confluent* if and only if, for all Σ-terms t_1, t_2, and t_3, if $t_1 \mapsto\!\!\!\rightarrow t_2$ and $t_1 \mapsto\!\!\!\rightarrow t_3$, then there exists a Σ-term t_4 such that $t_2 \mapsto\!\!\!\rightarrow t_4$ and $t_3 \mapsto\!\!\!\rightarrow t_4$.

The following theorem is a standard result in the theory of term rewriting systems, see e.g., (Klop, 1987).

Theorem 2.4.8 (Unique normal forms) Let $T = (\Sigma, R)$ be a term rewriting system. If T is strongly normalizing and confluent, then every term has a unique normal form.

A given term rewriting system can be turned into an equational theory by replacing every $\rightarrow$ symbol in its set of rewrite rules by the $=$ symbol. If the term rewriting system is strongly normalizing and confluent, the following is a decision procedure to establish derivability between two terms. First, reduce both terms to their normal forms. Since the term rewriting system is strongly normalizing, this can be achieved. Then, if the resulting normal forms are identical, the terms are derivably equal; if they are not, the terms are definitely not derivably equal. This is guaranteed by the fact that the term rewriting system has the property of unicity of normal forms.

Unfortunately, it is not possible to associate a strongly normalizing and confluent term rewriting system with every equational theory. The reason for this is that equality is not always decidable. This undecidability result is well-known as Gödel's incompleteness theorem. For more details, see e.g., (Van Heijenoort, 1967).

In some cases, some of the equations of an equational theory can readily be turned into rewrite rules, but others have no clear direction (such as axioms expressing the commutativity or associativity of an operator). Then, it may be useful to rewrite *modulo* these undirected equations, i.e., to rewrite not just single terms, but equivalence classes of terms. The details are beyond the scope of this book. The interested reader is referred to (Jouannaud & Muñoz, 1984).

Exercises

2.4.1 Prove for the term rewriting system in Table 2.3 that

$$\mathbf{m}(\mathbf{s}(\mathbf{s}(\mathbf{s}(\mathbf{0}))), \mathbf{s}(\mathbf{s}(\mathbf{0}))) \twoheadrightarrow \mathbf{s}(\mathbf{s}(\mathbf{s}(\mathbf{s}(\mathbf{s}(\mathbf{s}(\mathbf{0})))))).$$

2.4.2 Prove that the closed normal forms for the term rewriting system in Table 2.3 are the terms of the form $\mathbf{s}^n(\mathbf{0})$ (with $n \in \mathbf{N}$).

2.4.3 Consider the term rewriting system *Cnf* in Table 2.4. The reduction rules are given in infix notation, leaving out many brackets. Reduce the term $\neg(x \wedge \neg y) \wedge z$ to normal form. Notice that the normal forms of this term rewriting system are known in propositional logic as *conjunctive normal forms*.

2.4.4 Prove that the term rewriting system with the one rule

$$f(f(x)) \to f(g(f(x)))$$

is strongly normalizing.

2.4.5 Is the term rewriting system with the one rule

$$f(g(x, y)) \to g(g(f(f(x)), y), y)$$

strongly normalizing?

Cnf	
unary: $\neg$;	binary: $\vee$, $\wedge$;
x, y, z;	

$$\begin{array}{lcl}
\neg\neg x & \to & x \\
\neg(x \vee y) & \to & \neg x \wedge \neg y \\
\neg(x \wedge y) & \to & \neg x \vee \neg y \\
x \vee (y \wedge z) & \to & (x \vee y) \wedge (x \vee z) \\
(x \wedge y) \vee z & \to & (x \vee z) \wedge (y \vee z)
\end{array}$$

Table 2.4. Conjunctive normal forms.

2.5 Bibliographical remarks

This chapter gives an introduction to equational theories and their models. This is standard in universal algebra, see e.g., (Burris & Sankappanavar, 1981). The present presentation stems from (Klop, 1987), and was successively adapted in (Baeten, 1986) and (Baeten & Weijland, 1990).

In this book, it is made explicit when certain notions apply to ground terms only: thus, an axiomatization is called ground-complete if and only if all equations that hold in the model between closed terms can be derived from the axioms, and a conservative ground-extension preserves all equations between closed terms only. The notion of ground-extension deviates in one important aspect from the standard definition of an equational extension (Definition 2.2.14). Following (Mousavi & Reniers, 2005), it is not required that all axioms of the base theory are contained in the extended theory. This relaxation does not change the essence of the extension concept and the related conservativity notion, but it is convenient when for example considering extensions with time (Chapter 9). For further motivation and details, see (Mousavi & Reniers, 2005; Baeten *et al.*, 2005).

The section on term rewriting systems is mostly based on (Klop, 1987).

3

Transition systems

3.1 Transition-system spaces

This chapter introduces the semantic domain that is used throughout this book. The goal is to model reactive systems; the most important feature of such systems is the interaction between a system and its environment. To describe such systems, the well-known domain of *transition systems*, *process graphs*, or *automata* is chosen. In fact, it is the domain of non-deterministic (finite) automata known from formal language theory. An automaton models a system in terms of its states and the transitions that lead from one state to another state; transitions are labeled with the actions causing the state change. An automaton is said to describe the *operational* behavior of a system. An important observation is that, since the subject of study is interacting systems, not just the language generated by an automaton is important, but also the states traversed during a run or execution of the automaton. The term 'transition system' is the term most often used in reactive-systems modeling. Thus, also this book uses that term.

The semantic domain serves as the basis for the remainder of the book. The meaning of the various equational theories for reasoning about reactive systems developed in the remaining chapters is defined in terms of the semantic domain, in the way explained in the previous chapter. Technically, it turns out to be useful to embed all transition systems that are of interest in one large set of states and transitions, from which the individual transition systems can be extracted. Such a large set of states and transitions is called a *transition-system space*.

Definition 3.1.1 (Transition-system space) A *transition-system space* over a set of labels L is a set S of *states*, equipped with one ternary relation $\rightarrow$ and one subset $\downarrow$:

(i) $\rightarrow \subseteq S \times L \times S$ is the set of *transitions*;
(ii) $\downarrow \subseteq S$ is the set of *terminating* or *final* states.

The notation $s \overset{a}{\rightarrow} t$ is used for $(s, a, t) \in \rightarrow$. It is said that s has an a-step to t. Notation $s\downarrow$ is used for $s \in \downarrow$, and it is often said that s has a (successful) termination option; $s \notin \downarrow$ is denoted $s\not\downarrow$. The fact that for all states $t \in S$, it holds that $(s, a, t) \notin \rightarrow$, is abbreviated as $s \overset{a}{\nrightarrow}$. It is also said that s does not have an a-step.

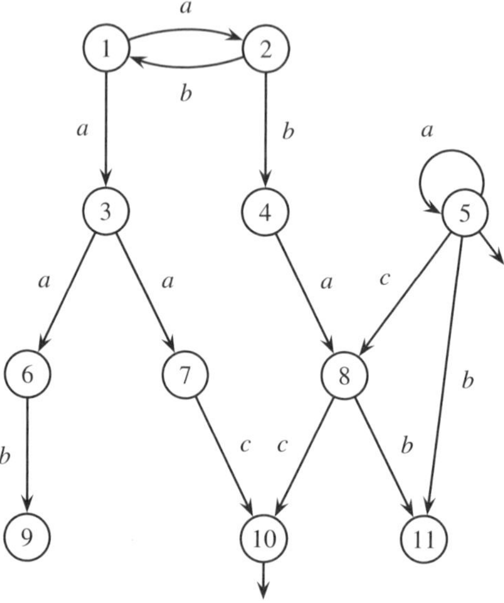

Fig. 3.1. An example of a transition-system space.

Example 3.1.2 (Transition-system space) Consider Figure 3.1. It visualizes a transition-system space with eleven states, depicted by circles. Terminating states are marked with a small outgoing arrow. Transitions are visualized by labeled arrows connecting two states.

In the remainder, assume that $(S, L, \rightarrow, \downarrow)$ is a transition-system space. Each state $s \in S$ can be identified with a transition system that consists of all states and transitions reachable from s. The notion of reachability is defined by generalizing the transition relation to sequences of labels, called words. The set of all words consisting of symbols from some set A is denoted A^*.

Definition 3.1.3 (Reachability) The reachability relation $\rightarrow^* \subseteq S \times L^* \times S$ is defined inductively by the following clauses:

(i) $s \xrightarrow{\epsilon}{}^* s$ for each $s \in S$, where $\epsilon \in L^*$ denotes the empty word;
(ii) for all $s, t, u \in S, \sigma \in L^*$, and $a \in L$, if $s \xrightarrow{\sigma}{}^* t$ and $t \xrightarrow{a} u$, then $s \xrightarrow{\sigma a}{}^* u$, where σa is the word obtained by appending a at the end of σ.

A state $t \in S$ is said to be *reachable* from state $s \in S$ if and only if there is a word $\sigma \in L^*$ such that $s \xrightarrow{\sigma}{}^* t$.

Example 3.1.4 (Reachability) Consider the transition-system space of Figure 3.1. From states 1 and 2, all states except state 5 are reachable; from state 3, states 3, 6, 7, 9, and 10 are reachable, et cetera.

Definition 3.1.5 (Transition system) For each state $s \in S$, the *transition system* induced by s consists of all states reachable from s, and it has the transitions and final states induced by the transition-system space. State s is called the *initial state* or *root* of the transition system associated with s. Note that often the terminology 'transition system s' is used to refer to the transition system *induced* by s.

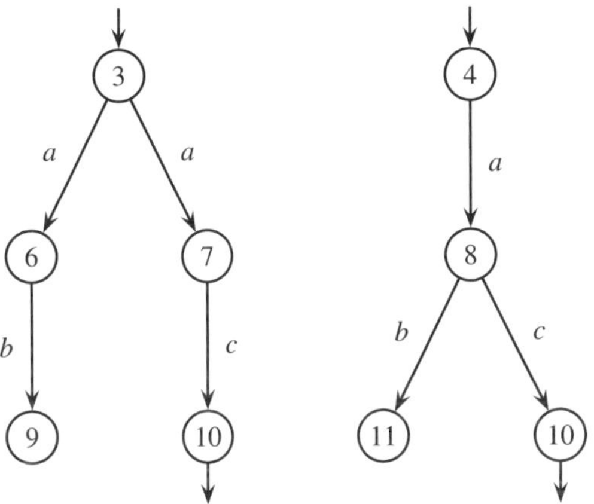

Fig. 3.2. Examples of simple transition systems.

Example 3.1.6 (Transition systems) Consider again Figure 3.1. The transition system with root state 3 consists of states 3, 6, 7, 9, and 10. Taking state 4 as the root yields a transition system consisting of states 4, 8, 10, and 11. Figure 3.2 visualizes these two transition systems; the root states are marked with small incoming arrows. The states are rearranged slightly to emphasize the similarity between the two transition systems.

It follows from the above definitions that the notion of a transition system coincides with the classical notion of an automaton. The classical notion of language equivalence on automata says that two automata are equivalent if and only if they have the same *runs* from the initial state to a final state.

Definition 3.1.7 (Run, language equivalence) A word $\sigma \in L^*$ is a *complete execution* or *run* of a transition system $s \in S$ if and only if there is some $t \in S$ with $s \xrightarrow{\sigma}^* t$ and $t\downarrow$.

Two transition systems are language equivalent if and only if they have the same set of runs.

Example 3.1.8 (Language equivalence) Consider once more the two transition systems depicted in Figure 3.2. Both transition systems have only one run, namely ac. The two systems are thus language equivalent. Note that ab is not a run of any of the two transition systems because states 9 and 11 are non-terminating.

Language equivalence turns out to be insufficient for our purposes. Since interaction of automata is considered, there is a need to consider all states of an automaton, not just the complete runs. This can be illustrated with Frank Stockton's story 'The Lady or the Tiger?' (see (Smullyan, 1982)).

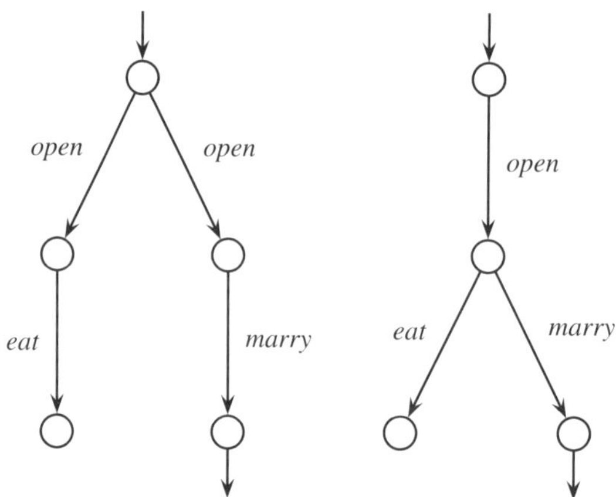

Fig. 3.3. The lady or the tiger?

Example 3.1.9 (The lady or the tiger?) A prisoner is confronted with two closed doors. Behind one of the doors is a dangerous tiger, and behind the other there is a beautiful lady. If the prisoner opens the door hiding the tiger he will be eaten. On the other hand, if he opens the door hiding the beautiful lady, the lady and he will get married and he will be free. Unfortunately, the prisoner does not know what hides behind what door.

This situation can be described as a transition system using the following actions:

(i) *open* representing the act of opening a door;
(ii) *eat* representing the act of (the tiger) eating the young man;
(iii) *marry* representing the act of the beautiful lady and the prisoner getting married.

The situation described above can be modeled by the left transition system depicted in Figure 3.3. This transition system models the fact that after a door has been opened the prisoner is confronted with either the tiger or the beautiful lady. He does not have the possibility to select his favorite, which conforms to the description above. The observant reader might notice the similarity with the left transition system of Figure 3.2. Note the subtle fact that transition *marry* ends in a terminating state, whereas transition *eat* does not. This can be interpreted to mean that the *marry* transition results in a *successful* termination of the process, and that the *eat* transition results in *unsuccessful* termination. A non-terminating state in which no actions are possible, such as the state resulting from the *eat* transition, is often called a *deadlock* state (see also Definition 3.1.14).

One might wonder whether the same process cannot be described by the slightly simpler transition system on the right of Figure 3.3, which strongly resembles the right transition system in Figure 3.2. However, there are good reasons why the situation modeled by the right transition system of Figure 3.3 is different from the situation described by the other transition system in that figure. In the right transition system, the choice between the tiger and the lady is only made after opening a door. It either describes a situation with only one door leading to both the tiger and the lady or a situation with two doors both leading to both the tiger and the lady; in either case, the prisoner still has a choice after opening a door. Clearly, these situations differ considerably from the situation described above.

The above example illustrates that there are good reasons to distinguish the two transition systems of Figure 3.2. Example 3.1.8 shows that these two transition systems are language equivalent, thus confirming the earlier remark that language equivalence does not suit our purposes. It does not in all cases distinguish transition systems that clearly model different situations. Two aspects are not sufficiently taken into account. First, two transition systems that are language equivalent may have completely different sets of ‘runs’ that end in a non-terminating state. As explained in the above example, terminating and non-terminating states may be used to model successful and unsuccessful termination of a process, respectively. In such cases, it is desirable to distinguish transition systems that have the same sets of runs ending in terminating states but that differ in executions leading to non-terminating states. Second, language equivalence does not distinguish transition systems that have the same runs but that are different in the moments that *choices* are made. To illustrate this, consider again the transition system on the right-hand side of Figure 3.2. It has a state in which both b and c are possible as the following action (state 8), whereas the system on the left only has states where exactly one of the two is possible (states 6 and 7). Thus, if for some reason action c is impossible, is blocked, then the transition system on the left can become stuck after the execution of an a action, whereas the one on the right cannot. The choice whether or not to execute b or c in the left transition system is made (implicitly) upon execution of the a action in the initial state, whereas the same choice is made only after execution of the initial a action in the right transition system. It is said that the transition systems have different *branching structure*.

A choice between alternatives that are initially identical, as in state 3 of the leftmost transition system of Figure 3.2, is called a *non-deterministic* choice. Such choices are the subject of many investigations in the theory of concurrency. A detailed treatment of non-determinism is beyond the scope of this book.

It is often desirable to be able to distinguish between transition systems with the same runs that have different termination behavior or that have different branching structure. In order to do this, a notion of equivalence is defined that is finer than language equivalence, in the sense that it distinguishes transition systems accepting the same language but with different termination behavior or branching structure. This notion is called bisimilarity or bisimulation equivalence.

Definition 3.1.10 (Bisimilarity) A binary relation R on the set of states S of a transition-system space is a *bisimulation* relation if and only if the following so-called *transfer conditions* hold:

(i) for all states $s, t, s' \in S$, whenever $(s, t) \in R$ and $s \xrightarrow{a} s'$ for some $a \in L$, then there is a state t' such that $t \xrightarrow{a} t'$ and $(s', t') \in R$;

(ii) vice versa, for all states $s, t, t' \in S$, whenever $(s, t) \in R$ and $t \xrightarrow{a} t'$ for some $a \in L$, then there is a state s' such that $s \xrightarrow{a} s'$ and $(s', t') \in R$;

(iii) whenever $(s, t) \in R$ and $s\downarrow$ then $t\downarrow$;

(iv) whenever $(s, t) \in R$ and $t\downarrow$ then $s\downarrow$.

The transfer conditions are illustrated in Figures 3.4 and 3.5. These figures show the transition systems starting from s and t as consisting of disjoint sets of states, but this is just done for clarity; it is possible that states are shared.

Two transition systems $s, t \in S$ are *bisimulation equivalent* or *bisimilar*, notation $s \leftrightarrow t$, if and only if there is a bisimulation relation R on S with $(s, t) \in R$.

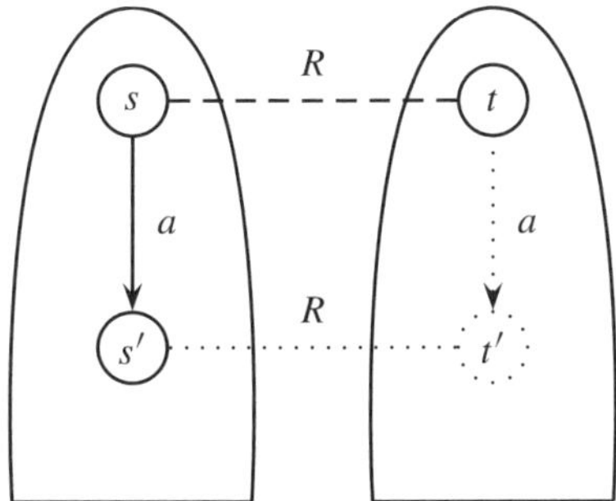

Fig. 3.4. Transfer condition (i) of a bisimulation.

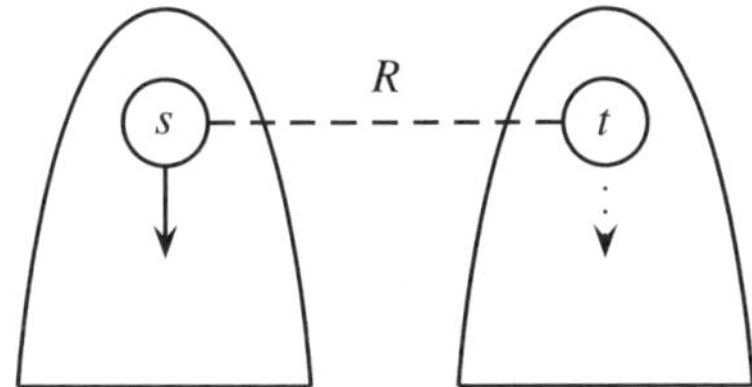

Fig. 3.5. Transfer condition (iii) of a bisimulation.

One can think of the notion of bisimilarity in terms of a two-person game. Suppose two players each have their own behavior, captured in the form of a transition system. The game is played as follows. First, one of the players makes a transition or move from the initial state of his or her transition system. The role of the other player is to match this move precisely, also starting from the initial state. Next, again one of the players makes a move. This does not have to be the same player as the one that made the first move. The other must try to match this move, and so on. If both players can play in such a way that at each point in the game any move by one of the players can be matched by a move of the other player, then the transition systems are bisimilar. Otherwise, they are not.

Example 3.1.11 (Bisimilarity) In Figure 3.6, an example of a bisimulation relation on transition systems is given. (Note that, technically, the two transition systems are embedded in one transition-system space.) Related states are connected by a dashed line. Since the initial states of the two transition systems are related, they are bisimilar.

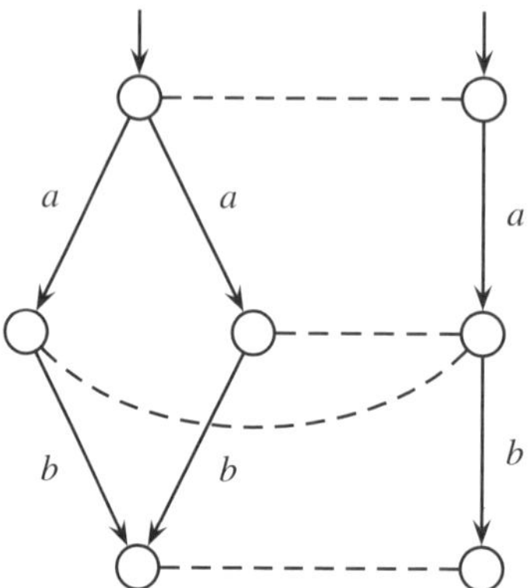

Fig. 3.6. Example of a bisimulation.

Example 3.1.12 (Bisimilarity) Figure 3.7 recalls two by now well-known transition systems. It should not come as a surprise that they are not bisimilar. States that can possibly be related are connected by a dashed line. The states where the behaviors of the two systems differ are indicated by dotted lines labeled with a question mark. None of the two indicated pairs of states satisfies the transfer conditions of Definition 3.1.10 (Bisimilarity).

So far, bisimilarity is just a relation on transition systems. However, it has already been mentioned that it is meant to serve as a notion of equality. For that purpose, it is necessary that bisimilarity is an equivalence relation. It is not difficult to show that bisimilarity is indeed an equivalence relation.

Theorem 3.1.13 (Equivalence) Bisimilarity is an equivalence.

Proof Let S be the set of states of a transition-system space. Proving that a relation is an equivalence means that it must be shown that it is reflexive, symmetric, and transitive. First, it is not hard to see that the relation $R = \{(s, s) \mid s \in S\}$ is a bisimulation relation. This implies that $s \leftrightarrow s$ for any (transition system induced by) state $s \in S$. Second, assume that $s \leftrightarrow t$ for states $s, t \in S$. If R is a bisimulation relation such that $(s, t) \in R$, then the relation

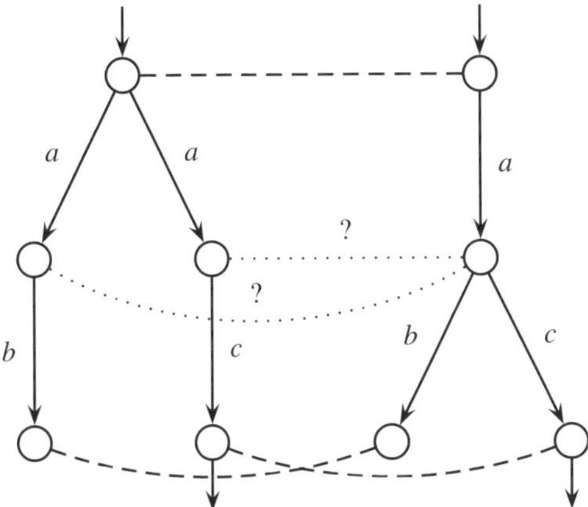

Fig. 3.7. Two transition systems that are not bisimilar.

$R' = \{(v, u) \mid (u, v) \in R\}$ is a bisimulation relation as well. Moreover, as $(s, t) \in R$, obviously $(t, s) \in R'$. Hence, $t \leftrightarrow s$, proving symmetry of $\leftrightarrow$. Finally, for transitivity of $\leftrightarrow$, it must be shown that the relation composition of two bisimulation relations results in a bisimulation relation again. Let s, t, and u be states in S, and let R_1 and R_2 be bisimulation relations with $(s, t) \in R_1$ and $(t, u) \in R_2$. The relation composition $R_1 \circ R_2$ is a bisimulation with $(s, u) \in R_1 \circ R_2$, implying transitivity of $\leftrightarrow$. The detailed proof is left as an exercise to the reader (Exercise 3.1.6). □

The discussion leading from the notion of language equivalence to the introduction of bisimilarity is illustrative for a more general problem. When designing a semantic framework based on transition systems, one has to choose a meaningful equivalence on transition systems. The question of what equivalence is most suitable depends on the context and is often difficult to answer. In fact, the question is considered so important that it has generated its own field of research, called comparative concurrency semantics. In Chapter 12, the problem of choosing an appropriate equivalence is investigated in more detail. In the other chapters of this book, bisimilarity serves as the main semantic equivalence.

To end this section, several relevant subclasses of transition systems are defined.

Definition 3.1.14 (Deadlock) A state s of a transition system as defined in Definition 3.1.5 (Transition system) is a *deadlock state* if and only if it does not have any outgoing transitions and it does not allow successful termination, i.e., if and only if for all $a \in L$, $s \stackrel{a}{\nrightarrow}$, and $s \notin \downarrow$. A transition system *has a deadlock* if and only if it has a deadlock state; it is *deadlock free* if and only if it does not have a deadlock.

An important property that has already been suggested when motivating the notion of bisimilarity is that bisimilarity preserves deadlocks. Exercise 3.1.5 asks for a proof of this fact.

Definition 3.1.15 (Regular transition system) A transition system is *regular* if and only if both its sets of states and of transitions are *finite*.

The reader familiar with automata theory will notice that a regular transition system is simply a finite automaton. The fact that finite automata define the class of regular languages explains the name 'regular transition system'.

Definition 3.1.16 (Finitely branching transition system) A transition system is *finitely branching* if and only if each of its states has only *finitely many outgoing transitions*; if any of its states has infinitely many outgoing transitions, the transition system is said to be infinitely branching.

Note that a regular transition system is by definition finitely branching.

So far, it has not been made precise what are the states in a transition-system space. In the remainder, however, the states in a transition-system space consist of terms from a particular equational theory, as introduced in the previous chapter.

Exercises

3.1.1 Consider the transition-system space of Figure 3.1. Draw the transition system with root 5.

3.1.2 Are the following pairs of transition systems bisimilar? If so, give a bisimulation between the two systems; otherwise, explain why they are not bisimilar.

(a)

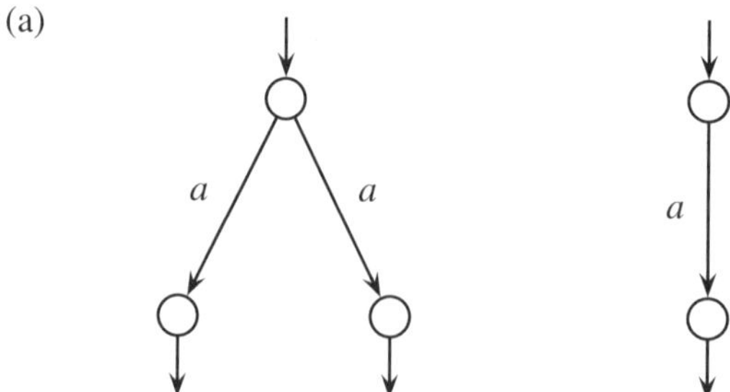

(b)

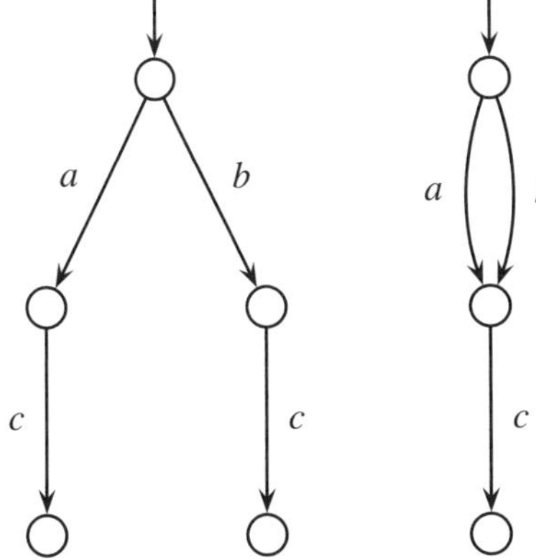

(c)

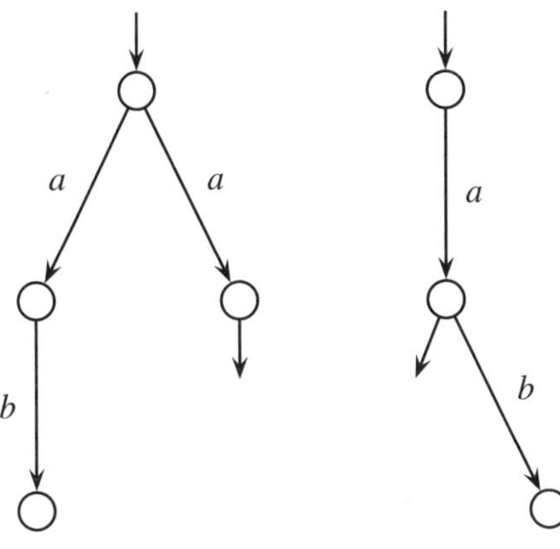

(d)

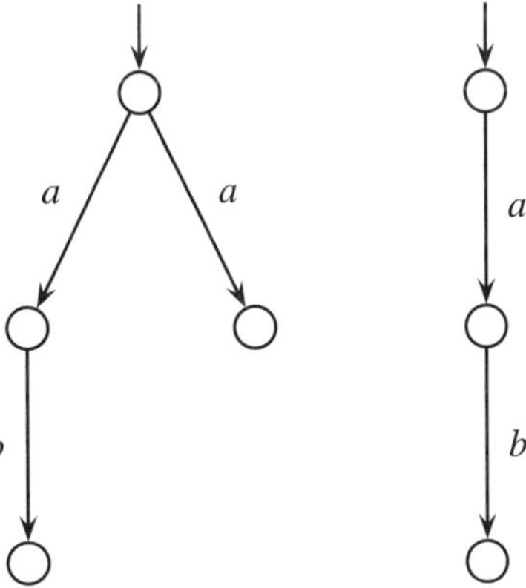

(e)

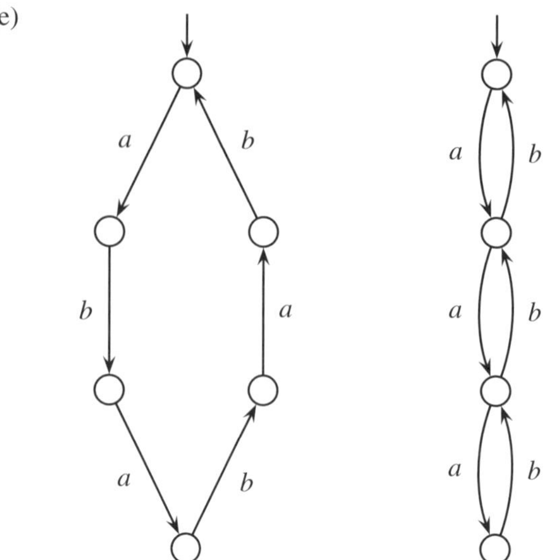

3.1.3 Give a bisimulation between any two of the following six transition systems.

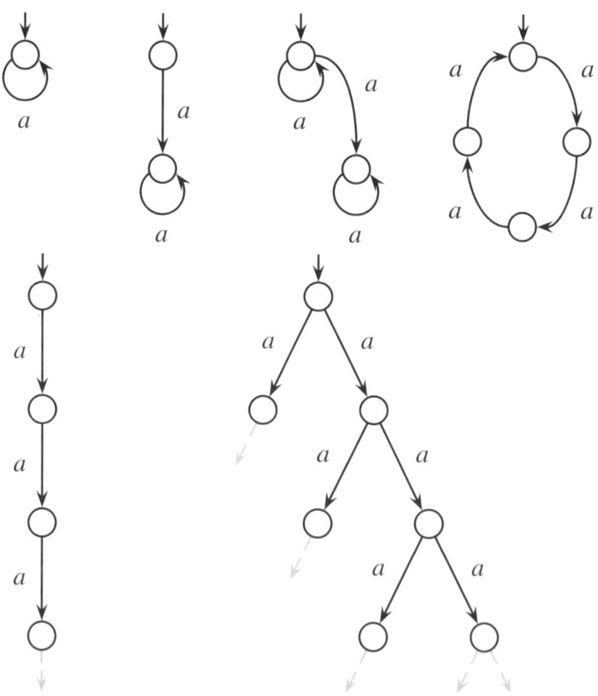

3.1.4 Recall Definitions 3.1.14 (Deadlock), 3.1.15 (Regular transition system), and 3.1.16 (Finitely branching transition system). Which of the transition systems of Exercises 3.1.2 and 3.1.3 are deadlock free? Which ones are regular? Which ones are finitely branching?

3.1.5 Recall Definition 3.1.14 (Deadlock). Let s and t be two *bisimilar* transition systems in some transition-system space. Show that s has a deadlock if and only if t has a deadlock.

3.1.6 Prove that the relation composition of two bisimulation relations is again a bisimulation.

3.1.7 Formalize the game-theoretic characterization of bisimilarity using concepts from game theory (see e.g. (Osborne & Rubinstein, 1994)).

3.1.8 Prove that the union of all possible bisimulation relations on a transition-system space is again a bisimulation relation. This is called the *maximal* bisimulation relation.

3.1.9 Let a set C be given, the set of *colors*. A *coloring* of a transition-system space $(S, L, \rightarrow, \downarrow)$ is a mapping from S to C, so each node has a color. A *colored trace* starting from $s \in S$ is a sequence $(c_0, a_1, c_1, \ldots, a_k, c_k)$ such that there are states $s_1, \ldots, s_k$ in S with $s \xrightarrow{a_1} s_1 \ldots \xrightarrow{a_k} s_k$, s has color c_0 and s_i has color c_i $(1 \leq i \leq k)$. A coloring is *consistent* if two nodes have the same color only if the same colored traces start from them and if they are both terminating or both non-terminating. Prove that two nodes are bisimilar exactly when there is a consistent coloring in which both nodes have the same color.

3.1.10 Recall Definition 2.3.26 (Isomorphism of algebras). On a transition-system space, the notion of isomorphism can be defined as follows: two transition systems s, t are isomorphic if and only if there is a bijective function f between the set of states reachable from s and the set of states reachable from t such that $u \xrightarrow{a} v \Leftrightarrow f(u) \xrightarrow{a} f(v)$ and $u\downarrow \Leftrightarrow f(u)\downarrow$. Prove that isomorphism is an equivalence relation on the transition-system space that is finer than bisimilarity, i.e., prove that isomorphic transition systems are bisimilar and give an example of two transition systems that are bisimilar but not isomorphic.

3.2 Structural operational semantics

In the previous section, the notion of a transition-system space was introduced. In this section, this is expanded upon by turning the set of states into a set of (closed) terms over some equational theory. Thus, it is shown how transition-system spaces can be used to provide equational theories with operational semantics.

Example 3.2.1 (Operational semantics) An illustration of what is involved is given by considering the equational theory $T_1 = (\Sigma_1, E_1)$ of Example 2.2.5. As shown in Example 2.2.11, each closed term over this theory is derivably equal to a closed term of the form $\mathbf{s}^m(\mathbf{0})$ for some natural number m. These terms $\mathbf{s}^m(\mathbf{0})$ can be transformed into a transition system as follows: the term $\mathbf{0}$ is a terminating state, and there is a transition from state $\mathbf{s}^{n+1}(\mathbf{0})$ to state $\mathbf{s}^n(\mathbf{0})$ for each natural number n. For simplicity, just one label is considered here, denoted 1. In this way, the state $\mathbf{s}^m(\mathbf{0})$ is characterized by having a sequence of exactly m transitions to a terminating state. Figure 3.8 shows the transition system induced by closed term $\mathbf{s}^2(\mathbf{0})$.

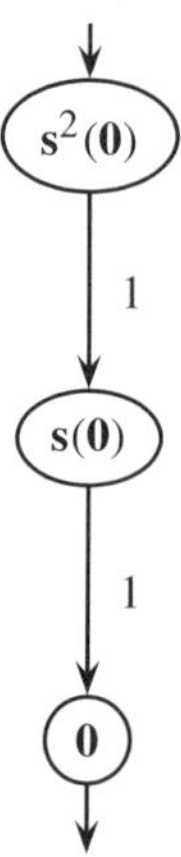

Fig. 3.8. The transition system corresponding to closed Σ_1-term $\mathbf{s}^2(\mathbf{0})$.

The general idea is to define transition systems for all closed Σ_1-terms of theory T_1 such that two closed terms, i.e., states, are bisimilar exactly when these terms are derivably equal in the equational theory. The desired transition-system space can be constructed in the following way: any transition for a certain closed term led by a certain function symbol is derived from the transitions of the arguments of the function symbol. The same holds for the termination predicate: whether or not a term is a terminating state is derived from the termination of the arguments of the leading function symbol. In other words, transitions and termination are determined based on the structure of terms. Since the transition-systems framework has an operational flavor, the resulting semantics of the equational theory is often referred to as a *structural operational semantics*. The rules defining all possible transitions and terminating states in a transition-system space constructed in this way are called *deduction rules*. The conditions on the arguments of the leading function symbol are called the *premises* of the deduction rule. Deduction rules without premises are often referred to as *axioms*.

For the example theory T_1, first, there are two axioms, corresponding to the two cases already described above: $\mathbf{0}$ is a terminating state, and each term that starts with a successor function symbol can do a step. Formally, for any Σ_1-term x,

$$\mathbf{0}\downarrow \qquad \mathbf{s}(x) \xrightarrow{1} x.$$

Note that the second axiom holds for arbitrary (open) Σ_1-terms; however, the transition-system space that will be derived from these rules is built from closed terms only.

Second, the addition function symbol is given an operational semantics. As mentioned, each closed Σ_1-term is derivably equal to a closed term of the form $\mathbf{s}^m(\mathbf{0})$ for some natural number m. The aim to obtain a semantics such that two derivably equal terms correspond to bisimilar transition systems can be achieved by ensuring that each closed term that is derivably equal to a closed term of the form $\mathbf{s}^m(\mathbf{0})$ has a single path of exactly m transitions to a terminating state. Deduction rules for the function symbol $\mathbf{a}$ can therefore be formulated as follows. For any Σ_1-terms x, x', y, y',

$$\frac{y \xrightarrow{1} y'}{\mathbf{a}(x, y) \xrightarrow{1} \mathbf{a}(x, y')} \quad \frac{x \xrightarrow{1} x',\ y\downarrow}{\mathbf{a}(x, y) \xrightarrow{1} x'} \quad \frac{x\downarrow,\ y\downarrow}{\mathbf{a}(x, y)\downarrow}.$$

The first rule says that whenever a term y has a transition to term y', then $\mathbf{a}(x, y)$ has a transition to $\mathbf{a}(x, y')$ for any arbitrary term x. The second rule states that whenever a term x can do a step to x' and term y cannot do a step, the term $\mathbf{a}(x, y)$ can do a step to x'. The idea of these two rules is that first the second argument of a term with leading symbol $\mathbf{a}$ does all its steps; if the second argument cannot do any further steps, then the first argument continues with its steps. Of course, it is also possible to first let the first argument do its steps and then the second. In principle, it is even possible to allow arbitrary interleavings of the steps of the two arguments. However, the above rules follow Axioms PA1 and PA2 given in Table 2.1. This choice simplifies the proofs of certain properties that are given in the remainder. The third and last rule given above says that $\mathbf{a}(x, y)$ is a terminating state if both x and y are terminating states.

By repeatedly applying the deduction rules given so far, it can be established that $\mathbf{a}(\mathbf{s}(\mathbf{0}), \mathbf{s}(\mathbf{0}))$ has the expected sequence of two transitions to a terminating state. From the leftmost axiom given above, for example, it is immediately clear that $\mathbf{0}\downarrow$. From the second axiom, it follows that $\mathbf{s}(\mathbf{0}) \xrightarrow{1} \mathbf{0}$. From these two facts, using the first deduction rule for the addition function symbol, it is obtained that $\mathbf{a}(\mathbf{s}(\mathbf{0}), \mathbf{0}) \xrightarrow{1} \mathbf{0}$. Continuing in this way results in the transition system given in Figure 3.9.

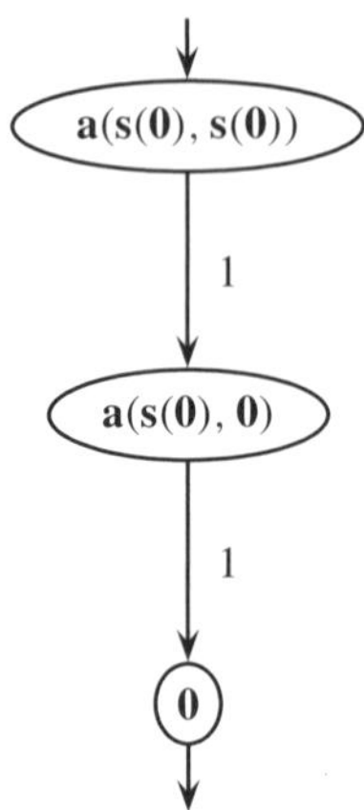

Fig. 3.9. The transition system corresponding to $\mathbf{a}(\mathbf{s}(\mathbf{0}), \mathbf{s}(\mathbf{0}))$.

In Example 2.2.9, it has already been shown that

$$T_1 \vdash \mathbf{a}(\mathbf{s}(\mathbf{0}), \mathbf{s}(\mathbf{0})) = \mathbf{s}(\mathbf{s}(\mathbf{0})).$$

From the two transition systems given in Figures 3.8 and 3.9, it immediately follows that

$$\mathbf{a}(\mathbf{s}(\mathbf{0}), \mathbf{s}(\mathbf{0})) \leftrightarrows \mathbf{s}(\mathbf{s}(\mathbf{0})),$$

where, as explained before, closed terms are interpreted as states in a transition-system space or initial states of a transition system. The above two results conform to the aim that two closed Σ_1-terms are bisimilar if and only if these terms are derivably equal in the equational theory T_1.

To complete the example, consider the following deduction rules that define the transitions involving the function symbol $\mathbf{m}$. For any Σ_1-terms x, x', y, and y',

$$\frac{x \xrightarrow{1} x',\ y \xrightarrow{1} y'}{\mathbf{m}(x, y) \xrightarrow{1} \mathbf{a}(\mathbf{m}(x, y'), x')} \quad \frac{x\downarrow}{\mathbf{m}(x, y)\downarrow} \quad \frac{y\downarrow}{\mathbf{m}(x, y)\downarrow}.$$

The reader is urged to try to understand these rules. Also in this case the rules guarantee that each closed term has a transition system consisting of a single path of transitions to a terminating state, where the length of the path is the 'natural-number interpretation' of the term.

The pair of a signature and a set of deduction rules for terms over this signature is called a *deduction system*. The deduction system developed in this example forms the basis for a transition-system space. The set of states of the transition-system space is the set of *closed* Σ_1-terms, $\mathcal{C}(\Sigma_1)$ (see Definition 2.2.3 (Terms)); the set of action labels is the singleton $\{1\}$. The transition relation is the *smallest* relation in $\mathcal{C}(\Sigma_1) \times \{1\} \times \mathcal{C}(\Sigma_1)$ satisfying the deduction rules given above. The requirement that it is the smallest relation guarantees that no transitions are present that cannot be derived from the deduction rules. Similarly, the set of terminating states is the smallest set of states satisfying the deduction rules.

Unfortunately, the transition-system space given in this example is not an algebra in the sense of Section 2.3, and it cannot be turned into a model for theory T_1 (see Definition 2.3.8 (Model)) without some additional work. In the remainder, it is shown how the transition-system space of this example can be turned into a model of T_1; then, it is also possible to formally prove the claim that two closed Σ_1-terms are bisimilar if and only if they are derivably equal.

The following definitions precisely introduce the notions of a deduction system and its induced transition-system space.

Definition 3.2.2 (Deduction system) A *term deduction system*, or simply a *deduction system*, is a pair (Σ, R), where Σ is a signature as defined in Definition 2.2.1 (Signature), and where R is a set of *rules*. A *rule* is of the form

$$\frac{\Phi}{\psi},$$

where ψ is a so-called *formula* (called the *conclusion* of the rule), and where Φ is a *set* of formulas (called the *premises* of the rule). A formula is either a *transition* $s \xrightarrow{a} t$ or a *termination* $t\downarrow$, for Σ-terms s, t and a label a taken from some given set of labels L. The term s in a transition $s \xrightarrow{a} t$ is called the *source* of the transition; term t is called the *target*. The term in a termination is referred to as the source of the termination. If the set of premises Φ is empty, then a rule is called an *axiom*.

Definition 3.2.3 (Transition-system space induced by a deduction system) Assume (Σ, R) is a term deduction system; furthermore, assume that L is the set of labels occurring in the set of rules R. The transition-system space induced by (Σ, R) is the quadruple $(\mathcal{C}(\Sigma), L, \rightarrow, \downarrow)$ where $\rightarrow \subseteq \mathcal{C}(\Sigma) \times L \times$

$\mathcal{C}(\Sigma)$ and $\downarrow \subseteq \mathcal{C}(\Sigma)$ contain a formula of (Σ, R) if and only if this formula is a closed substitution instance of a conclusion of a rule in R of which all the closed instances of the premises are also in $\rightarrow$ or $\downarrow$. In other words, a closed formula ϕ (i.e., a formula containing only closed terms) is an element of $\rightarrow$ or $\downarrow$ exactly when there is a rule $\frac{\Phi}{\psi}$ and a substitution σ such that $\phi \equiv \psi[\sigma]$ and the formulas $\chi[\sigma]$, for each $\chi \in \Phi$, are elements of $\rightarrow$ or $\downarrow$. (Recall the notion of substitution from Definition 2.2.6; also recall that $\equiv$ denotes syntactical identity on terms. In the current definition, both substitution and syntactical identity are overloaded to formulas, but that should not cause confusion.)

The example and the definitions given so far show that a deduction system is a way to turn the set of closed terms over a signature into a transition-system space and, thus, the individual closed terms into transition systems. The next step is to show how such a transition-system space can be transformed into a *model* of an equational theory over that signature, in the sense of Section 2.3. The key idea is to find an equivalence relation on the transition-system space that matches the notion of derivability in the equational theory, and to use this equivalence to construct a quotient algebra as defined in Definition 2.3.18; this quotient algebra is then a model of the equational theory. It should not come as a surprise that for the example theory T_1 bisimilarity is the equivalence notion matching derivability.

Consider Definition 2.3.18 (Quotient algebra). It reveals two important aspects. First, the starting point of a quotient algebra is an algebra (see Definition 2.3.1 (Algebra)); second, the equivalence relation must be a congruence on this algebra (see Definition 2.3.16 (Congruence)).

Concerning the first aspect, as already mentioned, a transition-system space is not an algebra. However, if a transition-system space is constructed from a term deduction system, as illustrated in Example 3.2.1, then it is straightforward to turn the space into an algebra of transition systems. Note that the set of closed terms over any signature with the constants and function symbols of the signature forms an algebra, often referred to as the term algebra. According to Definition 3.1.5 (Transition system), the closed terms over the signature of a term deduction system can be interpreted as transition systems in the transition-system space induced by the deduction system, which means that the algebra of these closed terms can be seen as an algebra of transition systems.

Example 3.2.4 (Algebra of transition systems) Consider again the example equational theory $T_1 = (\Sigma_1, E_1)$ of Example 2.2.5. Based on the transition-system space introduced in Example 3.2.1, the set of closed Σ_1-terms $\mathcal{C}(\Sigma_1)$

with constant **0** and functions **s**, **a**, and **m** forms an algebra of transition systems, referred to as $\mathbb{A}_1$.

Considering the second aspect mentioned above, it turns out that it is often also not too difficult to show that bisimilarity is a congruence on an algebra of transition systems constructed from a term deduction system. Theorem 3.1.13 implies that bisimilarity is an equivalence relation on transition systems. Thus, if it is possible to prove the second condition in Definition 2.3.16 (Congruence) for bisimilarity as well, it is possible to construct a quotient algebra from an algebra of transition systems and bisimilarity. In general, proving that a bisimilarity is a congruence on some algebra of transition systems can be quite tedious. However, it turns out that if the rules of the term deduction system used for constructing this algebra adhere to a certain simple format, then the desired congruence result follows automatically. The following definition introduces this format.

Definition 3.2.5 (Path format) Let (Σ, R) be a deduction system. Consider the following restrictions on a deduction rule in R:

(i) any target of any transition in the premises is just a single variable;
(ii) the source of the conclusion is either a single variable or it is of the form $f(x_1, \ldots, x_n)$, for some natural number n, with $f \in \Sigma$ an n-ary function symbol and the x_i variables;
(iii) the variables in the targets of the transitions in the premises and the variables in the source of the conclusion are all distinct, i.e., two targets of transitions in the premises are not the same variable and the variables in the source of the conclusion are all different, and no target of a premise occurs in the source of the conclusion.

If a rule satisfies these conditions, then it is said to be in *path* format. A deduction system is in path format if all its rules are.

Example 3.2.6 (Path format) It is easily seen that the deduction system for equational theory T_1 introduced in Example 3.2.1 is in path format.

The exercises at the end of this section contain some examples illustrating that the restrictions in the above definition are necessary in order to ensure that the desired congruence result holds. Almost all deduction systems given in this book turn out to be in path format.

The following theorem is given without proof. The interested reader can find a proof in (Baeten & Verhoef, 1993).

Theorem 3.2.7 (Congruence theorem) Consider a deduction system in path format. Bisimilarity is a congruence on the induced algebra of transition systems.

Example 3.2.8 (Congruence, quotient algebra) Consider once again the equational theory $T_1 = (\Sigma_1, E_1)$. It follows from the above congruence theorem and the fact that the deduction system for T_1 of Example 3.2.1 is in path format (Example 3.2.6) that bisimilarity is a congruence on the algebra $\mathbb{A}_1$ of transition systems introduced in Example 3.2.4. Thus, at this point, it is possible to construct a quotient algebra. Following Definition 2.3.18 (Quotient algebra), let $\mathbb{M}_1$ be the quotient algebra $\mathbb{A}_{1/\leftrightarrow}$ with domain $[\mathcal{C}(\Sigma_1)]_{\leftrightarrow}$, constant $[\mathbf{0}]_{\leftrightarrow}$ and functions $\mathbf{s}_{\leftrightarrow}$, $\mathbf{a}_{\leftrightarrow}$, and $\mathbf{m}_{\leftrightarrow}$. It turns out that this quotient algebra is a model of theory T_1, as defined in Definition 2.3.8; it can even be shown that this model is ground-complete, as defined in Definition 2.3.23.

Recall that it is our goal to prove that two closed Σ_1-terms are bisimilar if and only if they are derivably equal in T_1. The attentive reader might see that this result follows from the soundness and ground-completeness of theory T_1 for model $\mathbb{M}_1$ of the above example. Thus, the following two theorems formally prove these soundness and ground-completeness results. The proofs themselves can be skipped on a first reading (or on any reading, for that matter). They are included for the sake of completeness and to show the interested reader what is involved in soundness and ground-completeness proofs.

Theorem 3.2.9 (Soundness of T_1) Algebra $\mathbb{M}_1$ of Example 3.2.8 is a model of theory T_1 using the standard interpretation of constant $\mathbf{0}$ and functions $\mathbf{s}$, $\mathbf{a}$, and $\mathbf{m}$ explained in Definition 2.3.18 (Quotient algebra).

Proof Definition 2.3.8 (Model) implies that for each axiom $s = t$ of theory T_1 it must be shown that $\mathbb{M}_1 \models s = t$. Only the proof for Axiom PA2 is given; the proofs for the other axioms are left as Exercise 3.2.7.

Recall the notations concerning quotient algebras introduced in Section 2.3. Let p and q be arbitrary closed Σ_1-terms. Definition 2.3.6 (Validity) states that the following equality must be proven: $\mathbf{a}_{\leftrightarrow}([p]_{\leftrightarrow}, \mathbf{s}_{\leftrightarrow}([q]_{\leftrightarrow})) = \mathbf{s}_{\leftrightarrow}(\mathbf{a}_{\leftrightarrow}([p]_{\leftrightarrow}, [q]_{\leftrightarrow}))$. It follows from Definition 2.3.18 (Quotient algebra) that it therefore must be shown that $[\mathbf{a}(p, \mathbf{s}(q))]_{\leftrightarrow} = [\mathbf{s}(\mathbf{a}(p, q))]_{\leftrightarrow}$ and, thus, that $\mathbf{a}(p, \mathbf{s}(q)) \leftrightarrow \mathbf{s}(\mathbf{a}(p, q))$.

To prove the desired bisimilarity, it suffices to give a bisimulation relation that contains all the pairs $(\mathbf{a}(p, \mathbf{s}(q)), \mathbf{s}(\mathbf{a}(p, q)))$ for arbitrary closed terms p and q. Let $R = \{(\mathbf{a}(p, \mathbf{s}(q)), \mathbf{s}(\mathbf{a}(p, q))) \mid p, q \in \mathcal{C}(T_1)\} \cup \{(p, p) \mid p \in$

$\mathcal{C}(T_1)\}$. It needs to be proven that all pairs in R satisfy the transfer conditions of Definition 3.1.10 (Bisimilarity). These conditions trivially hold for all pairs (p, p) with p a closed Σ_1-term. This means that only elements of R of the form $(\mathbf{a}(p, \mathbf{s}(q)), \mathbf{s}(\mathbf{a}(p, q)))$ with p, q in $\mathcal{C}(T_1)$ need to be considered. Assume that $(\mathbf{a}(p, \mathbf{s}(q)), \mathbf{s}(\mathbf{a}(p, q)))$ is such an element.

(i) Assume that $\mathbf{a}(p, \mathbf{s}(q)) \xrightarrow{1} r$ for some $r \in \mathcal{C}(T_1)$. Inspection of the deduction rules given in Example 3.2.1 and the fact that $\mathbf{s}(q) \xrightarrow{1} q$ show that necessarily $r \equiv \mathbf{a}(p, q)$. Since also $\mathbf{s}(\mathbf{a}(p, q)) \xrightarrow{1} \mathbf{a}(p, q)$, the fact that $(\mathbf{a}(p, q), \mathbf{a}(p, q)) \in R$ proves that the first transfer condition is satisfied.

(ii) Assume that $\mathbf{s}(\mathbf{a}(p, q)) \xrightarrow{1} r$ for some $r \in \mathcal{C}(T_1)$. It easily follows from the deduction rules of Example 3.2.1 that $r \equiv \mathbf{a}(p, q)$. Since also $\mathbf{a}(p, \mathbf{s}(q)) \xrightarrow{1} \mathbf{a}(p, q)$ and $(\mathbf{a}(p, q), \mathbf{a}(p, q)) \in R$, also this transfer condition is satisfied.

(iii) Assume that $\mathbf{a}(p, \mathbf{s}(q))\downarrow$. Since $\mathbf{s}(q)$ cannot terminate, this yields a contradiction. Thus, $\mathbf{a}(p, \mathbf{s}(q))$ cannot terminate, which means that the third transfer condition is trivially satisfied.

(iv) Since also $\mathbf{s}(\mathbf{a}(p, q))$ cannot terminate, also the final transfer condition is satisfied, completing the proof.

□

Based on Proposition 2.3.9 (Soundness) and Definitions 2.3.15 (Equivalence classes) and 2.3.18 (Quotient algebra), the above theorem has two immediate corollaries. The second corollary shows that two closed Σ_1-terms that are derivably equal in theory T_1 are bisimilar.

Corollary 3.2.10 (Soundness) Let s and t be Σ_1-terms. If $T_1 \vdash s = t$, then $\mathbb{M}_1 \models s = t$.

Corollary 3.2.11 (Soundness) Let p and q be closed Σ_1-terms. If $T_1 \vdash p = q$, then $p \leftrightarrows q$.

As mentioned, it can be shown that the model $\mathbb{M}_1$ is ground-complete for theory T_1, and thus that two bisimilar closed Σ_1-terms are derivably equal in T_1. The proof of this completeness result needs two auxiliary properties. The first one states that a closed Σ_1-term that corresponds to a termination state is derivably equal to $\mathbf{0}$. The second one states that a closed Σ_1-term p that can make a step towards another closed term q is derivably equal to $\mathbf{s}(q)$. These two results are crucial in the ground-completeness result because they allow a reduction of the problem to basic Σ_1-terms as defined in Definition 2.2.10.

Lemma 3.2.12 For any closed Σ_1-term p, $p\downarrow$ implies that $T_1 \vdash p = \mathbf{0}$.

Proof The proof goes via structural induction on p. Assume that $p\downarrow$.

(i) Assume $p \equiv \mathbf{0}$. Obviously, $T_1 \vdash p = \mathbf{0}$, satisfying the property.

(ii) Assume $p \equiv \mathbf{s}(q)$ for some $q \in \mathcal{C}(T_1)$. Since under this assumption not $p\downarrow$, the property follows trivially in this case.

(iii) Assume $p \equiv \mathbf{a}(q, r)$ for some $q, r \in \mathcal{C}(T_1)$. From $p\downarrow$ and the deduction rules in Example 3.2.1, it follows that $q\downarrow$ and $r\downarrow$. Induction gives that $T_1 \vdash q = \mathbf{0}$ and $T_1 \vdash r = \mathbf{0}$. Hence, $T_1 \vdash p = \mathbf{a}(q, r) = \mathbf{a}(\mathbf{0}, \mathbf{0}) \overset{\text{PA1}}{=} \mathbf{0}$, completing the proof in this case.

(iv) Assume $p \equiv \mathbf{m}(q, r)$ for some $q, r \in \mathcal{C}(T_1)$. From $p\downarrow$ and the deduction rules of Example 3.2.1, it follows that (a) $q\downarrow$ or (b) $r\downarrow$.

  (a) Induction gives that $T_1 \vdash q = \mathbf{0}$. Hence, using Exercise 2.2.8 and the conservativity result of Proposition 2.2.17, $T_1 \vdash p = \mathbf{m}(q, r) = \mathbf{m}(r, q) = \mathbf{m}(r, \mathbf{0}) \overset{\text{PA3}}{=} \mathbf{0}$, completing this case.

  (b) Induction gives that $T_1 \vdash r = \mathbf{0}$. Hence, $T_1 \vdash p = \mathbf{m}(q, r) = \mathbf{m}(q, \mathbf{0}) \overset{\text{PA3}}{=} \mathbf{0}$, completing also this final case.

□

Lemma 3.2.13 For any closed Σ_1-terms p and p', $p \overset{1}{\to} p'$ implies that $T_1 \vdash p = \mathbf{s}(p')$.

Proof The proof goes via structural induction on p. Assume that $p \overset{1}{\to} p'$.

(i) Assume $p \equiv \mathbf{0}$. In this case $p \overset{1}{\not\to}$, so the property is satisfied.

(ii) Assume $p \equiv \mathbf{s}(q)$ for some $q \in \mathcal{C}(T_1)$. Since $\mathbf{s}(q) \overset{1}{\to} q$, it follows that $p' \equiv q$. Hence $T_1 \vdash p = \mathbf{s}(q) = \mathbf{s}(p')$, proving the property in this case.

(iii) Assume $p \equiv \mathbf{a}(q, r)$ for some $q, r \in \mathcal{C}(T_1)$. From $p \overset{1}{\to} p'$ and the deduction rules in Example 3.2.1, it follows that (a) $p' \equiv \mathbf{a}(q, r')$ with $r \overset{1}{\to} r'$ or (b) $p' \equiv q'$ with $q \overset{1}{\to} q'$ and $r\downarrow$.

  (a) Induction gives that $T_1 \vdash r = \mathbf{s}(r')$. Hence, $T_1 \vdash p = \mathbf{a}(q, r) = \mathbf{a}(q, \mathbf{s}(r')) \overset{\text{PA2}}{=} \mathbf{s}(\mathbf{a}(q, r')) = \mathbf{s}(p')$, completing this case.

  (b) Induction gives that $T_1 \vdash q = \mathbf{s}(q')$. Furthermore, Lemma 3.2.12 implies that $T_1 \vdash r = \mathbf{0}$. Hence, $T_1 \vdash p = \mathbf{a}(q, r) \overset{\text{PA1}}{=} q = \mathbf{s}(q') = \mathbf{s}(p')$, completing also this case.

(iv) Assume $p \equiv \mathbf{m}(q, r)$ for some $q, r \in \mathcal{C}(T_1)$. From $p \xrightarrow{1} p'$ and the deduction rules of Example 3.2.1, it follows that $p' \equiv \mathbf{a}(\mathbf{m}(q, r'), q')$ with $q \xrightarrow{1} q'$ and $r \xrightarrow{1} r'$. Induction yields that $T_1 \vdash q = \mathbf{s}(q')$ and $T_1 \vdash r = \mathbf{s}(r')$. Hence, $T_1 \vdash p = \mathbf{m}(q, r) = \mathbf{m}(q, \mathbf{s}(r')) \stackrel{\text{PA4}}{=} \mathbf{a}(\mathbf{m}(q, r'), q) = \mathbf{a}(\mathbf{m}(q, r'), \mathbf{s}(q')) \stackrel{\text{PA2}}{=} \mathbf{s}(\mathbf{a}(\mathbf{m}(q, r'), q')) = \mathbf{s}(p')$, completing the proof.

□

Theorem 3.2.14 (Ground-completeness of T_1) Theory T_1 is a ground-complete axiomatization of the model $\mathbb{M}_1$, i.e., for any closed Σ_1-terms p and q, $\mathbb{M}_1 \models p = q$ implies $T_1 \vdash p = q$.

Proof Assume that $\mathbb{M}_1 \models p = q$. It must be shown that $T_1 \vdash p = q$. In Example 2.2.13, it has been shown that each closed Σ_1-term can be written as a basic Σ_1-term, as defined in Definition 2.2.10. Thus, assume that p_1 and q_1 are basic Σ_1-terms such that $T_1 \vdash p = p_1$ and $T_1 \vdash q = q_1$. It follows from Corollary 3.2.11 that $p \leftrightarrow p_1$ and $q \leftrightarrow q_1$. Since $\mathbb{M}_1 \models p = q$, also $p \leftrightarrow q$. The fact that bisimilarity is an equivalence implies that $p_1 \leftrightarrow q_1$. Assuming that it can be shown that $T_1 \vdash p_1 = q_1$, it follows that $T_1 \vdash p = p_1 = q_1 = q$, which is the desired result.
The proof that $T_1 \vdash p_1 = q_1$ under the assumption that $p_1 \leftrightarrow q_1$ is a structural-induction proof on the structure of p_1. Since p_1 is a basic term, only two cases need to be considered.

(i) Assume $p_1 \equiv \mathbf{0}$. It follows both that $T_1 \vdash p_1 = \mathbf{0}$ and that $p_1 \downarrow$. Since $p_1 \leftrightarrow q_1$, the third transfer condition of Definition 3.1.10 (Bisimilarity) yields that $q_1 \downarrow$. Lemma 3.2.12 yields that $T_1 \vdash q_1 = \mathbf{0}$. Thus, $T_1 \vdash p_1 = \mathbf{0} = q_1$, proving the desired property in this case.

(ii) Assume $p_1 \equiv \mathbf{s}(r)$ for some basic Σ_1-term r. Then, $p_1 \xrightarrow{1} r$. Lemma 3.2.13 yields that $T_1 \vdash p_1 = \mathbf{s}(r)$. Since $p_1 \leftrightarrow q_1$, the first transfer condition of Definition 3.1.10 (Bisimilarity) yields that $q_1 \xrightarrow{1} s$ for some $s \in \mathcal{C}(T_1)$ such that $r \leftrightarrow s$. In fact, it follows from the structure of basic terms that s must be a basic Σ_1-term. Induction yields that $T_1 \vdash r = s$. From $q_1 \xrightarrow{1} s$ and Lemma 3.2.13, it follows that $T_1 \vdash q_1 = \mathbf{s}(s)$. Combining the results obtained so far gives $T_1 \vdash p_1 = \mathbf{s}(r) = \mathbf{s}(s) = q_1$, proving the desired property also in this case.

□

The ground-completeness result has an immediate corollary that proves the claim that two bisimilar closed Σ_1-terms are derivably equal in T_1.

Corollary 3.2.15 (Ground-completeness) Let p and q be closed Σ_1-terms. If $p \leftrightarrow q$, then $T_1 \vdash p = q$.

Consider again equational theory T_1 of Example 2.2.5. In Example 2.2.15, this theory has been extended with an extra binary function symbol **e**, yielding theory T_2. It has already been shown that this extension does not influence what equalities between closed terms can be derived from the original theory T_1 (Proposition 2.2.17 (Conservative extension)). In the context of the current section, which gives an operational semantics of T_1 in terms of transition systems, it is interesting to investigate to what extent the soundness and ground-completeness results for T_1 can be used to obtain similar results for the extended theory T_2, hopefully reducing the amount of work needed to obtain a ground-complete model for T_2.

In Definitions 2.2.16 and 2.2.19, a notion of equational conservativity is introduced. A similar notion can be defined for deduction systems, and it turns out that such an operational conservativity notion is useful in obtaining soundness and ground-completeness results for theories extending some other theory. Note that a deduction system can be extended by extending the signature and/or the deduction rules in question, but also by extending the set of labels that are used in the transitions. Furthermore, observe from Definition 3.2.3 (Transition-system space induced by a deduction system) that only transitions between closed terms over the signature of a deduction system are of interest. Hence, it is not necessary to distinguish two notions of extension and conservativity as in the equational context. Informally, a deduction system conservatively extends another deduction system if and only if it does not add any transitions or terminations with respect to closed terms of the original system compared to those already present in that original system.

Definition 3.2.16 (Operational conservative extension) Let $D_1 = (\Sigma_1, R_1)$ over a set of labels L_1 and $D_2 = (\Sigma_2, R_2)$ over a set of labels L_2 be deduction systems as defined in Definition 3.2.2. Deduction system D_2 is an *operational conservative extension* of system D_1 if and only if

(i) Σ_2 contains Σ_1, R_2 contains R_1 and L_2 contains L_1, and
(ii) a transition $p \xrightarrow{a} q$ or termination $p\downarrow$, with p a closed Σ_1-term, $a \in L_2$ and q a closed Σ_2-term, is in the transition-system space induced by D_1 exactly when it is in the transition-system space induced by D_2 (see Definition 3.2.3). This implies that if p is a Σ_1-term and $p \xrightarrow{a} q$, then necessarily $a \in L_1$ and q is a Σ_1-term.

In order to distinguish the notions of conservative extension for equational theories and deduction systems, a conservative extension of equational theories is sometimes called an *equational* conservative extension.

The notion of an operational conservative extension can be used in ground-completeness proofs for equational theories extending some base theory. The conditions of the definition can be weakened in two ways, still achieving these results, but the present definition suffices for most of the applications that are considered in this book. First of all, it is not needed that all transitions are preserved exactly, but only that the resulting transition systems are bisimilar (since the results are used to establish facts about bisimulation models), and secondly, in some restricted circumstances it can be allowed to add new transitions for some old terms.

Under certain assumptions it is possible to prove operational conservativity in a straightforward way, as shown by the theorem given below. The theorem uses the following notion of source-dependency. Informally, the meaning of source-dependency can be explained as follows. The conclusion of a rule in a deduction system defines a transition of its source term. The rule is said to be source-dependent when all the variables in the rule originate from the source of the conclusion.

Definition 3.2.17 (Source-dependency) Let (Σ, R) be a deduction system. It is defined inductively when a variable in a rule in R is *source-dependent*:

(i) all variables in the source of the conclusion are source-dependent;
(ii) if $s \xrightarrow{a} t$ is a premise of a rule, and all variables in s are source-dependent, then all variables in t are source-dependent.

If all variables in a rule are source-dependent, then the rule is said to be source-dependent.

Example 3.2.18 (Source-dependency) Consider the deduction system given in Example 3.2.1. Any of the rules with a termination as its conclusion is source-dependent based on item (i) of the above definition. The rule for **s** is source-dependent because the target of the conclusion contains only variable x which is introduced in the source. The first rule for the **a** function symbol is source-dependent because variables x and y are introduced in the source of the conclusion, implying that they are source-dependent, and variable y' is the target of a premise with only the source-dependent variable y in its source, implying that also y' is source-dependent. Similar reasoning shows that also the other two rules in the deduction system are source-dependent.

As an example of a rule which is not source-dependent, consider the rule $x\downarrow / \mathbf{0}\downarrow$. The variable x appearing in the premise is not source-dependent, as it does not appear in the (source of the) conclusion.

The following theorem is given without proof. The interested reader can find a proof in (Verhoef, 1994).

Theorem 3.2.19 (Operational conservativity) Let $D_1 = (\Sigma_1, R_1)$ and $D_2 = (\Sigma_2, R_2)$ be deduction systems such that Σ_2 contains Σ_1 and R_2 contains R_1. Deduction system D_2 is an *operational conservative extension* of system D_1 if

(i) all rules in R_1 are source-dependent, and
(ii) for each added rule $r \in R_2 \backslash R_1$, either the source of the conclusion is not a Σ_1-term, or the rule has a premise of the form $s \xrightarrow{a} t$ with s a Σ_1-term such that all variables of s occur in the source of the conclusion and either label a is new or t is not a Σ_1-term.

The second clause in this definition ensures that each new rule is 'fresh', i.e., cannot be applied to old terms. This means that new transitions cannot be added to old terms. When this is done in Chapter 9, Section 9.6, nevertheless, the present theory cannot be used any longer.

Example 3.2.20 (Operational conservativity) Consider theory T_2 of Example 2.2.15. It is possible to provide an operational semantics for this theory by extending the deduction system for T_1 given in Example 3.2.1 with deduction rules for the $\mathbf{e}$ function symbol. For any Σ_2-terms x, x', y, y', and z,

$$\frac{x \xrightarrow{1} x',\ y \xrightarrow{1} y',\ \mathbf{e}(x, y') \xrightarrow{1} z}{\mathbf{e}(x, y) \xrightarrow{1} \mathbf{a}(\mathbf{m}(\mathbf{e}(x, y'), x'), z)}$$

and

$$\frac{x\downarrow,\ y \xrightarrow{1} y'}{\mathbf{e}(x, y)\downarrow} \qquad \frac{y\downarrow}{\mathbf{e}(x, y) \xrightarrow{1} \mathbf{0}}.$$

In particular the first rule might be difficult to understand. It can be clarified by a comparison to the algebra of natural numbers $(\mathbf{N}, +, \times, exp, succ, 0)$, which is an extension of the algebra of Example 2.3.3 with the exponentiation function *exp*. (Note that it is straightforward to show that this algebra is a model of theory T_2; see Exercise 2.3.3.) Assume that for any $n, m \in \mathbf{N}$, $exp(n, m)$ is written n^m; further assume that multiplication is not explicitly written. In terms of the algebra of natural numbers, the first rule above could be formulated as follows: if $n = 1 + n'$, $m = 1 + m'$, and $n^{m'} = 1 + l$, then $n^m = 1 + (n^{m'} n' + l)$, for $l, n, n', m, m' \in \mathbf{N}$. The following simple calculation shows that this is correct: $n^m = n^{1+m'} = nn^{m'} = (1+n')n^{m'} = n^{m'} + n'n^{m'} = 1 + l + n'n^{m'} = 1 + (n^{m'}n' + l)$. Note that the second and third rule can be interpreted in a similar way: if $n = 0$ and $m = 1+m'$ (i.e., $m \neq 0$), then $n^m = 0$, and if $m = 0$, then $n^m = 1 + 0 = 1$ ($n, m, m' \in \mathbf{N}$). (At this point, it may be interesting to have another look at the deduction rules in Example 3.2.1.)

The rules given in this example extend the deduction system given in Example 3.2.1. Since all the deduction rules of Example 3.2.1 are source-dependent (see Example 3.2.18) and since the source of the conclusion in all the extra rules concerns the new function symbol **e**, it follows in a straightforward way from Theorem 3.2.19 (Operational conservativity) that the extended deduction system is an operational conservative extension of the deduction system of Example 3.2.1.

There are close connections between extensions of deduction systems and extensions of equational theories. Theorem 3.2.21 (Conservativity) formalizes this relation and Theorem 3.2.26 (Ground-completeness) given below builds on this result. The two theorems are used several times in the remainder of this book.

The following theorem establishes conditions under which structural operational semantics can be used to determine that one equational theory is a conservative ground-extension of another one.

Theorem 3.2.21 (Conservativity) Let $D_1 = (\Sigma_1, R_1)$ and $D_2 = (\Sigma_2, R_2)$ be deduction systems. Let $T_1 = (\Sigma_1, E_1)$ and $T_2 = (\Sigma_2, E_2)$ be equational theories over the same signatures with E_1 a subset of E_2. Then T_2 is an equational conservative ground-extension of T_1 if the following conditions are satisfied:

(i) D_2 is an operational conservative extension of D_1,
(ii) T_1 is a ground-complete axiomatization of the bisimulation model induced by D_1, and
(iii) T_2 is a sound axiomatization of the bisimulation model induced by D_2.

Example 3.2.22 (Conservativity) It is interesting to see how this theorem can be applied to the two example theories T_1 and T_2. The aim is to show that T_2 is a conservative ground-extension of T_1, as defined in Definition 2.2.19. In Examples 3.2.1 and 3.2.20, two deduction systems for T_1 and T_2 have been given. Example 3.2.20 furthermore has shown that the deduction system for T_2 is an operational conservative extension of the deduction system for T_1. Theorems 3.2.9 and 3.2.14 show that T_1 is a sound and ground-complete axiomatization of the algebra of transition systems induced by the term deduction system for T_1. Thus, only the third condition in the above theorem needs to be satisfied in order to prove that T_2 is an equational conservative extension of T_1.

Example 3.2.23 (Model) Consider again theory T_2 of Example 2.2.15 and its deduction system of Examples 3.2.1 and 3.2.20. It is not difficult to verify that this system is in path format, as defined in Definition 3.2.5. Thus, Theorem 3.2.7 (Congruence theorem) implies that bisimilarity is a congruence on the induced algebra of transition systems. This result, in turn, means that the quotient algebra modulo bisimilarity is well-defined. Let $\mathbb{M}_2$ be this quotient algebra. It turns out that this algebra is a model of T_2.

Theorem 3.2.24 (Soundness of T_2) Algebra $\mathbb{M}_2$ of the previous example is a model of theory T_2 using the standard interpretation of constant $\mathbf{0}$ and functions $\mathbf{s}$, $\mathbf{a}$, $\mathbf{m}$, and $\mathbf{e}$ explained in Definition 2.3.18 (Quotient algebra).

Proof According to Definition 2.3.8 (Model), it must be shown that, for each axiom $s = t$ of T_2, $\mathbb{M}_2 \models s = t$. The proof for the axioms already present in T_1 carries over directly from the proof of Theorem 3.2.9 (Soundness of T_1) and Exercise 3.2.7. The proof for Axioms PA5 and PA6 that are new in T_2 is based on the following two bisimulation relations:

$$\{(\mathbf{e}(p, \mathbf{0}), \mathbf{s}(\mathbf{0})) \mid p \in \mathcal{C}(T_2)\} \cup \{(\mathbf{0}, \mathbf{0})\}$$

and

$$\{(\mathbf{e}(p, \mathbf{s}(q)), \mathbf{m}(\mathbf{e}(p, q), p)) \mid p, q \in \mathcal{C}(T_2)\} \cup \{(p, p) \mid p \in \mathcal{C}(T_2)\}.$$

The proof that these two relations are indeed bisimulation relations as defined in Definition 3.1.10 is left as Exercise 3.2.8. □

Combining Theorem 3.2.24 with the observations made in Example 3.2.22 implies that all three conditions of Theorem 3.2.21 (Conservativity) are satisfied. Thus, the following proposition, which is a restatement of Proposition 2.2.17, follows immediately.

Proposition 3.2.25 (Conservativity) Theory T_2 of Table 2.2 is an equational conservative ground-extension of theory T_1 of Table 2.1.

When the extension is of a particular kind, namely when newly introduced syntax can be eliminated from closed terms, then ground-completeness of the extended theory can be established incrementally. This is formulated in the following theorem.

Theorem 3.2.26 (Ground-completeness) Assume that $D_1 = (\Sigma_1, R_1)$ and $D_2 = (\Sigma_2, R_2)$ are deduction systems. Let $T_1 = (\Sigma_1, E_1)$ and $T_2 = (\Sigma_2, E_2)$ be equational theories over the same signatures with E_1 a subset of E_2. Then T_2 is a ground-complete axiomatization of the model induced by D_2 if in addition to the conditions of Theorem 3.2.21 (Conservativity) the following condition is satisfied:

(iv) theory T_2 has the elimination property with respect to T_1, i.e., for each closed Σ_2-term p, there is a closed Σ_1-term q such that $T_2 \vdash p = q$.

Let us return one more time to the running example of theories T_1 of Table 2.1 and T_2 of Table 2.2. It has already been argued that these two theories with their deduction systems satisfy the conditions of Theorem 3.2.21 (Conservativity). Proposition 2.2.20 (Elimination) implies that theory T_2 has the elimination property with respect to T_1. Thus, the following completeness result follows immediately from the above theorem.

Theorem 3.2.27 (Ground-completeness of T_2) Theory T_2 is a ground-complete axiomatization of model $\mathbb{M}_2$, i.e., for any closed Σ_2-terms p and q, $\mathbb{M}_2 \models p = q$ implies $T_2 \vdash p = q$.

It goes without saying that a completeness result based on Theorem 3.2.26 (Ground-completeness), such as the one given for Theorem 3.2.27 (Ground-completeness of T_2), for example, is preferable over a completeness result from scratch. Thus, the results given in this section motivate a modular setup of equational theories, starting from some minimal theory and subsequently defining interesting extensions.

Exercises

3.2.1 Add to the deduction system given in Example 3.2.1 the rule

$$\frac{p \xrightarrow{1} \mathbf{0}}{\mathbf{s}(p) \xrightarrow{ok} \mathbf{0}} \,.$$

Show that $\mathbf{s}(\mathbf{a}(\mathbf{0}, \mathbf{0})) \leftrightarrow \mathbf{s}(\mathbf{0})$ but $\mathbf{s}(\mathbf{s}(\mathbf{a}(\mathbf{0}, \mathbf{0}))) \not\leftrightarrow \mathbf{s}(\mathbf{s}(\mathbf{0}))$. Thus, bisimilarity is not a congruence. Note that the added rule violates the first clause in the definition of the *path* format.

3.2.2 Add to the deduction system given in Example 3.2.1 the axiom

$$\mathbf{m}(x, x) \xrightarrow{ok} \mathbf{0} \,.$$

Show that $\mathbf{a}(\mathbf{0},\mathbf{0}) \leftrightarrow \mathbf{0}$ but $\mathbf{m}(\mathbf{a}(\mathbf{0},\mathbf{0}),\mathbf{0}) \not\leftrightarrow \mathbf{m}(\mathbf{0},\mathbf{0})$. Thus, bisimilarity is not a congruence. Note that the added rule violates the second clause in the definition of the *path* format.

3.2.3 Add to the deduction system given in Example 3.2.1 the axiom

$$\mathbf{a}(x, \mathbf{a}(y, z)) \xrightarrow{ok} \mathbf{0} \ .$$

Show that $\mathbf{a}(\mathbf{0},\mathbf{0}) \leftrightarrow \mathbf{0}$ but $\mathbf{a}(\mathbf{0},\mathbf{a}(\mathbf{0},\mathbf{0})) \not\leftrightarrow \mathbf{a}(\mathbf{0},\mathbf{0})$. Thus, bisimilarity is not a congruence. Note that the added rule violates the second clause in the definition of the *path* format.

3.2.4 Add to the deduction system given in Example 3.2.1 the rule

$$\frac{p \xrightarrow{1} x,\ q \xrightarrow{1} x}{\mathbf{a}(p, q) \xrightarrow{ok} \mathbf{0}} \ .$$

Show that $\mathbf{s}(\mathbf{a}(\mathbf{0},\mathbf{0})) \leftrightarrow \mathbf{s}(\mathbf{0})$ but $\mathbf{a}(\mathbf{s}(\mathbf{0}),\mathbf{s}(\mathbf{a}(\mathbf{0},\mathbf{0}))) \not\leftrightarrow \mathbf{a}(\mathbf{s}(\mathbf{0}),\mathbf{s}(\mathbf{0}))$. Thus, bisimilarity is not a congruence. Note that the added rule violates the third clause in the definition of the *path* format.

3.2.5 Add to the deduction system given in Example 3.2.1 the rule

$$\frac{x \xrightarrow{1} y}{\mathbf{m}(x, y) \xrightarrow{ok} \mathbf{0}} \ .$$

Show that $\mathbf{s}(\mathbf{a}(\mathbf{0},\mathbf{0})) \leftrightarrow \mathbf{s}(\mathbf{0})$ but $\mathbf{m}(\mathbf{s}(\mathbf{a}(\mathbf{0},\mathbf{0})),\mathbf{0}) \not\leftrightarrow \mathbf{m}(\mathbf{s}(\mathbf{0}),\mathbf{0})$. Thus, bisimilarity is not a congruence. Note that the added rule violates the third clause in the definition of the *path* format.

3.2.6 Add to the term deduction system with as only rule $x\!\downarrow \,/\, \mathbf{0}\!\downarrow$ a new constant **1**. Show that this extension is not operationally conservative.

3.2.7 Complete the proof of Theorem 3.2.9 (Soundness of T_1) by proving the validity of Axioms PA1, PA3, and PA4.

3.2.8 Complete the proof of Theorem 3.2.24 (Soundness of T_2) by showing that the two relations given for Axioms PA5 and PA6 are bisimulation relations as defined in Definition 3.1.10.

3.3 Bibliographical remarks

In the literature, the term transition system is used in two different meanings: the meaning that is given here, and in the meaning of a transition-system space. The notion of a transition system is closely related to an automaton in language theory (see e.g. (Linz, 2001)), the notion of a synchronization tree in CCS (see e.g. (Milner, 1980)), or the notion of a process graph (see e.g. (Bergstra & Klop, 1985)). The notion of bisimulation as given here is from (Park, 1981), and is closely related to the notion of strong equivalence from CCS (Hennessy & Milner, 1980). For more information on a game characterization of bisimulation, see (Oguztuzun, 1989). For further information on comparative concurrency semantics, see (Van Glabbeek, 1990).

The notion of choice as given in transition systems will, as becomes more clear further on, be subject to influence from outside, from the environment. Non-deterministic choice is a means to show a choice that cannot be influenced. Some theories, like CSP (Hoare, 1985), have two different constructs for the two types of choice.

This chapter gives an introduction to the theory of structural operational semantics (often abbreviated to SOS). This theory finds its origins in the article (Plotkin, 1981), later reprinted in the special issue (Aceto & Fokkink, 2004), where a lot more information on SOS theory can be found. A good overview of SOS theory is (Aceto *et al.*, 2001). The *path* format was introduced in (Baeten & Verhoef, 1993). The material on conservative extensions originates in (Verhoef, 1994). For some recent developments in this area, see (Mousavi *et al.*, 2007).

4

Basic process theory

4.1 Introduction

Chapter 3 has introduced the notion of transition systems both as an abstract operational model of reactive systems and as a means to give operational semantics to equational theories. The latter has been illustrated by giving an operational interpretation of the equational theory of natural numbers. The aim of this book, however, is to develop equational theories for reasoning about reactive systems. This chapter provides the first simple examples of such theories. Not surprisingly, the semantics of these theories is defined in terms of the operational framework of the previous chapter. For clarity, equational theories tailored towards reasoning about reactive systems are referred to as *process theories*. The objects being described by a process theory are referred to as *processes*. The next two sections introduce a *minimal* process theory with its semantics. This minimal theory is mainly illustrative from a conceptual point of view. Sections 4.4 and 4.5 provide some elementary extensions of the minimal theory, to illustrate the issues involved in extending process theories. Incremental development of process theories is crucial in tailoring a process theory to the specifics of a given design or analysis problem. The resulting framework is flexible and it allows designers to include precisely those aspects in a process theory that are relevant and useful for the problem at hand. Incremental design also simplifies many of the proofs needed for the development of a rich process theory. The remainder of this book builds upon the simple theory introduced in Sections 4.2 through 4.4. Sections 4.5 and 4.6 present extensions of this basic process theory that provide a basis for the next chapter on recursion. Recursion is essential in any practically useful theory. The final section of this chapter puts everything into the perspective of the relevant literature, and provides pointers for further reading.

4.2 The process theory MPT

This chapter starts from a very simple process theory MPT(A), where MPT is an abbreviation for Minimal Process Theory and where A is a set of actions (sometimes also referred to as *atomic* actions). The set of actions is a parameter of the theory. The idea is that terms over the signature of theory MPT(A) specify processes. The signature has one constant, one binary function, and a set of unary functions. Note that it is common practice to refer to functions in the signature of a process theory as *operators*.

(i) The constant in the signature of MPT(A) is the constant 0, denoting *inaction*. Process 0 cannot execute any action; in other words, 0 can only deadlock.

(ii) The signature also has a binary operator $+$, denoting *alternative composition* or *choice*. If x and y are terms over the signature of MPT(A), the process corresponding to term $x + y$ behaves either as x or as y, but not as both. A choice is resolved upon execution of the first action. The inaction constant 0 is the identity element (also called unit element or neutral element) of alternative composition.

(iii) Finally, the signature of theory MPT(A) has, for each action $a \in A$, a unary operator $a.\_$, denoting *action prefix*. If x is a term, the process corresponding to $a.x$ executes action a and then proceeds as x. Substituting the inaction constant 0 for x yields the basic process $a.0$ that can execute an a and then deadlocks.

From these descriptions, it is already clear that the theory MPT(A) allows for the specification of simple sequential processes with branching behavior. The latter is obtained via the choice operator. It remains to give the axioms of the equational theory MPT(A). The process theory is axiomatized by four axioms, namely A1, A2, A3, and A6, given in Table 4.1. The naming is not consecutive for historical reasons (see (Baeten & Weijland, 1990)). The table adheres to the format introduced in Section 2.2. Notation $(a.\_)_{a \in A}$ in the signature of theory MPT(A) means that MPT(A) has a function $a.\_$ for every $a \in A$.

Axioms A1, A2, and A3 express properties of alternative composition. The fact that a choice between x and y is the same as a choice between y and x is reflected by Axiom A1. Axiom A2 expresses that a choice between x and choosing between y and z is the same as a choice between choosing between x and y, and z. In both cases, a choice is made between three alternatives. If one has to choose between two identical alternatives, this is the same as not choosing at all; this is expressed by Axiom A3. The three properties of alternative composition reflected by Axioms A1, A2, and A3, are often referred to as *commutativity*, *associativity*, and *idempotency*, respectively. Axiom A6 expresses

MPT(A)		
constant: 0;	unary: $(a.\_)_{a \in A}$;	binary: $\_ + \_$;
x, y, z;		
	$x + y = y + x$	A1
	$(x + y) + z = x + (y + z)$	A2
	$x + x = x$	A3
	$x + 0 = x$	A6

Table 4.1. The process theory MPT(A).

that in the context of a choice deadlock is avoided as long as possible. It is not allowed to choose for inaction if there is still an alternative. Stated mathematically, the inaction constant is an *identity element* for alternative composition.

To improve readability, terms over the signature of some process theory T are simply referred to as T-terms. Furthermore, binding priorities are introduced. Action-prefix operators always bind stronger than other operators; the binary $+$ always binds weaker than other operators. Hence, the term $a.x + y$, with x and y arbitrary MPT(A)-terms and a an action in A, is in fact the term $(a.x) + y$; similarly, $a.a.x + a.y$ represents $(a.(a.x)) + (a.y)$.

Using the axioms of the theory MPT(A) and the rules of equational logic presented in Chapter 2, equalities between process terms can be derived.

Example 4.2.1 (Proofs in a process theory) The following derivation is a compact proof of the equality $a.x + (b.y + a.x) = a.x + b.y$, where a and b are actions in A and x and y are arbitrary MPT(A)-terms:

$$\begin{aligned} \text{MPT}(A) \vdash \; a.x + (b.y + a.x) &= a.x + (a.x + b.y) \\ &= (a.x + a.x) + b.y = a.x + b.y. \end{aligned}$$

The above example shows how a process theory can be used to reason about the equivalence of processes. This is one of the main objectives of a process theory. Another major objective of a process theory is that it serves as a means to specify processes.

Example 4.2.2 (The lady or the tiger?) Recall Example 3.1.9 from the previous chapter, describing a situation where a prisoner is confronted with two closed doors, one hiding a dangerous tiger and the other hiding a beautiful lady. The described situation can be modeled by a process term using the three actions introduced in Example 3.1.9, namely the term

$$\mathit{open}.\mathit{eat}.0 + \mathit{open}.\mathit{marry}.0. \tag{4.2.1}$$

This term describes that after opening a door the prisoner is confronted with either the tiger or the lady. He does not have a choice; in fact, the choice is made as soon as he chooses a door to open, which is the desired situation. In the previous chapter, such a choice was called a non-deterministic choice.

In Example 3.1.9, the described situation has been captured in the leftmost transition system of Figure 3.3. Term (4.2.1) corresponds to this transition system, except for the termination behavior. In Example 3.1.9, a distinction was made between successful and unsuccessful termination, expressed through a terminating state and a deadlock state, respectively. The process theory MPT(A) does not have the possibility to distinguish between these two kinds of termination behavior. Termination is specified by the inaction constant 0. In the next section, where a model of MPT(A) is given, it becomes clear that 0 corresponds to unsuccessful termination. In Section 4.4, theory MPT(A) is extended with a new constant that allows the specification of successful termination.

In Example 3.1.9, a second transition system is discussed, namely the rightmost transition system of Figure 3.3. Except for the termination behavior, also this transition system can be specified as an MPT(A)-term:

$$open.(eat.0 + marry.0). \tag{4.2.2}$$

For the same reasons as those given in Example 3.1.9, terms (4.2.1) and (4.2.2) describe different situations. Thus, it is desirable that the two terms are not derivably equal.

Generalizing the last observation in the above example means that terms of the form $a.(x+y)$ and $a.x+a.y$, where a is an action and x and y are arbitrary but different terms, should not be derivably equal (unless x and y are derivably equal). It turns out that the general equality $a.(x + y) = a.x + a.y$ is indeed not derivable from theory MPT(A) (see Exercise 4.3.7). In other words, action prefix does not distribute over alternative composition.

In term $a.x + a.y$, the choice between the eventual execution of x or y is made upon the execution of a, whereas in $a.(x+y)$ this choice is made after the execution of a. In the terminology of Section 3.1, the two terms specify processes with different branching structure. Thus, (at least some) processes with different branching structure cannot be proven equal in theory MPT(A). In the next section, a model of MPT(A) is given in terms of the semantic domain introduced in the previous chapter. It turns out that derivability in MPT(A) coincides with bisimilarity in the semantic domain.

In Section 3.1, it has already been mentioned that it is not always necessary to distinguish between processes that only differ in branching structure. In the semantic domain, this translates to choosing another equivalence on transition systems. In the framework of the process theory MPT(A), it is possible to add the distributivity of action prefix over choice as an axiom to the theory. In general, one has to design a process theory in such a way that derivability in the theory coincides with the desired semantic equivalence. In Chapter 3, bisimilarity has been chosen as the basic semantic equivalence. As a consequence, distributivity of action prefix over choice is not included as an axiom in theory MPT(A). Note that this conforms to the goal of this section that aims at developing a *minimal* process theory. By omitting distributivity of action prefix over choice from the minimal theory MPT(A), the freedom of adding it when necessary or desirable is retained. Of course, doing so has consequences for the semantic domain in the sense that a different equivalence on transition systems is needed in order to construct a model of the extended theory. Chapter 12 investigates a number of interesting axioms that lead to different semantic equivalences when they are included in a process theory.

Exercises

4.2.1 Prove that the three axioms A1, A2, and A3 of MPT(A) are equivalent to the following *two* axioms:

$$(x + y) + z = (y + z) + x \qquad \text{A2}'$$
$$x + x = x \qquad \text{A3}$$

(with x, y, z MPT(A)-terms).
(Hint: first show that commutativity (A1) is derivable from A2′ and A3.)

4.2.2 Prove that the three axioms A1, A2, and A3 of MPT(A) are equivalent to the following two axioms:

$$(x + y) + z = y + (z + x) \qquad \text{A2}''$$
$$x + x = x \qquad \text{A3}$$

(with x, y, z MPT(A)-terms).
(Hint: as in the previous exercise, show commutativity first. Use this several times in order to show associativity.)

4.2.3 For any (open) MPT(A)-terms x and y, define $x \leq y$ if and only if MPT(A) $\vdash x + y = y$; if $x \leq y$, it is said that x is a *summand* of y. The idea is that summand x describes a (not necessarily strict) subset of the alternatives of term y, and can thus be added to y without essentially changing the process.

(a) Prove that $x \leq y$, for terms x and y, if and only if there is a term z such that MPT(A) $\vdash x + z = y$.
(b) Prove that $\leq$ is a partial ordering, i.e., that

1. $\leq$ is reflexive (for all terms x, $x \leq x$),
2. $\leq$ is anti-symmetric (for all x, y, $x \leq y$ and $y \leq x$ implies $\text{MPT}(A) \vdash x = y$),
3. $\leq$ is transitive (for all x, y, z, $x \leq y$ and $y \leq z$ implies $x \leq z$).

(c) Give an example of two closed MPT(A)-terms p and q such that not $p \leq q$ and not $q \leq p$.

(d) Prove that for any terms x, y, z, $x \leq y$ implies $x + z \leq y + z$.

(e) Give an example of two closed MPT(A)-terms p and q such that $p \leq q$ but not $a.p \leq a.q$ (with $a \in A$).

4.3 The term model

In the previous section, the process theory MPT(A), with A a set of actions, has been introduced. This section presents a model of this equational theory, following the concepts explained in Section 2.3. The model is built using the semantic framework of Chapter 3.

The starting point of the construction of this model is a so-called *term algebra*. The term algebra for the theory MPT(A) has as its universe the set of all closed MPT(A)-terms. The constants and functions of the term algebra are the constants and functions of MPT(A). The identity on the domain of the algebra is the syntactical equivalence of terms (denoted $\equiv$; see Definition 2.2.3 (Terms)). The term algebra itself is not a model of MPT(A). The reason is that syntactical equivalence of terms does not coincide with derivability as defined by the axioms of MPT(A). The term algebra can be turned into a model by transforming its domain, the closed MPT(A)-terms, into a transition-system space, as defined in Definition 3.1.1. As a consequence, bisimilarity, as defined in Definition 3.1.10, becomes an equivalence relation on closed MPT(A)-terms. As already suggested before, it turns out that bisimilarity is a suitable equivalence that matches derivability in MPT(A). It is shown that bisimilarity is a congruence on the term algebra. The term algebra modulo bisimilarity is shown to be a model of MPT(A), referred to as the term model. Finally, it is shown that the process theory MPT(A) is a ground-complete axiomatization of the term model.

The remainder often uses the notation $\mathcal{C}(T)$ to denote the set of closed terms over the signature of a process theory T. (Note that this slightly generalizes the notation for closed terms introduced in Definition 2.2.3 (Terms).)

Definition 4.3.1 (Term algebra) The algebra $\mathbb{P}(\text{MPT}(A)) = (\mathcal{C}(\text{MPT}(A)), +, (a.\_)_{a \in A}, 0)$ is called the *term algebra* for theory MPT(A). Recall from

Definition 2.2.3 (Terms) that syntactical equivalence, $\equiv$, is the identity on the domain $\mathcal{C}(\text{MPT}(A))$ of this algebra.

The term algebra is not a model of the process theory $\text{MPT}(A)$, assuming the identity function as the interpretation of the signature of $\text{MPT}(A)$ into $\mathbb{P}(\text{MPT}(A))$. The term algebra does not capture the equalities defined by the axioms of $\text{MPT}(A)$. This can be easily seen as follows. Consider the equality $a.0 + a.0 = a.0$, with $a \in A$. Clearly, because of Axiom A3, $\text{MPT}(A) \vdash a.0 + a.0 = a.0$; however, $a.0 + a.0 \not\equiv a.0$. According to Definition 2.3.6 (Validity), this means that Axiom A3 is not valid in the term algebra $\mathbb{P}(\text{MPT}(A))$. As a direct consequence, the term algebra is not a model of $\text{MPT}(A)$ (see Definition 2.3.8 (Model)).

The second step in the construction of a model of the theory $\text{MPT}(A)$ is to turn the set of process terms $\mathcal{C}(\text{MPT}(A))$ into a transition-system space as defined in Definition 3.1.1. The sets of states and labels are the sets of closed terms $\mathcal{C}(\text{MPT}(A))$ and actions A, respectively. A direct consequence of this choice is that closed $\text{MPT}(A)$-terms are turned into transition systems. The termination predicate $\_\downarrow$ and the (ternary) transition relation $\_ \xrightarrow{\_} \_$ are defined through a term deduction system. Recall that deduction systems are discussed in Section 3.2. The transition relation is constructed from a family of binary transition relations $\_ \xrightarrow{a} \_$ for each atomic action $a \in A$. If p and p' are closed terms in $\mathcal{C}(\text{MPT}(A))$, intuitively, $p \xrightarrow{a} p'$ holds if and only if p can execute an action a and thereby transforms into p'. The deduction system defining the termination predicate and the transition relation is given in Table 4.2. The tabular presentation of the deduction system is similar to the presentation of equational theories as outlined in Chapter 2. The term deduction system corresponding to an equational theory T is referred to as $TDS(T)$. The first entry of Table 4.2 gives the signature of the term deduction system. The second entry contains the deduction rules. The termination predicate and the ternary transition relation of the transition-system space under construction are defined as the smallest set and relation satisfying these deduction rules, as explained in Definition 3.2.3 (Transition-system space induced by a deduction system).

The first deduction rule (which actually has an empty set of premises and is therefore also called an axiom, as explained in Section 3.2) states that any process term $a.p$, with a an action and p another process term, can execute the atomic action a and thereby transforms into process term p. The other two deduction rules explain that a process term $p + q$ can execute either an action from p or an action from q. As a consequence, the alternative disappears and can no longer be executed. Since the term deduction system for theory $\text{MPT}(A)$ does not have any rules for termination, the termination predicate

— *TDS*(MPT(A))		
constant: 0;	unary: $(a.\_)_{a \in A}$;	binary: $\_ + \_$;
x, x', y, y';		
$a.x \xrightarrow{a} x$	$\dfrac{x \xrightarrow{a} x'}{x + y \xrightarrow{a} x'}$	$\dfrac{y \xrightarrow{a} y'}{x + y \xrightarrow{a} y'}$

Table 4.2. Term deduction system for MPT(A) (with $a \in A$).

becomes the empty set. This means that successful termination is not possible, which corresponds to the intuitive explanations given earlier.

Example 4.3.2 (Transition systems for closed MPT(A)-terms) As an example, Figure 4.1 shows the transition systems induced by the process terms $a.b.0$ and $a.b.0+a.(b.0+b.0)$. Note that the two terms are derivably equal, whereas the two transition systems are obviously not the same. However, it is straightforward to show that the two transition systems are bisimilar (see Section 3.1). Notice that any transition system induced by a closed MPT(A)-term is a regular transition system (see Definition 3.1.15), that does not contain any cycles (i.e., from any state, that state is not reachable by a non-empty sequence of steps). The fact that closed MPT(A)-terms correspond to regular transition systems is an immediate consequence of Theorem 5.8.2 proven in Section 5.8. The fact that these transition systems cannot contain cycles follows from Theorem 4.5.4 proven later in this chapter.

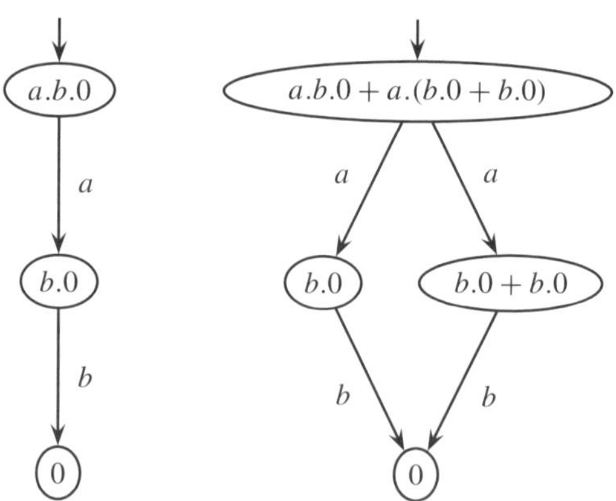

Fig. 4.1. Transition systems $a.b.0$ and $a.b.0 + a.(b.0 + b.0)$.

At this point, the term algebra $\mathbb{P}$(MPT(A)) of Definition 4.3.1 has been turned into a transition-system space. In the remainder, a term algebra such as $\mathbb{P}(\mathrm{MPT}(A))$ is also referred to as an algebra of transition systems. This implicitly assumes that the term algebra is accompanied by a term deduction system defining a transition-system space. It is always clear from the context which term deduction system is meant.

A consequence of the fact that term algebra $\mathbb{P}(\mathrm{MPT}(A))$ has been turned into a transition-system space is that bisimilarity is inherited as an equivalence relation on closed terms. It has already been suggested a number of times that derivability in $\mathrm{MPT}(A)$ captures the same notion of equivalence as bisimilarity. At this point, it is possible to be more precise. It can be shown that two closed terms are derivably equal if and only if the induced transition systems are bisimilar. Let us examine the relation between bisimilarity and derivability in some more detail.

Recall the context rule from Definition 2.2.8 (Derivability). This rule plays a crucial role in equational derivations. It implies that terms can be replaced by derivably equal terms in arbitrary contexts. If bisimilarity and derivability are supposed to be the 'same' notion of equivalence, the context rule from equational logic must in some sense also be valid for bisimilarity. It turns out that the notion of a *congruence relation*, as defined in Definition 2.3.16, is the desired equivalent of the context rule.

Theorem 4.3.3 (Congruence) Bisimilarity is a congruence on the algebra of transition systems $\mathbb{P}(\mathrm{MPT}(A))$.

Proof Using Theorem 3.2.7 (Congruence theorem), the proof is trivial because it is easy to see that the deduction system of Table 4.2 is in path format, as defined in Definition 3.2.5.

Unfortunately, deduction systems are not always in path format, which means that it sometimes may be necessary to prove a congruence result directly from the definition of a congruence relation, namely Definition 2.3.16. To illustrate such a proof, it is given here as well. Definition 2.3.16 states two requirements on a relation, bisimilarity in this case. The first requirement is that bisimilarity is an equivalence. From Theorem 3.1.13, it is already known that bisimilarity is an equivalence. Thus, in order to prove that bisimilarity is a congruence on $\mathbb{P}(\mathrm{MPT}(A))$, it suffices to show that for each n-ary ($n \geq 1$) function f of $\mathbb{P}(\mathrm{MPT}(A))$ and for all $p_1, \ldots, p_n, q_1, \ldots, q_n \in \mathcal{C}(\mathrm{MPT}(A))$, $p_1 \leftrightarrow q_1, \cdots, p_n \leftrightarrow q_n$ implies that $f(p_1, \ldots, p_n) \leftrightarrow f(q_1, \ldots, q_n)$.

Consider the binary function $+$. Assume that $p_1 \leftrightarrow q_1$ and $p_2 \leftrightarrow q_2$, with $p_1, p_2, q_1, q_2 \in \mathcal{C}(\mathrm{MPT}(A))$. By definition, this means that there exist bisimulation relations R_1 and R_2 such that $(p_1, q_1) \in R_1$ and $(p_2, q_2) \in R_2$. Define relation R as follows: $R = R_1 \cup R_2 \cup \{(p_1 + p_2, q_1 + q_2)\}$. It can be shown that relation R is a bisimulation relation. It needs to be shown that R satisfies for each pair of process terms in the relation the transfer conditions of Definition 3.1.10 (Bisimilarity). The pairs of process terms in R that are elements of R_1 or R_2 obviously satisfy the transfer conditions because R_1 and R_2 are bisimulation relations that satisfy those conditions. Thus, it remains to prove that the pair of process terms $(p_1 + p_2, q_1 + q_2)$ satisfies the transfer conditions. Only condition (i) is proven; condition (ii) follows from the symmetry in Definition 3.1.10 (Bisimilarity). Since terms in $\mathcal{C}(\mathrm{MPT}(A))$ cannot terminate successfully, transfer conditions (iii) and (iv) are trivially satisfied.

(i) Suppose that $p_1 + p_2 \xrightarrow{a} p'$ for some $a \in A$ and $p' \in \mathcal{C}(\mathrm{MPT}(A))$. It must be shown that there is a $q' \in \mathcal{C}(\mathrm{MPT}(A))$ such that $q_1 + q_2 \xrightarrow{a} q'$ and $(p', q') \in R$. Inspection of the deduction rules in Table 4.2 reveals that $p_1 + p_2 \xrightarrow{a} p'$ must follow from the fact that $p_1 \xrightarrow{a} p'$ or $p_2 \xrightarrow{a} p'$. In the first case, the fact that R_1 is a bisimulation relation that relates the terms p_1 and q_1 yields the existence of a term $q' \in \mathcal{C}(\mathrm{MPT}(A))$ such that $q_1 \xrightarrow{a} q'$ and $(p', q') \in R_1$; in the second case, for similar reasons, $q_2 \xrightarrow{a} q'$ for some q' such that $(p', q') \in R_2$. Thus, in both cases, $q_1 + q_2 \xrightarrow{a} q'$ for some $q' \in \mathcal{C}(\mathrm{MPT}(A))$ such that $(p', q') \in R$.

The proof that bisimilarity is a congruence with respect to the action-prefix operators is left as an exercise (Exercise 4.3.3). □

The above theorem implies that bisimilarity on closed terms respects the rules of equational logic. It provides the basis for the definition of the term model of the process theory MPT(A) of the previous section. The term model is in fact a quotient algebra, namely the term algebra modulo bisimilarity (see Definition 2.3.18 (Quotient algebra)).

Definition 4.3.4 (Term model) The term model of process theory MPT(A) is the quotient algebra $\mathbb{P}(\mathrm{MPT}(A))_{/\leftrightarroweq}$, where $\mathbb{P}(\mathrm{MPT}(A))$ is the term algebra defined in Definition 4.3.1.

The elements of the universe of the algebra $\mathbb{P}(\mathrm{MPT}(A))_{/\leftrightarroweq}$ are called *processes*. In the term model, a process is an equivalence class of closed terms under bisimilarity. It can be shown that there is a strong correspondence between bisimilarity and the equalities that can be obtained from the equations of the process theory MPT(A): (1) any two derivably equal MPT(A)-terms fall into the same equivalence class when interpreted in the term model, and (2) any two closed MPT(A)-terms that are bisimilar are also derivably equal. In Chapter 2, the first notion has been introduced as soundness (see Definition 2.3.8

(Model)), whereas the second property has been called ground-completeness (Definition 2.3.23). In order to prove soundness and ground-completeness of $\text{MPT}(A)$ for the term model, an interpretation of constants and functions of $\text{MPT}(A)$ into those of the term model is needed. The construction of the model allows a very straightforward interpretation. The constant 0 is mapped onto the equivalence class $[0]_{\leftrightarrow}$, whereas each of the operators is mapped onto the corresponding function in $\mathbb{P}(\text{MPT}(A))_{/\leftrightarrow}$ following Definition 2.3.18 (Quotient algebra). In the remainder, it is always assumed that this standard interpretation is used; thus, it is omitted in the various notations whenever possible.

Theorem 4.3.5 (Soundness) The process theory $\text{MPT}(A)$ is a sound axiomatization of the algebra $\mathbb{P}(\text{MPT}(A))_{/\leftrightarrow}$, i.e., $\mathbb{P}(\text{MPT}(A))_{/\leftrightarrow} \models \text{MPT}(A)$.

Proof According to Definition 2.3.8 (Model), it must be shown that, for each axiom $s = t$ of $\text{MPT}(A)$, $\mathbb{P}(\text{MPT}(A))_{/\leftrightarrow} \models s = t$. Below, the proof is given for Axiom A6; the proofs for the other axioms are left as an exercise (Exercise 4.3.4).

Recall the notations concerning quotient algebras introduced in Section 2.3. Let p be a closed term in $\mathcal{C}(\text{MPT}(A))$. It follows from Definition 2.3.6 (Validity) that it must be shown that $[p]_{\leftrightarrow} +_{\leftrightarrow} [0]_{\leftrightarrow} = [p]_{\leftrightarrow}$. Definition 2.3.18 (Quotient algebra) implies that it must be shown that $[p + 0]_{\leftrightarrow} = [p]_{\leftrightarrow}$ and, thus, that $p + 0 \leftrightarrow p$.

It suffices to give a bisimulation relation on process terms that contains all the pairs $(p + 0, p)$ for closed $\text{MPT}(A)$-term p. Let $R = \{(p + 0, p) \mid p \in \mathcal{C}(\text{MPT}(A))\} \cup \{(p, p) \mid p \in \mathcal{C}(\text{MPT}(A))\}$. It must be shown that all elements of R satisfy the transfer conditions of Definition 3.1.10 (Bisimilarity). The transfer conditions trivially hold for all pairs (p, p) with p a closed term. Hence, only elements of R of the form $(p + 0, p)$ with $p \in \mathcal{C}(\text{MPT}(A))$ need to be considered. Let $(p + 0, p)$ be such an element. Transfer conditions (iii) and (iv) are trivially satisfied because closed $\text{MPT}(A)$-terms cannot terminate successfully.

(i) Suppose that $p + 0 \xrightarrow{a} p'$ for some $a \in A$ and $p' \in \mathcal{C}(\text{MPT}(A))$. By inspection of the deduction rules in Table 4.2, it easily follows that necessarily $p \xrightarrow{a} p'$. The fact that $(p', p') \in R$ proves this case.

(ii) Suppose that $p \xrightarrow{a} p'$ for some $a \in A$ and $p' \in \mathcal{C}(\text{MPT}(A))$. The application of the bottom left deduction rule of Table 4.2 yields $p + 0 \xrightarrow{a} p'$. As $(p', p') \in R$, also this transfer condition is satisfied.

□

The above theorem has two immediate corollaries.

Corollary 4.3.6 (Soundness) Let s and t be MPT(A)-terms. If MPT$(A) \vdash s = t$, then $\mathbb{P}(\text{MPT}(A))_{/\leftrightarrow} \models s = t$.

Corollary 4.3.7 (Soundness) Let p and q be two closed MPT(A)-terms. If MPT$(A) \vdash p = q$, then $p \leftrightarrow q$.

This last corollary states that by using the process theory to reason about closed terms only bisimilar terms can be proved equivalent. Under the assumption that the model captures the appropriate intuitions about processes (such as, for example, operational intuitions concerning the execution of actions), this property guarantees that using the equational theory for deriving equalities cannot lead to mistakes. The converse of this property, ground-completeness, assures that the process theory is strong enough to derive all bisimilarities between closed terms. That is, assuming two closed MPT(A)-terms p and q that are bisimilar, it can be shown that p and q are also derivably equal, i.e., MPT$(A) \vdash p = q$. The idea behind the ground-completeness proof, given below, is to show MPT$(A) \vdash p = q$ via the intermediate results MPT$(A) \vdash p = p + q$ and MPT$(A) \vdash p + q = q$. Clearly, these intermediate results imply MPT$(A) \vdash p = p + q = q$. To understand the intuition behind this idea, recall the notion of summands as introduced in Exercise 4.2.3. The crucial idea of the ground-completeness proof is that, if p and q are bisimilar, it must be the case that every summand of p is a summand of q and vice versa. This implies that p as a whole can be seen as a summand of q and q as a whole as a summand of p, which corresponds to the above mentioned intermediate results.

The following two lemmas are needed in the ground-completeness proof.

Lemma 4.3.8 (Towards completeness) Let p be a closed MPT(A)-term. If $p \xrightarrow{a} p'$ for some closed term p' and $a \in A$, then MPT$(A) \vdash p = a.p' + p$.

Proof The property is proven by induction on the structure of p.

(i) $p \equiv 0$. This case cannot occur as $0 \not\xrightarrow{a}$.

(ii) $p \equiv b.p''$ for some $b \in A$ and closed term p''. The assumption that $p \xrightarrow{a} p'$ implies that $b \equiv a$ and $p'' \equiv p'$. Thus, MPT$(A) \vdash p = p + p = b.p'' + p = a.p' + p$.

(iii) $p \equiv p_1 + p_2$ for some closed terms p_1 and p_2. From $p \xrightarrow{a} p'$, it follows that $p_1 \xrightarrow{a} p'$ or $p_2 \xrightarrow{a} p'$. By induction, (1) $p_1 \xrightarrow{a} p'$ implies MPT$(A) \vdash p_1 = a.p' + p_1$, and (2) $p_2 \xrightarrow{a} p'$ implies MPT$(A) \vdash p_2 = a.p' + p_2$. If $p_1 \xrightarrow{a} p'$, then MPT$(A) \vdash p = p_1 + p_2 = (a.p' + p_1) + p_2 = a.p' + (p_1 + p_2) = a.p' + p$. If $p_2 \xrightarrow{a} p'$, then

$\text{MPT}(A) \vdash p = p_1 + p_2 = p_1 + (a.p' + p_2) = a.p' + (p_1 + p_2) = a.p' + p$. □

Lemma 4.3.9 Let p, q, and r be closed MPT(A)-terms. If $(p+q)+r \leftrightarrow r$, then $p + r \leftrightarrow r$ and $q + r \leftrightarrow r$.

Proof See Exercise 4.3.5. □

Theorem 4.3.10 (Ground-completeness) Theory MPT(A) is a ground-complete axiomatization of the term model $\mathbb{P}(\text{MPT}(A))_{/\leftrightarrow}$, i.e., for any closed MPT(A)-terms p and q, $\mathbb{P}(\text{MPT}(A))_{/\leftrightarrow} \models p = q$ implies $\text{MPT}(A) \vdash p = q$.

Proof Suppose that $\mathbb{P}(\text{MPT}(A))_{/\leftrightarrow} \models p = q$, i.e., $p \leftrightarrow q$. It must be shown that $\text{MPT}(A) \vdash p = q$. It suffices to prove that, for all closed MPT(A)-terms p and q,

$$p + q \leftrightarrow q \quad \text{implies} \quad \text{MPT}(A) \vdash p + q = q \tag{4.3.1}$$

and that, for all closed MPT(A)-terms p and q,

$$p \leftrightarrow p + q \quad \text{implies} \quad \text{MPT}(A) \vdash p = p + q. \tag{4.3.2}$$

That these properties are sufficient to prove the theorem can be seen as follows. Suppose that properties (4.3.1) and (4.3.2) hold. If $p \leftrightarrow q$, then, by the fact that bisimilarity is reflexive (i.e., $p \leftrightarrow p$ and $q \leftrightarrow q$) and the fact that bisimilarity is a congruence on $\mathbb{P}(\text{MPT}(A))$, $p + p \leftrightarrow p + q$ and $p + q \leftrightarrow q + q$. The soundness of MPT($A$) for $\mathbb{P}(\text{MPT}(A))_{/\leftrightarrow}$, more in particular the validity of Axiom A3, implies that $p + p \leftrightarrow p$ and $q + q \leftrightarrow q$. Using symmetry and transitivity of bisimilarity, $p \leftrightarrow p + q$ and $p + q \leftrightarrow q$ are obtained. Thus, properties (4.3.2) and (4.3.1), respectively, yield that $\text{MPT}(A) \vdash p = p + q$ and $\text{MPT}(A) \vdash p + q = q$. These last results can be combined to show that $\text{MPT}(A) \vdash p = p + q = q$.

Property (4.3.1), namely, for all closed MPT(A)-terms p and q, $p + q \leftrightarrow q$ implies $\text{MPT}(A) \vdash p + q = q$, is proven by induction on the total number of symbols (counting constants and action-prefix operators) in closed terms p and q. The proof of property (4.3.2) is similar and therefore omitted.

The induction proof goes as follows. Assume $p + q \leftrightarrow q$ for some closed MPT(A)-terms p and q. The base case of the induction corresponds to the case that the total number of symbols in p and q equals two, namely when p and q are both equal to 0. Using Axiom A3, it trivially follows that $\text{MPT}(A) \vdash 0 + 0 = 0$, proving the base case. The proof of the inductive step consists of a case analysis based on the structure of term p.

(i) Assume $p \equiv 0$. It follows directly from the axioms in Table 4.1 that $\text{MPT}(A) \vdash p + q = 0 + q = q + 0 = q$.

(ii) Assume $p \equiv a.p'$ for some $a \in A$ and closed term p'. Then, $p \xrightarrow{a} p'$ and thus $p + q \xrightarrow{a} p'$. As $p + q \leftrightarrow q$, also $q \xrightarrow{a} q'$ for some closed term q' such that $p' \leftrightarrow q'$. By Lemma 4.3.8 (Towards completeness), $\text{MPT}(A) \vdash q = a.q' + q$. From $p' \leftrightarrow q'$, as in the first part of the proof of this theorem, it follows that $p' + q' \leftrightarrow q'$ and $q' + p' \leftrightarrow p'$ and, hence, by induction, $\text{MPT}(A) \vdash p' + q' = q'$ and $\text{MPT}(A) \vdash q' + p' = p'$. Combining these last two results gives $\text{MPT}(A) \vdash p' = q' + p' = p' + q' = q'$. Finally, $\text{MPT}(A) \vdash p + q = a.p' + q = a.q' + q = q$.

(iii) Assume $p \equiv p_1 + p_2$ for some closed terms p_1 and p_2. As $(p_1 + p_2) + q \leftrightarrow q$, by Lemma 4.3.9, $p_1 + q \leftrightarrow q$ and $p_2 + q \leftrightarrow q$. Thus, by induction, $\text{MPT}(A) \vdash p_1 + q = q$ and $\text{MPT}(A) \vdash p_2 + q = q$. Combining these results gives $\text{MPT}(A) \vdash p + q = (p_1 + p_2) + q = p_1 + (p_2 + q) = p_1 + q = q$, which completes the proof. □

Corollary 4.3.11 (Ground-completeness) Let p and q be arbitrary closed $\text{MPT}(A)$-terms. If $p \leftrightarrow q$, then $\text{MPT}(A) \vdash p = q$.

An interesting observation at this point is that the term model constructed in this section is isomorphic (as defined in Definition 2.3.26) to the initial algebra of equational theory $\text{MPT}(A)$ (as defined in Definition 2.3.19). Exercise 4.3.6 asks to prove this fact.

Exercises

4.3.1 Consider the terms $a.(b.(c.0 + d.0))$, $a.(b.c.0 + b.d.0)$, and $a.b.c.0 + a.b.d.0$. Give the transition systems for these terms, following the example of Figure 4.1.

4.3.2 Consider the terms $a.c.0 + b.d.0$ and $a.c.0 + b.c.0$. Give the transition systems for these terms.

4.3.3 Prove that bisimilarity is a congruence with respect to the action-prefix operators $a.\_$ $(a \in A)$ on the term algebra $\mathbb{P}(\text{MPT}(A))$ defined in Definition 4.3.1, i.e., complete the second proof of Theorem 4.3.3 (Congruence).

4.3.4 Complete the proof of Theorem 4.3.5 (Soundness) by proving the validity of Axioms A1 through A3.

4.3.5 Prove Lemma 4.3.9.

4.3.6 Give the initial algebra (see Definition 2.3.19) of the process theory MPT(A). Show that this algebra is isomorphic to the term model given in Definition 4.3.4.

4.3.7 Consider the process theory MPT(A) of Table 4.1. Show that *not* MPT(A) $\vdash a.x + a.y = a.(x + y)$ (with $a \in A$ and x, y terms). (Hint: construct a model of theory MPT(A) that does not validate the equality.)

4.3.8 Show that the transition systems of the terms $a.(0 + 0) + a.0$ and $a.0 + a.0$ are not isomorphic (as defined in Exercise 3.1.10), whereas $a.(0 + 0)$ and $a.0$ are isomorphic. This implies that isomorphism is not a congruence relation on algebra $\mathbb{P}(\text{MPT}(A))$. Isomorphism can be turned into a congruence relation by allowing that states from a transition system are replaced by isomorphic states in the transition-system space. Show that turning isomorphism into a congruence in this way gives exactly bisimilarity, i.e., two transition systems are bisimilar if and only if they become isomorphic by replacing some of their reachable states by isomorphic states.

4.4 The empty process

The process theory MPT(A) is a *minimal* theory; not much can be expressed in it. One aspect that cannot be addressed is successful termination. The semantic framework of Chapter 3 distinguishes between terminating states and deadlock states; this distinction cannot be made in MPT(A). This issue was already addressed in Examples 3.1.9 and 4.2.2 (The lady or the tiger?), illustrating that the distinction is meaningful from a specification point of view. The distinction between successful and unsuccessful termination also turns out to be essential when sequential composition is introduced in Chapter 6.

To ease the description of processes, it is quite common to take an existing process theory and add a constant or an operator plus axioms. There are two types of extensions. First, there are extensions that only allow to describe certain processes more conveniently than before. Second, extensions may allow processes to be described that could not be described in the original theory. In Section 4.5, an extension of the first type is discussed; in this section, an extension of the second type is discussed, namely an extension that allows to distinguish successful and unsuccessful termination.

In order to express successful termination, the new constant 1, referred to as the empty process or the termination constant, is introduced. The extension of the process theory MPT(A) with the empty process 1 results in process theory BSP(A), the theory of Basic Sequential Processes. This section gives the equational theory as well as its term model.

Table 4.3 defines process theory BSP(A). The only difference between the signature of MPT(A) and the signature of BSP(A) is the constant 1. The axioms of BSP(A) are exactly the axioms of MPT(A), given in Table 4.1. The layout of Table 4.3 follows the rules set out in Chapter 2. The first entry formally states that BSP(A) is an extension of MPT(A). The second entry introduces the new constant, whereas the main part of the table gives additional axioms, none in this case.

BSP(A)
MPT(A);
constant: 1;
–

Table 4.3. The process theory BSP(A).

The extension of the process theory MPT(A) with the empty process resulting in the process theory BSP(A) has enlarged the set of terms that can be used to specify processes. The terms specifying processes are the closed terms in a process theory. Clearly, the set of closed BSP(A)-terms is strictly larger than the set of closed MPT(A)-terms. A question that needs answering is whether this extension has really enlarged the set of processes that can be specified in the process theory. If this is the case, the expressiveness of the process theory has increased. If this is not the case, the same set of processes can be specified, but in more syntactically different ways. The latter can thus be considered an extension for convenience.

In this case, it is not difficult to see that the expressiveness has increased. A term that contains an occurrence of 1 can never be equal to a term without a 1; inspection of the axioms (of MPT(A)) shows this easily. Thus, any term over the signature of BSP(A) that is not a term over the signature of MPT(A) cannot be derivably equal to a term over the signature of MPT(A). Observe that closed terms that are derivably equal must refer to the same process in some given model of an equational theory. Closed terms that are not derivably equal may be used to specify different processes. In fact, it is always possible to construct a model in which closed terms that are not derivably equal specify different processes (e.g., the initial algebra as defined in Definition 2.3.19). Thus, since any closed MPT(A)-term is a closed BSP(A)-term and since there are closed BSP(A)-terms that are not derivably equal to closed

MPT(A)-terms, the expressiveness of BSP(A) is strictly larger than the expressiveness of MPT(A). This fact is confirmed below by the fact that the term model of BSP(A) contains strictly more processes than the term model of MPT(A) given in the previous section.

Recall the notion of elimination as introduced in Section 2.2 in Example 2.2.13 and Proposition 2.2.20. An immediate consequence of the above discussion is that process theory BSP(A) does not have the elimination property for MPT(A); that is, it is not possible to eliminate the empty-process constant from BSP(A)-terms to obtain MPT(A)-terms. Nevertheless, it can be shown that the theory BSP(A) is a conservative ground-extension of the theory MPT(A), as defined in Definition 2.2.19. This assures that the theory BSP(A) can always be used to derive equalities between closed MPT(A)-terms.

Theorem 4.4.1 (Conservative ground-extension) Process theory BSP(A) is a conservative ground-extension of process theory MPT(A).

Proof Recall Definition 2.2.19 that states two proof obligations. By definition, the signature of BSP(A) includes the elements of the signature of MPT(A), and the axioms of BSP(A) are the axioms of MPT(A). This proves that BSP(A) is an extension of MPT(A), as defined in Definition 2.2.14, implying that it is also a ground-extension as defined in Definition 2.2.18. This satisfies the first proof obligation of Definition 2.2.19. Thus, it remains to be shown that for all closed MPT(A)-terms p and q, BSP(A) $\vdash p = q$ implies that MPT(A) $\vdash p = q$. Suppose that a proof of BSP(A) $\vdash p = q$ is given. Because neither p nor q contain any occurrences of 1 and because the axioms of BSP(A) are such that any term with an occurrence of 1 can only be equal to a term also containing an occurrence of 1, no term that occurs in the proof of BSP(A) $\vdash p = q$ contains an occurrence of 1. In other words, all terms that occur in the proof of BSP(A) $\vdash p = q$ are MPT(A)-terms. This means that the proof of BSP(A) $\vdash p = q$ is also a proof of MPT(A) $\vdash p = q$, completing the proof. □

Figure 4.2 visualizes the fact that theory BSP(A) is a conservative ground-extension of MPT(A). At this point, the figure is very simple and may be considered redundant. However, in the remainder, this figure is incrementally extended to show the relationships between the various process theories introduced in this book.

It remains to provide a model for BSP(A). In the same way as for the process theory MPT(A), a term model can be defined. Starting from the term algebra, the meaning of the constants and operators is defined using a term deduction

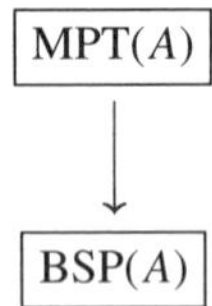

Fig. 4.2. BSP(A) is a conservative ground-extension of MPT(A).

system. This term deduction system is an extension of the term deduction system for MPT(A) given in Section 4.3. The term model is the quotient algebra of the term algebra modulo bisimilarity. The first step is to define the term algebra of closed BSP(A)-terms.

Definition 4.4.2 (Term algebra) The term algebra for BSP(A) is the algebra $\mathbb{P}(\text{BSP}(A)) = (\mathcal{C}(\text{BSP}(A)), +, (a.\_)_{a \in A}, 0, 1)$.

The next step in the construction of a model is to turn the set of closed terms into a transition-system space (see Definition 3.1.1). The sets of states and labels are the sets of closed terms $\mathcal{C}(\text{BSP}(A))$ and actions A, respectively. Both the ternary transition relation $\rightarrow \subseteq \mathcal{C}(\text{BSP}(A)) \times A \times \mathcal{C}(\text{BSP}(A))$ and the termination predicate $\downarrow \subseteq \mathcal{C}(\text{BSP}(A))$ are defined through the term deduction system in Table 4.4 that extends the term deduction system in Table 4.2. In other words, the transition relation and the termination predicate are the smallest relation and predicate satisfying the deduction rules in Tables 4.2 and 4.4. Note that the domain over which the variables range in Table 4.2 has (implicitly) been extended from the closed MPT(A)-terms to the set of closed BSP(A)-terms.

$TDS(\text{BSP}(A))$		
$TDS(\text{MPT}(A))$;		
constant: 1;		
x, y;		
$1 \downarrow$	$\dfrac{x \downarrow}{(x+y) \downarrow}$	$\dfrac{y \downarrow}{(x+y) \downarrow}$

Table 4.4. Term deduction system for BSP(A).

The term deduction system for BSP(A) has three extra deduction rules when compared to the term deduction system for MPT(A). The first rule is an axiom: it says that 1 can terminate. The other two rules state that an alternative-composition term has a termination option, as soon as one of the components has this option.

Example 4.4.3 (Transition systems of BSP(A)**-terms)** For any given closed term, a transition system can be obtained from the deduction system in Table 4.4 in the same way as before. The transition systems associated with the process terms $a.1 + b.0$ and $a.(b.0 + 1)$ are given in Figure 4.3. Recall that terminating states (such as the ones represented by the process terms 1 and $b.0 + 1$) are labeled by a small outgoing arrow.

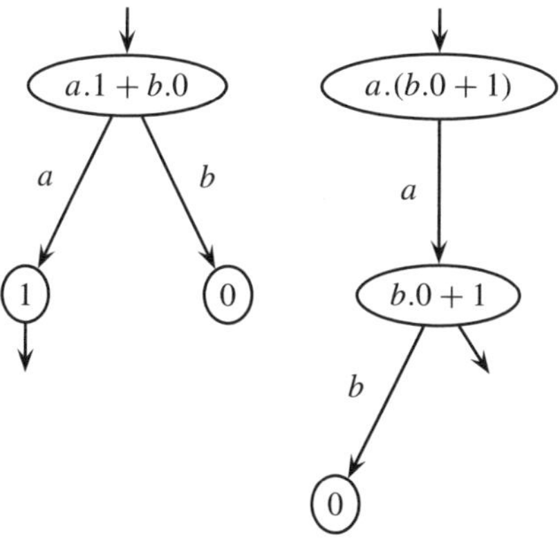

Fig. 4.3. Transition systems associated with $a.1 + b.0$ and $a.(b.0 + 1)$.

Example 4.4.4 (Transition systems) In drawing transition systems, it is often natural or convenient to abstract from the precise terms corresponding to a state. Usually, it is known from the context what terms are meant. Note that transition systems with identical graph structure are no longer distinguishable when terms are omitted from the nodes. For example, the transition systems associated with the processes $a.1$, $a.1 + 0$, and $a.1 + a.1$ are indistinguishable if the process terms are omitted, as illustrated in Figure 4.4. Note that transition systems with identical graph structure but different terms in the nodes are always bisimilar.

As in Section 4.3, bisimilarity is a congruence on the term algebra. This result forms the basis for the term model of BSP(A), which is the term algebra modulo bisimilarity. Note that the definition of bisimilarity (Definition 3.1.10) takes into account the termination relation. It is not difficult to see that transition systems that have termination options cannot be bisimilar to transition systems that do not have such options. Thus, transition systems with and

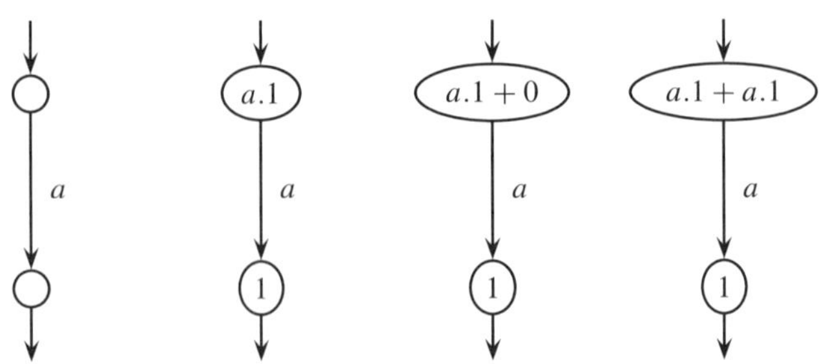

Fig. 4.4. Transition systems with identical graph structure.

without termination options end up in different equivalence classes in the term algebra modulo bisimilarity, i.e., they form different processes. Since all processes that can be specified in the theory MPT(A) of the previous section can also be specified in BSP(A), and since MPT(A) cannot be used to specify processes with termination options, the examples of Figure 4.3 confirm the earlier observation that BSP(A) is more expressive than MPT(A).

Proposition 4.4.5 (Congruence) Bisimilarity is a congruence on the term algebra $\mathbb{P}$(BSP(A)).

Proof The property follows immediately from the format of the deduction rules in Tables 4.2 and 4.4 and Theorem 3.2.7 (Congruence theorem). □

As mentioned, the resulting term model of BSP(A) is the term algebra of Definition 4.4.2 modulo bisimilarity (see Definition 2.3.18 (Quotient algebra)).

Definition 4.4.6 (Term model of BSP(A)**)** The term model of BSP(A) is the quotient algebra $\mathbb{P}(\mathrm{BSP}(A))_{/\leftrightarrow}$.

Theorem 4.4.7 (Soundness) The process theory BSP(A) is a sound axiomatization of the algebra $\mathbb{P}(\mathrm{BSP}(A))_{/\leftrightarrow}$, i.e., $\mathbb{P}(\mathrm{BSP}(A))_{/\leftrightarrow} \models \mathrm{BSP}(A)$.

Proof The proof of this theorem follows the same lines as the proof of the soundness of theory MPT(A) with respect to the algebra $\mathbb{P}(\mathrm{MPT}(A))_{/\leftrightarrow}$ (Theorem 4.3.5). It must be shown that, for each axiom $s = t$ of BSP(A), $\mathbb{P}(\mathrm{BSP}(A))_{/\leftrightarrow} \models s = t$. As the axioms of MPT($A$) and the axioms of BSP($A$) are identical, it may seem that there is nothing new to prove. This is not true, however, as deduction rules defining the termination predicate have been added to the term deduction system for MPT(A), and hence transfer conditions (iii) and (iv) of Definition 3.1.10 (Bisimilarity) that were trivially true in the proof of Theorem 4.3.5 are no longer satisfied trivially. The remainder gives the proof of Theorem 4.4.7 for Axiom A6; the proofs for the other axioms are left as Exercise 4.4.4.

Recall that it suffices to give a bisimulation that relates all pairs of left-hand- and right-hand sides of closed instantiations of Axiom A6. Let $R = \{(p + 0, p) \mid p \in \mathcal{C}(\text{BSP}(A))\} \cup \{(p, p) \mid p \in \mathcal{C}(\text{BSP}(A))\}$. It must be shown that all elements of R satisfy the transfer conditions of Definition 3.1.10 (Bisimilarity). Since the transfer conditions trivially hold for all pairs (p, p) with p a closed term, only elements of R of the form $(p + 0, p)$ need to be considered. Let $(p + 0, p)$ be such an element. For transfer conditions (i) and (ii), the proofs as given in Theorem 4.3.5 can be copied as no deduction rules involving the transition relation have been added.

(iii) Suppose that $(p + 0) \downarrow$. By inspection of the deduction rules in Table 4.4, it easily follows that necessarily $p \downarrow$, as it is impossible to derive $0 \downarrow$. This immediately proves this case.

(iv) Suppose that $p \downarrow$. The application of the middle deduction rule of Table 4.4 yields $(p + 0) \downarrow$, which proves also this case.

□

Corollary 4.4.8 (Soundness) Let s and t be two BSP(A)-terms. If $\text{BSP}(A) \vdash s = t$, then $\mathbb{P}(\text{BSP}(A))_{/\leftrightarrow} \models s = t$.

Corollary 4.4.9 (Soundness) Let p and q be two closed BSP(A)-terms. If $\text{BSP}(A) \vdash p = q$, then $p \leftrightarrow q$.

The soundness result shows that equational theory BSP(A) is a sound axiomatization of the term model $\mathbb{P}(\text{BSP}(A))_{/\leftrightarrow}$. It remains to see whether or not the axiomatization is also ground-complete. It turns out that this is the case. In order to prove this result, a similar approach is followed as the one leading to the ground-completeness result for MPT(A). The following lemmas provide steps towards the ground-completeness theorem.

Lemma 4.4.10 (Towards completeness) Let p be a closed BSP(A)-term. If $p \xrightarrow{a} p'$ for some closed term p' and $a \in A$, then $\text{BSP}(A) \vdash p = a.p' + p$. If $p \downarrow$, then $\text{BSP}(A) \vdash p = 1 + p$.

Proof The proof of the first property is similar to the proof of Lemma 4.3.8 (Towards completeness). There is one additional case in the induction.

This is the case that $p \equiv 1$. As $1 \overset{a}{\nrightarrow}$, for any $a \in A$, the property is trivially satisfied in this case. The proofs of the other cases can be copied as no deduction rules involving the binary transition relations $\_ \overset{a}{\rightarrow} \_$ have been added to the term deduction system.

The second property is proven by induction on the structure of p.

(i) $p \equiv 0$. The property is satisfied as $0 \not\downarrow$.

(ii) $p \equiv 1$. Using Axiom A3, obviously, $\text{BSP}(A) \vdash p = 1 = 1 + 1 = 1 + p$, which completes this case.

(iii) $p \equiv a.p'$ for some $a \in A$ and closed term p'. This case is satisfied as $a.p' \not\downarrow$.

(iv) $p \equiv p_1 + p_2$ for some closed terms p_1 and p_2. From $(p_1 + p_2)\downarrow$, it follows that $p_1\downarrow$ or $p_2\downarrow$. By induction, (1) $p_1\downarrow$ implies $\text{BSP}(A) \vdash p_1 = 1 + p_1$, and (2) $p_2\downarrow$ implies $\text{BSP}(A) \vdash p_2 = 1 + p_2$. If $p_1\downarrow$, then $\text{BSP}(A) \vdash p = p_1 + p_2 = (1 + p_1) + p_2 = 1 + (p_1 + p_2) = 1 + p$. If $p_2\downarrow$, then $\text{BSP}(A) \vdash p = p_1 + p_2 = p_1 + (1 + p_2) = (p_1 + 1) + p_2 = (1 + p_1) + p_2 = 1 + (p_1 + p_2) = 1 + p$. □

Lemma 4.4.11 Let p, q, and r be closed $\text{BSP}(A)$-terms. If $(p + q) + r \leftrightarrow r$, then $p + r \leftrightarrow r$ and $q + r \leftrightarrow r$.

Proof See Exercise 4.4.5. □

Theorem 4.4.12 (Ground-completeness) Theory $\text{BSP}(A)$ is a ground-complete axiomatization of the term model $\mathbb{P}(\text{BSP}(A))_{/\leftrightarrow}$, i.e., for any closed $\text{BSP}(A)$-terms p and q, $\mathbb{P}(\text{BSP}(A))_{/\leftrightarrow} \models p = q$ implies $\text{BSP}(A) \vdash p = q$.

Proof Suppose that $\mathbb{P}(\text{BSP}(A))_{/\leftrightarrow} \models p = q$, i.e., $p \leftrightarrow q$. It must be shown that $\text{BSP}(A) \vdash p = q$. Since bisimilarity is a congruence on $\mathbb{P}(\text{BSP}(A))$ (Proposition 4.4.5) and $\text{BSP}(A)$ is sound for $\mathbb{P}(\text{BSP}(A))_{/\leftrightarrow}$ (Theorem 4.4.7), as in the proof of Theorem 4.3.10, it suffices to prove that, for all closed $\text{BSP}(A)$-terms p and q, $p + q \leftrightarrow q$ implies $\text{BSP}(A) \vdash p + q = q$ and $p \leftrightarrow p + q$ implies $\text{BSP}(A) \vdash p = p + q$.

Only the first property is proven, by induction on the total number of symbols in closed terms p and q. Assume $p + q \leftrightarrow q$ for some closed $\text{BSP}(A)$-terms p and q. Three of the four cases in the induction proving that $\text{BSP}(A) \vdash p = p + q$ can be copied directly from the proof of Theorem 4.3.10. Thus, only the remaining case, when $p \equiv 1$, is detailed. If $p \equiv 1$, $p\downarrow$ and thus $(p + q)\downarrow$. As $p + q \leftrightarrow q$, also $q\downarrow$. By Lemma 4.4.10 (Towards completeness), $\text{BSP}(A) \vdash q = 1 + q$. Hence, since $p \equiv 1$, $\text{BSP}(A) \vdash p + q = 1 + q = q$. □

Corollary 4.4.13 (Ground-completeness) Let p and q be arbitrary closed BSP(A)-terms. If $p \leftrightarrow q$, then BSP(A) $\vdash p = q$.

Theory BSP(A) with alternative composition, prefixing and constants for successful and unsuccessful termination as presented in this section is the basic theory for the rest of this book. Almost all theories presented further on are extensions of BSP(A). This chapter started out from a still simpler theory, the theory MPT(A), in order to present a process theory that is as simple as possible, and also to facilitate comparisons to the literature, in which often only one termination constant is present.

The term model for BSP(A) constructed in this section is a quotient algebra, namely the term algebra of Definition 4.4.2 modulo bisimilarity. In Chapter 3 also language equivalence was introduced as an equivalence relation on transition systems, see Definition 3.1.7. It is interesting to note that the term algebra modulo language equivalence is also a model of theory BSP(A). However, BSP(A) is not a ground-complete axiomatization of this model, because action prefix does not distribute over choice (see the discussion in Section 4.2), but also because language equivalence identifies all sequences of actions that end in a non-terminating state (see Example 3.1.8 (Language equivalence)). The axioms of BSP(A) do not capture these equivalences. Note that language equivalence is not very meaningful in the context of theory MPT(A), because it only has the inaction constant and not the empty process. This means that the model of closed terms modulo language equivalence is a so-called one-point model, which has only one process. Chapter 12 considers different semantic equivalences in more detail.

To conclude this section, let us briefly reconsider the notion of deadlocks in processes. In Chapter 3, Definition 3.1.14 (Deadlock), it has been defined when a transition system has a deadlock, and when it is deadlock free. Since theory BSP(A) allows to distinguish successful and unsuccessful termination, it is possible to define when a process term is deadlock free and when it has a deadlock.

Definition 4.4.14 (Deadlocks in BSP(A)**-terms)** Let p be a closed BSP(A)-term. Term p is deadlock free if and only if there is a closed BSP(A)-term q without an occurrence of the inaction constant 0 such that BSP(A) $\vdash p = q$. Term p has a deadlock if and only if it is not deadlock free.

It is possible to prove that the model-independent notion of deadlocks for closed BSP(A)-terms introduced in the above definition is consistent with the notion of deadlocks for such terms that can be derived from the term model of theory BSP(A) of Definition 4.4.6. (Recall that the term model is based on an algebra of transition systems, namely the term algebra of Definition 4.4.2, in which each closed BSP(A)-term induces a transition system.)

Proposition 4.4.15 (Deadlocks) Let p be some closed BSP(A)-term. The transition system of p obtained from the deduction system in Table 4.4 is deadlock free if and only if p is deadlock free according to Definition 4.4.14.

Proof The proof goes via induction on the structure of p.

(i) $p \equiv 0$. It follows immediately from the deduction system in Table 4.4 and Definition 3.1.14 (Deadlock) that the transition system of p consists of a single deadlock state, and, hence, is not deadlock free. It remains to prove that p is not deadlock free according to Definition 4.4.14, i.e., that 0 is not derivably equal to a closed term without occurrence of 0. Assume towards a contradiction that there is a closed term q without occurrence of 0 such that BSP(A) $\vdash 0 = q$. It follows from Corollary 4.4.9 that $0 \leftrightarrow q$. Definition 3.1.10 (Bisimilarity) and the fact that the transition system of 0 is a single deadlock state then imply that also the transition system of q must be a single deadlock state. However, the only closed BSP(A)-terms resulting in such a transition system are 0, $0 + 0$, $0 + 0 + 0$, et cetera, i.e., any summation of inaction constants. Clearly this means that q always has a 0 occurrence, which yields a contradiction, and thus proves that term p is not deadlock free according to Definition 4.4.14.

(ii) $p \equiv 1$. It follows immediately from the deduction system in Table 4.4 that the transition system of p is deadlock free. Since $p \equiv 1$, also BSP(A)$\vdash p = 1$, which means that p is also deadlock free according to Definition 4.4.14.

(iii) $p \equiv a.p'$ for some $a \in A$ and closed term p'. The transition system of p is deadlock free if and only if the transition system of p' is deadlock free. By induction, it follows that there is a 0-free closed term q such that BSP(A) $\vdash p' = q$. Thus, $a.q$ does not contain a 0 occurrence and BSP(A) $\vdash p = a.p' = a.q$, which shows that p is deadlock free according to Definition 4.4.14, completing also this case.

(iv) $p \equiv p_1 + p_2$ for some closed terms p_1 and p_2. The transition system of p is deadlock free if and only if (a) the transition systems of both p_1 and p_2 are deadlock free or if (b) one of the two is deadlock free and the other one is the transition system consisting of a single deadlock state. Assume case (a). By induction, it follows that there are two 0-free closed terms q_1 and q_2 such that BSP(A)$\vdash p_1 = q_1$ and BSP(A)$\vdash$

$p_2 = q_2$. Hence, $q_1 + q_2$ is 0-free and $\text{BSP}(A) \vdash p = p_1 + p_2 = q_1 + q_2$, which shows that p is deadlock free according to Definition 4.4.14. Assume case (b), and assume without loss of generality that the transition system of p_1 is deadlock free. By induction, it follows that there is a 0-free closed term q_1 such that $\text{BSP}(A) \vdash p_1 = q_1$. Following the reasoning in the first item of this induction proof, it furthermore follows that p_2 is some arbitrary summation of inaction constants. Thus, based on Axiom A6, it follows that $\text{BSP}(A) \vdash p = p_1 + p_2 = q_1$, showing also in this final case that p is deadlock free according to Definition 4.4.14. □

The following corollary immediately follows from the above result and the fact that both in Definition 3.1.14 (Deadlock) and in Definition 4.4.14 (Deadlocks in BSP(A)-terms) the presence of deadlocks and deadlock freeness are defined as opposites.

Corollary 4.4.16 (Deadlocks) Let p be some closed BSP(A)-term. The transition system of p obtained from the deduction system in Table 4.4 has a deadlock if and only if p has a deadlock according to Definition 4.4.14.

Exercises

4.4.1 Draw transition systems for the following closed BSP(A)-terms:

(a) $a.(1 + 0)$
(b) $a.1 + a.0$
(c) $1 + a.1$
(d) $1 + a.0$

Show that there does not exist a bisimulation relation between any pair of these transition systems.

4.4.2 Prove that the term algebra of BSP(A) of Definition 4.4.2 modulo language equivalence, Definition 3.1.7, is a model of theory BSP(A).

4.4.3 Recall Definition 3.1.14 (Deadlock) and Definition 4.4.14 (Deadlocks in BSP(A)-terms). Let p and q be closed BSP(A)-terms, and let a be an action in A.

(a) Which of the terms of Exercise 4.4.1 has a deadlock?
(b) Show that, if p has a deadlock and $\text{BSP}(A) \vdash p = q$, then q has a deadlock.
(c) Show that, if p has a deadlock, then $a.p$ has a deadlock.

(d) Give an example showing that $p + q$ may be deadlock free even if one of the two terms p or q has a deadlock.

(e) Show that, if p has a deadlock, then $a.p + q$ has a deadlock.

(f) Give an inductive definition defining when a closed BSP(A)-term has a deadlock in a model-independent way, that is consistent with the earlier two definitions concerning deadlocks (Definitions 3.1.14 and 4.4.14).

(g) Give an inductive definition defining deadlock freeness in a model-independent way.

(h) Prove that a closed term has a deadlock according to the inductive definition of item (f) if and only if it is not deadlock free according to the inductive definition of item (g).

4.4.4 Complete the proof of Theorem 4.4.7 (Soundness) by proving the validity of Axioms A1 through A3.

4.4.5 Prove Lemma 4.4.11.

4.5 Projection

This section considers an extension of the process theory BSP(A). Contrary to the situation in the previous section, this extension does not allow to describe more processes, but rather allows to describe already present processes in more ways than before. Thus, it is an extension for convenience.

Theory BSP(A) can be extended with a family of so-called projection operators π_n, for each $n \in \mathbf{N}$. There are several reasons for introducing such operators. First, they are interesting in their own right. Second, they are a good candidate to explain what concepts play a role in extending a process theory with additional syntax and axioms. (Recall that the simple extension of MPT(A) to BSP(A) discussed in the previous section does not introduce any new axioms.) Third, the projection operators turn out to be useful in reasoning about iterative and recursive processes; a simple form of iteration is introduced later in this chapter, and recursion is the topic of the next chapter. A more general form of iteration is briefly discussed in Chapter 6.

Let x be some term in some process theory. Intuitively speaking, the term $\pi_n(x)$, for some $n \in \mathbf{N}$, corresponds to the behavior of x up to depth n, where the depth is measured in terms of the number of actions that have been executed. Table 4.5 gives process theory (BSP + PR)(A), the extension of theory BSP(A) with projection operators.

Table 4.5 expresses that (BSP+PR)(A) is an extension of BSP(A), and gives the additional syntax and axioms. Note that the five axioms are in fact *axiom*

(BSP + PR)(A)	
BSP(A);	
unary: $(\pi_n)_{n \in \mathbf{N}}$;	
x, y;	
$\pi_n(1) = 1$	PR1
$\pi_n(0) = 0$	PR2
$\pi_0(a.x) = 0$	PR3
$\pi_{n+1}(a.x) = a.\pi_n(x)$	PR4
$\pi_n(x + y) = \pi_n(x) + \pi_n(y)$	PR5

Table 4.5. The process theory (BSP + PR)(A) (with $a \in A$).

schemes. Consider PR1, PR2 and PR5, for example. There is one instance of PR1, PR2 and PR5 for each of the projection operators π_n, with $n \in \mathbf{N}$. For PR3, there is one instance for each action-prefix operator $a.\_$, with $a \in A$, and PR4 has an instance for each combination of a projection operator and an action-prefix operator. Despite the fact that PR1 through PR5 are in fact axiom schemes, they are usually referred to as simply axioms.

An interesting observation is that the five axioms follow the structure of BSP(A)-terms. This is often the case when extending a process theory for the ease of specification; it guarantees that the extension, in this case projection, is defined for all possible process terms in the theory that is being extended.

Axiom PR1 says that the behavior of the termination constant up to some arbitrary depth n equals termination, or, in other words, the empty process; this obviously corresponds to the fact that the empty process cannot execute any actions. Likewise, Axiom PR2 says that the behavior of the inaction constant up to arbitrary depth equals inaction. The third axiom, Axiom PR3, states that the behavior of a process up to depth 0, i.e., the behavior corresponding to the execution of no actions, simply equals inaction for processes that have no immediate successful termination option. The fourth axiom is the most interesting one; Axiom PR4 states that the behavior of a process with a unique initial action up to some positive depth m equals the initial action of this process followed by the behavior of the remainder up to depth $m - 1$. The final axiom simply says that projection operators distribute over choice.

Example 4.5.1 (Projection) Let a, b, and c be actions in A. It is not difficult to verify that (BSP + PR)(A) $\vdash$

$$\begin{aligned}
&\pi_0(a.b.1) = \pi_0(a.b.0) = 0, \\
&\pi_1(a.b.1) = \pi_1(a.b.0) = a.0, \\
&\pi_n(a.b.1) = a.b.1, \qquad \text{if } n \geq 2,
\end{aligned}$$

$$\begin{aligned}
&\pi_n(a.b.0) = a.b.0, && \text{if } n \geq 2,\\
&\pi_n(a.0 + b.1) = a.0 + b.1, && \text{if } n \geq 1,\\
&\pi_0(a.0 + b.c.1) = 0, &&\\
&\pi_1(a.0 + b.c.1) = a.0 + b.0, &&\\
&\pi_n(a.0 + b.c.1) = a.0 + b.c.1, && \text{if } n \geq 2,\\
&\pi_1(a.(a.0 + b.c.1)) = a.0, && \text{and}\\
&\pi_2(a.(a.0 + b.c.1)) = a.(a.0 + b.0). &&
\end{aligned}$$

As a note aside, observe that it is also possible to extend the theory MPT(A) of Section 4.2 with projection operators, resulting in (MPT + PR)(A). This extension follows the lines of the extension of BSP(A) with projection; the only difference is that Axiom PR1 is omitted. As theory (MPT + PR)(A) is not needed in the remainder, its elaboration is left as Exercise 4.5.7.

The extension of the process theory BSP(A) with the projection operators to the process theory (BSP + PR)(A) has enlarged the set of closed terms that can be used for specifying processes. The question whether this extension has also enlarged the set of processes that can be specified in the process theory still needs to be addressed; stated in other words, it must be investigated whether the expressiveness of the process theory has increased. If this is not the case, the same set of processes can be specified, but in more syntactically different ways. This can thus be considered an extension for convenience. The following elimination theorem expresses that every closed (BSP + PR)(A)-term is derivably equal to a closed BSP(A)-term. The consequence of this theorem is that the addition of the projection operators has not enlarged the expressiveness of the process theory, which conforms to the claim made in the introduction to this section. Example 4.5.1 shows that it is often straightforward to eliminate projection operators from (BSP + PR)(A)-terms. Recall the concept of elimination from Example 2.2.13 and Proposition 2.2.20. Note that closed BSP(A)-terms play the role of basic terms. Proposition 2.2.20 has been proven via induction (Exercise 2.2.5). Another way of proving an elimination result is through rewrite theory. The proof given below is based on rewrite theory because it provides the most insight in the working of equational theory (BSP + PR)(A). However, it is also possible to prove Theorem 4.5.2 through induction (Exercise 4.5.4).

Theorem 4.5.2 (Elimination) For every closed (BSP + PR)(A)-term p, there exists a closed BSP(A)-term q such that (BSP + PR)$(A) \vdash p = q$.

Proof Recall Definition 2.4.1 (Term rewriting system). The first step of the proof is to turn equational theory (BSP+PR)(A) into a rewriting system.

The signature of the rewriting system equals the signature of $(\mathrm{BSP} + \mathrm{PR})(A)$. The rewrite rules correspond to Axioms PR1–PR5 of Table 4.5 when read from left to right; for any $n \in \mathbf{N}$, $a \in A$, and $(\mathrm{BSP} + \mathrm{PR})(A)$-terms x, y:

$$\pi_n(1) \to 1$$
$$\pi_n(0) \to 0$$
$$\pi_0(a.x) \to 0$$
$$\pi_{n+1}(a.x) \to a.\pi_n(x)$$
$$\pi_n(x + y) \to \pi_n(x) + \pi_n(y)$$

The idea of the choice of rewrite rules is that for each rewrite rule $s \to t$ of the term rewriting system, $(\mathrm{BSP} + \mathrm{PR})(A) \vdash s = t$. This means that each rewrite step transforms a process term into a process term that is derivably equal.

The second step of the proof is to show that the above term rewriting system is strongly normalizing, i.e., that no process term allows an infinite reduction (see Definition 2.4.6). The details of this part of the proof are left as an exercise (Exercise 4.5.3) because they are not essential to the understanding of the proof of the elimination theorem. A consequence of the choice of the rewrite rules and the resulting strong-normalization property is that every $(\mathrm{BSP} + \mathrm{PR})(A)$-term has a normal form that is derivably equal.

The last part of the proof is to show that no *closed* normal form of the above term rewriting system contains a projection operator, i.e., the operators to be eliminated. Note that it is sufficient to prove the property for normal forms that are *closed terms* because the elimination theorem is formulated only for closed terms. (It is an interesting exercise for the reader to explain why the closed-term restriction is also necessary, implying that the elimination theorem cannot be extended to arbitrary open terms.)

Let closed $(\mathrm{BSP} + \mathrm{PR})(A)$-term u be a normal form of the above rewriting system. Suppose that u contains projection operators, i.e., it is not a (closed) BSP(A)-term. Thus, u must contain at least one subterm of the form $\pi_n(v)$, for some natural number n and closed $(\mathrm{BSP} + \mathrm{PR})(A)$-term v. Clearly, this subterm can always be chosen to be minimal, such that v is a closed BSP(A)-term containing no projection operators itself. It follows immediately from the structure of BSP(A)-terms that precisely one of the rewrite rules of the above term rewriting system can be applied to $\pi_n(v)$. As a consequence, u is not a normal form. This contradiction implies that u must be a closed BSP(A)-term.

Summarizing all the above, it has been shown that each closed $(\mathrm{BSP}+\mathrm{PR})(A)$-term p has a derivably equal normal form q that is a closed BSP(A)-term, thus completing the proof. □

Now that it has been established that the additions to the basic process theory have not increased expressiveness, it is time to consider conservativity. Besides the addition of operators to the signature of the process theory, also axioms (involving these operators) have been added. Thus, the collection of proofs in the process theory has grown. Nevertheless, it can be shown that theory $(\mathrm{BSP}+\mathrm{PR})(A)$ is a conservative ground-extension of $\mathrm{BSP}(A)$. That is, it is not possible to obtain new equalities between $\mathrm{BSP}(A)$-terms despite the addition of the extra axioms. Figure 4.5 extends Figure 4.2 to include this conservativity result; it also includes conservativity results for theory $(\mathrm{MPT}+\mathrm{PR})(A)$, which however are not explicitly formulated (see Exercise 4.5.7). Note that the combined elimination and conservativity results imply that the term models of $\mathrm{BSP}(A)$ and $(\mathrm{BSP}+\mathrm{PR})(A)$ have in fact the same number of processes.

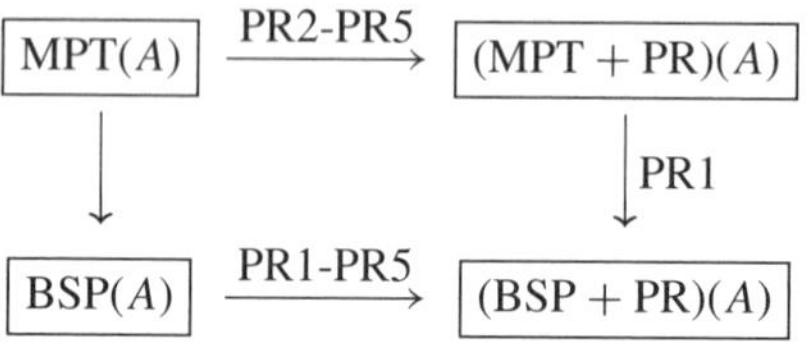

Fig. 4.5. Conservativity results for $(\mathrm{MPT}+\mathrm{PR})(A)$ and $(\mathrm{BSP}+\mathrm{PR})(A)$.

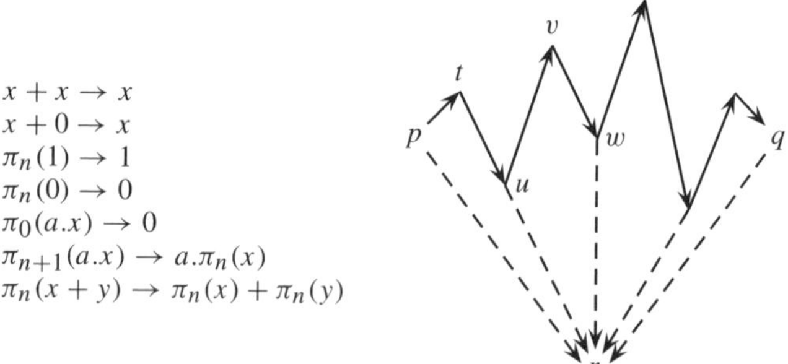

Fig. 4.6. Conservativity of the extension of $\mathrm{BSP}(A)$ with projection.

Theorem 4.5.3 (Conservative ground-extension) Theory $(\mathrm{BSP}+\mathrm{PR})(A)$ is a conservative ground-extension of process theory $\mathrm{BSP}(A)$.

Proof There are several ways to prove the above theorem. Two possibilities are outlined. The first possibility provides the most insight, whereas the second possibility is often technically more convenient.

Consider Definition 2.2.19 (Conservative ground-extension). Since the signature and axioms of theory $(\mathrm{BSP}+\mathrm{PR})(A)$ contain the signature and axioms of BSP(A), the ground-extension requirement is satisfied. Thus, it remains to prove that, for closed BSP(A)-terms p and q, $(\text{BSP}+\text{PR})(A) \vdash p = q$ implies $\text{BSP}(A) \vdash p = q$. Assume that $(\text{BSP} + \text{PR})(A) \vdash p = q$; it must be shown that $\text{BSP}(A) \vdash p = q$. In other words, a derivation in $(\text{BSP}+\text{PR})(A)$ must be transformed into a derivation in BSP(A).

The idea of the proof is visualized in Figure 4.6. The left part of this figure shows the rules of a term rewriting system, which correspond to the axioms of theory $(\text{BSP} + \text{PR})(A)$ read from left to right, excluding Axioms A1 (commutativity of choice) and A2 (associativity). The solid arrows in the right part of the figure visualize a derivation showing that p equals q. A downward arrow corresponds to a part of the derivation in which axioms are applied in the left-to-right direction, conform the rewrite rules in the left part of the figure, whereas an upward arrow corresponds to the application of axioms in the right-to-left direction. For the sake of simplicity, terms that differ only with respect to commutativity and associativity of choice are considered equal. Clearly, any derivation in $(\text{BSP} + \text{PR})(A)$ is of the form depicted in the figure.

Returning to the term rewriting system given in the figure, it can be shown that it is both strongly normalizing (see Definition 2.4.6) and confluent (see Definition 2.4.7), for the latter assuming that terms that differ only with respect to associativity and commutativity of choice may be considered equivalent. The proof of the confluence property uses the theory of term rewriting modulo a congruence relation. The reader interested in details is referred to (Dershowitz & Jouannaud, 1990). The confluence of the term rewriting system has some important consequences. Consider, for example, point t in Figure 4.6. It follows from the explanation of the meaning of the solid arrows given above that it is possible to rewrite t both into p and into u. Thus, the confluence property implies that it must be possible to rewrite both p and u into a single term r, as depicted by the dashed arrows in the figure. The strong-normalization property implies that r can be chosen to be a normal form. Next, consider term v. It is clear that it can be rewritten into r via u; it can also be rewritten into w. Thus, due to the confluence property, it must be possible to rewrite r and w into a common term. Since r is a normal form, this common term must be r, which explains the dashed arrow from w to r. Using similar reasoning, it can be shown that, in the end, also q can be rewritten into r.

It remains to show how this result can be used to turn the $(\text{BSP} + \text{PR})(A)$ derivation from p to q into a BSP(A) derivation. An important observation is that none of the rewrite rules introduces a projection operator and that both p and q are BSP(A)-terms and thus do not contain projection operators. An immediate consequence is that the dashed arrows from p to r and from q to r correspond to BSP(A) derivations. Clearly, the two derivations can be combined into one derivation showing that $\mathrm{BSP}(A) \vdash p = q$ and completing the proof.

The second, technically more convenient way to prove the conservativity theorem builds upon the framework of Chapter 3. An interesting observation is that this proof uses soundness and ground-completeness results with respect to the term models for $\mathrm{BSP}(A)$ (see Section 4.3) and $(\mathrm{BSP}+\mathrm{PR})(A)$ (see below), whereas the above proof is independent of any given model.

The desired conservativity result is a direct consequence of the application of Theorem 3.2.21 (Conservativity). It uses the facts that $\mathrm{BSP}(A)$ is a ground-complete axiomatization of the term model $\mathbb{P}(\mathrm{BSP}(A))_{/\leftrightarrow}$ (Theorem 4.4.12), that $(\mathrm{BSP}+\mathrm{PR})(A)$ is a sound axiomatization of the term model $\mathbb{P}((\mathrm{BSP}+\mathrm{PR})(A))_{/\leftrightarrow}$ (see Theorem 4.5.8 below), and that $TDS((\mathrm{BSP}+\mathrm{PR})(A))$ (see Table 4.6 below) is an *operational* conservative extension of $TDS(\mathrm{BSP}(A))$, as defined in Definition 3.2.16. This last fact follows immediately from the format of the deduction rules in Tables 4.2, 4.4 and 4.6, and Theorem 3.2.19 (Operational conservative extension). □

The following theorem shows an interesting application of projection operators. It proves that all closed $(\mathrm{BSP}+\mathrm{PR})(A)$-terms have a finite depth, or in other words, that processes specified by closed $(\mathrm{BSP}+\mathrm{PR})(A)$-terms cannot have unbounded executions. This implies among others that transition systems of closed $(\mathrm{BSP}+\mathrm{PR})(A)$-terms cannot have cycles. Note that process theories $(\mathrm{BSP}+\mathrm{PR})(A)$ and $\mathrm{BSP}(A)$ allow the same set of processes to be specified (due to the elimination theorem), and that $\mathrm{MPT}(A)$ allows a subset of those processes to be specified. As a result, also in $\mathrm{MPT}(A)$ and $\mathrm{BSP}(A)$ only processes with bounded-depth executions can be specified.

Theorem 4.5.4 (Bounded depth) For each closed $(\mathrm{BSP}+\mathrm{PR})(A)$-term p, there exists a natural number n such that for all $k \geq n$,

$$(\mathrm{BSP}+\mathrm{PR})(A) \vdash \pi_k(p) = p.$$

Proof Using Theorem 4.5.2 (Elimination), it suffices to prove the desired property for closed $\mathrm{BSP}(A)$-terms; see also Chapter 2, Example 2.2.21. Thus, it suffices to show that, for each closed $\mathrm{BSP}(A)$-term p_1, there exists a natural number n such that for all $k \geq n$, $(\mathrm{BSP}+\mathrm{PR})(A) \vdash \pi_k(p_1) = p_1$. The property is proven by induction on the structure of closed $\mathrm{BSP}(A)$-term p_1.

(i) Assume $p_1 \equiv 1$. Choose $n = 0$ and observe that $(\mathrm{BSP}+\mathrm{PR})(A) \vdash \pi_k(1) = 1$ for all $k \geq 0$.

(ii) Assume $p_1 \equiv 0$. Choose $n = 0$ and observe that $(\mathrm{BSP}+\mathrm{PR})(A) \vdash \pi_k(0) = 0$ for all $k \geq 0$.

(iii) Assume $p_1 \equiv a.q$, for some $a \in A$ and closed BSP(A)-term q. By induction, there exists an $m \in \mathbf{N}$ such that $(\mathrm{BSP}+\mathrm{PR})(A) \vdash \pi_l(q) = q$ for all $l \geq m$. Choose $n = m + 1$. It must be shown that $(\mathrm{BSP} + \mathrm{PR})(A) \vdash \pi_k(p_1) = p_1$ for all $k \geq n$. Observe that $n \geq 1$. Thus, for all $k - 1 \geq m$ and, hence, for all $k \geq n$, $(\mathrm{BSP} + \mathrm{PR})(A) \vdash \pi_k(p_1) = \pi_k(a.q) = a.\pi_{k-1}(q) = a.q = p_1$.

(iv) Assume $p_1 \equiv q_1 + q_2$ for some closed BSP(A)-terms q_1 and q_2. By induction, there exist m_1 and m_2 such that $(\mathrm{BSP} + \mathrm{PR})(A) \vdash \pi_{l_1}(q_1) = q_1$ and $(\mathrm{BSP} + \mathrm{PR})(A) \vdash \pi_{l_2}(q_2) = q_2$ for all $l_1 \geq m_1$ and $l_2 \geq m_2$. Choose n to be the maximum of m_1 and m_2: $n = \max(m_1, m_2)$. Then, for all $k \geq \max(m_1, m_2) = n$, $(\mathrm{BSP}+\mathrm{PR})(A) \vdash \pi_k(p) = \pi_k(q_1 + q_2) = \pi_k(q_1) + \pi_k(q_2) = q_1 + q_2 = p$. □

It remains to construct a model of theory $(\mathrm{BSP} + \mathrm{PR})(A)$. The model given in the remainder of this section is a term model, similar to the term model of BSP(A) given in Section 4.4. The first step is to define the term algebra of closed $(\mathrm{BSP} + \mathrm{PR})(A)$-terms.

Definition 4.5.5 (Term algebra) The *term algebra* for $(\mathrm{BSP} + \mathrm{PR})(A)$ is the algebra $\mathbb{P}((\mathrm{BSP}+\mathrm{PR})(A)) = (\mathcal{C}((\mathrm{BSP}+\mathrm{PR})(A)), +, (\pi_n)_{n\in\mathbf{N}}, (a.\_)_{a\in A}, 0, 1)$.

The next step in the construction of a model is to turn the set of closed terms $\mathcal{C}((\mathrm{BSP}+\mathrm{PR})(A))$ into a transition-system space. The sets of states and labels are the sets of closed terms $\mathcal{C}((\mathrm{BSP} + \mathrm{PR})(A))$ and actions A, respectively. The termination predicate and the ternary transition relation are defined via the term deduction system in Table 4.6, which extends the term deduction systems in Tables 4.2 and 4.4. In other words, the termination predicate and the transition relation are the smallest set and relation satisfying the deduction rules in Tables 4.2, 4.4 and 4.6.

TDS$((\mathrm{BSP} + \mathrm{PR})(A))$

TDS(BSP(*A*));

unary: $(\pi_n)_{n\in\mathbf{N}}$;

x, x';

$$\frac{x\downarrow}{\pi_n(x)\downarrow} \qquad \frac{x \xrightarrow{a} x'}{\pi_{n+1}(x) \xrightarrow{a} \pi_n(x')}$$

Table 4.6. Term deduction system for $(\mathrm{BSP} + \mathrm{PR})(A)$ (with $a \in A$).

The term deduction system for $(\mathrm{BSP}+\mathrm{PR})(A)$ has two extra deduction rules when compared to the term deduction system for BSP(A). The first rule implies that any closed term $\pi_n(p)$ has a termination option exactly when closed term p has. This expresses the fact that projection does not influence termination. The second rule assumes that some closed term p can execute an action a thereby transforming into some other closed term p' as a result. It then states that the execution of an action by a closed term $\pi_m(p)$ with $m \in \mathbf{N}$ is allowed if, and only if, the subscript of the projection operator m is not zero. Since the execution of an action increases the actual depth of a process by one, the result of the execution is term $\pi_{m-1}(p')$, i.e., closed term p' up to depth *m minus one*. The resulting term model is the term algebra of Definition 4.5.5 modulo bisimilarity.

Proposition 4.5.6 (Congruence) Bisimilarity is a congruence on term algebra $\mathbb{P}((\text{BSP} + \text{PR})(A))$.

Proof The property follows immediately from the format of the deduction rules given in Tables 4.2, 4.4 and 4.6 (see Theorem 3.2.7 (Congruence theorem)). □

Definition 4.5.7 (Term model of (BSP + PR)(A)**)** The term model of (BSP+PR)(A) is the quotient algebra $\mathbb{P}((\text{BSP} + \text{PR})(A))_{/\leftrightarrow}$.

Theorem 4.5.8 (Soundness) Theory (BSP + PR)(A) is a sound axiomatization of the algebra $\mathbb{P}((\text{BSP} + \text{PR})(A))_{/\leftrightarrow}$, i.e., $\mathbb{P}((\text{BSP} + \text{PR})(A))_{/\leftrightarrow} \models (\text{BSP} + \text{PR})(A)$.

Proof According to Definition 2.3.8 (Model), it must be shown that, for each axiom $s = t$ of (BSP + PR)(A), $\mathbb{P}((\text{BSP} + \text{PR})(A))_{/\leftrightarrow} \models s = t$. The proof for the axioms of BSP(A) carries over directly from the proof of Theorem 4.4.7 (Soundness of BSP(A)) and Exercise 4.4.4. The proof for the axioms that are new in (BSP + PR)(A) goes along the same lines and is left as Exercise 4.5.5. □

Having soundness, the question is addressed whether or not the axiomatization is also ground-complete. It turns out that this is the case. Informally, the ground-completeness of (BSP + PR)(A) follows from the fact that the addition of the projection operators to the basic theory BSP(A) does not increase the set of processes that can be expressed and the ground-completeness of BSP(A). There are two straightforward ways for proving the result formally. First, it is possible to apply Theorem 3.2.26 (Ground-completeness), which is a meta-result applicable to models fitting the operational framework of Chapter 3. However, the ground-completeness result also follows in a fairly straightforward way from the basic results developed in this chapter, namely the elimination theorem (Theorem 4.5.2), the conservativity theorem (Theorem 4.5.3), and the ground-completeness of BSP(A) (Theorem 4.4.12). For illustration purposes, both proofs are given below.

Theorem 4.5.9 (Ground-completeness) The process theory $(\mathrm{BSP}+\mathrm{PR})(A)$ is a ground-complete axiomatization of the term model $\mathbb{P}((\mathrm{BSP}+\mathrm{PR})(A))_{/\leftrightarrow}$, i.e., for any closed $(\mathrm{BSP}+\mathrm{PR})(A)$-terms p and q, $\mathbb{P}((\mathrm{BSP}+\mathrm{PR})(A))_{/\leftrightarrow} \models p = q$ implies $(\mathrm{BSP}+\mathrm{PR})(A) \vdash p = q$.

Proof The first way to prove the desired result is the application of Theorem 3.2.26 (Ground-completeness). In the proof of Theorem 4.5.3 (Conservative ground-extension), it has already been established that the two theories $(\mathrm{BSP}+\mathrm{PR})(A)$ and BSP(A) and their associated deduction systems and models satisfy the conditions of Theorem 3.2.21 (Conservativity). Thus, Theorem 4.5.2 (Elimination) immediately gives the desired result.

The second proof builds on the basic results for theories $(\mathrm{BSP}+\mathrm{PR})(A)$ and BSP(A) directly, without resorting to the meta-results of Chapter 3. Let p and q be closed $(\mathrm{BSP}+\mathrm{PR})(A)$-terms. Suppose that $\mathbb{P}((\mathrm{BSP}+\mathrm{PR})(A))_{/\leftrightarrow} \models p = q$. Then, by definition, $p \leftrightarrow q$. By Theorem 4.5.2 (Elimination), there exist closed BSP(A)-terms p_1 and q_1 such that $(\mathrm{BSP}+\mathrm{PR})(A) \vdash p = p_1$ and $(\mathrm{BSP}+\mathrm{PR})(A) \vdash q = q_1$. This implies $p \leftrightarrow p_1$ and $q \leftrightarrow q_1$. Since bisimilarity is an equivalence (Theorem 3.1.13), the fact that $p \leftrightarrow q$, $p \leftrightarrow p_1$, and $q \leftrightarrow q_1$ implies that $p_1 \leftrightarrow q_1$. From the facts that p_1 and q_1 are closed BSP(A)-terms and that BSP(A) is a ground-complete axiomatization of the term model $\mathbb{P}(\mathrm{BSP}(A))_{/\leftrightarrow}$, it follows that $\mathrm{BSP}(A) \vdash p_1 = q_1$ (Corollary 4.4.13). Since $(\mathrm{BSP}+\mathrm{PR})(A)$ is a conservative ground-extension of BSP(A) (Theorem 4.5.3) and since p_1 and q_1 are closed BSP(A)-terms, it follows that $(\mathrm{BSP}+\mathrm{PR})(A) \vdash p_1 = q_1$. Combining results yields that $(\mathrm{BSP}+\mathrm{PR})(A) \vdash p = p_1 = q_1 = q$, completing the proof. □

Exercises

4.5.1 Let p be the closed term $a.(b.1 + c.d.0) + a.b.1$. Calculate $\pi_n(p)$ (as a closed BSP(A)-term) for all $n \geq 0$.

4.5.2 Prove that, for all closed $(\mathrm{BSP}+\mathrm{PR})(A)$-terms p, it holds that $(\mathrm{BSP}+\mathrm{PR})(A) \vdash \pi_0(p) = 1$ if and only if $(\mathrm{BSP}+\mathrm{PR})(A) \vdash p = p + 1$ and that $(\mathrm{BSP}+\mathrm{PR})(A) \vdash \pi_0(p) = 0$ otherwise.

4.5.3 Prove that the term rewriting system that is given in the proof of Theorem 4.5.2 (Elimination) is strongly normalizing.
(Hint: use induction on the total number of symbols that occur in the term that is the operand of the projection operator.)

4.5.4 Give an inductive proof of Theorem 4.5.2 (Elimination).
(Hint: difficult.)

4.5.5 Complete the proof of Theorem 4.5.8 (Soundness) by proving the validity of Axioms PR1 through PR5 of Table 4.5.

4.5.6 Prove by structural induction that for all closed BSP(A)-terms p and all natural numbers $n, m \geq 0$ the following holds:

$$(\mathrm{BSP} + \mathrm{PR})(A) \vdash \pi_n(\pi_m(p)) = \pi_{\min(n,m)}(p).$$

4.5.7 Starting from theory MPT(A), develop the theory (MPT + PR)(A). That is, define the equational theory (MPT + PR)(A), prove an elimination and a conservativity result, and give a term model proving soundness and ground-completeness. Also, prove that theory (BSP + PR)(A) is a conservative ground-extension of (MPT + PR)(A).

4.6 Prefix iteration

Recall Theorem 4.5.4 (Bounded depth). A consequence of that theorem is the fact that none of the process theories considered so far allows us to specify behavior with unbounded depth. Most example processes that will be considered in the following chapters have unbounded depth. Thus, it is interesting to investigate extensions of basic process theory that remove this boundedness restriction. This section extends the process theory BSP(A) with prefix iteration. This will constitute a limited instantiation of much more general constructs to be discussed in the following chapter. For each action $a \in A$, a new unary operator $a^*\_$ called a *prefix-iteration* operator is added to the signature of BSP(A). The process a^*x can execute a any number of times before starting the execution of x. Note that this construction indeed allows unbounded-depth behavior; for instance, a^*0 will execute a an unbounded number of times.

The extension of BSP(A) with prefix-iteration operators is called BSP*(A). The axioms of BSP*(A) are the axioms of BSP(A) plus Axioms PI1 and PI2 given in Table 4.7. These axioms, and their names, are taken from (Fokkink, 1994). The first axiom explains that a process a^*x has a choice between executing a and repeating itself, and executing x. The second axiom expresses idempotency of prefix iteration, i.e., allowing two iterations before continuing with x is the same as allowing only one iteration.

It is straightforward to extend the term model of theory BSP(A) to a model

BSP*(A)
BSP(A);

unary: $(a^{*}\_)_{a \in A}$;

x;

$a.(a^{*}x) + x = a^{*}x$	PI1
$a^{*}(a^{*}x) = a^{*}x$	PI2

Table 4.7. The process theory BSP*(A).

of BSP*(A). The closed BSP*(A)-terms with the signature of theory BSP*(A) form the term algebra $\mathbb{P}$(BSP*(A)). This term algebra can be turned into a term model for BSP*(A) via the deduction system given in Table 4.8. Compared to the deduction system for theory BSP(A) (see Tables 4.2 and 4.4), it contains three new deduction rules, all three for prefix-iteration operators. The first prefix-iteration rule implies that a closed term $a^{*}p$ can execute action a an arbitrary number of times. The other two rules state that closed term $a^{*}p$ can mimic the behavior (action execution and termination) of closed term p.

TDS(BSP*(A))
TDS(BSP(A));

unary: $(a^{*}\_)_{a \in A}$;

x, x';

$$a^{*}x \xrightarrow{a} a^{*}x \qquad \frac{x \xrightarrow{b} x'}{a^{*}x \xrightarrow{b} x'} \qquad \frac{x\downarrow}{a^{*}x\downarrow}$$

Table 4.8. Term deduction system for BSP*(A) (with $a, b \in A$).

Example 4.6.1 (Transition systems) The transition systems that can be associated with terms $a^{*}1$, $a^{*}0$, and $a^{*}(b.1)$ are given in Figure 4.7. Note that transition systems induced by closed BSP*(A)-terms are still regular, but now, loops from a node to itself can occur. The relationship between (closed terms in) equational theories and regular transition systems is addressed in more detail in the next chapter. One of the results given in that chapter is an equational theory that precisely captures all regular transition systems.

Proposition 4.6.2 (Congruence) Bisimilarity is a congruence on term algebra $\mathbb{P}$(BSP*(A)).

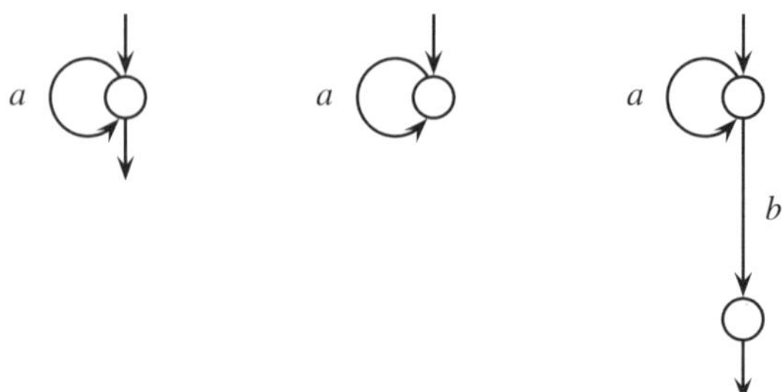

Fig. 4.7. Transition systems of a^*1, a^*0, and $a^*(b.1)$.

Proof Using Theorem 3.2.7 (Congruence theorem), the property follows immediately from the format of the deduction rules given in Tables 4.2, 4.4 and 4.8. □

Theorem 4.6.3 (Soundness) The process theory BSP*(A) is a sound axiomatization of the algebra $\mathbb{P}(\mathrm{BSP}^*(A))_{/\leftrightarrow}$.

Proof Exercise 4.6.2. □

In contrast with the extension of the process theory BSP(A) with projection operators, the extension with prefix iteration actually allows to define more processes. It is not possible to prove an elimination result similar to Theorem 4.5.2 (Elimination). It is possible though to prove a conservativity result, which implies that in the extended theory BSP*(A) it is not possible to prove any equalities between closed BSP(A)-terms that cannot be proven in BSP(A).

Theorem 4.6.4 (Conservative ground-extension) Theory BSP*(A) is a conservative ground-extension of process theory BSP(A).

Proof The result follows immediately from Theorem 3.2.21 (Conservativity) and the facts that BSP(A) is a ground-complete axiomatization of the term model $\mathbb{P}(\mathrm{BSP}(A))_{/\leftrightarrow}$ (Theorem 4.4.12), that BSP*(A) is a sound axiomatization of $\mathbb{P}(\mathrm{BSP}^*(A))_{/\leftrightarrow}$, and that *TDS*(BSP*$(A)$) is an operational conservative extension of *TDS*(BSP(A)) (Table 4.4). This last fact is a direct consequence of the format of the deduction rules in Tables 4.2, 4.4 and 4.8, and Theorem 3.2.19 (Operational conservative extension). □

Figure 4.8 visualizes the conservativity result proven by Theorem 4.6.4. For the sake of completeness, it also shows conservativity results regarding the

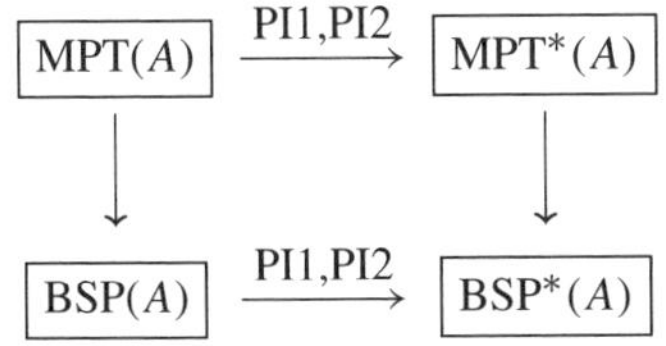

Fig. 4.8. Conservativity results for MPT*(A) and BSP*(A).

theory MPT*(A), the minimal process theory of Section 4.2 extended with prefix iteration. The details of this theory and the conservativity results do not play a role in the remainder and are therefore omitted.

It still remains to support the claim, made in the introduction to this section, that the extension of BSP(A) with prefix iteration allows us to describe unbounded processes. Consider the extension of theory BSP*(A) with projection operators, i.e., the theory (BSP* + PR)(A). Details of this extension are straightforward and left to the reader; see Exercise 4.6.3. The extension allows us to introduce a notion of boundedness for process terms, following the idea of Theorem 4.5.4 (Bounded depth).

Definition 4.6.5 (Bounded depth) Let p be a closed (BSP* + PR)(A)-term. Term p has a bounded depth if and only if there exists a natural number n such that for all $k \geq n$,

$$(\mathrm{BSP}^* + \mathrm{PR})(A) \vdash \pi_k(p) = p.$$

Note that this definition introduces a notion of boundedness for all process theories introduced so far, because theory (BSP* + PR)(A) contains all other theories.

Notation 4.6.6 (n-fold action prefix) For any atomic action $a \in A$, any natural number n, and any term x, the term $a^n x$ denotes the n-fold application of the action-prefix operator $a.\_$ to x. An inductive definition is as follows:

$$a^0 x = x, \qquad \text{and, for all } n \in \mathbf{N},$$
$$a^{n+1} x = a.a^n x.$$

Example 4.6.7 ((Un-)boundedness) Let a be an action in A. Consider the process term a^*0. It can easily be established that, for all natural numbers $n \in \mathbf{N}$,

$$(\mathrm{BSP}^* + \mathrm{PR})(A) \vdash \pi_n(a^*0) = a^n 0. \tag{4.6.1}$$

The proof is left as an exercise (see Exercise 4.6.5).

Since all the finite projections of a^*0 are different, by Definition 4.6.5, it cannot have bounded depth. To see this, assume that there is a natural number n such that for all $k \geq n$, $(\text{BSP}^* + \text{PR})(A) \vdash \pi_k(a^*0) = a^*0$. It then follows from property (4.6.1) that, for all $k \geq n$, $(\text{BSP}^* + \text{PR})(A) \vdash a^k 0 = a^*0$, which in turn implies that for all $k, l \geq n$ with $k \neq l$, $(\text{BSP}^* + \text{PR})(A) \vdash a^k 0 = a^l 0$. This contradicts the fact $a^k 0$ and $a^l 0$ correspond to different processes in the term model $\mathbb{P}(\text{BSP}^*(A))_{/\leftrightarrow}$. Hence, a^*0 has unbounded depth.

Note that by Theorem 4.5.4 (Bounded depth) all closed $(\text{BSP} + \text{PR})(A)$-terms are bounded according to Definition 4.6.5. Thus, this example illustrates that the extension of $\text{BSP}(A)$ with prefix iteration is a true extension that allows to describe unbounded-depth processes, as already claimed informally in the introduction to this section.

This section ends with a ground-completeness result.

Theorem 4.6.8 (Ground-completeness) Process theory $\text{BSP}^*(A)$ is a ground-complete axiomatization of the term model $\mathbb{P}(\text{BSP}^*(A))_{/\leftrightarrow}$.

Proof The proof is a straightforward adaptation of the proof given in (Fokkink, 1994) for a theory similar to BSP^* but without empty process. □

As a final remark, it is important to note that prefix iteration can be seen as a simple form of recursion, as process a^*p can be seen as the solution of the recursive equation $X = a.X + p$. The next chapter is fully devoted to recursion.

Exercises

4.6.1 Draw the transition system of the following closed $\text{BSP}^*(A)$-terms:

(a) a^*b^*1,
(b) $a^*(b^*0 + c.1)$, and
(c) $a^*b.c^*0$

(with $a, b, c \in A$).

4.6.2 Prove Theorem 4.6.3 (Soundness).

4.6.3 Develop the theory $(\text{BSP}^* + \text{PR})(A)$. That is, define $(\text{BSP}^* + \text{PR})(A)$ by extending $\text{BSP}^*(A)$ with the projection operators and axioms of Table 4.5, prove elimination and conservativity results, and give a term model proving soundness and ground-completeness.

4.6.4 Define by induction a series of closed BSP(A)-terms $(p_n)_{n \in \mathbf{N}}$ such that, for all $n \in \mathbf{N}$, $(\mathrm{BSP}^* + \mathrm{PR})(A) \vdash \pi_n(a^*1) = p_n$.

4.6.5 Recall Notation 4.6.6 (n-fold action prefix).

(a) Prove that, for all natural numbers $n \in \mathbf{N}$, $(\mathrm{BSP} + \mathrm{PR})(A) \vdash \pi_n(a^{n+1}0) = a^n 0$.

(b) Prove that, for all natural numbers $n \in \mathbf{N}$, $(\mathrm{BSP}^* + \mathrm{PR})(A) \vdash \pi_n(a^*0) = a^n 0$.

4.6.6 Consider the so-called *proper iteration* operators $a^{\oplus}\_$, with a an action in A. The process described by $a^{\oplus}x$, for some term x, is the process that executes a a number of times, but at least once, and then continues as the process described by x. Give deduction rules for the transition relations $\_ \xrightarrow{a} \_$ and the termination predicate $\_\downarrow$ that specify the expected operational semantics of proper iteration. Give also axioms for proper iteration without using prefix iteration. Finally, express proper iteration in terms of action prefix and prefix iteration, and express prefix iteration in terms of proper iteration.
(Hint: difficult.)

4.7 Bibliographical remarks

Minimal Process Theory is the same as basic CCS, see e.g. (Hennessy & Milner, 1980). The inaction constant is denoted 0 or *nil*. The present formulation of MPT is the theory MPA, minimal process algebra, from (Baeten, 2003). It is a subtheory of the theory BPA$_\delta$, Basic Process Algebra with inaction, of (Bergstra & Klop, 1984a). In both of these theories, the inaction constant is denoted δ. The system was called FINTREE in (Aceto *et al.*, 1994). The summand relation of Exercise 4.2.3 can be found in (Bergstra & Klop, 1985).

The material of Section 4.3 is based on (Van Glabbeek, 1987). Section 4.4 again follows (Baeten, 2003). The addition of the empty process 1 in ACP-style process algebra originates in (Koymans & Vrancken, 1985), and was continued in (Vrancken, 1997), (Baeten & Van Glabbeek, 1987). In all of these papers, the empty process is denoted ϵ. In CSP, the empty process is written SKIP; see (Hoare, 1985).

The theory BPA (Basic Process Algebra) of Bergstra and Klop (Bergstra & Klop, 1982) (later published as (Bergstra & Klop, 1992)), (Bergstra & Klop, 1984a; Bergstra & Klop, 1985) is related to BSP as follows: BPA has constants a for each atomic action a, which in BSP would be represented as $a.1$; furthermore, BPA has general sequential composition, introduced in the framework of this book in Chapter 6.

The operational semantics of BSP has an action relation and a termination predicate; there is no need for a mixed relation $\_ \xrightarrow{a} \surd$ as in (Baeten & Weijland, 1990) or (Baeten & Verhoef, 1995).

The material on presence and absence of deadlocks is based on (Baeten & Bergstra, 1988). Projection operators appear in many process algebras, see e.g. (De Bakker & Zucker, 1982b; Bergstra & Klop, 1982). Conservativity of the (ground-)extension is addressed e.g. in (Baeten & Verhoef, 1995).

Section 4.6 discusses an iteration operator. The origin of such an operator, and the star notation, dates back to (Kleene, 1956). The article (Copi *et al.*, 1958) introduced a unary variant of Kleene's operator, and later, (Bergstra *et al.*, 1994) went back to the binary variant (in the absence of the empty process 1). With the constants 0 and 1, there is no finite ground-complete axiomatization for iteration modulo bisimulation (Sewell, 1997), which led to the consideration of restricted iteration operators like the prefix iteration introduced in this chapter, see (Fokkink, 1994) and (Aceto *et al.*, 1998). A general (unary) iteration operator in the context of this book is discussed in Section 6.5. An overview of iteration concepts in a process-algebraic context is given in (Bergstra *et al.*, 2001).

5

Recursion

5.1 Introduction

Section 4.6 has introduced operators for describing unbounded processes. The collection of unbounded processes that can be described using the syntax presented so far is, however, still very limited. For example, it is not possible to describe the process given as a transition system in Figure 5.1: it executes an action a followed by a b any number of times before continuing with the execution of c. To extend the expressiveness of the algebraic framework developed up to this point, so that it is possible to describe more realistic processes, this chapter investigates the notion of recursion.

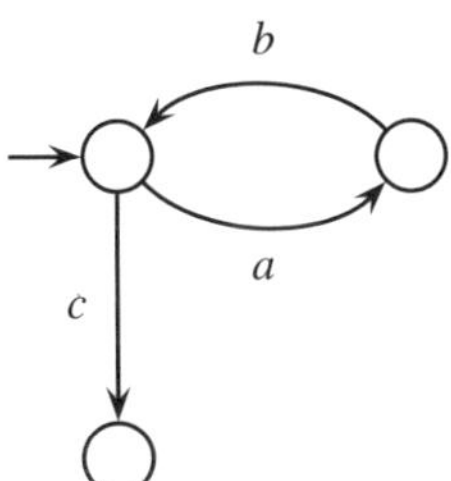

Fig. 5.1. Transition system that cannot be described by a process term so far.

Example 5.1.1 (Coffee machine) Consider a simple coffee machine that operates as follows: after the insertion of a quarter by a client, a cup of coffee is dispensed. A description of such a coffee machine (called *SCM*) could be given as follows:

$$SCM = quarter.coffee.1,$$

where the atomic action *quarter* represents the insertion of a quarter and the atomic action *coffee* represents the handing out of coffee. An objection to this description is that after one cup of coffee has been dispensed no coffee is handed out ever again. A better description therefore would be the following equation:

$$SCM = quarter.coffee.SCM.$$

In this equation, the object to be described, namely the simple coffee machine, is represented by a variable, namely *SCM*, that occurs not only as the left-hand side of the equation but again in the right-hand side of the equation. Such an equation is called a *recursive* equation and a variable such as *SCM* is called a *recursion variable*.

A set of recursive equations (that satisfies some simple requirements to be detailed below) is called a *recursive specification*. In the remainder of this chapter, an extension of the process theory BSP(A) with recursive specifications is presented. Recursion is needed in any practical algebraic framework. It turns out that with recursive specifications, in principle, any process can be described.

5.2 Recursive specifications

Definition 5.2.1 (Recursive specification) Let Σ be a signature and let V_R be a set of recursion variables. A *recursive equation* over Σ and V_R is an equation of the form $X = t$ where X is a recursion variable from V_R and t is a term over the signature Σ in which no other variables than those from V_R occur. A *recursive specification* E over Σ and V_R is a set of recursive equations that contains precisely one recursive equation $X = t$ over Σ and V_R for each recursion variable X from V_R. To denote the set of all recursion variables in specification E notation $V_R(E)$ is used.

The reader familiar with fixed point equations may recognize that recursive specifications are nothing but sets of fixed point equations. However, in the context of process algebra, the terminology recursive specification is preferred.

Observe from the above definition that recursion variables can be used in terms (see Definition 2.2.3) just like ordinary variables. However, recursion variables are not the same as ordinary variables. Intuitively, a recursion variable is meant to specify some specific process of interest, whereas ordinary variables are meant to denote arbitrary processes. To emphasize the special role of recursion variables, they are usually written with capitals. In the remainder, the role of recursion variables is investigated in some more detail. The signature and/or the set of recursion variables are often left implicit when they are clear from the context.

Example 5.2.2 (Recursive specifications) Let A be the set of actions that includes a, b, c, and d. The following are examples of recursive specifications:

(i) $E_1 = \{X = a.(b.1 + c.d.0)\}$. The only recursion variable is X. Observe that X does not appear in the right-hand side of the recursive equation. Nevertheless, although no recursion is present, the equation still is a recursive equation according to Definition 5.2.1.

(ii) $E_2 = \{X = a.(b.X + c.0)\}$. Again, X is the only recursion variable. It does occur in the right-hand side of the recursive equation.

(iii) $E_3 = \{X = a.Y, Y = b.X + a.Y\}$. This recursive specification has two recursion variables, namely X and Y.

(iv) $E_4 = \{X_0 = a.X_1, X_{i+1} = a.X_{i+2} + b.X_i \mid i \in \mathbf{N}\}$. This recursive specification has an infinite number of recursion variables, namely $X_0, X_1, \ldots$.

Example 5.2.3 (Recursive specifications) Intuitively, the transition system of Figure 5.1 can be specified by recursion variable X of the recursive specification $E = \{X = a.Y + c.0, Y = b.X\}$. Alternatively, the process can be specified by recursion variable Z in the recursive specification $E' = \{Z = a.b.Z + c.0\}$. Of course, it remains to formalize the claims that these recursive specifications represent the transition system of Figure 5.1. In other words, an operational semantics for recursive specifications in terms of transition systems is needed. Such a semantics is given in Section 5.4.

In deriving equalities between terms in a process theory with recursion, it seems natural to use the equations of recursive specifications as ordinary axioms. Actually, under certain assumptions, they are axioms. A recursive specification can be seen as an extension of some given process theory. The recursion variables should then be interpreted as *constants* in the signature of this process theory. This corresponds to the intuition that a recursion variable specifies a specific process in a model of the theory. Recall that the construction of a model of an equational theory from some algebra requires that constants from the signature of the theory are mapped onto precisely one element in the domain of the algebra (Definitions 2.3.6 (Validity) and 2.3.8 (Model)). Let E be some recursive specification. Table 5.1 gives the process theory BSP(A) extended with E.

Example 5.2.4 (Derivations) Consider the recursive specification $E = \{X = a.Y, Y = b.X\}$. Theory $(\mathrm{BSP} + E)(A)$ can be used to derive equation $X = a.(b.X)$ as

$$(\mathrm{BSP} + E)(A) \vdash X = a.Y = a.(b.X).$$

(BSP + E)(A)	
BSP(A);	
constant: $(X)_{X \in V_R(E)}$;	
$(X = t)_{X=t \in E}$	R

Table 5.1. The process theory (BSP + E)(A).

This result can, in turn, be used in for example the following derivation. For readability, redundant parentheses are omitted.

$$(\text{BSP} + E)(A) \vdash X = a.b.X = a.b.a.b.X.$$

Notation 5.2.5 (Recursion variables) Sometimes, it is desirable to emphasize the fact that recursion variables should be interpreted as constants, or it is necessary to explicitly provide the recursive specification in which a recursion variable occurs. Notation $\mu X.E$ denotes recursion variable X interpreted as a constant as defined by recursive specification E.

Notation 5.2.6 (Process theories with recursion) Table 5.1 shows the extension of a process theory with a single recursive specification. It is convenient to have a notation for a process theory extended with all recursive specifications of potential interest. In such a case, a subscript rec is used. For example, process theory BSP(A) extended with arbitrary recursive specifications of interest is denoted $\text{BSP}_{\text{rec}}(A)$. The set of all recursive specifications of interest is denoted *Rec*.

Exercises

5.2.1 A man is playing a game of Russian roulette. After pulling the trigger of the gun either a bang or a click follows. This game is repeated until the man dies due to the occurrence of a bang. Describe the process of playing this game with a recursive specification. Use the following atomic actions in the description:

- t for pulling the trigger;
- b for hearing a bang;
- c for hearing a click;
- d for the act of dying.

In this description, you can assume that the man is alive when he starts playing.

5.2.2 A more complicated vending machine than the one described in Example 5.1.1 (Coffee machine) charges 25 cents for coffee and 20 cents for hot chocolate. The machine accepts the following coins: 5 cents, 10 cents, and 20 cents. Give a recursive specification for this vending machine. In order to do this, several questions must be answered. For instance: Is it allowed to insert too much money? Can coins be inserted in arbitrary order? Can coins be inserted simultaneously? Can the machine ever terminate? Pay attention to the moments at which choices are made.

5.2.3 Consider a vending machine for refreshing drinks (coffee is not considered to be such a drink). This machine accepts 5 cent, 10 cent, and 20 cent coins only. The customer has to pay 25 cents for a refreshment. When a wrong coin is inserted, it is rejected by the machine. Sometimes the machine does not accept a good coin. Describe this vending machine using the following atomic actions:

- 5 for inserting a 5 cent coin;
- 10 for inserting a 10 cent coin;
- 20 for inserting a 20 cent coin;
- *re* for rejecting a wrong coin;
- *a* for accepting a coin;
- *na* for not accepting a good coin;
- *r* for returning a refreshment.

5.3 Solutions of recursive specifications

An operational semantics for a process theory with recursive specifications is, as before, based on a model built from transition systems. That is, it is an algebra of transition systems modulo bisimilarity. The semantics of a recursive specification in such a model is then a set of processes from the domain of this model, one for each recursion variable in the specification, that validates the equations in the specification when interpreted in the model. Such a set of processes is called a *solution* of the recursive specification. Before turning to the construction of a term model for BSP(A) with recursion in the next section, the concept of solutions is investigated in some more detail.

Definition 5.3.1 (Solution) Let T be a process theory with signature Σ, let E be a recursive specification over Σ and recursion variables V_R, and let $\mathbb{M}$ be a model of T with respect to interpretation ι. The signature consisting of Σ and the variables in V_R as additional constants is referred to as the *extended* *signature*. Let κ be an interpretation of this extended signature into algebra $\mathbb{M}$ that is identical to ι for elements of Σ. Interpretation κ is a *solution* of recursive specification E in $\mathbb{M}$ if and only if the equations from the recursive specification are valid in the model under interpretation κ: $\mathbb{M}, \kappa \models X = t$ for any equation $X = t \in E$.

Most of the time, one of the recursion variables in E represents the process of interest. In such cases, a process p in the domain of $\mathbb{M}$ is called a solution of X if and only if there exists a solution κ of E such that $\kappa(X) = p$.

As an aside, recall that a recursive specification can be seen as a set of fixed point equations. Consequently, solutions of recursive specifications are in fact fixed points.

Example 5.3.2 (Solutions) Consider again recursive specification $E' = \{Z = a.b.Z + c.0\}$ of Example 5.2.3 (Recursive specifications). It has been mentioned that the transition system of Figure 5.1 is a solution for Z. Based on Definition 5.3.1, it is only possible to talk about solutions in the context of some basic equational theory and a model for this theory. Process theory BSP(A) is our basic equational theory. For now, let us assume the existence of some operational model for BSP(A) with as its domain equivalence classes of arbitrary transition systems (assuming bisimilarity as the equivalence). Under this assumption, it is possible to prove the claim that the (equivalence class corresponding to the) transition system of Figure 5.1 is a solution for Z by showing that the transition system for the left-hand side of the equation $Z = a.b.Z+c.0$ equals (i.e., is bisimilar to) the transition system for the right-hand side of this equation. The transition system for Z is the transition system of Figure 5.1; the transition system for $a.b.Z + c.0$ can intuitively be constructed via the semantics of BSP(A)-terms (see Section 4.4) and substitution of the transition system for Z at the appropriate point, fusing the two deadlock states. The result is shown in Figure 5.2. It is not difficult to see that the two transition systems of Figures 5.1 and 5.2 are indeed bisimilar. The construction of a bisimulation is left as Exercise 5.3.1.

At this point it is useful to consider the special role of recursion variables in a bit more detail. It has already been mentioned that in the context of an equational theory, they should be considered as constants. Nevertheless, they are called recursion *variables*, and, intuitively, they also behave like variables in some aspects. Considering the above definition of a solution sheds some light on these two faces of recursion variables. Recall that validity (Definition 2.3.6) requires a *fixed* interpretation for the constants and operators of an equational theory in the model under consideration, and an *arbitrary* interpretation

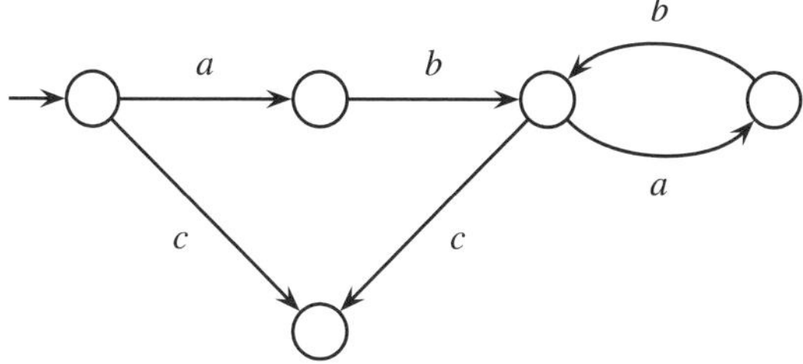

Fig. 5.2. A transition system for $a.b.Z + c.0$ using the transition system of Figure 5.1 for Z.

for all the normal variables in a term. Definition 5.3.1 (Solution) shows that a recursion variable can be interpreted *in any way that satisfies the recursive specification* defining the recursion variable. In that sense, recursion variables are in fact *constrained variables* that behave like variables in the context of a recursive specification but turn into constants when added to the signature of an equational theory.

A question that arises from the introduction of recursion is how to deal with equality between recursion variables, possibly from different recursive specifications. That is, when do two recursion variables specify the same process?

Example 5.3.3 (Equivalence of recursion variables) Consider the recursive specifications $E_1 = \{X_1 = a.X_1\}$ and $E_2 = \{X_2 = a.a.X_2\}$. It can be shown that any solution of X_1 is also a solution of X_2. Assume that BSP(A) is the basic equational theory, and that $\mathbb{M}$ with domain $\mathbf{M}$ is a model of BSP(A) with interpretation ι. Suppose that process p taken from $\mathbf{M}$ is a solution for recursion variable X_1, i.e., there exists an interpretation κ_1 of the signature of BSP(A) plus recursion variable X_1 consistent with interpretation ι such that $\kappa_1(X_1) = p$. According to Definitions 5.3.1 (Solution) and 2.3.6 (Validity), it follows that $p =_{\mathbf{M}} \kappa_1(X_1) =_{\mathbf{M}} \kappa_1(a.)(\kappa_1(X_1)) =_{\mathbf{M}} \kappa_1(a.)(p) =_{\mathbf{M}} \iota(a.)(p)$, i.e., $p =_{\mathbf{M}} \iota(a.)(p)$. Let κ_2 be the interpretation of the signature of BSP(A) consistent with ι and of recursion variable X_2 with $\kappa_2(X_2) = p$. It can be shown that κ_2 specifies a solution of X_2. Using the previous result and the assumption, it follows that $\kappa_2(X_2) =_{\mathbf{M}} p =_{\mathbf{M}} \iota(a.)(p) =_{\mathbf{M}} \iota(a.)(\iota(a.)(p)) =_{\mathbf{M}} \kappa_2(a.)(\kappa_2(a.)(\kappa_2(X_2)))$, i.e., $\mathbb{M}, \kappa_2 \models X_2 = a.a.X_2$. This shows that κ_2, and thus p, is indeed a solution of X_2. Since p was chosen as an arbitrary solution of X_1, this proves that any solution of X_1 is also a solution of X_2.

Using equational reasoning, the fact that any solution of recursion variable X_1 is a solution of X_2 can be achieved by deriving the equation defining X_2 in recursive specification E_2 with all occurrences of X_2 replaced by X_1 from the equation defining X_1 in E_1 in the equational theory $(\text{BSP} + E_1)(A)$:

$$(\text{BSP} + E_1)(A) \vdash X_1 = a.X_1 = a.a.X_1.$$

Note that this derivation does not assume that recursive specification E_2 is part of the equational theory. It is therefore not allowed to use the equation of E_2 as an axiom in the derivation. Despite the fact that E_2 is not a part of the equational theory, the above derivation proves a property of recursion variable X_2 of E_2, namely that any solution of X_1 is also a solution of X_2.

The results derived thus far in this example do not yet mean that X_1 and X_2 have the same solutions. It can still be the case that there are solutions of X_2 that are not solutions of X_1. In fact, an attempt to prove $(\text{BSP}+E_2)(A) \vdash X_2 = a.X_2$, which would imply that any solution of X_2 is also a solution of X_1, will not be successful.

As an aside, the above example shows that equational theory BSP(A) allows the derivation of a so-called *conditional* equation. The reasoning proves that $\text{BSP}(A) \vdash X = a.X \Rightarrow X = a.a.X$, for any action a and (recursion) variable X. Note that, from the validity point of view, variable X can be interpreted as a normal variable in this conditional equation. The equation has to be valid for *any* interpretation of X, which emphasizes the special role of recursion variables. This book does not study equational theories with conditional equations and axioms in detail. The interested reader is referred to, e.g., (Hussman, 1985).

An important consequence of the reasoning in the above example is the following useful theorem, stating that two recursive specifications E_1 and E_2 specify the same solutions if and only if there is a one-to-one mapping between the recursion variables from E_1 and E_2 such that both E_1 can be rewritten into E_2 with its variables replaced by the corresponding ones in E_1 and E_2 can be rewritten into E_1 with its variables substituted by those in E_2. The theorem uses the notion of substitution of variables of Definition 2.2.6 (Substitution) overloaded to recursion variables (which are strictly speaking constants in the context of an equational theory).

Theorem 5.3.4 (Equivalence of recursive specifications) Let E_1 and E_2 be two recursive specifications over the signature of theory BSP(A). These two specifications define the same solutions in any model of BSP(A) if and only if there is a bijective substitution $\sigma : V_R(E_1) \to V_R(E_2)$ with inverse σ^{-1} such that, for all $X_2 = t_2 \in E_2$, $(\text{BSP} + E_1)(A) \vdash \sigma^{-1}(X_2) = t_2[\sigma^{-1}]$ and for all $X_1 = t_1 \in E_1$, $(\text{BSP} + E_2)(A) \vdash \sigma(X_1) = t_1[\sigma]$.

Example 5.3.3 (Equivalence of recursion variables) illustrates some of the subtleties of recursive specifications and their solutions. The main idea is that a recursive specification *defines* a process that cannot be expressed as a closed term. (Recall that the major purpose of recursive specifications is to extend the expressiveness of basic process theories.) That is, in principle, a recursive specification is usually expected to have a single solution. However, the definitions of recursive specifications and their solutions allow that a recursive specification has no solutions at all in some model of the basic process theory under consideration, or that it has two or more different solutions. This is illustrated by the following examples.

Example 5.3.5 (No solutions) Consider the following recursive specification: $E = \{X = a.X\}$. In the term model for process theory BSP(A) given in Section 4.4, namely the algebra of transition systems $\mathbb{P}(\mathrm{BSP}(A))_{/\leftrightarrow}$, this recursive specification has no solutions. This can be seen as follows.

Suppose that some process p from the domain of $\mathbb{P}(\mathrm{BSP}(A))_{/\leftrightarrow}$ is a solution of X. The construction of the term model as a quotient algebra (see Definition 2.3.18) implies that there exists a closed BSP(A)-term t such that p is the equivalence class of t under bisimilarity: $p = [t]_{\leftrightarrow}$. In other words, t is a representative of the equivalence class p. From Definition 5.3.1 (Solution), it follows that there must be an interpretation κ such that $\kappa(X) = p$. The construction of the term model $\mathbb{P}(\mathrm{BSP}(A))_{/\leftrightarrow}$ and the interpretation of recursion variable X as a constant imply that X must be a representative of equivalence class p, and thus that X and t are representatives of the same equivalence class.

Consider term t again. As any closed BSP(A)-term is also a closed (BSP + PR)(A)-term, by Theorem 4.5.4 (Bounded depth), there exists a natural number n such that $(\mathrm{BSP}+\mathrm{PR})(A) \vdash \pi_k(t) = t$ for all $k \geq n$. Thus, the soundness result of Theorem 4.5.8 implies that $\pi_k(t) \leftrightarrow t$ for all $k \geq n$.

Next, recall the n-fold action prefix of Notation 4.6.6. It is not hard to prove that $(\mathrm{BSP} + \mathrm{PR} + E)(A) \vdash \pi_m(X) = a^m 0$ for any natural number m. Since term t and constant X are representatives of the same equivalence class under bisimilarity in the term model $\mathbb{P}(\mathrm{BSP}(A))_{/\leftrightarrow}$, it follows that $\pi_m(t) \leftrightarrow a^m 0$ for any natural number m.

Combining the facts derived in the last two paragraphs means that it must be the case that for all natural numbers $k, l \geq n$, $a^k 0 \leftrightarrow \pi_k(t) \leftrightarrow t \leftrightarrow \pi_l(t) \leftrightarrow a^l 0$. However, it is easily shown that the process terms $a^k 0$ and $a^l 0$ are not bisimilar for the cases that $k \neq l$. Hence, a contradiction results, which implies that there cannot be a process p in the algebra $\mathbb{P}(\mathrm{BSP}(A))_{/\leftrightarrow}$ that is a solution of E. Thus, this example shows that the algebra $\mathbb{P}(\mathrm{BSP}(A))_{/\leftrightarrow}$ cannot be turned into a model for $(\mathrm{BSP} + E)(A)$.

The observation made at the end of the above example relates solutions to models, and can be generalized as follows.

Theorem 5.3.6 (Solutions vs. models) A model $\mathbb{M}$ of BSP(A) has a solution for a recursive specification E if and only if $\mathbb{M}$ is also a model of the extended theory $(\text{BSP} + E)(A)$.

Proof Given the definition of theory $(\text{BSP} + E)(A)$ in Table 5.1, the result immediately follows from Definitions 5.3.1 (Solution) and 2.3.8 (Model). □

Example 5.3.7 (Multiple solutions) Consider recursive specification $\{X = X\}$. For any process theory and any model $\mathbb{M}$ of that theory, each element p of the domain $\mathbf{M}$ of that model is a solution for X. If $\mathbf{M}$ has at least two elements, the recursive specification has at least two different solutions. Thus, it does not uniquely define a process.

The first of the above examples indicates that there are recursive specifications that in some models of some given basic process theory do not have a solution at all. In some sense, this is a desirable result, as the goal of introducing recursion is to increase expressiveness. The second example indicates that in any model with two or more elements there is more than one solution for some recursive specifications. When constructing a model for a process theory with recursion, it is necessary to take these intricacies into account. It should also be investigated under what conditions a recursive specification precisely defines one unique process. Section 5.5 addresses these issues in more detail. First, the next section presents a term model for BSP(A) with recursive specifications.

Exercises

5.3.1 Give a bisimulation relation between the two transition systems of Figures 5.1 and 5.2.

5.3.2 Consider Example 5.3.2 (Solutions). Along the lines of this example, provide a solution for recursion variable *SCM* defined in the recursive specification of Example 5.1.1 (Coffee machine), including a correctness argument.

5.3.3 Find in the term model $\mathbb{P}(\text{BSP}(A))_{/\leftrightarrow}$ two different solutions of the recursive equation $X = X + a.0$.

5.3.4 Does the term model $\mathbb{P}(\text{BSP}(A))_{/\leftrightarrow}$ have a solution of the recursive equation $X = a.X + X$?

5.3.5 Show that any solution of X from $\{X = Y, Y = a.X\}$ is also a solution of Z from $\{Z = a.W, W = a.Z\}$.

5.4 The term model

This section presents a term model for BSP(A) with recursion. Recall Notations 5.2.5 (Recursion variables) and 5.2.6 (Process theories with recursion). Since recursion variables are interpreted as constants in the process theory BSP(A) with recursion, that is, $\mathrm{BSP}_{\mathrm{rec}}(A)$, note that $\mathcal{C}(\mathrm{BSP}_{\mathrm{rec}}(A))$ denotes all closed terms over the BSP(A) signature extended with all recursion variables of potential interest.

Definition 5.4.1 (Term algebra) The *term algebra* for $\mathrm{BSP}_{\mathrm{rec}}(A)$ is the algebra $\mathbb{P}(\mathrm{BSP}_{\mathrm{rec}}(A)) = (\mathcal{C}(\mathrm{BSP}_{\mathrm{rec}}(A)), +, (a.\_)_{a \in A}, (\mu X.E)_{E \in Rec, X \in V_R(E)}, 0, 1)$.

Notation 5.4.2 (Solutions of terms) Let E be a recursive specification over a set of recursion variables V_R. For convenience, the notation $\mu X.E$ for some variable X in V_R is generalized to $\mu t.E$ for some arbitrary term t in $\mathcal{C}((\mathrm{BSP} + E)(A))$. An inductive definition of this notation is given by:

(i) $\mu 1.E = 1$;
(ii) $\mu 0.E = 0$;
(iii) for any recursion variable $X \in V_R$, $\mu(\mu X.E).E = \mu X.E$;
(iv) for any $a \in A$ and $t \in \mathcal{C}((\mathrm{BSP} + E)(A))$, $\mu(a.t).E = a.(\mu t.E)$;
(v) for any $s, t \in \mathcal{C}((\mathrm{BSP} + E)(A))$, $\mu(s + t).E = \mu s.E + \mu t.E$.

The termination predicate and the ternary transition relation in the transition-system space underlying the model under construction are defined via the term deduction system in Table 5.2, which extends the term deduction systems in Tables 4.2 and 4.4. Essentially, the new deduction rules express that a solution for a recursion variable in a recursive specification behaves as the right-hand side of its defining recursive equation.

Proposition 5.4.3 (Congruence) Bisimilarity is a congruence on term algebra $\mathbb{P}(\mathrm{BSP}_{\mathrm{rec}}(A))$.

Proof The property follows immediately from the format of the deduction rules given in Tables 4.2, 4.4, and 5.2, and Theorem 3.2.7 (Congruence theorem). □

$TDS(\mathrm{BSP}_{\mathrm{rec}}(A))$	
$TDS(\mathrm{BSP}(A))$;	
constant: $(\mu X.E)_{E \in Rec, X \in V_R(E)}$;	
y;	
$\dfrac{\mu t.E\downarrow}{\mu X.E\downarrow}$	$\dfrac{\mu t.E \xrightarrow{a} y}{\mu X.E \xrightarrow{a} y}$

Table 5.2. Deduction rules for recursion (with $a \in A$ and $X = t \in E$).

Definition 5.4.4 (Term model of $\mathrm{BSP}_{\mathrm{rec}}(A)$) The term model of $\mathrm{BSP}_{\mathrm{rec}}(A)$ is the quotient algebra $\mathbb{P}(\mathrm{BSP}_{\mathrm{rec}}(A))_{/\leftrightarrow}$.

Theorem 5.4.5 (Soundness of $\mathrm{BSP}_{\mathrm{rec}}(A)$) Theory $\mathrm{BSP}_{\mathrm{rec}}(A)$ is a sound axiomatization of $\mathbb{P}(\mathrm{BSP}_{\mathrm{rec}}(A))_{/\leftrightarrow}$, i.e., $\mathbb{P}(\mathrm{BSP}_{\mathrm{rec}}(A))_{/\leftrightarrow} \models \mathrm{BSP}_{\mathrm{rec}}(A)$.

Proof According to Definition 2.3.8 (Model), it must be shown that, for each axiom $s = t$ of $\mathrm{BSP}_{\mathrm{rec}}(A)$, $\mathbb{P}(\mathrm{BSP}_{\mathrm{rec}}(A))_{/\leftrightarrow} \models s = t$. The proof for the axioms of BSP(A) carries over directly from the proof of Theorem 4.4.7 (Soundness of BSP(A)) and Exercise 4.4.4. The proof for the axioms that are new in $\mathrm{BSP}_{\mathrm{rec}}(A)$, i.e., all the *recursive equations* in all recursive specifications of interest, follows in a straightforward way from the deduction rules in Table 5.2. If $X = t$ is some recursive equation in recursive specification E, then $R = \{(\mu X.E, \mu t.E)\} \cup \{(p, p) \mid p \in C(\mathrm{BSP}_{\mathrm{rec}}(A))\}$ is the bisimulation relation showing the desired result. □

Example 5.4.6 (Solutions in term models) Solutions of recursive equations over the BSP(A) signature in the term model of $\mathrm{BSP}_{\mathrm{rec}}(A)$ are equivalence classes of closed $\mathrm{BSP}_{\mathrm{rec}}(A)$-terms under bisimilarity. Consider again recursive specification $E = \{X = a.Y + c.0, Y = b.X\}$ of Example 5.2.3. The solution of X in the term model of $\mathrm{BSP}_{\mathrm{rec}}(A)$ is $[\mu X.E]_{\leftrightarrow}$. The solution of Z of recursive specification $E' = \{Z = a.b.Z + c.0\}$ of the same example is $[\mu Z.E']_{\leftrightarrow}$. It is easy to show that $\mu X.E \leftrightarrow \mu Z.E'$. Figure 5.3 shows the transition systems for $\mu X.E$ and $\mu Z.E'$. Hence, $[\mu X.E]_{\leftrightarrow} = [\mu Z.E']_{\leftrightarrow}$, which means that X and Z specify the same process in the term model of $\mathrm{BSP}_{\mathrm{rec}}(A)$. These results confirm the claims made in Example 5.2.3.

For reasons of brevity, it is often said that a closed $\mathrm{BSP}_{\mathrm{rec}}(A)$-term is a solution of some recursive specification over the BSP(A) signature, meaning that the corresponding equivalence class under bisimilarity is a solution.

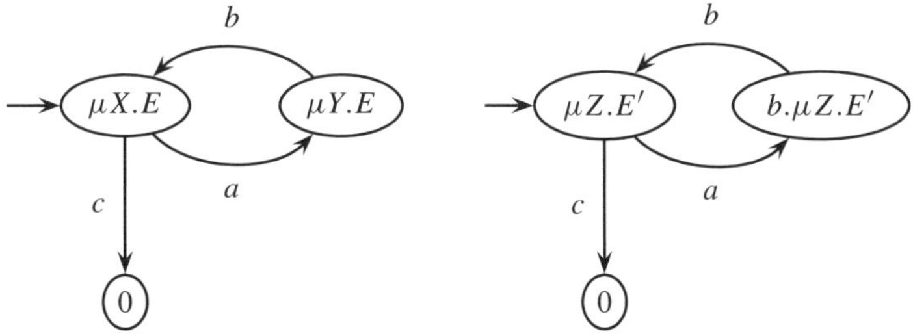

Fig. 5.3. Transition systems for $\mu X.E$ and $\mu Z.E'$ of Example 5.4.6.

It is interesting to observe that the term model $\mathbb{P}(\mathrm{BSP}_{\mathrm{rec}}(A))_{/\leftrightarrow}$ defines specific solutions for every recursive specification in the theory $\mathrm{BSP}_{\mathrm{rec}}(A)$, even for the ones that have multiple solutions. Recall that, following Definition 2.3.18 (Quotient algebra), the standard interpretation of constants and functions of theory $\mathrm{BSP}_{\mathrm{rec}}(A)$ in the term model $\mathbb{P}(\mathrm{BSP}_{\mathrm{rec}}(A))_{/\leftrightarrow}$ maps all constants, including the constants corresponding to recursion variables, onto their equivalence classes under bisimilarity, and each operator onto the corresponding function in the term model. For the recursive specification $\{X = X\}$, for example, which has all processes in $\mathbb{P}(\mathrm{BSP}_{\mathrm{rec}}(A))_{/\leftrightarrow}$ as solutions, the standard interpretation in the term model maps X onto (the equivalence class of) 0, because the term deduction system of Table 5.2 does not allow the derivation of any steps or the successful termination of X. This observation is consistent with the fact that any model of a process theory, and therefore also any model of $\mathrm{BSP}_{\mathrm{rec}}(A)$, is always accompanied with an interpretation that maps every closed term, and hence every recursion variable in the signature of $\mathrm{BSP}_{\mathrm{rec}}(A)$, to precisely one process in the model. These observations once again emphasize the dual role of recursion variables, as constrained variables when considering solutions in some given model of the basic theory under consideration and as constants when considering a model of the basic theory extended with recursion.

It is not possible to give a general ground-completeness result for $\mathrm{BSP}_{\mathrm{rec}}(A)$ and the term model introduced in this section, because in general it is not guaranteed that the recursive equations capture all equalities between recursion variables that are valid in the term model. The following example illustrates this fact.

Example 5.4.7 (Ground-completeness of $\mathrm{BSP}_{\mathrm{rec}}(A)$**)** Consider again Example 5.3.3 (Equivalence of recursion variables). Assume that the set of recursive specifications *Rec* equals $\{E_1, E_2\}$. It has been mentioned in Example 5.3.3

that it is not possible to prove that the two recursion variables X_1 and X_2 always have the same solutions. Thus, in particular, it is not possible to prove that $\mathrm{BSP_{rec}}(A) \vdash X_1 = X_2$. However, in the term model constructed in this section, the equality $X_1 = X_2$ is valid, i.e., $\mathbb{P}(\mathrm{BSP_{rec}}(A))_{/\leftrightarrow} \models X_1 = X_2$. The bisimulation relation proving this is the relation $\{(X_1, X_2), (X_1, a.X_2)\}$. This simple example proves that theory $\mathrm{BSP_{rec}}(A)$ is in general not ground-complete for the term model. Note that for specific instances of the set of recursive specifications *Rec* it may still be possible to obtain a ground-completeness result.

Given the results obtained so far, it is possible to prove that the extension of BSP(A) with recursion is conservative. In other words, using the extended theory, it is not possible to derive any new equalities between closed BSP(A)-terms. Note that it is not possible to prove an elimination result; that is, it is in general not possible to eliminate recursion variables from closed $\mathrm{BSP_{rec}}(A)$-terms resulting in BSP(A)-terms. This last observation should not be very surprising given the fact that recursion has been introduced in order to extend the expressiveness of the process theory BSP(A). It is also possible to show that $\mathrm{BSP_{rec}}(A)$ is a conservative ground-extension of theory $\mathrm{MPT_{rec}}(A)$, i.e., the minimal theory MPT(A) of Section 4.2 extended with recursion.

Theorem 5.4.8 (Conservative ground-extension) The theory $\mathrm{BSP_{rec}}(A)$ is a conservative ground-extension of theories BSP(A) and $\mathrm{MPT_{rec}}(A)$.

Proof The desired conservativity result for theory BSP(A) follows immediately from Theorem 3.2.21 (Conservativity), the fact that BSP(A) is a ground-complete axiomatization of the term model $\mathbb{P}(\mathrm{BSP}(A))_{/\leftrightarrow}$ (Theorem 4.4.12), the fact that $\mathrm{BSP_{rec}}(A)$ is a sound axiomatization of $\mathbb{P}(\mathrm{BSP_{rec}}(A))_{/\leftrightarrow}$, and the fact that *TDS*($\mathrm{BSP_{rec}}(A)$) is an operational conservative extension of *TDS*(BSP(A)) (Table 4.4). This last fact is a direct consequence of the format of the deduction rules in Tables 4.2, 4.4 and 5.2, and Theorem 3.2.19 (Operational conservative extension).

For theory $\mathrm{MPT_{rec}}(A)$, it is not possible to give a similar proof, because theory $\mathrm{MPT_{rec}}(A)$ is not a ground-complete axiomatization of the underlying term model (see Example 5.4.7 and Exercise 5.4.3). Instead, the proof goes along the lines of Theorem 4.4.1. The signature and axioms of $\mathrm{BSP_{rec}}(A)$ include the signature and axioms of $\mathrm{MPT_{rec}}(A)$, implying that $\mathrm{BSP_{rec}}(A)$ is a (ground-)extension of $\mathrm{MPT_{rec}}(A)$. Furthermore, since no axioms of $\mathrm{BSP_{rec}}(A)$ can introduce a completely new or entirely eliminate a 1 constant, any derivation in $\mathrm{BSP_{rec}}(A)$ showing the equality of two closed $\mathrm{MPT_{rec}}(A)$-terms is in fact a derivation in $\mathrm{MPT}_{\mathrm{rec}}(A)$, which yields the desired conservativity result. □

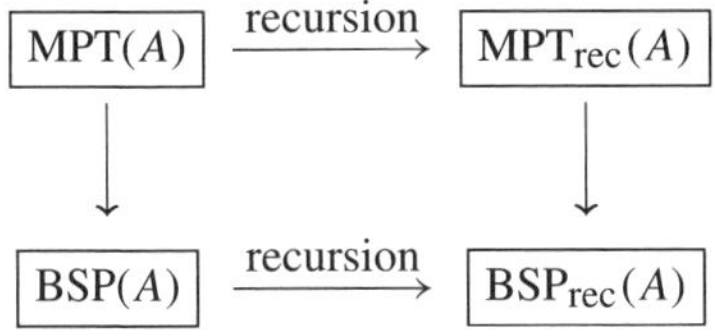

Fig. 5.4. Conservativity results for $\mathrm{MPT}_{\mathrm{rec}}(A)$ and $\mathrm{BSP}_{\mathrm{rec}}(A)$.

Figure 5.4 shows the conservativity results for theory $\mathrm{BSP}_{\mathrm{rec}}(A)$. It also shows that $\mathrm{MPT}_{\mathrm{rec}}(A)$ is a conservative ground-extension of $\mathrm{MPT}(A)$. The proof is left as an exercise.

Exercises

5.4.1 For each of the following terms, give the transition system associated with it by means of the deduction rules presented in this section.

(a) $\mu X.\{X = a.Y, Y = b.X\}$,
(b) $\mu X.\{X = 1 + a.Y, Y = b.X\}$,
(c) $\mu(a.X).\{X = a.b.X + b.Y + 0, Y = X + a.(Y + X)\}$,
(d) $\mu(b.X + 1).\{X = a.X + Y, Y = a.Y\}$.

5.4.2 Assume the standard interpretation of constants and functions of theory $\mathrm{BSP}_{\mathrm{rec}}(A)$ in its term model $\mathbb{P}(\mathrm{BSP}_{\mathrm{rec}}(A))_{/\leftrightarroweq}$, i.e., all constants are mapped onto their equivalence classes under bisimilarity, and each operator is mapped onto the corresponding function in the term model following Definition 2.3.18 (Quotient algebra).
Check that $\mathbb{P}(\mathrm{BSP}_{\mathrm{rec}}(A))_{/\leftrightarroweq} \models$

(a) $\mu X.\{X = X\} = 0$,
(b) $\mu X.\{X = a.0\} = a.0$,
(c) $\mu X.\{X = a.X + Y, Y = a.Y\} = \mu Z.\{Z = a.Z\}$,
(d) $\mu X.\{X = X + a.0\} = a.0$, and
(e) $\mu X.\{X = X + a.X\} = \mu Y.\{Y = a.Y\}$.

5.4.3 Develop the theory $\mathrm{MPT}_{\mathrm{rec}}(A)$ by extending theory $\mathrm{MPT}(A)$ with recursion. Define the equational theory $\mathrm{MPT}_{\mathrm{rec}}(A)$, provide a term model, prove soundness, and prove a conservativity result. Argue that there are no general elimination and ground-completeness results.

5.5 Recursion principles

It is a common situation that there is a need to add recursion to some given basic process theory without recursion. It is then interesting to know to what extent it is possible to build upon existing models of that basic theory when developing an operational semantics of the theory with recursion. The models of interest are those in which recursive specifications have precisely one solution. However, Example 5.3.7 (Multiple solutions) shows that it is in general impossible to find interesting models in which all recursive specifications have precisely one solution. Furthermore, Example 5.3.5 (No solutions) gives a recursive specification over the signature of theory BSP(A) that has no solutions in the term model $\mathbb{P}(\mathrm{BSP}(A))_{/\leftrightarrows}$.

These examples illustrate that it is interesting to study which models of process theories allow an easy extension of a theory with recursion. Example 5.3.7 (Multiple solutions) shows that the goal of precisely one solution for each recursive specification cannot be achieved without at least some restrictions. Section 5.4 has already shown the construction of a term model for a theory with recursion in such a way that every recursive specification has a solution. However, this term model does not address the issue that some recursive specifications have multiple solutions. To investigate these issues in a generic setting, this section introduces a number of so-called *recursion principles*. A recursion principle specifies characteristics of models and/or recursive specifications. A very elementary recursion principle is the *Recursive Definition Principle* (RDP), stating that, given a basic theory with some model, any recursive specification over the syntax of that theory has *at least one* solution in the given model.

Definition 5.5.1 (RDP) Assume some equational theory and some model of this theory. The *Recursive Definition Principle* (RDP) is the following assumption: every recursive specification over the signature of the theory has a solution in the given model.

The notion of validity for ordinary equations (see Definition 2.3.6) carries over to recursion principles. Given a model $\mathbb{M}$ of some equational theory and some recursion principle R, $\mathbb{M} \models R$ denotes that R is valid in model $\mathbb{M}$. Since a recursion principle must be valid in the algebra that is considered as a potential model for the process theory at hand, the introduction of a principle restricts the allowed models of the process theory.

It is interesting to consider the recursion principle RDP in a bit more detail in the context of process theories BSP(A) and $\mathrm{BSP}_{\mathrm{rec}}(A)$ and their term models.

An immediate consequence of Example 5.3.5 (No solutions) is that RDP is not valid in the term model of theory BSP(A), i.e., the algebra $\mathbb{P}(\mathrm{BSP}(A))_{/\leftrightarrow}$.

Theorem 5.5.2 (Invalidity of RDP for $\mathbb{P}(\mathrm{BSP}(A))_{/\leftrightarrow}$) Principle RDP is not valid in the term model of BSP(A), i.e., $\mathbb{P}(\mathrm{BSP}(A))_{/\leftrightarrow} \not\models \mathrm{RDP}$.

In the term model of theory $\mathrm{BSP}_{\mathrm{rec}}(A)$, however, which is also a model of theory BSP(A), RDP is valid.

Theorem 5.5.3 (Validity of RDP in $\mathbb{P}(\mathrm{BSP}_{\mathrm{rec}}(A))_{/\leftrightarrow}$) Recursion principle RDP is valid in the term model of $\mathrm{BSP}_{\mathrm{rec}}(A)$, i.e., $\mathbb{P}(\mathrm{BSP}_{\mathrm{rec}}(A))_{/\leftrightarrow} \models \mathrm{RDP}$.

Proof The validity of RDP follows immediately from the construction of the model $\mathbb{P}(\mathrm{BSP}_{\mathrm{rec}}(A))_{/\leftrightarrow}$. For any recursive specification E and recursion variable X in E, the equivalence class $[\mu X.E]_{/\leftrightarrow}$ is a solution for X. Hence, each recursive specification has a solution. □

Theorem 5.5.3 is not really surprising. Theory $\mathrm{BSP}_{\mathrm{rec}}(A)$ and its model $\mathbb{P}(\mathrm{BSP}_{\mathrm{rec}}(A))_{/\leftrightarrow}$ have been constructed in such a way that every recursive specification has at least one solution. In fact, given the construction of theory $\mathrm{BSP}_{\mathrm{rec}}(A)$, this observation straightforwardly yields the following result.

Theorem 5.5.4 ($\mathrm{BSP}_{\mathrm{rec}}(A)$ **and** RDP) An arbitrary algebra $\mathbb{M}$ is a model of $\mathrm{BSP}_{\mathrm{rec}}(A)$ if and only if it validates theory BSP(A) and recursion principle RDP, i.e., $\mathbb{M} \models \mathrm{BSP}_{\mathrm{rec}}(A)$ if and only if $\mathbb{M} \models \mathrm{BSP}(A)$ and $\mathbb{M} \models \mathrm{RDP}$.

As already mentioned before, the construction of theory $\mathrm{BSP}_{\mathrm{rec}}(A)$ does not enforce that a recursive specification has only one solution; recursive specifications may have multiple solutions in some given model. One solution to this problem would be to simply disallow all such models. However, as a direct consequence of Example 5.3.7 (Multiple solutions), this only leaves models in which all processes are equal, so-called *one-point models*. This is clearly undesirable. Other solutions are to restrict the recursive specifications that are allowed or considered relevant, or to select a unique default solution of a recursive specification in case it has more than one. The latter is done in for example CCS, where the notion of a least fixed point is used to select solutions (Milner, 1980; Milner, 1989). Also the deduction rules for recursion underlying a term model for a theory with recursion, as for example given in Table 5.2, generate one particular solution, as explained in the previous section and further illustrated by Exercise 5.4.2. However, choosing this generated solution as the default solution does not allow the interpretation of recursion variables as constrained variables, and is furthermore model-dependent. Therefore, a restriction of the set of the allowed recursive specifications is considered. This can be done independent of any particular model. To this end, the notion of *guardedness* of recursive specifications is introduced. The basic idea is that guarded recursive specifications have precisely one solution.

Definition 5.5.5 (Guardedness, part 1) Let s be a $BSP_{rec}(A)$-term. An occurrence of a (normal or recursion) variable x in term s is called *guarded* if and only if it occurs in the operand of an action-prefix operator, i.e., s has a subterm of the form $a.t$ for some $a \in A$ and $BSP_{rec}(A)$-term t, and this x occurs in t. Term s is called *completely guarded* if and only if all occurrences of all variables in s are guarded. A *recursive specification* E is called *completely guarded* if and only if all right-hand sides of all recursive equations of E are completely guarded.

Example 5.5.6 (Guardedness)

(i) Let $t_1 \equiv a.X + Y + c.(b.0 + X)$. In this term, both occurrences of recursion variable X are guarded: the first one because it is the operand of the action-prefix operator $a.\_$; the second one because it occurs in the operand of the action-prefix operator $c.\_$. The occurrence of Y is unguarded. Therefore, t_1 is not completely guarded.

(ii) Let $t_2 \equiv a.X + Y + a.(b.0 + Y)$. In this term, the occurrence of X is guarded and Y occurs both guarded and unguarded. As a result, t_2 is not completely guarded.

(iii) Let $t_3 \equiv a.(X + Y)$. The occurrences of X and Y are guarded and hence t_3 is completely guarded.

(iv) Recursive specification $E_1 = \{X_1 = a.X_1, Y_1 = a.X_1\}$ is completely guarded.

(v) Recursive specification $E_2 = \{X_2 = a.X_2, Y_2 = X_2\}$ is not completely guarded because X_2 occurs unguarded in equation $Y_2 = X_2$.

A closer look at the last two examples reveals that the notion of guardedness presented in Definition 5.5.5 is too restrictive. Recursive specification E_1 is completely guarded. Recall that a guarded specification is supposed to have a single solution in some appropriate model of the basic theory BSP(A). Assuming that this is the case, recursion variables X_1 and Y_1 in E_1 each determine precisely one process in that model. However, recursive specification E_2 is not completely guarded, suggesting that recursion variables X_2 and Y_2 do not determine precisely one process each. It can be shown that the latter is not true by proving that the two recursive specifications are equivalent in the sense of Theorem 5.3.4 (Equivalence of recursive specifications), meaning that all solutions of X_1 and Y_1 in some model of BSP(A) are also solutions of X_2 and Y_2 and vice versa. In other words, the two recursive specifications specify precisely the same processes.

Example 5.5.7 (Guardedness anomaly) Consider again recursive specifications $E_1 = \{X_1 = a.X_1, Y_1 = a.X_1\}$ and $E_2 = \{X_2 = a.X_2, Y_2 = X_2\}$ of Example 5.5.6. In order to obtain that all solutions of X_1 and Y_1 are also solutions of X_2 and Y_2 in some given model of BSP(A), it suffices to show that the recursive equations from E_2 with the occurrences of X_2 and Y_2 replaced by X_1 and Y_1, respectively, are derivable from the process theory $(\mathrm{BSP} + E_1)(A)$ (Theorem 5.3.4). This is easily achieved as follows:

$$(\mathrm{BSP} + E_1)(A) \vdash X_1 = a.X_1$$

and

$$(\mathrm{BSP} + E_1)(A) \vdash Y_1 = a.X_1 = X_1.$$

Similarly, the fact that all solutions of X_2 and Y_2 are solutions of X_1 and Y_1, can be seen as follows:

$$(\mathrm{BSP} + E_2)(A) \vdash X_2 = a.X_2$$

and

$$(\mathrm{BSP} + E_2)(A) \vdash Y_2 = X_2 = a.X_2.$$

But this means that X_1 and Y_1 determine unique processes if and only if X_2 and Y_2 determine unique processes, showing that the notion of guardedness introduced in Definition 5.5.5 (Guardedness, part 1) is not suitable for the intended purpose.

The reason for the anomaly observed in the above example is that the definition of guardedness is a purely syntactical one. It does not take into account that syntactically different process terms can be semantically equivalent. In the following definition, a notion of guardedness is defined that also includes E_2 of the above example as a guarded recursive specification; the definition builds upon the notion 'completely guarded' as defined in Definition 5.5.5 (Guardedness, part 1).

Definition 5.5.8 (Guardedness, part 2) Let s be a $\mathrm{BSP}_{\mathrm{rec}}(A)$-term. Term s is *guarded* if and only if there exists a $\mathrm{BSP}_{\mathrm{rec}}(A)$-term t that is completely guarded and derivably equal to s, i.e., $\mathrm{BSP}_{\mathrm{rec}}(A) \vdash s = t$. A recursive specification E is *guarded* if and only if it can be rewritten into a completely guarded recursive specification F, i.e., there exists a completely guarded recursive specification F with $V_R(E) = V_R(F)$ and for all $X = t \in F$, $(\mathrm{BSP} + E)(A) \vdash X = t$.

Example 5.5.9 (Guarded recursive specifications) Consider again recursive specification $E_2 = \{X_2 = a.X_2, Y_2 = X_2\}$. Although this recursive specification is not completely guarded, the derivations

$$(\mathrm{BSP} + E_2)(A) \vdash X_2 = a.X_2$$

and

$$(\mathrm{BSP} + E_2)(A) \vdash Y_2 = X_2 = a.X_2$$

show that it can be rewritten into the completely guarded recursive specification $F = \{X_2 = a.X_2, Y_2 = a.X_2\}$, indicating that it is guarded.

Note that, although the guardedness notions in the above definitions are defined in the context of theory BSP(A), they can be generalized to arbitrary process theories in a straightforward way.

The question remains whether the notion of guardedness defined in Definition 5.5.8 is satisfactory. To investigate this issue, a new recursion principle is introduced that disallows models in which guarded recursive specifications have more than one solution. This principle is called the *Recursive Specification Principle.*

Definition 5.5.10 (RSP) Assume some equational theory and some model of this theory. The *Recursive Specification Principle* (RSP) is the following assumption: a guarded recursive specification over the signature of the theory has at most one solution in the model.

In the context of process theory BSP(A) and its models $\mathbb{P}(\mathrm{BSP}(A))_{/\leftrightarrow}$ and $\mathbb{P}(\mathrm{BSP}_{\mathrm{rec}}(A))_{/\leftrightarrow}$, the following theorem holds.

Theorem 5.5.11 (Validity of RSP**)** Principle RSP is valid in both the term model of BSP(A) and the term model of $\mathrm{BSP}_{\mathrm{rec}}(A)$, i.e., $\mathbb{P}(\mathrm{BSP}(A))_{/\leftrightarrow} \models$ RSP and $\mathbb{P}(\mathrm{BSP}_{\mathrm{rec}}(A))_{/\leftrightarrow} \models$ RSP.

Proof The theorem is a consequence of Theorems 5.5.29 (Relation between the recursion principles) and 5.5.23 (Validity of AIP^-), proven later in this section. Note that these theorems are only proven for theories with projection operators. However, since extensions of BSP(A) and $\mathrm{BSP}_{\mathrm{rec}}(A)$ with projection operators are ground-conservative, any element in the term models of BSP(A) and $\mathrm{BSP}_{\mathrm{rec}}(A)$ is also an element of the term models of $(\mathrm{BSP}+\mathrm{PR})(A)$ and $(\mathrm{BSP}+\mathrm{PR})_{\mathrm{rec}}(A)$. Hence, if a recursive specification over the signature without projection operators has at most one solution in the term models of the theories with projection, it has also at most one solution in the term models of the theories without projection. □

Through the introduction of the recursion principles RSP and RDP, it has been shown that, in the term model $\mathbb{P}(\mathrm{BSP}_{\mathrm{rec}}(A))_{/\leftrightarrow}$, every *guarded* recursive specification over the signature of theory BSP(A) has at most one solution and that *every* recursive specification over the BSP(A)-signature has at least one solution. Together, this gives that *every guarded* recursive specification has *precisely one* solution. Thus, the notion of guardedness introduced in Definition 5.5.8 is meaningful indeed.

So how can recursion principles be used to reason about the equivalence of recursive specifications? In general, recursion principles may affect the notion of derivability, as defined in Definition 2.2.8. Thus, recursion principles may be used to derive equations between terms of some process theory that cannot be derived from the basic axioms of the theory, in particular equations involving recursion variables. Recursion principle RDP does not affect derivability. However, RSP does have an effect. The detailed redefinition of derivability is omitted, in this case and also in the remainder when other recursion principles are introduced. The use of recursion principles in the derivation of equations with recursion variables is illustrated through examples, as for instance Example 5.5.12 that follows below.

To clarify that a recursion principle is assumed to hold in derivations, its acronym is added to the name of the process theory being used. For example, the notation $(\mathrm{BSP}_{\mathrm{rec}} + \mathrm{RSP})(A)$ indicates that the theory $\mathrm{BSP}_{\mathrm{rec}}(A)$ is being used for derivations while assuming RSP to hold.

Example 5.5.12 (Recursion principle RSP) Consider again recursive specifications $E_1 = \{X_1 = a.X_1\}$ and $E_2 = \{X_2 = a.a.X_2\}$ of Example 5.3.3 (Equivalence of recursion variables). On intuitive grounds, it is expected that X_1 and X_2 define the same process. How can this (correct) intuition be captured in the equational theory? Observe that it is necessary to consider theory $(\mathrm{BSP} + E_1 + E_2)(A)$, or an extension of this theory. Only when E_1 and E_2 are part of the equational theory, the theory has a means to reason about the recursive specifications, and in particular about the equivalence of X_1 and X_2. As already mentioned in Example 5.3.3, an attempt to prove the equivalence of X_1 and X_2 using only the basic axioms of $(\mathrm{BSP}+E_1+E_2)(A)$ will not be successful. However, assuming recursion principle RSP, the desired equivalence can be proven.

First, it is shown that any solution of X_1 is a solution of X_2 by deriving the equation for X_2 with all occurrences of X_2 replaced by occurrences of X_1 from the process theory $(\mathrm{BSP} + E_1)(A)$ as shown before in Example 5.3.3:

$$(\mathrm{BSP} + E_1)(A) \vdash X_1 = a.X_1 = a.a.X_1.$$

Second, assume the validity of principle RSP. This means that only models of theory $(\text{BSP}+E_1+E_2)(A)$ that satisfy this principle, such as the term models $\mathbb{P}((\text{BSP}+E_1+E_2)(A))_{/\leftrightarrow}$ or $\mathbb{P}(\text{BSP}_{\text{rec}}(A))_{/\leftrightarrow}$, are considered. RSP, the fact that both E_1 and E_2 are guarded, and the fact that every model of $(\text{BSP}+E_1+E_2)(A)$ contains solutions for E_1 and E_2 by definition (see Theorem 5.3.6 (Solutions vs. models)) imply that both X_1 and X_2 have precisely one solution in any model considered. Since any solution for X_1 is a solution for X_2, the solutions for X_1 and X_2 must be the same. This shows that X_1 and X_2 are derivably equivalent in the process theory $(\text{BSP}+E_1+E_2+\text{RSP})(A)$:

$$(\text{BSP}+E_1+E_2+\text{RSP})(A) \vdash X_1 = X_2.$$

Note that the reasoning leading to this conclusion is completely model-independent. It illustrates how the recursion principle RSP can be used to derive equations involving recursion variables.

Example 5.5.13 (Recursion principle RSP**)** Consider the two recursive specifications

$$E = \left\{ \begin{array}{rcl} X_0 &=& a.X_1, \\ X_{n+1} &=& a.X_{n+2} + b.X_n \end{array} \middle| \, n \in \mathbf{N} \right\}$$

and

$$F = \left\{ \begin{array}{rcl} Y_{i,0} &=& a.Y_{i,1}, \\ Y_{i,j+1} &=& a.Y_{i,j+2} + b.Y_{i+1,j} \end{array} \middle| \, i, j \in \mathbf{N} \right\}.$$

These recursive specifications are guarded. Hence, each of them has precisely one solution in the term model $\mathbb{P}(\text{BSP}_{\text{rec}}(A))_{/\leftrightarrow}$. Using the principle RSP, it can be shown that $(\text{BSP}+E+F+\text{RSP})(A) \vdash X_n = Y_{i,n}$ for any natural numbers i and n. This shows that the recursive specification F where variables have a double index can be simplified to the recursive specification E where variables have only one index.

One way to arrive at the desired result is to show that the equations of F are derivable from the equations of E after replacing the occurrences of the $Y_{i,j}$ by occurrences of X_j. Hence, it has to be shown that $(\text{BSP}+E)(A) \vdash X_0 = a.X_1$ and, for any $j \in \mathbf{N}$, $(\text{BSP}+E)(A) \vdash X_{j+1} = a.X_{j+2} + b.X_j$. Obviously, this is the case. This result implies that any solution of X_j is also a solution of $Y_{i,j}$, for any $i \in \mathbf{N}$. Furthermore, both E and F have precisely one solution in any model of theory $(\text{BSP}+E+F+\text{RSP})(A)$, leading to the desired result that $(\text{BSP}+E+F+\text{RSP})(A) \vdash X_n = Y_{i,n}$ for any $i, n \in \mathbf{N}$.

A reasoning where the equations of E are shown to be derivable from the equations of F also leads to the desired result. In this approach, the occurrences of variables X_n in E can be replaced by occurrences of $Y_{0,n}$ (or any other $Y_{i,n}$). Hence, it has to be shown that $(\text{BSP}+F)(A) \vdash Y_{0,0} = a.Y_{0,1}$

and, for any $n \in \mathbf{N}$, $(\mathrm{BSP} + F)(A) \vdash Y_{0,n+1} = a.Y_{0,n+2} + b.Y_{0,n}$. This is much more elaborate than the above proof as it requires additional proofs of $(\mathrm{BSP} + F)(A) \vdash Y_{i,j} = Y_{i+1,j}$ for any $i, j \in \mathbf{N}$.

The above examples show that the principle RSP and the notion of guardedness are meaningful and useful. Guardedness of a recursive specification over the signature of BSP(A) implies that it has a unique solution in the term model $\mathbb{P}(\mathrm{BSP}_{\mathrm{rec}}(A))_{/\leftrightarrow}$, and RSP allows equational reasoning about guarded recursive specifications. It turns out that guardedness is also exactly the notion needed to characterize recursive specifications with unique solutions when considering the theory $\mathrm{BSP}_{\mathrm{rec}}(A)$ and its term model $\mathbb{P}(\mathrm{BSP}_{\mathrm{rec}}(A))_{/\leftrightarrow}$. Every unguarded recursive specification over the signature of BSP(A) with a finite or infinite but countable number of equations has multiple solutions in $\mathbb{P}(\mathrm{BSP}_{\mathrm{rec}}(A))_{/\leftrightarrow}$ when A is not empty. The proof for finite unguarded recursive specifications is as follows.

Proposition 5.5.14 (Guardedness) Every finite unguarded recursive specification over the signature of theory BSP(A) has multiple solutions in the model $\mathbb{P}(\mathrm{BSP}_{\mathrm{rec}}(A))_{/\leftrightarrow}$ when A is not empty.

Proof Suppose E is an unguarded recursive specification over the signature of BSP(A) with a finite number of equations. As E is unguarded, then either there is a variable X in $V_R(E)$ that occurs unguarded in the equation of X or there is a number $n \geq 1$ and a sequence of variables $X_0, \ldots, X_n$ in $V_R(E)$ such that X_{i+1} occurs unguarded in the equation of X_i $(i < n)$ and X_0 occurs unguarded in the equation of X_n (i.e., there is a 'cycle of unguardedness'). Consider the second case. The first case can be treated similarly.
Let p be an arbitrary closed BSP(A)-term. Consider the recursive specification E_p that is obtained from E by adding an extra summand p to each of the equations of $X_0, \ldots, X_n$, so, if $X_i = t_i$ is the equation in E, then $X_i = t_i + p$ becomes the equation in E_p.
Let $X_i = t_i + p$ and $X_{i+1} = t_{i+1} + p$ (for $i < n$) be equations in E_p. Recall that X_{i+1} occurs unguarded in t_i, which means that t_i is derivably equal to a term of the form $s + X_{i+1}$, for some term s. This implies that $(\mathrm{BSP}+E_p)(A) \vdash X_i = t_i + p = s + X_{i+1} + p = s + X_{i+1} + X_{i+1} + p = t_i + X_{i+1} + p$, i.e., X_i has an X_{i+1} summand. It follows that $(\mathrm{BSP}+E_p)(A) \vdash X_i = t_i + p = t_i + X_{i+1} + p = t_i + (t_{i+1} + p) + p = t_i + t_{i+1} + p = t_i + X_{i+1} = s + X_{i+1} + X_{i+1} = s + X_{i+1} = t_i$, i.e., $(\mathrm{BSP} + E_p)(A) \vdash X_i = t_i$. In a similar way, it is possible to show that $(\mathrm{BSP} + E_p)(A) \vdash X_n = t_n$. Thus, it follows that $(\mathrm{BSP} + E_p)(A) \vdash E$, and that any solution of E_p is also a solution of E. When A is not empty there are

infinitely many different instantiations that can be chosen for p (e.g., choosing $1, a.1, a.a.1, \ldots$ for some $a \in A$).

Next, consider the deduction system of Table 5.2. It implies that every state of the transition system defined by any recursion constant $\mu X.E$ is a subterm of one of the right-hand sides of the equations in E. As E has only finitely many equations, there are finitely many such subterms. The deduction rules imply that, as a consequence, the number of states of any transition system of a recursion variable of a finite recursive specification is finite. Note that the deduction system of Table 5.2 also shows that processes $\mu X_i.E_p$ $(i \leq n)$ among others allow the behavior of p. Only finitely many of these behaviors can already be present in each of the $\mu X_i.E$, as the corresponding transition systems have only finitely many states. Since there are infinitely many choices for p and any solution for $\mu X_i.E_p$ is also a solution for $\mu X_i.E$, infinitely many different solutions are obtained for each of the $\mu X_i.E$ and thus for E. □

The above property assumes that the action set is not empty. It is not difficult to give an unguarded recursive specification over the signature of BSP(A) with only one solution if the action set can be empty; see Exercise 5.5.3.

It seems that there are no general conditions independent of the basic process theory and the precise model that guarantee that guarded recursive specifications are always precisely the recursive specifications with one solution. In Chapter 10, the so-called inaccessible process is introduced. This process can be used to construct unguarded recursive specifications with only a single solution, even in the presence of actions (see Exercise 10.3.2). There are also models in which guarded recursive specifications have multiple solutions. In the initial algebra $\mathbb{I}(\mathrm{BSP}_{\mathrm{rec}}(A))$ of theory $\mathrm{BSP}_{\mathrm{rec}}(A)$, see Definition 2.3.19 (Initial algebra), in general many guarded recursive specifications have multiple solutions. Consider for example the two guarded recursive specifications $E_1 = \{X = a.X\}$ and $E_2 = \{Y = a.Y\}$, for some $a \in A$. Because theory $\mathrm{BSP}_{\mathrm{rec}}(A)$ – without assuming RSP – has no means to derive equalities between X and Y, the initial algebra $\mathbb{I}(\mathrm{BSP}_{\mathrm{rec}}(A))$ contains two equivalence classes $[\mu X.E_1]_{\vdash}$ and $[\mu Y.E_2]_{\vdash}$ that are both solutions of both X and Y. Furthermore, Example 4.5.2 in (Usenko, 2002) introduces an algebra that can be used to construct models for theories including sequential composition, as presented later in this book, in which every guarded recursive specification with at least one recursion variable in the right-hand side of one of its equations has infinitely many solutions. However, these models capture no longer the intuitive semantics of process theories and their operators. They exploit the large freedom in constructing models for equational theories, but have no meaning in process specification and modeling. In conclusion, the discussed examples show that guardedness does not capture uniqueness of solutions of recursive specifications under all possible circumstances. However, all the examples are exceptional or counterintuitive cases. In practice, guardedness is an appropriate and commonly used way to capture the uniqueness of solutions of recursive specifications, in a model-independent way.

An interesting observation is that principle RDP is stronger than strictly necessary for the purpose of capturing all recursive specifications with precisely one solution: it suffices to assume that *guarded* recursive specifications have a solution. This weaker principle is called the *Restricted Recursive Definition Principle*.

Definition 5.5.15 (RDP$^-$) Assume some equational theory and some model of this theory. The *Restricted Recursive Definition Principle* (RDP$^-$) is the following assumption: every guarded recursive specification over the signature of the theory has a solution in the model of that theory.

Theorem 5.5.16 ((In-)validity of RDP$^-$**)** Assuming BSP(A) as the basic process theory, principle RDP$^-$ is valid in $\mathbb{P}(\text{BSP}_{\text{rec}}(A))_{/\leftrightarrows}$ but it is not valid in $\mathbb{P}(\text{BSP}(A))_{/\leftrightarrows}$, i.e., $\mathbb{P}(\text{BSP}_{\text{rec}}(A))_{/\leftrightarrows} \models \text{RDP}^-$ and $\mathbb{P}(\text{BSP}(A))_{/\leftrightarrows} \not\models \text{RDP}^-$.

Proof The validity of RDP$^-$ in term model $\mathbb{P}(\text{BSP}_{\text{rec}}(A))_{/\leftrightarrows}$ is a direct consequence of the facts that RDP is valid in $\mathbb{P}(\text{BSP}_{\text{rec}}(A))_{/\leftrightarrows}$ (Theorem 5.5.3) and that RDP implies RDP$^-$. The invalidity of RDP$^-$ in model $\mathbb{P}(\text{BSP}(A))_{/\leftrightarrows}$ follows from the same example that proved the invalidity of the principle RDP for this term model (Example 5.3.5 (No solutions)). □

Theorems 5.5.2 (Invalidity of RDP), 5.5.3 (Validity of RDP), and 5.5.16 ((In-)validity of RDP$^-$) show that both RDP and RDP$^-$ are invalid in the term model $\mathbb{P}(\text{BSP}(A))_{/\leftrightarrows}$ and valid in the term model $\mathbb{P}(\text{BSP}_{\text{rec}}(A))_{/\leftrightarrows}$. It is also possible to construct models for BSP(A) that satisfy RDP$^-$ but not RDP, for example the term model $\mathbb{P}(\text{BSP}(A))_{/\leftrightarrows}$ extended with bisimilarity equivalence classes for all constants $\mu X.E$ for arbitrary recursion variables X and *guarded* recursive specifications E.

The validity of the recursion principles RSP and RDP$^-$ in the term model $\mathbb{P}(\text{BSP}_{\text{rec}}(A))_{/\leftrightarrows}$ reconfirms that every guarded recursive specification over the signature of BSP(A) has precisely one solution in $\mathbb{P}(\text{BSP}_{\text{rec}}(A))_{/\leftrightarrows}$.

Recall that the proof of Theorem 5.5.11, claiming the validity of principle RSP in the term models of BSP(A) and BSP$_{\text{rec}}$(A), was in effect postponed. The given proof uses the validity of another recursion principle, namely the

Restricted Approximation Induction Principle (AIP$^-$). This recursion principle is based on the idea that a solution of a recursive specification, which is a potentially infinite process, can be approximated by its series of finite projections, using the projection operators introduced in Section 4.5. Each such a finite projection can be considered as an approximation of the solution itself. In computing science and mathematics in general, and in process algebra in particular, it is quite common to describe an infinite object in terms of a series of approximations. The essence of AIP$^-$ is that two processes – for example, but not necessarily, two solutions of some recursive specification(s) – can be considered equal if all their finite projections are equal. However, as the name already suggests, AIP$^-$ restricts this essential idea to some extent. It is in fact a restricted version of a more general recursion principle that precisely captures this idea, namely the *Approximation Induction Principle* (AIP). Note that the principles AIP and AIP$^-$ explicitly refer to projections of processes. Hence, it is required that the basic theory under consideration contains projection operators. Therefore, in the following, the basic theories considered are (BSP + PR)(A) and (BSP + PR)$_{\text{rec}}(A)$ instead of BSP(A) and BSP$_{\text{rec}}(A)$.

Definition 5.5.17 (AIP) The *Approximation Induction Principle* (AIP) is the following assumption: for arbitrary (BSP+PR)$_{\text{rec}}(A)$-terms s and t, if (BSP+PR)$_{\text{rec}}(A) \vdash \pi_n(s) = \pi_n(t)$ for all natural numbers $n \in \mathbf{N}$, then ((BSP + PR)$_{\text{rec}}$ + AIP)$(A) \vdash s = t$.

An equivalent formulation of AIP is obtained by also allowing the use of the principle AIP in the derivation of $\pi_n(s) = \pi_n(t)$, i.e., (BSP + PR)$_{\text{rec}}(A) \vdash \pi_n(s) = \pi_n(t)$ can be replaced by ((BSP+PR)$_{\text{rec}}$+AIP)$(A) \vdash \pi_n(s) = \pi_n(t)$. Furthermore, note that the above definition is formulated in terms of the theory (BSP + PR)$_{\text{rec}}(A)$. However, the principle can be defined for arbitrary process theories that contain projection operators, also theories without recursion. In the remainder, it is used without further notice for other theories as well.

Example 5.5.18 (AIP) Consider again recursive specifications $\{X_1 = a.X_1\}$ and $\{X_2 = a.a.X_2\}$. Using AIP, it can be shown that X_1 and X_2 denote the same process, i.e., it can be shown that ((BSP + PR)$_{\text{rec}}$ + AIP)$(A) \vdash X_1 = X_2$.

Recall Notation 4.6.6 (n-fold action prefix). Using natural induction, it is not difficult to show that, for any natural number $n \in \mathbf{N}$,

$$(\text{BSP} + \text{PR})_{\text{rec}}(A) \vdash \pi_n(X_1) = a^n 0$$

and

$$(\text{BSP} + \text{PR})_{\text{rec}}(A) \vdash \pi_n(X_2) = a^n 0.$$

Thus, for any natural number $n \in \mathbf{N}$,

$$(\text{BSP} + \text{PR})_{\text{rec}}(A) \vdash \pi_n(X_1) = a^n 0 = \pi_n(X_2).$$

Using AIP gives

$$((\text{BSP} + \text{PR})_{\text{rec}} + \text{AIP})(A) \vdash X_1 = X_2.$$

Unfortunately, the principle AIP is not valid in the term model of theory $(\text{BSP} + \text{PR})_{\text{rec}}(A)$. It does hold in the term model of $(\text{BSP} + \text{PR})(A)$, but that model is not very interesting because not all recursive specifications have a solution in that model. The proof of the following theorem uses a new notation, $\sum$, which generalizes the choice operator $+$ to a choice between an arbitrary number of processes.

Notation 5.5.19 (Generalized choice) Let $I \subset \mathbf{N}$ be some finite index set of natural numbers, $j \in \mathbf{N} \setminus I$ a fresh index not in I, and t_i, for all $i \in I \cup \{j\}$, arbitrary terms in some process theory containing the choice operator $+$.

$$\sum_{i \in \emptyset} t_i \equiv 0 \text{ and } \sum_{i \in I \cup \{j\}} t_i \equiv t_j + \sum_{i \in I} t_i.$$

At this point, the above notation is simply an abbreviation. In Chapter 10, a true choice quantifier, i.e., the quantifier corresponding to the binary operator $+$ with 0 as its identity element, is added as an operator in process theories.

Theorem 5.5.20 ((In-)validity of AIP**)** Principle AIP is valid in $\mathbb{P}((\text{BSP} + \text{PR})(A))_{/\leftrightarrow}$ and it is not valid in $\mathbb{P}((\text{BSP}+\text{PR})_{\text{rec}}(A))_{/\leftrightarrow}$. That is, $\mathbb{P}((\text{BSP}+\text{PR})(A))_{/\leftrightarrow} \models \text{AIP}$ and $\mathbb{P}((\text{BSP} + \text{PR})_{\text{rec}}(A))_{/\leftrightarrow} \not\models \text{AIP}$.

Proof First, it is proven that recursion principle AIP holds in the term model $\mathbb{P}((\text{BSP} + \text{PR})(A))_{/\leftrightarrow}$.
Let p and q be closed $(\text{BSP} + \text{PR})(A)$-terms such that $\pi_n(p) \leftrightarrow \pi_n(q)$, for all natural numbers $n \in \mathbf{N}$. It has to be proven that $p \leftrightarrow q$. From Theorem 4.5.4 (Bounded depth), it follows that there exist natural numbers n_1 and n_2 such that, for all $k_1 \geq n_1$ and $k_2 \geq n_2$, $(\text{BSP} + \text{PR})(A) \vdash \pi_{k_1}(p) = p$ and $(\text{BSP}+\text{PR})(A) \vdash \pi_{k_2}(q) = q$. Hence, for all $k \geq \max(n_1, n_2)$, $\pi_k(p) \leftrightarrow p$ and $\pi_k(q) \leftrightarrow q$. Recall the assumption that $\pi_n(p) \leftrightarrow \pi_n(q)$ for all $n \in \mathbf{N}$. Taking an arbitrary $n' \geq \max(n_1, n_2)$, it follows that $p \leftrightarrow \pi_{n'}(p) \leftrightarrow \pi_{n'}(q) \leftrightarrow q$. Hence, the principle AIP is valid in the model $\mathbb{P}((\text{BSP} + \text{PR})(A))_{/\leftrightarrow}$.
Second, it is shown that principle AIP is not valid in the term model $\mathbb{P}((\text{BSP}+\text{PR})_{\text{rec}}(A))_{/\leftrightarrow}$.
Consider the recursive specifications $\{X_n = a^n 0 + X_{n+1} \mid n \in \mathbf{N}\}$ and $\{Y = a.Y\}$. As in Example 5.5.18 (AIP), it can be shown that $(\text{BSP} + \text{PR})_{\text{rec}}(A) \vdash$

$\pi_n(Y) = a^n0$ for all $n \in \mathbf{N}$. Furthermore, obviously $(\mathrm{BSP}+\mathrm{PR})(A) \vdash a^n0 = \pi_n(a^n0)$ for all $n \in \mathbf{N}$.
By induction, it can be shown that, for any natural number $n \in \mathbf{N}$,

$$(\mathrm{BSP}+\mathrm{PR})_{\mathrm{rec}}(A) \vdash X_0 = \sum_{i=0}^{n} a^i0 + X_{n+1}.$$

This results in

$$(\mathrm{BSP}+\mathrm{PR})_{\mathrm{rec}}(A) \vdash X_0 = X_0 + a^n0$$

as follows, using Axiom A3 in the second step:

$$\begin{aligned}(\mathrm{BSP}+\mathrm{PR})_{\mathrm{rec}}(A) \vdash X_0 &= \sum_{i=0}^{n} a^i0 + X_{n+1}\\ &= \sum_{i=0}^{n} a^i0 + a^n0 + X_{n+1}\\ &= X_0 + a^n0.\end{aligned}$$

Consequently, for any natural number $n \in \mathbf{N}$,

$$\begin{aligned}(\mathrm{BSP}+\mathrm{PR})_{\mathrm{rec}}(A) \vdash \pi_n(X_0+Y) &= \pi_n(X_0) + \pi_n(Y)\\ &= \pi_n(X_0) + a^n0\\ &= \pi_n(X_0) + \pi_n(a^n0)\\ &= \pi_n(X_0 + a^n0)\\ &= \pi_n(X_0).\end{aligned}$$

Applying AIP then gives

$$((\mathrm{BSP}+\mathrm{PR})_{\mathrm{rec}} + \mathrm{AIP})(A) \vdash X_0 + Y = X_0.$$

Assume now that AIP is valid in model $\mathbb{P}((\mathrm{BSP}+\mathrm{PR})_{\mathrm{rec}}(A))_{/\leftrightarrow}$. This yields that $X_0 + Y \leftrightarrow X_0$. The term $X_0 + Y$, however, exhibits an infinite path of a executions as follows:

$$X_0 + Y \xrightarrow{a} Y \xrightarrow{a} Y \xrightarrow{a} \cdots \xrightarrow{a} Y \xrightarrow{a} \cdots.$$

On the other hand, the process term X_0 only allows finite paths of a executions. Each such path is of the form

$$X_0 \xrightarrow{a} a^n0 \xrightarrow{a} a^{n-1}0 \xrightarrow{a} \cdots \xrightarrow{a} 0,$$

for some $n \geq 1$. However, this means that $X_0 + Y$ and X_0 cannot be bisimilar, i.e.,

$$X_0 + Y \not\leftrightarrow X_0.$$

When playing the bisimulation game as explained in Chapter 3, it is clear that the player playing with X_0 can at some point no longer match the moves of the infinite a sequence of process $X_0 + Y$, no matter what execution path of X_0 is chosen in the initial state. This implies a contradiction, and, as a conclusion, principle AIP is not valid in $\mathbb{P}((\mathrm{BSP}+\mathrm{PR})_{\mathrm{rec}}(A))_{/\leftrightarrow}$. □

The problem with the Approximation Induction Principle is that it is only capable of discriminating processes that differ in a finite initial part of their behavior. The two process terms $X_0 + Y$ and X_0 in the above proof do not differ in any finite initial part of their behaviors. Hence, AIP is too strong: It is not valid in the standard term model of the basic process theory with recursion. Principle AIP$^-$ restricts the applicability of AIP by requiring that one of the process terms under consideration should be guarded, solving the observed problem. This restricted version turns out to be valid in the standard term model. It can also be used, as intended, to prove the validity of RSP in the standard term model.

Definition 5.5.21 (AIP$^-$) The *Restricted Approximation Induction Principle* (AIP$^-$) is the following assumption: for arbitrary $(\mathrm{BSP} + \mathrm{PR})_{\mathrm{rec}}(A)$-terms s and t such that s is guarded, if $(\mathrm{BSP} + \mathrm{PR})_{\mathrm{rec}}(A) \vdash \pi_n(s) = \pi_n(t)$ for all natural numbers $n \in \mathbf{N}$, then $((\mathrm{BSP} + \mathrm{PR})_{\mathrm{rec}} + \mathrm{AIP}^-)(A) \vdash s = t$.

As for AIP, also in this case, the hypothesis $(\mathrm{BSP} + \mathrm{PR})_{\mathrm{rec}}(A) \vdash \pi_n(s) = \pi_n(t)$ can be replaced by $((\mathrm{BSP} + \mathrm{PR})_{\mathrm{rec}} + \mathrm{AIP}^-)(A) \vdash \pi_n(s) = \pi_n(t)$. Also AIP$^-$ can be defined straightforwardly in the context of other process theories.

Example 5.5.22 (AIP$^-$) Consider once more recursive specifications $\{X_1 = a.X_1\}$ and $\{X_2 = a.a.X_2\}$. As explained in Example 5.5.18 (AIP), $(\mathrm{BSP} + \mathrm{PR})_{\mathrm{rec}}(A) \vdash \pi_n(X_1) = a^n 0$ and $(\mathrm{BSP} + \mathrm{PR})_{\mathrm{rec}}(A) \vdash \pi_n(X_2) = a^n 0$, and hence $(\mathrm{BSP} + \mathrm{PR})_{\mathrm{rec}}(A) \vdash \pi_n(X_1) = \pi_n(X_2)$, for all natural numbers $n \in \mathbf{N}$. As X_1 and X_2 are guarded, applying AIP$^-$ yields $((\mathrm{BSP}{+}\mathrm{PR})_{\mathrm{rec}}{+}\mathrm{AIP}^-)(A) \vdash X_1 = X_2$.

Theorem 5.5.23 (Validity of AIP$^-$**)** The principle AIP$^-$ is valid in both term model $\mathbb{P}((\mathrm{BSP}+\mathrm{PR})(A))_{/\leftrightarrows}$ and term model $\mathbb{P}((\mathrm{BSP}+\mathrm{PR})_{\mathrm{rec}}(A))_{/\leftrightarrows}$. That is, $\mathbb{P}((\mathrm{BSP} + \mathrm{PR})(A))_{/\leftrightarrows} \models \mathrm{AIP}^-$ and $\mathbb{P}((\mathrm{BSP} + \mathrm{PR})_{\mathrm{rec}}(A))_{/\leftrightarrows} \models \mathrm{AIP}^-$.

Proof The fact that $\mathbb{P}((\mathrm{BSP}+\mathrm{PR})(A))_{/\leftrightarrows} \models \mathrm{AIP}^-$ follows immediately from the observation that AIP implies AIP$^-$ and the fact that $\mathbb{P}((\mathrm{BSP} + \mathrm{PR})(A))_{/\leftrightarrows} \models \mathrm{AIP}$ (Theorem 5.5.20).

The second part of the theorem is proven as follows. Let $p, q \in \mathcal{C}((\mathrm{BSP} + \mathrm{PR})_{\mathrm{rec}}(A))$ be such that p is guarded and $\pi_n(p) \leftrightarrows \pi_n(q)$ for all natural numbers $n \in \mathbf{N}$. It has to be proven that $p \leftrightarrows q$. By definition of guardedness there exists a completely guarded term $p' \in \mathcal{C}((\mathrm{BSP} + \mathrm{PR})_{\mathrm{rec}}(A))$ such that $p \leftrightarrows p'$. It suffices to prove that $p' \leftrightarrows q$. Define the relation R on closed $(\mathrm{BSP} + \mathrm{PR})_{\mathrm{rec}}(A)$-terms as follows:

$$R = \{(u, v) \in (\mathcal{C}((\text{BSP} + \text{PR})_{\text{rec}}(A)))^2 \mid \\ \pi_n(u) \leftrightarrow \pi_n(v) \text{ for all } n \in \mathbf{N} \text{ and } u \text{ is completely guarded}\}.$$

Clearly, $(p', q) \in R$. It remains to prove that R is a bisimulation relation. Consider an arbitrary pair $(u, v) \in R$. For technical reasons the parts of the proof are presented in a different order than usual.

- Suppose that $v \xrightarrow{a} v'$ for some $a \in A$ and closed term $v' \in \mathcal{C}((\text{BSP} + \text{PR})_{\text{rec}}(A))$. It has to be proven that there exists a $u' \in \mathcal{C}((\text{BSP} + \text{PR})_{\text{rec}}(A))$ such that $u \xrightarrow{a} u'$ and $(u', v') \in R$.
  Define, for any natural number $m \in \mathbf{N}$,

  $$S_m = \{u^* \in \mathcal{C}((\text{BSP} + \text{PR})_{\text{rec}}(A)) \mid \\ u \xrightarrow{a} u^* \text{ and } \pi_m(u^*) \leftrightarrow \pi_m(v')\}.$$

  The set S_m represents all processes that are reachable from u by performing a once and that are bisimilar to v' up to depth m.
  Then, the following observations can be made:

  (i) For any natural number $i \in \mathbf{N}$, $S_i \supseteq S_{i+1}$. This follows from the observation that, for any closed $(\text{BSP} + \text{PR})_{\text{rec}}(A)$-terms p and q and natural number $k \in \mathbf{N}$, $\pi_{k+1}(p) \leftrightarrow \pi_{k+1}(q)$ implies that $\pi_k(p) \leftrightarrow \pi_k(q)$ (see Exercise 5.5.8).

  (ii) For any natural number $i \in \mathbf{N}$, $S_i \neq \emptyset$. To see this, let $i \in \mathbf{N}$ be some natural number. From $v \xrightarrow{a} v'$ and the deduction rules for projection operators in Table 4.6 in Section 4.5, it follows that $\pi_{i+1}(v) \xrightarrow{a} \pi_i(v')$ for any $i \in \mathbf{N}$. From this, and the fact that $\pi_{i+1}(u) \leftrightarrow \pi_{i+1}(v)$ (assumption $(u, v) \in R$), it follows that there exists a closed $(\text{BSP} + \text{PR})_{\text{rec}}(A)$-term u' such that $\pi_{i+1}(u) \xrightarrow{a} u'$ and $u' \leftrightarrow \pi_i(v')$. Inspection of the deduction rules for projection operators reveals that necessarily $u' \equiv \pi_i(u'')$ for some closed $(\text{BSP}+\text{PR})_{\text{rec}}(A)$-term u'' such that $u \xrightarrow{a} u''$. Hence, $\pi_i(u'') \leftrightarrow \pi_i(v')$ for some u''. Then, by definition of S_i, $u'' \in S_i$. Hence $S_i \neq \emptyset$.

  (iii) For any natural number $i \in \mathbf{N}$, S_i is finite. This follows immediately from the fact that u is completely guarded and the property of the deduction rules that in one transition only a finite number of terms can be reached from a completely guarded term (see Exercise 5.5.9).

  From these observations, it can be concluded that $\bigcap_{i \in \mathbf{N}} S_i \neq \emptyset$. Take some $u' \in \bigcap_{i \in \mathbf{N}} S_i$. Observe that by the definition of the sets S_i necessarily $u \xrightarrow{a} u'$. As $u' \in S_i$ for all natural numbers $i \in \mathbf{N}$, it follows that $\pi_i(u') \leftrightarrow \pi_i(v')$ for all natural numbers $i \in \mathbf{N}$. It follows from the definition of R that $(u', v') \in R$, which completes this case of the proof.

- Suppose that $u \xrightarrow{a} u'$ for some action $a \in A$ and closed term $u' \in \mathcal{C}((\mathrm{BSP} + \mathrm{PR})_{\mathrm{rec}}(A))$. It has to be proven that there exists a $v' \in \mathcal{C}((\mathrm{BSP} + \mathrm{PR})_{\mathrm{rec}}(A))$ such that $v \xrightarrow{a} v'$ and $(u', v') \in R$.

  Define, similar to the previous case, for any natural number $m \in \mathbf{N}$,

  $$T_m = \{v^* \in \mathcal{C}((\mathrm{BSP} + \mathrm{PR})_{\mathrm{rec}}(A)) \mid \\ v \xrightarrow{a} v^* \text{ and } \pi_m(u') \leftrightarrow \pi_m(v^*)\}.$$

  Observe that the sequence $(T_i)_{i \in \mathbf{N}}$ is decreasing and that all T_i are non-empty. For each $i \in \mathbf{N}$, pick a term $v_i \in T_i$. Then, $v \xrightarrow{a} v_i$ by definition. By the previous item, there are u_i such that $u \xrightarrow{a} u_i$ and $(u_i, v_i) \in R$ for all $i \in \mathbf{N}$. As before, since u is completely guarded, it follows that only a finite number of terms can be reached from u. Therefore, the sequence $(u_i)_{i \in \mathbf{N}}$ must contain at least one element infinitely often. Let u^* be a term that occurs infinitely often in $(u_i)_{i \in \mathbf{N}}$ and k a natural number such that $u^* \equiv u_k$. It is claimed that $(u', v_k) \in R$, thus finishing the proof. To see that this claim indeed holds, one needs to prove that $\pi_n(u') \leftrightarrow \pi_n(v_k)$ for all $n \in \mathbf{N}$. Let n be an arbitrary natural number. Let l be a natural number such that $l \geq n$ and $u^* \equiv u_l$. Then $\pi_n(u') \leftrightarrow \pi_n(v_l)$ follows from the facts that $v_l \in T_l$ and $T_l \subseteq T_n$. Furthermore $(u^*, v_l) \in R$ and $(u^*, v_k) \in R$ are obtained from $(u_l, v_l) \in R$ and $u^* \equiv u_l$, and $(u_k, v_k) \in R$ and $u^* \equiv u_k$. Therefore, $\pi_n(u') \leftrightarrow \pi_n(v_l) \leftrightarrow \pi_n(u^*) \leftrightarrow \pi_n(v_k)$. Thus, $\pi_n(u') \leftrightarrow \pi_n(v_k)$ for all $n \in \mathbf{N}$ and thus $(u', v_k) \in R$.
- Suppose that $u\downarrow$. From the term deduction rules for projection operators, see Table 4.6, it follows that $\pi_n(u)\downarrow$ for all $n \in \mathbf{N}$. Since $\pi_n(u) \leftrightarrow \pi_n(v)$, it follows that $\pi_n(v)\downarrow$ for all $n \in \mathbf{N}$. Suppose that $v\not\downarrow$. Then, by the term deduction rules in Table 4.6, $\pi_n(v)\not\downarrow$ for all $n \in \mathbf{N}$. This results in a contradiction and therefore $v\downarrow$.
- Suppose that $v\downarrow$. Using a reasoning similar to the previous case, it can be shown that $u\downarrow$, completing the proof.

□

At this point, five recursion principles have been discussed: RDP, RSP, RDP$^-$, AIP, and AIP$^-$. It is interesting to consider the relations between these principles. Obviously, by their definitions, RDP implies RDP$^-$ and AIP implies AIP$^-$. The most interesting relation is the one already hinted at earlier, namely that validity of AIP$^-$ implies validity of RSP. The latter is only true under the assumption that the equational theory under consideration has the so-called head-normal-form (HNF) property. This is usually the case. The relations between the recursion principles are visualized in Figure 5.5, where an arrow connecting two principles indicates a logical implication. To formally prove these relations, the HNF property needs to be introduced, and some intermediate results are needed.

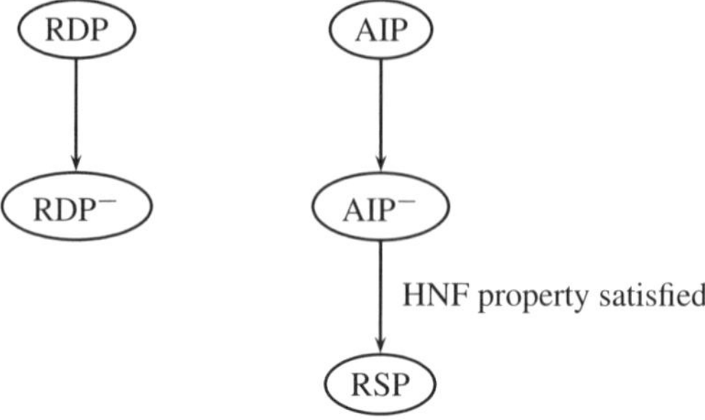

Fig. 5.5. Relation between the recursion principles.

Definition 5.5.24 (Head normal form) Consider an equational theory $T(A)$ that extends BSP(A), as defined in Definition 2.2.14. The set of *head normal forms* of theory $T(A)$ is inductively defined as follows. The constants 0 and 1 are head normal forms; for any action $a \in A$ and $T(A)$-term t, $a.t$ is a head normal form; for any head normal forms s and t, $s + t$ is a head normal form.

Theory $T(A)$ is said to satisfy the *head-normal-form (HNF) property* if and only if every *guarded* $T(A)$-term can be rewritten into a head normal form, i.e., for every guarded $T(A)$-term s, there is a head normal form t such that $T(A) \vdash s = t$.

Head normal forms can always be rewritten into a very specific form.

Proposition 5.5.25 (Head normal forms) Consider a theory $T(A)$ that extends BSP(A). For any head normal form t of $T(A)$, there is a natural number $n \in \mathbf{N}$ such that, for any $i < n$, there are $a_i \in A$ and $T(A)$-terms t_i such that

$$T(A) \vdash t = \sum_{i<n} a_i.t_i (+1),$$

where the $\sum$ notation is the generalized choice notation introduced in Notation 5.5.19 and the notation '$(+s)$' for some term s denotes an optional s-summand which may or may not be present.

Proof Straightforward via induction on the structure of head normal form t. □

Proposition 5.5.26 (HNF property) Process theory $(\text{BSP} + \text{PR})_{\text{rec}}(A)$ satisfies the HNF property.

Proof It needs to be proven that every guarded $(\text{BSP}+\text{PR})_{\text{rec}}(A)$-term s can be rewritten into a head normal form. By Definition 5.5.8 (Guardedness, part 2), it can be assumed without loss of generality that s is completely guarded. The proof goes via induction on the structure of s.

- $s \equiv 1$ or $s \equiv 0$. Term s is a head normal form by definition.
- $s \equiv a.s'$ for some $a \in A$ and $(\text{BSP} + \text{PR})_{\text{rec}}(A)$-term s'. Again, term s is a head normal form by definition.
- $s \equiv s' + s''$ for some completely guarded process terms s' and s''. By induction, there exist head normal forms t' and t'' such that
  $$(\text{BSP} + \text{PR})_{\text{rec}}(A) \vdash s' = t'$$
  and
  $$(\text{BSP} + \text{PR})_{\text{rec}}(A) \vdash s'' = t''.$$
  Hence, $t'+t''$ is a head normal form such that $(\text{BSP}+\text{PR})_{\text{rec}}(A) \vdash s = s' + s'' = t' + t''$, which proves this case.
- $s \equiv \pi_n(s')$ for some natural number $n \in \mathbf{N}$ and some completely guarded process term s'. By induction, there is a head normal form t such that
  $$(\text{BSP} + \text{PR})_{\text{rec}}(A) \vdash s' = t.$$
  By Proposition 5.5.25 (Head normal forms), there exists a natural number $m \in \mathbf{N}$ such that for any $i < m$, there are $a_i \in A$ and terms t_i such that
  $$(\text{BSP} + \text{PR})_{\text{rec}}(A) \vdash s' = \sum_{i<m} a_i.t_i(+1).$$
  If $m = 0$, then either $(\text{BSP} + \text{PR})_{\text{rec}}(A) \vdash s = \pi_n(s') = 0$ or $(\text{BSP} + \text{PR})_{\text{rec}}(A) \vdash s = \pi_n(s') = 1$. In both cases, s is therefore derivably equal to a head normal form. Assume that $m > 0$.
  $$(\text{BSP} + \text{PR})_{\text{rec}}(A) \vdash$$
  $$s = \pi_n(s') = \pi_n(\sum_{i<m} a_i.t_i(+1)) = \sum_{i<m} \pi_n(a_i.t_i)(+\pi_n(1)).$$
  If $n = 0$, then
  $$(\text{BSP} + \text{PR})_{\text{rec}}(A) \vdash s = \sum_{i<m} \pi_n(a_i.t_i)(+\pi_n(1)) = 0(+1).$$
  If $n > 0$,
  $$(\text{BSP} + \text{PR})_{\text{rec}}(A) \vdash$$
  $$s = \sum_{i<m} \pi_n(a_i.t_i)(+\pi_n(1)) = \sum_{i<m} a_i.\pi_{n-1}(t_i)(+1).$$
  The last term in the last two derivations is in both cases a head normal form, which completes the proof for this case.

- $s \equiv x$ for some (normal or recursion) variable x. Then s is not completely guarded, which means this case cannot occur.

□

The next proposition states that any projection of any solution of a recursion variable specified by a guarded recursive specification can be rewritten into an equivalent closed $(\text{BSP} + \text{PR})(A)$-term, i.e., a term without any variables. The intuition behind this result is that any guarded recursive specification can be rewritten such that the recursion variables in the right-hand sides of the equation in the specifications occur in the scope of any desirable number of nested action-prefix operators, in particular a number larger than the depth of the projection. Recall Definition 2.2.6 (Substitution). Let, for any term t over some arbitrary signature and variable x, t/x denote the substitution that maps x to t and all other variables onto themselves.

Proposition 5.5.27 (Projections of guarded recursive specifications) Let E be a guarded recursive specification and X a recursion variable in $V_R(E)$. For any natural number n, there is a closed $(\text{BSP} + \text{PR})(A)$-term p, such that for any $(\text{BSP} + \text{PR})_{\text{rec}}(A)$-term t satisfying the recursive specification of X, i.e., $(\text{BSP} + \text{PR})_{\text{rec}}(A) \vdash E[t/X]$, $(\text{BSP} + \text{PR})_{\text{rec}}(A) \vdash \pi_n(t) = p$.

Proof Assume without loss of generality that recursive specification E is completely guarded.
Let $X = t_X$ be the recursive equation defining X in E. Since E is guarded, based on Propositions 5.5.26 (HNF property) and 5.5.25 (Head normal forms), it follows that

$$(\text{BSP} + \text{PR})_{\text{rec}}(A) \vdash t = t_X[t/X] = \sum_{i<m} a_i.t_i[t/X](+1),$$

for some natural number $m \in \mathbf{N}$ and actions a_i and terms t_i for any $i < m$. It follows immediately that

$$(\text{BSP} + \text{PR})_{\text{rec}}(A) \vdash \pi_n(t) = \pi_n(\sum_{i<m} a_i.t_i[t/X](+1)),$$

for any natural number $n \in \mathbf{N}$.
Therefore, in the remainder, a slightly more general property is proven, namely that, for any natural number n, and any head normal form $\sum_{i<l} b_i.s_i(+1)$ with $l \in \mathbf{N}$ and, for any $i < l$, actions b_i and $(\text{BSP} + \text{PR})_{\text{rec}}(A)$-terms s_i, such that the s_i contain only recursion variables in $V_R(E)$, there is a closed $(\text{BSP} + \text{PR})(A)$-term q, such that

$$(\text{BSP} + \text{PR})_{\text{rec}}(A) \vdash \pi_n(\sum_{i<l} b_i.s_i[t/X](+1)) = q.$$

This generalized property can be proven via induction on n.
First, suppose $n = 0$. Then,

$$(\mathrm{BSP}+\mathrm{PR})_{\mathrm{rec}}(A)\vdash \\ \pi_0(\sum_{i<l} b_i.s_i[t/X](+1)) = \sum_{i<l} \pi_0(b_i.s_i[t/X])(+\pi_0(1)) = 0(+1),$$

which satisfies the base case.
Second, suppose $n > 0$. Then,

$$(\mathrm{BSP}+\mathrm{PR})_{\mathrm{rec}}(A)\vdash \\ \pi_n(\sum_{i<l} b_i.s_i[t/X](+1)) = \sum_{i<l} b_i.\pi_{n-1}(s_i[t/X])(+1).$$

Recall that the s_i contain only recursion variables from $V_R(E)$ and no other variables, and that E is completely guarded. It follows that all the s_i are guarded because any unguarded variable occurrences in an s_i can be replaced by the right-hand side of the defining equation of that variable. Therefore, by Proposition 5.5.26 (HNF property), each s_i can be rewritten into a head normal form $\sum_{j<k} b'_j.s'_j(+1)$ with $k \in \mathbf{N}$ and, for any $j < k$, actions b'_j and $(\mathrm{BSP}+\mathrm{PR})_{\mathrm{rec}}(A)$-terms s'_j, which contain no other variables than those from $V_R(E)$. Induction yields that for each s_i, there is a closed $(\mathrm{BSP}+\mathrm{PR})(A)$-term q_i, such that

$$(\mathrm{BSP}+\mathrm{PR})_{\mathrm{rec}}(A)\vdash \\ \pi_{n-1}(s_i[t/X]) = \pi_{n-1}(\sum_{j<k} b'_j.s'_j[t/X](+1)) = q_i.$$

Substituting this in the earlier result yields,

$$(\mathrm{BSP}+\mathrm{PR})_{\mathrm{rec}}(A)\vdash \pi_n(\sum_{i<l} b_i.s_i[t/X](+1)) = \sum_{i<l} b_i.q_i(+1),$$

which also completes this case. □

The following theorem is now straightforward to derive. It implies the derivable equality of all the finite projections of any two solutions of a guarded recursive specification.

Theorem 5.5.28 (Projection Theorem) Let E be a guarded recursive specification and X a recursion variable in $V_R(E)$. For any $(\mathrm{BSP}+\mathrm{PR})_{\mathrm{rec}}(A)$-terms s and t satisfying the recursive specification of X and any natural number n, $(\mathrm{BSP}+\mathrm{PR})_{\mathrm{rec}}(A)\vdash \pi_n(s) = \pi_n(t)$.

Proof From Proposition 5.5.27 above, it follows immediately that for any natural number n, there is a closed $(\mathrm{BSP}+\mathrm{PR})(A)$-term p such that $(\mathrm{BSP}+\mathrm{PR})_{\mathrm{rec}}(A)\vdash \pi_n(s) = p = \pi_n(t)$. □

Note that the Projection Theorem does not use any essential aspects of the theory $(\text{BSP}+\text{PR})_{\text{rec}}(A)$, other than the fact that it satisfies the HNF property. It can be generalized to arbitrary process theories extending $(\text{BSP}+\text{PR})_{\text{rec}}(A)$ that satisfy this property.

Theorem 5.5.29 (Relation between the recursion principles) Let $T(A)$ be some equational theory without recursion extending $(\text{BSP} + \text{PR})(A)$. Let $T_{\text{rec}}(A)$ be the corresponding theory with recursion.

(i) RDP implies RDP$^-$;
(ii) AIP implies AIP$^-$;
(iii) if $T_{\text{rec}}(A)$ satisfies the HNF property, then AIP$^-$ implies RSP.

Proof The first two implications follow immediately from the definitions of the principles.
The third one is more involved. Let $\mathbb{M}$ with domain $\mathbf{M}$ be some model of process theory $T_{\text{rec}}(A)$. Suppose that $\mathbb{M} \models \text{AIP}^-$. It has to be proven that $\mathbb{M} \models \text{RSP}$. Let E be an arbitrary guarded recursive specification and X a recursion variable in $V_R(E)$. Suppose that s and t are two $T_{\text{rec}}(A)$-terms satisfying the recursive specification of X. Note that, since E is guarded, this implies that both s and t are guarded. By the generalization of Theorem 5.5.28 (Projection Theorem) to $T_{\text{rec}}(A)$, which is allowed because $T_{\text{rec}}(A)$ satisfies the HNF property, $T_{\text{rec}}(A) \vdash \pi_n(s) = \pi_n(t)$, for all natural numbers $n \in \mathbf{N}$. Applying AIP$^-$ then gives $T_{\text{rec}}(A) \vdash s = t$. Suppose now that ι and κ are two solutions of E. Since s and t can among others be arbitrary variables, without loss of generality, assume that $\iota(X) = \iota_\alpha(s)$ and $\kappa(X) = \kappa_\alpha(t)$ for some variable valuation α. Then, $T_{\text{rec}}(A) \vdash s = t$ implies that $\mathbb{M} \models s = t$ and hence that $\iota_\alpha(s) =_{\mathbf{M}} \kappa_\alpha(t)$. Since E, X, s and t were all chosen arbitrarily, a guarded recursive specification has therefore at most one solution, which means that $\mathbb{M} \models \text{RSP}$. □

Note that Theorem 5.5.11 (Validity of RSP), given earlier in this section, can be derived in a straightforward way from this last result and Theorem 5.5.23 (Validity of AIP$^-$), as explained in the proof of Theorem 5.5.11.

At the end of this section, it is interesting to consider whether the recursion principles affect the equalities that can be derived between closed terms of the basic theory $(\text{BSP} + \text{PR})(A)$. It turns out that this is not the case.

Theorem 5.5.30 (Conservative ground-extension) Theory $(\text{BSP}+\text{PR})_{\text{rec}}(A)$ extended with any combination of the five recursion principles considered in this section is a conservative ground-extension of theory $(\text{BSP} + \text{PR})(A)$.

Proof Along the lines of the proof of Theorem 5.4.8 (Conservative ground-extension BSP$_{\text{rec}}(A)$), it can be proven that $(\text{BSP} + \text{PR})_{\text{rec}}(A)$ is a conservative ground-extension of $(\text{BSP} + \text{PR})(A)$. Since RDP does not affect derivability, the desired conservativity result follows immediately for any extension of $(\text{BSP} + \text{PR})_{\text{rec}}(A)$ with RDP. It follows from Theorem 4.5.4 (Bounded depth) that any two closed $(\text{BSP} + \text{PR})(A)$-terms that satisfy the condition of AIP are already derivably equal in the theory $(\text{BSP} + \text{PR})(A)$. Hence, also any extension of $(\text{BSP}+\text{PR})_{\text{rec}}(A)$ with principle AIP is a conservative ground-extension of $(\text{BSP}+\text{PR})(A)$. Theorem 5.5.29 (Relation between the recursion principles) completes the proof. □

Note that the extension of $(\text{BSP}+\text{PR})_{\text{rec}}(A)$ with any of the principles AIP, AIP$^-$, or RSP is not a conservative ground-extension of $(\text{BSP} + \text{PR})_{\text{rec}}(A)$. It is in fact the purpose of these recursion principles to derive equalities between terms with recursion variables that cannot be derived in the basic theory $(\text{BSP}+\text{PR})_{\text{rec}}(A)$. The extension of $(\text{BSP}+\text{PR})_{\text{rec}}(A)$ with RDP or RDP$^-$ is identical to $(\text{BSP} + \text{PR})_{\text{rec}}(A)$, and so these extensions are trivially conservative.

Exercises

5.5.1 Determine whether in the following terms the occurrences of the recursion variable X are guarded, unguarded, or both: $a.X$, $Y + b.X$, $b.(X + Y)$, $a.Y + X$.

5.5.2 Determine whether the following recursive specifications are guarded or unguarded: $\{X = Y, Y = a.X\}$, $\{X = a.Y + Z, Y = b.Z + X, Z = c.X + Y\}$.

5.5.3 Consider BSP$_{\text{rec}}(A)$ with its model $\mathbb{P}(\text{BSP}_{\text{rec}}(A))_{/\leftrightarrow}$, and assume that $A = \emptyset$. Give an unguarded recursive specification with only one solution.

5.5.4 Consider the recursive specification $\{X = a.X + b.c.X\}$. Calculate $\pi_0(X)$, $\pi_1(X)$, and $\pi_2(X)$.

5.5.5 Consider the recursive specification $E = \{X = a.X\}$. Prove that $(\text{BSP} + \text{PR} + E)(A) \vdash \pi_n(X) = a^n 0$ for any natural number $n \in \mathbf{N}$.

5.5.6 Consider the recursive specification $\{X = a.X + b.X\}$. Determine $\pi_n(X)$ for every natural number $n \in \mathbf{N}$.

5.5.7 Consider the recursive specifications $E_1 = \{X = a.X + b.X\}$ and $E_2 = \{Y = a.Y + b.Z, Z = a.Z + b.Y\}$. Prove that $(\text{BSP} + E_1 + E_2 + \text{RSP})(A) \vdash X = Y$.

5.5.8 Prove that for any closed $(\text{BSP}+\text{PR})_{\text{rec}}(A)$-terms p and q and natural number $n \in \mathbf{N}$, $\pi_{n+1}(p) \leftrightarrow \pi_{n+1}(q)$ implies that $\pi_n(p) \leftrightarrow \pi_n(q)$.

5.5.9 Consider the term deduction system underlying the standard term model of $(BSP + PR)_{rec}(A)$. Given a guarded $(BSP + PR)_{rec}(A)$-term t, prove that in one transition only a finite number of terms can be reached from t.
(Hint: use Proposition 5.5.26 (HNF property).)

5.6 Describing a stack

This section illustrates the use of recursion via an example of a specification of a data stack using the process theory $BSP_{rec}(A)$. The stack example is used at several points throughout the book to illustrate some of the concepts.

Consider an arbitrary, finite set of data elements $D = \{d_1, d_2, \cdots, d_n\}$, for some natural number $n \in \mathbf{N}$. Using recursion, a data stack with an unlimited capacity can be described in a straightforward way. Such a stack consists of a sequence of data elements from the set D. Elements from D can be added to or removed from the stack at only one end of the sequence. Usually, this end of the stack is called the top of the stack. The first element of the sequence modeling the stack is considered the top. The operation of adding an element d to the stack is modeled as the atomic action $push(d)$. Removing an element d from the stack is denoted $pop(d)$. In the recursive specification of the stack process, the following notations are used:

- The empty sequence of elements from D is denoted as ϵ.
- The set of all finite sequences of elements from D is denoted D^*.
- Concatenation of data elements and sequences into new sequences is denoted by juxtaposition. For example, for an element d from D and a sequence σ in D^*, the concatenation of d and σ is denoted $d\sigma$.
- The stack containing only one datum d, formally denoted by $d\epsilon$, is written as d.

A stack can be described in $BSP_{rec}(A)$, with an infinite set of recursive equations.

$$
\begin{aligned}
Stack1 &= S_\epsilon, \\
S_\epsilon &= 1 + \sum_{d \in D} push(d).S_d, \quad \text{and, for all } d \in D, \sigma \in D^*, \\
S_{d\sigma} &= pop(d).S_\sigma + \sum_{e \in D} push(e).S_{ed\sigma}.
\end{aligned}
$$

Note that the stack process can terminate if it is empty. This is particularly useful and meaningful if the stack is considered in the context of an environment. If the environment using the stack terminates after emptying the stack, then also the stack can terminate with it. In a theory with parallel composition, developed in Chapter 7, this can be made more precise; see Exercise 7.6.7.

In theory $\mathrm{BSP}_{\mathrm{rec}}(A)$, it is not possible to specify a stack with a finite number of recursive equations (see Exercise 5.8.1). In Chapter 6, a theory is introduced that does allow a finite recursive specification of a stack.

Observe that the above recursive specification is not completely guarded. It is guarded though, as it is derivably equal to the specification

$$\begin{aligned} Stack1 &= 1 + \sum_{d \in D} push(d).S_d, \\ S_\epsilon &= 1 + \sum_{d \in D} push(d).S_d, \quad \text{and, for all } d \in D, \sigma \in D^*, \\ S_{d\sigma} &= pop(d).S_\sigma + \sum_{e \in D} push(e).S_{ed\sigma}, \end{aligned}$$

which is completely guarded. Note that each right-hand side in this recursive specification consists of a sum of terms where each term is either an empty-process constant or a prefix operator applied to a recursion variable. Such a form is convenient, because guardedness immediately follows. This specific form of recursive specification is called a *linear* recursive specification, and it occurs often in equational verifications.

Figure 5.6 shows part of the stack's transition system, for the case that $D = \{0, 1\}$. For simplicity, $push(d)$ and $pop(d)$ are written $\overline{d}$ and $\underline{d}$, respectively.

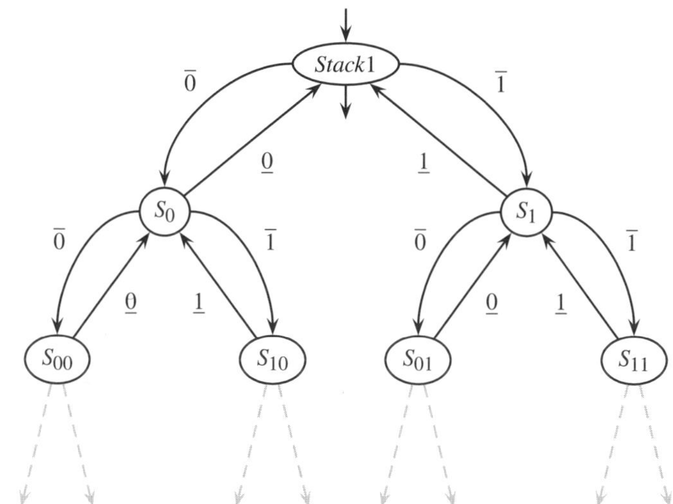

Fig. 5.6. Visualization of (part of) the stack with $D = \{0, 1\}$.

Exercises

5.6.1 Calculate, for the stack process described in this section, $\pi_0(Stack1)$, $\pi_1(Stack1)$, and $\pi_2(Stack1)$.

5.6.2 Give a recursive specification describing a stack with capacity C, i.e., a stack that contains at most C elements. You can assume that C is a given constant. Draw the transition system for the stack with capacity $C = 2$ and data elements from $D = \{0, 1\}$.

5.6.3 Consider the recursive specification $\{C_0 = 1 + plus.C_1, C_{n+1} = minus.C_n + plus.C_{n+2} \mid n \in \mathbf{N}\}$ that specifies a counter (that can terminate at the count of zero). Using RSP, prove that the counter (variable C_0) and the stack ($Stack1$) with $D = \{0\}$ are equal when assuming that $plus \equiv push(0)$ and $minus \equiv pop(0)$.

5.6.4 Prove that the counter of the previous exercise and the stack with $D = \{0\}$ are equal when assuming that $plus \equiv push(0)$ and $minus \equiv pop(0)$ but now using AIP^-.

5.7 Expressiveness and definability

At this point, it is interesting to consider the expressiveness of process theories in a bit more detail. In Chapter 4, expressiveness of a process theory was introduced as the class of processes that can be described by the closed terms over the signature of that process theory. It was shown for example that the addition of the 1 constant to the minimal theory of Section 4.2 increases expressiveness, but that the addition of projection operators in general does not increase expressiveness.

The extension of the basic process theory of the previous chapter with recursion in the current chapter was motivated from the expressiveness point of view. With the addition of recursion, however, and in particular given the special role of recursion variables, it is necessary to carefully consider the notion of expressiveness. Given that, in a process theory such as $\mathrm{BSP}_{\mathrm{rec}}(A)$, the recursion variables are simply constants in the signature, one could consider to define expressiveness of such a theory as the class of all processes in any model of the theory that are the interpretation of any closed term over the signature of that process theory. However, Example 5.3.7 (Multiple solutions) shows that this definition does not make much sense, because any process in any model can be the interpretation of constant $\mu X.\{X = X\}$. As an alternative, it is possible to consider the class of processes that can be specified via a closed term in a theory with recursion for a specific model with a specific interpretation. The standard term models and the operational framework of Chapter 3 are of particular interest in this context.

The transition-system framework of Chapter 3 and the standard term models of process theories essentially introduce equivalence classes of transition systems under bisimilarity as processes. Therefore, it is interesting to consider the universe of all equivalence classes of transition systems as the semantic context for studying the expressiveness of process theories. Given the standard interpretation for term models of process theories, the question then is which of these equivalence classes has a transition system corresponding to a closed term over the signature of some given theory as a representative.

Only one assumption is made, namely that, given a transition system, its set of states can be determined, and that given a state, its set of transitions and the existence of a termination option can be determined. This is an assumption that is not always fulfilled. Consider for example the following definition of transition system p (using the inaction and empty-process constants 0 and 1):

$$p = \begin{cases} 0, & \text{if the decimal expansion of the number } \pi \text{ contains a} \\ & \quad \text{sequence of nine consecutive 9s;} \\ 1, & \text{otherwise.} \end{cases}$$

The definition of p implies that it has exactly one state, but it cannot be determined whether or not this state has a termination option. (It is not possible to define an algorithm that can conclusively decide for any arbitrary sequence of numbers whether or not the decimal expansion of π contains that sequence; the part of the decimal expansion of π known to date does not contain a sequence of nine consecutive 9s.) Transition system p is an example of a *non-computable* transition system. In the remainder, only *computable* transition systems are considered. The formal definition of a computable transition system is omitted. The reader interested in a formal definition of computability is referred to any textbook on automata theory, e.g., (Linz, 2001). Informally, the definition of a computable transition system is that the behavior of the transition system can be determined by an algorithm. This corresponds to the above assumption that the set of states of a transition system can be determined, and that for each state the set of transitions and the existence of a termination option can be determined. Observe that the notion of computability is not limited to transition systems, but carries over to other concepts such as for example recursive specifications and processes, where a recursive specification is computable if and only if its set of equations can be determined by an algorithm, and a process is computable if and only if it is an equivalence class under bisimilarity of computable transition systems.

One final important notion used in the remainder is that of a *countable* set. A set is countable if and only if it has the same number of elements as some subset of the natural numbers, i.e., if it can be indexed using the natural numbers. The definition given here also considers finite sets to be countable. A countable set is also said to have countably many elements.

Definition 5.7.1 ((Countable) computable process) A computable process is an equivalence class under bisimilarity of computable transition systems. A (computable) process is countable if and only if it has a countable transition system as a representative (where a transition system is countable if and only if it has countably many states and countably many transitions).

Note that there are computable processes that are not countable and vice versa. The above example of a non-computable transition system leads to a process that is not computable, but since it has only one state and no transitions, it is countable. Also observe that the definition allows that a countable process may have a representative with an uncountable number of states or transitions. However, any such a transition system is bisimilar to a countable one, which implies that the corresponding process essentially has countably many states and transitions.

Definition 5.7.2 (Expressiveness) A computable process can be specified in a process theory T if and only if it has a transition system corresponding to a closed T-term as defined by the standard term model, as a representative.

The following two results show that in a context with all (computable) recursive specifications, already the basic process theory is sufficient to specify all *countable* computable processes.

Theorem 5.7.3 (Countable computable transition systems) Let the set of recursive specifications contain all computable recursive specifications. A transition system p is an element of the term algebra $\mathbb{P}(\text{BSP}_{\text{rec}}(A))$ if and only if p is computable and countable.

Proof First, consider the implication from left to right. A general element p of $\mathbb{P}(\text{BSP}_{\text{rec}}(A))$ corresponds to an arbitrary closed $\text{BSP}_{\text{rec}}(A)$-term. Such a term is by definition finite and may contain a finite number of recursion constants. Since also the right-hand side of the equation defining any recursion constant $\mu X.E$ is a finite term, by following the deduction rules of the term deduction system of Table 5.2, every transition and every state of the transition system defined by p can be determined and counted. As a consequence, transition system p is computable and countable.
Second, consider the implication from right to left. Let p be a countable computable transition system. Since p is countable, it has countably many states and countably many transitions. Enumerate the states of p as s_i with index $i = 0, 1, \ldots$. Enumerate the transitions of each state s_i with index k, $k = 0, 1, \ldots$. Assume that transition k leaving state s_i has label a_{ik}, and that

it goes to state $s_{j(i,k)}$. Define a recursive specification E over variables X_{ik} as follows, where variable X_{i0} corresponds to state s_i. For each variable X_{ik}, E contains equation

$$X_{ik} = a_{ik}.X_{j(i,k)0} + X_{i(k+1)}.$$

In case either the set of states or the set of transitions of a state is finite, just put $X_{ik} = 0$ for all remaining variables. If a state s_i has a termination option, which can be determined because p is computable, then a 1 summand has to be added to the equation of X_{i0}.
It is easy to see that the rules of the deduction system of Table 5.2 yield the transition system p for the recursive specification E, which means p is an element of the term algebra $\mathbb{P}(\mathrm{BSP}_{\mathrm{rec}}(A))$. □

Corollary 5.7.4 (Expressiveness of $\mathrm{BSP}_{\mathrm{rec}}(A)$**)** Theory $\mathrm{BSP}_{\mathrm{rec}}(A)$ with all computable recursive specifications as the set of recursive specifications allows to specify precisely all countable computable processes, i.e., the term model $\mathbb{P}(\mathrm{BSP}_{\mathrm{rec}}(A))_{/\leftrightarrow}$ contains precisely all countable computable processes.

Note that this corollary implies that the algebra $\mathbb{P}(\mathrm{BSP}_{\mathrm{rec}}(A))_{/\leftrightarrow}$ can be considered as an algebra of all countable computable processes, when the set of recursive specifications is the set of all computable recursive specifications. Given this observation, in the remainder, it is always assumed that the set of recursive specifications of interest is the set of all computable recursive specifications, or, when stated explicitly, a subset of those.

An important observation is that the notion of expressiveness introduced by Definition 5.7.2 is model-dependent. It assumes the operational framework of Chapter 3. Furthermore, it assumes the standard interpretation of process terms in term models. This implies, among others, that all recursion variables are interpreted as one specific process, which is not really in line with the interpretation of recursion variables as constrained variables. Recall that in Section 5.5, guardedness was introduced as a model-independent way to characterize uniqueness of solutions for recursive specifications, in line with the interpretation of recursion variables as constrained variables. A guarded recursive specification is supposed to *define* a process. Also observe that any closed term in a process theory without recursion can be turned into an equivalent (guarded) recursive specification in the theory extended with recursion by taking that closed term as the right-hand side of an equation in a recursive specification with only that one equation (see, for example, recursive specification E_1 of Example 5.2.2 (Recursive specifications)). These considerations suggest another notion of expressiveness, called *definability*, which is not depending on any particular model, and is consistent with the interpretation of recursion variables as constrained variables. This latter notion of expressiveness originates from ACP-style process algebra, whereas the notion of expressiveness defined in Definition 5.7.2 finds its origins in CCS-style process theory.

Definition 5.7.5 (Definability) Let T be a process theory without recursion. A process in some model of theory T is *definable* (over T) if and only if it is the unique solution of (some designated recursion variable of) a *guarded* recursive specification over the signature of theory T. A process is *finitely definable* if and only if it is the unique solution of a *finite guarded* recursive specification over the signature of T, i.e., a guarded recursive specification with a finite number of equations.

In the remainder, for simplicity, the recursion variable of the considered recursive specification for which a process is a solution is sometimes left implicit.

Finite definability is introduced because it is of particular interest whether or not a process can be defined via a finite guarded recursive specification. In the previous section, it was for example claimed that the stack process is not finitely definable over BSP(A). The next section returns to the notion of finite definability in some more detail.

Definition 5.7.5 (Definability) raises the question whether, when returning to the algebra of countable computable processes $\mathbb{P}(\mathrm{BSP}_{\mathrm{rec}}(A))_{/\leftrightarrows}$, all these processes are definable over BSP(A). It turns out that this is not the case. Observe that the proof of Theorem 5.7.3 (Countable computable transition systems) uses unguarded recursion. It can be shown that this use of unguarded recursion is essential.

Recall Definition 3.1.16 (Finitely branching transition system).

Definition 5.7.6 (Finitely branching process) A finitely branching process is an equivalence class of computable transition systems under bisimilarity containing at least one finitely branching transition system as a representative.

Note that this definition allows that infinitely branching transition systems are elements of the equivalence class defining a finitely branching process. Since any such infinitely branching transition system is bisimilar to a finitely branching one, the corresponding process essentially has finitely many outgoing transitions in each state. Also observe that a finitely branching process is necessarily countable. This follows from the fact that a transition system is defined as a reachable subspace of a transition-system space (see Definition 3.1.5). With finitely many outgoing transitions per state, only a countable number of states can be reached.

Theorem 5.7.7 (Processes definable over BSP(A)**)** A computable process is definable over BSP(A) if and only if it is finitely branching.

Proof First, consider the implication from left to right. Assume a process p is the unique solution of a guarded recursive specification E over the signature of BSP(A). By Exercise 5.5.9, the state corresponding to any $\mu X.E$ for some recursion variable X of E has only finitely many outgoing transitions. As a consequence, the transition system corresponding to any $\mu X.E$ is finitely branching, which means that process p is finitely branching.

Second, consider the implication from right to left. If a process is finitely branching, then it follows that the process has a finitely branching transition system s as a representative, which has countably many states with finitely many outgoing transitions per state. It is straightforward to define a guarded recursive specification corresponding to transition system s. Enumerate the states of s as s_i with index $i = 0, 1, \ldots$. Enumerate the transitions of each state s_i with index k, $k = 0, 1, \ldots, n_i - 1$, where n_i is the number of outgoing transitions of state s_i. Assume that transition k leaving state s_i has label a_{ik}, and that it goes to state $s_{j(i,k)}$. Define a linear recursive specification E over variables X_i as follows, where variable X_i corresponds to state s_i. For each variable X_i, E contains equation

$$X_i = \sum_{k=0}^{n_i-1} a_{ik}.X_{j(i,k)},$$

where the $\sum$ notation is the generalized choice notation of Notation 5.5.19. If s_i has a termination option, then a 1 summand is added to the equation.

It is straightforward to see that the deduction system of Table 5.2 yields the transition system s for the recursive specification E. Since E is guarded and defined over the signature of theory BSP(A), and since the term model $\mathbb{P}(\mathrm{BSP}_{\mathrm{rec}}(A))_{/\leftrightarrow}$ satisfies RSP, the process represented by s is a unique solution for E and therefore definable over BSP(A). □

As a final note, observe, in the context of the algebra of countable computable processes $\mathbb{P}(\mathrm{BSP}_{\mathrm{rec}}(A))_{/\leftrightarrow}$, the subtle difference between the phrases that 'a process can be expressed' or 'specified' and 'that a process can be defined'. The former means that there is a closed $\mathrm{BSP}_{\mathrm{rec}}(A)$-term with that process as its standard interpretation. The latter means that there is a guarded recursive specification over BSP(A) with that process as a unique solution, where this solution of course is the standard interpretation of this recursive specification.

Exercises

5.7.1 Consider the following recursive specifications. Recall the n-fold action-prefix notation of Notation 4.6.6.

(a) $E = \{X_n = X_{n+1} + a^n Y \mid n \in \mathbf{N}\} \cup \{Y = 1\}$;
(b) $F = \{X_n = X_{n+1} + a^n Y \mid n \in \mathbf{N}\} \cup \{Y = a.Y\}$.

These recursive specifications specify processes $\mu X_0.E$ and $\mu X_0.F$ in the standard term model of $\text{BSP}_{\text{rec}}(A)$ (which means that both these processes are expressible in theory $\text{BSP}_{\text{rec}}(A)$). Which of these processes are also finitely definable over theory BSP(A)? Either give a guarded finite recursive specification to show that a process is definable, or give an (informal) argument why such a specification does not exist.

5.8 Regular processes

The previous section has introduced the notion of finite definability. A process is finitely definable over some given theory if and only if it is the unique solution of a finite guarded recursive specification over the signature of that theory. In Chapter 3, the notion of a regular transition system has been introduced, see Definition 3.1.15, which captures precisely all finite transition systems. In light of Theorem 5.7.7 (Processes definable over BSP(A)), note that the regular transition systems form a subset of the finitely branching transition systems, and that finite definability is a restriction of definability. These observations suggest that it is interesting to have a closer look at the relation between regular transition systems and finite definability. It turns out that the regular transition systems can be captured precisely by all finite guarded recursive specifications.

Definition 5.8.1 (Regular process) A regular process is an equivalence class of computable transition systems under bisimilarity containing at least one regular transition system as a representative.

The definition allows non-regular transition systems as representatives of regular processes, which is in line with the earlier definitions of countable and finitely branching processes. Since any such non-regular transition system is bisimilar to a regular one, the corresponding process has finitely many states and transitions, which is the essence of regularity.

Theorem 5.8.2 (Regular processes) A computable process is regular if and only if it is finitely definable over BSP(A).

Proof Consider the implication from left to right. A regular process has a regular transition system s as a representative. Enumerate the states of s as s_i with index $i = 0, 1, \ldots, n-1$, where n is the number of states of s. Enumerate the transitions of each state s_i with index k, $k = 0, 1, \ldots, n_i - 1$, where n_i is the number of outgoing transitions of state s_i. Assume that transition k leaving state s_i has label a_{ik} and that it goes to state $s_{j(i,k)}$. Let recursive specification E over variables X_i, where variable X_i corresponds to state s_i, contain for each variable X_i, equation

$$X_i = \sum_{k=0}^{n_i-1} a_{ik}.X_{j(i,k)},$$

with an additional 1 summand if s_i has a termination option. The deduction system of Table 5.2 yields transition system s for recursive specification E. Since E is guarded, finite, and defined over the signature of BSP(A), and since $\mathbb{P}(\text{BSP}_{\text{rec}}(A))_{/\leftrightarrow}$ satisfies RSP, the process represented by s is a unique solution for E and therefore finitely definable over BSP(A).
Consider the implication from right to left. Assume a process p is the unique solution of a finite guarded recursive specification E over the signature of BSP(A). It follows from Theorem 5.7.7 (Processes definable over BSP(A)) that p is finitely branching. The deduction system of Table 5.2 implies that every state of the transition system defined by E is a subterm of one of the right-hand sides of the equations in E. As E has only finitely many equations, there are finitely many such subterms, and hence the transition system has finitely many states. As a consequence, the transition system is regular, which means that process p is regular. □

Consider again the stack process of Section 5.6. Since the given recursive specification is guarded, the stack is definable over BSP(A). However, it is not finitely definable, as already claimed in Section 5.6 and shown in Exercise 5.8.1. This implies that a stack is not a regular process.

Given the importance of regular processes, let process theory $\text{BSP}_{\text{gfrec}}(A)$, term algebra $\mathbb{P}(\text{BSP}_{\text{gfrec}}(A))$, and process algebra $\mathbb{P}(\text{BSP}_{\text{gfrec}}(A))_{/\leftrightarrow}$ be the theory, term algebra, and term model obtained by extending the basic theory BSP(A) with constants only for guarded finite recursive specifications. Theory $\text{BSP}_{\text{gfrec}}(A)$ and its model $\mathbb{P}(\text{BSP}_{\text{gfrec}}(A))_{/\leftrightarrow}$ can be considered as an equational theory and an algebra of regular processes. Note that the proof of Theorem 5.8.2 implies that all the processes in the algebra of regular processes $\mathbb{P}(\text{BSP}_{\text{gfrec}}(A))_{/\leftrightarrow}$ contain in fact only regular transition systems as representatives, leading to the following corollary.

Corollary 5.8.3 (Regular transition systems) A transition system p is an element of the term algebra $\mathbb{P}(\mathrm{BSP}_{\mathrm{gfrec}}(A))$ if and only if p is regular.

This corollary confirms the observation made in Example 4.3.2 (Transition systems for closed MPT(A)-terms) that all transition systems corresponding to closed MPT(A)-terms are regular, because all closed MPT(A)-terms are closed $\mathrm{BSP}_{\mathrm{gfrec}}(A)$-terms. Note that the algebra of countable computable processes $\mathbb{P}(\mathrm{BSP}_{\mathrm{rec}}(A))_{/\leftrightarrows}$, obviously, contains all regular processes, but that in $\mathbb{P}(\mathrm{BSP}_{\mathrm{rec}}(A))_{/\leftrightarrows}$, different from $\mathbb{P}(\mathrm{BSP}_{\mathrm{gfrec}}(A))_{/\leftrightarrows}$, regular processes may contain non-regular transition systems as representatives.

Since regularity and (finite) definability are so closely related, it is interesting to have a look at the validity of the recursion principles of Section 5.5 in the algebra of regular processes $\mathbb{P}(\mathrm{BSP}_{\mathrm{gfrec}}(A))_{/\leftrightarrows}$. Since principles AIP and AIP$^-$ are only meaningful in a context with projection operators, consider theory $(\mathrm{BSP} + \mathrm{PR})_{\mathrm{gfrec}}(A)$, basic process theory with projection and guarded finite recursion, and its term model $\mathbb{P}((\mathrm{BSP} + \mathrm{PR})_{\mathrm{gfrec}}(A))_{/\leftrightarrows}$. The proof of Theorem 5.8.2 (Regular processes) carries over to this setting, showing that $\mathbb{P}((\mathrm{BSP} + \mathrm{PR})_{\mathrm{gfrec}}(A))_{/\leftrightarrows}$ is isomorphic to the algebra of regular processes $\mathbb{P}(\mathrm{BSP}_{\mathrm{gfrec}}(A))_{/\leftrightarrows}$. Obviously, $\mathbb{P}((\mathrm{BSP} + \mathrm{PR})_{\mathrm{gfrec}}(A))_{/\leftrightarrows}$ is a model of BSP(A). It does not satisfy RDP and RDP$^-$, however, because the guarded recursive specification given for the stack in Section 5.6 does not have a solution in $\mathbb{P}((\mathrm{BSP}+\mathrm{PR})_{\mathrm{gfrec}}(A))_{/\leftrightarrows}$ (see Exercise 5.8.1). In fact, the observation that the algebra of regular processes does not satisfy principles RDP$^-$ and RDP corresponds to the observation that regular processes form a strict subclass of the definable and countable computable processes, respectively. The algebra of regular processes does satisfy AIP, AIP$^-$, and RSP. Since any regular process in $\mathbb{P}((\mathrm{BSP} + \mathrm{PR})_{\mathrm{gfrec}}(A))_{/\leftrightarrows}$ can be specified via a (finite) *guarded* recursive specification, Theorem 5.5.23, that shows the validity of recursion principle AIP$^-$ in the term model $\mathbb{P}((\mathrm{BSP} + \mathrm{PR})_{\mathrm{rec}}(A))_{/\leftrightarrows}$, shows that the more general principle AIP, formulated for all $(\mathrm{BSP} + \mathrm{PR})_{\mathrm{gfrec}}(A)$-terms, is valid in the algebra $\mathbb{P}((\mathrm{BSP}+\mathrm{PR})_{\mathrm{gfrec}}(A))_{/\leftrightarrows}$. Theorem 5.5.29 (Relation between the recursion principles) then implies that algebra $\mathbb{P}((\mathrm{BSP} + \mathrm{PR})_{\mathrm{gfrec}}(A))_{/\leftrightarrows}$ also satisfies AIP$^-$ and RSP.

Theorem 5.8.4 (Regular processes and the recursion principles) The algebra of regular processes $\mathbb{P}((\mathrm{BSP} + \mathrm{PR})_{\mathrm{gfrec}}(A))_{/\leftrightarrows}$ does not satisfy recursion principles RDP and RDP$^-$ but it does satisfy AIP, AIP$^-$, and RSP.

For readers familiar with automata theory (see e.g. (Linz, 2001)), the results of this section can be rephrased as follows. Finite non-deterministic automata under bisimulation equivalence correspond to right-linear grammars. This confirms that it is meaningful to speak of regular processes. Note that left-linear grammars cannot be formulated in the present setting. When such a notion can be formulated (in Chapter 6, Section 6.6), it turns out that it can be used to specify also non-regular processes. Also, in Section 6.5, a notion of regular expressions can be formulated. But then it turns out that not all regular processes are equivalent to a regular expression under bisimulation equivalence. The conclusion is that some results of automata theory remain valid in the current algebraic setting, when language equivalence is replaced by bisimilarity, but most do not.

It is also possible to consider equivalence classes of closed $\mathrm{BSP}_{\mathrm{gfrec}}(A)$-terms under language equivalence as a model of equational theory $\mathrm{BSP}_{\mathrm{gfrec}}(A)$. As expected, this yields the usual algebra of finite automata with language equivalence. In Section 6.5, the relation between regular processes as defined in this section and finite automata is considered in a bit more detail.

Exercises

5.8.1 Prove that the stack process of Section 5.6 is not finitely definable over $\mathrm{BSP}(A)$, which shows that the stack process is not regular.

5.9 Recursion and $\mathrm{BSP}^*(A)$

In the introduction to this chapter, it was already indicated that prefix iteration only allows for the description of a limited class of unbounded processes. To solve this expressiveness problem, recursion has been introduced. In a setting with recursive specifications, prefix-iteration operators are redundant in the sense that every process described by a closed term from the process theory $\mathrm{BSP}^*(A)$ can easily be described by recursion in the process theory $\mathrm{BSP}_{\mathrm{rec}}(A)$. This is achieved by replacing all occurrences of a^*p, for some action $a \in A$ and closed $\mathrm{BSP}^*(A)$-term p, by a recursion variable X with recursive equation $X = a.X + p$, resulting in a recursive specification.

Example 5.9.1 (Prefix iteration and recursion) The closed $\mathrm{BSP}^*(A)$-term $a.(b^*(c.0) + 1)$ defines the same process as the closed $\mathrm{BSP}_{\mathrm{rec}}(A)$-term $a.(X + 1)$ where X is defined by the recursive specification $\{X = b.X + c.0\}$.

The closed $\mathrm{BSP}^*(A)$-term $a^*(b.1 + c^*0)$ can be represented by the recursion variable X where $X = a.X + b.1 + c^*0$. In turn, c^*0 can be replaced by Y with $Y = c.Y + 0$. As a result, $a^*(b.1 + c^*0)$ defines the same process as X with $\{X = a.X + b.1 + Y, Y = c.Y\}$.

Although the expressiveness of the process theory $\mathrm{BSP}^*(A)$ is less than the expressiveness of the process theory $\mathrm{BSP}_{\mathrm{rec}}(A)$, the latter is not a (conservative) extension of the former. The reason for this is the fact that the signature of $\mathrm{BSP}^*(A)$ is not contained in the signature of $\mathrm{BSP}_{\mathrm{rec}}(A)$. It is interesting to observe that in fact $\mathrm{BSP}^*(A)$ is not more expressive than the theory of regular processes $\mathrm{BSP}_{\mathrm{gfrec}}(A)$ of the previous section. Using Axiom PI1 in Table 4.7, every occurrence of $a^* p$ in some closed $\mathrm{BSP}^*(A)$-term can first be rewritten into $a.(a^* p) + p$, after which the action-prefix occurrence can be replaced by a recursion variable as sketched in the above example. Since any closed $\mathrm{BSP}^*(A)$-term can only contain a finite number of prefix-iteration operators, this conversion results in a finite guarded recursive specification. Thus, theory $\mathrm{BSP}^*(A)$ allows only specifications of regular processes, which confirms the observation made in Example 4.6.1 (Transition systems of $\mathrm{BSP}^*(A)$-terms). It is in fact easy to see that $\mathrm{BSP}^*(A)$ is strictly less expressive than $\mathrm{BSP}_{\mathrm{gfrec}}(A)$; the process in Figure 5.1 is regular but cannot be described in $\mathrm{BSP}^*(A)$.

If for whatever reason it is needed to have both prefix iteration and recursion as means to describing unbounded processes, the addition of recursion to the process theory $\mathrm{BSP}^*(A)$ goes along the same lines as for the process theory $\mathrm{BSP}(A)$, resulting in theory $\mathrm{BSP}^*_{\mathrm{rec}}(A)$. The term model $\mathbb{P}(\mathrm{BSP}^*(A))_{/\leftrightarrow}$ is not a model of theory $\mathrm{BSP}^*_{\mathrm{rec}}(A)$ if the set of recursive specifications is sufficiently rich specifying processes that cannot be described by prefix iteration. The extended term model $\mathbb{P}(\mathrm{BSP}^*_{\mathrm{rec}}(A))_{/\leftrightarrow}$ does result in a model of $\mathrm{BSP}^*_{\mathrm{rec}}(A)$. Furthermore, theory $\mathrm{BSP}^*_{\mathrm{rec}}(A)$ is a conservative ground-extension of theory $\mathrm{BSP}^*(A)$. The notion of guardedness does not change: the occurrence of recursion variable X in a term $a^* X$ cannot be considered guarded because of the possibility that X starts executing immediately. In the extended term model $\mathbb{P}(\mathrm{BSP}^*_{\mathrm{rec}}(A))_{/\leftrightarrow}$, the principles RSP, RDP, and RDP^- are valid. Principle AIP^- is valid if also projection is included.

Example 5.9.2 (Prefix iteration and recursion) Consider again the closed $\mathrm{BSP}^*(A)$-term $a.(b^*(c.0) + 1)$ and the recursive specification $E_1 = \{X = b.X + c.0\}$. It can be shown that

$$(\mathrm{BSP}^* + E_1 + \mathrm{RSP})(A) \vdash a.(b^*(c.0) + 1) = a.(X + 1),$$

which confirms the claim made in Example 5.9.1 that the two terms in the equality define the same process. To show this equality, it suffices to show that $(\mathrm{BSP}^* + E_1 + \mathrm{RSP})(A) \vdash X = b^*(c.0)$. It follows from Axiom PI1 in Table 4.7 that $\mathrm{BSP}^*(A) \vdash b^*(c.0) = b.(b^*(c.0)) + c.0$. This implies that $b^*(c.0)$ is a solution of X. Assuming RSP implies that (the process specified by) $b^*(c.0)$ is the only solution, showing that $(\mathrm{BSP}^* + E_1 + \mathrm{RSP})(A) \vdash X = b^*(c.0)$.

Consider now closed BSP$^*(A)$-term $a^*(b.1 + c^*0)$ and recursive specification $E_2 = \{X = a.X + b.1 + Y, Y = c.Y\}$. It is not difficult to show that

$$(\mathrm{BSP}^* + E_2 + \mathrm{RSP})(A) \vdash a^*(b.1 + c^*0) = X,$$

which confirms also the second claim in Example 5.9.1.

Exercises

5.9.1 Show that $\mathbb{P}(\mathrm{BSP}^*_{\mathrm{rec}}(A))_{/\leftrightarrow} \models \mu X.\{X = a.X\} = a^*0$.

5.9.2 Show that $(\mathrm{BSP}^* + E_2 + \mathrm{RSP})(A) \vdash a^*(b.1 + c^*0) = X$, with E_2 as specified in Example 5.9.2.

5.9.3 Find two different solutions of the recursive equation $X = a^*X$ in the term model $\mathbb{P}(\mathrm{BSP}^*_{\mathrm{rec}}(A))_{/\leftrightarrow}$.

5.9.4 Consider the proper-iteration operators of Exercise 4.6.6. Give an argument that recursion variable X in term $a^{\oplus}X$ can be considered guarded. Show that recursive equation $X = a^{\oplus}X$ has a unique solution in the term model of theory BSP(A) with proper iteration and recursion.

5.10 The projective limit model

An important motivation for equational reasoning is that it is model-independent. That is, any derivation in an equational theory yields an equality that is valid in any model of that theory. Recursion principles have been introduced for similar reasons. They allow us to reason about certain meaningful classes of models in the context of recursion, without limiting ourselves to specific models.

So far, term models have been the most important models that were considered, but also the initial algebra (see Definition 2.3.19) has been mentioned. Considering process theory $(\mathrm{BSP} + \mathrm{PR})(A)$ as the basic theory, an interesting observation is that none of the term models $\mathbb{P}((\mathrm{BSP}+\mathrm{PR})(A))_{/\leftrightarrow}$, $\mathbb{P}((\mathrm{BSP}+\mathrm{PR})_{\mathrm{gfrec}}(A))_{/\leftrightarrow}$ and $\mathbb{P}((\mathrm{BSP}+\mathrm{PR})_{\mathrm{rec}}(A))_{/\leftrightarrow}$, and none of the initial algebras of the various considered equational theories $\mathbb{I}((\mathrm{BSP} + \mathrm{PR})(A))$, $\mathbb{I}((\mathrm{BSP} + \mathrm{PR})_{\mathrm{gfrec}}(A))$, and $\mathbb{I}((\mathrm{BSP} + \mathrm{PR})_{\mathrm{rec}}(A))$ validates both RDP and AIP, the two strongest recursion principles (see Theorem 5.5.29).

Table 5.3 gives an overview of the validity of the recursion principles in the various models. The results for the three term models have been proven in Sections 5.5 and 5.8. Note that the inclusion of the projection operators in the theories does not affect the results derived for principles RDP and RDP$^-$. The fact that the initial algebras $\mathbb{I}((\mathrm{BSP}+\mathrm{PR})(A))$ and $\mathbb{I}((\mathrm{BSP}+\mathrm{PR})_{\mathrm{gfrec}}(A))$

do not satisfy RDP$^-$ and RDP follows from the same examples used to show the invalidity of these principles in the corresponding term models. The fact that $\mathbb{I}((\mathrm{BSP}+\mathrm{PR})_{\mathrm{rec}}(A))$ satisfies RDP and RDP$^-$ follows from the simple observation that theory $(\mathrm{BSP}+\mathrm{PR})_{\mathrm{rec}}(A)$ contains a constant for each recursion variable in each recursive specification. Initial algebra $\mathbb{I}((\mathrm{BSP}+\mathrm{PR})(A))$ satisfies AIP (and therefore AIP$^-$ and RSP) because the model only contains bounded-depth processes, whereas $\mathbb{I}((\mathrm{BSP}+\mathrm{PR})_{\mathrm{gfrec}}(A))$ and $\mathbb{I}((\mathrm{BSP}+\mathrm{PR})_{\mathrm{rec}}(A))$ do not satisfy RSP, AIP$^-$, or AIP simply because without recursion principles the equational theories $(\mathrm{BSP}+\mathrm{PR})_{\mathrm{gfrec}}(A)$ and $(\mathrm{BSP}+\mathrm{PR})_{\mathrm{rec}}(A)$ do not have any generally applicable means to derive equalities between recursion variables specified by different recursive specifications. As already explained on Page 132, this implies that it is easy to construct guarded recursive specifications with multiple solutions. Note that AIP and AIP$^-$ are valid in the models $\mathbb{I}((\mathrm{BSP}+\mathrm{PR})(A))$ and $\mathbb{P}((\mathrm{BSP}+\mathrm{PR})(A))_{/\leftrightarrow}$ for arbitrary $(\mathrm{BSP}+\mathrm{PR})(A)$-terms, i.e., terms of the basic theory without recursion. The results in Table 5.3 for the term models and initial algebras of $(\mathrm{BSP}+\mathrm{PR})_{\mathrm{gfrec}}(A)$ and $(\mathrm{BSP}+\mathrm{PR})_{\mathrm{rec}}(A)$ refer to AIP and AIP$^-$ formulated for arbitrary closed $(\mathrm{BSP}+\mathrm{PR})_{\mathrm{gfrec}}(A)$- and $(\mathrm{BSP}+\mathrm{PR})_{\mathrm{rec}}(A)$-terms, respectively, i.e., for terms including recursion variables. An interesting observation is the fact that the initial algebra $\mathbb{I}((\mathrm{BSP}+\mathrm{PR})_{\mathrm{gfrec}}(A))$ does not satisfy any of the five recursion principles.

	RDP$^-$	RDP	RSP	AIP$^-$	AIP
$\mathbb{I}((\mathrm{BSP}+\mathrm{PR})(A))$	no	no	yes	yes	yes
$\mathbb{P}((\mathrm{BSP}+\mathrm{PR})(A))_{/\leftrightarrow}$	no	no	yes	yes	yes
$\mathbb{I}((\mathrm{BSP}+\mathrm{PR})_{\mathrm{gfrec}}(A))$	no	no	no	no	no
$\mathbb{P}((\mathrm{BSP}+\mathrm{PR})_{\mathrm{gfrec}}(A))_{/\leftrightarrow}$	no	no	yes	yes	yes
$\mathbb{I}((\mathrm{BSP}+\mathrm{PR})_{\mathrm{rec}}(A))$	yes	yes	no	no	no
$\mathbb{P}((\mathrm{BSP}+\mathrm{PR})_{\mathrm{rec}}(A))_{/\leftrightarrow}$	yes	yes	yes	yes	no
$\mathbb{I}(((\mathrm{BSP}+\mathrm{PR})_{\mathrm{rec}}+\mathrm{AIP})(A))$	yes	yes	yes	yes	yes
$\mathbb{I}^{\infty}((\mathrm{BSP}+\mathrm{PR})(A))$	yes	yes	yes	yes	yes

Table 5.3. Validity of recursion principles in models for $(\mathrm{BSP}+\mathrm{PR})(A)$.

So, is it possible to create a model that satisfies all five recursion principles introduced in Section 5.5? It is in fact relatively straightforward to do so. The initial algebra $\mathbb{I}(((\text{BSP} + \text{PR})_{\text{rec}} + \text{AIP})(A))$ satisfies RDP and AIP by definition, and hence by Theorem 5.5.29 (Relation between the recursion principles) also the other principles. However, it could be that this model is a one-point model, which contains only one process and in which everything is equal. It has already been mentioned before that these models are not very interesting.

This section introduces another model that satisfies all five recursion principles, namely the so-called projective limit model $\mathbb{I}^\infty((\text{BSP} + \text{PR})(A))$. This model is not trivial in the sense that it contains many processes, and it provides a meaningful and intuitive interpretation of process specifications. Since in the initial algebra $\mathbb{I}(((\text{BSP} + \text{PR})_{\text{rec}} + \text{AIP})(A))$ the valid equalities are precisely those that are derivably equal, any equality valid in this initial algebra must be valid in any other model of $(\text{BSP} + \text{PR})_{\text{rec}}(A)$ that satisfies AIP as well. In particular, if $\mathbb{I}(((\text{BSP} + \text{PR})_{\text{rec}} + \text{AIP})(A))$ is a one-point model, any other model of $(\text{BSP} + \text{PR})_{\text{rec}}(A)$ that satisfies AIP must be a one-point model. The existence of the projective limit model therefore implies that also the initial algebra $\mathbb{I}(((\text{BSP}+\text{PR})_{\text{rec}}+\text{AIP})(A))$ is not a trivial model. Note that for both $\mathbb{I}(((\text{BSP} + \text{PR})_{\text{rec}} + \text{AIP})(A))$ and $\mathbb{I}^\infty((\text{BSP} + \text{PR})(A))$, AIP and AIP$^-$ are valid for arbitrary $(\text{BSP} + \text{PR})_{\text{rec}}(A)$-terms, i.e., for terms including recursion variables of arbitrary recursive specifications.

Besides the fact that the projective limit model is interesting from the point of view of recursion, it is also an example of a model for process theories that is constructed in an entirely different way than the term models and the initial algebras seen so far. The basic idea behind the projective limit model is that behavior is something that evolves over time. As there is no explicit notion of time in the process theories and algebras considered so far, the abstract notion of counting actions that have been executed is used to represent evolution. For this purpose, the projection operators are very useful. In the projective limit model, a process is an infinite sequence of finite projections. Two processes are considered equal if and only if their sequences of projections are the same.

Definition 5.10.1 (Projective limit model) Recall Definition 2.3.19 (Initial algebra). Consider the initial algebra $\mathbb{I}((\text{BSP} + \text{PR})(A))$ of the process theory $(\text{BSP} + \text{PR})(A)$. Let $\mathbf{I}$ denote the universe of the equivalence classes of closed $(\text{BSP} + \text{PR})(A)$-terms under derivability, and let $+_\vdash$, $(\pi_{n\vdash})_{n\in\mathbf{N}}$, $(a._\vdash)_{a\in A}$, $0_\vdash$, and $1_\vdash$ denote the operators and constants of the algebra. An infinite sequence $(p_0, p_1, p_2, \ldots)$ of elements of $\mathbf{I}$ is called a *projective sequence* if and only if it satisfies the following: $\pi_{n\vdash}(p_{n+1}) =_\mathbf{I} p_n$, for all natural numbers $n \in \mathbf{N}$.

Define $\mathbb{I}^\infty((\text{BSP} + \text{PR})(A))$ as the algebra with as its universe $\mathbf{I}^\infty$ the set of projective sequences of elements of $\mathbf{I}$. By definition, $(p_0, p_1, p_2, \ldots) =_{\mathbf{I}^\infty} (q_0, q_1, q_2, \ldots)$ if and only if $p_n =_\mathbf{I} q_n$ for all $n \in \mathbf{N}$.

The operators $+^\infty$, π_n^∞ (for each $n \in \mathbf{N}$), and $a.^\infty$ (for each $a \in A$) are defined as follows:

$$(p_0, p_1, \ldots) +^\infty (q_0, q_1, \ldots) = (p_0 +_\vdash q_0, p_1 +_\vdash q_1, \ldots),$$
$$\pi_n^\infty(p_0, p_1, \ldots) = (\pi_{n\vdash}(p_0), \pi_{n\vdash}(p_1), \ldots), \text{ and}$$
$$a.^\infty(p_0, p_1, \ldots) = (0_\vdash, a._\vdash p_0, a._\vdash p_1, \ldots).$$

The proof that these defining equations are sound, i.e., that the right-hand sides are projective sequences, is left as Exercise 5.10.1.

Finally, the constants 0^∞ and 1^∞ are defined as the projective sequences $(0_\vdash, 0_\vdash, 0_\vdash, \ldots)$ and $(1_\vdash, 1_\vdash, 1_\vdash, \ldots)$, respectively.

Algebra $\mathbb{I}^\infty((\text{BSP}+\text{PR})(A)) = (\mathbf{I}^\infty, +^\infty, (\pi_n^\infty)_{n\in\mathbf{N}}, (a.^\infty)_{a\in A}, 0^\infty, 1^\infty)$ is called the *projective limit model* of theory $(\text{BSP} + \text{PR})(A)$.

The above definition defines the projective limit model for the basic theory $(\text{BSP}+\text{PR})(A)$, but it can be defined in a similar way for any other theory with projection operators. It turns out that the projective limit model of (BSP + PR)(A) is in fact a model of $(\text{BSP} + \text{PR})_{\text{rec}}(A)$ that satisfies all five recursion principles.

As a first step, it is shown that $\mathbb{I}^\infty((\text{BSP} + \text{PR})(A))$ is a model of (BSP + PR)(A). The expected interpretation of the signature of $(\text{BSP}+\text{PR})(A)$ into the functions and constants of the algebra $\mathbb{I}^\infty((\text{BSP}+\text{PR})(A))$ is used, namely the interpretation that maps every operator or constant symbol f in the signature of $(\text{BSP}+\text{PR})(A)$ to the function or constant f^∞ of $\mathbb{I}^\infty((\text{BSP}+\text{PR})(A))$. Let ι denote this interpretation.

The following proposition shows that the projective sequence of a closed $(\text{BSP} + \text{PR})(A)$-term can be calculated by deriving all its projections. Each such a projection is the representative of one of the equivalence classes in the projective sequence.

Proposition 5.10.2 (Projective sequences) Let p be a closed $(\text{BSP}+\text{PR})(A)$-term. Projective sequence $\iota(p)$ is equal to $([\pi_0(p)]_\vdash, [\pi_1(p)]_\vdash, [\pi_2(p)]_\vdash, \ldots)$.

Proof The proof is straightforward via induction on the structure of closed $(\text{BSP} + \text{PR})(A)$-term p.

- $p \equiv 1$. It follows from Axiom PR1 in Table 4.5 that $(\text{BSP}+\text{PR})(A) \vdash \pi_n(1) = 1$ for all $n \in \mathbf{N}$. Hence, it is straightforward to show the desired result: $\iota(1) = 1^\infty = (1_\vdash, 1_\vdash, 1_\vdash, \ldots) =_{\mathbf{I}^\infty} ([\pi_0(1)]_\vdash, [\pi_1(1)]_\vdash, [\pi_2(1)]_\vdash, \ldots)$.
- $p \equiv 0$. It follows from Axiom PR2 that $(\text{BSP} + \text{PR})(A) \vdash \pi_n(0) = 0$ for all $n \in \mathbf{N}$, which makes the proof straightforward also in this case.

- $p \equiv a.q$ for some $a \in A$ and closed $(\mathrm{BSP} + \mathrm{PR})(A)$-term q. It follows that $(\mathrm{BSP} + \mathrm{PR})(A) \vdash \pi_0(p) = 0$ and $\pi_{n+1}(p) = a.\pi_n(q)$, for all $n \in \mathbf{N}$. It also follows that $\iota(p) = a.^{\infty}\iota(q)$. By induction, $\iota(q) = ([\pi_0(q)]_{\vdash}, [\pi_1(q)]_{\vdash}, [\pi_2(q)]_{\vdash}, \ldots)$. Hence, $a.^{\infty}\iota(q) =_{\mathbf{I}^\infty} ([0]_{\vdash}, [a.\pi_0(q)]_{\vdash}, [a.\pi_1(q)]_{\vdash}, \ldots)$, which proves this case.
- $p \equiv q + r$ for some closed $(\mathrm{BSP} + \mathrm{PR})(A)$-terms q and r. $(\mathrm{BSP} + \mathrm{PR})(A) \vdash \pi_n(p) = \pi_n(q) + \pi_n(r)$, for all $n \in \mathbf{N}$. By induction, $\iota(q) = ([\pi_0(q)]_{\vdash}, [\pi_1(q)]_{\vdash}, [\pi_2(q)]_{\vdash}, \ldots)$ and $\iota(r) = ([\pi_0(r)]_{\vdash}, [\pi_1(r)]_{\vdash}, [\pi_2(r)]_{\vdash}, \ldots)$. It follows that $\iota(p) = \iota(q) +^{\infty} \iota(r) =_{\mathbf{I}^\infty} ([\pi_0(q) + \pi_0(r)]_{\vdash}, [\pi_1(q) + \pi_1(r)]_{\vdash}, [\pi_2(q) + \pi_2(r)]_{\vdash}, \ldots) =_{\mathbf{I}^\infty} ([\pi_0(q+r)]_{\vdash}, [\pi_1(q+r)]_{\vdash}, [\pi_2(q+r)]_{\vdash}, \ldots)$.
- $p \equiv \pi_n(q)$ for natural number $n \in \mathbf{N}$ and closed $(\mathrm{BSP} + \mathrm{PR})(A)$-term q. It follows from Exercise 4.5.6 that $(\mathrm{BSP} + \mathrm{PR})(A) \vdash \pi_k(p) = \pi_k(q)$, for all natural numbers $k < n$, and $(\mathrm{BSP} + \mathrm{PR})(A) \vdash \pi_l(p) = \pi_n(q)$, for all natural numbers $l \geq n$. By induction, $\iota(q) = ([\pi_0(q)]_{\vdash}, [\pi_1(q)]_{\vdash}, [\pi_2(q)]_{\vdash}, \ldots)$. Thus, again using the result of Exercise 4.5.6, it follows that $\iota(p) =_{\mathbf{I}^\infty} ([\pi_n(\pi_0(q))]_{\vdash}, [\pi_n(\pi_1(q))]_{\vdash}, \ldots, [\pi_n(\pi_n(q))]_{\vdash}, [\pi_n(\pi_{n+1}(q))]_{\vdash}, \ldots) =_{\mathbf{I}^\infty} ([\pi_0(q)]_{\vdash}, [\pi_1(q)]_{\vdash}, \ldots, [\pi_n(q)]_{\vdash}, [\pi_n(q)]_{\vdash}, \ldots)$, which completes also this last case.

□

Example 5.10.3 (Projective sequences) The projective sequence associated to the $(\mathrm{BSP} + \mathrm{PR})(A)$-term $p \equiv a.(b.0 + c.a.1)$ can be obtained in two ways, namely directly via the definition of the projective limit model and the accompanying interpretation ι or via Proposition 5.10.2.

(i) Interpretation of the operators and constants:

$$
\begin{aligned}
& \iota(a.(b.0 + c.a.1)) \\
= \;& a.^{\infty}(b.^{\infty}0^{\infty} +^{\infty} c.^{\infty}a.^{\infty}1^{\infty}) \\
=_{\mathbf{I}^\infty} \;& a.^{\infty}(b.^{\infty}(0_{\vdash}, 0_{\vdash}, \ldots) +^{\infty} c.^{\infty}a.^{\infty}(1_{\vdash}, 1_{\vdash}, \ldots)) \\
=_{\mathbf{I}^\infty} \;& a.^{\infty}((0_{\vdash}, b._{\vdash}0_{\vdash}, b._{\vdash}0_{\vdash}, \ldots) +^{\infty} \\
& \qquad c.^{\infty}(0_{\vdash}, a._{\vdash}1_{\vdash}, a._{\vdash}1_{\vdash}, \ldots)) \\
=_{\mathbf{I}^\infty} \;& a.^{\infty}((0_{\vdash}, b._{\vdash}0_{\vdash}, b._{\vdash}0_{\vdash}, \ldots) +^{\infty} \\
& \qquad (0_{\vdash}, c._{\vdash}0_{\vdash}, c._{\vdash}a._{\vdash}1_{\vdash}, c._{\vdash}a._{\vdash}1_{\vdash}, \ldots)) \\
=_{\mathbf{I}^\infty} \;& a.^{\infty}(0_{\vdash} +_{\vdash} 0_{\vdash}, b._{\vdash}0_{\vdash} +_{\vdash} c._{\vdash}0_{\vdash}, b._{\vdash}0_{\vdash} +_{\vdash} c._{\vdash}a._{\vdash}1_{\vdash}, \\
& \qquad b._{\vdash}0_{\vdash} +_{\vdash} c._{\vdash}a._{\vdash}1_{\vdash}, \ldots) \\
=_{\mathbf{I}^\infty} \;& a.^{\infty}([0]_{\vdash}, [b.0 + c.0]_{\vdash}, [b.0 + c.a.1]_{\vdash}, [b.0 + c.a.1]_{\vdash}, \ldots) \\
=_{\mathbf{I}^\infty} \;& ([0]_{\vdash}, a._{\vdash}[0]_{\vdash}, a._{\vdash}[b.0 + c.0]_{\vdash}, a._{\vdash}[b.0 + c.a.1]_{\vdash}, \\
& \qquad a._{\vdash}[b.0 + c.a.1]_{\vdash}, \ldots) \\
=_{\mathbf{I}^\infty} \;& ([0]_{\vdash}, [a.0]_{\vdash}, [a.(b.0 + c.0)]_{\vdash}, [a.(b.0 + c.a.1)]_{\vdash}, \\
& \qquad [a.(b.0 + c.a.1)]_{\vdash}, \ldots).
\end{aligned}
$$

(ii) Via projections: it is straightforward to see that

$$\begin{aligned}
&(\mathrm{BSP}+\mathrm{PR})(A) \vdash \\
&\quad \pi_0(p) = 0, \\
&\quad \pi_1(p) = a.0, \\
&\quad \pi_2(p) = a.\pi_1(b.0 + c.a.1) = a.(\pi_1(b.0) + \pi_1(c.a.1)) \\
&\quad = a.(b.0 + c.0), \\
&\quad \pi_n(p) = a.(b.0 + c.a.1) = p \text{ (for } n \geq 3).
\end{aligned}$$

Hence, the projective sequence $\iota(p)$ equals

$$([0]_{\vdash}, [a.0]_{\vdash}, [a.(b.0 + c.0)]_{\vdash}, [a.(b.0 + c.a.1)]_{\vdash}, [a.(b.0 + c.a.1)]_{\vdash}, \ldots),$$

which is the same result as derived in the previous case.

The example shows that the projective sequence corresponding to a bounded-depth closed term (i.e., any closed (BSP + PR)(A)-term, see Theorem 4.5.4 (Bounded depth)) 'converges' in the sense that the projections at some point in the sequence do not change anymore.

Theorem 5.10.4 (Soundness of (BSP + PR)(A) **for** $\mathbb{I}^\infty((\mathrm{BSP}+\mathrm{PR})(A))$**)** Theory $(\mathrm{BSP}+\mathrm{PR})(A)$ is a sound axiomatization of the projective limit model $\mathbb{I}^\infty((\mathrm{BSP}+\mathrm{PR})(A))$, i.e., $\mathbb{I}^\infty((\mathrm{BSP}+\mathrm{PR})(A)) \models (\mathrm{BSP}+\mathrm{PR})(A)$.

Proof It must be shown that $\mathbb{I}^\infty((\mathrm{BSP}+\mathrm{PR})(A))$ validates all axioms of $(\mathrm{BSP}+\mathrm{PR})(A)$.
Consider Axiom A1, $x + y = y + x$. Let p_n, q_n, for all $n \in \mathbf{N}$, be closed $(\mathrm{BSP}+\mathrm{PR})(A)$-terms such that $s_1 = ([p_0]_{\vdash}, [p_1]_{\vdash}, [p_2]_{\vdash}, \ldots)$ and $s_2 = ([q_0]_{\vdash}, [q_1]_{\vdash}, [q_2]_{\vdash}, \ldots)$ are projective sequences. It needs to be shown that $s_1 +^\infty s_2 =_{\mathbb{I}^\infty} s_2 +^\infty s_1$. From the definitions of a projective sequence and an initial algebra, it follows that

$$\begin{aligned}
& s_1 +^\infty s_2 \\
= \;& ([p_0]_{\vdash}, [p_1]_{\vdash}, [p_2]_{\vdash}, \ldots) +^\infty ([q_0]_{\vdash}, [q_1]_{\vdash}, [q_2]_{\vdash}, \ldots) \\
=_{\mathbb{I}^\infty} \;& ([p_0]_{\vdash} +_{\vdash} [q_0]_{\vdash}, [p_1]_{\vdash} +_{\vdash} [q_1]_{\vdash}, [p_2]_{\vdash} +_{\vdash} [q_2]_{\vdash}, \ldots) \\
=_{\mathbb{I}^\infty} \;& ([p_0 + q_0]_{\vdash}, [p_1 + q_1]_{\vdash}, [p_2 + q_2]_{\vdash}, \ldots).
\end{aligned}$$

Similarly, $s_2 +^\infty s_1 =_{\mathbb{I}^\infty} ([q_0 + p_0]_{\vdash}, [q_1 + p_1]_{\vdash}, [q_2 + p_2]_{\vdash}, \ldots)$. Obviously, $(\mathrm{BSP}+\mathrm{PR})(A) \vdash p + q = q + p$ for any closed $(\mathrm{BSP}+\mathrm{PR})(A)$-terms p and q. This implies that for all $n \in \mathbf{N}$, $(\mathrm{BSP}+\mathrm{PR})(A) \vdash p_n + q_n = q_n + p_n$, and thus that $[p_n + q_n]_{\vdash} =_{\mathbb{I}} [q_n + p_n]_{\vdash}$. Hence, $s_1 +^\infty s_2 =_{\mathbb{I}^\infty} s_1 +^\infty s_2$, completing the proof for Axiom A1.
The other axioms are left as an exercise. □

The next step is to show that the projective limit model of (BSP + PR)(A) satisfies recursion principle RDP. For this purpose, it needs to be shown that every recursive specification has a solution in this model. Proposition 5.5.27

(Projections of guarded recursive specifications) implies that the projections of recursion variables of guarded recursive specifications correspond to closed $(\text{BSP} + \text{PR})(A)$ terms. Thus, a recursion variable of such a specification can be interpreted as the projective sequence of these projections.

Example 5.10.5 (Interpretation of recursion constants) Consider the recursion constant X defined by the guarded recursive specification $E = \{X = a.X\}$. Then, $(\text{BSP} + \text{PR} + E)(A) \vdash \pi_0(X) = 0$, $\pi_1(X) = a.0$, and $\pi_2(X) = a.\pi_1(X) = a.(a.0)$. In general, $(\text{BSP} + \text{PR} + E)(A) \vdash \pi_n(X) = a^n 0$, where a^n is the n-fold action prefix of Notation 4.6.6.

Let $s = ([0]_\vdash, [a.0]_\vdash, [a.a.0]_\vdash, \ldots, [a^n 0]_\vdash, [a^{n+1} 0]_\vdash, \ldots)$ be the projective sequence associated with X. To show that s is indeed a solution of X, it needs to be shown that $s =_{\mathbb{I}^\infty} a.^\infty s$. This follows immediately from the definition of $a.^\infty$, see Definition 5.10.1 (Projective limit model).

The construction of solutions for *unguarded* recursive specifications is more involved. The details are beyond the scope of this book. The interested reader is referred to (Bergstra & Klop, 1982). Given solutions for arbitrary recursive specifications, the following theorem follows.

Theorem 5.10.6 (Validity of RDP**)** Assuming theory $(\text{BSP} + \text{PR})(A)$ as the basic process theory, recursion principle RDP is valid in $\mathbb{I}^\infty((\text{BSP} + \text{PR})(A))$, i.e., $\mathbb{I}^\infty((\text{BSP} + \text{PR})(A)) \models \text{RDP}$.

Proof See (Bergstra & Klop, 1982), where the result is proven for a slightly different theory. □

Theorem 5.5.4 ($\text{BSP}_{\text{rec}}(A)$ and RDP), which generalizes to process theory $(\text{BSP} + \text{PR})_{\text{rec}}(A)$, yields immediately the following corollary.

Corollary 5.10.7 (Soundness $(\text{BSP} + \text{PR})_{\text{rec}}(A)$ **for** $\mathbb{I}^\infty((\text{BSP} + \text{PR})(A))$**)** Theory $(\text{BSP} + \text{PR})_{\text{rec}}(A)$ is a sound axiomatization of the projective limit model $\mathbb{I}^\infty((\text{BSP} + \text{PR})(A))$, i.e., $\mathbb{I}^\infty((\text{BSP} + \text{PR})(A)) \models (\text{BSP} + \text{PR})_{\text{rec}}(A)$.

The final step is to prove the validity of AIP.

Theorem 5.10.8 (Validity of AIP**)** Recursion principle AIP, as formulated in Definition 5.5.17 for all $(\text{BSP}+\text{PR})_{\text{rec}}(A)$-terms, is valid in the projective limit model of $(\text{BSP} + \text{PR})(A)$, i.e., $\mathbb{I}^\infty((\text{BSP} + \text{PR})(A)) \models \text{AIP}$.

Proof Let s_1 and s_2 be projective sequences such that, for all $n \in \mathbf{N}$, $\pi_n^\infty(s_1) =_{\mathbb{I}^\infty} \pi_n^\infty(s_2)$. It needs to be shown that $s_1 =_{\mathbb{I}^\infty} s_2$.

Let p_n, q_n, for all $n \in \mathbf{N}$, be equivalence classes of closed (BSP + PR)(A)-terms such that $s_1 = (p_0, p_1, p_2, \ldots)$ and $s_2 = (q_0, q_1, q_2, \ldots)$. It follows from the definition of the π_n^∞ operators that $\pi_n^\infty(s_1) =_{\mathbf{I}^\infty} (\pi_{n\vdash}(p_0), \pi_{n\vdash}(p_1), \pi_{n\vdash}(p_2), \ldots)$ and $\pi_n^\infty(s_2) =_{\mathbf{I}^\infty} (\pi_{n\vdash}(q_0), \pi_{n\vdash}(q_1), \pi_{n\vdash}(q_2), \ldots)$. It follows from the definition of projective sequences that $\pi_{n\vdash}(p_{n+1}) =_{\mathbf{I}} p_n$ and that $\pi_{n\vdash}(q_{n+1}) =_{\mathbf{I}} q_n$. The assumption that $\pi_n^\infty(s_1) =_{\mathbf{I}^\infty} \pi_n^\infty(s_2)$ implies that $p_n =_{\mathbf{I}} \pi_{n\vdash}(p_{n+1}) =_{\mathbf{I}} \pi_{n\vdash}(q_{n+1}) =_{\mathbf{I}} q_n$. Hence, for all $n \in \mathbf{N}$, $p_n =_{\mathbf{I}} q_n$, which means that $s_1 =_{\mathbf{I}^\infty} s_2$. □

Since (BSP + PR)$_{\mathrm{rec}}(A)$ satisfies the HNF property (Proposition 5.5.26), Theorem 5.5.29 (Relation between the recursion principles) yields the following corollary.

Corollary 5.10.9 (Recursion principles and the projective limit model) Projective limit model $\mathbb{I}^\infty((\mathrm{BSP}+\mathrm{PR})(A))$ satisfies recursion principles RDP, RDP$^-$, AIP, AIP$^-$, and RSP.

At the end of this section, it is interesting to once more consider the nature of the projective limit model. Many facts about processes in this book (for instance the notion of a regular process in Section 5.8) are stated in terms of transition systems, and so do not directly apply to other models such as the projective limit model considered here. However, any model can be turned into a transition-system space. The following definition illustrates this transformation for the projective limit model. The transition-system space can be turned into a model for theory (BSP + PR)$_{\mathrm{rec}}(A)$, that is isomorphic to the projective limit model, and therefore satisfies all five recursion principles. Note however that the notion of equivalence on this transition-system space induced by the identity in the projective limit model is not bisimilarity, but simply identity, because there is a one-to-one correspondence between projective sequences and transition systems.

Definition 5.10.10 (Transition-system space of the projective limit model) The projective limit model $\mathbb{I}^\infty((\mathrm{BSP}+\mathrm{PR})(A))$ with set of projective sequences $\mathbf{I}^\infty$ induces the transition-system space $(\mathbf{I}^\infty, A, \;\rightarrow\;, \downarrow)$ with, for any projective sequences $s, t \in \mathbf{I}^\infty$, $s \xrightarrow{a} t$ if and only if $s =_{\mathbf{I}^\infty} a.^\infty t +^\infty s$ and $s\downarrow$ if and only if $s =_{\mathbf{I}^\infty} 1^\infty +^\infty s$.

This definition can be used to define a notion of regular processes in the context of the projective limit model. Recall Definitions 3.1.15 (Regular transition system) and 5.8.1 (Regular process). The first definition is still valid in the current setting. The second definition defines a regular process in the context of the standard operational framework with bisimulation equivalence as an equivalence class of transition systems under bisimilarity that contains at least one regular transition system as a representative. Adapting this definition to the current context with identity as the equivalence yields the following straightforward definition of a regular projective sequence.

Definition 5.10.11 (Regular projective sequence) A projective sequence is regular if and only if its corresponding transition system is regular.

Exercise 5.10.6 investigates the possibility to give a direct definition of regularity of projective sequences, not using a transformation to a transition-system space.

Exercises

5.10.1 Prove that for an arbitrary projective sequence s from the projective limit model $\mathbb{I}^\infty((\mathrm{BSP} + \mathrm{PR})(A))$, the sequences $a.^\infty s$ (for any $a \in A$) and $\pi_n^\infty(s)$ (for any natural number $n \in \mathbf{N}$) are again projective sequences. Also, prove that for any two projective sequences s_1 and s_2, the sequence $s_1 +^\infty s_2$ is a projective sequence.

5.10.2 Complete the proof of Theorem 5.10.4 (Soundness).

5.10.3 Consider the recursive specification $\{X_n = a^n 0 + X_{n+1} \mid n \in \mathbf{N}\}$, used in the proof of Theorem 5.5.20 ((In-)validity of AIP). Show that the solution for variable X_0 in the projective limit model $\mathbb{I}^\infty((\mathrm{BSP} + \mathrm{PR})(A))$ is the process $([0]_\vdash, [a.0]_\vdash, [a.0 + a^2 0]_\vdash, \ldots)$.

5.10.4 The algebra $\mathbb{I}^n(\mathrm{BSP}(A))$, for some $n \in \mathbf{N}$, has as its domain $\mathbf{I}_n = \{\pi_{n\vdash}(p) | p \in \mathbf{I}\}$, where $\mathbf{I}$ is the domain of the initial algebra $\mathbb{I}((\mathrm{BSP} + \mathrm{PR})(A))$, operators $+_n$, $(a._n)_{a \in A}$ defined by $p +_n q = p +_\vdash q$ and $a._n p = \pi_{n\vdash}(a._\vdash p)$, and constants $0_n = 0_\vdash$ and $1_n = 1_\vdash$.

(a) Show that $\mathbb{I}^n(\mathrm{BSP}(A)) \models \mathrm{BSP}(A)$.
(b) Define projection operators on $\mathbf{I}_n$, with algebra $\mathbb{I}^n((\mathrm{BSP}+\mathrm{PR})(A))$ as a result, such that $\mathbb{I}^n((\mathrm{BSP} + \mathrm{PR})(A)) \models (\mathrm{BSP} + \mathrm{PR})(A)$.
(c) What process in $\mathbb{I}^n((\mathrm{BSP} + \mathrm{PR})(A))$ is a solution of $X = a.X$?
(d) Show that recursion principles AIP, RDP$^-$, and RSP are valid in $\mathbb{I}^n((\mathrm{BSP} + \mathrm{PR})(A))$.
(e) In what sense is $\mathbb{I}^\infty((\mathrm{BSP} + \mathrm{PR})(A))$ the limit of the algebras $\mathbb{I}^n((\mathrm{BSP} + \mathrm{PR})(A))$, for all $n \in \mathbf{N}$?

5.10.5 The so-called *Limit Rule* is the statement that all equations (containing variables) that are derivable from some given process theory when closed terms are substituted for the variables, are derivable from that theory in general. Formulate this Limit Rule in a formal way and show, by using AIP and Proposition 5.5.26 (HNF property), that it holds for theory $((\mathrm{BSP}+\mathrm{PR})_{\mathrm{rec}}+\mathrm{AIP})(A)$. (Note that this implies that theory $((\mathrm{BSP}+\mathrm{PR})_{\mathrm{rec}}+\mathrm{AIP})(A)$ is ω-complete, as defined in Section 2.3; observe that the projective limit model introduced in this section is a model of that theory, but that, due to the assumption of AIP, the standard term model is not a model.)

5.10.6 Definition 5.10.11 (Regular projective sequence) shows how to define regularity of projective sequences via a transformation to a transition-system space. Define regularity directly in terms of projective sequences and argue that your definition gives the same notion of regularity as the one defined in Definition 5.10.11.
(Hint: the number of outgoing transitions of every state, the branching degree, stabilizes.)

5.11 Bibliographical remarks

Recursion is an essential ingredient of every concurrency theory. There are algebraic treatments in CCS (Milner, 1980), CSP (Hoare, 1985), ACP (Baeten & Weijland, 1990), topological process theory (De Bakker & Zucker, 1982a) and in other places. The present treatment owes most to (Bergstra & Klop, 1984b).

The notation $\mu X.E$ is inspired by the notation for least fixed points, and similar notations used in CCS and CSP. The CCS notation $\mu X.t$, where t is a term (potentially) containing recursion variable X, is generalized in the current notation to $\mu X.\{X = t\}$. Notation $\mu X.E$ corresponds to the notation $\langle X \mid E\rangle$ in ACP-style process algebra, that originates from (Bergstra & Klop, 1988).

A closer look at recursion in process algebra is found in (Kranakis, 1987; Usenko, 2002). The deduction rules in Table 5.2 are from (Van Glabbeek, 1987), and based on (Milner, 1980). The results in Section 5.4 are based on (Van Glabbeek, 1987; Baeten & Verhoef, 1995). For Section 5.8, see (Bergstra & Klop, 1984b) and (Mauw & Mulder, 1994). The dual role of recursion variables, as both constants and constrained variables, is also discussed in (Baeten & Bravetti, 2006); see also (Baeten & Bravetti, 2005).

The notion of guardedness is found in (Milner, 1980; Milne, 1982), but is derived from older ideas. In the present setting, guardedness comes down to having a right-linear grammar, see e.g. (Linz, 2001).

The principle RSP was formulated in (Bergstra & Klop, 1986c). Principles RDP, RDP^-, AIP, and AIP^-, as well as the proof of Theorem 5.5.23, are from (Baeten *et al.*, 1987b). A slightly less restrictive form of AIP^-, using the notion of bounded non-determinism, can be found in (Van Glabbeek, 1987). Proposition 5.5.26 (HNF property) is from (Baeten & Van Glabbeek, 1987). The Projection Theorem is from (Baeten *et al.*, 1987a).

For the material on the projective limit model, see (Bergstra & Klop, 1982; De Bakker & Zucker, 1982a). For the Limit Rule, see (Baeten & Bergstra, 1988).

6

Sequential processes

6.1 Sequential composition

In the process theory BSP(A) discussed in Chapter 4, the only way of combining two processes is by means of alternative composition. For the specification of more complex systems, additional composition mechanisms are useful. This chapter treats the extension with a *sequential-composition* operator. Given two process terms x and y, the term $x \cdot y$ denotes the sequential composition of x and y. The intuition of this operation is that upon the *successful* termination of process x, process y is started. If process x ends in a deadlock, also the sequential composition $x \cdot y$ deadlocks. Thus, a pre-requisite for a meaningful introduction of a sequential-composition operator is that successful and unsuccessful termination can be distinguished. As already explained in Chapter 4, this is not possible in the theory MPT(A) as all processes end in deadlock. Thus, as before, as a starting point the theory BSP(A) of Chapter 4 is used. This theory is extended with sequential composition to obtain the *Theory of Sequential Processes* TSP(A). It turns out that the empty process is an identity element for sequential composition: $x \cdot 1 = 1 \cdot x = x$.

6.2 The process theory TSP

This section introduces the process theory TSP, the Theory of Sequential Processes. The theory has, as before, a set of actions A as its parameter. The signature of the process theory TSP(A) is the signature of the process theory BSP(A) extended with the sequential-composition operator.

To obtain the axioms of TSP(A), the axioms from Table 6.1 are added to the axioms of the process theory BSP(A) from Table 4.3. Axiom A5 states that sequential composition is associative. As mentioned before, and now formally captured in Axioms A8 and A9, the empty process is an identity element with respect to sequential composition. Axiom A7 states that after a deadlock has been reached no continuation is possible. Note that the theory does not contain the axiom $x \cdot 0 = 0$; so the inaction constant 0 is not a 'true' zero for sequential composition. Axiom A4 describes the distribution of sequential composition over alternative composition from the right. The other distributivity property is not desired as it does not respect the moment of choice (recall Example 4.2.2 (The lady or the tiger?)). Finally, Axiom A10 describes the relation between sequential composition and action prefixes. The unary action-prefix operators bind stronger than the binary sequential composition.

TSP(A)			
BSP(A)			
binary: $\cdot$;			
x, y, z;			
$(x + y) \cdot z = x \cdot z + y \cdot z$	A4	$0 \cdot x = 0$	A7
$(x \cdot y) \cdot z = x \cdot (y \cdot z)$	A5	$x \cdot 1 = x$	A8
$a.x \cdot y = a.(x \cdot y)$	A10	$1 \cdot x = x$	A9

Table 6.1. The process theory TSP(A) (with $a \in A$).

Axiom A5 (associativity of sequential composition) is redundant in the sense that for closed TSP(A)-terms, it can be proven from the other axioms (see Exercise 6.2.8). This means that the axiom is not necessary to obtain a ground-complete axiomatization of the standard term model for TSP(A). This could be a reason not to include the axiom in the theory. However, as soon as recursion comes into play, it is needed to allow all derivations of interest.

The addition of the sequential-composition operator to the process syntax has been motivated from a user's perspective. From the expressiveness point of view, with respect to the description of processes by means of closed process terms (see Definition 5.7.2 (Expressiveness)), the addition of this operator is not needed. This is shown in the following *elimination theorem*. It states that for any closed term described using sequential composition, there is also an equivalent description in which sequential composition is not used.

Theorem 6.2.1 (Elimination) For any closed TSP(A)-term p, there exists a closed BSP(A)-term q such that TSP(A) $\vdash p = q$.

Proof The property is proven by providing a term rewriting system with the same signature as TSP(A) such that

(i) each rewrite step transforms a process term into a process term that is derivably equal,
(ii) the term rewriting system is strongly normalizing, and
(iii) no closed normal form of the term rewriting system contains a sequential-composition operator.

Consider the term rewriting system that has the following rewrite rules, obtained directly from the axioms of TSP(A) (Table 6.1) by replacing $=$ by $\to$; for any $a \in A$, and TSP(A)-terms x, y, z:

$$
\begin{aligned}
&(x + y) \cdot z \to x \cdot z + y \cdot z,\\
&(x \cdot y) \cdot z \to x \cdot (y \cdot z),\\
&0 \cdot x \to 0,\\
&x \cdot 1 \to x,\\
&1 \cdot x \to x,\\
&a.x \cdot y \to a.(x \cdot y).
\end{aligned}
$$

A consequence of the construction of the rules from the axioms of TSP(A) is that each rewrite step transforms a term into a term that is derivably equal.
The second step of the proof, the strong normalization of the term rewriting system, is left to the reader, as an exercise (Exercise 6.2.4).
The last part of the proof is to show that no closed normal form of the term rewriting system contains a sequential-composition operator. Thereto, let u be a normal form of the above term rewriting system. Suppose that u contains at least one sequential-composition operator. Then, u must contain a subterm of the form $v \cdot w$ for some closed TSP(A)-terms v and w. This subterm can always be chosen in such a way that v is a closed BSP(A)-term. It follows immediately from the structure of closed BSP(A)-terms that one of the above rewrite rules can be applied to $v \cdot w$. As a consequence, u is not a normal form. This contradiction implies that u must be a closed BSP(A)-term. □

Exercises

6.2.1 Give a derivably equivalent closed BSP(A)-term for each of the following TSP(A)-terms:

(a) $a.1 \cdot b.1$;
(b) $(a.1 + b.1) \cdot (a.1 + b.1)$;
(c) $(a.1 + b.1) \cdot (a.1 + b.1) \cdot (a.1 + b.1)$.

6.2.2 From Theorem 6.2.1 (Elimination), it follows immediately that for any two closed BSP(A)-terms p and q, there exists a closed BSP(A)-term r such that TSP(A) $\vdash p \cdot q = r$. Prove this result, without using the elimination theorem.

6.2.3 Define the n-fold sequential composition $\_^n$ as an operator in TSP(A), by induction on n, in a similar way as in Notation 4.6.6 (n-fold action prefix). Show that $(a.1)^n = a^n 1$ for any $a \in A$, where $a^n\_$ is the n-fold action prefix.

6.2.4 Prove that the term rewriting system used in the proof of the elimination theorem (Theorem 6.2.1) is strongly normalizing.
(Hint: try induction on the weighted number of symbols in a term, where symbols in the left operand of a sequential composition operator have a higher weight than other symbols.)

6.2.5 Prove Theorem 6.2.1 (Elimination) by induction on the structure of closed TSP(A)-term p.

6.2.6 Show that in TSP(A), the axiom $x + x = x$ (A3) is equivalent to the equation $1 + 1 = 1$. More precisely, show that TSP(A) $\vdash 1 + 1 = 1$ and that A1, A2, $1 + 1 = 1$, A4 – A10 $\vdash x + x = x$.

6.2.7 Show that in TSP(A) the axiom $x + 0 = x$ (A6) is equivalent to the equation $1 + 0 = 1$. More precisely, show that TSP(A) $\vdash 1 + 0 = 1$ and that A1 – A5, $1 + 0 = 1$, A7 – A10 $\vdash x + 0 = x$.

6.2.8 Prove that, for closed TSP(A)-terms p, q, and r, the associativity of sequential composition, i.e., $(p \cdot q) \cdot r = p \cdot (q \cdot r)$, is derivable from the other axioms of TSP(A).

6.3 The term model

The term model for the process theory TSP(A) is obtained in a similar way as earlier term models have been obtained. Starting from the term algebra $\mathbb{P}(\text{TSP}(A))$, first the term deduction system for TSP(A) is defined, and then the quotient algebra $\mathbb{P}(\text{TSP}(A))_{/\leftrightarrow}$ is obtained. It is shown that the process theory TSP(A) is indeed a sound and complete axiomatization of the term model $\mathbb{P}(\text{TSP}(A))_{/\leftrightarrow}$.

Definition 6.3.1 (Term algebra) The *term algebra* for theory TSP(A) is the algebra $\mathbb{P}(\text{TSP}(A)) = (\mathcal{C}(\text{TSP}(A)), +, \cdot, (a.\_)_{a \in A}, 0, 1)$.

The term algebra is not a model of the process theory TSP(A). The set of closed terms $\mathcal{C}(\text{TSP}(A))$ is turned into a transition-system space by means of a term deduction system. The term deduction system for TSP(A), given in Table 6.2, is obtained by extending the term deduction system for BSP(A) of Table 4.4 with deduction rules for the sequential-composition operator.

The first of these rules describes that the sequential composition of two processes p and q in the transition-system space has an option to terminate if both

$TDS(\text{TSP}(A))$		
$TDS(\text{BSP}(A))$;		
binary: $\cdot$;		
x, x', y, y';		
$\dfrac{x\downarrow \quad y\downarrow}{(x \cdot y)\downarrow}$	$\dfrac{x \overset{a}{\rightarrow} x'}{x \cdot y \overset{a}{\rightarrow} x' \cdot y}$	$\dfrac{x\downarrow \quad y \overset{a}{\rightarrow} y'}{x \cdot y \overset{a}{\rightarrow} y'}$

Table 6.2. Term deduction system for TSP(A) (with $a \in A$).

p and q have this option; the second deduction rule states that actions from p can be executed; and the third deduction rule explains that actions from q can be executed in case p has an option to terminate.

Proposition 6.3.2 (Congruence) Bisimilarity is a congruence on $\mathbb{P}(\text{TSP}(A))$.

Proof The property follows immediately from the format of the deduction rules in Tables 4.2, 4.4, and 6.2 by application of Theorem 3.2.7 (Congruence theorem). □

Definition 6.3.3 (Term model of TSP(A)**)** The term model of theory TSP(A) is the quotient algebra $\mathbb{P}(\text{TSP}(A))_{/\leftrightarrow}$, see Definition 2.3.18 (Quotient algebra), where $\mathbb{P}(\text{TSP}(A))$ is the term algebra defined in Definition 6.3.1.

Theorem 6.3.4 (Soundness) The process theory TSP(A) is a sound axiomatization of the algebra $\mathbb{P}(\text{TSP}(A))_{/\leftrightarrow}$, i.e., $\mathbb{P}(\text{TSP}(A))_{/\leftrightarrow} \models \text{TSP}(A)$.

Proof The proof of this statement follows the same lines as the proof of soundness of BSP(A) with respect to $\mathbb{P}(\text{BSP}(A))_{/\leftrightarrow}$ (Theorem 4.4.7). It must be shown that, for each axiom $s = t$ of TSP(A), $\mathbb{P}(\text{TSP}(A))_{/\leftrightarrow} \models s = t$. The axioms of BSP($A$) form a subset of the axioms of TSP(A) and no deduction rules have been added for the operators from the signature of BSP(A). Therefore, the validity proof of the BSP(A) axioms remains valid. Hence, only the validity of the additional axioms A4, A5, and A7–A10 has to be proven. This is left as an exercise (Exercise 6.3.3). □

The above theorem has two immediate corollaries.

Corollary 6.3.5 (Soundness) Let s and t be two TSP(A)-terms. If $\text{TSP}(A) \vdash s = t$, then $\mathbb{P}(\text{TSP}(A))_{/\leftrightarrow} \models s = t$.

Corollary 6.3.6 (Soundness) Let p and q be two closed TSP(A)-terms. If TSP(A) $\vdash p = q$, then $p \leftrightarrow q$.

Theorem 6.3.7 (Conservative ground-extension) Process theory TSP(A) is a conservative ground-extension of process theory BSP(A).

Proof See Exercise 6.3.2. □

Theory TSP(A) is a conservative ground-extension of BSP(A). This is visualized in Figure 6.1. Obviously, by Theorem 4.4.1, TSP(A) is also a conservative ground-extension of MPT(A).

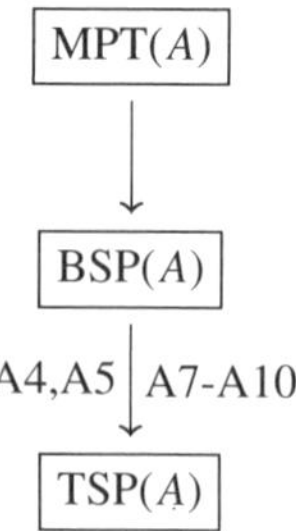

Fig. 6.1. TSP(A) is a conservative ground-extension of BSP(A).

Corollary 6.3.8 (Conservative ground-extension) Theory TSP(A) is a conservative ground-extension of theory MPT(A).

Theorem 6.3.9 (Ground-completeness) Process theory TSP(A) is a ground-complete axiomatization of the term model $\mathbb{P}(\text{TSP}(A))_{/\leftrightarrow}$, i.e., for any closed TSP(A)-terms p and q, $\mathbb{P}(\text{TSP}(A))_{/\leftrightarrow} \models p = q$ implies TSP(A) $\vdash p = q$.

Proof Using Theorem 3.2.19 (Operational conservativity), obviously *TDS*(TSP(A)) is an operational conservative extension of *TDS*(BSP(A)). As additionally BSP(A) is a ground-complete axiomatization of the model induced by *TDS*(BSP(A)) (Theorem 4.4.12), TSP(A) is a sound axiomatization of the model induced by *TDS*(TSP(A)) (Theorem 6.3.4), and TSP(A) has the elimination property with respect to BSP(A) (Theorem 6.2.1), from Theorem 3.2.26 (Ground-completeness), the desired result follows immediately. □

Corollary 6.3.10 (Ground-completeness) Let p and q be arbitrary closed TSP(A)-terms. If $p \leftrightarrow q$, then TSP(A) $\vdash p = q$.

Exercises

6.3.1 Draw the transition system of the following TSP(A)-terms:

(a) $(a.1 + 1) \cdot 0$;
(b) $(a.1 + 1) \cdot 1$;
(c) $(a.1 + 1) \cdot (a.1 + 1)$.

6.3.2 Prove Theorem 6.3.7 (Conservative ground-extension).

6.3.3 Finish the proof of soundness of theory TSP(A) for the term model $\mathbb{P}(\mathrm{TSP}(A))_{/\leftrightarrows}$ (Theorem 6.3.4), i.e., prove that $\mathbb{P}(\mathrm{TSP}(A))_{/\leftrightarrows} \models$ A4, A5, A7–A10.

6.4 Projection in TSP(A)

In Chapter 4, the process theory BSP(A) has been extended with projection operators to obtain (BSP + PR)(A). In this section, the extension of process theory TSP(A) along these lines is discussed. This extension of TSP(A) with the family of projection operators $(\pi_n)_{n \in \mathbf{N}}$ is called (TSP + PR)(A). The process theory (TSP + PR)(A) is obtained by extending the process theory TSP(A) with Axioms PR1 through PR5 of Table 4.5, or by extending (BSP + PR)(A) with the axioms of Table 6.1. In both cases, the same process theory results. Due to Theorem 6.2.1 (Elimination), no additional axioms are needed for the projection operators in combination with sequential composition. Given two closed TSP(A)-terms p and q, the projection $\pi_n(p \cdot q)$ can be computed by first reducing $p \cdot q$ to a closed BSP(A)-term and then applying the axioms for projection from the process theory (BSP + PR)(A). This observation implies several elimination results.

Theorem 6.4.1 (Elimination) For any closed (TSP + PR)(A)-term p, there exists a closed TSP(A)-term q such that TSP(A) $\vdash p = q$.

Proof Exercise 6.4.1 □

In addition, (TSP + PR)(A) has the elimination property with respect to theories BSP(A) and (BSP + PR)(A), i.e., closed (TSP + PR)(A)-terms can be reduced to BSP(A)- and (BSP + PR)(A)-terms, respectively.

The term deduction system underlying the standard term model of theory (TSP + PR)(A) consists of the deduction rules from the term deduction system for TSP(A) and the deduction rules from the term deduction system for (BSP + PR)(A). Furthermore, bisimilarity is a congruence on the term algebra of closed (TSP + PR)(A)-terms. The process theory (TSP + PR)(A) is a sound and ground-complete axiomatization of the corresponding term model

$\mathbb{P}((\text{TSP}+\text{PR})(A))_{/\leftrightarrow}$. Finally, $(\text{TSP}+\text{PR})(A)$ is a conservative ground-extension of both TSP(A) and (BSP + PR)(A), and hence also of theories BSP(A), MPT(A) and (MPT + PR)(A), as illustrated below.

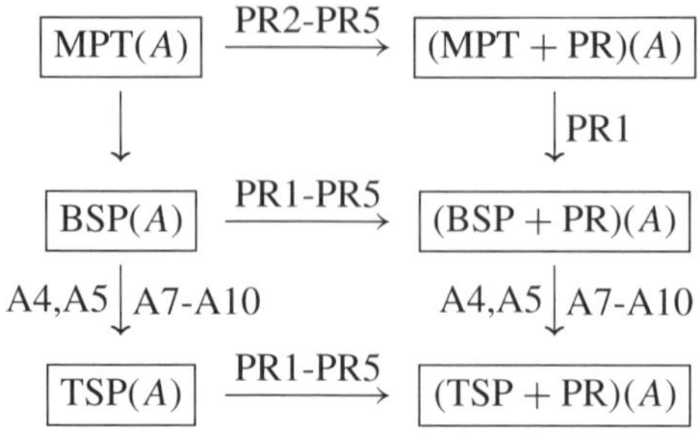

$$
\begin{array}{ccc}
\boxed{\text{MPT}(A)} & \xrightarrow{\text{PR2-PR5}} & \boxed{(\text{MPT}+\text{PR})(A)} \\
\downarrow & & \downarrow \text{PR1} \\
\boxed{\text{BSP}(A)} & \xrightarrow{\text{PR1-PR5}} & \boxed{(\text{BSP}+\text{PR})(A)} \\
\text{A4,A5} \downarrow \text{A7-A10} & & \text{A4,A5} \downarrow \text{A7-A10} \\
\boxed{\text{TSP}(A)} & \xrightarrow{\text{PR1-PR5}} & \boxed{(\text{TSP}+\text{PR})(A)}
\end{array}
$$

Exercises

6.4.1 Prove Theorem 6.4.1 (Elimination). Thereto provide a term rewriting system such that

(a) each rewrite step transforms a process term into a process term that is derivably equal,
(b) the term rewriting system is strongly normalizing, and
(c) no closed normal form of the term rewriting system contains a projection operator.

(Hint: have a look at the proofs of Theorems 4.5.2 and 6.2.1.)

6.4.2 Prove by structural induction that for all closed TSP(A)-terms p and q and $n \geq 0$,

$$(\text{TSP}+\text{PR})(A) \vdash \pi_n(p \cdot q) = \pi_n(\pi_n(p) \cdot \pi_n(q)).$$

6.5 Iteration

6.5.1 Prefix iteration

Another extension of basic process theories that has been discussed before is the introduction of a family of prefix-iteration operators $(a^*\_)_{a\in A}$. Analogous to the extension discussed in the previous section, it is possible to extend the process theory TSP(A) with these operators. The resulting theory is abbreviated TSP$^*(A)$. The axioms of TSP$^*(A)$ are the axioms of the process theory TSP(A), with additionally the prefix-iteration axioms PI1 and PI2 of Table 4.7 and Axiom PI3 given in Table 6.3. The unary prefix-iteration operators bind stronger than the binary sequential-composition operator.

TSP*(A)	
TSP(A), BSP*(A);	
-	
x, y;	
$a^*(x \cdot y) = a^*x \cdot y$	PI3

Table 6.3. The process theory TSP*(A) (with $a \in A$).

The process theory TSP*(A) does not have the elimination property for TSP(A), but it has the elimination property for BSP*(A).

The term deduction system underlying the term model for TSP*(A) consists of the rules of the term deduction systems for TSP(A) and BSP*(A). Bisimilarity is a congruence on the term algebra of closed TSP*(A)-terms. Theory TSP*(A) is a sound and ground-complete axiomatization of the term model $\mathbb{P}(\text{TSP}^*(A))_{/\leftrightarrow}$. TSP*(A) is a conservative ground-extension of both TSP(A) and BSP*(A).

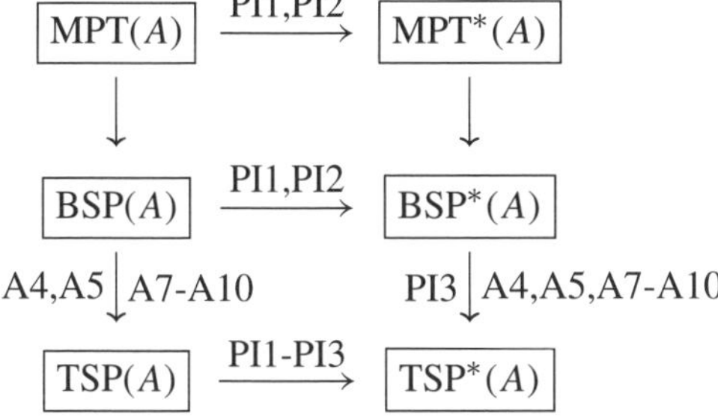

6.5.2 General iteration

The sequential-composition operator can be considered as a generalization of the action-prefix operators, allowing to prefix a process with an arbitrary process. Similarly, the prefix-iteration operator can be generalized to a general *iteration operator*. Thus, the theory (TSP + IT)(A), the Theory of Sequential Processes with Iteration, is introduced. The signature of (TSP + IT)(A) is the signature of the process theory TSP(A) extended with the unary iteration operator $\_^*$. The axioms of (TSP + IT)(A) are obtained by adding the axioms of Table 6.4 to the axioms of the process theory TSP(A) of Table 6.1. As before, the unary iteration operator binds stronger than the binary sequential-composition operator.

Axiom IT1 can be compared to Axiom PI1 for prefix iteration: it states that x^* can execute its body at least once (followed by the iterated process

(TSP + IT)(A)	
TSP(A);	
unary: $\_^*$;	
x, y;	
$x^* = x \cdot x^* + 1$	IT1
$(x + 1)^* = x^*$	IT2
$(x + y)^* = x^* \cdot (y \cdot (x + y)^* + 1)$	IT3

Table 6.4. The process theory $(\text{TSP} + \text{IT})(A)$.

again), or terminate immediately. Axiom IT2 states that a 1 summand inside an iteration does not make a difference, as this is not something that can be executed and, by IT1, any iteration term can terminate already. Finally, Axiom IT3 is a difficult axiom due to Troeger (Troeger, 1993), that is not discussed here any further.

The axioms of $(\text{TSP} + \text{IT})(A)$ do not state anything explicitly about iterations of the basic inaction and empty processes. From IT1, however, it can easily be derived that $(\text{TSP} + \text{IT})(A) \vdash 0^* = 1$. Using IT2, it can then be inferred that $(\text{TSP} + \text{IT})(A) \vdash 1^* = 1$. Both results are as intuitively expected.

The iteration operator cannot be eliminated from closed terms in all circumstances, so there is no elimination theorem. This becomes more clear when the term model is considered.

A term deduction system for $(\text{TSP} + \text{IT})(A)$ is constructed by extending the term deduction system for TSP(A) of Table 6.2 with deduction rules for the iteration operator. Table 6.5 gives the term deduction system. The additional deduction rules should not come as a surprise.

TDS((TSP + IT)(A))	
TDS(TSP(A));	
unary: $\_^*$;	
x, x';	
$x^* \downarrow$	$\dfrac{x \overset{a}{\to} x'}{x^* \overset{a}{\to} x' \cdot x^*}$

Table 6.5. Term deduction system for $(\text{TSP} + \text{IT})(A)$ (with $a \in A$).

Based on the term deduction system, the term model $\mathbb{P}((\text{TSP} + \text{IT})(A))_{/\leftrightarrow}$ can be constructed, because, as before, bisimilarity is a congruence on the term algebra by the format of the deduction rules. Theory $(\text{TSP} + \text{IT})(A)$ is a sound axiomatization of the term model, and the theory is a conservative ground-extension of TSP(A), but it is not a ground-complete axiomatization of the term model (see (Sewell, 1997)).

The theory (TSP + IT)(A) is more expressive than the theory TSP*(A). In the term model of TSP*(A), a loop can only occur from a certain state to itself. Or in other words, a loop can only consist of one action. On the other hand, in the term model of (TSP + IT)(A), processes can have loops consisting of multiple actions and states. Consider for example the process $(a.b.1)^*$, which has a cycle consisting of two states (see Exercise 6.5.2).

An interesting observation is that equational theory (TSP + IT)(A) can be viewed as a theory of regular expressions. When eliminating the action-prefix operators $a.\_$ in favor of action constants $a.1$, (TSP + IT)(A) has the same constants and operators as the algebra of regular expressions known from automata theory (see e.g. (Linz, 2001)). The model of closed (TSP + IT)(A)-terms modulo language equivalence known from automata theory (see Definition 3.1.7) is in fact the algebra of finite automata. In this book, theory (TSP + IT)(A), however, builds upon bisimulation equivalence instead of language equivalence. In automata theory, every finite automaton (regular process in the context of this book, see Section 5.8) can be expressed as a regular expression (closed (TSP + IT)(A)-term). In the current context, it is not possible to represent all regular processes as closed (TSP + IT)(A)-terms. Figure 6.2 shows a transition system for which it can be shown that there is no closed (TSP + IT)(A)-term with a transition system in the term algebra $\mathbb{P}((\text{TSP} + \text{IT})(A))$ that is bisimilar to this transition system. The proof of this fact is beyond the scope of this text; the interested reader is referred to e.g. (Bergstra *et al.*, 2001). This example also shows that the theory (TSP + IT)(A) is less expressive than theory $\text{BSP}_{\text{gfrec}}(A)$ of Section 5.8. In other words, iteration is less expressive than general guarded finite recursion, which is not very surprising. It is interesting to observe that theories (TSP + IT)(A) and $\text{BSP}_{\text{gfrec}}(A)$ are equally expressive when language equivalence is the basic semantic equivalence. It follows from the results in Section 5.8 and language theory that both equational theories capture precisely all finite automata (regular transition systems in the terminology of this book).

Exercises

6.5.1 Prove that $(\text{TSP} + \text{IT})(A) \vdash 0^* = 1 = 1^*$.

6.5.2 Draw the transition system of the following (TSP + IT)(A)-terms: $(a.b.1)^*$, $(a.0)^*$, $(a.b.1)^* \cdot 0$, $(a.1 + b.1)^*$.

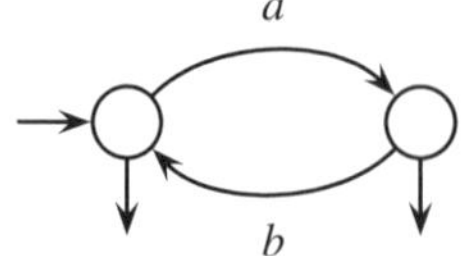

Fig. 6.2. A transition system that is not bisimilar to the transition system of any closed (TSP + IT)(A)-term.

6.6 Recursion

In Section 6.2, it has been shown that from each closed TSP(A)-term all occurrences of the sequential-composition operator can be eliminated (thus obtaining a closed BSP(A)-term). This, however, does not mean that the addition of sequential composition is without consequences. In a setting with recursion, the elimination property for sequential composition does not hold anymore. This section discusses the extension of TSP(A) with recursion.

6.6.1 The theory

The theory $\mathrm{TSP}_{\mathrm{rec}}(A)$, the Theory of Sequential Processes with Recursion, is obtained by extending the signature of theory TSP(A) with constants corresponding to all recursion variables in all recursive specifications of interest, and by adding all the recursive equations of these specifications as axioms to the theory, along the lines of Section 5.2. The term model $\mathbb{P}(\mathrm{TSP}_{\mathrm{rec}}(A))_{/\leftrightarrow}$ of $\mathrm{TSP}_{\mathrm{rec}}(A)$ is based on the term deduction system $\mathit{TDS}(\mathrm{TSP}_{\mathrm{rec}}(A))$, obtained by combining the term deduction systems of Tables 6.2 (Term deduction system of TSP(A)) and 5.2 (Term deduction system of $\mathrm{BSP}_{\mathrm{rec}}(A)$). It is straightforward to prove that $\mathrm{TSP}_{\mathrm{rec}}(A)$ is a sound axiomatization of $\mathbb{P}(\mathrm{TSP}_{\mathrm{rec}}(A))_{/\leftrightarrow}$.

There is no ground-completeness result, because in general the recursive equations do not capture all equalities between recursion variables that are valid in the term model. It is in general also not possible to eliminate recursion variables, and as a consequence, sequential-composition occurrences, from closed $\mathrm{TSP}_{\mathrm{rec}}(A)$-terms. However, the extension of TSP(A) with recursion is conservative, i.e., theory $\mathrm{TSP}_{\mathrm{rec}}(A)$ is a conservative ground-extension of process theory TSP(A). Intuitively, $\mathrm{TSP}_{\mathrm{rec}}(A)$ should also be a conservative ground-extension of $\mathrm{BSP}_{\mathrm{rec}}(A)$. However, none of the standard proof techniques, via term rewriting or the theory of structural operational semantics, can be applied to prove this result. Figure 6.3 shows the conservativity result and conjecture for theory $\mathrm{TSP}_{\mathrm{rec}}(A)$, extending Figures 5.4 and 6.1.

Recursion principles are needed to allow meaningful equational reasoning

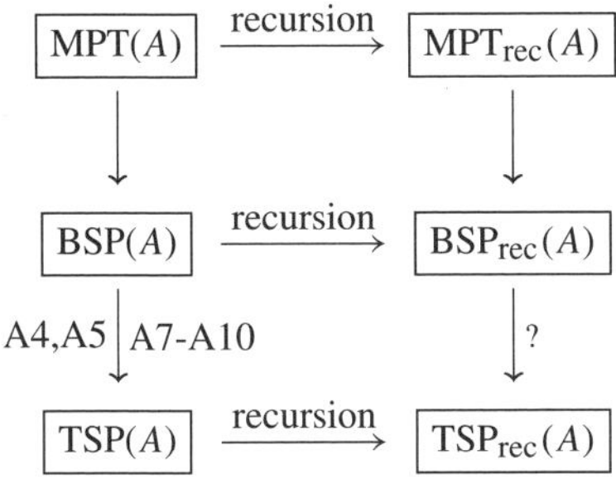

Fig. 6.3. Conservativity results for $\mathrm{TSP}_{\mathrm{rec}}(A)$.

in a context with recursion. Recall that principles AIP and AIP^- are only meaningful in a context with projection operators. Note that the definition of guardedness, Definition 5.5.8, carries over to $(\mathrm{TSP} + \mathrm{PR})_{\mathrm{rec}}(A)$-terms.

Theorem 6.6.1 (Recursion principles) Recursion principles RDP, RDP^-, RSP, and AIP^- are valid in the term model $\mathbb{P}((\mathrm{TSP} + \mathrm{PR})_{\mathrm{rec}}(A))_{/\leftrightarrow}$. Principle AIP is not valid in this model. RDP, RDP^-, and RSP are also valid in model $\mathbb{P}(\mathrm{TSP}_{\mathrm{rec}}(A))_{/\leftrightarrow}$.

The validity of principle RDP, and hence RDP^-, in both mentioned models follows immediately from the construction of the process theories and their term models. The proof of Theorem 5.5.23 (Validity of AIP^- in $\mathbb{P}((\mathrm{BSP} + \mathrm{PR})_{\mathrm{rec}}(A))_{/\leftrightarrow}$) carries over to the context of theory $(\mathrm{TSP} + \mathrm{PR})_{\mathrm{rec}}(A)$, showing the validity of principle AIP^- in $\mathbb{P}((\mathrm{TSP} + \mathrm{PR})_{\mathrm{rec}}(A))_{/\leftrightarrow}$. The invalidity of AIP in $\mathbb{P}((\mathrm{TSP} + \mathrm{PR})_{\mathrm{rec}}(A))_{/\leftrightarrow}$ follows from the same example as used to show the invalidity of AIP in model $\mathbb{P}((\mathrm{BSP} + \mathrm{PR})_{\mathrm{rec}}(A))_{/\leftrightarrow}$ (see Theorem 5.5.20). Assuming the validity of RSP in model $\mathbb{P}((\mathrm{TSP} + \mathrm{PR})_{\mathrm{rec}}(A))_{/\leftrightarrow}$, its validity in $\mathbb{P}(\mathrm{TSP}_{\mathrm{rec}}(A))_{/\leftrightarrow}$ follows from the fact that $(\mathrm{TSP} + \mathrm{PR})_{\mathrm{rec}}(A)$ is a ground-conservative extension of $\mathrm{TSP}_{\mathrm{rec}}(A)$, following the reasoning in the proof of Theorem 5.5.11 (Validity of RSP in $\mathrm{BSP}_{\mathrm{rec}}(A)$). Finally, the validity of RSP in $\mathbb{P}(\mathrm{TSP}_{\mathrm{rec}}(A))_{/\leftrightarrow}$ follows from Theorem 5.5.29 (Relation between the recursion principles) and the following proposition.

Proposition 6.6.2 (HNF property) Process theory $(\mathrm{TSP} + \mathrm{PR})_{\mathrm{rec}}(A)$ satisfies the HNF property, as defined in Definition 5.5.24 (Head normal form).

Proof The proof goes via induction on the structure of a completely guarded $(\mathrm{TSP} + \mathrm{PR})_{\mathrm{rec}}(A)$-term s, similar to the proof of Proposition 5.5.26 (HNF property for $(\mathrm{BSP} + \mathrm{PR})_{\mathrm{rec}}(A)$). Five out of six cases in the current proof are straightforward adaptations of the corresponding cases in the proof of Proposition 5.5.26. The sixth case is the case that $s \equiv s' \cdot s''$, for two completely guarded $(\mathrm{TSP}+\mathrm{PR})_{\mathrm{rec}}(A)$-terms s' and s''. It then follows by induction that both s' and s'' can be rewritten into head normal forms, say t' and t'', respectively. Proposition 5.5.25 (Head normal forms) implies that there exists a natural number $n \in \mathbf{N}$ such that, for any $i < n$, there are $a_i \in A$ and $(\mathrm{TSP}+\mathrm{PR})_{\mathrm{rec}}(A)$-terms t_i such that

$$(\mathrm{TSP}+\mathrm{PR})_{\mathrm{rec}}(A) \vdash t' = \sum_{i<n} a_i.t_i(+1).$$

Then, applying the axioms of $(\mathrm{TSP}+\mathrm{PR})_{\mathrm{rec}}(A)$,

$$(\mathrm{TSP}+\mathrm{PR})_{\mathrm{rec}}(A) \vdash s = t' \cdot t'' =$$
$$(\sum_{i<n} a_i.t_i(+1)) \cdot t'' = \sum_{i<n}(a_i.t_i) \cdot t''(+1 \cdot t'') = \sum_{i<n} a_i.(t_i \cdot t'')(+t'').$$

The last term in this derivation is a head normal form, which completes the proof. □

6.6.2 The stack revisited

In Section 5.6, a stack has been specified using BSP(A) with recursion. For this purpose, an infinite number of recursive equations was needed, even if the set D of data is finite. Using the additional syntax presented in this chapter, alternative specifications of a stack can be given and proven equal to the original one. These specifications are finite as long as the set D from which the elements in the stack are taken is finite, showing the usefulness of sequential composition.

Recall from Definition 5.5.19 (Generalized choice) that the use of the $\sum$-notation is only allowed for finite index sets. Using the syntax of $\mathrm{TSP}_{\mathrm{rec}}(A)$ and given a finite data set D, a recursive specification E for the stack can be given as follows:

$$Stack2 = 1 + \sum_{d \in D} push(d).Stack2 \cdot pop(d).Stack2.$$

Notice that this specification is guarded. In the equation, when an element d is pushed on the stack, a return is made to *Stack*2, which can push additional elements on the stack or terminate immediately. Eventually, d can be popped from the stack, and then the stack is empty, after which it can terminate or start over. Notice that, using the iteration operator of Section 6.5.2, this specification can also be given as follows:

$$Stack2 = (\sum_{d \in D} push(d).Stack2 \cdot pop(d).1)^*.$$

The two descriptions of the stack given in Section 5.6 and above are derivably equivalent.

Proposition 6.6.3 (Stacks) $(\mathrm{TSP}_{\mathrm{rec}} + \mathrm{RSP})(A) \vdash \mathit{Stack}1 = \mathit{Stack}2$.

To prove this proposition, introduce the following notation: for any $d \in D$ and arbitrary sequence $\sigma \in D^*$,

$$\begin{aligned} X_\epsilon &\equiv \mathit{Stack}2, \\ X_{d\sigma} &\equiv \mathit{Stack}2 \cdot pop(d).X_\sigma. \end{aligned}$$

Inspired by the transition systems of *Stack*1 and *Stack*2, it is proven that X_ϵ is a solution for *Stack*1 and X_σ is a solution for S_σ for all σ. Thereto, the following equations have to be proven:

$$\begin{aligned} &(\mathrm{TSP} + E)(A) \vdash X_\epsilon = X_\epsilon, \\ &(\mathrm{TSP} + E)(A) \vdash X_\epsilon = 1 + \sum_{d \in D} push(d).X_d, \\ &(\mathrm{TSP} + E)(A) \vdash X_{d\sigma} = pop(d).X_\sigma + \sum_{e \in D} push(e).X_{ed\sigma}. \end{aligned}$$

The first equation is trivial. The derivations for the second and third equation are as follows.

$$\begin{aligned} &(\mathrm{TSP} + E)(A) \vdash \\ &\quad X_\epsilon = \mathit{Stack}2 \\ &\quad\quad = 1 + \sum_{d \in D} push(d).\mathit{Stack}2 \cdot pop(d).\mathit{Stack}2 \\ &\quad\quad = 1 + \sum_{d \in D} push(d).(\mathit{Stack}2 \cdot pop(d).X_\epsilon) \\ &\quad\quad = 1 + \sum_{d \in D} push(d).X_d \end{aligned}$$

and

$$\begin{aligned} &(\mathrm{TSP} + E)(A) \vdash \\ &\quad X_{d\sigma} = \mathit{Stack}2 \cdot pop(d).X_\sigma \\ &\quad\quad = \left(1 + \sum_{e \in D} push(e).\mathit{Stack}2 \cdot pop(e).\mathit{Stack}2\right) \cdot pop(d).X_\sigma \\ &\quad\quad = 1 \cdot pop(d).X_\sigma + \\ &\quad\quad\quad\quad \left(\sum_{e \in D} push(e).\mathit{Stack}2 \cdot pop(e).\mathit{Stack}2\right) \cdot pop(d).X_\sigma \\ &\quad\quad = pop(d).X_\sigma + \\ &\quad\quad\quad\quad \sum_{e \in D} (push(e).\mathit{Stack}2 \cdot pop(e).\mathit{Stack}2) \cdot pop(d).X_\sigma \\ &\quad\quad = pop(d).X_\sigma + \\ &\quad\quad\quad\quad \sum_{e \in D} push(e).\mathit{Stack}2 \cdot (pop(e).\mathit{Stack}2 \cdot pop(d).X_\sigma) \\ &\quad\quad = pop(d).X_\sigma + \\ &\quad\quad\quad\quad \sum_{e \in D} push(e).\mathit{Stack}2 \cdot pop(e).(\mathit{Stack}2 \cdot pop(d).X_\sigma) \end{aligned}$$

$$= pop(d).X_\sigma + \sum_{e\in D} push(e).Stack2 \cdot pop(e).X_{d\sigma}$$
$$= pop(d).X_\sigma + \sum_{e\in D} push(e).(Stack2 \cdot pop(e).X_{d\sigma})$$
$$= pop(d).X_\sigma + \sum_{e\in D} push(e).X_{ed\sigma}.$$

At this point, it has been shown that any solution for *Stack*2 is also a solution for *Stack*1. As both recursive specifications involved are guarded, using RSP, each of them has precisely one solution in the model $\mathbb{P}(\text{TSP}_{\text{rec}}(A))_{/\leftrightarrow}$. Consequently, $(\text{TSP}_{\text{rec}}+\text{RSP})(A)\vdash Stack1 = Stack2$, proving the above proposition.

Observe that the above derivations use associativity of sequential composition on terms containing recursion variables. This cannot be avoided, showing that, in a context with recursion, associativity axiom A5 is meaningful, whereas it could be omitted from the basic theory TSP(A) without many consequences, as explained in Section 6.2.

6.6.3 Some expressiveness aspects

In Section 5.8, the theory $\text{BSP}_{\text{gfrec}}(A)$ was introduced, and it was shown that guarded finite recursion in the context of BSP(A) coincides with regular processes. The stack process is not finitely definable over BSP(A) (see Definition 5.7.5 (Definability)). It cannot be specified as a closed $\text{BSP}_{\text{gfrec}}(A)$-term, and it is not regular. The guarded finite recursive specification for *Stack*2 in this section therefore shows that TSP with guarded finite recursion is more expressive than $\text{BSP}_{\text{gfrec}}(A)$. In fact, the specification for *Stack*2 shows that finite guarded recursive specifications over TSP(A) allow the specification of non-regular processes, or, in other words, that non-regular processes are finitely definable over TSP(A). It is interesting to look a bit closer into these expressiveness aspects, particularly in relation with guardedness (which is required by the definition of definability).

Note that the general theories $\text{BSP}_{\text{rec}}(A)$ and $\text{TSP}_{\text{rec}}(A)$ allowing arbitrary recursion are equally expressive, as defined in Definition 5.7.2 (Expressiveness). Process theory $\text{BSP}_{\text{rec}}(A)$ is already sufficiently powerful to specify all countable computable processes, see Section 5.7. The extension with sequential composition does not affect the expressiveness of the theory, because of the fundamental restriction that computable recursive specifications can only specify countable processes. Recall furthermore Theorem 5.7.7 (Processes definable over BSP(A)) that states that a process is definable over BSP(A) if and only if it is finitely branching. Also this result carries over to the context with sequential composition, i.e., a process is definable over TSP(A) if and only if it is finitely branching. However, when allowing unguarded recursive specifications, already a finite specification is sufficient to specify an infinitely branching process.

Consider the recursive specification

$$\{X = X \cdot (a.1) + a.1\}.$$

Using the deduction rules for recursion constants of Table 5.2, for any natural number n, the following transition can be derived:

$$X \xrightarrow{a} (a.1)^n,$$

where $\_^n$ is the n-fold sequential composition of Exercise 6.2.3. This can be proven by induction on the natural number n as follows:

(i) $n = 0$. Since $a.1 \xrightarrow{a} 1$, also $X \cdot (a.1) + a.1 \xrightarrow{a} 1$ and $X \xrightarrow{a} 1 \equiv (a.1)^0$.

(ii) $n > 0$. By induction, $X \xrightarrow{a} (a.1)^{n-1}$. Then, $X \cdot (a.1) \xrightarrow{a} (a.1)^{n-1} \cdot (a.1)$, i.e., $X \cdot (a.1) \xrightarrow{a} (a.1)^n$. This means that $X \cdot (a.1) + a.1 \xrightarrow{a} (a.1)^n$ and therefore also $X \xrightarrow{a} (a.1)^n$.

As for different natural numbers m and n, process terms $(a.1)^m$ and $(a.1)^n$ are not bisimilar, it must be concluded that the transition system associated with X has an infinite number of different successor states for the state associated with X. Hence, the process specified by recursion variable X is infinitely branching, showing that finite unguarded recursion can describe infinitely branching processes. (Note that the recursive specification does not *define* the process that X specifies via the default interpretation in the term model; since the recursive specification is unguarded, it has many other solutions as well (see Exercise 6.6.8).)

Another interesting observation is based on the following specification taken from (Bosscher, 1997):

$$\{X = a.(Y \cdot a.1), Y = a.(Y \cdot Z) + a.1, Z = a.1 + 1\}.$$

This finite guarded recursive specification over the signature of TSP(A) *defines*, as argued above, a finitely branching process, but interestingly there is no bound on the number of outgoing transitions that any single state of the process might have; the process exhibits so-called *unbounded* branching. This can be verified by drawing the transition system for recursion variable X, see Exercise 6.6.6. Thus, this example shows that unbounded branching processes are finitely definable over TSP(A). As shown in (Bosscher, 1997), it is not possible to finitely define processes with unbounded branching over theory BSP(A).

Finally, it is interesting to consider the expressiveness results in this subsection in the context of automata theory. Observe that recursive specification $E = \{X = X \cdot (a.1) + a.1\}$ discussed above corresponds to a left-linear grammar in the automata-theoretic context. In that context, left-linear grammars, right-linear grammars, finite automata, and regular languages are all equivalent notions. However, in the current context, the process specified by specification E is infinitely branching, and thus non-regular.

Exercises

6.6.1 Prove, using AIP^-, that any solution of $X = a.X \cdot b.1$ is also a solution of $X = a.X$.

6.6.2 Prove that $((\mathrm{TSP} + \mathrm{PR})_{\mathrm{rec}} + \mathrm{AIP}^-)(A) \vdash \mu X.\{X = a.X\} \cdot \mu Y.\{Y = b.Y\} = \mu X.\{X = a.X\}$.

6.6.3 Given the syntax of $\mathrm{TSP}_{\mathrm{rec}}(A)$ and a finite data set D, a recursive specification for the stack using three equations can be given as follows:

$$\begin{aligned} \mathit{Stack3} &= 1 + T \cdot \mathit{Stack3}, \\ T &= \sum_{d \in D} \mathit{push}(d).(U \cdot \mathit{pop}(d).1), \\ U &= 1 + T \cdot U. \end{aligned}$$

In this set of equations, *Stack*3 is specified as an iteration of T, which represents a terminating stack. In the specification of T, $U \cdot \mathit{pop}(d)$ can be seen as a stack element d, where U may or may not put new elements on top of the element, and where $\mathit{pop}(d)$ removes the element from the stack. Show that this recursive specification is guarded. Prove that $(\mathrm{TSP}_{\mathrm{rec}} + \mathrm{RSP})(A) \vdash \mathit{Stack2} = \mathit{Stack3}$.

6.6.4 Consider yet another recursive specification for the stack, consisting of $|D| + 2$ equations, for data set D:

$$\begin{aligned} \mathit{Stack4} &= 1 + T \cdot \mathit{Stack4}, \\ T &= \sum_{d \in D} \mathit{push}(d).T_d, \quad \text{and, for all } d \in D, \\ T_d &= \mathit{pop}(d).1 + T \cdot T_d. \end{aligned}$$

Show that this recursive specification is guarded. Prove that $(\mathrm{TSP}_{\mathrm{rec}} + \mathrm{RSP})(A) \vdash \mathit{Stack2} = \mathit{Stack4}$.

6.6.5 A specification of a counter can be obtained by considering a stack that can only contain elements from a data set with one element. When, additionally, the atomic actions representing putting this element on the stack and taking it from the stack are represented by *plus* and *minus*, respectively, the following specification can be derived from the specification for *Stack*4 of the previous exercise:

$$\begin{aligned} \mathit{Counter} &= 1 + T \cdot \mathit{Counter}, \\ T &= \mathit{plus}.T', \\ T' &= \mathit{minus}.1 + T \cdot T'. \end{aligned}$$

Give a transition system for the process *Counter*. Show that this counter specification is derivably equivalent to the counter specification of Exercises 5.6.3 and 5.6.4.

6.6.6 Consider the recursive specification $\{X = a.(Y \cdot a.1), Y = a.(Y \cdot Z) + a.1, Z = a.1 + 1\}$. Draw the transition system of X (and observe that it is a transition system with unbounded branching).

6.6.7 Find two non-bisimilar transition systems that are both solutions of the (unguarded!) recursive equation $X = X \cdot a.1 + X \cdot b.1$.

6.6.8 Consider again recursive specification $\{X = X \cdot a.1 + a.1\}$ of the last subsection. Give a different solution for this recursive specification than the one already given. Give a plausible argument why any solution of this recursive specification must be infinitely branching.

6.6.9 Prove or disprove that $\mathrm{TSP}_{\mathrm{rec}}(A)$ is a conservative ground-extension of $\mathrm{BSP}_{\mathrm{rec}}(A)$. (Please inform the authors of any solution to this exercise.)

6.7 Renaming, encapsulation, and skip operators

In Exercises 5.6.3, 5.6.4 and 6.6.5, a counter was considered that can also be specified as a stack over a trivial singleton data type. However, for the stack, different action names are used (*push*, *pop*) than for the counter (*plus*, *minus*). In the exercises, the names were just changed without any further consideration. Often, it is desirable to have such a renaming inside the theory, in order to be able to deal with this in a more formal and precise way. This is not difficult to do. This section briefly presents the extension of the basic theory BSP(A) with renaming and two related families of operators, namely encapsulation and skip operators. The extension of TSP(A) with renaming is left as Exercise 6.7.7.

Suppose f is a renaming function, i.e., f is a function on atomic actions, $f : A \to A$. Then, a renaming operator ρ_f can be defined on process terms. Table 6.6 shows the extension of BSP(A) with renaming operators.

It is straightforward to obtain an elimination theorem and a conservativity theorem. Also the operational rules are not difficult; see Table 6.7. Again, it is a useful exercise to show that the resulting term model admits a soundness and a ground-completeness theorem.

The remainder of this section covers two other operators that turn out to be very useful: an operator that can block a certain action, and an operator that can skip a certain action. The former can be considered a renaming into 0, the latter a renaming into 1. Suppose H is a set of atomic actions, i.e., $H \subseteq A$. The operator ∂_H blocks execution of actions from H, and leaves other actions

(BSP + RN)(A)	
BSP(A);	
unary: $(\rho_f)_{f:A\to A}$;	
x, y;	
$\rho_f(1) = 1$	RN1
$\rho_f(0) = 0$	RN2
$\rho_f(a.x) = f(a).\rho_f(x)$	RN3
$\rho_f(x + y) = \rho_f(x) + \rho_f(y)$	RN4

Table 6.6. BSP(A) with renaming (with $a \in A$ and $f : A \to A$).

TDS((BSP + RN)(A))

TDS(BSP(A));

unary: $(\rho_f)_{f:A\to A}$;

x, x';

$$\frac{x\downarrow}{\rho_f(x)\downarrow} \qquad \frac{x \xrightarrow{a} x'}{\rho_f(x) \xrightarrow{f(a)} \rho_f(x')}$$

Table 6.7. Term deduction system for BSP(A) with renaming (with $a \in A$ and $f : A \to A$).

unchanged. For reasons that become clear in the next chapter, this operator is called the *encapsulation operator*. Axioms are presented in Table 6.8.

(BSP + DH)(A)		
BSP(A);		
unary: $(\partial_H)_{H\subseteq A}$;		
x, y;		
$\partial_H(1) = 1$		D1
$\partial_H(0) = 0$		D2
$\partial_H(a.x) = 0$	if $a \in H$	D3
$\partial_H(a.x) = a.\partial_H(x)$	otherwise	D4
$\partial_H(x + y) = \partial_H(x) + \partial_H(y)$		D5

Table 6.8. BSP(A) plus encapsulation (with $a \in A$, $H \subseteq A$).

Example 6.7.1 (Encapsulation) As an example, consider, on the one hand, the behavior of a machine performing process $a.(b.1 + c.1)$, that, for some reason, is unable to execute the atomic action c. Then, after having performed a, it will continue with b, as it does not have any other choice available.

On the other hand, consider a similar machine performing $a.b.1 + a.c.1$. Assuming again that c cannot be executed, this second machine will perform an a-step and next it will either perform b, or it will be in the position that it can only continue with the blocked c, which means it will end in a deadlock.

Using the encapsulation operator, this example can be modeled by blocking c in the above two specifications; thus, $H = \{c\}$. As a consequence,

$$\begin{aligned}&(\text{BSP} + \text{DH})(A) \vdash \\ &\quad \partial_H(a.(b.1 + c.1)) = a.\partial_H(b.1 + c.1) = a.(\partial_H(b.1) + \partial_H(c.1)) \\ &\qquad = a.(b.\partial_H(1) + 0) = a.b.1,\end{aligned}$$

and, on the other hand,

$$\begin{aligned}&(\text{BSP} + \text{DH})(A) \vdash \\ &\quad \partial_H(a.b.1 + a.c.1) = \partial_H(a.b.1) + \partial_H(a.c.1) \\ &\qquad = a.\partial_H(b.1) + a.\partial_H(c.1) = a.b.1 + a.0.\end{aligned}$$

Notice that process $a.b.1 + a.0$ has a deadlock, whereas $a.b.1$ does not (see Definition 4.4.14).

Next, suppose I is a set of atomic actions, $I \subseteq A$. The operator ε_I skips the execution of actions from I, and leaves other actions unchanged. It is therefore called a *skip* operator. Axioms are presented in Table 6.9.

(BSP + EI)(A)		
BSP(A);		
unary: $(\varepsilon_I)_{I \subseteq A}$;		
x, y;		
$\varepsilon_I(1) = 1$		E1
$\varepsilon_I(0) = 0$		E2
$\varepsilon_I(a.x) = \varepsilon_I(x)$	if $a \in I$	E3
$\varepsilon_I(a.x) = a.\varepsilon_I(x)$	otherwise	E4
$\varepsilon_I(x + y) = \varepsilon_I(x) + \varepsilon_I(y)$		E5

Table 6.9. BSP(A) with skip operators (with $a \in A$, $I \subseteq A$).

Also for the extensions with encapsulation and skip operators standard results can be established. Without further comment, Table 6.10 presents the operational rules for encapsulation. The rules for the skip operators are given in Table 6.11. The two rules in the bottom row of the table may need some explanation. As usual, the steps and the termination option for term $\varepsilon_I(p)$ are derived from the steps and termination option of p. The bottom left rule states that $\varepsilon_I(p)$ may terminate if p can do an a-step that is skipped and p', the result of executing a in p, can terminate *after* skipping all actions in I in p'. The last provision is necessary because skipping actions can create extra termination options. The bottom right rule states that $\varepsilon_I(p)$ may do a b-step if p can do some a-step that is skipped followed by a b-step that is not skipped. Thus, the rules look ahead at the behavior of the p process after skipping the a action to determine the behavior of $\varepsilon_I(p)$.

TDS((BSP + DH)(A))
TDS(BSP(A));
unary: $(\partial_H)_{H \subseteq A}$;
x, x';

$$\frac{x\downarrow}{\partial_H(x)\downarrow} \qquad \frac{x \xrightarrow{a} x' \quad a \notin H}{\partial_H(x) \xrightarrow{a} \partial_H(x')}$$

Table 6.10. Term deduction system for encapsulation (with $a \in A$, $H \subseteq A$).

TDS((BSP + EI)(A))
TDS(BSP(A));
unary: $(\varepsilon_I)_{I \subseteq A}$;
x, x', y;

$$\frac{x\downarrow}{\varepsilon_I(x)\downarrow} \qquad \frac{x \xrightarrow{a} x' \quad a \notin I}{\varepsilon_I(x) \xrightarrow{a} \varepsilon_I(x')}$$

$$\frac{x \xrightarrow{a} x' \quad a \in I \quad \varepsilon_I(x')\downarrow}{\varepsilon_I(x)\downarrow} \qquad \frac{x \xrightarrow{a} x' \quad a \in I \quad \varepsilon_I(x') \xrightarrow{b} y}{\varepsilon_I(x) \xrightarrow{b} y}$$

Table 6.11. The term deduction system for skip operators (with $a, b \in A$ and $I \subseteq A$).

As a final remark, the extensions of TSP(A) with encapsulation and skip operators, (TSP + DH)(A) and (TSP + EI)(A), respectively, are obtained by simply combining the signatures and axiom sets of TSP(A) with those of (BSP + DH)(A) and (BSP + EI)(A), respectively. All standard results can be obtained as expected.

Exercises

6.7.1 Generalizing Definition 4.4.14 (Deadlock in BSP(A)-terms), a closed (BSP + DH)(A)-term is deadlock free if and only if it is derivably equal to a closed BSP(A)-term without 0 occurrence.

Simplify $\partial_{\{a\}}(a.0 + b.1)$. Note that the process $a.0 + b.1$ has a deadlock, but $\partial_{\{a\}}(a.0+b.1)$ does not. Hence, encapsulation can cause the loss of deadlock possibilities. Conversely, it is easy to find a closed BSP(A)-term p such that p is without deadlock, whereas $\partial_{\{a\}}(p)$ is not. Give such an example.

6.7.2 Give an example of a closed BSP(A)-term p such that p has a deadlock and $\varepsilon_I(p)$ for some appropriate I does no longer have a deadlock (assuming a generalization of Definition 4.4.14 (Deadlock in BSP(A)-terms) to closed (BSP + EI)(A)-terms).

6.7.3 Consider the behavior of the vending machine of Exercise 5.2.2 under the assumption that due to some mechanical defect it is impossible to insert any 10 cent coins. Does this machine have any deadlock?

6.7.4 Let *id* be the identity function on A and let $\circ$ denote function composition. Show that for all closed BSP(A)-terms p and renaming functions $f, g : A \to A$,

(a) $(\mathrm{BSP} + \mathrm{RN})(A) \vdash \rho_{id}(p) = p$,
(b) $(\mathrm{BSP} + \mathrm{RN})(A) \vdash \rho_f(\rho_g(p)) = \rho_{f\circ g}(p)$.

6.7.5 Consider theory $(\mathrm{BSP} + \mathrm{EI})(A)$ with recursion.

(a) Given the equation $X = \varepsilon_{\{a\}}(a.X)$, show that in the term model $\mathbb{P}((\mathrm{BSP} + \mathrm{EI})_{\mathrm{rec}}(A))_{/\leftrightarrow} \models X = 0$.
(b) Find two different solutions of the equation $X = \varepsilon_{\{a\}}(a.X)$ in the term model of $(\mathrm{BSP} + \mathrm{EI})(A)$ with recursion.
(c) Find two different solutions of the equation $X = a.\varepsilon_{\{a\}}(X)$ in the term model of $(\mathrm{BSP} + \mathrm{EI})(A)$ with recursion.
(d) Can you formulate a notion of guardedness in the presence of skip operators?

6.7.6 Consider the extensions of theory TSP(A) with encapsulation and skip operators, (TSP+DH)(A) and (TSP+EI)(A). Show by structural induction that for all closed TSP(A)-terms p, q and $H, I \subseteq A$,

(a) $(\mathrm{TSP} + \mathrm{DH})(A) \vdash \partial_H(p \cdot q) = \partial_H(p) \cdot \partial_H(q)$,
(b) $(\mathrm{TSP} + \mathrm{EI})(A) \vdash \varepsilon_I(p \cdot q) = \varepsilon_I(p) \cdot \varepsilon_I(q)$.

6.7.7 Develop the theory (TSP + RN)(A), TSP with renaming, i.e., the equational theory obtained by extending (BSP + RN)(A) with the sequential-composition operator and the axioms of Table 6.1. Prove elimination and conservativity results, and give a term model proving soundness and ground-completeness.

6.8 Bibliographical remarks

Taking the equational theory TSP(A), replacing processes $a.1$ by constants a, and subsequently removing action prefixing and the constants 0 and 1, results in the theory BPA(A) of (Bergstra & Klop, 1984a). The present treatment is from (Baeten, 2003), which in turn is based on (Koymans & Vrancken, 1985; Vrancken, 1997). The term deduction system of theory TSP(A) is due to (Baeten & Van Glabbeek, 1987).

Section 6.5 is based on (Bergstra *et al.*, 2001). Further work can be found in (Baeten *et al.*, 2007).

The specification of the stack in one equation is new here. The specification of the stack in three equations of Exercise 6.6.3 is due to (Koymans & Vrancken, 1985). The (earlier) one in $|D| + 2$ equations, where D is the data set, given in Exercise 6.6.4 is from (Bergstra & Klop, 1986a). The specification in one equation is possible due to the termination option of the empty stack. The specifications of (Koymans & Vrancken, 1985) and (Bergstra & Klop, 1986a) do not have such an initial termination option, and the specifications given in the current chapter have been adapted to include this termination option.

Section 6.7 is based on (Baeten & Bergstra, 1988). Renaming operators occur in most concurrency theories, see e.g. (Milner, 1980; Hoare, 1985). Encapsulation, and the notation ∂_H, is from (Bergstra & Klop, 1984a). For skipping, see (Baeten & Weijland, 1990).

7

Parallel and communicating processes

7.1 Interleaving

So far, the focus has been on *sequential* processes: actions can be executed, or alternatives can be explored, starting from a single point of control. In this chapter, the step is taken towards the treatment of parallel or distributed systems: it is allowed that activities exist in parallel. Just allowing separate activity of different components is not enough. A genuine treatment of parallel activity requires in addition a description of interaction between parallel activities.

Suppose there are two sequential processes x and y that can execute actions, and choose alternatives, independently. The *merge* operator $\|$ denotes parallel composition. Thus, the parallel composition of x and y is denoted $x \parallel y$. To illustrate the intuition behind the algebraic treatment of parallel composition, consider an external observer $\mathcal{O}$ that observes process $x \parallel y$. Observations can be made of executions of actions. Assume that these observations are instantaneous. Then, it can be seen that the observations of actions of x and actions of y will be *merged* or *interleaved* in time.

Consider the example $a.0 \parallel b.0$. This process involves the execution of two actions, one from each component. Observer $\mathcal{O}$ might see the execution of a first, and then the execution of b. After this, no further activity is possible. On the other hand, observer $\mathcal{O}$ might see the execution of b first, then the execution of a followed by inaction. Finally, the observer might observe the two actions simultaneously.

The simultaneous observation of two actions is reserved for the interaction between the two processes, i.e., processes achieve interaction through *synchronization*; the occurrence of interaction between two processes is the result of the simultaneous execution of matching actions. By a judicious choice of atomic actions, *communication* can be achieved with synchronization, i.e., a message can be passed from one process to another.

Returning to the simple example, assume the interaction that is achieved by the simultaneous execution of a and b is denoted by c. Summarizing the above discussions, the execution of $a.0 \parallel b.0$ has three possibilities: first a and then b, first b and then a, or c (denoting a and b together). In terms of an equation, this can be stated as follows. The merge operator $\parallel$ binds stronger than choice and weaker than action prefix.

$$a.0 \parallel b.0 = a.b.0 + b.a.0 + c.0.$$

The sketched approach to parallel composition is called *arbitrary interleaving* or *shuffle* in the literature. Note that the *observations* of the action executions are interleaved, not necessarily the actions themselves. So, the actions themselves can have duration (and will have duration in practice). It is also not necessarily the case that the first action has finished when the second action starts. If necessary, it can be made explicit that actions can overlap in time, by allowing observations of the beginning and the ending of an action:

$$begin_a.end_a.0 \parallel begin_b.end_b.0.$$

This process has $begin_a.begin_b.end_a.end_b.0$ as one of its possible execution sequences.

This chapter expands the theories BSP and TSP of the earlier chapters with the interleaving merge operator, presenting equational theories and the underlying models for communicating parallel processes.

7.2 An operational view

Before turning to an equational theory, parallel processing and communication is first studied from an operational point of view, to provide insight in some of the aspects involved.

Considering parallel processing without interaction or communication, the basic idea is that a component in a parallel composition can execute an action by itself, independent of other components. This can be described in a straightforward way by the following deduction rules (as defined in the context of term deduction systems), where x, x', y, and y' are arbitrary process terms and a is an action:

$$\frac{x \xrightarrow{a} x'}{x \parallel y \xrightarrow{a} x' \parallel y} \quad \text{and} \quad \frac{y \xrightarrow{a} y'}{x \parallel y \xrightarrow{a} x \parallel y'}.$$

Interaction is more involved. As mentioned, interaction is the simultaneous execution of actions that match in some sense. An example of communication through synchronization has already been given in the previous section where the synchronized execution of actions a and b resulted in an action c. More concretely, one could consider a process that can perform a *send* action, and that is executing in parallel with another process that can perform a *receive* action. If it is assumed that these actions match, then the simultaneous executions of these two actions could be defined to result in a *communicate* action, thus achieving communication between parallel processes.

Communication resulting from the simultaneous execution of matching actions is *synchronous*, as opposed to asynchronous communication in which a message might be sent at one point in time and received at a different, later point in time. Synchronous communication is the basic form of communication in this book. Asynchronous communication can be achieved by explicitly specifying buffers or communication channels.

In elementary synchronous communication, every communication has two parts. Actions that may communicate can be specified through a *communication function* γ, that takes a pair of communicating actions and returns the result of the communication, which is also an action. Suppose an atomic action $communicate(5)$ represents the communication of a data value 5. Intuitively, when communication is reliable, this communication action should be the result of the synchronized execution of a $send(5)$ action and a $receive(5)$ action; that is, the data value that is received should match the value that is sent. This can be defined as follows:

$$\gamma(send(5), receive(5)) = communicate(5).$$

If two actions do *not* communicate, e.g., continuing the example, when the sent and received values do not match, then their communication is not defined. For example,

$$\gamma(send(5), receive(6)) \text{ is not defined.}$$

Not every function is a meaningful communication function. For example, $\gamma(send(5), receive(5))$ and $\gamma(receive(5), send(5))$ are typically expected to give the same result. These ideas lead to the following definition of a communication function.

Definition 7.2.1 (Communication function) As always, set A is the set of atomic actions. A *communication function* on A is a partial, binary function $\gamma : A \times A \to A$ satisfying the following conditions:

(i) for all $a, b \in A$: $\gamma(a, b) = \gamma(b, a)$, i.e., communication is *commutative*;

(ii) for all $a, b, c \in A$: $\gamma(\gamma(a, b), c) = \gamma(a, \gamma(b, c))$, i.e., communication is *associative*.

Note that equations as above for partial functions imply that one side of the equation is defined exactly when the other side is. If $\gamma(a, b)$ for certain $a, b \in A$ is not defined, it is said that a and b *do not communicate*. An action $c \in A$ such that $c = \gamma(a, b)$ for certain a, b is called a *communication action*. A communication $\gamma(a, b)$ is called a *binary* communication.

A communication function in principle specifies communication between two actions, the binary communications. The result of such a communication can itself be allowed to communicate with other actions, which means that it is possible to specify communication among more than two actions. The associativity property in the definition of a communication function implies that the result of such communications is always the same, independent of the order in which the binary communications among pairs of actions are resolved. In fact, it follows from the commutativity and associativity requirements that it is possible to simplify expressions like $\gamma(a, \gamma(\gamma(b, c), d))$, and simply write $\gamma(a, b, c, d)$.

Having introduced the notion of a communication function, interaction between two components in a parallel composition can be described by the following deduction rule, where x, x', y, and y' are arbitrary process terms, γ is a communication function, and a, b, and c are actions:

$$\frac{x \overset{a}{\rightarrow} x' \quad y \overset{b}{\rightarrow} y' \quad \gamma(a, b) = c}{x \parallel y \overset{c}{\rightarrow} x' \parallel y'} \ .$$

Sometimes, one would like to express that communication is restricted. For example, it could be the case that only binary communications, i.e., communications involving only two actions, are possible. An action $\gamma(a, b, c)$ involves three actions, and is therefore called a *ternary* communication. It is an example of so-called higher-order communication. In many applications, higher-order communication is not possible and only binary communication occurs. This is called *handshaking* and can be expressed as follows.

Definition 7.2.2 (Handshaking communication) Let $\gamma : A \times A \rightarrow A$ be a communication function. If for all $a, b, c \in A$, $\gamma(a, b, c)$ is not defined, then γ is said to be a *handshaking* communication function.

In some applications, there is no communication whatsoever between the components. In such cases, no two atomic actions $a, b \in A$ communicate, i.e., $\gamma(a, b)$ is undefined for all $a, b \in A$. This is indicated by writing $\emptyset$ for γ, thus referring to the characterization of γ as the set $\{(a, b, c) \in A^3 \mid \gamma(a, b) = c\}$.

These two examples illustrate that the concept of a communication function is rather flexible. The deduction rule for communication does not change when restricting the allowed communication functions beyond Definition 7.2.1 as in the above two examples. Note however, that the deduction rule for communication does not allow the derivation of any communication actions if $\gamma = \emptyset$, and is therefore redundant in that case, which is the expected result.

Finally, it is necessary to consider termination. Assume some parallel composition $x \parallel y$, with x and y process terms. Successful termination of the composition can be observed when both x and y are able to terminate. If one component still needs to execute actions, or cannot terminate successfully, then the composite process cannot terminate, and, for example, cannot pass control to a process following $x \parallel y$ (composed sequentially). This can be captured in the following deduction rule, with x and y arbitrary process terms:

$$\frac{x\downarrow \quad y\downarrow}{x \parallel y\downarrow} \; .$$

The next section presents a simple example illustrating the concepts introduced so far in this chapter. Section 7.4 then follows with the development of a basic equational theory for communicating processes.

Exercises

7.2.1 On the basis of the intuition given in this section, try to reason which of the following identities are correct. Assume there is no communication, i.e., $\gamma = \emptyset$.

(a) $a.1 \parallel b.1 = a.b.1 + b.a.1$.
(b) $a.b.1 \parallel c.1 = a.b.c.1 + a.c.b.1 + c.a.b.1$.
(c) $a.b.1 \parallel c.1 = a.(b.c.1 + c.b.1) + c.a.b.1$.
(d) $(a.1 + b.1) \parallel c.1 = a.c.1 + b.c.1 + c.(a.1 + b.1)$.
(e) $a.1 \parallel 0 = a.0$.
(f) $a.1 \parallel 0 = a.1$.

7.2.2 Formally describe the situation where only binary and ternary communication are possible, and none of higher order.

7.2.3 Is it possible to describe the situation where *only* ternary communication is possible, and not binary?

7.3 Standard communication

Many examples of communication involve the transmission of data at ports. It turns out to be useful to have some standardized notation for so-called *standard communication*.

Assume a number of *locations*, that are interconnected by *ports* or *channels*. Figure 7.1 gives an example. The system in the example has locations A, B, and C and ports ia, ab, ac, and co. Locations correspond to processes (represented by a closed term or a guarded recursive specification). Standard communication allows only binary communication, i.e., handshaking is assumed. Ports that connect two locations are called *internal*, ports attached to one location only are *external*. External ports can be used for communication between the system of processes and its environment. In the example of Figure 7.1, ports ab and ac are internal, and ia and co are external. The communication aspects of systems like those in Figure 7.1 can be captured via the following definition.

Definition 7.3.1 (Standard communication) Let D be a set of data elements; let P be a set of port names. Assume, for each port $p \in P$ and each $d \in D$, the presence of the following atomic actions in the set of actions A:

- $p!d$ (send data element d at port p);
- $p?d$ (receive d at p);
- $p?\!\!\!!\,d$ (communicate d at p).

The *standard communication function* $\gamma_S : A \times A \to A$ is given by the following equation:

$$\gamma_S(p!d, p?d) = \gamma_S(p?d, p!d) = p?\!\!\!!\,d,$$

for any $p \in P$ and $d \in D$; γ_S is not defined otherwise.

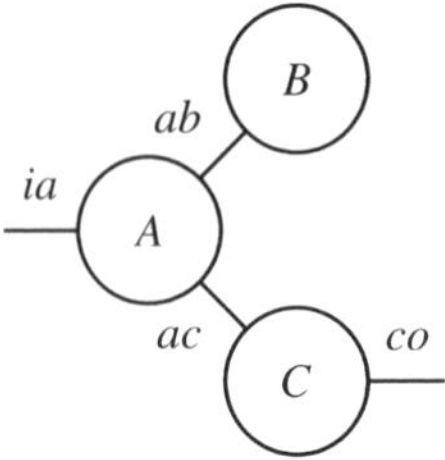

Fig. 7.1. A network of communicating processes.

Consider again the example of Figure 7.1. Using the actions predefined in Definition 7.3.1, process A might for example be specified by the term $ia?d.(ab!d.1 \parallel ac!d.1)$, for some data element d. Processes B and C might be defined as $ab?d.1$ and $ac?d.co!d.1$, respectively.

The system of Figure 7.1 as a whole can be described as a parallel composition of the processes involved:

$$ia?d.(ab!d.1 \parallel ac!d.1) \parallel ab?d.1 \parallel ac?d.co!d.1.$$

Following the intuition of the merge operator and its operational description discussed in the previous sections, this parallel composition allows arbitrary interleavings of the actions of the constituent processes, including communication actions of synchronizing processes. However, communication is not enforced. It could be desirable to enforce communication over the internal ports *ab* and *ac*. This can be done using the encapsulation operator of Section 6.7 by blocking isolated send and receive actions over these internal ports, see Exercise 7.3.1:

$$\partial_{\{p?d,\, p!d \mid p \in \{ab,ac\}, d \in D\}} \\ (ia?d.(ab!d.1 \parallel ac!d.1) \parallel ab?d.1 \parallel ac?d.co!d.1).$$

Exercises

7.3.1 Assume that a complete execution sequence of a system is a sequence of actions that can be performed by the system and that leads to successful termination. Provide three complete execution sequences of the example system discussed in this section when it is not assumed that any form of communication is enforced. Provide a complete execution sequence when assuming that communication over the internal ports *ab* and *ac* is enforced.

7.3.2 Provide a recursive specification for a stack with input port i and output port o using the actions of Definition 7.3.1 (Standard communication).

7.4 The process theory BCP

Coming up with a set of axioms that fully captures the intuition of communicating parallel processes given in the previous sections is no easy matter. In fact, Moller proved in (Moller, 1989) that no finite direct axiomatization exists. This means that there is no finite ground-complete axiomatization in the signature of the basic theory BSP(A) of Section 4.4 extended with the merge operator only of the standard term model based on bisimilarity obtained from the deduction rules of Section 7.2. In order to give a finite axiomatization nonetheless, an artifice is needed in the form of auxiliary operators.

First, consider the four deduction rules given in Section 7.2. The first rule says that $x \parallel y$ can start by executing a step from x, and the second rule says that $x \parallel y$ can start by executing a step from y. The last two rules concern joint activity. Either x and y execute an interaction, or they join in termination.

Thus, it can be seen that parallel composition is broken up into three alternatives, namely the part where the first step comes from x, the part where the first step comes from y, and the part where x and y execute together. Two new operators are introduced in order to express these options: $x \mathbin{⌊\!⌊} y$ denotes the parallel composition of x and y with the restriction that the first step comes from x; $x \mid y$ denotes the parallel composition of x and y starting with a joint activity. Using this so-called *left-merge* operator $⌊\!⌊$ and *communication-merge* operator $\mid$, the alternatives of parallel composition can be presented as follows. It is assumed that $⌊\!⌊$ and $\mid$ have the same binding priority as $\parallel$, i.e., they bind stronger than choice and weaker than action prefix.

$$x \parallel y = x \mathbin{⌊\!⌊} y + y \mathbin{⌊\!⌊} x + x \mid y.$$

Implicitly, it is assumed here that the operators $\parallel$ and $\mid$ will be commutative, so that the order in which the components are presented is not relevant. Using the above equality, the problem of axiomatizing the $\parallel$ operator is replaced by the problem of axiomatizing the $⌊\!⌊$ and $\mid$ operators. Surprisingly, the latter problem is relatively straightforward.

First, the left-merge operator is considered. A case analysis following the structure of the left-hand argument provides the desired axioms. Let x, y, z be processes, and $a \in A$ an action.

First of all, the case of the prefix operators is not difficult:

$$a.x \mathbin{⌊\!⌊} y = a.(x \parallel y).$$

In words, in a parallel composition of processes $a.x$ and y where the first step is from $a.x$, this first step must be an a. What remains is the parallel composition of x and y (without restriction).

Second, alternative composition is also straightforward.

$$(x + y) \mathbin{⌊\!⌊} z = x \mathbin{⌊\!⌊} z + y \mathbin{⌊\!⌊} z.$$

It is crucial to notice that the moment of choice on both sides is the same: the choice is made by the execution of the first action. This is in contrast to the situation with the $\parallel$ operator where $(x + y) \parallel z$ is not equal to $x \parallel z + y \parallel z$, as the first step might be a step from z which means that the choice in the left argument of $(x + y) \parallel z$ is not decided whereas the choice in $x \parallel z + y \parallel z$ is decided.

Finally, what remains is the behavior of the left merge with respect to the termination constants 0 and 1. The termination behavior of a parallel composition is coded into the communication-merge operator, because termination and communication both require some form of synchronization, which means they fit naturally together. Therefore, termination behavior is of no concern for the left merge. The following axioms follow the intuition that a (successfully or unsuccessfully) terminated process cannot perform a step, which implies that these constants as the left operand of a left merge lead to inaction.

$$0 \mathbin{\|\!\!\lfloor} x = 0 \quad \text{and} \quad 1 \mathbin{\|\!\!\lfloor} x = 0.$$

Next, the communication-merge operator is considered. A case analysis following the structure of the two arguments of the communication merge yields the axioms. Let x, y, z be processes, and $a, b, c \in A$ actions.

As the communication merge involves activity from both sides, it distributes over choice:

$$(x + y) \mid z = x \mid z + y \mid z \quad \text{and} \quad x \mid (y + z) = x \mid y + x \mid z.$$

Obviously, an inaction constant 0 on one side of a communication merge allows no joint activity whatsoever:

$$0 \mid x = 0 \quad \text{and} \quad x \mid 0 = 0.$$

What remains are the cases where both sides are action-prefix terms or empty processes 1. Successful termination, i.e., both sides of the communication merge are 1, is simple:

$$1 \mid 1 = 1.$$

If both sides are action prefixes, the result is based on the communication function γ. If γ is defined for the involved actions, then the communicating process can actually perform the defined communication action, and then proceed as an unconstrained parallel composition of the remaining behaviors of both operands of the communication merge; if γ is undefined, the communicating process cannot perform any action at all.

$$\begin{array}{ll} a.x \mid b.y = c.(x \parallel y) & \text{if } \gamma(a, b) = c \\ a.x \mid b.y = 0 & \text{if } \gamma(a, b) \text{ is not defined.} \end{array}$$

Finally, communication-merge expressions combining an action prefix and an empty process lead to inaction, because both a joint action and synchronized successful termination are impossible:

$$a.x \mid 1 = 0 \quad \text{and} \quad 1 \mid a.x = 0.$$

Note that the axiom system presented below contains an axiom stipulating the commutativity of the communication merge. This allows to save on the number of axioms required for the communication-merge operator. From the three cases with symmetric axioms discussed above, only one axiom for each case is needed. Assuming commutativity of the communication merge does not influence the equalities that can be derived for closed terms in the theory presented below. However, it does allow the derivation of equalities between open terms that cannot be derived from the theory without this axiom (and containing all six axioms for the above three symmetric cases).

The formal definition of process theory BCP, the theory of Basic Communicating Processes, is given in Table 7.1. It extends theory $(\mathrm{BSP} + \mathrm{DH})(A)$ of Table 6.8. The theory thus includes the encapsulation operator because this operator is essential in describing communication between processes, as illustrated by the example in Section 7.3. As before, the theory has as a parameter the set of actions A. Besides this, it has as a second parameter a communication function $\gamma : A \times A \to A$ satisfying the conditions of Definition 7.2.1 (Communication function). The signature of process theory $\mathrm{BCP}(A, \gamma)$ extends the signature of the process theory $(\mathrm{BSP} + \mathrm{DH})(A)$ with the merge operator $\parallel$, the left-merge operator $⫦$ and the communication-merge operator $\mid$. The three new operators bind stronger than choice but weaker than action prefix. The axioms of $\mathrm{BCP}(A, \gamma)$ are the axioms in Table 7.1 added to the axioms of theory $(\mathrm{BSP} + \mathrm{DH})(A)$ of Table 6.8. Note that Axioms LM3 and CM4–6 are actually *axiom schemes*: there is such an axiom for each combination of atomic actions $a, b, c \in A$ occurring in them.

$\mathrm{BCP}(A, \gamma)$			
$(\mathrm{BSP} + \mathrm{DH})(A)$;			
binary: $\_ \parallel \_,\ \_ ⫦ \_,\ \_ \mid \_$;			
x, y, z;			
$x \parallel y = x ⫦ y + y ⫦ x + x \mid y$	M	$x \mid y = y \mid x$	SC1
$0 ⫦ x = 0$	LM1		
$1 ⫦ x = 0$	LM2	$x \parallel 1 = x$	SC2
$a.x ⫦ y = a.(x \parallel y)$	LM3	$1 \mid x + 1 = 1$	SC3
$(x + y) ⫦ z = x ⫦ z + y ⫦ z$	LM4		
$0 \mid x = 0$	CM1	$(x \parallel y) \parallel z = x \parallel (y \parallel z)$	SC4
$(x + y) \mid z = x \mid z + y \mid z$	CM2	$(x \mid y) \mid z = x \mid (y \mid z)$	SC5
$1 \mid 1 = 1$	CM3	$(x ⫦ y) ⫦ z = x ⫦ (y \parallel z)$	SC6
$a.x \mid 1 = 0$	CM4	$(x \mid y) ⫦ z = x \mid (y ⫦ z)$	SC7
$a.x \mid b.y = c.(x \parallel y)$ if $\gamma(a, b) = c$	CM5		
$a.x \mid b.y = 0$ if $\gamma(a, b)$ is not defined	CM6		

Table 7.1. The process theory $\mathrm{BCP}(A, \gamma)$ (with $a, b, c \in A$).

Axioms M, LM1–4, and CM1–6 of $\mathrm{BCP}(A, \gamma)$ have been discussed above. They serve to rewrite each closed term involving parallel composition operators into a closed $\mathrm{BSP}(A)$-term (see the elimination theorem below). Besides these axioms, the theory $\mathrm{BCP}(A, \gamma)$ contains seven additional axioms denoting properties of parallel composition, the so-called *Axioms of Standard Concurrency*. These properties are often convenient.

The commutativity and associativity of the merge operator, and the fact that

1 is an identity element, are the most important properties. Commutativity of the merge follows from SC1 and the commutativity of the choice operator (see Exercise 7.4.3). Associativity is posed as Axiom SC4. The fact that 1 is an identity element is stated by SC2. SC3 captures the fact that a communication with the empty process either results in inaction or successful termination and that no actions are possible, see Proposition 7.4.2 (Communication with the empty process) below. This axiom illustrates that the communication merge is used to capture the termination options of a parallel composition. The other axioms of standard concurrency are variants of SC4 involving the left-merge and communication-merge operators.

Example 7.4.1 (Communication) Consider a relay race with two runners, Alice and Bob. First, Alice runs some distance, then she passes the baton to Bob. Bob first takes the baton, and next runs some more. The processes executed can be given via closed BCP(A, γ)-terms as follows:

$$A = \mathit{runA}.\mathit{give}.1 \quad \text{and} \quad B = \mathit{take}.\mathit{runB}.1.$$

The only defined communication is $\gamma(\mathit{give}, \mathit{take}) = \mathit{pass}$ (and its commutative variant, of course). Applying the axioms of BCP(A, γ) gives the following result:

$$\begin{aligned}
&\mathrm{BCP}(A,\gamma)\vdash \\
&\quad A \parallel B = \mathit{runA}.(\mathit{give}.\mathit{take}.\mathit{runB}.1 + \mathit{pass}.\mathit{runB}.1 \\
&\qquad\qquad\qquad + \mathit{take}.(\mathit{give}.\mathit{runB}.1 + \mathit{runB}.\mathit{give}.1) \\
&\qquad\qquad\quad) + \\
&\qquad\qquad \mathit{take}.\ (\mathit{runB}.\mathit{runA}.\mathit{give}.1 \\
&\qquad\qquad\qquad + \mathit{runA}.(\mathit{give}.\mathit{runB}.1 + \mathit{runB}.\mathit{give}.1) \\
&\qquad\qquad\quad).
\end{aligned}$$

Obviously, many unwanted action sequences occur in this term, where 'halves' of communication actions occur by themselves. Communication can be enforced by the encapsulation operator, as already illustrated in Section 7.3. Defining $H = \{\mathit{give}, \mathit{take}\}$, it can be shown that

$$\mathrm{BCP}(A,\gamma) \vdash \partial_H(A \parallel B) = \mathit{runA}.\mathit{pass}.\mathit{runB}.1.$$

Thus, by blocking the separate components of communication actions, only the successful communications remain. This use of the encapsulation operator in fact explains its name: the operator prevents actions within its scope to communicate with actions outside.

Axiom SC3 of BCP(A, γ) may need some clarification. Recall the notion of summands introduced in Exercise 4.2.3. The following can be derived, for any process term x: $\mathrm{BCP}(A,\gamma) \vdash x = x \parallel 1 = x \mathbin{⌊\!⌊} 1 + 1 \mathbin{⌊\!⌊} x + x \mid 1 = x \mathbin{⌊\!⌊} 1 +$

$1 \mid x$. In other words, any process x breaks down into two parts, namely $x \mathbin{\|\!\lfloor} 1$, being all of x except a possibly occurring 1 summand (see Axioms LM1–4, in particular LM2), and $1 \mid x$, capturing this possibly occurring 1 summand. As a consequence, $1 \mid x$ is either equal to 1 (if x has a 1 summand) or 0 (otherwise). This is what Axiom SC3 expresses: $1 \mid x$ is a summand of 1, so it is either 1 or 0. Formally, the following can be derived.

Proposition 7.4.2 (Communication with the empty process) For any term x, if $\mathrm{BCP}(A, \gamma) \vdash x = x + 1$, then $\mathrm{BCP}(A, \gamma) \vdash 1 \mid x = 1$; if $\mathrm{BCP}(A, \gamma) \vdash x = x \mathbin{\|\!\lfloor} 1$, then $\mathrm{BCP}(A, \gamma) \vdash 1 \mid x = 0$.

Proof The two properties can be proven via straightforward equational reasoning, see Exercise 7.4.5. □

Thus, when a process contains a 1 summand, it can be derived from the axioms of $\mathrm{BCP}(A, \gamma)$ that $\mathrm{BCP}(A, \gamma) \vdash 1 \mid x = 1$. However, the general result that $1 \mid x$ is equal to 0 if x does not have a 1 summand cannot be derived from the axioms of $\mathrm{BCP}(A, \gamma)$ for general open $\mathrm{BCP}(A, \gamma)$-terms. It is only possible to derive the above conditional property (the second property in Proposition 7.4.2) and an instance of it for guarded terms (see Proposition 7.6.3, in Section 7.6 which covers recursion).

The next theorem shows that the newly introduced operators can be eliminated from closed $\mathrm{BCP}(A, \gamma)$-terms. This means that the introduction of parallel composition does not increase expressiveness; the same set of processes can be specified as in the theory $\mathrm{BSP}(A)$, but in more different, often more intuitive and more compact, ways. In fact, the number of symbols in a term can increase exponentially when rewriting a $\mathrm{BCP}(A, \gamma)$-term to an equivalent $\mathrm{BSP}(A)$-term, see Exercise 7.4.11.

Theorem 7.4.3 (Elimination) For any closed $\mathrm{BCP}(A, \gamma)$-term p, there exists a closed $\mathrm{BSP}(A)$-term q such that $\mathrm{BCP}(A, \gamma) \vdash p = q$.

Proof Axioms M, LM1–4, and CM1–6 in Table 7.1 can be ordered from left to right as a term rewriting system. It is necessary to add rewrite rules corresponding to CM1, CM2, and CM4 where the arguments of the communication merge are swapped. This is harmless due to Axiom SC1. Furthermore, rewrite rules corresponding to the axioms of encapsulation (see Table 6.8) need to be added. Then, this proof follows the same pattern as earlier proofs of elimination theorems. Details are left for Exercise 7.4.6. □

The Axioms of Standard Concurrency SC1 through SC7 of $\mathrm{BCP}(A, \gamma)$ are basic axioms of the theory of parallel processes, and they cannot be derived from the other axioms. However, except for SC1, they can be derived for all closed terms. (If the counterparts of CM1, CM2, and CM4 are added to the theory as in the proof of Theorem 7.4.3, then also SC1 can be derived for closed terms.)

Theorem 7.4.4 (Standard concurrency) For closed BCP(A, γ)-terms, the Axioms of Standard Concurrency SC2–7 are derivable from the other axioms of BCP(A, γ).

Proof The property for Axiom SC2 is proven by structural induction. In view of Theorem 7.4.3 (Elimination), assume that p is a closed BSP(A)-term.

(i) Assume $p \equiv 0$. Consequently, BCP$(A, \gamma) \vdash p \parallel 1 = 0 \mathbin{⌊\!⌊} 1 + 1 \mathbin{⌊\!⌊} 0 + 0 \mid 1 = 0 + 0 + 0 = 0 = p$.
(ii) Assume $p \equiv 1$. BCP$(A, \gamma) \vdash p \parallel 1 = 1 \mathbin{⌊\!⌊} 1 + 1 \mathbin{⌊\!⌊} 1 + 1 \mid 1 = 0 + 0 + 1 = 1 = p$.
(iii) Assume $p \equiv a.q$, for some $a \in A$ and closed BSP(A)-term q. It follows that BCP$(A, \gamma) \vdash p \parallel 1 = a.q \mathbin{⌊\!⌊} 1 + 1 \mathbin{⌊\!⌊} a.q + a.q \mid 1 = a.(q \parallel 1) + 0 + 0 = a.q = p$.
(iv) Assume $p \equiv p_1 + p_2$, for some closed BSP(A)-terms p_1 and p_2. Then, BCP$(A, \gamma) \vdash p \parallel 1 = p \mathbin{⌊\!⌊} 1 + 1 \mathbin{⌊\!⌊} p + p \mid 1 = p_1 \mathbin{⌊\!⌊} 1 + p_2 \mathbin{⌊\!⌊} 1 + 0 + p_1 \mid 1 + p_2 \mid 1 = p_1 \mathbin{⌊\!⌊} 1 + p_2 \mathbin{⌊\!⌊} 1 + 1 \mathbin{⌊\!⌊} p_1 + 1 \mathbin{⌊\!⌊} p_2 + p_1 \mid 1 + p_2 \mid 1 = p_1 \parallel 1 + p_2 \parallel 1 = p_1 + p_2 = p$.

The proof for Axiom SC3 is equally straightforward. Assume again that p is a closed BSP(A)-term.

(i) Assume $p \equiv 0$. Consequently, BCP$(A, \gamma) \vdash 1 \mid p + 1 = 1 \mid 0 + 1 = 0 \mid 1 + 1 = 0 + 1 = 1$.
(ii) Assume $p \equiv 1$. BCP$(A, \gamma) \vdash 1 \mid p + 1 = 1 \mid 1 + 1 = 1 + 1 = 1$.
(iii) Assume $p \equiv a.q$, for some action $a \in A$ and closed BSP(A)-term q. BCP$(A, \gamma) \vdash 1 \mid p + 1 = 1 \mid a.q + 1 = a.q \mid 1 + 1 = 0 + 1 = 1$.
(iv) Assume $p \equiv p_1 + p_2$, for some closed BSP(A)-terms p_1 and p_2. It then follows that BCP$(A, \gamma) \vdash 1 \mid p + 1 = 1 \mid (p_1 + p_2) + 1 = 1 \mid p_1 + 1 \mid p_2 + 1 = 1 \mid p_1 + 1 + 1 \mid p_2 + 1 = 1 + 1 = 1$.

For the other four axioms, the theorem is proved simultaneously by natural induction on the total number of symbols in closed BCP(A, γ)-terms p, q, and r. Assume that this number of symbols is k. Based on Theorem 7.4.3 (Elimination), assume again that p, q, and r are BSP(A)-terms.
The base case of the proof, where the number of symbols is three, and thus

all three terms are 1 or 0, is left to the reader. In the induction step, it can be assumed that all four equalities hold for all triples of closed terms containing in total fewer than k symbols, for some natural number k. As p is a closed BSP(A)-term, it follows from Proposition 5.5.25 (HNF property) that it may be assumed that p can be written as follows:

$$p \equiv \sum_{i<n} a_i . p_i \ (+1),$$

for a certain natural number $n \geq 0$, atomic actions a_i and closed terms p_i with fewer symbols than p, and a 1 summand which may or may not be present. For Axiom SC6, consider the following derivation, using induction (with respect to Axiom SC4) in the fifth step:

$$\begin{aligned}
\mathrm{BCP}(A,\gamma) \vdash (p \mathbin{\lfloor\!\lfloor} q) \mathbin{\lfloor\!\lfloor} r &= \left(\left(\sum_{i<n} a_i . p_i \ (+1)\right) \mathbin{\lfloor\!\lfloor} q\right) \mathbin{\lfloor\!\lfloor} r \\
&= \left(\sum_{i<n} a_i . p_i \mathbin{\lfloor\!\lfloor} q \ (+1 \mathbin{\lfloor\!\lfloor} q)\right) \mathbin{\lfloor\!\lfloor} r \\
&= \sum_{i<n} a_i . (p_i \parallel q) \mathbin{\lfloor\!\lfloor} r \\
&= \sum_{i<n} a_i . ((p_i \parallel q) \parallel r) \\
&= \sum_{i<n} a_i . (p_i \parallel (q \parallel r)) \\
&= \sum_{i<n} a_i . p_i \mathbin{\lfloor\!\lfloor} (q \parallel r) \\
&= \sum_{i<n} a_i . p_i \mathbin{\lfloor\!\lfloor} (q \parallel r)(+1 \mathbin{\lfloor\!\lfloor} (q \parallel r)) \\
&= (\sum_{i<n} a_i . p_i (+1)) \mathbin{\lfloor\!\lfloor} (q \parallel r) \\
&= p \mathbin{\lfloor\!\lfloor} (q \parallel r).
\end{aligned}$$

For Axiom SC7, besides p also q is written in sum notation:

$$q \equiv \sum_{j<m} b_j . q_j \ (+1),$$

for natural number $m \geq 0$, actions $b_j \in A$, and simpler closed terms q_j. The following derivation uses the induction hypothesis in the sixth step. Note that a communication merge has only a termination option (a 1 summand) if both its arguments have a termination option. Therefore, in the one-but-last step of the derivation, the optional 1 summands can be added because the resulting right argument of the communication-merge operator does not have a termination option due to the occurrence of the left-merge operator.

$$\begin{aligned}
&\mathrm{BCP}(A,\gamma) \vdash (p \mid q) \mathbin{\lfloor\!\lfloor} r \\
&\qquad = \left((\sum_{i<n} a_i . p_i \ (+1)) \mid (\sum_{j<m} b_j . q_j \ (+1)) \right) \mathbin{\lfloor\!\lfloor} r
\end{aligned}$$

$$= \left(\sum_{i<n} \sum_{j<m} a_i.p_i \mid b_j.q_j \right) \mathbin{\|\!\!\lfloor} r \ (+1 \mathbin{\|\!\!\lfloor} r)$$
$$= \left(\sum_{i,\,j \text{ with } \gamma(a_i,\,b_j) \text{ defined}} \gamma(a_i, b_j).(p_i \parallel q_j) \right) \mathbin{\|\!\!\lfloor} r$$
$$= \sum_{i,\,j \text{ with } \gamma(a_i,\,b_j) \text{ defined}} \gamma(a_i, b_j).(p_i \parallel q_j) \mathbin{\|\!\!\lfloor} r$$
$$= \sum_{i,\,j \text{ with } \gamma(a_i,\,b_j) \text{ defined}} \gamma(a_i, b_j).((p_i \parallel q_j) \parallel r)$$
$$= \sum_{i,\,j \text{ with } \gamma(a_i,\,b_j) \text{ defined}} \gamma(a_i, b_j).(p_i \parallel (q_j \parallel r))$$
$$= (\sum_{i<n} a_i.p_i) \mid (\sum_{j<m} b_j.(q_j \parallel r))$$
$$= (\sum_{i<n} a_i.p_i) \mid (\sum_{j<m} b_j.q_j \mathbin{\|\!\!\lfloor} r)$$
$$= (\sum_{i<n} a_i.p_i (+1)) \mid (\sum_{j<m} (b_j.q_j (+1)) \mathbin{\|\!\!\lfloor} r)$$
$$= p \mid (q \mathbin{\|\!\!\lfloor} r).$$

For Axiom SC5, all three terms are written in sum notation, so in addition to the earlier assumptions,

$$r \equiv \sum_{k<l} c_k.r_k \ (+1),$$

for natural number $l \geq 0$, $c_k \in A$, and simpler closed terms r_k. Notice that terms of the form $(p \mid q) \mid r$ and $p \mid (q \mid r)$ only contain a 1 summand if all three of p, q, and r contain a 1 summand. The following derivation uses in the fourth step the induction hypothesis and the associativity of the communication function.

$$\text{BCP}(A, \gamma) \vdash (p \mid q) \mid r$$
$$= \left(\sum_{i<n} a_i.p_i \ (+1) \mid \sum_{j<m} b_j.q_j \ (+1) \right) \mid r$$
$$= \left(\sum_{i,\,j \text{ with } \gamma(a_i,\,b_j) \text{ defined}} \gamma(a_i, b_j).(p_i \parallel q_j) \ (+1) \right) \mid r$$
$$= \sum_{i,\,j,\,k \text{ with } \gamma(a_i,\,b_j,\,c_k) \text{ defined}} \gamma(\gamma(a_i, b_j), c_k).((p_i \parallel q_j) \parallel r_k) \ (+1)$$
$$= \sum_{i,\,j,\,k \text{ with } \gamma(a_i,\,b_j,\,c_k) \text{ defined}} \gamma(a_i, \gamma(b_j, c_k)).(p_i \parallel (q_j \parallel r_k)) \ (+1)$$
$$= (\sum_{i<n} a_i.p_i (+1)) \mid \left(\sum_{j,\,k \text{ with } \gamma(b_j,\,c_k) \text{ defined}} \gamma(b_j, c_k).(q_j \parallel r_k) \ (+1) \right)$$
$$= p \mid (q \mid r).$$

Thus, SC5–7 are proved for all triples of closed terms with total number of symbols k. This fact is now used in the following derivation, proving the theorem for SC4 for all triples of closed terms with total number of symbols k:

$$
\begin{aligned}
\mathrm{BCP}(A,\gamma) \vdash{}& (p \parallel q) \parallel r \\
&= (p \parallel q) \mathbin{\|\!\lfloor} r + r \mathbin{\|\!\lfloor} (p \parallel q) + (p \parallel q) \mid r \\
&= (p \mathbin{\|\!\lfloor} q + q \mathbin{\|\!\lfloor} p + p \mid q) \mathbin{\|\!\lfloor} r + r \mathbin{\|\!\lfloor} (p \parallel q) + r \mid (p \parallel q) \\
&= (p \mathbin{\|\!\lfloor} q) \mathbin{\|\!\lfloor} r + (q \mathbin{\|\!\lfloor} p) \mathbin{\|\!\lfloor} r + (p \mid q) \mathbin{\|\!\lfloor} r + r \mathbin{\|\!\lfloor} (p \parallel q) \\
&\qquad + r \mid (p \mathbin{\|\!\lfloor} q) + r \mid (q \mathbin{\|\!\lfloor} p) + r \mid (p \mid q) \\
&= p \mathbin{\|\!\lfloor} (q \parallel r) + q \mathbin{\|\!\lfloor} (p \parallel r) + p \mid (q \mathbin{\|\!\lfloor} r) + r \mathbin{\|\!\lfloor} (q \parallel p) \\
&\qquad + (r \mid p) \mathbin{\|\!\lfloor} q + (r \mid q) \mathbin{\|\!\lfloor} p + (p \mid q) \mid r \\
&= p \mathbin{\|\!\lfloor} (q \parallel r) + q \mathbin{\|\!\lfloor} (r \parallel p) + p \mid (q \mathbin{\|\!\lfloor} r) + (r \mathbin{\|\!\lfloor} q) \mathbin{\|\!\lfloor} p \\
&\qquad + (p \mid r) \mathbin{\|\!\lfloor} q + (q \mid r) \mathbin{\|\!\lfloor} p + p \mid (q \mid r) \\
&= p \mathbin{\|\!\lfloor} (q \parallel r) + (q \mathbin{\|\!\lfloor} r) \mathbin{\|\!\lfloor} p + p \mid (q \mathbin{\|\!\lfloor} r) + (r \mathbin{\|\!\lfloor} q) \mathbin{\|\!\lfloor} p \\
&\qquad + p \mid (r \mathbin{\|\!\lfloor} q) + (q \mid r) \mathbin{\|\!\lfloor} p + p \mid (q \mid r) \\
&= p \mathbin{\|\!\lfloor} (q \parallel r) + (q \parallel r) \mathbin{\|\!\lfloor} p + p \mid (q \parallel r) \\
&= p \parallel (q \parallel r).
\end{aligned}
$$

Induction then proves the theorem for SC4–7 for all closed $\mathrm{BCP}(A,\gamma)$-terms. □

Because of Axiom SC4, it is not necessary to write parentheses in expressions like $x \parallel y \parallel z$. Therefore, a notation for generalized parallel composition is introduced, similar to Notation 5.5.19 (Generalized choice). Considering Axiom SC2, the parallel composition of an empty set of process terms results in the empty process.

Notation 7.4.5 (Generalized merge) Let $I \subset \mathbf{N}$ be some finite index set of natural numbers, $j \in \mathbf{N} \setminus I$ a fresh index not in I, and t_i, for all $i \in I \cup \{j\}$, arbitrary terms in some process theory containing the merge operator $\parallel$.

$$\mathop{\parallel}_{i \in \emptyset} t_i \equiv 1 \text{ and } \mathop{\parallel}_{i \in I \cup \{j\}} t_i \equiv t_j \parallel \mathop{\parallel}_{i \in I} t_i.$$

Similarly, based on Axiom SC5, a generalized notation for the communication merge can be introduced, where it is important to observe that the communication merge does not have an identity element (which implies that the notation cannot be defined for an empty index set).

Notation 7.4.6 (Generalized communication merge) Let $I \subset \mathbf{N}$ be some finite, non-empty index set of natural numbers, $j \in \mathbf{N} \setminus I$ a fresh index not in I, and t_i, for all $i \in I \cup \{j\}$, arbitrary terms in some process theory containing the communication merge operator $\mid$.

$$\mathop{\mid}_{i \in \{j\}} t_i \equiv t_j \text{ and } \mathop{\mid}_{i \in I \cup \{j\}} t_i \equiv t_j \mid \mathop{\mid}_{i \in I} t_i.$$

Using these notations, the following expansion theorem can be formulated.

This theorem is the main tool in breaking down the parallel composition of a number of processes, and it is often used in the remainder.

Theorem 7.4.7 (Expansion theorem) Let $I \subset \mathbf{N}$ be some finite, non-empty index set of natural numbers, and t_i, for all $i \in I$, arbitrary BCP(A, γ)-terms.

$$\mathrm{BCP}(A,\gamma) \vdash \mathop{\|}\limits_{i \in I} t_i = \sum_{\emptyset \neq J \subset I} \Big(\mathop{|}\limits_{j \in J} t_j\Big) \mathbin{\lfloor\!\lfloor} \Big(\mathop{\|}\limits_{i \in I \setminus J} t_i\Big) + \mathop{|}\limits_{i \in I} t_i .$$

Proof The proof is by induction on the cardinality of index set I. In the base case where the cardinality is 1, say the index set is singleton $\{0\}$, the theorem reduces to a trivial equality: $\mathrm{BCP}(A, \gamma) \vdash t_0 \parallel 1 = t_0 = 0 + t_0$. For the induction step, assume that the theorem is proven for all index sets of cardinality k, with $k \geq 1$, and assume that index set I of cardinality $k + 1$ is equal to $K \cup \{k\}$ with $K = \{0, 1, \ldots, k - 1\}$. The following derivation inductively applies the expansion theorem in the third step. The first four summands in the expression after the fourth step correspond to the cases where the set of indices (1) is a non-empty, strict subset of K, (2) equals K, (3) equals singleton $\{k\}$, and (4) contains index k and some non-empty, strict subset of K. Together, these four cases cover all non-empty, strict subsets of $I (= K \cup \{k\})$. These observations clarify the last two steps of the derivation.

$$
\begin{aligned}
&\mathrm{BCP}(A,\gamma) \vdash \\
&\quad \mathop{\|}\limits_{i \in I} t_i = \Big(\mathop{\|}\limits_{i \in K} t_i\Big) \parallel t_k \\
&\qquad = \Big(\mathop{\|}\limits_{i \in K} t_i\Big) \mathbin{\lfloor\!\lfloor} t_k + t_k \mathbin{\lfloor\!\lfloor} \Big(\mathop{\|}\limits_{i \in K} t_i\Big) + \Big(\mathop{\|}\limits_{i \in K} t_i\Big) \mid t_k \\
&\qquad = \left(\sum_{\emptyset \neq J \subset K} \Big(\mathop{|}\limits_{j \in J} t_j\Big) \mathbin{\lfloor\!\lfloor} \Big(\mathop{\|}\limits_{i \in K \setminus J} t_i\Big) + \mathop{|}\limits_{i \in K} t_i \right) \mathbin{\lfloor\!\lfloor} t_k \\
&\qquad\quad + t_k \mathbin{\lfloor\!\lfloor} \Big(\mathop{\|}\limits_{i \in K} t_i\Big) \\
&\qquad\quad + \left(\sum_{\emptyset \neq J \subset K} \Big(\mathop{|}\limits_{j \in J} t_j\Big) \mathbin{\lfloor\!\lfloor} \Big(\mathop{\|}\limits_{i \in K \setminus J} t_i\Big) + \mathop{|}\limits_{i \in K} t_i \right) \mid t_k \\
&\qquad = \sum_{\emptyset \neq J \subset K} \Big(\mathop{|}\limits_{j \in J} t_j\Big) \mathbin{\lfloor\!\lfloor} \Big(\Big(\mathop{\|}\limits_{i \in K \setminus J} t_i\Big) \parallel t_k\Big) \\
&\qquad\quad + \Big(\mathop{|}\limits_{i \in K} t_i\Big) \mathbin{\lfloor\!\lfloor} t_k \\
&\qquad\quad + t_k \mathbin{\lfloor\!\lfloor} \Big(\mathop{\|}\limits_{i \in K} t_i\Big) \\
&\qquad\quad + \sum_{\emptyset \neq J \subset K} \Big(\Big(\mathop{|}\limits_{j \in J} t_j\Big) \mid t_k\Big) \mathbin{\lfloor\!\lfloor} \Big(\mathop{\|}\limits_{i \in K \setminus J} t_i\Big) \\
&\qquad\quad + \Big(\mathop{|}\limits_{i \in K} t_i\Big) \mid t_k
\end{aligned}
$$

$$
\begin{aligned}
&= \sum_{\emptyset \neq J \subset K} (\mid_{j \in J} t_j) \mathbin{⌊\!⌊} (\|_{i \in I \setminus J} t_i) \\
&\quad + \sum_{J = K} (\mid_{j \in J} t_j) \mathbin{⌊\!⌊} (\|_{i \in I \setminus J} t_i) \\
&\quad + \sum_{J = \{k\}} (\mid_{j \in J} t_j) \mathbin{⌊\!⌊} (\|_{i \in I \setminus J} t_i) \\
&\quad + \sum_{\{k\} \subset J \subset I} (\mid_{j \in J} t_j) \mathbin{⌊\!⌊} (\|_{i \in I \setminus J} t_i) \\
&\quad + \mid_{i \in I} t_i \\
&= \sum_{\emptyset \neq J \subset I} (\mid_{j \in J} t_j) \mathbin{⌊\!⌊} (\|_{i \in I \setminus J} t_i) + \mid_{i \in I} t_i .
\end{aligned}
$$

The desired result now follows by induction. □

The expansion theorem is an important means to rewrite a parallel composition into sequential behaviors. Therefore, it is important to understand what it says. In the proof of the theorem, it was already noted that for an index set of size one, it is a trivial statement. For an index set of cardinality two, the expansion theorem reduces exactly to Axiom M of theory BCP(A, γ). For an index set of size three, it can be written out as follows:

$$
\begin{aligned}
&\text{BCP}(A, \gamma) \vdash \\
&\quad x \parallel y \parallel z = x \mathbin{⌊\!⌊} (y \parallel z) + y \mathbin{⌊\!⌊} (x \parallel z) + z \mathbin{⌊\!⌊} (y \parallel z) \\
&\qquad\qquad + (x \mid y) \mathbin{⌊\!⌊} z + (x \mid z) \mathbin{⌊\!⌊} y + (y \mid z) \mathbin{⌊\!⌊} x \\
&\qquad\qquad + x \mid y \mid z .
\end{aligned}
$$

In words, in a parallel composition of three processes, the first step is a step from one of the three processes (the first three summands of the right-hand term) or a communication step between two of the three processes (the next three summands) or a synchronization between all processes (the last summand).

The remainder of this section briefly considers two special cases of parallel processes, the case when communication is absent and the case when only handshaking communication (see Definition 7.2.2 (Handshaking communication)) is allowed. These special cases lead to additional axioms in the equational theory to capture the appropriate restrictions on communication, and to specialized versions of the expansion theorem.

First, consider the case without interaction between processes. This can be captured by assuming that the communication function is nowhere defined, i.e., $\gamma = \emptyset$. Parallel composition without interaction between processes is often called a *free merge*. In this case, Axiom SC3 of theory BCP(A, γ) can be strengthened to the *Free-Merge Axiom*, given in Table 7.2. The axiom states that the synchronization of two processes either results in inaction (0) or in successful termination (1). Thus, communication actions are indeed no longer possible. The role of the communication merge in the resulting equational theory reduces to capturing the termination options of parallel processes.

(BCP + FMA)$(A, \emptyset)$	
BCP$(A, \emptyset)$;	
-	
x, y;	
$x \mid y + 1 = 1$	FMA

Table 7.2. Basic communicating processes with a free merge.

For closed terms, the Free-Merge Axiom is derivable from the axioms of the equational theory BCP$(A, \emptyset)$.

Proposition 7.4.8 (Free-Merge Axiom) For closed BCP$(A, \emptyset)$-terms p and q, BCP$(A, \emptyset) \vdash p \mid q + 1 = 1$.

Proof Exercise 7.4.7. □

In the presence of the Free-Merge Axiom, the expansion theorem of Theorem 7.4.7 can be simplified. All terms containing both a communication merge and a left merge can be omitted, because they result in inaction. The summand in the expansion corresponding to the communication merge of all terms in the parallel composition only denotes a possible termination option, i.e., this summand is either 1 or 0.

Theorem 7.4.9 (Expansion theorem for free merge) Let $I \subset \mathbf{N}$ be some finite, non-empty index set of natural numbers, and t_i, for all $i \in I$, arbitrary (BCP + FMA)$(A, \emptyset)$-terms.

$$(\mathrm{BCP} + \mathrm{FMA})(A, \emptyset) \vdash \mathop{\|}_{i \in I} t_i = \sum_{i \in I} t_i \mathbin{\|\!\!\lfloor} (\mathop{\|}_{j \in I \setminus \{i\}} t_j) + \mathop{|}_{i \in I} t_i .$$

Proof The desired result follows directly from the general expansion theorem, Theorem 7.4.7, by observing that Axiom FMA implies that (BCP + FMA)$(A, \emptyset) \vdash (x \mid y) \mathbin{\|\!\!\lfloor} z = 0$ for arbitrary terms x, y, and z (Exercise 7.4.8). □

The second special case that is considered is the case where there is only binary communication, called handshaking before, i.e., the communication function γ satisfies that $\gamma(a, b, c)$ is not defined, for any atomic actions a, b, c (see Definition 7.2.2 (Handshaking communication)). This case can also be formulated in terms of an extra axiom, called the *Handshaking Axiom*, given in Table 7.3. The axiom states that any communication involving three (or more) processes results either in inaction or in successful termination.

(BCP + HA)(A, γ)	
BCP(A, γ);	
-	
x, y, z;	
$x \mid y \mid z + 1 = 1$	HA

Table 7.3. Basic communicating processes with handshaking communication (with γ a handshaking communication function).

The Handshaking Axiom is derivable for all closed terms when assuming a handshaking communication function. Furthermore, the following expansion theorem is obtained.

Theorem 7.4.10 (Expansion theorem, handshaking communication) Let $I \subset \mathbf{N}$ be some finite, non-empty index set of natural numbers, and t_i, for all $i \in I$, arbitrary (BCP + HA)(A, γ)-terms.

$$\begin{aligned}(\mathrm{BCP} + \mathrm{HA})(A, \gamma) \vdash \mathop{\|}_{i \in I} t_i = \\ \sum_{i \in I} t_i \mathbin{\|\!\!\lfloor} \Big(\mathop{\|}_{j \in I \setminus \{i\}} t_j\Big) + \sum_{i, j \in I, i \neq j} (t_i \mid t_j) \mathbin{\|\!\!\lfloor} \Big(\mathop{\|}_{k \in I \setminus \{i, j\}} t_k\Big) + \mathop{|}_{i \in I} t_i .\end{aligned}$$

Proof The result follows from the expansion theorem of Theorem 7.4.7 and the observation that Axiom HA implies that (BCP + HA)$(A, \gamma) \vdash (x \mid y \mid z) \mathbin{\|\!\!\lfloor} w = 0$ for terms x, y, z, and w. □

Exercises

7.4.1 Use the axioms of BCP(A, γ) to write the following terms without parallelism and encapsulation operators (i.e., eliminate $\|$, $\|\!\!\lfloor$, $\mid$ and ∂_H). The only defined communication is $\gamma(a, b) = c$ and $H = \{a, b\}$.

(a) $a.a.1 \parallel b.b.1$;
(b) $\partial_H(a.a.1 \parallel b.b.1)$;
(c) $(a.1 + b.1) \parallel (a.1 + b.1)$;
(d) $\partial_H((a.1 + b.1) \parallel (a.1 + b.1))$;
(e) $a.a.a.1 \parallel a.a.a.1$.

7.4.2 Let $\gamma(a, b) = c$ be the only defined communication and let $H = \{a, b\}$. Show that $\partial_H(c.(a.1 + b.1) \parallel b.1)$ is deadlock free, where a closed BCP(A, γ)-term is deadlock free if and only if it is derivably equal to a closed BSP(A)-term without 0 occurrence. Show that $\partial_H((c.a.1 + c.b.1) \parallel b.1)$ does have a deadlock. This again illustrates the difference between terms like $c.a.1 + c.b.1$ and $c.(a.1 + b.1)$.

7.4.3 Prove that BCP(A, γ) $\vdash x \parallel y = y \parallel x$.

7.4.4 Prove that, for each atomic action $a \in A$ and natural numbers $m, n \in \mathbf{N}$, BCP(A, γ) $\vdash a^m 1 \parallel a^n 1 = a^{m+n} 1$, where a^k for any $k \in \mathbf{N}$ is the k-fold action prefix of Notation 4.6.6.

7.4.5 Prove Proposition 7.4.2 (Communication with the empty process).

7.4.6 Complete the proof of Theorem 7.4.3 (Elimination).

7.4.7 Prove Proposition 7.4.8 (Free-Merge Axiom).

7.4.8 Prove that the following identities follow from (BCP + FMA)($A, \emptyset$), for arbitrary terms x, y, and z:

(a) $(x \mid y) \mathbin{⌊\!⌊} z = 0$;
(b) if $x = x + 1$ and $y = y + 1$, then $x \mid y = 1$;
(c) if $x = x \mathbin{⌊\!⌊} 1$ or $y = y \mathbin{⌊\!⌊} 1$, then $x \mid y = 0$;
(d) $1 \mid x = 1 \mid x + 1 \mid x \mid y$.

7.4.9 In (BCP + FMA)($A, \emptyset$), prove the following identities for all closed terms p and q, and action a.

(a) $a.p \mid q = 0$;
(b) $1 \mid p = 1 \mid p \mid p$;
(c) $p + p \mid q = p$;
(d) $p \mid p \mid q = p \mid q$;
(e) $p + p \parallel (1 \mid q) + p \parallel 0 = p + p \parallel 0$.

7.4.10 Write out the proofs of Theorems 7.4.9 (Expansion theorem for free merge) and 7.4.10 (Expansion theorem for handshaking communication) in full detail.

7.4.11 Consider Theorem 7.4.3 (Elimination). Argue that the elimination of parallelism operators from a closed BCP(A, γ)-term may result in a BSP(A)-term with a length that is exponential in the number of symbols of the original term. Write a computer program that implements the rewriting system used in the proof of Theorem 7.4.3. Use this program to eliminate the parallelism operators from term $a^3 1 \parallel b^3 1 \parallel c^3 1$, where d^n for action d and natural number n is the n-fold action prefix of Notation 4.6.6. For simplicity, assume there is no communication (take $\gamma = \emptyset$).

7.4.12 Give an axiomatization of the theory BCP(A, $\emptyset$) without communication-merge operator, where the termination behavior is coded into the left-merge operator.

7.5 The term model

In the previous section, the process theory BCP(A, γ), with A a set of actions and γ a communication function on A, has been introduced. This section considers a model of this equational theory, using a set of operational rules as in the earlier chapters. The basis is the term algebra $\mathbb{P}(\text{BCP}(A,\gamma)) = (\mathcal{C}(\text{BCP}(A,\gamma)), +, \parallel, \lfloor\!\lfloor, \mid, (a.\_)_{a\in A}, (\partial_H)_{H\subseteq A}, 0, 1)$.

The term deduction system for BCP(A, γ) is obtained by extending the term deduction system for (BSP + DH)(A) with deduction rules for the parallelism operators merge, left merge, communication merge, and is given in Table 7.4. The rules for the parallelism operators were already informally introduced in Section 7.2. The rules for left merge and communication merge each show a different part of the behavior of the merge operator.

TDS(BCP(A, γ))

TDS((BSP + DH)(A));

binary: $\_ \parallel \_$, $\_ \lfloor\!\lfloor \_$, $\_ \mid \_$;

x, x', y, y';

$$\frac{x\downarrow \quad y\downarrow}{x \parallel y\downarrow} \qquad \frac{x\downarrow \quad y\downarrow}{x \mid y\downarrow}$$

$$\frac{x \xrightarrow{a} x'}{x \parallel y \xrightarrow{a} x' \parallel y} \qquad \frac{y \xrightarrow{a} y'}{x \parallel y \xrightarrow{a} x \parallel y'} \qquad \frac{x \xrightarrow{a} x'}{x \lfloor\!\lfloor y \xrightarrow{a} x' \parallel y}$$

$$\frac{x \xrightarrow{a} x' \quad y \xrightarrow{b} y' \quad \gamma(a,b) = c}{x \parallel y \xrightarrow{c} x' \parallel y'} \qquad \frac{x \xrightarrow{a} x' \quad y \xrightarrow{b} y' \quad \gamma(a,b) = c}{x \mid y \xrightarrow{c} x' \parallel y'}$$

Table 7.4. Term deduction system for BCP(A, γ) (with $a, b, c \in A$).

Given the equational theory and the term deduction system, the development of the model and soundness, conservativity, and completeness results goes along the same lines as earlier. Figure 7.2 visualizes the conservativity results, introducing the Minimal Theory of Communicating Processes, MTCP (see Exercise 7.5.9).

Proposition 7.5.1 (Congruence) Bisimilarity is a congruence on term algebra $\mathbb{P}(\text{BCP}(A,\gamma))$.

Proof The result follows immediately from the format of the deduction rules in Tables 4.2, 4.4, 6.10, and 7.4, and Theorem 3.2.7 (Congruence theorem). □

Definition 7.5.2 (Term model of BCP(A, γ)**)** The term model of BCP(A, γ) is the quotient algebra $\mathbb{P}(\text{BCP}(A, \gamma))_{/\leftrightarrow}$.

Theorem 7.5.3 (Soundness) Theory BCP(A, γ) is a sound axiomatization of the algebra $\mathbb{P}(\text{BCP}(A, \gamma))_{/\leftrightarrow}$, i.e., $\mathbb{P}(\text{BCP}(A, \gamma))_{/\leftrightarrow} \models \text{BCP}(A, \gamma)$.

Proof Exercise 7.5.6. □

Theorem 7.5.4 (Conservative ground-extension) Process theory BCP(A, γ) is a conservative ground-extension of process theory BSP(A).

Proof Exercise 7.5.7. □

Theorem 7.5.5 (Ground-completeness) The process theory BCP(A, γ) is a ground-complete axiomatization of the term model $\mathbb{P}(\text{BCP}(A, \gamma))_{/\leftrightarrow}$, i.e., for any two closed BCP(A, γ)-terms p and q, $\mathbb{P}(\text{BCP}(A, \gamma))_{/\leftrightarrow} \models p = q$ implies $\text{BCP}(A, \gamma) \vdash p = q$.

Proof Exercise 7.5.8. □

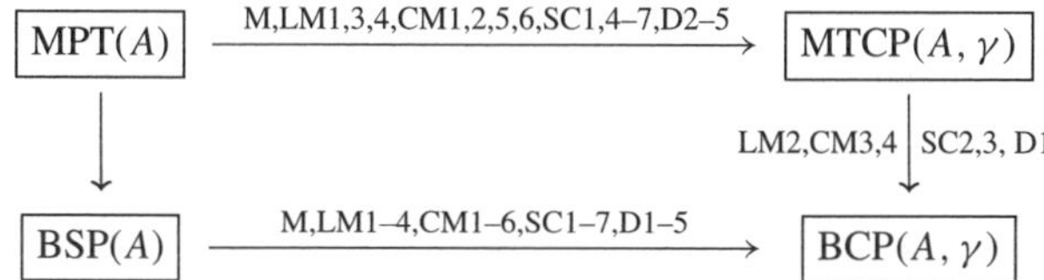

Fig. 7.2. Conservativity results for BCP(A, γ).

Exercises

7.5.1 Draw the transition system of the following BCP(A, γ)-terms, using the operational rules of Tables 4.2, 4.4, 6.10 and 7.4. Assume that $\gamma(a, b) = c$ is the only defined communication and that $H = \{a, b\}$.

(a) $a.a.1 \parallel b.b.1$;
(b) $\partial_H(a.a.1 \parallel b.b.1)$;

(c) $(a.1 + b.1) \parallel (a.1 + b.1)$;
(d) $\partial_H((a.1 + b.1) \parallel (a.1 + b.1))$;
(e) $a.a.a.1 \parallel a.a.a.1$.

7.5.2 Use the definition of bisimilarity and the operational rules of the term deduction system of BCP(A, γ) to show that $a.1 \mathbin{\|\!\_} p \leftrightarroweq a.p$, for any action $a \in A$ and closed BCP(A, γ)-term p.

7.5.3 Let x, y, and z be arbitrary process terms. Give an example to show that equation $(x+y) \parallel z = x \parallel z + y \parallel z$ is not valid in $\mathbb{P}(\text{BCP}(A, \emptyset))_{/\leftrightarroweq}$. Note that the communication function is assumed to be empty, i.e., communication is not allowed.

7.5.4 Let x and y be process terms. Give an example to show that $\partial_H(x \parallel y) = \partial_H(x) \parallel \partial_H(y)$ is not valid in $\mathbb{P}(\text{BCP}(A, \gamma))_{/\leftrightarroweq}$. Is this equation valid if $\gamma = \emptyset$?

7.5.5 Define the n-fold parallel-composition operator $\_^{\parallel n}$ in the process theory BCP$(A, \emptyset)$, with $n \in \mathbf{N}$, inductively as follows:

$$\begin{array}{lll} x^{\parallel 0} & = 1 & \text{and, for all } n \in \mathbf{N}, \\ x^{\parallel n+1} & = x^{\parallel n} \parallel x. & \end{array}$$

Prove that for any action $a \in A$, BCP$(A, \emptyset) \vdash (a.1)^{\parallel n} = a^n 1$, for all $n \in \mathbf{N}$, with a^n the n-fold action prefix of Notation 4.6.6. Show that BCP$(A, \emptyset) \nvdash (a.b.1)^{\parallel n} = a^n b^n 1$.

7.5.6 Prove Theorem 7.5.3 (Soundness of BCP(A, γ)).

7.5.7 Prove Theorem 7.5.4 (Conservative ground-extension).

7.5.8 Prove Theorem 7.5.5 (Ground-completeness of BCP(A, γ)).

7.5.9 Develop the process theory MTCP(A, γ). That is, define the equational theory, prove an elimination and a conservativity result, and give a term model proving both soundness and ground-completeness. Also, prove that theory BCP(A, γ) is a conservative ground-extension of MTCP(A, γ).

7.6 Recursion, buffers, and bags

The fact that all occurrences of the parallel-composition operators can be eliminated from each closed BCP(A, γ)-term does not imply that the addition of parallel composition is without consequences in a context with recursion. In fact, using parallel composition (even without communication), it is possible to give a finite guarded recursive specification over the signature of the theory BCP(A, γ) of a process that is not finitely definable over any of the earlier theories.

To extend BCP(A, γ) with recursion, the theory is extended with constants

$\mu X.E$ for any recursion variable X in a recursive specification E, and with axioms corresponding to the equations in all the recursive specifications of interest. The resulting theory is theory $\mathrm{BCP_{rec}}(A, \gamma)$. The term deduction system *TDS*($\mathrm{BCP_{rec}}(A, \gamma)$) is obtained by merging the term deduction systems *TDS*($\mathrm{BSP_{rec}}(A)$) of Table 5.2 and *TDS*(BCP(A, γ)) of Table 7.4. The resulting term model is $\mathbb{P}(\mathrm{BCP_{rec}}(A, \gamma))_{/\leftrightarrow}$. There are no elimination and ground-completeness results, but the extension with recursion is conservative.

Recursion principles are needed to allow for meaningful equational reasoning in a context with recursion. The development goes along the lines of Section 6.6, which discusses the extension of TSP(A) with recursion. The extension of BCP(A, γ) and $\mathrm{BCP_{rec}}(A, \gamma)$ with projection, needed for AIP and AIP^-, is straightforward. Definition 5.5.8 (Guardedness) carries over to the current context. The reasoning leading to Theorem 7.6.2 (Recursion principles) uses the following generalization of Proposition 5.5.26 (HNF property), which shows that every guarded $(\mathrm{BCP} + \mathrm{PR})_{\mathrm{rec}}(A, \gamma)$-term can be rewritten into a head normal form (see Definition 5.5.24).

Proposition 7.6.1 (HNF property) Process theory $(\mathrm{BCP} + \mathrm{PR})_{\mathrm{rec}}(A, \gamma)$ satisfies the HNF property.

Proof It needs to be shown that every guarded $(\mathrm{BCP} + \mathrm{PR})_{\mathrm{rec}}(A, \gamma)$-term can be rewritten into a head normal form. It may be assumed that this term, say s, is completely guarded. The proof is by induction on the structure of s. Compared to Proposition 5.5.26, there are four extra cases to consider:

- $s \equiv \partial_H(s')$, for some completely guarded $(\mathrm{BCP} + \mathrm{PR})_{\mathrm{rec}}(A, \gamma)$-term s' and subset of actions $H \subseteq A$;
- $s \equiv s' \mathbin{⌊\!⌊} s''$, for completely guarded $(\mathrm{BCP} + \mathrm{PR})_{\mathrm{rec}}(A, \gamma)$-terms s' and s'';
- $s \equiv s' \mid s''$, for completely guarded $(\mathrm{BCP} + \mathrm{PR})_{\mathrm{rec}}(A, \gamma)$-terms s' and s'';
- $s \equiv s' \parallel s''$, for completely guarded $(\mathrm{BCP} + \mathrm{PR})_{\mathrm{rec}}(A, \gamma)$-terms s' and s''.

These cases are not difficult. See Exercise 7.6.1. □

Theorem 7.6.2 (Recursion principles) The principles RDP, RDP^-, RSP, and AIP^- are valid in the term model $\mathbb{P}((\mathrm{BCP} + \mathrm{PR})_{\mathrm{rec}}(A, \gamma))_{/\leftrightarrow}$. Principle AIP is not valid in this model. RDP, RDP^-, and RSP are also valid in model $\mathbb{P}(\mathrm{BCP_{rec}}(A, \gamma))_{/\leftrightarrow}$.

A few results derived earlier deserve attention in a context with recursion. First, recall Proposition 7.4.2 (Communication with the empty process). It shows under what conditions a communication with the empty process results in successful or unsuccessful termination. If a process has a 1 summand, then it can be derived that the communication of that process with the empty process results in the empty process, i.e., in successful termination. It cannot in general be derived that the absence of a 1 summand in the process results in inaction. However, the second part of Proposition 7.4.2, concerning the absence of a 1 summand, holds for guarded terms.

Proposition 7.6.3 (Communication with the empty process) Assume that s is a guarded $\mathrm{BCP}_{\mathrm{rec}}(A, \gamma)$-term. If term s does not contain a 1 summand, then $\mathrm{BCP}_{\mathrm{rec}}(A, \gamma) \vdash 1 \mid s = 0$.

Proof Based on Proposition 7.6.1 (HNF property), let t be a head normal form such that $\mathrm{BCP}_{\mathrm{rec}}(A, \gamma) \vdash s = t$. It follows from Proposition 5.5.25 (Head normal forms) and the fact that s does not have a 1 summand, that there is a natural number n, and that there are, for any $i < n$, $a_i \in A$ and $\mathrm{BCP}(A, \gamma)$-terms t_i such that $\mathrm{BCP}_{\mathrm{rec}}(A, \gamma) \vdash t = \sum_{i<n} a_i.t_i$. It is now possible to prove that s satisfies the condition in the second property in Proposition 7.4.2. However, it also follows directly that $\mathrm{BCP}_{\mathrm{rec}}(A, \gamma) \vdash 1 \mid s = 1 \mid t = 1 \mid \sum_{i<n} a_i.t_i = \sum_{i<n} 1 \mid a_i.t_i = \sum_{i<n} 0 = 0$. □

Second, recall Proposition 7.4.8 (Free-Merge Axiom), stating that the Free-Merge Axiom can be derived from the axioms of theory $\mathrm{BCP}(A, \emptyset)$ for all closed $\mathrm{BCP}(A, \emptyset)$-terms. This proposition can be generalized to all guarded $\mathrm{BCP}_{\mathrm{rec}}(A, \emptyset)$-terms in the current context with recursion. Also the Handshaking Axiom (see Table 7.3) is derivable for all guarded $\mathrm{BCP}_{\mathrm{rec}}(A, \gamma)$-terms when γ is a handshaking communication function.

As an example of calculations with recursive specifications in $\mathrm{BCP}_{\mathrm{rec}}(A, \gamma)$, let us consider *buffers* of finite capacity. Recall Definition 7.3.1 (Standard communication). Assume that the set of data elements D is the set of bits $\{0, 1\}$. In the minimal theory $\mathrm{MPT}(A)$ with recursion, a *one-bit buffer* with input port i and output port o can be specified as follows:

$$Buf1 = 1 + i?0.o!0.Buf1 + i?1.o!1.Buf1.$$

Note that in this specification, an empty buffer has an option to terminate. The reason to include this option is that an environment using the buffer can decide to terminate. Absence of this initial termination option would prevent such termination; see Exercise 7.6.7.

In general, a one-place buffer over a finite data set D is given as follows:

$$Buf1 = 1 + \sum_{d \in D} i?d.o!d.Buf1.$$

To describe a buffer with capacity two, a specification with two equations is needed (one parameterized with a data element, meaning that the actual number of equations in the recursive specification equals the cardinality of D plus one):

$$\begin{aligned} Buf2 &= 1 + \sum_{d \in D} i?d.B_d \quad \text{and, for all } d \in D, \\ B_d &= o!d.Buf2 + \sum_{e \in D} i?e.o!d.B_e. \end{aligned}$$

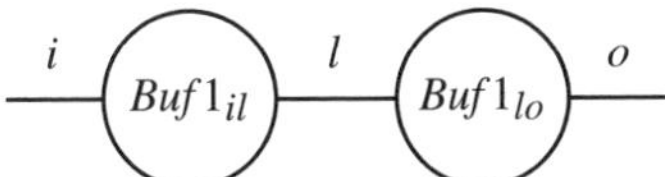

Fig. 7.3. A sequence of two one-place buffers.

Consider now a communication network consisting of two buffers of capacity one, $Buf1_{il}$ with input port i and output port l (short for *link*), and $Buf1_{lo}$ with input port l and output port o; see Figure 7.3. The two components are specified as above:

$$\begin{aligned} Buf1_{il} &= 1 + \sum_{d \in D} i?d.l!d.Buf1_{il} \quad \text{and} \\ Buf1_{lo} &= 1 + \sum_{d \in D} l?d.o!d.Buf1_{lo}. \end{aligned}$$

It is interesting to consider the parallel composition of the two processes $Buf1_{il}$ and $Buf1_{lo}$. Assume communication is specified by the standard communication function γ_S of Definition 7.3.1. To enforce communication in the parallel composition, encapsulation of halves of internal communication actions is required. Thus, put $H = \{l?d, l!d \mid d \in D\}$ and consider the process $\partial_H\,(Buf1_{il} \parallel Buf1_{lo})$. This process can be interpreted as a two-place buffer, with an internal communication port l. Values from D are passed along this port, using the synchronous communication mechanism of the theory. A guarded recursive specification can be derived for this process. Let $X = \partial_H\,(Buf1_{il} \parallel Buf1_{lo})$ and, for each $d \in D$, let $X_d = \partial_H\,(Buf1_{il} \parallel o!d.Buf1_{lo})$.

$$\begin{aligned} &\mathrm{BCP}_{\mathrm{rec}}(A, \gamma_S) \vdash \\ &\quad X = \partial_H\left(Buf1_{il} \mathbin{\|\!\lfloor} Buf1_{lo}\right) + \partial_H\left(Buf1_{lo} \mathbin{\|\!\lfloor} Buf1_{il}\right) \\ &\qquad\quad + \partial_H\,(Buf1_{il} \mid Buf1_{lo}) \\ &\quad\;\; = \partial_H\left(\sum_{d \in D} i?d.(l!d.Buf1_{il} \parallel Buf1_{lo})\right) + 0 + 1 \end{aligned}$$

$$
\begin{aligned}
&= 1 + \sum_{d \in D} i?d.\partial_H(l!d.Buf1_{il} \mathbin{⌊\!⌊} Buf1_{lo} \\
&\qquad\qquad + Buf1_{lo} \mathbin{⌊\!⌊} l!d.Buf1_{il} \\
&\qquad\qquad + l!d.Buf1_{il} \mid Buf1_{lo} \\
&\qquad)\\
&= 1 + \sum_{d \in D} i?d.(0 + 0 + l?\!d.\partial_H(Buf1_{il} \parallel o!d.Buf1_{lo})) \\
&= 1 + \sum_{d \in D} i?d.l?\!d.X_d
\end{aligned}
$$

and

$$
\begin{aligned}
&\mathrm{BCP}_{\mathrm{rec}}(A, \gamma_S) \vdash X_d \\
&\quad = \partial_H\left(Buf1_{il} \mathbin{⌊\!⌊} o!d.Buf1_{lo}\right) + \partial_H\left(o!d.Buf1_{lo} \mathbin{⌊\!⌊} Buf1_{il}\right) \\
&\qquad\quad + \partial_H\left(Buf1_{il} \mid o!d.Buf1_{lo}\right) \\
&\quad = \sum_{e \in D} i?e.\partial_H\left(l!e.Buf1_{il} \parallel o!d.Buf1_{lo}\right) \\
&\qquad\qquad + o!d.\partial_H\left(Buf1_{il} \parallel Buf1_{lo}\right) + 0 \\
&\quad = \sum_{e \in D} i?e.(0 + o!d.\partial_H\left(l!e.Buf1_{il} \parallel Buf1_{lo}\right) + 0) + o!d.X \\
&\quad = \sum_{e \in D} i?e.o!d.(0 + 0 + l?\!e.\partial_H\left(Buf1_{il} \parallel o!e.Buf1_{lo}\right)) + o!d.X \\
&\quad = \sum_{e \in D} i?e.o!d.l?\!e.X_e + o!d.X.
\end{aligned}
$$

Thus, a system of two connected one-place buffers is given by recursive specification:

$$
\begin{aligned}
X &= 1 + \sum_{d \in D} i?d.l?\!d.X_d \quad \text{and, for all } d \in D, \\
X_d &= o!d.X + \sum_{e \in D} i?e.o!d.l?\!e.X_e.
\end{aligned}
$$

Recall from Section 6.7 the concept of skip operators. It can be seen that skipping the internal communication actions in this specification gives the two-place buffer between ports i and o, i.e., with $I = \{l?\!d \mid d \in D\}$,

$$
\begin{aligned}
&((\mathrm{BCP} + \mathrm{EI})_{\mathrm{rec}} + \mathrm{RSP})(A, \gamma_S) \vdash \\
&\qquad \varepsilon_I(\partial_H(Buf1_{il} \parallel Buf1_{lo})) = Buf2.
\end{aligned}
$$

The next chapter introduces a notion of abstraction, which can be used to obtain a similar result (in a conceptually more elegant way); see Exercise 8.8.1.

This example once more shows the general form of a system describing a communication network: a number of component processes, in the scope of an encapsulation operator that blocks isolated send and receive actions on internal ports. This allows only communication actions on these internal ports and blocks interaction with the environment over these ports.

The following considers an example of a recursive specification of a process in $\mathrm{BCP}_{\mathrm{rec}}(A, \emptyset)$, i.e., the theory with a free merge where communication is not possible. Notwithstanding, standard notation for inputs and outputs (send and receive actions) established earlier is used. The process *bag* of unbounded capacity is able to input arbitrary elements of a finite data set D at port i and output elements that have been input previously in any order, at port o. Thus, input order is not important, but the number of specific elements present has to be kept track of. To keep things simple, first consider only bits, so $D = \{0, 1\}$. This means there are input actions $i?0$ and $i?1$, and output actions $o!0$ and $o!1$.

An (infinite) recursive specification over the signature of the minimal theory MPT(A) has variables $B_{n,m}$ that denote the state of the bag with n zeroes and m ones. The following equations exist for all $n, m \geq 0$, and together form the (linear) recursive specification E.

$$\begin{aligned}
B_{0,0} &= 1 + i?0.B_{1,0} + i?1.B_{0,1}, \\
B_{0,m+1} &= o!1.B_{0,m} + i?0.B_{1,m+1} + i?1.B_{0,m+2}, \\
B_{n+1,0} &= o!0.B_{n,0} + i?0.B_{n+2,0} + i?1.B_{n+1,1}, \\
B_{n+1,m+1} &= o!0.B_{n,m+1} + o!1.B_{n+1,m} + \\
&\qquad + i?0.B_{n+2,m+1} + i?1.B_{n+1,m+2}.
\end{aligned}$$

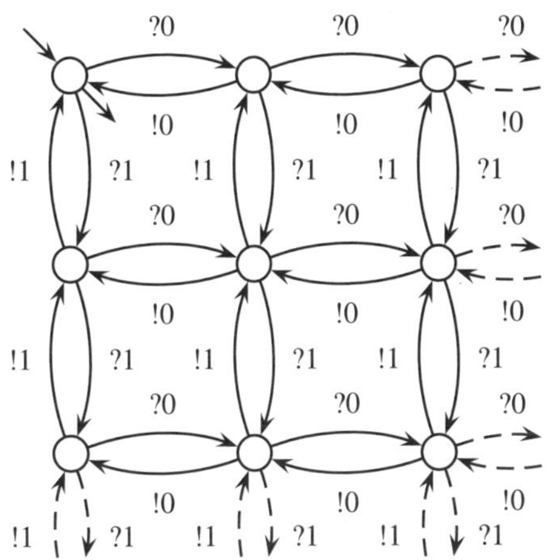

Fig. 7.4. The transition system of a bag of bits.

Figure 7.4 visualizes the transition system of the above specification of the bag of bits, using obvious abbreviations for input and output actions.

The following gives a *finite* recursive specification F of a bag, in BCP(A, ∅) with recursion. This specification has just one variable, *Bag*.

$$Bag = 1 + i?0.(Bag \parallel o!0.1) + i?1.(Bag \parallel o!1.1).$$

It can be seen immediately that this is a guarded recursive specification.

Proposition 7.6.4 (Bags)

$$(\text{BCP} + \text{FMA} + E + F + \text{RSP})(A, \emptyset) \vdash Bag = B_{0,0}.$$

Proof Define the processes $D_{n,m}$, for $n, m \geq 0$, as follows:

$$D_{n,m} = Bag \parallel (o!0)^n 1 \parallel (o!1)^m 1,$$

where as before a^n for action a is the n-fold action prefix of Notation 4.6.6. The first steps in the first derivation below show that (BCP+FMA+F)$(A, \emptyset)\vdash$ $D_{0,0} = Bag$. Therefore, to prove the theorem, it is sufficient to show that the processes $D_{n,m}$ form a solution of E. Consider the equations one by one. First,

$$\begin{aligned}
&(\mathrm{BCP} + \mathrm{FMA} + F)(A, \emptyset)\vdash \\
&\quad D_{0,0} = Bag \parallel (o!0)^0 1 \parallel (o!1)^0 1 \\
&\qquad = Bag \parallel 1 \parallel 1 \\
&\qquad = Bag \\
&\qquad = 1 + i?0.(Bag \parallel o!0.1) + i?1.(Bag \parallel o!1.1) \\
&\qquad = 1 + i?0.(Bag \parallel (o!0)^1 1 \parallel 1) + i?1.(Bag \parallel 1 \parallel (o!1)^1 1) \\
&\qquad = 1 + i?0.D_{1,0} + i?1.D_{0,1}.
\end{aligned}$$

The second derivation uses Axiom M. Since communication is not possible and one of the terms does not contain a 1 summand, the communication-merge term is skipped. This derivation also uses laws of standard concurrency and the fact that, for each atomic action $a \in A$ and natural number $k \in \mathbf{N}$, the equality $a^k 1 \parallel a.1 = a^{k+1} 1$ is derivable (see Exercise 7.4.4).

$$\begin{aligned}
&(\mathrm{BCP} + \mathrm{FMA} + F)(A, \emptyset)\vdash \\
&\quad D_{0,m+1} = Bag \parallel 1 \parallel (o!1)^{m+1} 1 \\
&\qquad = Bag \parallel (o!1)^{m+1} 1 \\
&\qquad = Bag \mathbin{⫦\!\!\!_} (o!1)^{m+1} 1 + (o!1)^{m+1} 1 \mathbin{⫦\!\!\!_} Bag \\
&\qquad = (1 + i?0.D_{1,0} + i?1.D_{0,1}) \mathbin{⫦\!\!\!_} (o!1)^{m+1} 1 \\
&\qquad\qquad + (o!1)^{m+1} 1 \mathbin{⫦\!\!\!_} Bag \\
&\qquad = i?0.(D_{1,0} \parallel (o!1)^{m+1} 1) + i?1.(D_{0,1} \parallel (o!1)^{m+1} 1) \\
&\qquad\qquad + o!1.((o!1)^m 1 \parallel Bag) \\
&\qquad = i?0.D_{1,m+1} + i?1.D_{0,m+2} + o!1.D_{0,m}.
\end{aligned}$$

The third derivation, for $D_{n+1,0}$, is left as an exercise to the reader, because it is similar to the previous one.

Finally, the last derivation starts with an application of the expansion theorem for the free merge (Theorem 7.4.9). Again, the communication-merge term is skipped, as no termination is possible.

$$\begin{aligned}
&(\mathrm{BCP} + \mathrm{FMA} + F)(A, \emptyset) \vdash D_{n+1,m+1} \\
&\quad = Bag \parallel (o!0)^{n+1} 1 \parallel (o!1)^{m+1} 1 \\
&\quad = Bag \mathbin{⫦\!\!\!_} ((o!0)^{n+1} 1 \parallel (o!1)^{m+1} 1) \\
&\qquad + (o!0)^{n+1} 1 \mathbin{⫦\!\!\!_} (Bag \parallel (o!1)^{m+1} 1) \\
&\qquad + (o!1)^{m+1} 1 \mathbin{⫦\!\!\!_} (Bag \parallel (o!0)^{n+1} 1)
\end{aligned}$$

$$
\begin{aligned}
&= (1 + i?0.D_{1,0} + i?1.D_{0,1}) \mathbin{⌊⌊} ((o!0)^{n+1}1 \parallel (o!1)^{m+1}1) \\
&\qquad + (o!0)^{n+1}1 \mathbin{⌊⌊} (Bag \parallel (o!1)^{m+1}1) \\
&\qquad + (o!1)^{m+1}1 \mathbin{⌊⌊} (Bag \parallel (o!0)^{n+1}1) \\
&= i?0.(D_{1,0} \parallel (o!0)^{n+1}1 \parallel (o!1)^{m+1}1) \\
&\qquad + i?1.(D_{0,1} \parallel (o!0)^{n+1}1 \parallel (o!1)^{m+1}1) \\
&\qquad + o!0.((o!0)^{n}1 \parallel Bag \parallel (o!1)^{m+1}1) \\
&\qquad + o!1.((o!1)^{m}1 \parallel Bag \parallel (o!0)^{n+1}1) \\
&= i?0.D_{n+2,m+1} + i?1.D_{n+1,m+2} + o!0.D_{n,m+1} + o!1.D_{n+1,m}.
\end{aligned}
$$

The above derivations show that processes $D_{n,m}$ form a solution of specification E. Hence, by RSP, it follows that $(\mathrm{BCP}+\mathrm{FMA}+E+F+\mathrm{RSP})(A,\emptyset) \vdash D_{n,m} = B_{n,m}$, and in particular that $(\mathrm{BCP}+\mathrm{FMA}+E+F+\mathrm{RSP})(A,\emptyset) \vdash Bag = B_{0,0}$. □

The above proposition shows that there is a specification for a bag over a data set of two elements in the theory $\mathrm{BCP}_{\mathrm{rec}}(A,\emptyset)$ using just one guarded recursive equation. Such a finite guarded recursive specification does not exist in the theory $\mathrm{TSP}_{\mathrm{rec}}(A)$. For a proof of this fact, the interested reader is referred to (Bergstra & Klop, 1984b). Recall Definition 5.7.5 (Definability). An interesting consequence of these observations is that the parallel composition does add expressive power, even in the absence of communication. It is possible to finitely define a process that cannot be finitely defined when parallel composition is absent, not even when sequential composition is present. More precisely, when A contains at least four actions, there are processes that are finitely definable over $\mathrm{BCP}(A,\emptyset)$ that are not finitely definable over $\mathrm{TSP}(A)$; the requirement on A is necessary because the mentioned proof in (Bergstra & Klop, 1984b) essentially uses the fact that the specification of the bag with two data elements uses four actions.

The expressive power of finite guarded recursive specifications over the signatures of theories $\mathrm{BCP}(A,\gamma)$ and $\mathrm{TSP}(A)$ is probably incomparable. To show this, it remains to give a finite guarded recursive specification over the signature of $\mathrm{TSP}(A)$ that defines a process that cannot be finitely defined over $\mathrm{BCP}(A,\gamma)$; see Exercise 7.6.10. Note that the theories with general recursion, $\mathrm{BCP}_{\mathrm{rec}}(A,\gamma)$ and $\mathrm{TSP}_{\mathrm{rec}}(A)$, are equally expressive (as defined in Definition 5.7.2 (Expressiveness)). Already in the basic theory $\mathrm{BSP}_{\mathrm{rec}}(A)$, it is possible to specify all countable computable processes; this does not change with the extensions with sequential composition or parallel composition. Without recursion, $\mathrm{BCP}(A,\gamma)$ and $\mathrm{TSP}(A)$ are also equally expressive. Both theories extend the basic theory $\mathrm{BSP}(A)$ and all closed $\mathrm{BCP}(A,\gamma)$- and $\mathrm{TSP}(A)$-terms can be rewritten into equivalent $\mathrm{BSP}(A)$-terms, which makes these three theories equally expressive.

In case the data set D is a finite set, not necessarily containing only two elements, the generalized-choice notation can be used to obtain an even more compact equation for the specification of a bag over D:

$$Bag = 1 + \sum_{d \in D} i?d.(Bag \parallel o!d.1).$$

The equation for a bag can be specialized to the case where the data type contains exactly one element, say d. The bag in this case is just a counter, which can be specified as follows when assuming that $i?d \equiv plus$ and $o!d \equiv minus$:

$$Counter2 = 1 + plus.(Counter2 \parallel minus.1).$$

Recall that Exercise 6.6.5 also introduced a specification of a counter, using sequential composition. In order to reason about the relation between these two counter specifications, a theory is needed where both sequential composition and parallel composition are present. This theory, TCP, the Theory of Communicating Processes, is treated in the following section.

Exercises

7.6.1 Prove Proposition 7.6.1 (HNF property).

7.6.2 Let $n \geq 1$. Give a specification of an n-place buffer $Buf n$.

7.6.3 Describe a biscuit-tin (with unbounded capacity) with two kinds of biscuits by means of a guarded recursive specification over theory BCP$(A, \emptyset)$ with recursion.

7.6.4 Consider the extension of BCP(A, γ) with projection. For the process Bag defined above (for an arbitrary finite data set D), calculate $\pi_1(Bag)$, $\pi_2(Bag)$, and $\pi_3(Bag)$.

7.6.5 Sketch the transition system of a bag over data set $D = \{0, 1, 2\}$.

7.6.6 Verify that

$$((\mathrm{BCP} + \mathrm{EI})_{\mathrm{rec}} + \mathrm{RSP})(A, \gamma_S) \vdash \varepsilon_I(\partial_H(Buf1_{il} \parallel Buf1_{lo})) = Buf2,$$

using among others the axioms of Table 6.9.

7.6.7 Consider two users that communicate via the one-place buffer $Buf1$ specified in this section. One user sends two data items 0 over port i and one receives these two data items over port o. Both users terminate successfully after sending resp. receiving their data. Specify this system, and prove that it can terminate successfully. Show that it cannot terminate successfully if the termination option in the defining equation for *Buf*1 is omitted. Argue that the system even with the initial termination option of the buffer cannot terminate when the buffer is not empty.

7.6.8 Consider again the communication network of Figure 7.3, but now with the processes S and R instead of $Buf1_{il}$ and $Buf1_{lo}$, given by the equations:

$$S = 1 + \sum_{d \in D} i?d.l!d.l?ack.S,$$
$$R = 1 + \sum_{d \in D} l?d.o!d.l!ack.R.$$

In these equations, $ack \notin D$ is a special element denoting an *acknowledgement*. Let $H = \{l!d, l?d \mid d \in D \cup \{ack\}\}$. Find a recursive equation for process $\partial_H (S \parallel R)$.

7.6.9 Let p be a closed BCP$(A, \emptyset)$-term. The *replication* of p, in the literature on process algebra often denoted $!p$, is the process term $p \parallel p \parallel p \parallel \ldots$. This process cannot be defined (in the sense of Definition 5.7.5 (Definability)) by equation $X = p \parallel X$ with X some recursion variable, as this equation is unguarded, and has infinitely many solutions in the term model of theory $\text{BCP}_{\text{rec}}(A, \emptyset)$. However, the equation $X = p \mathbin{⌊\!⌊} X + p \mid 1$ can be used for the intended purpose (in the theory without communication). Argue that this equation is guarded, and yields the replication of p.

7.6.10 Recall Definition 5.7.5 (Definability). Give a finite guarded recursive specification over the signature of theory TSP(A) that defines a process that cannot be finitely defined over theory BCP(A, γ), or, alternatively, prove that TSP(A) allows to finitely define strictly fewer processes than BCP(A, γ). Inform the authors about your answer.

7.7 The process theory TCP and further extensions

It is often useful to have both sequential composition and parallel composition present in the same theory. The process theory TCP, the Theory of Communicating Processes, is the union of the process theories BCP and TSP; see Table 7.5. The axioms of TCP(A, γ) are the axioms of BCP(A, γ) and TSP(A), see Tables 7.1 and 6.1, with one additional Axiom of Standard Concurrency.

It is straightforward to obtain elimination and conservativity results with respect to theory BSP(A). Figure 7.5 visualizes the conservativity results for the basic theories with parallel composition. As before, the extra Axiom of Standard Concurrency is derivable for closed terms.

TCP(A, γ)	
TSP(A), BCP(A, γ);	
-	
x;	
$x \mathbin{\|\!\!\lfloor} 0 = x \cdot 0$	SC8

Table 7.5. The process theory TCP(A, γ).

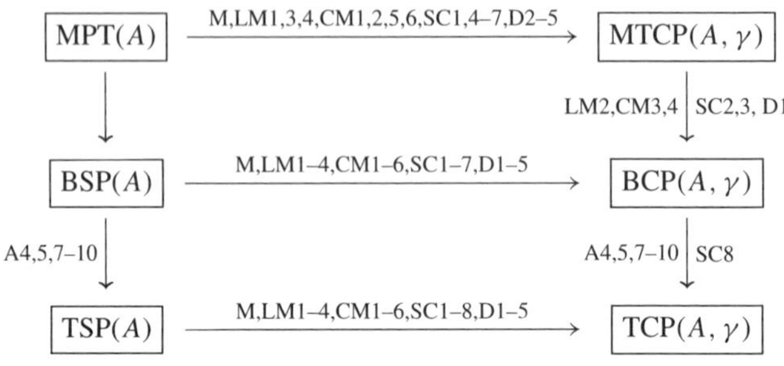

Fig. 7.5. Conservativity results for TCP(A, γ).

Theorem 7.7.1 (Standard concurrency) For closed TCP(A, γ)-terms, Axiom SC8 is derivable from the other axioms of TCP(A, γ).

Proof By structural induction. See Exercise 7.7.2. □

The term deduction system underlying the term model of theory TCP(A, γ) is just the union of the two term deduction systems for TSP(A) and BCP(A, γ). It is a useful exercise to show that the resulting term model admits a soundness and a ground-completeness theorem.

Extension of TCP(A, γ) with other features does not present difficulties. For instance, it is straightforward to extend the theory with projection operators π_n for all $n \in \mathbf{N}$, resulting in the theory (TCP + PR)(A, γ), or with renaming (see Section 6.7), resulting in (TCP + RN)(A, γ).

Example 7.7.2 (CSP **parallel composition and communication)** As an example of a definition in the theory (TCP + RN)(A, γ), consider the parallel composition operator of CSP, see (Hoare, 1985). For a given set of action names S, the actions in S must synchronize as much as possible, where different actions with the same name may synchronize, resulting in one occurrence of the same action. The difficulty is to ensure that these actions do not occur by themselves when they should synchronize. In order to achieve this, assume that the set of actions A is divided into two parts: a set of names N and a set of communications N_c such that for each $n \in N$ there is exactly one $n_c \in N_c$. Now take the communication function γ that has $\gamma(n, n) = n_c$ and is not defined otherwise, and the renaming function f with $f(n_c) = n$. Then, CSP-style parallel composition $\|_S^{\mathrm{CSP}}$, with $S \subseteq N$, can be defined by axiom

$$x \|_S^{\mathrm{CSP}} y = \rho_f(\partial_{S \cup (N_c \setminus S_c)}(x \parallel y)),$$

where $S_c = \{n_c \mid n \in S\}$. As an example, if $S = \{a\}$ and $a, b, c \in N$, then it can be derived that

$$b.a.b.a.1 \|_S^{\mathrm{CSP}} a.c.1 = b.a.(b.c.0 + c.b.0).$$

Also the extension with recursion follows the standard steps. To illustrate reasoning in TCP(A, γ), consider the counter specifications given in the previous section and in Exercise 6.6.5. Since there is no communication and the counter specifications use recursion, and because the equational reasoning uses projection operators, the precise context is the theory $(\mathrm{TCP} + \mathrm{PR})_{\mathrm{rec}}(A, \emptyset)$. In the previous section, the following recursive equation for a counter was given:

$$\mathit{Counter2} = 1 + \mathit{plus}.(\mathit{Counter2} \parallel \mathit{minus}.1).$$

In Exercise 6.6.5, a different specification was given, namely,

$$\begin{aligned} \mathit{Counter} &= 1 + T \cdot \mathit{Counter}, \\ T &= \mathit{plus}.T', \\ T' &= \mathit{minus}.1 + T \cdot T'. \end{aligned}$$

It can be shown that these two specifications are equal. Recall that also Exercise 5.6.3 gives a(n infinite) recursive specification of a counter. One way to prove the equality of the above two specifications is by showing that the two processes both satisfy this infinite specification and to apply RSP, which is essentially the technique applied most often so far. To illustrate a different proof technique, the desired equality can also be proven via AIP^-.

Proposition 7.7.3 (Counters) $((\mathrm{TCP} + \mathrm{PR})_{\mathrm{rec}} + \mathrm{AIP}^-)(A, \emptyset) \vdash \mathit{Counter} = \mathit{Counter2}$.

Proof The proof shows that

$$\begin{aligned} &((\mathrm{TCP} + \mathrm{PR})_{\mathrm{rec}} + \mathrm{AIP}^-)(A, \emptyset) \vdash \\ &\qquad (T')^k \cdot \mathit{Counter} = \mathit{Counter2} \parallel \mathit{minus}^k 1, \end{aligned}$$

for every natural number $k \in \mathbf{N}$, where x^k for any term x is the k-fold sequential composition of Exercise 6.2.3. Note that this equation reduces to

$$((\mathrm{TCP} + \mathrm{PR})_{\mathrm{rec}} + \mathrm{AIP}^-)(A, \emptyset) \vdash \mathit{Counter} = \mathit{Counter2},$$

if k equals zero. By AIP$^-$, it is sufficient to show that all finite projections of the processes in the desired equations are derivably equal. This can be proven by induction. Observe that the recursive specification of *Counter* can be rewritten as follows:

$$\begin{aligned}&(\mathrm{TCP}+\mathrm{PR})_{\mathrm{rec}}(A,\emptyset)\vdash\\&\qquad Counter = 1 + plus.T'\cdot Counter,\\&\qquad T' \qquad\;\; = minus.1 + plus.(T')^2.\end{aligned}$$

The basis of the induction considers projections of depth 0. First, assume $k = 0$. Then,

$$\begin{aligned}&(\mathrm{TCP}+\mathrm{PR})_{\mathrm{rec}}(A,\emptyset)\vdash\\&\quad \pi_0(Counter) = \pi_0(1 + plus.T'\cdot Counter) = 1\end{aligned}$$

and

$$\begin{aligned}&(\mathrm{TCP}+\mathrm{PR})_{\mathrm{rec}}(A,\emptyset)\vdash\\&\quad \pi_0(Counter2) = \pi_0(1 + plus.(Counter2 \parallel minus.1)) = 1.\end{aligned}$$

Similarly, if $k > 0$, then

$$\begin{aligned}&(\mathrm{TCP}+\mathrm{PR})_{\mathrm{rec}}(A,\emptyset)\vdash\\&\quad \pi_0((T')^k\cdot Counter) = 0 = \pi_0(Counter2 \parallel minus^k 1).\end{aligned}$$

For the inductive step, assume that the desired result holds for some $n \in \mathbf{N}$. Then, the following derivation can be made for $n+1$ if k equals 0:

$$\begin{aligned}&(\mathrm{TCP}+\mathrm{PR})_{\mathrm{rec}}(A,\emptyset)\vdash\\&\quad \pi_{n+1}(Counter) = \pi_{n+1}(1 + plus.T'\cdot Counter)\\&\qquad\qquad\qquad\quad = 1 + plus.\pi_n(T'\cdot Counter)\\&\qquad\qquad\qquad\quad = 1 + plus.\pi_n(Counter2 \parallel minus.1)\\&\qquad\qquad\qquad\quad = \pi_{n+1}(1 + plus.(Counter2 \parallel minus.1))\\&\qquad\qquad\qquad\quad = \pi_{n+1}(Counter2).\end{aligned}$$

The final part of the proof uses the equality proven in Exercise 7.4.4. If $k = l+1 > 0$ for some natural number $l \in \mathbf{N}$,

$$\begin{aligned}&(\mathrm{TCP}+\mathrm{PR})_{\mathrm{rec}}(A,\emptyset)\vdash \pi_{n+1}((T')^{l+1}\cdot Counter)\\&\quad = \pi_{n+1}(minus.(T')^l\cdot Counter + plus.(T')^{l+2}\cdot Counter)\\&\quad = minus.\pi_n((T')^l\cdot Counter) + plus.\pi_n((T')^{l+2}\cdot Counter\\&\quad = minus.\pi_n(Counter2 \parallel minus^l 1)\\&\qquad\qquad + plus.\pi_n(Counter2 \parallel minus^{l+2} 1)\\&\quad = \pi_{n+1}(minus.(Counter2 \parallel minus^l 1)\\&\qquad\qquad + plus.(Counter2 \parallel minus^{l+2} 1))\\&\quad = \pi_{n+1}(minus^{l+1} 1 \mathbin{⫗} Counter2\\&\qquad\qquad + plus.((Counter2 \parallel minus.1) \parallel minus^{l+1} 1))\end{aligned}$$

$$
\begin{aligned}
&= \pi_{n+1}(minus^{l+1}1 \mathbin{\lfloor\!\lfloor} Counter2 \\
&\qquad\qquad + plus.(Counter2 \parallel minus.1) \mathbin{\lfloor\!\lfloor} minus^{l+1}1) \\
&= \pi_{n+1}(minus^{l+1}1 \mathbin{\lfloor\!\lfloor} Counter2 + Counter2 \mathbin{\lfloor\!\lfloor} minus^{l+1}1) \\
&= \pi_{n+1}(Counter2 \parallel minus^{l+1}1).
\end{aligned}
$$

□

At this point, it is interesting to consider some expressiveness aspects. The results of (Bergstra & Klop, 1984b) imply that there are processes that can be defined by a finite guarded recursive specification over the signature of theory TCP(A, γ), for a certain γ, but that cannot be defined by a finite guarded recursive specification over the signature of TCP$(A, \emptyset)$. Also an unbounded FIFO (First-In-First-Out) queue is an example of a process that is finitely definable over TCP(A, γ) when general communication is allowed but not over TCP$(A, \emptyset)$. The queue example is discussed in more detail below; in particular, Exercise 7.7.10 gives a finite guarded recursive specification over the signature of theory TCP(A, γ). These observations imply that finite guarded recursive specifications over the signature of theory TCP(A, γ) for a general communication function have more expressive power than those over the signature of TCP$(A, \emptyset)$. This illustrates the added value of communication when compared to parallel composition without communication. As before, when general recursion is allowed, the two variants TCP$_{\text{rec}}(A, \gamma)$ and TCP$_{\text{rec}}(A, \emptyset)$ with and without communication are equally expressive in the sense of Definition 5.7.2 (Expressiveness); they both allow the specification of all countable computable processes. Also TCP(A, γ) and TCP$(A, \emptyset)$, i.e., the theories without recursion, are equally expressive in the sense of this definition, because, independent of the definition of γ, the set of closed TCP(A, γ)-terms contains all closed BSP(A)-terms, and, again independent of the definition of γ, all closed TCP(A, γ)-terms can always be rewritten into a closed BSP(A)-term. Hence, both the generic theory TCP(A, γ) and the variant with the free merge are equally expressive as BSP(A) (and therefore equally expressive as theories such as TSP(A) and BCP(A, γ)).

As already suggested, an interesting example in the current context is the FIFO queue. Consider such a queue with unbounded capacity, with input port i and output port o. An infinite guarded recursive specification over the signature of the minimal theory MPT(A) is not hard to give. Suppose D is a finite data set, and notation of sequences over D is as before (see Section 5.6). The following recursive specification has a variable for each sequence over D.

$$
\begin{aligned}
Queue1 &= Q_\epsilon, \\
Q_\epsilon &= 1 + \sum_{d \in D} i?d.Q_d, \quad \text{and, for all } d \in D, \sigma \in D^*, \\
Q_{\sigma d} &= o!d.Q_\sigma + \sum_{e \in D} i?e.Q_{e\sigma d}.
\end{aligned}
$$

The last equation gives the behavior of the non-empty queue. Comparing the present specification with the one of the stack in Section 5.6 shows obvious similarity. In Section 6.6.2, it has been shown that theory TSP(A) allows a finite guarded recursive specification of the stack. Therefore, it may come as a surprise that there is no finite guarded recursive specification for the queue over the signature of theory TCP(A, γ) when communication is restricted to handshaking communication, which is an extension of the signature of TSP(A). The proof of this fact is outside the scope of this text. The interested reader is referred to (Baeten & Bergstra, 1988). Exercise 7.7.10 shows that the queue is finitely definable over TCP(A, γ) when arbitrary communication is allowed, showing that the restriction to handshaking in the above is essential.

Another interesting aspect is that some extensions of theory TCP(A, γ) are more expressive than the basic theory TCP(A, γ) itself when considering finite guarded recursion. It turns out that there is a finite guarded recursive specification for the queue in the basic theory BCP$_{\mathrm{rec}}(A, \gamma)$ with handshaking communication *extended with renaming operators* (see Section 6.7), as the following shows. That is, the queue is finitely definable over theory (BCP+HA+RN)(A, γ). The specification assumes the standard communication function γ_S of Definition 7.3.1.

Consider two renaming functions $f, g : A \to A$. For all data elements $d \in D$, $f(o!d) = l!d$, and f leaves all other atomic actions unchanged; $g(l?d) = o!d$, for each $d \in D$, and g leaves all other atomic actions unchanged. Consider the following recursive specification with variables *Queue*2 and Z, with $H = \{l!d, l?d \mid d \in D\}$:

$$\begin{aligned} \mathit{Queue2} &= 1 + \sum_{d \in D} i?d.\rho_g(\partial_H(\rho_f(\mathit{Queue2}) \parallel o!d.Z)), \\ Z &= 1 + \sum_{d \in D} l?d.Z. \end{aligned}$$

The proposition below proves that $((\mathrm{BCP} + \mathrm{HA} + \mathrm{RN})_{\mathrm{rec}} + \mathrm{RSP})(A, \gamma_S) \vdash \mathit{Queue1} = \mathit{Queue2}$. In order to gain some more intuition about the specification of *Queue*2, consider the following. An unbounded queue can be imagined as a one-element buffer connected to an unbounded (sub)queue. Although this may seem strange at a first glance, it does work. The fact that the queue is unbounded is crucial. The first element put into the queue (through an $i?d$ action) is put into the one-place buffer; all following elements are put into the subqueue. The output port of the subqueue is some internal port l (which explains the renaming via function f of the recursive occurrence of *Queue*2 in the specification). This port is watched over by a guard Z, that becomes activated only if the one-element buffer is emptied (through an $o!d$ action). By encapsulating isolated communication actions over the internal port l and renaming successful communications over this internal port to $o!d$ actions, this guard makes sure that the elements of the subqueue are forwarded to the outside world over port o as $o!d$ actions in the right order. Of course, the subqueue is itself again built from a one-element buffer and a subqueue ..., see Figure 7.6.

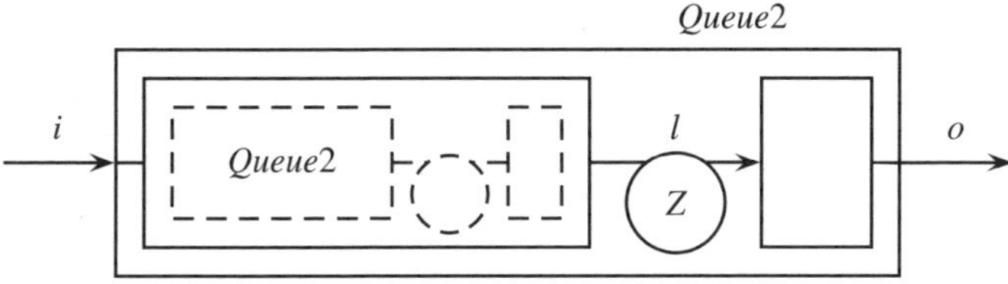

Fig. 7.6. The intuition behind the specification of *Queue*2.

Proposition 7.7.4 (Queues)

$$((\mathrm{BCP} + \mathrm{HA} + \mathrm{RN})_{\mathrm{rec}} + \mathrm{RSP})(A, \gamma_S) \vdash \mathit{Queue}1 = \mathit{Queue}2.$$

Proof By RSP, it is enough to show that process *Queue*2 is a solution of the recursive specification of *Queue*1. In order to do so, it is necessary to find an expression in terms of *Queue*2 for each variable Q_σ (with $\sigma \in D^*$) in the specification of *Queue*1. These expressions are defined inductively as follows.

Expressions R^n_σ, for each $n \in \mathbf{N}$ and each $\sigma \in D^*$, are defined by induction on n. So, first of all, the expressions R^0_σ are defined, by induction on σ:

$$\begin{aligned} R^0_\epsilon &= \mathit{Queue}2, \quad \text{and, for all } \sigma \in D^*, d \in D,\\ R^0_{\sigma d} &= \rho_g(\partial_H(\rho_f(R^0_\sigma) \parallel o!d.Z)). \end{aligned}$$

Next, given the expressions R^n_σ, for all $n \in \mathbf{N}$ and $\sigma \in D^*$, expressions R^{n+1}_σ are defined as follows:

$$R^{n+1}_\sigma = \rho_g(\partial_H(\rho_f(R^n_\sigma) \parallel Z)).$$

Using the equations in the specification for *Queue*2, the following can be derived, for each $n \in \mathbf{N}$ and each $d \in D, \sigma \in D^*$:

$$\begin{aligned} &(\mathrm{BCP} + \mathrm{HA} + \mathrm{RN})_{\mathrm{rec}}(A, \gamma_S) \vdash\\ &\qquad R^n_\epsilon = 1 + \sum_{d \in D} i?d.R^n_d,\\ &\qquad R^n_{\sigma d} = o!d.R^{n+1}_\sigma + \sum_{e \in D} i?e.R^n_{e\sigma d}. \end{aligned}$$

Following the reasoning in Example 5.5.13 (Recursion principle RSP), it can be inferred that $((\mathrm{BCP} + \mathrm{HA} + \mathrm{RN})_{\mathrm{rec}} + \mathrm{RSP})(A, \gamma_S) \vdash R^n_\sigma = Q_\sigma$ for all

$n \in \mathbf{N}, \sigma \in D^*$, and so in particular $((\mathrm{BCP} + \mathrm{HA} + \mathrm{RN})_{\mathrm{rec}} + \mathrm{RSP})(A, \gamma_S) \vdash$ $Queue2 = R^0_\epsilon = Q_\epsilon = Queue1$. □

Exercises

7.7.1 Develop theory $\mathrm{TCP}(A, \gamma)$. That is, prove elimination and conservativity results, and give a term model proving soundness and ground-completeness.

7.7.2 Prove Theorem 7.7.1 (Standard concurrency).

7.7.3 Prove that the following identities can be derived from $\mathrm{TCP}(A, \gamma)$:

(a) $x \parallel 0 = x \cdot 0$;
(b) $x \mathbin{\lfloor\!\lfloor} y \cdot 0 = x \cdot 0 \mathbin{\lfloor\!\lfloor} y = (x \mathbin{\lfloor\!\lfloor} y) \cdot 0$;
(c) $x \parallel y \cdot 0 = x \cdot 0 \parallel y = (x \parallel y) \cdot 0$.

7.7.4 Prove that, for all closed $\mathrm{TCP}(A, \emptyset)$-terms p and actions $a \in A$, $\mathrm{TCP}(A, \emptyset) \vdash p \cdot a.1 \parallel a.1 = (p \parallel a.1) \cdot a.1$.
(Note that this equality expresses a property about the free merge (i.e., without communication) and its interaction with sequential composition. It cannot be derived from the other axioms of $\mathrm{TCP}(A, \emptyset)$ for arbitrary open terms, not even in the presence of the Free-Merge Axiom FMA of Table 7.2. This is similar to the earlier results obtained for the Axioms of Standard Concurrency. A consequence of this result is that $(\mathrm{TCP} + \mathrm{FMA})(A, \emptyset)$ is not ω-complete (see Section 2.3).)

7.7.5 Consider Example 7.7.2 (CSP parallel composition and communication). Show that the given equality $b.a.b.a.1 \parallel^{\mathrm{CSP}}_S a.c.1 = b.a.(b.c.0 + c.b.0)$ can be derived from the theory $(\mathrm{TCP} + \mathrm{RN})(A, \gamma)$ extended with the defining axiom for CSP parallel composition.

7.7.6 Consider the so-called *laws* of CSP in (Hoare, 1985). Which of the laws concerning parallel composition can be derived in the theory $(\mathrm{TCP} + \mathrm{RN})(A, \gamma)$ extended with the defining axiom for CSP parallel composition in Example 7.7.2 (CSP parallel composition and communication)?

7.7.7 Consider a vending machine K, where coffee costs 35 cents. Three coins, of 20, 10, and 5 cents, need to be inserted (in arbitrary order) and then coffee is dispensed. Describe K by means of a recursive equation, using the merge operator without communication.

7.7.8 Sketch the transition system of the queue for the case $D = \{0, 1\}$.

7.7.9 Derive the recursive specification for the expressions R^n_σ given in the proof of Proposition 7.7.4 (Queues) from the equations of the specification for $Queue2$.

7.7.10 The queue is finitely definable over theory BCP(A, γ) when non-binary communication is allowed. Suppose there are actions $k(d)$, $m(d) \in A$ (for $d \in D$) such that $\gamma(o!d, k(d)) = m(d)$ and $\gamma(m(d), k(d)) = o!d$; let $H = \{o!d, m(d) \mid d \in D\}$ and $K = \{m(d), k(d) \mid d \in D\}$. Show that the queue can be defined by the following recursive specification:

$$\begin{aligned} \mathit{Queue3} &= 1 + \sum_{d \in D} i?d.\partial_K(Z \parallel \partial_H(\mathit{Queue3} \parallel m(d).Z)), \\ Z &= 1 + \sum_{d \in D} k(d).Z. \end{aligned}$$

7.8 Specifying the Alternating-Bit Protocol

This section presents a more elaborate example of an algebraic specification, namely the specification of a communication protocol. This protocol is often referred to as the Alternating-Bit Protocol in the literature. It concerns the transmission of data through an unreliable channel in such a way that – despite the unreliability – no information will get lost. The communication network used in the example is shown in Figure 7.7.

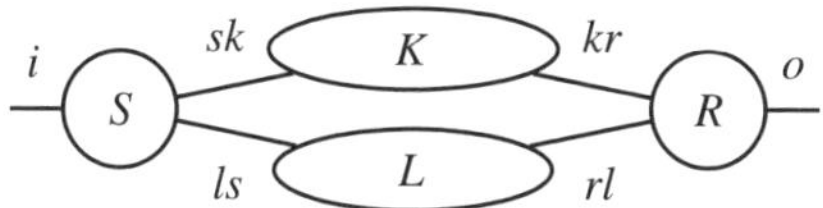

Fig. 7.7. The Alternating-Bit Protocol: communication network.

The following describes the components of this network. In Figure 7.7, S is the sender, sending data elements $d \in D$, with D a finite data domain, to the receiver R via the unreliable channel K. After having received a certain data element, R will send an acknowledgement to S via channel L which is unreliable as well. (In practice, K and L are usually physically the same medium.) The problem now is to define processes S and R such that no information will get lost; that is, the behavior of the entire process, apart from the communications at the internal ports *sk*, *kr*, *rl*, and *ls*, satisfies the equation

$$\mathit{Buf1}_{io} = 1 + \sum_{d \in D} i?d.o!d.\mathit{Buf1}_{io},$$

i.e., the process behaves externally as a one-place buffer with input port i and output port o (see Section 7.6).

A solution can be formulated as follows. The sender S reads a datum d at port i and passes on a sequence $d0, d0, d0, \ldots$ of copies of this datum with an appended bit 0 to K until an acknowledgement 0 is received at port *ls*. Then, the next datum is read, and sent on together with a bit 1; the acknowledgement then is the reception of a 1. The following data element has, in turn, 0 as an appended bit. Thus, 0 and 1 form the alternating bit. A datum with an appended bit is called a *frame*.

The process K denotes the data transmission channel, passing on frames of the form $d0$ and $d1$. K may corrupt data, however, passing on $\perp$ (an error message; thus, it is assumed that the incorrect transmission of d can be recognized, for instance, using a checksum).

Receiver R gets frames $d0$, $d1$ from K, sending on d to port o (if this was not already done earlier), and sending the acknowledgement 0 resp. 1 to L.

The process L is the acknowledgement transmission channel, and passes bits 0 or 1, received from R, on to S. L is also unreliable, and may send on $\perp$ instead of 0 or 1.

The processes S, K, R, and L can be specified by means of recursive specifications. Let D be a finite data set, and define the set of frames by $F = \{d0, d1 \mid d \in D\}$. The following specification uses the standard communication function γ_S of Definition 7.3.1 (Standard communication), with $F \cup \{0, 1, \perp\}$ as the set of data elements.

Let t be some atomic action. The channels K and L are given by the following equations.

$$
\begin{aligned}
K &= 1 + \sum_{x \in F} sk?x.(t.kr!x.K + t.kr!\perp.K), \\
L &= 1 + \sum_{n \in \{0,1\}} rl?n.(t.ls!n.L + t.ls!\perp.L).
\end{aligned}
$$

The actions t serve to make the choices non-deterministic: the decision whether or not the frame will be corrupted is internal to the channels, and cannot be influenced by the environment. The protocol to be specified is still functioning correctly, nonetheless, if the occurrences of internal action t are removed. Exercise 7.8.2 addresses this point in more detail.

The sender S and the receiver R are given by the following recursive specifications, for all $n \in \{0, 1\}$ and $d \in D$. Intuitively, Sn specifies the (possibly repeated) attempt to transmit a datum with appended bit n; Rn corresponds to the situation that the last properly received frame contained bit n, which means that the expected frame contains bit $1 - n$. The sender S iteratively executes behaviors $S0$ and $S1$, and the receiver R repeats $R1$ followed by $R0$.

$$
\begin{aligned}
S &= 1 + S0 \cdot S1 \cdot S, \\
Sn &= 1 + \sum_{d \in D} i?d.Sn_d, \\
Sn_d &= sk!dn.Tn_d, \\
Tn_d &= ls?(1-n).Sn_d + ls?\perp.Sn_d + ls?n.1,
\end{aligned}
$$

and

$$
\begin{aligned}
R \;\; &= 1 + R1 \cdot R0 \cdot R, \\
Rn &= 1 + kr?\bot.rl!n.Rn + \sum_{d \in D} kr?dn.rl!n.Rn \\
&\qquad + \sum_{d \in D} kr?d(1-n).o!d.rl!(1-n).1.
\end{aligned}
$$

The composition of the four processes of the Alternating-Bit Protocol, enforcing communication, is represented by

$$\partial_H(S \parallel K \parallel L \parallel R),$$

where $H = \{p?x,\, p!x \mid x \in F \cup \{0, 1, \bot\},\ p \in \{sk, kr, rl, ls\}\}$.

The next step is to derive a recursive specification for this process. Consider the following recursive specification, using variables $X, X1_d, X2_d, Y, Y1_d$, and $Y2_d$ (for each $d \in D$).

$$
\begin{aligned}
X \;\; &= 1 + \sum_{d \in D} i?d.X1_d, \\
X1_d &= sk\text{‽}d0.\,(t.kr\text{‽}\bot.rl\text{‽}1.(t.ls\text{‽}\bot.X1_d + t.ls\text{‽}1.X1_d) \\
&\qquad\qquad + t.kr\text{‽}d0.o!d.X2_d)\,, \\
X2_d &= rl\text{‽}0.\,(t.ls\text{‽}\bot.sk\text{‽}d0.(t.kr\text{‽}\bot.X2_d + t.kr\text{‽}d0.X2_d) + t.ls\text{‽}0.Y)\,, \\
Y \;\; &= 1 + \sum_{d \in D} i?d.Y1_d, \\
Y1_d &= sk\text{‽}d1.\,(t.kr\text{‽}\bot.rl\text{‽}0.(t.ls\text{‽}\bot.Y1_d + t.ls\text{‽}0.Y1_d) \\
&\qquad\qquad + t.kr\text{‽}d1.o!d.Y2_d)\,, \\
Y2_d &= rl\text{‽}1.\,(t.ls\text{‽}\bot.sk\text{‽}d1.(t.kr\text{‽}\bot.Y2_d + t.kr\text{‽}d1.Y2_d) + t.ls\text{‽}1.X)\,.
\end{aligned}
$$

It can be proved that process $\partial_H(S \parallel K \parallel L \parallel R)$ is a solution of this recursive specification, i.e., that it satisfies the equation for X. The following list shows the processes that should be substituted for the variables in the above specification.

$$
\begin{aligned}
X \;\; &= \partial_H(S \parallel K \parallel L \parallel R), \\
X1_d &= \partial_H(S0_d \cdot S1 \cdot S \parallel K \parallel L \parallel R), \\
X2_d &= \partial_H(T0_d \cdot S1 \cdot S \parallel K \parallel L \parallel rl!0.R0 \cdot R), \\
Y \;\; &= \partial_H(S1 \cdot S \parallel K \parallel L \parallel R0 \cdot R), \\
Y1_d &= \partial_H(S1_d \cdot S \parallel K \parallel L \parallel R0 \cdot R), \\
Y2_d &= \partial_H(T1_d \cdot S \parallel K \parallel L \parallel rl!1.R).
\end{aligned}
$$

The expansion theorem for handshaking communication, Theorem 7.4.10, can be used to show that these processes form a solution. Part of the calculations are given in the following. In fact, these calculations show how the above specification and the process expressions to be substituted for the variables are *derived*. It is not necessary to 'invent' them beforehand.

The transition system for X is depicted in Figure 7.8. Here, the sum over different data elements in the nodes of X and Y is not shown, but just one,

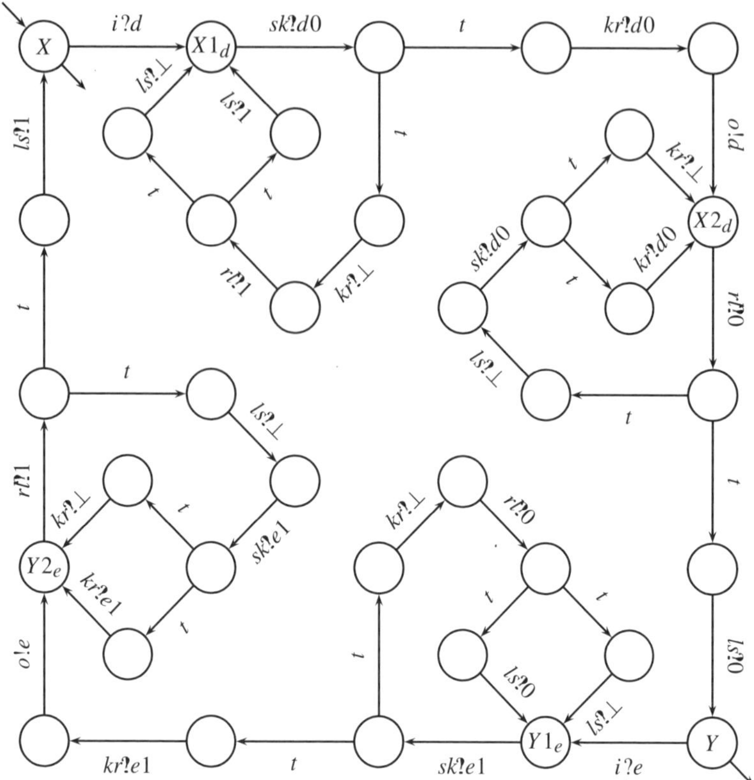

Fig. 7.8. Alternating-Bit Protocol.

arbitrary element is shown (d resp. e). To help the reader, variable names are given inside states.

For the first equation in the above list, observe that

$$\begin{aligned}&(\mathrm{TCP}+\mathrm{HA})_{\mathrm{rec}}(A, \gamma_S) \vdash \\ &\quad \partial_H(S \parallel K \parallel L \parallel R) = 1 + \sum_{d \in D} i?d.\partial_H(S0_d \cdot S1 \cdot S \parallel K \parallel L \parallel R) \\ &\quad = 1 + \sum_{d \in D} i?d.X1_d.\end{aligned}$$

Note that the Handshaking Axiom is strictly speaking not necessary to arrive at the desired result. However, it is convenient in the derivation, because it allows to use the expansion theorem for handshaking, Theorem 7.4.10.

For the second equation, assume $d \in D$. In the following, two abbreviations are used, for $x \in F$ and $n \in \{0, 1\}$:

$$K'_x = t.kr!x.K + t.kr!\bot.K,$$
$$L'_n = t.ls!n.L + t.ls!\bot.L.$$

Consider

$$\begin{aligned}
&(\mathrm{TCP} + \mathrm{HA})_{\mathrm{rec}}(A, \gamma_S) \vdash \\
&\quad \partial_H(S0_d \cdot S1 \cdot S \parallel K \parallel L \parallel R) \\
&\quad = sk?d0.\partial_H(T0_d \cdot S1 \cdot S \parallel K'_{d0} \parallel L \parallel R) \\
&\quad = sk?d0.(t.\partial_H(T0_d \cdot S1 \cdot S \parallel kr!d0.K \parallel L \parallel R) \\
&\qquad\quad + t.\partial_H(T0_d \cdot S1 \cdot S \parallel kr!\bot.K \parallel L \parallel R)) \\
&\quad = sk?d0.(t.kr?d0.\partial_H(T0_d \cdot S1 \cdot S \parallel K \parallel L \parallel o!d.rl!0.R0 \cdot R) \\
&\qquad\quad + t.kr?\bot.\partial_H(T0_d \cdot S1 \cdot S \parallel K \parallel L \parallel rl!1.R1 \cdot R0 \cdot R)) \\
&\quad = sk?d0.(t.kr?d0.o!d.\partial_H(T0_d \cdot S1 \cdot S \parallel K \parallel L \parallel rl!0.R0 \cdot R) \\
&\qquad\quad + t.kr?\bot.rl?1.\partial_H(T0_d \cdot S1 \cdot S \parallel K \parallel L'_1 \parallel R)) \\
&\quad = sk?d0.(t.kr?d0.o!d.\partial_H(T0_d \cdot S1 \cdot S \parallel K \parallel L \parallel rl!0.R0 \cdot R) \\
&\qquad\quad + t.kr?\bot.rl?1.(t.\partial_H(T0_d \cdot S1 \cdot S \parallel K \parallel ls!1.L \parallel R) \\
&\qquad\qquad\quad + t.\partial_H(T0_d \cdot S1 \cdot S \parallel K \parallel ls!\bot.L \parallel R))) \\
&\quad = sk?d0.(t.kr?d0.o!d.\partial_H(T0_d \cdot S1 \cdot S \parallel K \parallel L \parallel rl!0.R0 \cdot R) \\
&\qquad\quad + t.kr?\bot.rl?1.(t.ls?1.\partial_H(S0_d \cdot S1 \cdot S \parallel K \parallel L \parallel R) \\
&\qquad\qquad\quad + t.ls?\bot.\partial_H(S0_d \cdot S1 \cdot S \parallel K \parallel L \parallel R))).
\end{aligned}$$

The appropriate substitutions yield the second equation. Continuing with the third, assume again $d \in D$.

$$\begin{aligned}
&(\mathrm{TCP} + \mathrm{HA})_{\mathrm{rec}}(A, \gamma_S) \vdash \\
&\quad \partial_H(T0_d \cdot S1 \cdot S \parallel K \parallel L \parallel rl!0.R0 \cdot R) \\
&\quad = rl?0.\partial_H(T0_d \cdot S1 \cdot S \parallel K \parallel L'_0 \parallel R0 \cdot R) \\
&\quad = rl?0.(t.\partial_H(T0_d \cdot S1 \cdot S \parallel K \parallel ls!0.L \parallel R0 \cdot R) \\
&\qquad + t.\partial_H(T0_d \cdot S1 \cdot S \parallel K \parallel ls!\bot.L \parallel R0 \cdot R)) \\
&\quad = rl?0.(t.ls?0.\partial_H(S1 \cdot S \parallel K \parallel L \parallel R0 \cdot R) \\
&\qquad + t.ls?\bot.\partial_H(S0_d \cdot S1 \cdot S \parallel K \parallel L \parallel R0 \cdot R)) \\
&\quad = rl?0.(t.ls?0.\partial_H(S1 \cdot S \parallel K \parallel L \parallel R0 \cdot R) \\
&\qquad + t.ls?\bot.sk?d0.\partial_H(T0_d \cdot S1 \cdot S \parallel K'_{do} \parallel L \parallel R0 \cdot R)) \\
&\quad = rl?0.(t.ls?0.\partial_H(S1 \cdot S \parallel K \parallel L \parallel R0 \cdot R) \\
&\qquad + t.ls?\bot.sk?d0. \\
&\qquad\qquad (t.\partial_H(T0_d \cdot S1 \cdot S \parallel kr!d0.K \parallel L \parallel R0 \cdot R) \\
&\qquad\qquad + t.\partial_H(T0_d \cdot S1 \cdot S \parallel kr!\bot.K \parallel L \parallel R0 \cdot R))) \\
&\quad = rl?0.(t.ls?0.\partial_H(S1 \cdot S \parallel K \parallel L \parallel R0 \cdot R) \\
&\qquad + t.ls?\bot.sk?d0. \\
&\qquad\qquad (t.kr?d0.\partial_H(T0_d \cdot S1 \cdot S \parallel K \parallel L \parallel rl!0.R0 \cdot R) \\
&\qquad\qquad + t.kr?\bot.\partial_H(T0_d \cdot S1 \cdot S \parallel K \parallel L \parallel rl!0.R0 \cdot R))).
\end{aligned}$$

In this way, the first three equations have been obtained. The remaining three equations are dealt with in the same way.

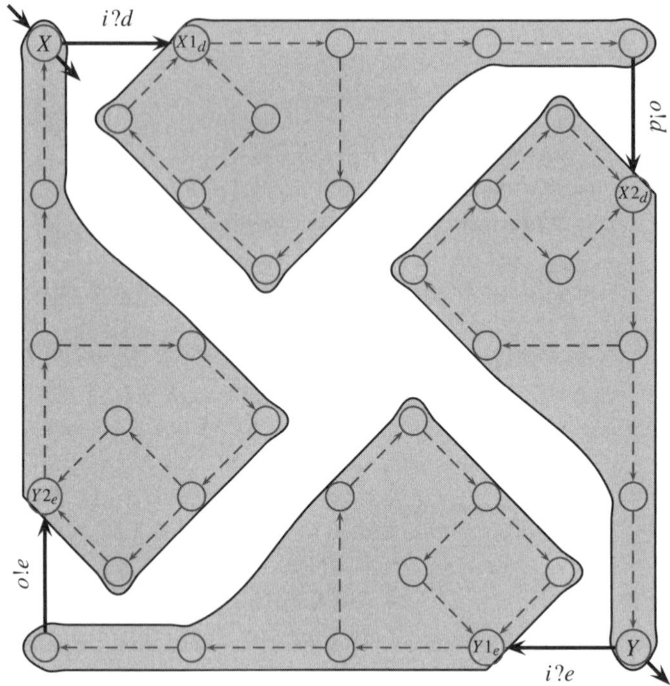

Fig. 7.9. Clustering of states in the Alternating-Bit Protocol.

Next, as indicated in the beginning of this section, it remains to be shown that process $\partial_H(S \parallel K \parallel L \parallel R)$, after abstraction of internal actions, satisfies the specification of the one-place buffer $Buf1_{io}$. The set of internal steps is $I = \{p?\!\!!x \mid x \in F \cup \{0, 1, \perp\},\ p \in \{sk, kr, rl, ls\}\} \cup \{t\}$, i.e., all communications over internal ports and the internal actions t; only the actions $i?d$ and $o!d$, for any $d \in D$, that occur at external ports and are meant to communicate with the environment, are external. Thus, there is need of an abstraction operator τ_I, making internal steps in the parameter set I invisible, such that

$$\tau_I(\partial_H(S \parallel K \parallel L \parallel R)) = Buf1_{io}$$

is derivable from the theory extended with abstraction. Such a parameterized class of abstraction operators is defined in the following chapter. For now, a plausibility argument is given by means of a picture showing that, after abstraction, $\partial_H(S \parallel K \parallel L \parallel R)$ shows the intended behavior. In Figure 7.9, the shaded areas of the graph represent clusters, containing sets of internal states that are equivalent from the point of view of the environment.

Exercises

7.8.1 In this exercise, a simple communication protocol is considered. Data (from some finite data set D) are to be transmitted from a sender S to a receiver R through some unreliable channel K (see Figure 7.10).

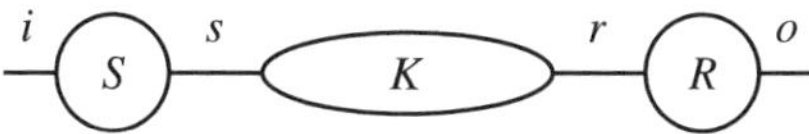

Fig. 7.10. A simple communication network.

The channel may forward the data correctly, or it may completely destroy data. The sender will send a data element until an acknowledgement *ack* is received. Consider the following specifications for S, K, and R:

$$\begin{aligned}
S &= 1 + \sum_{d \in D} i?d.S_d, \qquad \text{with for all } d \in D,\\
S_d &= s!d.S_d + s?ack.S,\\
R &= 1 + \sum_{d \in D} r?d.o!d.R + r!ack.R,\\
K &= 1 + \sum_{d \in D} s?d.(t.K + t.r!d.L),\\
L &= r?ack.(t.L + t.s!ack.K).
\end{aligned}$$

In this specification, t is some internal action. Assume standard communication, and let $H = \{s!x, s?x, r!x, r?x \mid x \in D \cup \{ack\}\}$.

(a) Derive a recursive specification for the process $\partial_H(S \parallel K \parallel R)$, and draw the transition system.

(b) Does this communication protocol behave correctly?

7.8.2 Consider, in the Alternating-Bit Protocol, alternative channel specifications *without* the internal t-steps:

$$\begin{aligned}
Ka &= 1 + \sum_{x \in F} sk?x.(kr!x.Ka + kr!\bot.Ka),\\
La &= 1 + \sum_{n \in \{0,1\}} rl?n.(ls!n.La + ls!\bot.La).
\end{aligned}$$

Show that the receiver can *force* channel Ka to behave correctly, by refusing to accept errors, i.e., consider

$$Ra = \partial_{\{kr?\bot\}}(R)$$

and similarly

$$Sa = \partial_{\{ls?\bot\}}(S)$$

and show that in the process $\partial_H(Sa \parallel Ka \parallel La \parallel Ra)$ (with $H = \{p?x, p!x \mid x \in F \cup \{0, 1, \bot\}, p \in \{sk, kr, rl, ls\}\}$ as above), errors $kr?\bot$ and $ls?\bot$ never occur, and that the protocol behaves correctly.
On the other hand, show that *with* the t actions, an occurrence of an error with the alternative sender and receiver specifications Sa and Ra results in deadlock, i.e., process $\partial_H(Sa \parallel K \parallel L \parallel Ra)$ has a deadlock (see Definition 4.4.14, adapted to the current setting).

7.9 Bibliographical remarks

The formulation of the theory TCP(A, γ) first appeared in (Baeten *et al.*, 2005). Earlier versions of TCP(A, γ) appear in (Baeten, 2003; Baeten & Reniers, 2004; Baeten & Bravetti, 2005); for older versions of similar theories with different names, see (Koymans & Vrancken, 1985; Vrancken, 1997; Baeten & Van Glabbeek, 1987). Replacing processes $a.1$ by constants a and removing action prefixing and the constant 1 yields the theory PA(A) of (Bergstra & Klop, 1982) when assuming a free merge (i.e., absence of communication, $\gamma = \emptyset$) and the theory ACP(A, γ) of (Bergstra & Klop, 1984a) for general communication functions. The theory MTCP(A, γ) corresponds to the theory of Basic Parallel Processes introduced in (Christensen, 1993) when the communication function γ is empty.

Communication and interaction occur in all concurrency theories. In (Hennessy, 1981), there is a communication function that has an identity element. Communication in CCS assumes both the presence of a so-called silent action τ (see the next chapter) and that all actions a have a so-called conjugate action $\bar{a}$. CCS communication is a special kind of handshaking with $\gamma(a, \bar{a}) = \tau$ for all a (see (Milner, 1980)). Since silent actions are related to abstraction; CCS communication combines these two concepts to some extent. In the current framework, communication and abstraction are separated, as discussed in more detail in the next chapter. CSP enforces communication of actions of the same name (see (Hoare, 1985)), a form of communication that is close to pure synchronization. Example 7.7.2 originates from (Baeten & Bravetti, 2006). In (Winskel, 1982), various communication formats are discussed.

The auxiliary operator $\mathbin{\|\!\_}$ is from (Bergstra & Klop, 1982) (although something similar can be found in (Bekič, 1984)); the auxiliary operator $\mid$ was introduced in (Bergstra & Klop, 1984a). In (Hennessy, 1988b), a single auxiliary operator is used for an axiomatization of parallel composition.

The standard communication function is from (Bergstra & Klop, 1986c), here in a notation inspired by CSP. Example 7.4.1 (Communication) is from (Baeten & Weijland, 1990). The earliest version of the Axioms of Standard

Concurrency, the Handshaking Axiom and the expansion theorem can be found in (Bergstra & Tucker, 1984). The specification of the bag in one equation, and the proof that the bag has no finite guarded recursive specification over the signature of TSP(A), can be found in (Bergstra & Klop, 1984b). The specification of the queue in Section 7.7 is from (Baeten & Bergstra, 1988). It is owed to earlier work in (Bergstra & Tiuryn, 1987). For further work on queues, see (Van Glabbeek & Vaandrager, 1989; Denvir *et al.*, 1985; Broy, 1987; Hoare, 1985; Pratt, 1982). The Alternating-Bit Protocol of (Bartlett *et al.*, 1969) was verified in ACP-style process algebra in (Bergstra & Klop, 1986c). For further information, see (Koymans & Mulder, 1990; Van Glabbeek & Vaandrager, 1989; Larsen & Milner, 1987; Milner, 1989; Halpern & Zuck, 1987).

8
Abstraction

8.1 Introduction

In the previous chapter, Sections 7.6 and 7.8, the need arose to abstract from certain actions. Assume that the actions that need to be abstracted from are defined by a set $I \subseteq A$. Using skip operators ε_I (see Section 6.7) in some cases yields the desired result. With skipping, abstraction from an action b in the process described by $a.b.c.1$ is denoted as $\varepsilon_{\{b\}}(a.b.c.1)$. Using the previously given axioms (see Table 6.9), the result of this form of abstraction for this example is

$$\varepsilon_{\{b\}}(a.b.c.1) = a.c.1.$$

It does not always work out well to use a skip operator ε_I for the purpose of abstraction. This can be illustrated as follows. Consider the process described by the process term $a.1 + b.0$. Abstraction from the action b through the application of $\varepsilon_{\{b\}}$ to this process term results in

$$\varepsilon_{\{b\}}(a.1 + b.0) = a.1 + 0 = a.1.$$

The problem with this form of abstraction is that, before abstraction, it was evident that the process described has a deadlock whereas after abstraction the potential deadlock has disappeared. For practical use of the process theories in this book, a form of abstraction needs to be defined that does not lose so much information while abstracting from unimportant activity. This means that the abstraction mechanism should allow for the hiding of certain actions but it should not hide the consequences of the execution of those. An example of such a consequence is a potential deadlock.

This motivates the introduction of the silent step τ in this chapter. The silent step cannot be observed explicitly by an observer that is observing the behavior of a process. A silent step can be removed in some cases, but in other cases it cannot. In the process theories to be introduced, the silent step appears as an action-prefix operator $\tau.\_$. Abstraction, through abstraction operators τ_I (for $I \subseteq A$), then means the renaming of each occurrence of an action-prefix operation $a.\_$ with $a \in I$ into a silent-step prefix operation.

The abstractions intended in the above examples can then be formulated as

$$\tau_{\{b\}}(a.b.c.1) = a.\tau.c.1$$

and

$$\tau_{\{b\}}(a.1 + b.0) = a.1 + \tau.0.$$

The occurrence of the silent step in the first example can be removed, because it cannot be observed by an external observer in any way, but in the second example it cannot be removed, because it can implicitly be observed via the deadlock resulting from its execution:

$$\tau_{\{b\}}(a.b.c.1) = a.\tau.c.1 = a.c.1$$

and

$$\tau_{\{b\}}(a.1 + b.0) = a.1 + \tau.0 \neq a.1 + 0 = a.1.$$

This chapter formally introduces abstraction and abstraction operators in the process-algebraic framework, and it is investigated when occurrences of silent steps are redundant and can hence be removed.

8.2 Transition systems with silent steps

The introduction of silent steps implies that it is necessary to reconsider the semantic framework used throughout this book. This section considers transition systems in which silent steps may occur. The resulting framework is an extension of the operational framework of Chapter 3. In the remainder, assume that $(S, L, \rightarrow, \downarrow)$ is a transition-system space, as defined in Definition 3.1.1. It is assumed that τ is a label, i.e., $\tau \in L$. Based on the observations in the introduction to this chapter, the following intuition can be formulated: if during the execution of a process a τ transition can be taken *without* discarding any of the options that were present before that transition, then this τ transition is redundant and can be removed. Figure 8.1 illustrates this situation. Observe that, assuming silent transitions are not externally visible, the process sketched on the left cannot be distinguished from the process on the right. After execution of the a action, the process on the left has the possibility of performing a step from x, or, after a silent step, a step from x or y. Assuming that an external observer cannot directly 'see' the silent step, this is equivalent to a process simply choosing between x and y as depicted on the right.

From the above discussion and examples, it should be clear that silent actions differ from other actions. This different behavior could potentially be

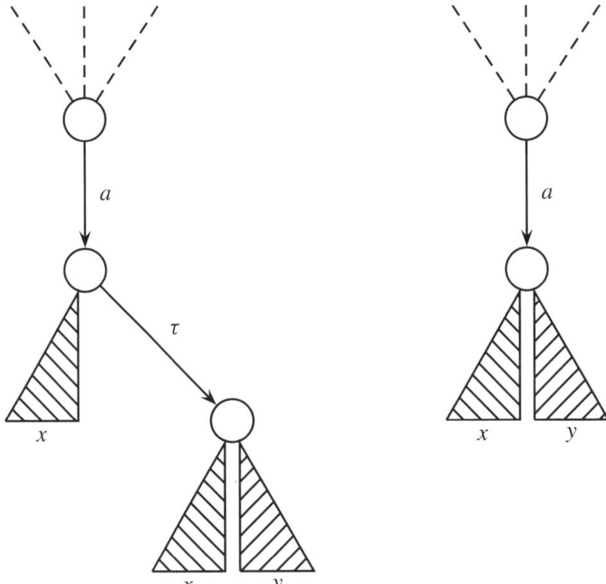

Fig. 8.1. Discarding silent steps.

realized by extra rules in a term deduction system that is used in the construction of a term model for some given process theory. However, a more generic and more elegant solution is to change the notion of equivalence on transition systems. The semantic equivalence in this chapter is no longer bisimilarity as considered before, but instead, (rooted) branching bisimilarity. In order to distinguish the various semantic equivalences, bisimilarity as considered up to this point, is sometimes called *strong* bisimilarity from now on.

To define branching bisimilarity, two auxiliary notions are needed. The following definition introduces the concept of reachability via silent steps.

Definition 8.2.1 (Reachable with τ-steps) The binary relation $\twoheadrightarrow$ on the states S of a transition-system space, denoting reachability via silent steps, is the smallest relation satisfying, for all states $s, t, u \in S$,

(i) $s \twoheadrightarrow s$;
(ii) whenever $s \xrightarrow{\tau} t$, then $s \twoheadrightarrow t$;
(iii) whenever $s \twoheadrightarrow t$ and $t \twoheadrightarrow u$, then $s \twoheadrightarrow u$.

Stated differently, relation $\twoheadrightarrow$ is the reflexive and transitive closure of the relation $\xrightarrow{\tau}$.

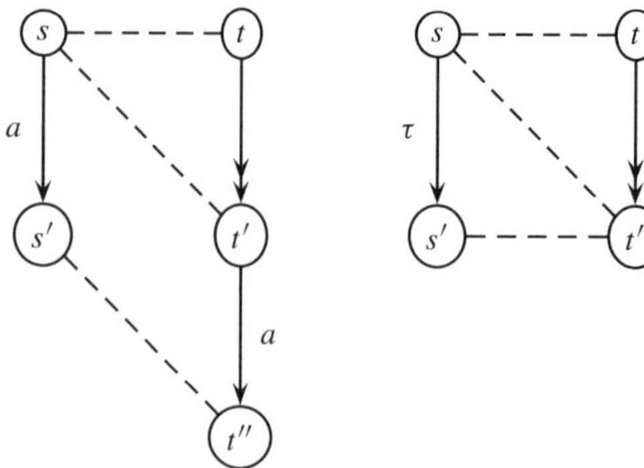

Fig. 8.2. Visualization of transfer condition (i) of a branching bisimulation.

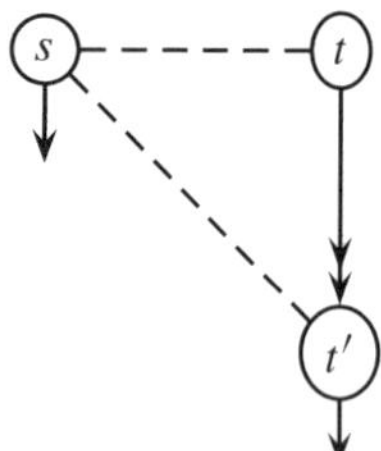

Fig. 8.3. Visualization of transfer condition (iii) of a branching bisimulation.

The following notational abbreviation is introduced to allow shorter formulations.

Notation 8.2.2 Let for any states $s, t \in S$ of a transition-system space and action $a \in L$, notation $s \stackrel{(a)}{\rightarrow} t$ be an abbreviation of $s \stackrel{a}{\rightarrow} t$, or $a = \tau$ and $s = t$. That is, $s \stackrel{(\tau)}{\rightarrow} t$ means that either one or zero τ-steps are performed; $s \stackrel{(a)}{\rightarrow} t$ with $a \neq \tau$ means that a single a-step is performed.

Definition 8.2.3 (Branching bisimilarity) A binary relation R on the set of states S of a transition-system space is a *branching bisimulation* relation if and only if the following so-called transfer conditions hold:

(i) for all states $s, t, s' \in S$, whenever $(s, t) \in R$ and $s \stackrel{a}{\rightarrow} s'$ for some $a \in L$, then there are states t' and t'' in S such that $t \twoheadrightarrow t'$ and $t' \stackrel{(a)}{\rightarrow} t''$ and both $(s, t') \in R$ and $(s', t'') \in R$;

(ii) vice versa, for all states $s, t, t' \in S$, whenever $(s, t) \in R$ and $t \stackrel{a}{\rightarrow} t'$ for some $a \in L$, then there are states s' and s'' in S such that $s \twoheadrightarrow s'$ and $s' \stackrel{(a)}{\rightarrow} s''$ and both $(s', t) \in R$ and $(s'', t') \in R$;

(iii) whenever $(s, t) \in R$ and $s\downarrow$, then there is a state $t' \in S$ such that $t \twoheadrightarrow t'$, $t'\downarrow$, and $(s, t') \in R$;

(iv) whenever $(s, t) \in R$ and $t\downarrow$, then there is a state $s' \in S$ such that $s \twoheadrightarrow s'$, $s'\downarrow$, and $(s', t) \in R$.

The first and third conditions are visualized in Figures 8.2 and 8.3. The branching bisimulation relations are indicated by the dashed lines connecting the states.

Two transition systems $s, t \in S$ are *branching bisimulation equivalent* or *branching bisimilar*, notation $s \leftrightarrow_b t$, if and only if there is a branching bisimulation relation R on S with $(s, t) \in R$.

Example 8.2.4 (Branching bisimilarity) In Figure 8.4, two pairs of branching bisimilar transition systems are depicted.

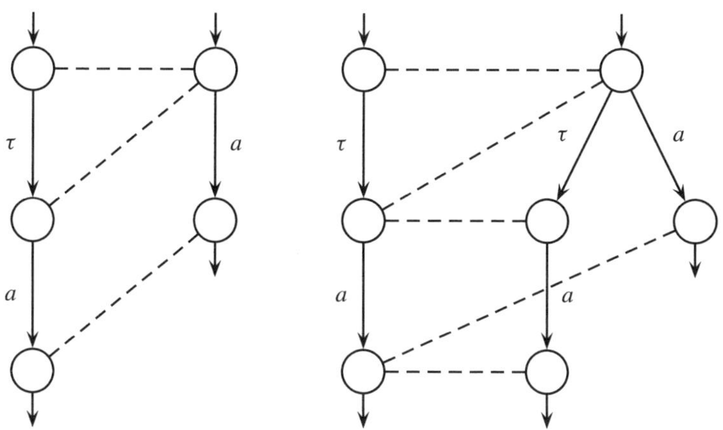

Fig. 8.4. Examples of branching bisimilar transition systems.

Theorem 8.2.5 (Equivalence) Branching bisimilarity is an equivalence.

Proof Let S be the set of states of a transition-system space. First, the relation $R = \{(s, s) \mid s \in S\}$ is obviously a branching bisimulation relation. This proves that $s \leftrightarrow_b s$ for any transition system induced by any state $s \in S$, showing reflexivity of branching bisimilarity. Second, assume that $s \leftrightarrow_b t$ for states $s, t \in S$. If R is a branching bisimulation relation witnessing $s \leftrightarrow_b t$, then the relation $R' = \{(v, u) \mid (u, v) \in R\}$ is a branching bisimulation relation as well. This implies that $t \leftrightarrow_b s$, showing symmetry of branching bisimilarity. Third, assume that $s \leftrightarrow_b t$ and $t \leftrightarrow_b u$ for states $s, t, u \in S$. Let

R_1 and R_2 be branching bisimulation relations witnessing $s \leftrightarrow_b t$ and $t \leftrightarrow_b u$, respectively. Then the relation composition $R_1 \circ R_2$ is a branching bisimulation relation witnessing $s \leftrightarrow_b u$, showing transitivity and completing the proof. The interested reader is referred to (Basten, 1998) for a more detailed proof. □

In order to define a process theory for a semantic equivalence, it is important that such an equivalence is a congruence with respect to the operators that are in the signature of that equational theory. (In other words, the equivalence should be a congruence on the term algebra.) This also applies to branching bisimilarity. So, to define a process theory with silent actions that extends the process theory BSP(A), it is required that the equivalence to be axiomatized is a congruence for the action-prefix operators and alternative composition.

It turns out that the notion of branching bisimilarity is lacking in this respect, as it is not a congruence with respect to alternative composition, assuming that the deduction rules for the alternative-composition operator remain as they are (see Table 4.2). Consider the process terms $a.1$ and $\tau.a.1$. To these process terms, the transition systems from Figure 8.5 can be associated. A branching

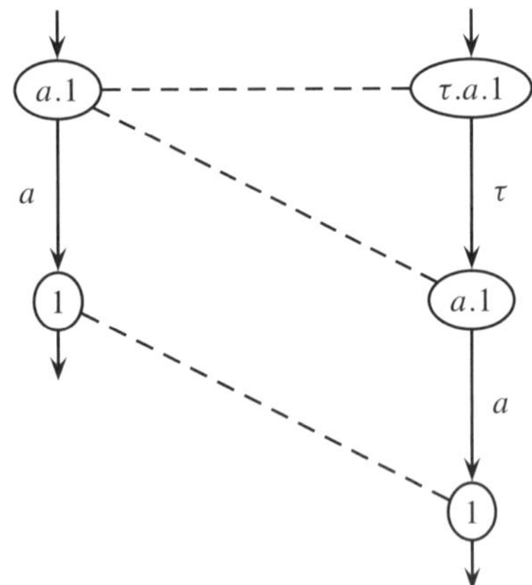

Fig. 8.5. Transition systems $a.1$ and $\tau.a.1$.

bisimulation relation on the states is drawn in the figure as well. Hence, the states represented by these two process terms are branching bisimilar. (Note the correspondence between the transition systems of Figure 8.5 and the two leftmost transition systems in Figure 8.4.) Now consider the transition systems associated to the process terms $a.1 + b.1$ and $\tau.a.1 + b.1$ in Figure 8.6. If branching bisimilarity would be a congruence with respect to alternative composition, then the states represented by these two process terms would be branching bisimilar as well. This is not the case. By definition, the two

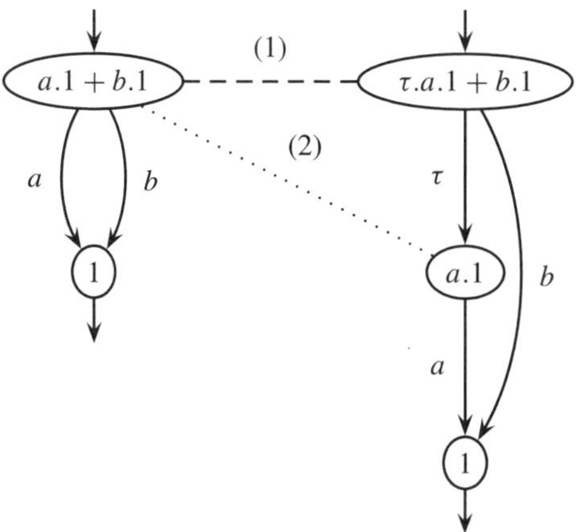

Fig. 8.6. Transition systems $a.1 + b.1$ and $\tau.a.1 + b.1$.

initial states of the transition systems should be related (1). As the right initial state has a τ transition to the state $a.1$, necessarily (by transfer condition (ii) of Definition 8.2.3 (Branching bisimilarity)) this state must be related to the initial state of the left transition system (2). But, this cannot be, as the one only allows an *a* transition, whereas the other one also allows a *b* transition.

Thus, the notion of branching bisimilarity turns out not to be a congruence with respect to the alternative composition and it will be necessary to define an extra condition, by which a notion that is a congruence can be formulated. The extra condition should ensure that processes $a.1$ and $\tau.a.1$ are considered different.

It is possible to give an intuitive explanation as to why pairs of processes like $a.1$ and $\tau.a.1$ should be considered different. Assume that a machine performing atomic actions is observed and that the beginning of an atomic step is observable. With this interpretation, the silent step can be interpreted as some action of which also the beginning cannot be observed. It follows from this intuition that the processes $a.1$ and $\tau.a.1$ are not equivalent, whereas they are branching bisimilar. The one process will immediately start by performing *a* whereas the other process will wait some time before showing its first observable action.

The extra condition that is formulated next amounts to saying that the pair of initial states should be treated differently, when relating them by a branching bisimulation: the initial step of a process cannot be matched by a step of the other process that has preceding silent steps, and the relation is therefore like a strong bisimulation initially.

Definition 8.2.6 (Rooted branching bisimilarity) Two transition systems s and t in S are *rooted branching bisimulation equivalent* or *rooted branching bisimilar*, notation $s \leftrightarrow_{rb} t$, if and only if there is a branching bisimulation relation R on S with $(s, t) \in R$ such that

(i) for all states $s' \in S$, whenever $s \xrightarrow{a} s'$ for some $a \in L$, then there is a state t' such that $t \xrightarrow{a} t'$ and $(s', t') \in R$;
(ii) vice versa, for all states $t' \in S$, whenever $t \xrightarrow{a} t'$ for some $a \in L$, then there is a state s' such that $s \xrightarrow{a} s'$ and $(s', t') \in R$;
(iii) whenever $s\downarrow$, then $t\downarrow$;
(iv) whenever $t\downarrow$, then $s\downarrow$.

Usually, a branching bisimulation relation that satisfies the above so-called root conditions with respect to the states s and t is called a rooted branching bisimulation relation for s and t.

Example 8.2.7 (Rooted branching bisimilarity) The two transition systems of Figure 8.5 are not rooted branching bisimilar; in particular, the branching bisimulation given in Figure 8.5 is not a rooted branching bisimulation.

Figure 8.7 depicts two pairs of rooted branching bisimilar transition systems. The rooted branching bisimulation relations are as usual indicated by the dashed lines. In Figure 8.8, a rooted branching bisimulation relation is drawn for two slightly more complex transition systems.

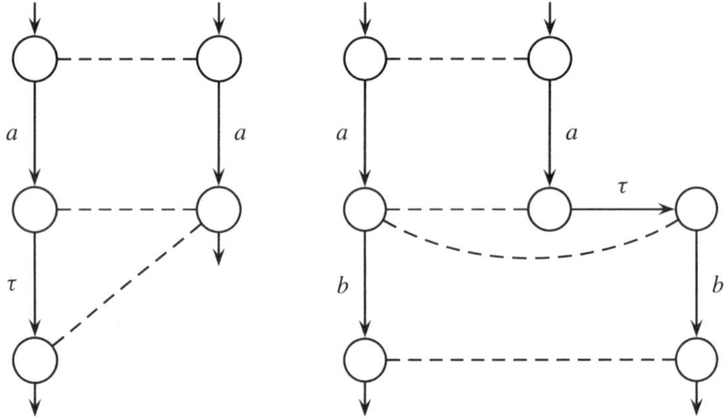

Fig. 8.7. Examples of rooted branching bisimilar transition systems.

Before, it was shown that branching bisimilarity is not a congruence with respect to alternative composition by means of a counterexample. For rooted branching bisimilarity, this is not a counterexample since the transition systems from Figure 8.5 are not rooted branching bisimilar.

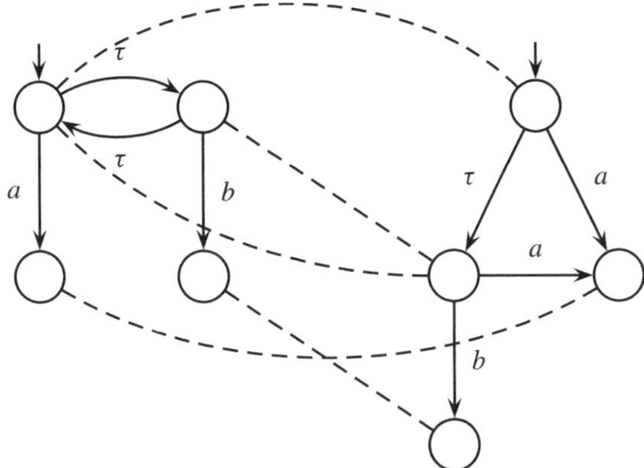

Fig. 8.8. Another example of rooted branching bisimilar transition systems.

Rooted branching bisimilarity turns out to be an equivalence relation.

Theorem 8.2.8 (Equivalence) Rooted branching bisimilarity is an equivalence relation.

Proof The relations that prove that branching bisimilarity is an equivalence also prove that rooted branching bisimilarity is an equivalence. □

Theorem 8.2.9 (Relation between bisimilarity notions) The following relations hold between the three semantic equivalences introduced so far in Chapter 3 and this chapter:

$$\leftrightarrow \subseteq \leftrightarrow_{\mathrm{rb}} \subseteq \leftrightarrow_{\mathrm{b}}.$$

Proof Suppose that $p \leftrightarrow q$, i.e., p and q are strongly bisimilar. By definition this means that there exists a strong bisimulation relation R such that $(p, q) \in R$. Using the facts that $s \xrightarrow{a} t$ implies $s \xrightarrow{(a)} t$ and that $t \twoheadrightarrow t$ always holds, every strong bisimulation relation is also a branching bisimulation relation. Equally obvious is that every strong bisimulation relation R satisfies the root conditions for each of its elements. Therefore, the strong bisimulation relation R witnessing the bisimilarity of p and q is also a rooted branching bisimulation relation for p and q. This proves $\leftrightarrow \subseteq \leftrightarrow_{\mathrm{rb}}$.
Suppose that $p \leftrightarrow_{\mathrm{rb}} q$, i.e., p and q are rooted branching bisimilar. Then, by definition, there is a rooted branching bisimulation relation R such that $(p, q) \in R$. Since R is also a branching bisimulation, p and q are branching bisimilar: $p \leftrightarrow_{\mathrm{b}} q$. This proves that $\leftrightarrow_{\mathrm{rb}} \subseteq \leftrightarrow_{\mathrm{b}}$. □

The theorem cannot in general be strengthened. For transition-system spaces without silent steps, the three semantic equivalences are equal, so none of the subset relations in the theorem is strict in general. However, the examples involving silent steps given so far show that the three semantic equivalences are in general all different, in the sense that they relate different transition systems for most non-trivial transition-system spaces with silent actions, so none of the subset relations in the theorem are equalities in general.

Exercises

8.2.1 Are the following transition systems branching bisimilar? If so, give a branching bisimulation relation between the two systems; otherwise, explain why they are not branching bisimilar.

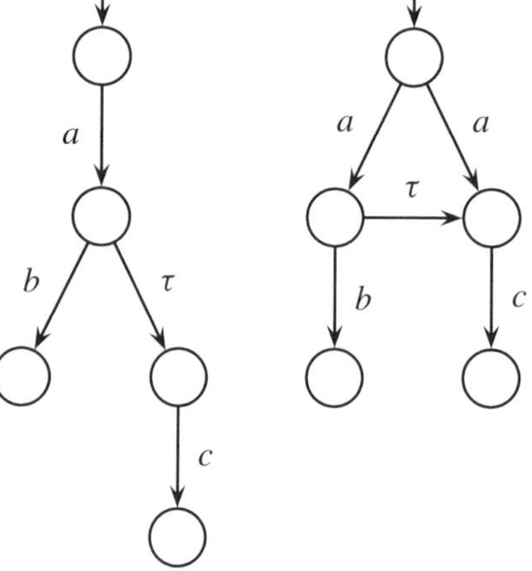

8.2.2 Are the following pairs of transition systems rooted branching bisimilar? If so, give a rooted branching bisimulation relation between the two systems; otherwise, explain why they are not rooted branching bisimilar.

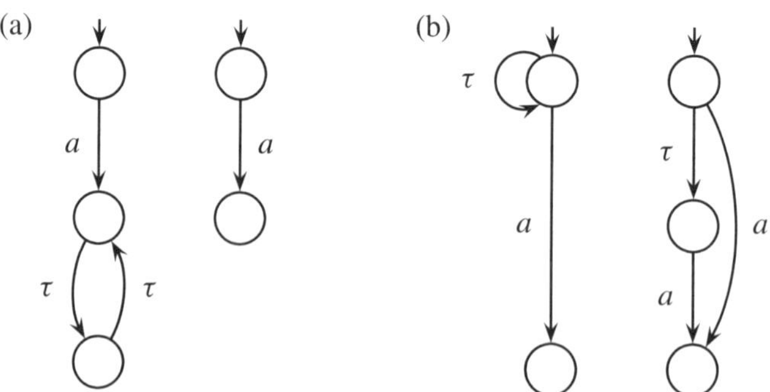

(c)

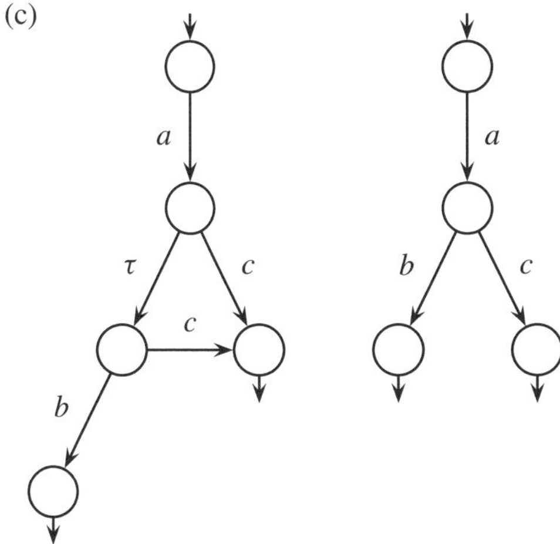

8.2.3 Starting from Exercise 3.1.9, try to develop a notion of coloring for branching bisimilarity. That is, develop the concepts of abstract colored traces and coloring schemes that precisely capture branching bisimilarity and rooted branching bisimilarity.

8.2.4 A binary relation R on the set of states S of a transition-system space is called a *weak bisimulation* relation if and only if the following conditions hold:

(a) for all states $s, t, s' \in S$, whenever $(s, t) \in R$ and $s \stackrel{a}{\rightarrow} s'$ for some $a \in L$, then there are states t_1, t_2, t' in S such that $t \twoheadrightarrow t_1$, $t_1 \stackrel{(a)}{\rightarrow} t_2$ and $t_2 \twoheadrightarrow t'$, such that $(s', t') \in R$;

(b) vice versa, for all states $s, t, t' \in S$, whenever $(s, t) \in R$ and $t \stackrel{a}{\rightarrow} t'$ for some $a \in L$, then there are states s_1, s_2, s' in S such that $s \twoheadrightarrow s_1$, $s_1 \stackrel{(a)}{\rightarrow} s_2$ and $s_2 \twoheadrightarrow s'$ such that $(s', t') \in R$;

(c) whenever $(s, t) \in R$ and $s\downarrow$, then there is a state $t' \in S$ such that $t \twoheadrightarrow t'$ and $t'\downarrow$;

(d) whenever $(s, t) \in R$ and $t\downarrow$, then there is a state $s' \in S$ such that $s \twoheadrightarrow s'$ and $s'\downarrow$.

Prove that weak bisimilarity is an equivalence relation on the set of states S. Prove that, whenever two states are branching bisimilar, they are also weakly bisimilar. Give an example of two transition systems that are weakly bisimilar but not branching bisimilar.

8.2.5 Two transition systems s and t in S are *rooted weak bisimulation equivalent* or *rooted weakly bisimilar* if and only if there is a weak bisimulation relation R on S with $(s, t) \in R$ such that

(a) for all states $s' \in S$, whenever $s \stackrel{a}{\to} s'$ for some $a \in L, a \neq \tau$, then there is a state t' such that $t \stackrel{a}{\to} t'$ and $(s', t') \in R$;
(b) vice versa, for all states $t' \in S$, whenever $t \stackrel{a}{\to} t'$ for some $a \in L, a \neq \tau$, then there is a state s' such that $s \stackrel{a}{\to} s'$ and $(s', t') \in R$;
(c) whenever $s\downarrow$, then $t\downarrow$;
(d) whenever $t\downarrow$, then $s\downarrow$.

Prove that rooted weak bisimilarity is an equivalence relation on S. Prove that, whenever two states are rooted branching bisimilar, they are also rooted weakly bisimilar. Give an example of two transition systems that are rooted weakly bisimilar but not branching bisimilar.

8.3 BSP with silent steps

This section introduces the process theory $\mathrm{BSP}_\tau(A)$. This theory is the extension of BSP(A) with the previously mentioned τ-prefix operator $\tau.\_$. The axioms of the process theory $\mathrm{BSP}_\tau(A)$ are the axioms of the process theory BSP(A) (given in Table 4.3) and the axiom given in Table 8.1. All atomic actions a that occur in the axioms are from now on assumed to be from the set $A_\tau = A \cup \{\tau\}$, unless explicitly stated otherwise.

$\mathrm{BSP}_\tau(A)$	
BSP(A);	
unary: $\tau.\_$;	
x, y;	
$a.(\tau.(x + y) + x) = a.(x + y)$	B

Table 8.1. The process theory $\mathrm{BSP}_\tau(A)$ (with $a \in A_\tau$).

The one and only new axiom in $\mathrm{BSP}_\tau(A)$ is Axiom B, the so-called *Branching Axiom*. It captures precisely which occurrences of the silent step are without consequences and can therefore be omitted. This is illustrated by means of the schematic representation of the Branching Axiom in Figure 8.9. The execution of the internal step τ only adds alternatives. In other words, the alternatives that could have been chosen instead of executing the internal step, are still alternatives once this internal step has been executed.

Example 8.3.1 (A derivation) A derivation of

$$\mathrm{BSP}_\tau(A) \vdash c.(\tau.(b.1 + a.1) + \tau.(a.1 + b.1)) = c.(a.1 + b.1)$$

using Axiom B can be given as follows:

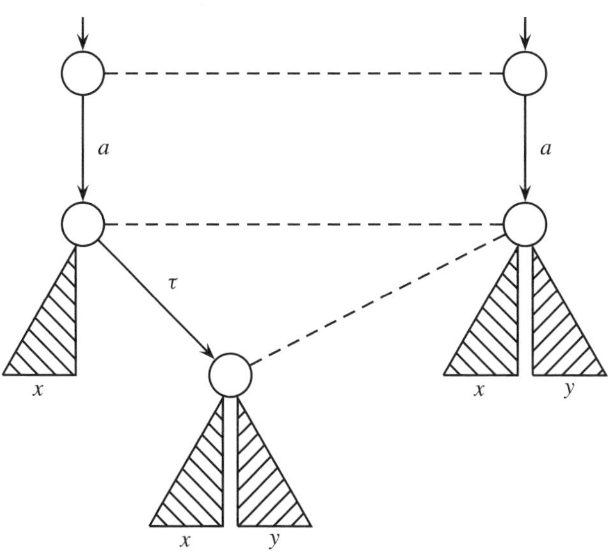

Fig. 8.9. Schematic representation of the Branching Axiom.

$$\begin{aligned}\mathrm{BSP}_\tau(A) \vdash c.(\tau.(b.1 + a.1) + \tau.(a.1 + b.1)) \\ = c.(\tau.(a.1 + b.1) + \tau.(a.1 + b.1)) \\ = c.(\tau.(a.1 + b.1)) = c.(\tau.(0 + a.1 + b.1) + 0) \\ = c.(0 + a.1 + b.1) = c.(a.1 + b.1).\end{aligned}$$

For obvious reasons, it is impossible to obtain an elimination theorem, i.e., it is impossible to reduce an arbitrary closed $\mathrm{BSP}_\tau(A)$-term to a $\mathrm{BSP}(A)$-term. Nevertheless, it can be shown that $\mathrm{BSP}_\tau(A)$ is a conservative ground-extension of $\mathrm{BSP}(A)$.

Theorem 8.3.2 (Conservative ground-extension) Process theory $\mathrm{BSP}_\tau(A)$ is a conservative ground-extension of process theory $\mathrm{BSP}(A)$.

Proof Exercise 8.3.4. □

Exercises

8.3.1 Prove that $\mathrm{BSP}_\tau(A) \vdash a.(\tau.b.1 + b.1) = a.\tau.(\tau.b.1 + \tau.\tau.b.1)$.

8.3.2 Prove that $\mathrm{BSP}_\tau(A) \vdash a.\tau.x = a.x$ for all $a \in A_\tau$.

8.3.3 Prove that $\mathrm{BSP}_\tau(A) \vdash a.(\tau.x + x) = a.x$ for all $a \in A_\tau$.

8.3.4 Prove Theorem 8.3.2 (Conservative ground-extension).

(Hint: construct a proof based on a term rewriting system, as illustrated in the proof of Theorem 4.5.3 (Conservative ground-extension of projection). The term rewriting system needs three variants of Axiom B. A proof via the results developed in Section 3.2 is not possible since this meta-theory assumes strong bisimilarity as a semantic equivalence, and therefore does not apply to the current setting with (rooted) branching bisimilarity as the equivalence notion.)

8.4 The term model

A term model for the process theory $\mathrm{BSP}_\tau(A)$ can be developed along the same lines as in earlier chapters. First, the term algebra $\mathbb{P}(\mathrm{BSP}_\tau(A))$ is defined.

Definition 8.4.1 (Term algebra) The *term algebra* for $\mathrm{BSP}_\tau(A)$ is the algebra $\mathbb{P}(\mathrm{BSP}_\tau(A)) = (\mathcal{C}(\mathrm{BSP}_\tau(A)), +, (a.\_)_{a\in A}, \tau.\_, 0, 1)$.

The term deduction system for $\mathrm{BSP}_\tau(A)$ consists of the same deduction rules as the deduction rules for $\mathrm{BSP}(A)$ of Tables 4.2 and 4.4 with the only difference that now $a \in A_\tau$.

As already mentioned in Section 8.2, rooted branching bisimilarity is an equivalence. It is not hard to prove that it is also a congruence on the term algebra for $\mathrm{BSP}_\tau(A)$. Recall that branching bisimilarity is not a congruence with respect to alternative composition. Note that it is not possible to prove the desired result via Theorem 3.2.7 (Congruence theorem), because that only applies to strong bisimilarity and not to rooted branching bisimilarity.

Theorem 8.4.2 (Congruence) Rooted branching bisimilarity is a congruence on the term algebra $\mathbb{P}(\mathrm{BSP}_\tau(A))$.

Proof To prove that rooted branching bisimilarity is a congruence on $\mathbb{P}(\mathrm{BSP}_\tau(A))$, it is necessary to show that for each n-ary ($n \geq 1$) function f of $\mathbb{P}(\mathrm{BSP}_\tau(A))$ and for all $p_1, \ldots, p_n, q_1, \ldots, q_n \in \mathcal{C}(\mathrm{BSP}_\tau(A))$, $p_1 \leftrightarroweq_{\mathrm{rb}} q_1, \cdots, p_n \leftrightarroweq_{\mathrm{rb}} q_n$ implies that $f(p_1, \ldots, p_n) \leftrightarroweq_{\mathrm{rb}} f(q_1, \ldots, q_n)$.

(i) Alternative composition. Suppose that $p_1 \leftrightarroweq_{\mathrm{rb}} q_1$ and $p_2 \leftrightarroweq_{\mathrm{rb}} q_2$. By definition, this means that there exist branching bisimulation relations R_1 and R_2 such that the pairs $(p_1, q_1) \in R_1$ and $(p_2, q_2) \in R_2$ satisfy the root conditions of Definition 8.2.6 (Rooted branching bisimilarity). It needs to be shown that $p_1 + p_2 \leftrightarroweq_{\mathrm{rb}} q_1 + q_2$.
Define $R = R_1 \cup R_2 \cup \{(p_1 + p_2, q_1 + q_2)\}$. The pairs in R that are

also in R_1 or in R_2 trivially satisfy the transfer conditions of Definition 8.2.3 (Branching bisimilarity). Thus, it remains to check whether the pair $(p_1 + p_2, q_1 + q_2) \in R$ satisfies the transfer conditions of Definition 8.2.3 and the root conditions of Definition 8.2.6 (Rooted branching bisimilarity). Since the root conditions imply the transfer conditions, in effect, this means that only the root conditions have to be checked.

First, consider root condition (i) of Definition 8.2.6. Suppose that $p_1 + p_2 \xrightarrow{a} r_1$ for some $a \in A_\tau$ and $r_1 \in \mathcal{C}(\mathrm{BSP}_\tau(A))$. Then, by the deduction rules of Table 4.2, $p_1 \xrightarrow{a} r_1$ or $p_2 \xrightarrow{a} r_1$. The two cases are similar; hence only the first case is elaborated. From the assumptions that $p_1 \leftrightarrow_{\mathrm{rb}} q_1$ and that this rooted branching bisimilarity relationship is witnessed by the relation R_1, it follows that $q_1 \xrightarrow{a} s_1$ for some s_1 in $\mathcal{C}(\mathrm{BSP}_\tau(A))$ such that $(r_1, s_1) \in R_1$. Using the deduction rules of Table 4.2 then also $q_1 + q_2 \xrightarrow{a} s_1$. Furthermore, as $R_1 \subseteq R$, $(r_1, s_1) \in R$, this completes the proof for condition (i).

The proof for root condition (ii) is omitted as it is similar to the proof for condition (i).

Consider root condition (iii). Suppose that $(p_1 + p_2)\downarrow$. Then $p_1\downarrow$ or $p_2\downarrow$. From the assumption that $p_1 \leftrightarrow_{\mathrm{rb}} q_1$ and $p_2 \leftrightarrow_{\mathrm{rb}} q_2$, it follows that $q_1\downarrow$ or $q_2\downarrow$. Thus, in either case $(q_1 + q_2)\downarrow$.

The proof for root condition (iv) is again omitted as it is similar to the previous proof.

(ii) Action prefix. Suppose that $p \leftrightarrow_{\mathrm{rb}} q$ is witnessed by the rooted branching bisimulation relation R. Define $R' = R \cup \{(a.p, a.q)\}$. It has to be shown that R' is a branching bisimulation and that the pair $(a.p, a.q)$ satisfies the root conditions.

As R is assumed to be a branching bisimulation, all pairs in R' that are also in R satisfy the transfer conditions. Hence, it remains to check whether the pair $(a.p, a.q)$ satisfies the transfer conditions. Since in addition for $(a.p, a.q)$ the root conditions must be satisfied, it suffices to establish only the root conditions. Both $a.p$ and $a.q$ cannot terminate: $(a.p)\not\downarrow$ and $(a.q)\not\downarrow$. Each of these process terms can perform an a transition only: $a.p \xrightarrow{a} p$ and $a.q \xrightarrow{a} q$. It must be shown that the resulting states (process terms, i.e., p and q) are related by R'. As R is a (rooted) branching bisimulation relation witnessing $p \leftrightarrow_{\mathrm{rb}} q$, by definition $(p, q) \in R$. As $R \subseteq R'$, then also $(p, q) \in R'$.

(iii) τ-prefix. Suppose that $p \leftrightarrow_{\mathrm{rb}} q$ is witnessed by the rooted branching bisimulation relation R. Define $R' = R \cup \{(\tau.p, \tau.q)\}$. It has to be shown that R' is a branching bisimulation relation and that $(\tau.p, \tau.q)$

satisfies the root conditions. Again, proving that $(\tau.p, \tau.q)$ satisfies the root conditions suffices. This part is trivial and therefore omitted. □

The term model of $\mathrm{BSP}_\tau(A)$ is obtained in the standard way by considering the rooted branching bisimilarity quotient of the term algebra. It can be shown that $\mathrm{BSP}_\tau(A)$ is indeed a sound axiomatization of rooted branching bisimilarity on closed process terms. It turns out that it is also ground-complete.

Definition 8.4.3 (Term model of $\mathrm{BSP}_\tau(A)$**)** The term model of process theory $\mathrm{BSP}_\tau(A)$ is the quotient algebra $\mathbb{P}(\mathrm{BSP}_\tau(A))_{/\leftrightarrows_{rb}}$, with $\mathbb{P}(\mathrm{BSP}_\tau(A))$ the term algebra of Definition 8.4.1.

Theorem 8.4.4 (Soundness) Theory $\mathrm{BSP}_\tau(A)$ is a sound axiomatization of algebra $\mathbb{P}(\mathrm{BSP}_\tau(A))_{/\leftrightarrows_{rb}}$, i.e., $\mathbb{P}(\mathrm{BSP}_\tau(A))_{/\leftrightarrows_{rb}} \models \mathrm{BSP}_\tau(A)$.

Proof It must be shown that, for each axiom $s = t$ of $\mathrm{BSP}_\tau(A)$, $\mathbb{P}(\mathrm{BSP}_\tau(A))_{/\leftrightarrows_{rb}} \models s = t$. Hence, for each axiom $s = t$ it must be shown that $p \leftrightarrows_{rb} q$ for any closed instantiation $p = q$ of $s = t$.
For each axiom $s = t$ of $\mathrm{BSP}_\tau(A)$ that is also an axiom of $\mathrm{BSP}(A)$, it has already been shown that $p \leftrightarrows q$ for any closed instantiation $p = q$ of $s = t$; see the proofs of Theorems 4.3.5 (Soundness of MPT(A)) and 4.4.7 (Soundness of BSP(A)). Note that these proofs carry over to the current setting where closed terms may contain τ-prefix operators. As $\leftrightarrows \subseteq \leftrightarrows_{rb}$ (see Theorem 8.2.9 (Relation between bisimilarity notions)), it follows immediately that $p \leftrightarrows_{rb} q$ for any closed instantiation $p = q$ of any axiom $s = t$ of $\mathrm{BSP}_\tau(A)$ that is also an axiom of BSP(A). Hence, $\mathbb{P}(\mathrm{BSP}_\tau(A))_{/\leftrightarrows_{rb}} \models s = t$ for all these axioms.
For the soundness of Axiom B, it has to be shown that $a.(\tau.(p+q)+p) \leftrightarrows_{rb} a.(p+q)$ for any action $a \in A_\tau$ and closed terms $p, q \in C(\mathrm{BSP}_\tau(A))$. Let $R = \{(a.(\tau.(p+q)+p), a.(p+q)), (\tau.(p+q)+p, p+q), (p, p) \mid a \in A_\tau, p, q \in C(\mathrm{BSP}_\tau(A))\}$. It must be shown that all elements of R satisfy the transfer conditions for branching bisimulation relations of Definition 8.2.3 (Branching bisimilarity) and that the pair $(a.(\tau.(p+q)+p), a.(p+q))$ in addition satisfies the root conditions of Definition 8.2.6 (Rooted branching bisimilarity). For all pairs (p, p) the transfer conditions are satisfied trivially. Next, consider the pairs in R of the form $(\tau.(p+q)+p, p+q)$.

(i) Suppose that $\tau.(p+q)+p \xrightarrow{a} p'$ for some $a \in A_\tau$ and $p' \in C(\mathrm{BSP}_\tau(A))$. By inspection of the deduction rules, it easily follows that necessarily (1) $p \xrightarrow{a} p'$ or (2) $a \equiv \tau$ and $p' \equiv p+q$. In the first case, then also $p + q \twoheadrightarrow p + q$ and $p + q \stackrel{(a)}{\rightarrow} p'$, and $(\tau.(p+q) + p, p + q) \in R$ and $(p', p') \in R$. Visually,

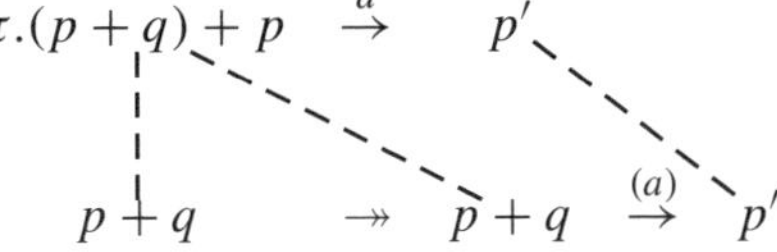

In the second case, obviously, $p + q \twoheadrightarrow p + q$, $p + q \stackrel{(\tau)}{\rightarrow} p + q$, $(\tau.(p+q) + p, p + q) \in R$ and $(p + q, p + q) \in R$. Visually,

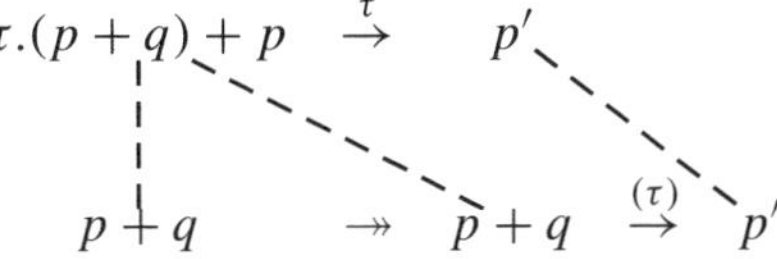

(ii) Suppose that $p + q \stackrel{a}{\rightarrow} q'$ for some $a \in A_\tau$ and $q' \in \mathcal{C}(\mathrm{BSP}_\tau(A))$. From the deduction rules, it follows that $\tau.(p + q) + p \stackrel{\tau}{\rightarrow} p + q$. Therefore, $\tau.(p + q) + p \twoheadrightarrow p + q$. Also, $p + q \stackrel{(a)}{\rightarrow} q'$ follows from $p+q \stackrel{a}{\rightarrow} q'$. This means that this case is proven since $(p+q, p+q) \in R$ and $(q', q') \in R$.

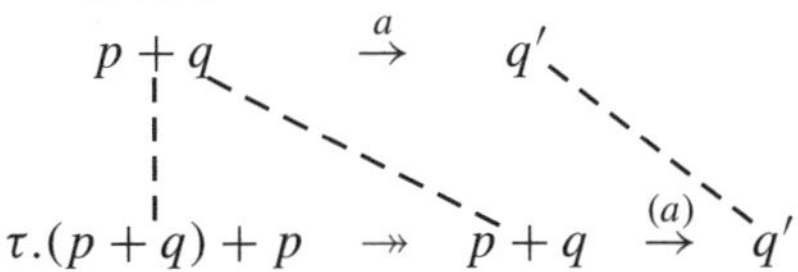

(iii) Suppose that $(\tau.(p + q) + p)\downarrow$. Then, necessarily, $p\downarrow$. Then also, $p+q \twoheadrightarrow p+q$ and $(p + q)\downarrow$. Note that $(\tau.(p+q)+p, p+q) \in R$, which proves this case.

(iv) Suppose that $(p + q)\downarrow$. By the deduction rules, $\tau.(p + q) + p \stackrel{\tau}{\rightarrow} p+q$. Therefore, $\tau.(p+q)+p \twoheadrightarrow p+q$. Combined with $(p + q)\downarrow$ and $(p + q, p + q) \in R$ this case is also proven.

Finally, consider the pairs of the form $(a.(\tau.(p+q)+p), a.(p+q))$. As both $(a.(\tau.(p + q) + p))\not\downarrow$ and $(a.(p + q))\not\downarrow$, obviously the root conditions regarding termination are satisfied. The root conditions for transitions are satisfied as the only possible transitions are $a.(\tau.(p + q) + p) \stackrel{a}{\rightarrow} \tau.(p + q) + p$ and $a.(p + q) \stackrel{a}{\rightarrow} p + q$ and $(\tau.(p + q) + p, p + q) \in R$. Visually,

$$\begin{array}{ccc} a.(\tau.(p+q)+p) & \stackrel{a}{\rightarrow} & \tau.(p+q)+p \\ | & & | \\ a.(p+q) & \stackrel{a}{\rightarrow} & p+q \end{array}$$

□

Theorem 8.4.5 (Ground-completeness) Theory $\mathrm{BSP}_\tau(A)$ is a ground-complete axiomatization of the term model $\mathbb{P}(\mathrm{BSP}_\tau(A))_{/\leftrightarrow_{\mathrm{rb}}}$, i.e., for any closed

$\text{BSP}_\tau(A)$-terms p and q, $\mathbb{P}(\text{BSP}_\tau(A))_{/\leftrightarrow_{\text{rb}}} \models p = q$ implies that $\text{BSP}_\tau(A) \vdash p = q$.

The proof of this ground-completeness result needs an alternative characterization of the notion of rooted branching bisimilarity, based on colorings, in line with the characterization of strong bisimilarity given in Exercise 3.1.9.

Definition 8.4.6 (Coloring) A *coloring* of a transition-system space is a mapping from the states of the space to a set of colors. A coloring is *canonical* if two states have the same color if and only if they can be related by a rooted branching bisimulation. A transition system is in *transition-system normal form* if and only if there exists a canonical coloring such that each state of the transition system has a different color and the transition system has no τ-loop $s \xrightarrow{\tau} s$ for any of its states s.

The following property is useful for the proof of Theorem 8.4.5. Two transition systems are isomorphic if and only if there is a one-to-one mapping between their states that preserves transitions and termination options. Let $\cong$ denote isomorphism of transition systems. Recall that transition systems are named by their initial states.

Lemma 8.4.7 For transition systems g and h that are in transition-system normal form, $g \leftrightarrow_{\text{rb}} h$ if and only if $g \cong h$.

Proof The implication from right to left is trivial as the bijection that witnesses the isomorphism is also a rooted branching bisimulation relation. In the other direction, the rooted branching bisimulation relation that proves that g and h are rooted branching bisimilar, is a bijection. It is surjective since any branching bisimulation between two transition systems relates every state of any of the two transition systems to some state in the other transition system. It is injective since every state is related with at most one other state. If two different states in g (h) are related to the same state in h (g), then these two states are rooted branching bisimilar. But then these states have the same color in a canonical coloring, which contradicts the assumption that g (h) is in transition-system normal form. □

Recall the notions of regular transition systems (Definition 3.1.15), regular processes (Definition 5.8.1), and bounded-depth processes (Section 4.5). In line with the reasoning in Sections 4.5, 4.6, and 5.8, it can be shown that closed $\text{BSP}_\tau(A)$-terms can be used to precisely specify all bounded-depth regular processes. As a consequence, it is sufficient to consider only regular transition systems without any cycles in the remainder of this section. Under this assumption, it is possible to define a rewriting system on transition systems that has the following properties:

(i) normal forms with respect to the rewriting system are transition-system normal forms;
(ii) every rewrite step preserves rooted branching bisimilarity;
(iii) every rewrite step corresponds to a proof in the equational theory $BSP_\tau(A)$.

Definition 8.4.8 (Double states, manifestly inert transitions) Two states s and t in a transition system are called *double states* if and only if $s \neq t$, $s\downarrow$ if and only if $t\downarrow$, and for all states u and labels a, $s \xrightarrow{a} u$ if and only if $t \xrightarrow{a} u$. A transition $s \xrightarrow{\tau} t$ is *manifestly inert* if and only if s is not the root of the transition system, if $s\downarrow$, then $t\downarrow$, and for all states u and labels a such that $a \neq \tau$ or $u \neq t$, if $s \xrightarrow{a} u$, then $t \xrightarrow{a} u$.

Definition 8.4.9 (Rewriting system) The rewriting system consists of the following one-step reductions. Let g and h be transition systems.

(i) Contracting a pair of double states s and t in g: Transition system h is obtained from g by replacing all transitions that lead to s by transitions that lead to t and removing s and all its outgoing transitions from the transition system. Since g and h are both embedded in the underlying transition-system space, this means that g and h both have their own set of states but that there is a bijection between the states of g excluding s and the states of h that preserves transitions and termination options when considering states s and t in g as identical.
(ii) Contracting a manifestly inert transition $s \xrightarrow{\tau} t$ in g: Transition system h is obtained from g by replacing all transitions that lead to s by transitions that lead to t and removing s and all its outgoing transitions from the transition system. As in the previous case, this implies a bijection between the states of g excluding s and the states of h preserving transitions and termination options when considering s and t as identical.

In line with Definitions 2.4.3 (One-step reduction) and 2.4.4 (Reduction relation), a rewrite step is denoted with $\mapsto$ and sequences of rewrites are captured by the reduction relation denoted $\mapsto\!\!\!\!\rightarrow$.

Definition 8.4.10 (Term of a transition system) A function $\langle \_ \rangle$ is defined that associates with a transition system a closed $BSP_\tau(A)$-term as follows. Let r be (the root state of) a transition system.

$$\langle r\rangle = \begin{cases} \sum_{r \xrightarrow{a} s} a.\langle s\rangle & \text{if } r \not\downarrow, \\ \sum_{r \xrightarrow{a} s} a.\langle s\rangle + 1 & \text{if } r\downarrow. \end{cases}$$

Note that this definition is only well-defined for acyclic, regular transition systems. From the definition, it follows immediately that the closed terms associated to isomorphic transition systems are identical and hence derivably equal in $\mathrm{BSP}_\tau(A)$.

Corollary 8.4.11 For transition systems g and h, if $g \cong h$, then $\mathrm{BSP}_\tau(A) \vdash \langle g\rangle = \langle h\rangle$.

The rewriting system on transition systems of Definition 8.4.9 has the following properties:

(i) Normal forms of the rewriting system are transition-system normal forms.

It can be shown that any acyclic regular transition system with branching bisimilar states has at least one pair of states that either form a pair of double states or a manifestly inert τ-transition. Any two bisimilar states closest to (successful or unsuccessful) termination are a pair of double states or a manifestly inert transition. Hence, such a transition system is not a normal form of the rewriting system. Furthermore, any acyclic transition system remains acyclic during rewriting. Therefore, any normal form of the rewriting system has no branching bisimilar states and no τ-loops, which implies that it is in transition-system normal form.

(ii) Every rewrite step preserves rooted branching bisimilarity. That is, for any transition systems g and h,

$$\text{if } g \mapsto h, \text{ then } g \leftrightarrow_{\mathrm{rb}} h. \tag{8.4.1}$$

From $g \mapsto h$, it follows that there exist states s and t such that s and t are double states or such that there is a manifestly inert transition $s \xrightarrow{\tau} t$ and h is the result of replacing all incoming transitions of s by incoming transitions of t and the subsequent removal of s and all associated transitions from g. Let R be the bijection between the states of g minus s and the states of h mentioned in Definition 8.4.9 (Rewriting system). Then, the relation $\{(s, R(t))\} \cup R$ is obviously a rooted branching bisimulation relation between g and h. Hence, $g \leftrightarrow_{\mathrm{rb}} h$.

(iii) Each transition system has a unique normal form (up to isomorphism) with respect to the rewriting system.

Suppose that a transition system g has two normal forms with respect to the rewriting system, say h and h'. Then, by item (i) above this means that h and h' are transition-system normal forms. From property (8.4.1), it follows that $g \leftrightarrow_{\mathrm{rb}} h$ and $g \leftrightarrow_{\mathrm{rb}} h'$. Therefore, also $h \leftrightarrow_{\mathrm{rb}} h'$. Thus, by Lemma 8.4.7, $h \cong h'$.

Now, the following property can be proven.

Lemma 8.4.12 Every rewrite step corresponds to a proof in the theory. For any transition systems g and h,

$$\text{if } g \mapsto h, \text{ then } \mathrm{BSP}_\tau(A) \vdash \langle g \rangle = \langle h \rangle.$$

Proof The rewriting of g into h is due to either the contraction of double states or the contraction of a manifestly inert transition. Suppose that the states involved are s and t. Transition system h is obtained from g by moving all incoming transitions of s to t and by removing s. Let R be the bijection between the states of g minus s and the states of h mentioned in Definition 8.4.9 (Rewriting system). It can be shown that $\mathrm{BSP}_\tau(A) \vdash a.\langle s \rangle = a.\langle t \rangle = a.\langle R(t) \rangle$ for any $a \in A_\tau$. This is trivial for the case that s and t are a pair of double states since the outgoing transitions of s and t have the same label and target states, also $R(t)$ has the same outgoing transitions up to isomorphism of states, and s, t, and $R(t)$ have the same termination options. For the case that $s \xrightarrow{\tau} t$ is a manifestly inert transition, all outgoing transitions of s are also outgoing transitions of t. Then, $\mathrm{BSP}_\tau(A) \vdash a.\langle s \rangle = a.(\tau.\langle t \rangle + p)$ and $\mathrm{BSP}_\tau(A) \vdash \langle t \rangle = p + q$, where p is the result of applying $\langle\rangle$ to s without this manifestly inert transition and where q represents the outgoing transitions of t. Then, $\mathrm{BSP}_\tau(A) \vdash a.\langle s \rangle = a.(\tau.\langle t \rangle + p) = a.(\tau.(p+q)+p) = a.(p+q) = a.\langle t \rangle$. Since $R(t)$ is isomorphic to t, also in this case, it follows by Corollary 8.4.11 that $\mathrm{BSP}_\tau(A) \vdash a.\langle s \rangle = a.\langle t \rangle = a.\langle R(t) \rangle$ for any $a \in A_\tau$.

For states v that are not in between the root state g and state s, obviously $\langle v \rangle \equiv \langle R(v) \rangle$, i.e., the terms are syntactically equal (and hence derivably equal). For any other state v (excluding s), by induction on the distance from state s, it can be proven that $\mathrm{BSP}_\tau(A) \vdash \langle v \rangle = \langle R(v) \rangle$.

- The distance between v and s is one. Assume, $[w\downarrow]$ denotes 1 if w is a terminating state, and 0, otherwise. Then,

$$\begin{aligned}
\mathrm{BSP}_\tau(A) \vdash & \\
\langle v \rangle &= \sum_{v \xrightarrow{a} s} a.\langle s \rangle + \sum_{v \xrightarrow{a} v', v' \neq s} a.\langle v' \rangle + [v\downarrow] \\
&= \sum_{v \xrightarrow{a} s} a.\langle t \rangle + \sum_{v \xrightarrow{a} v', v' \neq s} a.\langle v' \rangle + [v\downarrow] \\
&= \sum_{R(v) \xrightarrow{a} R(t)} a.\langle R(t) \rangle + \\
&\qquad \sum_{R(v) \xrightarrow{a} R(v'), v' \neq t} a.\langle R(v') \rangle + [R(v)\downarrow] \\
&= \langle R(v) \rangle.
\end{aligned}$$

- The distance between v and s is more than one. By induction, for all states w such that $v \xrightarrow{a} w$ for some a, $\mathrm{BSP}_\tau(A) \vdash \langle w \rangle = \langle R(w) \rangle$. Then,

$$\begin{aligned}
\mathrm{BSP}_\tau(A) \vdash \langle v \rangle &= \sum_{v \xrightarrow{a} w} a.\langle w \rangle + [v\downarrow] \\
&= \sum_{v \xrightarrow{a} w} a.\langle R(w) \rangle + [v\downarrow] \\
&= \sum_{R(v) \xrightarrow{a} R(w)} a.\langle R(w) \rangle + [R(v)\downarrow] \\
&= \langle R(v) \rangle.
\end{aligned}$$

This last result implies that also $\mathrm{BSP}_\tau(A) \vdash \langle g \rangle = \langle R(g) \rangle = \langle h \rangle$, completing the proof. □

So far in this book, closed terms have been used both to refer to syntactical objects in an equational theory and to the transition systems obtained from them in an operational semantics. In the remainder of this section, it is desirable to distinguish these two meanings of a closed term. Therefore, let $[\![p]\!]$ denote the transition system obtained from closed $\mathrm{BSP}_\tau(A)$-term p via the term deduction system of $\mathrm{BSP}_\tau(A)$ defined earlier in this section.

Lemma 8.4.13 For closed $\mathrm{BSP}_\tau(A)$-term p, $\mathrm{BSP}_\tau(A) \vdash \langle [\![p]\!] \rangle = p$.

Proof Via induction on the structure of term p; see Exercise 8.4.4. □

Finally, it is possible to establish the desired ground-completeness result.

Proof (of Theorem 8.4.5 (Ground-completeness)).
Let p and q be closed $\mathrm{BSP}_\tau(A)$-terms. Assume that $\mathbb{P}(\mathrm{BSP}_\tau(A))_{/\leftrightarrow_{\mathrm{rb}}} \models p = q$. Then, by definition, $[\![p]\!] \leftrightarrow_{\mathrm{rb}} [\![q]\!]$. Let g and h be the unique normal forms with respect to the rewriting system of Definition 8.4.9 (Rewriting system) of the transition systems $[\![p]\!]$ and $[\![q]\!]$, respectively:

$$[\![p]\!] \mapsto\!\!\!\rightarrow g \qquad \text{and} \qquad [\![q]\!] \mapsto\!\!\!\rightarrow h.$$

Then, as a direct consequence of Property (8.4.1), $[\![p]\!] \leftrightarrow_{\text{rb}} g$ and $[\![q]\!] \leftrightarrow_{\text{rb}} h$. Since $[\![p]\!] \leftrightarrow_{\text{rb}} [\![q]\!]$, the properties of $\leftrightarrow_{\text{rb}}$ imply that $g \leftrightarrow_{\text{rb}} h$.
Since g and h are in normal form with respect to the rewriting system and since they are also rooted branching bisimilar, it follows (by Lemma 8.4.7) that g and h are isomorphic: $g \cong h$. Therefore, by Corollary 8.4.11, $\text{BSP}_\tau(A) \vdash \langle g \rangle = \langle h \rangle$.
Using Lemma 8.4.12, from $[\![p]\!] \mapsto\!\!\!\rightarrow g$ and $[\![q]\!] \mapsto\!\!\!\rightarrow h$, it follows that $\text{BSP}_\tau(A) \vdash \langle [\![p]\!] \rangle = \langle g \rangle$ and $\text{BSP}_\tau(A) \vdash \langle [\![q]\!] \rangle = \langle h \rangle$. Then,

$$\text{BSP}_\tau(A) \vdash p = \langle [\![p]\!] \rangle = \langle g \rangle = \langle h \rangle = \langle [\![q]\!] \rangle = q,$$

where the first and last equalities are due to Lemma 8.4.13. □

Exercises

8.4.1 Draw the transition systems associated with the following pairs of process terms and construct a rooted branching bisimulation between each of the pairs of transition systems.

(a) $a.(\tau.b.1 + b.1)$ and $a.b.1$;
(b) $a.(\tau.(b.1 + c.1) + b.1)$ and $a.(b.1 + c.1)$;
(c) $a.\tau.(\tau.b.1 + \tau.\tau.b.1)$ and $a.b.1$.

8.4.2 Consider rooted weak bisimilarity as introduced in Exercise 8.2.5. Prove that rooted weak bisimilarity is a congruence on the term algebra $\mathbb{P}(\text{BSP}_\tau(A))$.

8.4.3 Building upon the previous exercise, prove the following, for all closed $\text{BSP}_\tau(A)$-terms p, q:

(a) $\tau.p + p$ is rooted weakly bisimilar to $\tau.p$;
(b) $a.(\tau.p + q)$ is rooted weakly bisimilar to $a.p + a.(\tau.p + q)$.

Are these pairs of terms also rooted branching bisimilar? Motivate your answer.

8.4.4 Prove Lemma 8.4.13.

8.5 Some extensions of $\text{BSP}_\tau(A)$

This section presents extensions of $\text{BSP}_\tau(A)$ with useful operators for abstraction, encapsulation, and projection. Moreover, the choice operators of the process algebra CSP are considered. The treatment is concise, as such extensions follow the same lines as before. However, to prove the various results for these extended theories, the results of Section 3.2 cannot be used, because these assume strong bisimilarity as the underlying semantic equivalence. Therefore, in the next subsection, all the relevant propositions and theorems are listed, and proofs are asked in the form of exercises. The interested reader is advised to consult the proofs given in Chapter 4 that do not use the framework of Section 3.2. The proofs expected for the results in this section go along the same lines. In Sections 8.5.2, 8.5.3, and 8.5.4, the main results are summarized but for reasons of brevity not explicitly listed.

8.5.1 Abstraction

Recall the calculations for a two-place buffer from Section 7.6. The derivations show that a two-place buffer can be seen as a composition of two one-place buffers, as illustrated in Figure 7.3. The final step of the derivations used a skip operator to skip the execution of internal actions. However, as already explained in the introduction to this chapter, it is more elegant to rename internal actions into unobservable silent actions. Such a renaming, in contrast to the skipping of internal actions, preserves moments of choice. This subsection introduces such a renaming into silent actions, called *abstraction* or *hiding*.

The process theory $(\mathrm{BSP}_\tau + \mathrm{ABS})(A)$ is the extension of the process theory $\mathrm{BSP}_\tau(A)$ with a family of abstraction or hiding operators τ_I for each $I \subseteq A$. The set I contains the atomic actions that need to be abstracted from. The axioms in Table 8.2 closely reflect the operational intuition that all occurrences of prefix operators $a.\_$ for which the atomic action is to be hidden ($a \in I$) are replaced by τ-prefix operators.

$(\mathrm{BSP}_\tau + \mathrm{ABS})(A)$		
$\mathrm{BSP}_\tau(A)$;		
unary: $(\tau_I)_{I \subseteq A}$;		
x, y;		
$\tau_I(1) = 1$		TI1
$\tau_I(0) = 0$		TI2
$\tau_I(a.x) = a.\tau_I(x)$	if $a \notin I$	TI3
$\tau_I(a.x) = \tau.\tau_I(x)$	if $a \in I$	TI4
$\tau_I(x + y) = \tau_I(x) + \tau_I(y)$		TI5

Table 8.2. Axioms for abstraction ($a \in A_\tau$, $I \subseteq A$).

From the observation that the axioms in Table 8.2 closely follow the structure of $\mathrm{BSP}_\tau(A)$ terms, it follows easily that all occurrences of the abstraction operators can be eliminated.

Theorem 8.5.1 (Elimination) For every $(\mathrm{BSP}_\tau + \mathrm{ABS})(A)$-term p, there is a closed $\mathrm{BSP}_\tau(A)$-term q such that $(\mathrm{BSP}_\tau + \mathrm{ABS})(A) \vdash p = q$.

Proof Exercise 8.5.5. □

The theory also allows the expected conservativity result.

Theorem 8.5.2 (Conservative ground-extension) Theory $(\mathrm{BSP}_\tau + \mathrm{ABS})(A)$ is a conservative ground-extension of process theory $\mathrm{BSP}_\tau(A)$.

Proof Exercise 8.5.6. □

The term model is based on the term algebra for theory $(\mathrm{BSP}_\tau + \mathrm{ABS})(A)$, $\mathbb{P}((\mathrm{BSP}_\tau + \mathrm{ABS})(A)) = (\mathcal{C}((\mathrm{BSP}_\tau + \mathrm{ABS})(A)), +, (a.\_)_{a \in A}, \tau.\_, (\tau_I)_{I \subseteq A}, 0, 1)$. The term deduction system for $(\mathrm{BSP}_\tau + \mathrm{ABS})(A)$ is obtained by extending the term deduction system for $\mathrm{BSP}_\tau(A)$ with deduction rules for the abstraction operators as defined in Table 8.3. The first deduction rule means that applying abstraction to a process does not alter its termination behavior. The second deduction rule simply states that all behavior that is not abstracted from is still present. The third deduction rule states that all action names that occur in the set I are made unobservable by replacing them by the silent step.

TDS$((\mathrm{BSP}_\tau + \mathrm{ABS})(A))$
TDS$(\mathrm{BSP}_\tau(A))$;

unary: $(\tau_I)_{I \subseteq A}$;

x, x';

$$\frac{x\downarrow}{\tau_I(x)\downarrow} \qquad \frac{x \xrightarrow{a} x' \quad a \notin I}{\tau_I(x) \xrightarrow{a} \tau_I(x')} \qquad \frac{x \xrightarrow{a} x' \quad a \in I}{\tau_I(x) \xrightarrow{\tau} \tau_I(x')}$$

Table 8.3. Term deduction system for $(\mathrm{BSP}_\tau + \mathrm{ABS})(A)$ (with $a \in A_\tau$, $I \subseteq A$).

Proposition 8.5.3 (Congruence) Rooted branching bisimilarity is a congruence on $\mathbb{P}((\mathrm{BSP}_\tau + \mathrm{ABS})(A))$.

Proof Exercise 8.5.7. □

Definition 8.5.4 (Term model of $(\mathrm{BSP}_\tau + \mathrm{ABS})(A)$**)** The term model of theory $(\mathrm{BSP}_\tau + \mathrm{ABS})(A)$ is the quotient algebra $\mathbb{P}((\mathrm{BSP}_\tau + \mathrm{ABS})(A))_{/\leftrightarrow_{\mathrm{rb}}}$.

Theorem 8.5.5 (Soundness) Theory $(\mathrm{BSP}_\tau + \mathrm{ABS})(A)$ is a sound axiomatization of $\mathbb{P}((\mathrm{BSP}_\tau + \mathrm{ABS})(A))_{/\leftrightarrow_{\mathrm{rb}}}$, i.e., $\mathbb{P}((\mathrm{BSP}_\tau + \mathrm{ABS})(A))_{/\leftrightarrow_{\mathrm{rb}}} \models (\mathrm{BSP}_\tau + \mathrm{ABS})(A)$.

Proof Exercise 8.5.8. □

Theorem 8.5.6 (Ground-completeness) Theory $(\mathrm{BSP}_\tau + \mathrm{ABS})(A)$ is a ground-complete axiomatization of the term model $\mathbb{P}((\mathrm{BSP}_\tau + \mathrm{ABS})(A))_{/\leftrightarrow_{\mathrm{rb}}}$, i.e., for any closed $(\mathrm{BSP}_\tau + \mathrm{ABS})(A)$-terms p and q, $\mathbb{P}((\mathrm{BSP}_\tau + \mathrm{ABS})(A))_{/\leftrightarrow_{\mathrm{rb}}} \models p = q$ implies $(\mathrm{BSP}_\tau + \mathrm{ABS})(A) \vdash p = q$.

Proof Exercise 8.5.9. □

8.5.2 *Encapsulation*

In Chapter 6, encapsulation operators have been introduced in order to block certain actions from being executed. In Chapter 7, this operator has been used to force certain actions to communicate. In this section, the extension of the process theory $\mathrm{BSP}_\tau(A)$ with such encapsulation operators is discussed. The only relevant difference between the process theories $\mathrm{BSP}(A)$ and $\mathrm{BSP}_\tau(A)$ is the τ-prefix operator. Before, it was assumed that $H \subseteq A$. Now, it should be decided whether it is also allowed to block internal actions, i.e., whether H should be allowed to include τ.

Example 8.5.7 (Encapsulation and silent steps) Assume that it is allowed to block internal actions. Consider the process term $\partial_{\{\tau\}}(a.\tau.1)$. If it is allowed to block silent actions, then the following equality can be established by using the axioms for encapsulation from Table 6.8:

$$\partial_{\{\tau\}}(a.\tau.1) = a.0.$$

However, it is also possible to derive

$$\partial_{\{\tau\}}(a.\tau.1) = \partial_{\{\tau\}}(a.1) = a.1,$$

by applying (a derivative of) the Branching Axiom of Table 8.1 first. Thus, allowing the encapsulation of internal steps leads to the identity

$$a.0 = a.1.$$

Consequently, allowing encapsulation of internal actions results in a process theory that equates successful and unsuccessful termination, and is therefore not a conservative (ground-)extension of $\mathrm{BSP}_\tau(A)$.

As indicated by the example, it is not desirable to allow the encapsulation of internal steps. Therefore, the set of action names to be blocked must still be a subset of A: $H \subseteq A$. Theory $(\mathrm{BSP}_\tau + \mathrm{DH})(A)$ is precisely the union of $(\mathrm{BSP} + \mathrm{DH})(A)$ from Table 6.8 (but assuming $a \in A_\tau$) and theory $\mathrm{BSP}_\tau(A)$ from Table 8.1.

Encapsulation operators can be eliminated from closed $(\mathrm{BSP}_\tau + \mathrm{DH})(A)$-terms to yield a derivably equal closed $\mathrm{BSP}_\tau(A)$-term. Process theory $(\mathrm{BSP}_\tau + \mathrm{DH})(A)$ is furthermore a conservative ground-extension of $\mathrm{BSP}_\tau(A)$. The term deduction system for $(\mathrm{BSP}_\tau + \mathrm{DH})(A)$ is the union of the term deduction systems for $(\mathrm{BSP} + \mathrm{DH})(A)$ (Table 6.10) and $\mathrm{BSP}_\tau(A)$, with $a \in A_\tau$. Theory $(\mathrm{BSP}_\tau + \mathrm{DH})(A)$ is a sound and ground-complete axiomatization of the resulting term model $\mathbb{P}((\mathrm{BSP}_\tau + \mathrm{DH})(A))_{/\leftrightarrow_{\mathrm{rb}}}$.

8.5.3 Projection

Process theory $(\mathrm{BSP}_\tau + \mathrm{PR})(A)$ is the extension of $\mathrm{BSP}_\tau(A)$ with the family of projection operators π_n (for each natural number n). In order to obtain $(\mathrm{BSP}_\tau + \mathrm{PR})(A)$ as a conservative ground-extension of $\mathrm{BSP}_\tau(A)$, it is not possible to simply adopt the axioms of $(\mathrm{BSP} + \mathrm{PR})(A)$ of Table 4.5 with $a \in A_\tau$. This can be illustrated as follows. Consider the following derivations, applying the axioms of $(\mathrm{BSP} + \mathrm{PR})(A)$ on $\mathrm{BSP}_\tau(A)$-terms:

$$\pi_1(a.\tau.1) = a.\pi_0(\tau.1) = a.0$$

and

$$\pi_1(a.\tau.1) = \pi_1(a.1) = a.\pi_0(1) = a.1.$$

Hence, as in Example 8.5.7 (Encapsulation and silent steps), it can be derived that $a.0 = a.1$. As this is an identity between closed $\mathrm{BSP}_\tau(A)$-terms that is not derivable in $\mathrm{BSP}_\tau(A)$, $(\mathrm{BSP}_\tau + \mathrm{PR})(A)$ cannot have the axiom $\pi_0(\tau.x) = 0$. For similar reasons, the axiom $\pi_{n+1}(\tau.x) = \tau.\pi_n(x)$ is not acceptable.

The axioms of $(\mathrm{BSP}_\tau + \mathrm{PR})(A)$ are the axioms of $\mathrm{BSP}_\tau(A)$ with $a \in A_\tau$, the axioms of $(\mathrm{BSP}+\mathrm{PR})(A)$ with $a \in A$, and in addition the axiom presented in Table 8.4.

Theory $(\mathrm{BSP}_\tau + \mathrm{PR})(A)$ allows an elimination result, stating that projection operators can be eliminated from closed $(\mathrm{BSP}_\tau + \mathrm{PR})(A)$-terms. Theory $(\mathrm{BSP}_\tau + \mathrm{PR})(A)$ is also a conservative ground-extension of $\mathrm{BSP}_\tau(A)$.

The term deduction system for $(\mathrm{BSP}_\tau + \mathrm{PR})(A)$ consists of the deduction rules of the term deduction system for $\mathrm{BSP}_\tau(A)$ with $a \in A_\tau$, the deduction rules for $(\mathrm{BSP} + \mathrm{PR})(A)$ with $a \in A$ (Table 4.6), and in addition the

(BSP$_\tau$ + PR)(A)
BSP$_\tau(A)$, (BSP + PR)(A);
-
x;
$\pi_n(\tau.x) = \tau.\pi_n(x)$ PR6

Table 8.4. BSP$_\tau(A)$ with projection ($n \in \mathbf{N}$).

deduction rule given in Table 8.5. Theory (BSP$_\tau$ + PR)(A) is a sound and ground-complete axiomatization of the term model $\mathbb{P}((\text{BSP}_\tau + \text{PR})(A))_{/\leftrightarrow_{\text{rb}}}$.

TDS((BSP$_\tau$ + PR)(A))
TDS(BSP$_\tau$(A)), *TDS*((BSP + PR)(A));
-
x, x';
$\dfrac{x \xrightarrow{\tau} x'}{\pi_n(x) \xrightarrow{\tau} \pi_n(x')}$

Table 8.5. Term deduction system for (BSP$_\tau$ + PR)(A) (with $n \in \mathbf{N}$).

Note that, in the presence of projection operators, one can consider a projective limit model for (BSP$_\tau$ + PR)(A), similar to the model for theory (BSP + PR)(A) presented in Section 5.10. It turns out that the notion of projective sequences and the derived model can be adapted to the current setting with silent steps. However, such a model is not possible in a setting with abstraction operators, because abstraction operators cannot be defined on projective sequences. Exercise 8.5.12 investigates this further.

8.5.4 Non-determinism in CSP

In the CSP framework of (Hoare, 1985), bisimilarity is not the preferred notion of equivalence, but rather failures equivalence, to be considered in Section 12.2. As a consequence, the law $a.x + a.y = a.(\tau.x + \tau.y)$ holds in CSP, which means all non-determinism can be reduced to *silent non-determinism* (non-deterministic choices between silent steps).

CSP has two choice operators: $\sqcap$ denoting non-deterministic or *internal* choice, and $\Box$ denoting *external* choice. The internal-choice operator denotes a non-deterministic choice that cannot be influenced by the environment (other processes in parallel) and can simply be defined in the present setting by the defining axiom

$$x \sqcap y = \tau.x + \tau.y.$$

The definition of $\Box$ in the current context with rooted branching bisimilarity as the semantic equivalence is more subtle. It denotes a choice that can be influenced by the environment. If the arguments of the operator have initial silent non-determinism, then these silent steps can be executed without making the choice, and the choice will be made as soon as a visible action occurs. This intuition leads to the operational rules in the two middle rows of Table 8.6, which defines the term deduction system for theory $(\mathrm{BSP}_\tau \sqcap \Box)(A)$, $\mathrm{BSP}_\tau(A)$ extended with CSP choice operators, introduced below.

$TDS((\mathrm{BSP}_\tau \sqcap \Box)(A))$		
$TDS(\mathrm{BSP}_\tau(A))$		
-		
$x, y, x', y';$		
	$x \sqcap y \xrightarrow{\tau} x$	$x \sqcap y \xrightarrow{\tau} y$
$\dfrac{x\downarrow}{x \Box y\downarrow}$	$\dfrac{x \xrightarrow{a} x'}{x \Box y \xrightarrow{a} x'}$	$\dfrac{y \xrightarrow{a} y'}{x \Box y \xrightarrow{a} y'}$
$\dfrac{y\downarrow}{x \Box y\downarrow}$	$\dfrac{x \xrightarrow{\tau} x'}{x \Box y \xrightarrow{\tau} x' \Box y}$	$\dfrac{y \xrightarrow{\tau} y'}{x \Box y \xrightarrow{\tau} x \Box y'}$
$\dfrac{x\downarrow}{x \sqsubset y\downarrow}$	$\dfrac{x \xrightarrow{a} x'}{x \sqsubset y \xrightarrow{a} x'}$	$\dfrac{x \xrightarrow{\tau} x'}{x \sqsubset y \xrightarrow{\tau} x' \Box y}$

Table 8.6. Term deduction system for $(\mathrm{BSP}_\tau \sqcap \Box)(A)$ (with $a \in A$).

An axiomatization of the external-choice operator is not straightforward: similar to the situation with the parallel-composition operator, an auxiliary operator is needed. Let $\sqsubset$ denote the so-called *left-external-choice operator*. It satisfies the operational rules for the external choice that apply to the left operand of the external choice, but not those that apply to the right operand, as can be seen in the bottom row of Table 8.6.

Table 8.7 shows the theory $(\mathrm{BSP}_\tau \sqcap \Box)(A)$. It contains besides the defining axiom for the non-deterministic choice, an axiomatization of the CSP external-choice operator, using the left-external-choice operator.

The term deduction system of Table 8.6 can be used to provide a standard term model for theory $(\mathrm{BSP}_\tau \sqcap \Box)(A)$ based on rooted branching bisimilarity. Based on the axiomatization of Table 8.7, commutativity and associativity

(BSP$_\tau$ $\sqcap\Box$)(A)	
BSP$_\tau(A)$;	
binary: $\_\sqcap\_$, $\_\Box\_$, $\_\sqsubset\_$;	
x, y, z;	
$x \sqcap y = \tau.x + \tau.y$	$x \Box y = x \sqsubset y + y \sqsubset x$
$0 \sqsubset x = 0$	$x \sqsubset 0 = x$
$1 \sqsubset x = 1$	$(x \sqsubset y) \sqsubset z = x \sqsubset (y \Box z)$
$a.x \sqsubset y = a.x$	
$\tau.x \sqsubset y = \tau.(x \Box y)$	
$(x + y) \sqsubset z = x \sqsubset z + y \sqsubset z$	

Table 8.7. BSP$_\tau(A)$ extended with CSP choice operators (with $a \in A$).

of the external-choice operator can be easily derived. Also, 0 is an identity element of external choice. However, external choice is not idempotent. The internal-choice operator is commutative, but not associative or idempotent. It does not have an identity element.

The axiomatization of the CSP choice operators in the present setting based on bisimilarity uses silent actions. An interesting observation is that the extra τ-identities that are valid in failures semantics, together with the presence of two choice operators allows the elimination of all τ-occurrences from every expression, see (Bergstra *et al.*, 1987), which means that CSP can do without the silent step altogether.

Exercises

8.5.1 Give a derivably equal closed BSP$_\tau(A)$-term, eliminating silent steps whenever possible, for each of the following process terms:

(a) $\tau_{\{d\}}(a.(d.(b.d.0 + c.d.0) + b.d.0))$;
(b) $\tau_{\{d\}}(a.(d.(b.0 + c.0) + b.1))$;
(c) $\tau_{\{b,c\}}(a.b.0 + a.c.b.1)$;
(d) $\tau_{\{a\}}(b.a.0 + a.c.b.1)$;
(e) $\tau_{\{d\}}(a.(d.b.c.1 + b.c.0))$.

8.5.2 Prove that $(\text{BSP}_\tau + \text{ABS})(A) \vdash \tau_I(\tau_J(p)) = \tau_{I\cup J}(p)$ for any closed $(\text{BSP}_\tau + \text{ABS})(A)$-term p and any $I, J \subseteq A$.

8.5.3 Prove that $(\text{BSP}_\tau + \text{DH})(A) \vdash \partial_G(\partial_H(p)) = \partial_{G\cup H}(p)$ for any closed $(\text{BSP}_\tau + \text{DH})(A)$-term p and any $G, H \subseteq A$.

8.5.4 Give an example to show that $(\text{BSP}_\tau + \text{ABS} + \text{PR})(A) \nvdash \pi_n(\tau_I(x)) = \tau_I(\pi_n(x))$, for $n \in \mathbf{N}$, $I \subseteq A$, and term x.

8.5.5 Prove Theorem 8.5.1 (Elimination of abstraction operators).

8.5.6 Prove Theorem 8.5.2 (Conservativity of $(\mathrm{BSP}_\tau + \mathrm{ABS})(A)$).

8.5.7 Prove Proposition 8.5.3 (Congruence).

8.5.8 Prove Theorem 8.5.5 (Soundness of $(\mathrm{BSP}_\tau + \mathrm{ABS})(A)$).

8.5.9 Prove Theorem 8.5.6 (Ground-completeness of $(\mathrm{BSP}_\tau + \mathrm{ABS})(A)$).

8.5.10 Develop theory $(\mathrm{BSP}_\tau + \mathrm{DH})(A)$. That is, prove elimination and conservativity results, and give a term model proving soundness and ground-completeness.

8.5.11 Develop theory $(\mathrm{BSP}_\tau + \mathrm{PR})(A)$, proving elimination and conservativity results, as well as soundness and ground-completeness results for the standard term model.

8.5.12 Develop a projective limit model for theory $(\mathrm{BSP}_\tau + \mathrm{PR})(A)$, following the developments in Section 5.10. Investigate also the validity of recursion principles. Argue that it is not possible to define abstraction operators on projective sequences.

8.5.13 Develop theory $(\mathrm{BSP}_\tau \sqcap \Box)(A)$, proving elimination and conservativity results, as well as soundness and ground-completeness results for the standard term model based on rooted branching bisimilarity.

8.5.14 Show that theory $(\mathrm{BSP}_\tau \sqcap \Box)(A)$ is a sound axiomatization of the standard term model based on strong bisimilarity, when τ is treated as a normal action. (Note that any identity valid in a term model based on strong bisimilarity is also valid in a term model based on (rooted) branching bisimilarity.)

8.5.15 Derive the following equations from $(\mathrm{BSP}_\tau \sqcap \Box)(A)$:

(a) $x \sqcap y = y \sqcap x$;

(b) $x \Box y = y \Box x$;

(c) $x \Box (y \Box z) = (x \Box y) \Box z$;

(d) $x \Box 0 = x$.

Provide counterexamples to show that the following equations are not derivable:

(a) $x \sqcap x = x$;

(b) $x \sqcap (y \sqcap z) = (x \sqcap y) \sqcap z$;

(c) $x \Box x = x$;

(d) $x \Box (y \sqcap z) = (x \Box y) \sqcap (x \Box z)$;

(e) $x \sqcap (y \Box z) = (x \sqcap y) \Box (x \sqcap z)$.

8.6 TCP with silent steps

The basic theory $\text{BSP}_\tau(A)$ developed in this chapter can be extended with the various features introduced so far throughout this book. This section introduces process theory $\text{TCP}_\tau(A, \gamma)$, which extends $\text{BSP}_\tau(A)$ with sequential composition, parallel composition, encapsulation, and abstraction, providing a rich process theory, called the Theory of Communicating Processes with silent steps, that includes many useful ingredients for specifying and reasoning about processes. The axioms of theory $\text{TCP}_\tau(A, \gamma)$ are the axioms of process theory $\text{TCP}(A, \gamma)$ of Chapter 7 with $a \in A_\tau$ and $H \subseteq A$, the axioms of theory $(\text{BSP}_\tau + \text{ABS})(A)$ of the previous section, and two additional Axioms of Standard Concurrency SC9 and SC10. For readability, Table 8.8 gives a complete overview of the signature and the axioms of process theory $\text{TCP}_\tau(A, \gamma)$. Communications involving the silent step τ are always assumed to be undefined. This is captured axiomatically by Axiom SC10. (Exercise 8.6.8 illustrates why this assumption is necessary.) Axiom SC9 is a counterpart of the Branching Axiom B for the auxiliary left-merge operator. From Axiom SC9, the equality $x \mathbin{\lfloor\!\lfloor} (\tau.(y + z) + y) = x \mathbin{\lfloor\!\lfloor} (y + z)$ can be proven (see Exercise 8.6.4).

The extensions of $\text{TCP}_\tau(A, \gamma)$ with respect to theory $\text{BSP}_\tau(A)$ allow for the convenient specification of communicating processes but do not add to the expressiveness of the theory.

Theorem 8.6.1 (Elimination) For any closed $\text{TCP}_\tau(A, \gamma)$-term p, there is a closed $\text{BSP}_\tau(A)$-term q such that $\text{TCP}_\tau(A, \gamma) \vdash p = q$.

Proof Exercise 8.6.9. □

Theorem 8.6.2 (Conservative ground-extension) Theory $\text{TCP}_\tau(A, \gamma)$ is a conservative ground-extension of theory $\text{BSP}_\tau(A)$.

Proof Exercise 8.6.10. □

Theorem 8.6.3 (Standard concurrency) For closed $\text{TCP}_\tau(A, \gamma)$-terms, the Axioms of Standard Concurrency SC2–SC10 are derivable from the other axioms of $\text{TCP}_\tau(A, \gamma)$.

Proof For Axioms SC2–SC8, the proofs of Theorems 7.4.4 and 7.7.1 (Standard concurrency in $\text{BCP}(A, \gamma)$ and $\text{TCP}(A, \gamma)$) carry over to the current setting. The proof for the two new axioms goes via structural induction. First, the result for SC10 is proven, and then this can be used in the proof of SC9. See Exercise 8.6.3. □

$\mathrm{TCP}_\tau(A, \gamma)$			
constant: $0, 1$;			
unary: $(a.\_)_{a \in A_\tau}$, $(\partial_H)_{H \subseteq A}$, $(\tau_I)_{I \subseteq A}$;			
binary: $\_ + \_$, $\_ \cdot \_$, $\_ \parallel \_$, $\_ ⌊⌊ \_$, $\_ \mid \_$;			
x, y, z;			
$x + y = y + x$	A1	$x + 0 = x$	A6
$(x + y) + z = x + (y + z)$	A2	$0 \cdot x = 0$	A7
$x + x = x$	A3	$x \cdot 1 = x$	A8
$(x + y) \cdot z = x \cdot z + y \cdot z$	A4	$1 \cdot x = x$	A9
$(x \cdot y) \cdot z = x \cdot (y \cdot z)$	A5	$a.x \cdot y = a.(x \cdot y)$	A10
$a.(\tau.(x + y) + x) = a.(x + y)$	B		
$\partial_H(1) = 1$	D1	$\tau_I(1) = 1$	TI1
$\partial_H(0) = 0$	D2	$\tau_I(0) = 0$	TI2
$\partial_H(a.x) = 0$ if $a \in H$	D3	$\tau_I(a.x) = a.\tau_I(x)$ if $a \notin I$	TI3
$\partial_H(a.x) = a.\partial_H(x)$ if $a \notin H$	D4	$\tau_I(a.x) = \tau.\tau_I(x)$ if $a \in I$	TI4
$\partial_H(x + y) = \partial_H(x) + \partial_H(y)$	D5	$\tau_I(x + y) = \tau_I(x) + \tau_I(y)$	TI5
$x \parallel y = x ⌊⌊ y + y ⌊⌊ x + x \mid y$	M	$x \mid y = y \mid x$	SC1
		$x \parallel 1 = x$	SC2
$0 ⌊⌊ x = 0$	LM1	$1 \mid x + 1 = 1$	SC3
$1 ⌊⌊ x = 0$	LM2	$(x \parallel y) \parallel z = x \parallel (y \parallel z)$	SC4
$a.x ⌊⌊ y = a.(x \parallel y)$	LM3	$(x \mid y) \mid z = x \mid (y \mid z)$	SC5
$(x + y) ⌊⌊ z = x ⌊⌊ z + y ⌊⌊ z$	LM4	$(x ⌊⌊ y) ⌊⌊ z = x ⌊⌊ (y \parallel z)$	SC6
$0 \mid x = 0$	CM1	$(x \mid y) ⌊⌊ z = x \mid (y ⌊⌊ z)$	SC7
$(x + y) \mid z = x \mid z + y \mid z$	CM2	$x ⌊⌊ 0 = x \cdot 0$	SC8
$1 \mid 1 = 1$	CM3	$x ⌊⌊ \tau.y = x ⌊⌊ y$	SC9
$a.x \mid 1 = 0$	CM4	$x \mid \tau.y = 0$	SC10
$a.x \mid b.y = c.(x \parallel y)$ if $\gamma(a, b) = c$	CM5		
$a.x \mid b.y = 0$ if $\gamma(a, b)$ is not defined	CM6		

Table 8.8. The process theory $\mathrm{TCP}_\tau(A, \gamma)$ (with $a, b, c \in A_\tau$, $H, I \subseteq A$).

As in Section 7.4, an expansion theorem can be proven that allows reasoning about parallel compositions.

Theorem 8.6.4 (Expansion theorem) Let set $I \subset \mathbf{N}$ be a finite, non-empty set of natural numbers, and t_i, for all $i \in I$, arbitrary $\mathrm{TCP}_\tau(A, \gamma)$-terms.

$$\mathrm{TCP}_\tau(A, \gamma) \vdash \mathop{\parallel}_{i \in I} t_i = \sum_{\emptyset \neq J \subset I} (\mathop{\mid}_{j \in J} t_j) ⌊⌊ (\mathop{\parallel}_{i \in I \setminus J} t_i) + \mathop{\mid}_{i \in I} t_i.$$

Proof The proof is similar to the proof of the expansion theorem in the previous chapter. See Exercise 8.6.11. □

Also in line with the development of theory $\mathrm{BCP}(A, \gamma)$ of the previous chapter, it is possible to add the Free-Merge and Handshaking Axioms to the theory, resulting in theories $(\mathrm{TCP}_\tau + \mathrm{FMA})(A, \emptyset)$ and $(\mathrm{TCP}_\tau + \mathrm{HA})(A, \gamma)$, respectively. Each of these two theories has its own variant of the expansion theorem.

Theorem 8.6.5 (Expansion theorem for free merge) Let set $I \subset \mathbf{N}$ be some finite, non-empty index set of natural numbers, and t_i, for all $i \in I$, arbitrary $(\mathrm{TCP}_\tau + \mathrm{FMA})(A, \emptyset)$-terms.

$$(\mathrm{TCP}_\tau + \mathrm{FMA})(A, \emptyset) \vdash \mathop{\|}_{i \in I} t_i = \sum_{i \in I} t_i \mathbin{⫦} (\mathop{\|}_{j \in I \setminus \{i\}} t_j) + \mathop{|}_{i \in I} t_i .$$

Proof Exercise 8.6.12. □

Theorem 8.6.6 (Expansion theorem for handshaking communication) Let $I \subset \mathbf{N}$ be some finite, non-empty index set of natural numbers, and t_i, for all $i \in I$, arbitrary $(\mathrm{TCP}_\tau + \mathrm{HA})(A, \gamma)$-terms.

$$(\mathrm{TCP}_\tau + \mathrm{HA})(A, \gamma) \vdash \mathop{\|}_{i \in I} t_i =$$
$$\sum_{i \in I} t_i \mathbin{⫦} (\mathop{\|}_{j \in I \setminus \{i\}} t_j) + \sum_{i, j \in I, i \neq j} (t_i \mid t_j) \mathbin{⫦} (\mathop{\|}_{k \in I \setminus \{i, j\}} t_k) + \mathop{|}_{i \in I} t_i .$$

Proof Exercise 8.6.13. □

The development of the standard term model for $\mathrm{TCP}_\tau(A, \gamma)$ follows the usual pattern. The relevant definitions and results are summarized for the sake of completeness.

The term algebra is the algebra $\mathbb{P}(\mathrm{TCP}_\tau(A, \gamma)) = (\mathcal{C}(\mathrm{TCP}_\tau(A, \gamma)), +, \cdot, \|, ⫦, \mid, (a.\_)_{a \in A}, \tau.\_, (\partial_H)_{H \subseteq A}, (\tau_I)_{I \subseteq A}, 0, 1)$. The term deduction system for $\mathrm{TCP}_\tau(A, \gamma)$ is the union of the term deduction systems for $\mathrm{TCP}(A, \gamma)$ and $(\mathrm{BSP}_\tau + \mathrm{ABS})(A)$.

Proposition 8.6.7 (Congruence) Rooted branching bisimilarity is a congruence on the algebra $\mathbb{P}(\mathrm{TCP}_\tau(A, \gamma))$.

Proof Exercise 8.6.14. □

Definition 8.6.8 (Term model) The term model of $\mathrm{TCP}_\tau(A, \gamma)$ is the quotient algebra $\mathbb{P}(\mathrm{TCP}_\tau(A, \gamma))_{/\leftrightarrows_{\mathrm{rb}}}$.

Theorem 8.6.9 (Soundness) Theory $\mathrm{TCP}_\tau(A, \gamma)$ is a sound axiomatization of the algebra $\mathbb{P}(\mathrm{TCP}_\tau(A, \gamma))_{/\leftrightarrows_{\mathrm{rb}}}$, i.e., $\mathbb{P}(\mathrm{TCP}_\tau(A, \gamma))_{/\leftrightarrows_{\mathrm{rb}}} \models \mathrm{TCP}_\tau(A, \gamma)$.

Proof Exercise 8.6.15. □

Theorem 8.6.10 (Ground-completeness) Theory $\mathrm{TCP}_\tau(A,\gamma)$ is a ground-complete axiomatization of model $\mathbb{P}(\mathrm{TCP}_\tau(A,\gamma))_{/\leftrightarrow_{\mathrm{rb}}}$, i.e., for any closed $\mathrm{TCP}_\tau(A,\gamma)$-terms p and q, $\mathbb{P}(\mathrm{TCP}_\tau(A,\gamma))_{/\leftrightarrow_{\mathrm{rb}}} \models p = q$ implies $\mathrm{TCP}_\tau(A,\gamma) \vdash p = q$.

Proof Exercise 8.6.16. □

Exercises

8.6.1 Let $A = \{a, b, c\}$ with $\gamma(a, b) = c$ be the only defined communication. Eliminate all occurrences of the communication operators $\parallel$, $\lfloor\!\lfloor$, and $\mid$, and as many τ-prefix operator occurrences as possible from the process term $\tau.a.b.1 \parallel \tau.(\tau.a.1 + \tau.b.1)$.

8.6.2 Prove the following equalities, for $a \in A_\tau$ and $\mathrm{TCP}_\tau(A,\gamma)$-terms x, y:

(a) $\mathrm{TCP}_\tau(A,\gamma) \vdash a.(\tau.1 \parallel x) = a.x$;
(b) $\mathrm{TCP}_\tau(A,\gamma) \vdash a.(\tau.x \parallel y) = a.(x \parallel y)$.

8.6.3 Prove Theorem 8.6.3 (Standard concurrency) for Axioms SC9 and SC10.

8.6.4 Prove the following equalities, for $\mathrm{TCP}_\tau(A,\gamma)$-terms x, y, z:

(a) $\mathrm{TCP}_\tau(A,\gamma) \vdash x \parallel \tau.y = \tau.(x \parallel y) + x \lfloor\!\lfloor y$;
(b) $\mathrm{TCP}_\tau(A,\gamma) \vdash x \lfloor\!\lfloor (\tau.y + y) = x \lfloor\!\lfloor y$;
(c) $\mathrm{TCP}_\tau(A,\gamma) \vdash x \lfloor\!\lfloor (\tau.(y + z) + y) = x \lfloor\!\lfloor (y + z)$.

8.6.5 Assume that $I \subseteq A$ and that no element of I can communicate, i.e., $\gamma(i, a)$ and $\gamma(a, i)$ are undefined for any $a \in A$ and $i \in I$. Prove that for all closed $\mathrm{TCP}_\tau(A,\gamma)$-terms p and q:

$$\mathrm{TCP}_\tau(A,\gamma) \vdash \tau_I(p \parallel q) = \tau_I(\tau_I(p) \parallel \tau_I(q)).$$

Assume, in addition, that none of the elements in I is the result of a communication, i.e., $\gamma(a, b) \notin I$ for any $a, b \in A$. Prove that for all closed $\mathrm{TCP}_\tau(A,\gamma)$-terms p and q:

$$\mathrm{TCP}_\tau(A,\gamma) \vdash \tau_I(p \parallel q) = \tau_I(p) \parallel \tau_I(q).$$

8.6.6 Prove, for arbitrary $\mathrm{TCP}_\tau(A,\gamma)$-terms x and y, closed $\mathrm{TCP}_\tau(A,\gamma)$-term p, and action $a \in A_\tau$ that $\mathrm{TCP}_\tau(A,\gamma) \vdash a.p \cdot (\tau.(x + y) + x) = a.p \cdot (x + y)$. As a generalization, prove, for arbitrary $\mathrm{TCP}_\tau(A,\gamma)$-terms x and y, that $\mathrm{TCP}_\tau(A,\gamma) \vdash p \cdot (\tau.(x + y) + x) = p \cdot (x + y)$

for any closed $\mathrm{TCP}_\tau(A, \gamma)$-term p of the form $p = \sum_{i<n} a_i . p_i$ with $a_i \in A_\tau$ and p_i a closed $\mathrm{TCP}_\tau(A, \gamma)$-term for some $n \in \mathbf{N}$.

8.6.7 Let x, y, z be $\mathrm{TCP}_\tau(A, \gamma)$-terms. Prove that Axiom B can be derived from $x \mathbin{⌊⌊} (\tau.(y + z) + y) = x \mathbin{⌊⌊} (y + z)$ and the other axioms of $\mathrm{TCP}_\tau(A, \gamma)$.

8.6.8 Consider the assumption that communication with τ is always undefined. Show that without this assumption Axiom SC10 is not valid in the standard term model. Consider theory $\mathrm{TCP}_\tau(A, \gamma)$ without Axiom SC10 and without the assumption that communication with τ is impossible. Where does the standard development of this theory go wrong?

8.6.9 Prove Theorem 8.6.1 (Elimination).

8.6.10 Prove Theorem 8.6.2 (Conservative ground-extension).

8.6.11 Prove Theorem 8.6.4 (Expansion theorem).

8.6.12 Prove Theorem 8.6.5 (Expansion theorem for free merge).

8.6.13 Prove Theorem 8.6.6 (Expansion theorem for handshaking communication).

8.6.14 Prove Proposition 8.6.7 (Congruence).

8.6.15 Prove Theorem 8.6.9 (Soundness).

8.6.16 Prove Theorem 8.6.10 (Ground-completeness).

8.6.17 Specialize the set of actions A into a set of names N, a set of co-names $\bar{N}$, and a set of communications C such that for each $n \in N$, there is exactly one $\bar{n} \in \bar{N}$ and exactly one $n_c \in C$. The communication function γ has $\gamma(n, \bar{n}) = \gamma(\bar{n}, n) = n_c$ and is not defined otherwise. Now define the CCS parallel composition operator $\|^{\mathrm{CCS}}$ by the following defining axiom, with x and y arbitrary terms:

$$x \|^{\mathrm{CCS}} y = \tau_C(x \parallel y).$$

Derive the CCS *expansion law* (see (Milner, 1980; Milner, 1989)) from the theory $\mathrm{TCP}_\tau(A, \gamma)$ extended with this defining axiom, and where A and γ are defined as in this exercise.

8.7 Iteration and divergence

In Section 4.6, prefix iteration a^*x for action a and term x has been considered. The introduction of the silent step τ implies an additional action-prefix operator $\tau.\_$; so, it is natural to also have a look at τ-prefix iteration $\tau^*\_$, sometimes called *divergence*, capturing the fact that it allows an infinite sequence of τ actions to occur. The theory $\mathrm{BSP}^*_\tau(A)$ is the union of theories $\mathrm{BSP}^*(A)$ of Section 4.6 and $\mathrm{BSP}_\tau(A)$, extended with the τ-prefix iteration; see Table 8.9.

The term deduction system for $\mathrm{BSP}^*_\tau(A)$ is simply the term deduction system of $\mathrm{BSP}^*(A)$ but with $a \in A_\tau$.

$\mathrm{BSP}^*_\tau(A)$
$\mathrm{BSP}^*(A)$, $\mathrm{BSP}_\tau(A)$
unary: $\tau^*\_$;
–

Table 8.9. The process theory $\mathrm{BSP}^*_\tau(A)$.

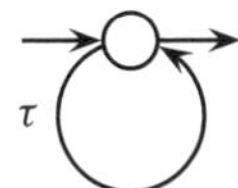

Fig. 8.10. τ^*1.

However, more can be said about τ-prefix iteration. Consider the process τ^*1, depicted in Figure 8.10. This process is branching bisimilar to the process 1 (but not rooted branching bisimilar!). This suggests that τ-loops can be removed. Since the standard term model is based on rooted branching bisimilarity, in the term model, only τ-loops not at the root can be removed entirely; τ-loops at the root can be reduced to a single τ-step. This fact can be captured as the *Fair-Iteration* Axiom; see Table 8.10. It can be shown, see Exercise 8.7.1, that the Fair-Iteration Axiom implies that $(\mathrm{BSP}^*_\tau + \mathrm{FI})(A) \vdash a.p \cdot \tau^* x = a.p \cdot x$ for all $(\mathrm{BSP}^*_\tau + \mathrm{FI})(A)$-terms x and closed $(\mathrm{BSP}^*_\tau + \mathrm{FI})(A)$-terms p. The Fair-Iteration Axiom expresses that τ-prefix iteration behaves fairly, in the sense that no infinite sequence of τ-steps occurs, or in other words that divergence does not occur. However, it needs to be stressed that the Fair-Iteration Axiom happens to hold in the standard term model of $\mathrm{BSP}^*_\tau(A)$ with rooted branching bisimilarity as the underlying equivalence, which means that this model is also a model of $(\mathrm{BSP}^*_\tau + \mathrm{FI})(A)$. Other models of $\mathrm{BSP}^*_\tau(A)$ exist where fair iteration does not hold, which means that these models are not models of $(\mathrm{BSP}^*_\tau + \mathrm{FI})(A)$.

It is interesting to consider a model that does not allow to remove τ-loops. Abstracting from τ-loops implies that processes without divergence are equivalent to processes with divergence. This is not always desirable. A model for BSP^*_τ that does not abstract from divergence can be constructed in the same way as the standard term model, but using a different semantic equivalence at the basis.

$(\mathrm{BSP}^*_\tau + \mathrm{FI})(A)$	
$\mathrm{BSP}^*_\tau(A)$	
-	
x;	
$\tau.\tau^*x = \tau.x$	FI

Table 8.10. Fair iteration.

Definition 8.7.1 (Branching bisimilarity with explicit divergence) A binary relation R on the set of states S of a transition-system space is a *branching bisimulation relation with explicit divergence* if and only if R is a branching bisimulation relation on S and in addition the following conditions hold:

(i) for all states $s, t \in S$, whenever $(s, t) \in R$ and $s \xrightarrow{\tau} s_0 \xrightarrow{\tau} s_1 \cdots$ is an infinite τ-path such that $(s_i, t) \in R$ for all $i \in \mathbf{N}$, then there are states $t_0, t_1, \ldots$ such that $t \xrightarrow{\tau} t_0 \xrightarrow{\tau} t_1 \cdots$ and $(s_i, t_j) \in R$ for all $i, j \in \mathbf{N}$;

(ii) vice versa, for all states $s, t \in S$, whenever $(s, t) \in R$ and $t \xrightarrow{\tau} t_0 \xrightarrow{\tau} t_1 \cdots$ is an infinite τ-path such that $(s, t_i) \in R$ for all $i \in \mathbf{N}$, then there are states $s_0, s_1, \ldots$ such that $s \xrightarrow{\tau} s_0 \xrightarrow{\tau} s_1 \cdots$ and $(s_j, t_i) \in R$ for all $i, j \in \mathbf{N}$.

This definition might seem very restrictive, but this is not really the case. As before, it is possible to define a rootedness condition for this notion, so that rooted branching bisimilarity with explicit divergence becomes a congruence relation on the term algebra. As a consequence, a model of $\mathrm{BSP}^*_\tau(A)$ is obtained where the Fair-Iteration Axiom does not hold; divergence cannot be abstracted away.

It is also possible to proceed in another way, by treating divergence as chaos. This is an extreme standpoint that states that, as soon as divergent behavior is possible, nothing more can be said about the process, no observation is possible. This means that any process with divergence is identified with the completely arbitrary process that can only do internal actions, called the *chaos* process. This situation is characterized by the axiom given in Table 8.11.

Proposition 8.7.2 (Chaos) The following equalities are derivable from theory $(\mathrm{BSP}^*_\tau + \mathrm{CH})(A)$, for any $(\mathrm{BSP}^*_\tau + \mathrm{CH})(A)$-terms x and y.

(i) $\tau^*x = x + \tau^*0$;

(ii) $\tau^*x + y = \tau^*0$.

— $(\mathrm{BSP}^*_\tau + \mathrm{CH})(A)$ —	
$\mathrm{BSP}^*_\tau(A)$	
-	
x;	
$\tau^*x = \tau^*0$	CH

Table 8.11. Catastrophic divergence.

Proof The derivations are as follows, where the second derivation uses the first identity in the second step. $(\mathrm{BSP}^*_\tau + \mathrm{CH})(A) \vdash$

(i) $\tau^*x = x + \tau.\tau^*x = x + x + \tau.\tau^*x = x + \tau^*x = x + \tau^*0$;
(ii) $\tau^*x + y = \tau^*0 + y = \tau^*y = \tau^*0$. □

This proposition, in particular the second identity, characterizes process τ^*x as chaos, that makes any determination of the subsequent or alternative process behavior impossible. The standard term model of $\mathrm{BSP}^*_\tau(A)$ does not validate the Chaos Axiom CH, but it is possible to find a model for the theory $\mathrm{BSP}^*_\tau(A)$ that does satisfy this axiom, and which is therefore a model of $(\mathrm{BSP}^*_\tau+\mathrm{CH})(A)$ (see Exercise 8.7.6).

Exercises

8.7.1 Show that the Fair-Iteration Axiom can be used to prove that $(\mathrm{BSP}^*_\tau + \mathrm{FI})(A) \vdash a.p\cdot\tau^*x = a.p\cdot x$ for all $(\mathrm{BSP}^*_\tau+\mathrm{FI})(A)$-terms x and closed $(\mathrm{BSP}^*_\tau + \mathrm{FI})(A)$-terms p. As a generalization, prove that $(\mathrm{BSP}^*_\tau + \mathrm{FI})(A) \vdash p \cdot \tau^*x = p \cdot x$ for all $(\mathrm{BSP}^*_\tau + \mathrm{FI})(A)$-terms x and closed terms p of the form $\sum_{i<n} a_i . p_i$ with $a_i \in A_\tau$ and closed terms p_i for some $n \in \mathbf{N}$.

8.7.2 In a transition system, a *divergent* state is a state from which an infinite series of τ-steps is possible. Find two transition systems that are branching bisimilar, by a branching bisimulation that relates divergent states to divergent states only, but such that the transition systems are not branching bisimilar with explicit divergence.

8.7.3 Verify that rooted branching bisimilarity with explicit divergence is a congruence relation on the term algebra for $\mathrm{BSP}^*_\tau(A)$. Verify that the resulting quotient algebra is a model for $\mathrm{BSP}^*_\tau(A)$, but that this algebra does not validate the Fair-Iteration Axiom FI (and is hence not a model of $(\mathrm{BSP}^*_\tau + \mathrm{FI})(A)$).

8.7.4 A weaker version of the Fair-Iteration Axiom is the equation

$$\tau^*\tau.x = \tau.x$$

that only removes so-called *unstable* divergence (i.e., divergence can only be escaped by means of a process that starts with a silent step). Show that the Fair-Iteration Axiom implies this equation. On the other hand, try to come up with a model for BSP^*_τ that satisfies this equation but not the Fair-Iteration Axiom.

8.7.5 Prove that $(\mathrm{BSP}^*_\tau + \mathrm{CH})(A) \vdash$

(a) $\tau^*(x + y) = \tau^*x + \tau^*y$;
(b) $\tau^*x + y = \tau^*x$.

8.7.6 Construct a model for $(\mathrm{BSP}^*_\tau + \mathrm{CH})(A)$.

8.8 Recursion and fair abstraction

The previous section illustrates that recursive and silent behavior form an interesting combination. This section investigates the extension of the general theory $\mathrm{TCP}_\tau(A, \gamma)$ with general recursion.

A crucial concept in any context with recursion is the concept of guardedness. In Chapter 5, an occurrence of a recursion variable in a term has been defined to be guarded if it occurs in a subterm of the form $a.s$ for some action $a \in A$ and term s. Now that a prefix operator $\tau.\_$ has been added, it should be discussed whether this operator can also act as a guard of a recursion variable.

To this end, consider the recursive equation $X = \tau.X$. Considering the term model of $\mathrm{TCP}_\tau(A, \gamma)$ of Section 8.6, all processes $[\tau.p]_{\leftrightarrow_{\mathrm{rb}}}$ are solutions for X, for any closed $\mathrm{TCP}_\tau(A, \gamma)$-term p, since $\tau.p \leftrightarrow_{\mathrm{rb}} \tau.\tau.p$. Hence, the silent step cannot be considered a guard for an occurrence of a recursion variable.

Also, the abstraction operator, as introduced in Section 8.5.1, can cause problems when considering recursion, and guardedness in particular.

Example 8.8.1 (Direct abstraction from a guard) Consider the recursive specification $E = \{X = \tau_I(i.X)\}$ where $i \in I$. With the definition of guardedness as given before, this recursive specification is guarded. Nevertheless, this equation has many different solutions: for all distinct actions a and b not in I, processes $[\tau.a.1]_{\leftrightarrow_{\mathrm{rb}}}$ and $[\tau.b.1]_{\leftrightarrow_{\mathrm{rb}}}$ are solutions for X. The reason for this problem is the occurrence of the abstraction operator, which is problematic because it abstracts from an atomic action that acts as a guard for a recursion variable.

Example 8.8.2 (Indirect abstraction from a guard) Consider the recursive specification $E = \{X = i.\tau_I(X)\}$ where $i \in I$. Although initially, the action i

acts as a guard for the occurrence of X on the right-hand side, all subsequent occurrences of i are abstracted away, as the recursive call to X is in the scope of the abstraction operator. Also this recursive specification has many solutions. For example, for different a and b not in I, the processes $[i.a.1]_{\leftrightarrow_{\mathrm{rb}}}$ and $[i.b.1]_{\leftrightarrow_{\mathrm{rb}}}$ are solutions for X.

These difficulties make it necessary to restrict the notion of guardedness. A recursive specification will only be said to be guarded if it can be brought into a form (by applying the equations and axioms of the theory) where all variables on the right-hand side are guarded by an atomic action different from τ and in which no abstraction operator occurs. The following definition replaces the corresponding part of Definition 5.5.5 (Guardedness, part 1). The other parts of Definitions 5.5.5 and 5.5.8 (Guardedness, parts 1 and 2) carry over to the current context without change.

Definition 8.8.3 (Guardedness in $\mathrm{TCP}_{\tau,\mathrm{rec}}(A,\gamma)$**)** An occurrence of a variable x in a $\mathrm{TCP}_{\tau,\mathrm{rec}}(A,\gamma)$-term s is *guarded* if and only if the abstraction operator does not occur in s and x occurs in a subterm of the form $a.t$ for some action $a \in A$ (so not equal to τ) and $\mathrm{TCP}_{\tau,\mathrm{rec}}(A,\gamma)$-term t.

With this restricted definition of guardedness, the familiar results can be established. The term model of the theory extended with recursion constants is defined as before. Proofs are left to the reader. They go along the lines of similar proofs given earlier in this book and proofs in (Baeten *et al.*, 1987b).

Theorem 8.8.4 (Validity of RDP**)** Recursion principle RDP is not valid in the standard term model but it is valid in the term model for the theory extended with recursion constants: $\mathbb{P}(\mathrm{TCP}_\tau(A,\gamma))_{/\leftrightarrow_{\mathrm{rb}}} \not\models \mathrm{RDP}$ and $\mathbb{P}(\mathrm{TCP}_{\tau,\mathrm{rec}}(A,\gamma))_{/\leftrightarrow_{\mathrm{rb}}} \models \mathrm{RDP}$.

Theorem 8.8.5 (Validity of RDP$^-$**)** The principle RDP$^-$ is not valid in the standard term model but it is valid in the term model with recursion constants: $\mathbb{P}(\mathrm{TCP}_\tau(A,\gamma))_{/\leftrightarrow_{\mathrm{rb}}} \not\models \mathrm{RDP}^-$ and $\mathbb{P}(\mathrm{TCP}_{\tau,\mathrm{rec}}(A,\gamma))_{/\leftrightarrow_{\mathrm{rb}}} \models \mathrm{RDP}^-$.

Theorem 8.8.6 (Validity of RSP**)** Recursion principle RSP is valid in both the term models with and without recursion constants: $\mathbb{P}(\mathrm{TCP}_\tau(A,\gamma))_{/\leftrightarrow_{\mathrm{rb}}} \models \mathrm{RSP}$ and $\mathbb{P}(\mathrm{TCP}_{\tau,\mathrm{rec}}(A,\gamma))_{/\leftrightarrow_{\mathrm{rb}}} \models \mathrm{RSP}$.

The extension of theory $\mathrm{TCP}_{\tau,\mathrm{rec}}(A,\gamma)$ with projection operators, needed for the formulation of the recursion principles AIP and AIP$^-$, can be obtained as outlined in Section 8.5.3.

Theorem 8.8.7 (Validity of AIP**)** Recursion principle AIP is valid in the standard term model but it is not valid in the term model with recursion constants: $\mathbb{P}((\mathrm{TCP}_\tau + \mathrm{PR})(A,\gamma))_{/\leftrightarrows_{\mathrm{rb}}} \models \mathrm{AIP}$ and $\mathbb{P}((\mathrm{TCP}_\tau + \mathrm{PR})_{\mathrm{rec}}(A,\gamma))_{/\leftrightarrows_{\mathrm{rb}}} \not\models \mathrm{AIP}$.

Theorem 8.8.8 (Validity of AIP^-**)** Principle AIP^- is valid in both the term models with and without recursion constants: $\mathbb{P}((\mathrm{TCP}_\tau + \mathrm{PR})(A,\gamma))_{/\leftrightarrows_{\mathrm{rb}}} \models \mathrm{AIP}^-$ and $\mathbb{P}((\mathrm{TCP}_\tau + \mathrm{PR})_{\mathrm{rec}}(A,\gamma))_{/\leftrightarrows_{\mathrm{rb}}} \models \mathrm{AIP}^-$.

Recall that AIP^- requires that at least one of the two considered terms is guarded. In the course of establishing the validity of AIP^-, the following theorem is needed. It characterizes a solution of a guarded recursive specification, or, in other words, a definable process (see Definition 5.7.5). As such, it replaces Theorem 5.7.7 (Processes definable over BSP(A)) in theories with silent steps, and it provides the properties of the process specified by the guarded term in the AIP^- formulation. A transition system is called *divergence free* if and only if from no state of the system, an infinite series of consecutive τ-steps can be taken. An equivalence class of transition systems under rooted branching bisimilarity, i.e., a process in the current context, is divergence free if and only if at least one element is.

Theorem 8.8.9 (Processes definable over $\mathrm{TCP}_\tau(A,\gamma)$**)** A process in the algebra of processes $\mathbb{P}(\mathrm{TCP}_{\tau,\mathrm{rec}}(A,\gamma))_{/\leftrightarrows_{\mathrm{rb}}}$ is definable over $\mathrm{TCP}_\tau(A,\gamma)$ if and only if it contains a transition system as an element that is both finitely branching and divergence free.

The proof of this result can be found in (Baeten *et al.*, 1987b). It should be stressed that this theorem states that a transition system is needed that has both properties at the same time. It is not so that a process is definable if and only if it is finitely branching and divergence free. The latter would allow that some transition systems in the equivalence class are finitely branching and some divergence free but that no single transition system is both finitely branching and divergence free. Consider for example the unguarded recursive specification, using the k-fold action prefix of Notation 4.6.6, that has equations $X_n = \tau.X_{n+1} + \sum_{0\le i\le n} a^i 1$ for each natural number n. The transition system for X_0 obtained by the operational rules is finitely branching but not divergence free, while after removing all τ-steps after the initial one a rooted branching bisimilar transition system is obtained that is divergence free but not finitely branching. The process containing among others these two transition systems is therefore finitely branching and divergence free but it is *not* definable over $\mathrm{TCP}_\tau(A,\gamma)$.

Let us take a closer look at transition systems with divergence that cannot be removed under (rooted) branching bisimilarity. As an example, consider the *unguarded* recursive specification $E = \{X_n = \tau.X_{n+1} + a^n 1 \mid n \in \mathbf{N}\}$. The transition system corresponding to recursion variable X_0 has divergence, and none of the τ-steps can be removed under branching bisimilarity, all states being different. Nevertheless, the process containing the transition system of X_0 is expressible in $\mathrm{BSP}_{\tau,\mathrm{rec}}(A)$ (and hence in $\mathrm{TCP}_{\tau,\mathrm{rec}}(A, \gamma)$), as defined in Definition 5.7.2 (Expressiveness). This is demonstrated by recursive specification E. However, the process is not *definable* over $\mathrm{BSP}_\tau(A)$ or $\mathrm{TCP}_\tau(A, \gamma)$, as this would contradict Theorem 8.8.9 above. This means that it is not the solution of a guarded recursive specification over the corresponding signature (see again (Baeten *et al.*, 1987b)). What can be done however is the following. Consider the guarded recursive specification $F = \{Y_n = i.X_{n+1} + a^n 1 \mid n \in \mathbf{N}\}$, where $i \in A$ is some atomic action. This recursive specification is guarded, so variable Y_0 has a unique solution, in the form of a definable process. Now process $\mu X_0.E$ can be obtained as $\tau_{\{i\}}(\mu Y_0.F)$, i.e., the process specified by unguarded specification E can be obtained as an abstraction applied to a definable process. It turns out that abstraction applied to definable processes is a powerful concept. Abstraction applied to *finitely* definable processes already allows to define *all countable computable* processes. Note that, when assuming that τ is an allowed transition label, the definition of a (countable) computable process as defined in Definition 5.7.1 carries over to the current setting. A process in the current context is an equivalence class of transition systems under rooted branching bisimilarity, but this results in the same set of (countable) computable processes. Based on Theorem 5.7.3 (Countable computable transition systems), this implies that all countable computable processes can be specified by means of $\mathrm{BSP}_{\tau,\mathrm{rec}}(A)$-terms. The following theorem states the universality of theory $\mathrm{TCP}_\tau(A, \gamma)$, meaning that every countable computable process can be defined via a finite expression over the signature of that theory with finite guarded recursion. A proof of the theorem is omitted. The interested reader is referred to (Baeten *et al.*, 1987b).

Theorem 8.8.10 (Universality of $\mathrm{TCP}_\tau(A, \gamma)$**)** Let p be a countable computable process, and $\mathrm{BSP}_{\tau,\mathrm{rec}}(A)$-term t the term specifying p. Then, there is a (finite) set of actions $I \subseteq A$ and a finite guarded recursive specification E over $\mathrm{TCP}_\tau(A, \gamma)$ with recursion variable X, such that $(\mathrm{TCP}_{\tau,\mathrm{rec}} + \mathrm{RSP})(A, \gamma) \vdash \tau_I(\mu X.E) = t$.

Recall from the previous section that divergence is tightly coupled to the notion of fairness. The Fair-Iteration Axiom given in the previous section expresses the assumption that τ-prefix iteration behaves fairly and divergence does not occur. It is therefore interesting to consider fairness in the current context with general recursion. Consider the following example.

Example 8.8.11 (Tossing a coin) Suppose a statistician carries out an experiment: he tosses a coin until head comes up. Assuming that the probability of tossing heads is between 0 and 1 (so, not equal to 0 or to 1), this process can be described by the following recursive equation.

$$S = toss.(\tau.tail.S + \tau.head.1).$$

In this specification, a non-deterministic choice is used to indicate that the choice cannot be influenced by another process (for instance, by blocking one alternative, or only offering a synchronization with one alternative). It is unclear at what point the outcome is determined: presumably after the moment the coin is thrown into the air, but before the moment the outcome is observed. The moment of choice itself cannot be observed, and this is why silent steps are used. In Section 11.2, a theory with probabilities is discussed that allows for a better description of examples in which probabilities play a role.

Assume now that the experiment is carried out in a closed room. Standing outside, an observer cannot observe anything occurring. However, if head comes up, the statistician yells: 'Head!', which means that the outside observer can 'observe' the *head* action, whereas actions from $I = \{toss, tail\}$ are still hidden from the observer. Thus, the observer observes the process $\tau_I(S)$. Because the coin is *fair*, after a number of tails (zero or more), head will come up. So, following this intuition, one would expect the following equality:

$$\tau_I(S) = \tau.head.1,$$

saying that after some internal activity *head* is observed. Figure 8.11 shows that the transition system associated with S where all actions from I are replaced by the silent step and the transition system associated with $\tau.head.1$ are indeed rooted branching bisimilar.

The question now arises whether the expected equality can also be derived from the axioms of the equational theories considered so far. The Fair-Iteration Axiom of the previous section only considers a τ-loop consisting of a single τ action, and not a cycle consisting of more than one τ-step. This axiom cannot be applied to prove the above equality. In fact, none of the axioms considered so far allows the derivation of the equality. Still, it is preferable to be able to derive this identity equationally.

The Fair-Iteration Axiom can be rephrased in a setting with recursion in the form of the following conditional axiom (see also Section 5.3). The axiom is

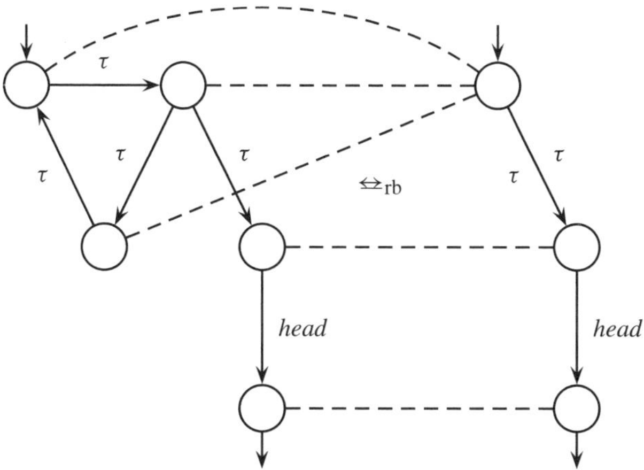

Fig. 8.11. Statistician.

given as a deduction rule, with x and y process terms, $i \in A$ an action, and $I \subseteq A$ some set of actions.

$$\frac{x = i.x + y,\ i \in I}{\tau.\tau_I(x) = \tau.\tau_I(y)} \qquad (\mathrm{KFAR}_1^{\mathrm{b}}).$$

Notice that in the equation $x = i.x + y$, the occurrence of recursion variable x is guarded, so the process x is uniquely defined and it makes sense to write $\tau_I(x)$.

In general, when there is a cycle of internal steps i_k of length n, conditional axioms, one for each n, can be formulated as follows.

$$\frac{\begin{array}{l} x_1 = i_1.x_2 + y_1 \\ x_2 = i_2.x_3 + y_2 \\ \vdots \\ x_{n-1} = i_{n-1}.x_n + y_{n-1} \\ x_n = i_n.x_1 + y_n \\ i_1, i_2, \cdots, i_n \in I \cup \{\tau\}, \text{ with at least one } i_k \not\equiv \tau \end{array}}{\tau.\tau_I(x_1) = \tau.(\tau_I(y_1) + \tau_I(y_2) + \cdots + \tau_I(y_n))} \qquad (\mathrm{KFAR}_n^{\mathrm{b}}).$$

The i_k actions in the equations for x_k form a cycle; the y_k specify the behaviors that leave the cycle. Figure 8.12 illustrates $\mathrm{KFAR}_4^{\mathrm{b}}$. Note that some of the i_k may be equal to τ, but not all of them, since that would make the specification of the x_k unguarded.

The given deduction rules are collectively called *Koomen's Fair Abstraction Rules*, abbreviated as $\mathrm{KFAR}^{\mathrm{b}}$. The 'b' in this name indicates that this

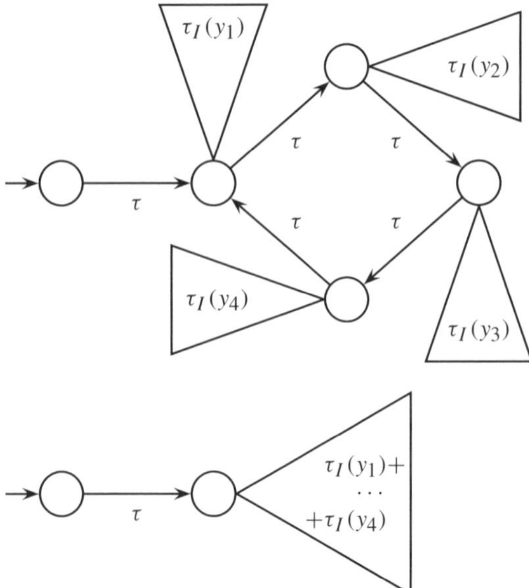

Fig. 8.12. An illustration of $\mathrm{KFAR}^{\mathrm{b}}$.

formulation holds in the context of (rooted) branching bisimilarity. The original formulation of Koomen's Fair Abstraction Rules only works in the context of another semantic equivalence called weak bisimulation (see (Baeten *et al.*, 1987b)). $\mathrm{KFAR}^{\mathrm{b}}$ says that, in abstracting from a set of internal actions, eventually (i.e., after performing a number of internal steps) an external step will be chosen (unless no such steps exist).

Theorem 8.8.12 (Validity of $\mathrm{KFAR}^{\mathrm{b}}$) Principle $\mathrm{KFAR}^{\mathrm{b}}$ is valid in both the term models with and without recursion constants: $\mathbb{P}(\mathrm{TCP}_\tau(A,\gamma))_{/\underline{\leftrightarrow}_{\mathrm{rb}}} \models \mathrm{KFAR}^{\mathrm{b}}$ and $\mathbb{P}(\mathrm{TCP}_{\tau,\mathrm{rec}}(A,\gamma))_{/\underline{\leftrightarrow}_{\mathrm{rb}}} \models \mathrm{KFAR}^{\mathrm{b}}$.

The proof of this result is straightforward and left to the reader. The theorem states that the collective set of $\mathrm{KFAR}^{\mathrm{b}}$ deduction rules is valid in the standard term models. However, it is interesting to observe that the individual rules are independent. For any n, there is a model for $\mathrm{TCP}_{\tau,\mathrm{rec}}(A,\gamma)$ that validates $\mathrm{KFAR}^{\mathrm{b}}_{n+1}$ but not $\mathrm{KFAR}^{\mathrm{b}}_n$. A proof of this fact is outside the scope of this text, but can be found in (Baeten & Weijland, 1990).

Example 8.8.13 (Tossing a coin) Consider the following description of the statistician tossing a coin until head comes up, that is equivalent to the one used in Example 8.8.11:

$$S = toss.S' + 0,$$
$$S' = \tau.S'' + \tau.head.1,$$
$$S'' = tail.S + 0.$$

Recall that $I = \{toss, tail\}$. Then, using KFAR^{b}, the following derivation can be obtained. Note that communication does not play a role, so γ can be chosen arbitrarily.

$$\begin{aligned}(\mathrm{TCP}_{\tau,\mathrm{rec}} + \mathrm{KFAR}^{\mathrm{b}})(A,\gamma) \vdash \\ \tau.\tau_I(S') &= \tau.(\tau_I(\tau.head.1) + \tau_I(0) + \tau_I(0)) \\ &= \tau.\tau.head.1 \\ &= \tau.head.1.\end{aligned}$$

It then follows easily that

$$\begin{aligned}&(\mathrm{TCP}_{\tau,\mathrm{rec}} + \mathrm{KFAR}^{\mathrm{b}})(A,\gamma) \vdash \\ &\quad \tau_I(S) = \tau_I(toss.S') = \tau.\tau_I(S') = \tau.\tau.head.1 = \tau.head.1,\end{aligned}$$

which proves the desired result.

Example 8.8.14 (Throwing a die) The statistician of Example 8.8.11 now decides to throw a die until six comes up. This is described by

$$\begin{aligned}S_2 = throw.(&\tau.one.S_2 + \tau.two.S_2 + \tau.three.S_2 \\ &+ \tau.four.S_2 + \tau.five.S_2 + \tau.six.1).\end{aligned}$$

Again, the experiment is carried out in a room, and the observer outside can only hear the yell 'Six!'. Abstracting from actions $I = \{throw, one, two, three, four, five\}$, one would expect that the identity $\tau_I(S_2) = \tau.six.1$ is derivable from the equational theory. However, the proof principle KFAR^{b} cannot be used directly to prove this expected result. (Try it.)

The reason that KFAR^{b} cannot be applied in the above example is that the structure of the recursive equation does not lead to a simple cycle, as illustrated in Figure 8.13. Using a trick, based on renaming of actions (see Section 6.7), it is possible to apply KFAR^{b} nonetheless, see Exercise 8.8.5. This trick can be used in some cases to extend the applicability of the proof principle, but also fails for more complicated structures of transition systems (although even then, with a more general theory of renaming, KFAR^{b} is sufficient (Baeten & Weijland, 1990; Vaandrager, 1986)). Therefore, it is useful to have a version of KFAR^{b} that is applicable to arbitrary so-called *clusters* of internal steps: the *Cluster Fair Abstraction Rule* CFAR^{b}.

Definition 8.8.15 (Cluster) Let E be a recursive specification, and let $I \subseteq A$. A subset C of variables from E is called a *cluster of I in $\mu X.E$* if variable X of E is in C and if the following condition holds: for all $Z \in C$, there

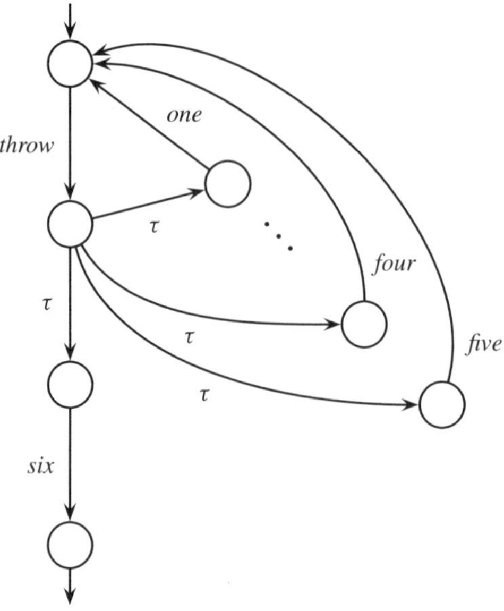

Fig. 8.13. The statistician throwing dice.

exist actions $i_1, \cdots, i_m \in I \cup \{\tau\}$, recursion variables $X_1, \cdots, X_m \in C$, and recursion variables $Y_1, \cdots, Y_n \notin C$ for some $m \geq 1$ and $n \geq 0$ such that the equation for Z in E is of the form

$$Z = \sum_{k=1}^{m} i_k.X_k + \sum_{j=1}^{n} Y_j.$$

The variables Y_j in this equation are called the *exits* of Z and denoted $U(Z)$. Furthermore, the exit set of the cluster C is $U(C) = \bigcup_{Z \in C} U(Z)$. A cluster is called *conservative* if every exit $Y \in U(C)$ is accessible from every variable in the cluster by doing a number of steps from $I \cup \{\tau\}$ to a cluster-variable which has exit Y.

Example 8.8.16 (Cluster) Reconsider process S_2 of Example 8.8.14. This process can be defined by the following guarded recursive specification E:

$$\begin{aligned}
S_2 &= \mathit{throw}.X_0 + 0\\
X_0 &= \tau.X_1 + \tau.X_2 + \tau.X_3 + \tau.X_4 + \tau.X_5 + X_6\\
X_1 &= \mathit{one}.S_2 + 0\\
X_2 &= \mathit{two}.S_2 + 0\\
X_3 &= \mathit{three}.S_2 + 0\\
X_4 &= \mathit{four}.S_2 + 0
\end{aligned}$$

$$X_5 = \mathit{five}.S_2 + 0$$
$$X_6 = \tau.\mathit{six}.1.$$

Then, $C = \{S_2, X_0, X_1, X_2, X_3, X_4, X_5\}$ is a conservative cluster of $I = \{\mathit{throw}, \mathit{one}, \mathit{two}, \mathit{three}, \mathit{four}, \mathit{five}\}$ with exit X_6 in any of the processes $\mu X.E$ with X in C. Note that the 0 summands in the equations correspond to empty summations. They are included to illustrate how the equations fit Definition 8.8.15.

Definition 8.8.17 (CFAR^b) Let E be a guarded recursive specification in which the recursion variable X occurs and let $I \subseteq A$. Let C be a finite conservative cluster of I in $\mu X.E$ and let U be the set of exits from the cluster C. Then, the following identity is derivable.

$$\tau.\tau_I(X) = \tau.\left(\sum_{Y \in U} \tau_I(Y)\right) \qquad (\text{CFAR}^b).$$

Note that CFAR^b is, like KFAR^b, a conditional axiom. It is valid for the standard term model of theory $\text{TCP}_{\tau,\text{rec}}(A, \gamma)$ (Baeten & Weijland, 1990; Vaandrager, 1986).

Example 8.8.18 (Application of CFAR^b**)** Return to Example 8.8.16. The given cluster C is finite. Consider the process specified by X_0. By CFAR^b, it follows that

$$(\text{TCP}_{\tau,\text{rec}} + \text{CFAR}^b)(A, \gamma) \vdash \tau.\tau_I(X_0) = \tau.\tau_I(X_6) = \tau.\mathit{six}.1.$$

This result easily leads to the result that

$$(\text{TCP}_{\tau,\text{rec}} + \text{CFAR}^b)(A, \gamma) \vdash \tau_I(S_2) = \tau.\mathit{six}.1,$$

which is the desired result, as explained in Example 8.8.14.

Exercises

8.8.1 Recall the specification and calculations for a two-place buffer from Section 7.6. A two-place buffer with input channel i and output channel o is given by the following equations:

$$\mathit{Buf2} = 1 + \sum_{d \in D} i?d.B_d \quad \text{and, for all } d \in D,$$
$$B_d = o!d.\mathit{Buf2} + \sum_{e \in D} i?e.o!d.B_e.$$

Assuming that $\mathit{Buf1}_{pq}$ is a one-place buffer with input port p and output port q, i.e.,

$$\mathit{Buf1}_{pq} = 1 + \sum_{d \in D} p?d.q!d.\mathit{Buf1}_{pq},$$

and assuming the standard communication function γ_S (see Definition 7.3.1), prove that

$$(\mathrm{TCP}_{\tau,\mathrm{rec}} + \mathrm{RSP})(A, \gamma_S) \vdash \\ Buf2 = \tau_I(\partial_H(Buf1_{il} \parallel Buf1_{lo})),$$

where $H = \{l!d, l?d \mid d \in D\}$ and $I = \{l?d \mid d \in D\}$.

8.8.2 Prove that the recursive specification $\{X = i.\tau_{\{j\}}(Y),\ Y = j.\tau_{\{i\}}(X)\}$ has more than one solution in the standard term model of theory $\mathrm{TCP}_{\tau,\mathrm{rec}}(A, \gamma)$ based on rooted branching bisimilarity.

8.8.3 Try to define the notion of guardedness for recursive specifications that, in contrast to what is allowed by Definition 8.8.3 (Guardedness in $\mathrm{TCP}_{\tau,\mathrm{rec}}(A, \gamma)$), may contain abstraction operators. As usual, the definition should guarantee that every guarded recursive specification has a unique solution in the standard term model, based on rooted branching bisimilarity in the current context. Consider only finite specifications.

8.8.4 Show that the conclusion of the $\mathrm{KFAR}^{\mathrm{b}}_n$ deduction rule can equivalently be formulated as follows:

$$\tau_I(x_1) = \tau_I(y_1) + \tau.(\tau_I(y_1) + \cdots + \tau_I(y_n)).$$

8.8.5 Let $I \subseteq A$ be some set of actions, and let $t \in A$ be some action. Define a renaming function (see Section 6.7) f by $f(a) = t$, if $a \in I$, and $f(a) = a$, otherwise. The renaming operator ρ_f is denoted t_I and called the *pre-abstraction* operator. Prove for all closed $\mathrm{TCP}_\tau(A, \gamma)$-terms p that

$$\mathrm{TCP}_\tau(A, \gamma) \vdash \tau_I(p) = \tau_{\{t\}}(t_I(p)),$$

whenever t does not occur in p.

Assume this equation also holds for recursively defined processes and reconsider Example 8.8.14 (Throwing a die). Use this equation to derive $\tau_I(S_2) = \tau.six.1$, using only the axioms of $\mathrm{TCP}_{\tau,\mathrm{rec}}(A, \gamma)$ and $\mathrm{KFAR}^{\mathrm{b}}$.

8.8.6 Show that $\mathrm{KFAR}^{\mathrm{b}}$ can be derived from $\mathrm{CFAR}^{\mathrm{b}}$.

8.8.7 Suppose someone starts a random walk in the lower left-hand corner of the 3×3 grid shown below. When arriving in the upper right-hand corner, the person stops walking. The process P describing this random walk has actions *begin*, *north*, *west*, *south*, *east*, *end*. Give a recursive specification for P. Let $I = \{north, west, south, east\}$ and calculate $\tau_I(P)$ using $\mathrm{CFAR}^{\mathrm{b}}$. Does this result conform to your intuition?

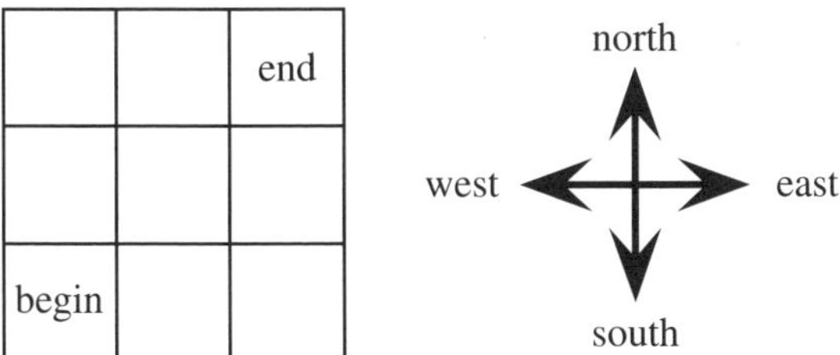

8.8.8 Formulate a variant of the KFAR^b principle that is suitable for the abstraction of unstable divergence, as treated in Exercise 8.7.4. Use the resulting rule to establish the identity desired in Example 8.8.11 (Tossing a coin).

8.9 Verification of the ABP and queues revisited

Consider again the Alternating-Bit Protocol from Section 7.8. In that section, it was already mentioned that the process $\partial_H(S \parallel K \parallel L \parallel R)$ after abstraction of internal actions, satisfies the specification of the one-place buffer $Buf1_{io}$. In this chapter, these claims are backed with a formal derivation of the following theorem.

Theorem 8.9.1 (Alternating-Bit Protocol) The Alternating-Bit Protocol is a *correct* communication protocol, i.e.,

$$((\mathrm{TCP}_\tau + \mathrm{HA})_{\mathrm{rec}} + \mathrm{CFAR}^{\mathrm{b}} + \mathrm{RSP})(A, \gamma_S) \vdash \tau_I(\partial_H(S \parallel K \parallel L \parallel R)) = Buf1_{io},$$

where $H = \{p?x, p!x \mid x \in F \cup \{0, 1, \bot\},\ p \in \{sk, kr, rl, ls\}\}$ and $I = \{p?\!\!\!?x \mid x \in F \cup \{0, 1, \bot\},\ p \in \{sk, kr, rl, ls\}\} \cup \{t\}$.

Proof In Section 7.8, the following recursive specification has been derived for the process $\partial_H(S \parallel K \parallel L \parallel R)$, using among others the Handshaking Axiom HA. The specification uses the recursion variables X, $X1_d$, $X2_d$, Y, $Y1_d$, and $Y2_d$ (for each $d \in D$), with process X equal to $\partial_H(S \parallel K \parallel L \parallel R)$:

$$\begin{aligned}
X &= 1 + \sum_{d \in D} i?d.X1_d,\\
X1_d &= sk?\!\!\!?d0.\,(t.kr?\!\!\!?\bot.rl?\!\!\!?1.(t.ls?\!\!\!?\bot.X1_d + t.ls?\!\!\!?1.X1_d)\\
&\qquad + t.kr?\!\!\!?d0.o!d.X2_d)\,,\\
X2_d &= rl?\!\!\!?0.\,(t.ls?\!\!\!?\bot.sk?\!\!\!?d0.(t.kr?\!\!\!?\bot.X2_d + t.kr?\!\!\!?d0.X2_d) + t.ls?\!\!\!?0.Y)\,,\\
Y &= 1 + \sum_{d \in D} i?d.Y1_d,\\
Y1_d &= sk?\!\!\!?d1.\,(t.kr?\!\!\!?\bot.rl?\!\!\!?0.(t.ls?\!\!\!?\bot.Y1_d + t.ls?\!\!\!?0.Y1_d)\\
&\qquad + t.kr?\!\!\!?d1.o!d.Y2_d)\,,\\
Y2_d &= rl?\!\!\!?1.\,(t.ls?\!\!\!?\bot.sk?\!\!\!?d1.(t.kr?\!\!\!?\bot.Y2_d + t.kr?\!\!\!?d1.Y2_d) + t.ls?\!\!\!?1.X)\,.
\end{aligned}$$

As the next step, for the process $X1_d$, an alternative recursive specification is given using additional recursion variables $Z_1, \cdots, Z_6$. The reason for doing so is that the above recursive specification does not fit well with the format required for applying CFAR^{b}. The equivalence of the two recursive specifications can be shown in a straightforward way.

$$\begin{aligned}
X1_d &= sk\text{‽}d0.Z_1,\\
Z_1 &= t.Z_2 + t.kr\text{‽}d0.o!d.X2_d,\\
Z_2 &= kr\text{‽}\bot.Z_3,\\
Z_3 &= rl\text{‽}1.Z_4,\\
Z_4 &= t.Z_5 + t.Z_6,\\
Z_5 &= ls\text{‽}1.X1_d,\\
Z_6 &= ls\text{‽}\bot.X1_d.
\end{aligned}$$

Then, $\{X1_d, Z_1, Z_2, Z_3, Z_4, Z_5, Z_6\}$ is a finite conservative cluster of I, with exit $t.kr\text{‽}d0.o!d.X2_d$. (Note that, when strictly following Definition 8.8.15 (Cluster), the exit should have been defined using an additional recursion variable.) From CFAR^{b}, it then follows that

$$\begin{aligned}
&(\mathrm{TCP}_{\tau,\mathrm{rec}} + \mathrm{CFAR}^{\mathrm{b}})(A, \gamma_S) \vdash\\
&\quad \tau_I(X1_d) = \tau.\tau_I(t.kr\text{‽}d0.o!d.X2_d) = \tau.o!d.\tau_I(X2_d).
\end{aligned}$$

So, the first cluster of internal steps, as visualized in Figure 7.9, has disappeared. The same procedure is followed for the cluster around $X2_d$. The alternative recursive specification is the following:

$$\begin{aligned}
X2_d &= rl\text{‽}0.Z_1,\\
Z_1 &= t.Z_2 + t.ls\text{‽}0.Y,\\
Z_2 &= ls\text{‽}\bot.Z_3,\\
Z_3 &= sk\text{‽}d0.Z_4,\\
Z_4 &= t.Z_5 + t.Z_6,\\
Z_5 &= kr\text{‽}d0.X2_d,\\
Z_6 &= kr\text{‽}\bot.X2_d.
\end{aligned}$$

Again, from the fact that $\{X2_d, Z_1, Z_2, Z_3, Z_4, Z_5, Z_6\}$ is a finite conservative cluster of I, it follows that:

$$\begin{aligned}
&(\mathrm{TCP}_{\tau,\mathrm{rec}} + \mathrm{CFAR}^{\mathrm{b}})(A, \gamma_S) \vdash\\
&\quad \tau_I(X2_d) = \tau.\tau_I(t.ls\text{‽}d0.Y) = \tau.\tau_I(Y).
\end{aligned}$$

Combining these results leads to

$$
\begin{aligned}
&(\mathrm{TCP}_{\tau,\mathrm{rec}} + \mathrm{CFAR}^{\mathrm{b}})(A, \gamma_S) \vdash \\
&\quad \tau_I(X) = 1 + \sum_{d \in D} i?d.\tau_I(X1_d) \\
&\qquad = 1 + \sum_{d \in D} i?d.\tau.o!d.\tau_I(X2_d) \\
&\qquad = 1 + \sum_{d \in D} i?d.o!d.\tau.\tau_I(Y) \\
&\qquad = 1 + \sum_{d \in D} i?d.o!d.\tau_I(Y).
\end{aligned}
$$

In the same way, one can derive

$$
\begin{aligned}
&(\mathrm{TCP}_{\tau,\mathrm{rec}} + \mathrm{CFAR}^{\mathrm{b}})(A, \gamma_S) \vdash \\
&\quad \tau_I(Y) = 1 + \sum_{d \in D} i?d.o!d.\tau_I(X).
\end{aligned}
$$

Now, consider the guarded recursive specification:

$$
\begin{aligned}
W_1 &= 1 + \sum_{d \in D} i?d.o!d.W_2, \\
W_2 &= 1 + \sum_{d \in D} i?d.o!d.W_1.
\end{aligned}
$$

It is straightforward that the equations for W_1 and W_2 can be derived from $(\mathrm{TCP}_{\tau,\mathrm{rec}} + \mathrm{CFAR}^{\mathrm{b}})(A, \gamma_S)$ for both the following substitutions for W_1 and W_2:

$$
\begin{aligned}
W_1 &\mapsto \tau_I(X), \\
W_2 &\mapsto \tau_I(Y),
\end{aligned}
\qquad \text{and} \qquad
\begin{aligned}
W_1 &\mapsto \mathit{Buf}1_{io}, \\
W_2 &\mapsto \mathit{Buf}1_{io}.
\end{aligned}
$$

Using RSP, it follows that

$$
(\mathrm{TCP}_{\tau,\mathrm{rec}} + \mathrm{CFAR}^{\mathrm{b}} + \mathrm{RSP})(A, \gamma_S) \vdash \tau_I(X) = \mathit{Buf}1_{io}.
$$

□

Observe that the use of $\mathrm{CFAR}^{\mathrm{b}}$ in the verification of the Alternating-Bit Protocol means in fact that the choice made by the channels is fair. Doing this, the possibility that any of the channels is completely defective is excluded.

To finish this section, consider again the two specifications of the process queue proven equal in Proposition 7.7.4 (Queues). Here, another specification of the unbounded FIFO queue is given, that uses abstraction in an essential way. The idea behind the following specification is that two queues chained together in sequence behave exactly like one single queue, as long as the internal communications are hidden. The idea is illustrated in Figure 8.14. Here, Q^{pq} stands for the queue with input port p and output port q.

Define $H_p = \{p?d, p!d \mid d \in D\}$ and $I_p = \{p?d \mid d \in D\}$ for $p = i, l, o$. Consider the following recursive specification of Q^{io}. This specification has six variables Q^{pq}, for each pair of distinct values from $\{i, l, o\}$, and Q^{pq} uses auxiliary port r, such that $\{p, q, r\} = \{i, l, o\}$.

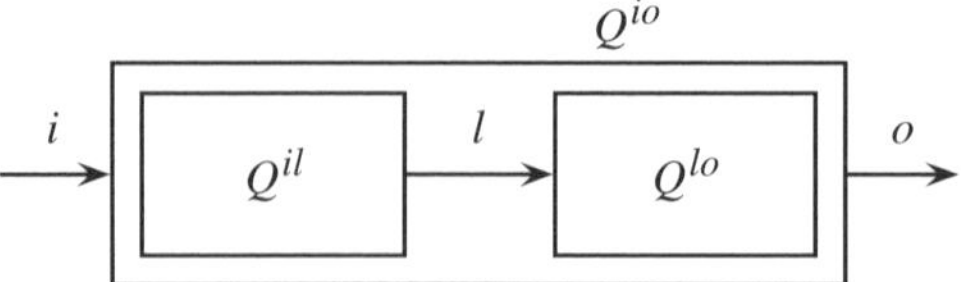

Fig. 8.14. Queue with abstraction.

$$
\begin{aligned}
Q^{io} &= 1 + \sum_{d \in D} i?d.\tau_{I_l}(\partial_{H_l}(Q^{il} \parallel l!d.Q^{lo})),\\
Q^{il} &= 1 + \sum_{d \in D} i?d.\tau_{I_o}(\partial_{H_o}(Q^{io} \parallel l!d.Q^{ol})),\\
Q^{lo} &= 1 + \sum_{d \in D} l?d.\tau_{I_i}(\partial_{H_i}(Q^{li} \parallel o!d.Q^{io})),\\
Q^{ol} &= 1 + \sum_{d \in D} o?d.\tau_{I_i}(\partial_{H_i}(Q^{oi} \parallel l!d.Q^{il})),\\
Q^{li} &= 1 + \sum_{d \in D} l?d.\tau_{I_o}(\partial_{H_o}(Q^{lo} \parallel i!d.Q^{oi})),\\
Q^{oi} &= 1 + \sum_{d \in D} o?d.\tau_{I_l}(\partial_{H_l}(Q^{ol} \parallel i!d.Q^{li})).
\end{aligned}
$$

Note that this is not a guarded recursive specification. Nevertheless, it has a unique solution in the term model that coincides with the solution of the specification *Queue*1 from Proposition 7.7.4 (Queues). This result is not proven here. The reader interested in a proof is referred to (Van Glabbeek & Vaandrager, 1993). The proof in (Van Glabbeek & Vaandrager, 1993) uses auxiliary operators. It is unknown whether a direct proof using only the framework developed in this chapter exists.

Exercises

8.9.1 Let the processes S, K, and R, and the set of blocked actions H be defined as in Exercise 7.8.1. Derive a recursive equation for the process $\tau_I(\partial_H(S \parallel K \parallel R))$, where $I = \{s?x, r?x \mid x \in D \cup \{ack\}\} \cup \{t\}$. Is this communication protocol correct?

8.10 Bibliographical remarks

The silent step τ was introduced in CCS, see (Milner, 1980), to abstract from unobservable behavior. Notation τ is used in that work to stand for the residual trace of a communication. As a semantic equivalence, originally, the notion of (rooted) weak bisimilarity was used both in CCS-style (Milner, 1989) and in ACP-style process algebras (Bergstra & Klop, 1985).

The present treatment is based on the semantic equivalence of (rooted) branching bisimilarity from (Van Glabbeek & Weijland, 1996; Van Glabbeek & Weijland, 1989). Note that the definition presented here differs from the original definition. The current definition, leading to the same equivalence, was called *semi*-branching bisimilarity earlier, and makes the proof of Theorem 8.2.5 (Equivalence) easier (Basten, 1996). A comparison between branching and weak bisimilarity can be found in (Van Glabbeek, 1994). Branching bisimilarity was also used in (Baeten & Weijland, 1990).

The abstraction operator τ_I was introduced in (Bergstra & Klop, 1985). The axiomatization of CSP's external choice is new here. Earlier axiomatizations can be found in (Brookes, 1983; D'Argenio, 1995; Van Glabbeek, 1997). For a definition in the absence of the empty process, see (Baeten & Bravetti, 2006).

The material on divergence is based on (Bergstra *et al.*, 1987), see also (Baeten & Weijland, 1990). Other references covering divergence are (Aceto & Hennessy, 1992; Walker, 1990). A reference to fair iteration is (Bergstra *et al.*, 2001). For bisimilarity with explicit divergence, see (Van Glabbeek, 1993), and further work in (Van Glabbeek *et al.*, 2008). The notion of catastrophic divergence is due to (Brookes *et al.*, 1984).

The material on recursion is based on (Baeten *et al.*, 1987b). Koomen's Fair Abstraction Rule was first applied by C.J. Koomen in a formula manipulation package based on CCS (see (Koomen, 1985)) and first formulated as a conditional equation in (Bergstra & Klop, 1986a). The present formulation of $KFAR^b$ and $CFAR^b$ for branching bisimilarity is from (Baeten & Weijland, 1990). The generalization of KFAR to CFAR is from (Vaandrager, 1986). Other references concerning fairness are (Francez, 1986; Parrow, 1985).

The verification of the Alternating-Bit Protocol is from (Bergstra & Klop, 1986c). For further information on algebraic verification, see (Groote & Reniers, 2001). The specification of the queue is from (Bergstra & Klop, 1986b), see also (Van Glabbeek & Vaandrager, 1993).

9
Timing

9.1 Introduction

The process theories introduced so far describe the main features of imperative concurrent programming without the explicit mention of time. Implicitly, time is present in the interpretation of many of the operators introduced before. In the process $a.x$, the action a must be executed *before* the execution of process x. The process theories introduced so far allow for the description of the ordering of actions relative to each other. This way of describing the execution of actions through time is called *qualitative time*. Many systems though rely on time in a more quantitative way.

Consider for example the following caller process. A caller takes a phone off the hook. If she hears a certain tone, she dials some number. It does not matter which one. If she does not hear the tone, she puts the phone back on the hook. After dialing the number, the caller waits some time for the other side to pick up the phone. After some conversation, the caller puts the phone back on the hook. In case the call is not answered within some given time, the caller gives up and also puts the phone back on the hook.

To be able to describe such systems in process theory in the same framework as untimed systems, many process theories have been extended with a quantitative notion of timing. In extending the untimed process theories with timing a number of fundamental choices have to be made with respect to the nature of the time domain, the way time appears syntactically in the equational theory, and the way time is incorporated semantically.

Linear time versus branching time Different time domains that are used in modeling real-life applications are the natural numbers and the non-negative real numbers. These time domains have in common that any two moments in time can be compared using some total ordering $\leq$ on that time domain. Time domains for which such an ordering is given (and used in comparing moments in time) are called *linear* time domains. In principle, one could also consider a time domain where only some of the moments in time can be compared, e.g., to express the lack of a globally synchronized clock, or to model relativistic space/time. These are the *branching* time domains. The time domains that appear in the process algebra literature, but also in almost any case study, are of the first type. In this chapter, therefore, a *linear*-time process theory is developed.

Discrete versus dense time A difference between the naturals and the non-negative reals is that in the latter between any two reals another one can be found, whereas for the naturals this is not possible. The naturals form an instance of a so-called *discrete* time domain; the non-negative reals are called a *dense* time domain. In this chapter, a *discrete*-time process theory is developed. A reason for selecting this type of time domain is that the relation with the untimed theory is easier to establish. In a discrete time domain, time is divided in so-called *time slices*: actions take place within a certain time slice, and within a certain time slice, ordering of actions is only qualitative. In moving to the next time slice, a special 'tick' event takes place, resembling the notion of a clock tick.

As a remark aside, note that the use of an uncountable, dense time domain such as the non-negative reals would provide means to specify uncountable processes, which is not possible with any of the techniques worked out in detail in this book; for more details, see the discussion and results in Section 5.7.

Absolute versus relative time Depending on the type of applications one wishes to describe using the timed process theory, either the passage of time is described relatively to a global clock, or relative to the previous action. The first way of describing time is called *absolute* time, the latter *relative* time. Process theories where both paradigms are combined also exist in the literature; these are called *parametric*-time process theories. In this chapter, a relative-time process theory is developed.

Timed action execution In the untimed process theory, it has been assumed that actions occur instantaneously. In developing a timed process theory, one has to decide whether actions have a duration or are still considered to occur instantaneously. In this chapter, the execution of an action in the timed process theory is assumed to be instantaneous, or maybe it is better to say that the *observation* of action execution is instantaneous. Thus, the interleaving approach to parallel composition can still be followed, and simultaneous occurrence of actions is reserved for the description of communication. In a discrete-time theory, action execution within a certain time slice can be dealt with as in untimed process algebra, but in a dense-time theory, a closer look has to be given to simultaneous execution of actions, as actions in unrelated parts of a system might occur at the same moment of time. Then, the usual choice in process algebra is to allow actions to execute consecutively at the same moment of time, rather than the alternative of using so-called multi-actions for such an occurrence.

Time-stamped versus two-phase description Capturing the timing aspects of a process can essentially be done in two ways. One way is to attach to each action a moment in time, or a time slice. This way of describing time is called *time-stamping*. The other way is to denote the passage of time itself in between actions explicitly. This way of describing time is paraphrased as the *two-phase* description of time. To stay as close as possible to the untimed transition systems and the syntax of the process theories in the previous chapters, in this chapter, a two-phase approach is used at the syntactical level of description. On the other hand, semantically, a time-stamped treatment is followed. The latter allows a better treatment of time determinism (to be treated next), and allows easier extensions.

Time determinism versus time non-determinism In the previous chapters, the execution of an action resulted in resolving a possible choice between alternatives. Thus, in a term $a.1 + b.1$, it is possible to execute a and thereby not do b, or to execute b and thereby not do a. As long as neither action has occurred, the choice is not determined. Now it can be the case that a and b are constrained in time; for example, it might happen that a can only occur in the following time slice (after one 'tick' event has occurred), and that b can only occur in the time slice thereafter (after two ticks). Then, when the first tick occurs, no choice is made, as both actions are still possible. This is called *time determinism*: it is not possible that time evolves in different ways. Thus, the tick event is different from an action in this respect. Most timed process algebras adopt the principle of time determinism, but there are exceptions.

Continuing the example, after the first tick, the action a can be executed, thereby disabling b. In this book, it is also allowed that a second tick event occurs, thereby moving to the following time slice, in which the choice for b can be effectuated. The occurrence of the second tick disables the occurrence of a, as the time slice in which it should occur has passed. Thus, the passage of time can disable a choice. This is called *weak time determinism*. When the principle of *strong time determinism* is adopted, on the other hand, then the second tick cannot be executed, and in this example, necessarily a must occur, and action execution has priority over passage of time. Adopting weak time determinism as is done here adheres to the intuition of alternative composition. Moreover, it makes it easier to describe timeouts.

Interpretation of untimed processes A crucial point in the development of the timed process theory in this chapter is the relation between the untimed process theories of the previous chapters and the timed process theory of this chapter. The view adopted in this book is that the timed process theory should be an equationally conservative ground-extension of the untimed process theory. As a consequence, every untimed process term should be interpreted in the timed setting in a consistent and meaningful way, especially, taking care to respect the identities between untimed processes. Basically, there are two ways of interpreting an untimed process. The first one is to assume all action execution to take place in one and the same time slice. The second one is to assume all action execution to take place arbitrarily dispersed over time though still respecting the ordering of actions as described in the untimed process term. This last interpretation fits better with an engineering discipline where first an untimed model is given, and after verification of the functional behavior, timing information is added to perform some timeliness verification. Hence, in this chapter, a timed process theory is developed that is a conservative ground-extension of the untimed theory under the interpretation that untimed actions can take place at an arbitrary moment in time.

9.2 Timed transition systems

Definition 9.2.1 (Timed transition-system space) In order to extend a transition-system space to take timing into account, both action execution and termination are extended with an extra parameter, a natural number that indicates after how many ticks the action or termination takes place. Moreover, there is an extra predicate $\leadsto$ that indicates how many ticks are possible from a given state.

A *timed transition-system space* over a set of labels L is a set S of states, equipped with one quaternary relation $\rightarrow$ and two binary relations $\downarrow$ and $\leadsto$:

(i) $\rightarrow \subseteq S \times \mathbf{N} \times L \times S$ is the set of *transitions*;
(ii) $\downarrow \subseteq S \times \mathbf{N}$ is the set of *terminating* states;
(iii) $\leadsto \subseteq S \times \mathbf{N}$ is the set of possible *delays*.

The notation $s \ {}_{n}\!\xrightarrow{a}\ t$ is used for $(s, n, a, t) \in \ \rightarrow$, and means intuitively that from state s, after n ticks, action a can be executed resulting in state t;

next, $s\downarrow_n$ is used for $(s, n) \in \downarrow$, and means that from state s, after n ticks, termination is possible; finally, $s \rightsquigarrow_n$, notation for $(s, n) \in \rightsquigarrow$, means that n ticks are possible from state s. The following implication is assumed to hold: whenever $s \;{}_n\!\xrightarrow{a} t$ or $s\downarrow_n$, then $s \rightsquigarrow_n$. Note that a state may satisfy other $\rightsquigarrow_n$ predicates in addition to those that are implied by the transitions and termination options. These can be used to specify timing behavior independent of actions or termination.

In the rest of this chapter, assume that $(S, L, \rightarrow, \downarrow, \rightsquigarrow)$ is a timed transition-system space. Each state $s \in S$ can be identified with a timed transition system that consists of all states and transitions reachable from s. The notion of reachability is defined by generalizing the transition relations.

Definition 9.2.2 (Reachability) The reachability relation $\rightarrow^* \subseteq S \times S$ is defined inductively as follows:

(i) $s \rightarrow^* s$ for each $s \in S$;
(ii) for all $s, t, u \in S$, $n \in \mathbf{N}$, and $a \in L$, if $s \rightarrow^* t$ and $t \;{}_n\!\xrightarrow{a} u$, then $s \rightarrow^* u$.

A state $t \in S$ is said to be *reachable* from state $s \in S$ if and only if $s \rightarrow^* t$.

Definition 9.2.3 (Timed transition system) For each state $s \in S$, the *timed transition system* associated with s consists of all states reachable from s, and has the transitions and terminating states induced by the timed transition-system space. State s is called the *initial state* or *root* of the timed transition-system associated with s. Usually, 'timed transition system s' is used to refer to the timed transition system *associated with* s.

The graphical representation of timed transition systems is similar to the graphical representation of transition systems in the previous chapters. The arrows and terminations have a natural number as an additional label. The $\rightsquigarrow$ predicates are omitted if these are implied by other arrows or terminations, and are denoted with dotted arrows annotated with natural numbers otherwise.

Example 9.2.4 (Timed transition system of the caller process) The timed transition system in Figure 9.1 represents the caller process described in the introduction to this chapter. From state 0, there is a transition for every $n \in \mathbf{N}$; state 4 has a transition for every $m \in \mathbf{N}$.

Example 9.2.5 (Timed transition system) Figure 9.2 shows another example of a timed transition system. In the initial state, it has among others an

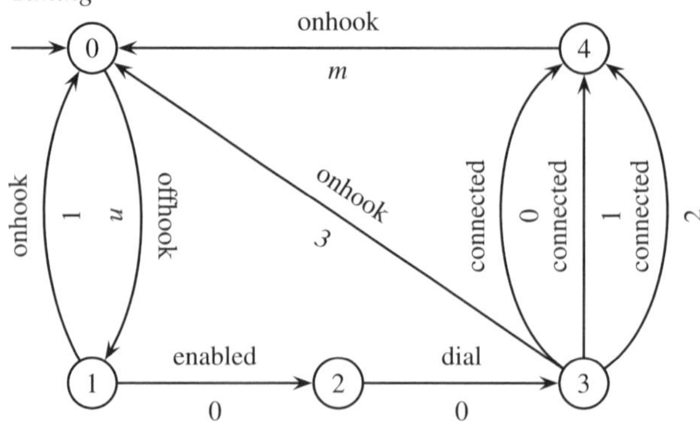

Fig. 9.1. An example of a timed transition system: the caller process.

option to allow the passage of time for two time units, after which time cannot progress any further, the process cannot terminate successfully, and it can no longer continue anymore with any action (i.e., it deadlocks).

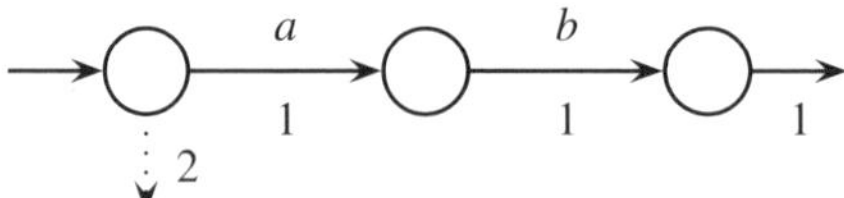

Fig. 9.2. Another example of a timed transition system.

Definition 9.2.6 (Timed bisimilarity) A binary relation R on the set of states S of a timed transition-system space is a *timed bisimulation relation* if and only if the following transfer conditions hold:

(i) for all states $s, t, s' \in S$, whenever $(s, t) \in R$ and $s \,{}_n\!\xrightarrow{a} s'$ for some $a \in L$ and $n \in \mathbf{N}$, then there is a state t' such that $t \,{}_n\!\xrightarrow{a} t'$ and $(s', t') \in R$;

(ii) vice versa, for all states $s, t, t' \in S$, whenever $(s, t) \in R$ and $t \,{}_n\!\xrightarrow{a} t'$ for some $a \in L$ and $n \in \mathbf{N}$, then there is a state s' such that $s \,{}_n\!\xrightarrow{a} s'$ and $(s', t') \in R$;

(iii) whenever $(s, t) \in R$ and $s{\downarrow_n}$ for some $n \in \mathbf{N}$, then $t{\downarrow_n}$;

(iv) vice versa, whenever $(s, t) \in R$ and $t{\downarrow_n}$ for some $n \in \mathbf{N}$, then $s{\downarrow_n}$;

(v) whenever $(s, t) \in R$ and $s \leadsto_n$ for some $n \in \mathbf{N}$, then $t \leadsto_n$;

(vi) vice versa, whenever $(s, t) \in R$ and $t \leadsto_n$ for some $n \in \mathbf{N}$, then $s \leadsto_n$.

Two transition systems $s, t \in S$ are *timed-bisimulation equivalent* or *timed bisimilar*, notation $s \leftrightarroweq_{\mathrm{t}} t$, if and only if there is a timed bisimulation relation R on S with $(s, t) \in R$.

Theorem 9.2.7 (Equivalence) Timed bisimilarity is an equivalence.

Proof The proof that bisimilarity is an equivalence can be followed exactly, in order to show that timed bisimilarity is an equivalence. □

9.3 Discrete time, relative time

This section presents theory $\text{BSP}^{\text{drt}}(A)$, which is a variant of BSP(A) with discrete, relative time. It is formally not an extension of BSP(A) as defined in Definition 2.2.14, because the signature of BSP(A) is not included in the signature of $\text{BSP}^{\text{drt}}(A)$. Although earlier it was argued that the 'any-time-slice' interpretation of the untimed atomic actions is more interesting, this section first presents an elementary theory with actions that take place in the *current time slice*. The signature of theory $\text{BSP}^{\text{drt}}(A)$ contains, besides the alternative-composition operator $+$, a *current-time-slice action-prefix* operator $\underline{a}.\_$, for any $a \in A$, and the constants *current-time-slice time stop* $\underline{0}$ and *current-time-slice termination* $\underline{1}$. The process $\underline{a}.x$ executes the action a in the current time slice and continues as the process x. The constant $\underline{0}$ expresses that time cannot progress beyond the current time slice, and no termination can take place. The current-time-slice time-stop constant is the identity element for alternative composition. The constant $\underline{1}$ expresses that time cannot progress beyond the current time slice, and that termination takes place. The current-time-slice termination constant is the identity element for sequential composition (to be added in Section 9.7). As all the atomic actions take place in the current time slice, the signature of the process theory contains the *time-prefix* operator $\sigma.\_$ to describe the passage to the next time slice explicitly. The process $\sigma.x$ passes to the next time slice and then executes x. In order to be able to distinguish between action execution and passage of time, it is assumed that $\sigma \notin A$.

As an example, the process term $\sigma.(\underline{a}.\underline{1} + \sigma.\underline{b}.\underline{1})$ specifies the process that can execute an a action in the second time slice followed by termination in that second time slice, or a b action followed by termination in the third time slice. This process term conforms to the example used in the introduction of this chapter to illustrate time determinism.

The axioms of $\text{BSP}^{\text{drt}}(A)$ are given in Table 9.1. They capture the properties of the operators mentioned before. Axiom DRTF, for *Discrete Relative Time Factorization*, captures the intuition that the passage of time by itself does not determine a choice, i.e., the already mentioned (weak) time determinism. Mathematically, DRTF can be paraphrased as the distribution of time prefix over alternative composition.

Example 9.3.1 (Derivation) The process terms $(\sigma.\underline{a}.\underline{1} + \sigma.\underline{b}.\underline{1}) + \sigma.\underline{0}$ and $\sigma.(\underline{a}.\underline{1} + \underline{b}.\underline{1})$ are equal in $\text{BSP}^{\text{drt}}(A)$, as can be seen as follows:

$\text{BSP}^{\text{drt}}(A)$		
constant: $\underline{0}, \underline{1}$;	unary: $(\underline{a}.\_)_{a \in A}, \sigma.\_$;	binary: $\_ + \_$;
x, y, z;		
	$x + y = y + x$	A1
	$(x + y) + z = x + (y + z)$	A2
	$x + x = x$	A3
	$x + \underline{0} = x$	A6DR
	$\sigma.(x + y) = \sigma.x + \sigma.y$	DRTF

Table 9.1. The process theory $\text{BSP}^{\text{drt}}(A)$ (with $a \in A$).

$$\begin{aligned}\text{BSP}^{\text{drt}}(A) \vdash\ (\sigma.\underline{a}.\underline{1} + \sigma.\underline{b}.\underline{1}) + \sigma.\underline{0} &= \sigma.(\underline{a}.\underline{1} + \underline{b}.\underline{1}) + \sigma.\underline{0} \\ &= \sigma.((\underline{a}.\underline{1} + \underline{b}.\underline{1}) + \underline{0}) = \sigma.(\underline{a}.\underline{1} + \underline{b}.\underline{1}).\end{aligned}$$

The process theory $\text{BSP}^{\text{drt}}(A)$ is not an equational conservative ground-extension of the process theory BSP(A), since the signature of BSP(A) is not included in the signature of $\text{BSP}^{\text{drt}}(A)$. Nevertheless, there is a strong relation between these process theories. If one interprets the operators 0, 1, and $a.\_$ of BSP(A) as the current-time-slice variants $\underline{0}$, $\underline{1}$ and $\underline{a}.\_$ of $\text{BSP}^{\text{drt}}(A)$, respectively, then it turns out that all equalities of BSP(A) are also equalities of $\text{BSP}^{\text{drt}}(A)$. This kind of relation between two process theories is also called an *embedding*. The intuition of the embedding described above is the previously mentioned embedding of untimed process theory into timed process theory where all activities take place in the first time slice.

Further on, there is a need to consider closed $\text{BSP}^{\text{drt}}(A)$-terms in a particular form, called *basic terms*, in line with the notion of basic terms as already used in Chapter 2. In the following definition, analogous to Notation 4.6.6 (n-fold action prefix), notation $\sigma^n x$ is used for the n-fold time prefix.

Definition 9.3.2 (Basic $\text{BSP}^{\text{drt}}(A)$-terms) The set of *basic terms* over the signature of $\text{BSP}^{\text{drt}}(A)$ is defined inductively as follows:

(i) terms $\sigma^n \underline{0}$ and $\sigma^n \underline{1}$ are basic terms, for each $n \in \mathbf{N}$;
(ii) for each basic term p, action $a \in A$, and $n \in \mathbf{N}$, $\sigma^n \underline{a}.p$ is a basic term;
(iii) if p, q are basic terms, then $p + q$ is a basic term.

The following is a kind of elimination theorem: a time prefix occurring before a choice is eliminated.

Proposition 9.3.3 (Reduction to basic terms) Let p be a closed $\text{BSP}^{\text{drt}}(A)$-term. Then there is a basic $\text{BSP}^{\text{drt}}(A)$-term q such that $\text{BSP}^{\text{drt}}(A) \vdash p = q$.

Proof Straightforward, by using Axiom DRTF as a rewrite rule from left to right. □

Exercises

9.3.1 Complete the proof of Proposition 9.3.3 (Reduction to basic terms).

9.4 The term model

In this section, a model is constructed for $\mathrm{BSP}^{\mathrm{drt}}(A)$, by associating a timed transition system with each closed process term and then considering timed-bisimilarity equivalence classes of these timed transition systems.

Definition 9.4.1 (Term algebra) Algebra $\mathbb{P}(\mathrm{BSP}^{\mathrm{drt}}(A)) = (\mathcal{C}(\mathrm{BSP}^{\mathrm{drt}}(A)), +, (\underline{a}.\_)_{a \in A}, \sigma.\_, \underline{0}, \underline{1})$ is the term algebra for theory $\mathrm{BSP}^{\mathrm{drt}}(A)$.

A timed transition system is associated with each process term by means of the term deduction system presented in Table 9.2.

$TDS(\mathrm{BSP}^{\mathrm{drt}}(A))$

constant: $\underline{0}$, $\underline{1}$;	unary: $(\underline{a}.\_)_{a \in A}$, $\sigma.\_$;	binary: $\_ + \_$;
x, x', y, y';		
$x \rightsquigarrow_0$	$\underline{1}\downarrow_0$	$\underline{a}.x \ {}_{0}\!\overset{a}{\rightarrow} x$
$\dfrac{x \rightsquigarrow_n}{\sigma.x \rightsquigarrow_{n+1}}$	$\dfrac{x\downarrow_n}{\sigma.x\downarrow_{n+1}}$	$\dfrac{x \ {}_{n}\!\overset{a}{\rightarrow} x'}{\sigma.x \ {}_{n+1}\!\overset{a}{\rightarrow} x'}$
$\dfrac{x \rightsquigarrow_n}{x + y \rightsquigarrow_n}$	$\dfrac{x\downarrow_n}{(x + y)\downarrow_n}$	$\dfrac{y\downarrow_n}{(x + y)\downarrow_n}$
$\dfrac{y \rightsquigarrow_n}{x + y \rightsquigarrow_n}$	$\dfrac{x \ {}_{n}\!\overset{a}{\rightarrow} x'}{x + y \ {}_{n}\!\overset{a}{\rightarrow} x'}$	$\dfrac{y \ {}_{n}\!\overset{a}{\rightarrow} y'}{x + y \ {}_{n}\!\overset{a}{\rightarrow} y'}$

Table 9.2. Term deduction system for $\mathrm{BSP}^{\mathrm{drt}}(A)$ (with $a \in A, n \in \mathbf{N}$).

Example 9.4.2 (Timed transition system of a $\mathrm{BSP}^{\mathrm{drt}}(A)$-term) The timed transition system of Figure 9.2 is the transition system associated to the process term $\sigma.(\underline{a}.\sigma.\underline{b}.\sigma.\underline{1} + \sigma.\underline{0})$.

The first axiom of the term deduction system of Table 9.2 says that every process in the present theory satisfies the predicate $\leadsto_0$, i.e., every process allows zero time ticks to occur. In some theories with timing, processes occur that denote an inconsistency, e.g., a timing inconsistency in an absolute-time theory. Such inconsistencies can be operationally characterized by the absence of the predicate $\leadsto_0$.

As already mentioned, the predicates $\leadsto_n$ can in general be used to specify timing behavior independent of actions and termination. In the present context, they are needed to distinguish processes that only differ in their timing behavior. To give an example, the processes specified by terms $\underline{0}$ and $\sigma.\underline{0}$ are only distinguished by the predicate $\leadsto_1$.

With the given term deduction system, the construction of a term model goes along the lines as before.

Theorem 9.4.3 (Congruence) Timed bisimilarity is a congruence on the algebra $\mathbb{P}(\mathrm{BSP}^{\mathrm{drt}}(A))$.

Proof The results presented in Chapter 3 do not apply directly to prove the desired congruence result, because the notion of transition systems used in the current chapter is different. However, (Baeten & Verhoef, 1995) shows that the meta-theory of Chapter 3 generalizes to transition-system spaces with multiple types of transitions and multiple predicates on states. The timed transition systems of the present setting fit into the framework of (Baeten & Verhoef, 1995), and the congruence result follows from the path format, as defined in (Baeten & Verhoef, 1995) for the general setting, of the deduction rules of Table 9.2. □

Definition 9.4.4 (Term model of $\mathrm{BSP}^{\mathrm{drt}}(A)$) The term model of process theory $\mathrm{BSP}^{\mathrm{drt}}(A)$ is the quotient algebra $\mathbb{P}(\mathrm{BSP}^{\mathrm{drt}}(A))_{/\leftrightarrows_{\mathrm{t}}}$.

Theorem 9.4.5 (Soundness) Theory $\mathrm{BSP}^{\mathrm{drt}}(A)$ is a sound axiomatization of the algebra $\mathbb{P}(\mathrm{BSP}^{\mathrm{drt}}(A))_{/\leftrightarrows_{\mathrm{t}}}$, i.e., $\mathbb{P}(\mathrm{BSP}^{\mathrm{drt}}(A))_{/\leftrightarrows_{\mathrm{t}}} \models \mathrm{BSP}^{\mathrm{drt}}(A)$.

Proof See Exercise 9.4.1. □

Next, it is shown that $\mathrm{BSP}^{\mathrm{drt}}(A)$ is a ground-complete axiomatization of the term model $\mathbb{P}(\mathrm{BSP}^{\mathrm{drt}}(A))_{/\leftrightarrows_{\mathrm{t}}}$. Thereto, the following two lemmas are introduced. Note the correspondence with the Lemmas 4.4.10 (Towards completeness) and 4.4.11 used in obtaining the ground-completeness of $\mathrm{BSP}(A)$ (Theorem 4.4.12).

Lemma 9.4.6 (Towards completeness) For arbitrary closed $\mathrm{BSP}^{\mathrm{drt}}(A)$-terms p and p' and arbitrary $a \in A, n \in \mathbf{N}$:

(i) if $p \rightsquigarrow_n$, then $\mathrm{BSP}^{\mathrm{drt}}(A) \vdash p = \sigma^n \underline{0} + p$;
(ii) if $p{\downarrow}_n$, then $\mathrm{BSP}^{\mathrm{drt}}(A) \vdash p = \sigma^n \underline{1} + p$;
(iii) if $p \;{}_n\!\xrightarrow{a}\; p'$, then $\mathrm{BSP}^{\mathrm{drt}}(A) \vdash p = \sigma^n \underline{a}.p' + p$.

Proof These three properties are proven by induction on n. In the inductive step, induction on the structure of closed $\mathrm{BSP}^{\mathrm{drt}}(A)$-term p is used. Details are left as an exercise to the reader (Exercise 9.4.2). □

Lemma 9.4.7 Let p, q, and r be closed $\mathrm{BSP}^{\mathrm{drt}}(A)$-terms. If $(p+q)+r \leftrightarroweq_{\mathrm{t}} r$, then $p + r \leftrightarroweq_{\mathrm{t}} r$ and $q + r \leftrightarroweq_{\mathrm{t}} r$.

Proof See Exercise 9.4.3. □

Theorem 9.4.8 (Ground-completeness) Equational theory $\mathrm{BSP}^{\mathrm{drt}}(A)$ is a ground-complete axiomatization of the term model $\mathbb{P}(\mathrm{BSP}^{\mathrm{drt}}(A))_{/\leftrightarroweq_{\mathrm{t}}}$, i.e., for any closed $\mathrm{BSP}^{\mathrm{drt}}(A)$-terms p and q, $\mathbb{P}(\mathrm{BSP}^{\mathrm{drt}}(A))_{/\leftrightarroweq_{\mathrm{t}}} \models p = q$ implies $\mathrm{BSP}^{\mathrm{drt}}(A) \vdash p = q$.

Proof Due to Proposition 9.3.3 (Reduction to basic terms) and the soundness of the axioms of $\mathrm{BSP}^{\mathrm{drt}}(A)$ (Theorem 9.4.5), it suffices to prove this theorem for basic $\mathrm{BSP}^{\mathrm{drt}}(A)$-terms.
Let p and q be basic terms. Suppose that $\mathbb{P}(\mathrm{BSP}^{\mathrm{drt}}(A))_{/\leftrightarroweq_{\mathrm{t}}} \models p = q$, i.e., $p \leftrightarroweq_{\mathrm{t}} q$. It must be shown that $\mathrm{BSP}^{\mathrm{drt}}(A) \vdash p = q$. Since bisimilarity is a congruence on $\mathbb{P}(\mathrm{BSP}^{\mathrm{drt}}(A))$ (Theorem 9.4.3) and $\mathrm{BSP}^{\mathrm{drt}}(A)$ is sound for $\mathbb{P}(\mathrm{BSP}^{\mathrm{drt}}(A))_{/\leftrightarroweq_{\mathrm{t}}}$ (Theorem 9.4.5), in line with the reasoning in the proof of Theorem 4.3.10 (Ground-completeness of MPT(A)), it suffices to prove that, for all basic $\mathrm{BSP}^{\mathrm{drt}}(A)$-terms p and q,

$$p + q \leftrightarroweq_{\mathrm{t}} q \quad \text{implies} \quad \mathrm{BSP}^{\mathrm{drt}}(A) \vdash p + q = q \tag{9.4.1}$$

and

$$p \leftrightarroweq_{\mathrm{t}} p + q \quad \text{implies} \quad \mathrm{BSP}^{\mathrm{drt}}(A) \vdash p = p + q. \tag{9.4.2}$$

Property (9.4.1) is proven by induction on the total number of symbols in terms p and q. The proof of property (9.4.2) is similar and therefore omitted. Assume $p + q \leftrightarroweq_{\mathrm{t}} q$ for basic terms p and q. The base case of the induction corresponds to the case that the total number of symbols in p and q equals two, namely when p and q are both equal to $\underline{0}$ or $\underline{1}$. In the case that $p \equiv \underline{0}$, using Axiom A6DR, it trivially follows that $\mathrm{BSP}^{\mathrm{drt}}(A) \vdash p + q = q$. In the case that $p \equiv \underline{1}$, $p{\downarrow_0}$ and thus $(p+q){\downarrow_0}$. As $p+q \leftrightarroweq_{\mathrm{t}} q$, also $q{\downarrow_0}$. By Lemma 9.4.6 (Towards completeness), $\mathrm{BSP}^{\mathrm{drt}}(A) \vdash q = \underline{1} + q$. Hence, $\mathrm{BSP}^{\mathrm{drt}}(A) \vdash p + q = \underline{1} + q = q$. The proof of the inductive step consists of a case analysis based on the structure of term p.

(i) Assume $p \equiv \sigma^n \underline{0}$ for some $n \in \mathbf{N}$. By Table 9.2, it follows that $p \rightsquigarrow_n$, and so also $p + q \rightsquigarrow_n$. As $p + q \leftrightarroweq_{\mathrm{t}} q$, also $q \rightsquigarrow_n$. By Lemma 9.4.6 (Towards completeness), $\mathrm{BSP}^{\mathrm{drt}}(A) \vdash q = \sigma^n \underline{0} + q$. Then, $\mathrm{BSP}^{\mathrm{drt}}(A) \vdash p + q = \sigma^n \underline{0} + q = q$.

(ii) Assume $p \equiv \sigma^n \underline{1}$ for some $n \in \mathbf{N}$. It follows from Table 9.2 that $p{\downarrow_n}$, and therefore also $(p+q){\downarrow_n}$. As $p + q \leftrightarroweq_{\mathrm{t}} q$, also $q{\downarrow_n}$. By Lemma 9.4.6 (Towards completeness), $\mathrm{BSP}^{\mathrm{drt}}(A) \vdash q = \sigma^n \underline{1} + q$. Thus, $\mathrm{BSP}^{\mathrm{drt}}(A) \vdash p + q = \sigma^n \underline{1} + q = q$.

(iii) Assume $p \equiv \sigma^n \underline{a}.p'$ for some $a \in A, n \in \mathbf{N}$ and basic term p'. Then, $p \;{}_n\!\xrightarrow{a}\; p'$ and thus $p + q \;{}_n\!\xrightarrow{a}\; p'$. As $p + q \leftrightarroweq_{\mathrm{t}} q$, also $q \;{}_n\!\xrightarrow{a}\; q'$ for some basic term q' such that $p' \leftrightarroweq_{\mathrm{t}} q'$. By Lemma 9.4.6 (Towards completeness), $\mathrm{BSP}^{\mathrm{drt}}(A) \vdash q = \sigma^n \underline{a}.q' + q$. From $p' \leftrightarroweq_{\mathrm{t}} q'$, following the reasoning in the first part of the proof of Theorem 4.3.10 (Ground-completeness of MPT(A)), it follows that $p' + q' \leftrightarroweq_{\mathrm{t}} q'$ and $q' + p' \leftrightarroweq_{\mathrm{t}} p'$ and, hence, by induction, $\mathrm{BSP}^{\mathrm{drt}}(A) \vdash p' + q' = q'$ and $\mathrm{BSP}^{\mathrm{drt}}(A) \vdash q' + p' = p'$. Combining these last two results gives $\mathrm{BSP}^{\mathrm{drt}}(A) \vdash p' = q' + p' = p' + q' = q'$. Finally, $\mathrm{BSP}^{\mathrm{drt}}(A) \vdash p + q = \sigma^n \underline{a}.p' + q = \sigma^n \underline{a}.q' + q = q$.

(iv) Assume $p \equiv p_1 + p_2$ for basic terms p_1 and p_2. As $(p_1 + p_2) + q \leftrightarroweq_{\mathrm{t}} q$, by Lemma 9.4.7, $p_1 + q \leftrightarroweq_{\mathrm{t}} q$ and $p_2 + q \leftrightarroweq_{\mathrm{t}} q$. Thus, by induction, $\mathrm{BSP}^{\mathrm{drt}}(A) \vdash p_1 + q = q$ and $\mathrm{BSP}^{\mathrm{drt}}(A) \vdash p_2 + q = q$. Combining these results gives $\mathrm{BSP}^{\mathrm{drt}}(A) \vdash p + q = (p_1 + p_2) + q = p_1 + (p_2 + q) = p_1 + q = q$, which completes the proof. □

Exercises

9.4.1 Prove Theorem 9.4.5 (Soundness of $\mathrm{BSP}^{\mathrm{drt}}(A)$).

9.4.2 Prove Lemma 9.4.6 (Towards completeness).

9.4.3 Prove Lemma 9.4.7.

9.5 Time iteration and delayable actions

In this section, the timed process algebra $\mathrm{BSP}^{\mathrm{drt}}(A)$ from the previous two sections is extended with the constants *any-time-slice deadlock* 0 and *any-time-slice termination* 1, the *any-time-slice action-prefix* operators $a.\_$ (for $a \in A$)

and the auxiliary *time-iteration prefix* operator $\sigma^*\_$ to obtain the process theory $\mathrm{BSP}^{\mathrm{drt}*}(A)$. The constants 0 and 1 are delayable versions of $\underline{0}$ and $\underline{1}$ which can take effect in any time slice (present or future). Similarly, $a.p$ denotes the execution of a in an arbitrary time slice followed by execution of p, and σ^*p denotes that the execution of p can be started in any time slice. Note that the intuitions of 0, 1 and $a.\_$ are in line with the 'any-time-slice' interpretation of the untimed constants and action-prefix operators.

$\mathrm{BSP}^{\mathrm{drt}*}(A)$			
$\mathrm{BSP}^{\mathrm{drt}}(A)$			
constant: 0, 1; unary: $(a.\_)_{a\in A}, \sigma^*\_$;			
x, y;			
$0 = \sigma^*\underline{0}$	DD	$\sigma^*x = x + \sigma.\sigma^*x$	ATS
$1 = \sigma^*\underline{1}$	DT	$\sigma^*x + \sigma^*y = \sigma^*(x+y)$	DRTIF
$a.x = \sigma^*\underline{a}.x$	DA	$\sigma^*\sigma.x = \sigma.\sigma^*x$	DRTA
		$\sigma^*\sigma^*x = \sigma^*x$	TITI

Table 9.3. The process theory $\mathrm{BSP}^{\mathrm{drt}*}(A)$ (with $a \in A$).

The axioms of theory $\mathrm{BSP}^{\mathrm{drt}*}(A)$ are given in Table 9.3. Axioms DD (Delayable Deadlock), DT (Delayable Termination) and DA (Delayable Actions) define the any-time-slice constants and action-prefix operators in terms of their current-time-slice counterparts and time iteration. Axiom DA illustrates that the any-time-slice action prefix can be interpreted as a *delayable action*. Axiom ATS (Any Time Slice) recursively defines time iteration. Axiom DRTIF (Discrete Relative Time Iteration Factorization) expresses that time factorization, i.e., the equational equivalent of (weak) time determinism, also applies to time iteration. Axiom DRTA (Discrete Relative Time Axiom) explains that also for time iteration time is measured relative to the previous action execution. Axiom TITI (Time Iteration Time Iteration) says that two consecutive time iterations are equivalent to only one time iteration. As a consequence, any number of consecutive time iterations is considered to be equivalent to a single one.

It is not the case that the newly introduced operators can all be eliminated. Nevertheless, the newly introduced syntax has some redundancy in the sense that either the time-iteration operator or the other newly introduced operators can be eliminated from closed terms. Definition 9.3.2 (Basic $\mathrm{BSP}^{\mathrm{drt}}(A)$-terms) is extended in order to incorporate the delayable constants and actions. Note that it uses the n-fold time prefix notation introduced just before Definition 9.3.2.

Definition 9.5.1 (Basic BSP$^{\mathrm{drt}*}(A)$-terms) The set of *basic terms* over the signature of theory BSP$^{\mathrm{drt}*}(A)$ is defined inductively as follows:

(i) terms $\sigma^n\underline{0}$, $\sigma^n 0$, $\sigma^n\underline{1}$, and $\sigma^n 1$ are basic terms, for each $n \in \mathbf{N}$;
(ii) for each basic term p, action $a \in A$, and $n \in \mathbf{N}$, $\sigma^n\underline{a}.p$ and $\sigma^n a.p$ are basic terms;
(iii) if p, q are basic terms, then $p + q$ is a basic term.

Again, a closed term can be reduced to a basic term, thereby eliminating the time-iteration operator.

Proposition 9.5.2 (Reduction to basic terms) Let p be a closed BSP$^{\mathrm{drt}*}(A)$-term. There is a basic BSP$^{\mathrm{drt}*}(A)$-term q such that BSP$^{\mathrm{drt}*}(A) \vdash p = q$.

Proof See Exercise 9.5.2. □

Theorem 9.5.3 (Conservative ground-extension) Theory BSP$^{\mathrm{drt}*}(A)$ is a conservative ground-extension of theory BSP$^{\mathrm{drt}}(A)$.

Proof The theorem follows from meta-results in the style of the results of Chapter 3, in particular Theorem 3.2.21 (Conservativity), for the generalized operational framework with transition systems with multiple types of transitions and/or state predicates as treated in (Baeten & Verhoef, 1995). The proof is based on the term model given below (although the result is model independent). □

A model is constructed for theory BSP$^{\mathrm{drt}*}(A)$ by associating a timed transition system with each closed term and then considering timed-bisimilarity equivalence classes of these timed transition systems. The term algebra for theory BSP$^{\mathrm{drt}*}(A)$ is the algebra $\mathbb{P}(\mathrm{BSP}^{\mathrm{drt}*}(A)) = (\mathcal{C}(\mathrm{BSP}^{\mathrm{drt}*}(A)), +, (a.\_)_{a\in A}, (\underline{a}.\_)_{a\in A}, \sigma.\_, 0, \underline{0}, 1, \underline{1})$. The term deduction system of Table 9.4 gives a timed transition system for each term in this algebra.

Proposition 9.5.4 (Congruence) Timed bisimilarity is a congruence on algebra $\mathbb{P}(\mathrm{BSP}^{\mathrm{drt}*}(A))$.

Proof As before, it follows from the format of the deduction rules; see also the proof of Theorem 9.4.3. □

The term model of BSP$^{\mathrm{drt}*}(A)$ is the quotient algebra $\mathbb{P}(\mathrm{BSP}^{\mathrm{drt}*}(A))_{/\leftrightarrow_t}$.

Theorem 9.5.5 (Soundness) Theory BSP$^{\mathrm{drt}*}(A)$ is a sound axiomatization of the algebra $\mathbb{P}(\mathrm{BSP}^{\mathrm{drt}*}(A))_{/\leftrightarrow_t}$, i.e., $\mathbb{P}(\mathrm{BSP}^{\mathrm{drt}*}(A))_{/\leftrightarrow_t} \models \mathrm{BSP}^{\mathrm{drt}*}(A)$.

$TDS(\mathrm{BSP}^{\mathrm{drt}*}(A))$		
$TDS(\mathrm{BSP}^{\mathrm{drt}}(A))$		
constant: 0, 1; unary: $(a.\_)_{a\in A}, \sigma^*\_$;		
x, x';		
$1\downarrow_n$	$1 \rightsquigarrow_n$	$0 \rightsquigarrow_n$
$a.x \;{}_n\xrightarrow{a}\; x$	$a.x \rightsquigarrow_n$	
$\sigma^* x \rightsquigarrow_n$	$\dfrac{x\downarrow_n}{\sigma^* x\downarrow_{n+m}}$	$\dfrac{x \;{}_n\xrightarrow{a}\; x'}{\sigma^* x \;{}_{n+m}\xrightarrow{a}\; x'}$

Table 9.4. Term deduction system for $\mathrm{BSP}^{\mathrm{drt}*}(A)$ ($a \in A, n, m \in \mathbf{N}$).

Proof See Exercise 9.5.3. □

Also ground-completeness can be shown as before. The following lemma is in line with the lemmas for earlier ground-completeness proofs.

Lemma 9.5.6 (Towards completeness) For any closed $\mathrm{BSP}^{\mathrm{drt}*}(A)$-terms p and p' and arbitrary $a \in A, n \in \mathbf{N}$:

(i) if $p \rightsquigarrow_n$, then $\mathrm{BSP}^{\mathrm{drt}*}(A) \vdash p = \sigma^n \underline{0} + p$;
(ii) if for all $m \geq n$, $p \rightsquigarrow_m$, then $\mathrm{BSP}^{\mathrm{drt}*}(A) \vdash p = \sigma^n 0 + p$;
(iii) if $p\downarrow_n$, then $\mathrm{BSP}^{\mathrm{drt}*}(A) \vdash p = \sigma^n \underline{1} + p$;
(iv) if for all $m \geq n$, $p\downarrow_m$, then $\mathrm{BSP}^{\mathrm{drt}*}(A) \vdash p = \sigma^n 1 + p$;
(v) if $p \;{}_n\xrightarrow{a}\; p'$, then $\mathrm{BSP}^{\mathrm{drt}*}(A) \vdash p = \sigma^n \underline{a}.p' + p$;
(vi) if for all $m \geq n$, $p \;{}_m\xrightarrow{a}\; p'$, then $\mathrm{BSP}^{\mathrm{drt}*}(A) \vdash p = \sigma^n a.p' + p$.

Proof As in the proof of Lemma 9.4.6, these properties are proven via induction on n, using structural induction in the inductive step. Based on Proposition 9.5.2 (Reduction to basic terms) and Theorem 9.5.5 (Soundness of $\mathrm{BSP}^{\mathrm{drt}*}(A)$), it is sufficient to prove the properties for basic terms. The proofs need the following fact: if p is a basic $\mathrm{BSP}^{\mathrm{drt}*}(A)$-term and $p \;{}_n\xrightarrow{a}\; p'$ for some $a \in A, n \in \mathbf{N}$, then also p' is a basic $\mathrm{BSP}^{\mathrm{drt}*}(A)$-term. This can easily be established by induction on the depth of the derivation of the transition. □

Lemma 9.5.7 Let p, q, and r be closed $\mathrm{BSP}^{\mathrm{drt}*}(A)$-terms. If $(p+q)+r \leftrightarrow_{\mathrm{t}} r$, then $p + r \leftrightarrow_{\mathrm{t}} r$ and $q + r \leftrightarrow_{\mathrm{t}} r$.

Proof See Exercise 9.5.4. □

Theorem 9.5.8 (Ground-completeness) Theory $BSP^{drt*}(A)$ is a ground-complete axiomatization of the term model $\mathbb{P}(BSP^{drt*}(A))_{/\leftrightarrow_t}$, i.e., for any closed $BSP^{drt*}(A)$-terms p and q, $\mathbb{P}(BSP^{drt*}(A))_{/\leftrightarrow_t} \models p = q$ implies $BSP^{drt*}(A) \vdash p = q$.

Proof Due to Proposition 9.5.2 (Reduction to basic terms) and the soundness of the axioms of $BSP^{drt*}(A)$ (Theorem 9.5.5), it suffices to prove this theorem for basic terms. Let p and q be basic $BSP^{drt*}(A)$-terms. Suppose that $\mathbb{P}(BSP^{drt*}(A))_{/\leftrightarrow_t} \models p = q$, i.e., $p \leftrightarrow_t q$. It must be shown that $BSP^{drt*}(A) \vdash p = q$. Since bisimilarity is a congruence on $\mathbb{P}(BSP^{drt*}(A))$ (Proposition 9.5.4) and $BSP^{drt*}(A)$ is sound for $\mathbb{P}(BSP^{drt*}(A))_{/\leftrightarrow_t}$ (Theorem 9.5.5), it suffices to prove that, for all basic terms p and q,

$$p + q \leftrightarrow_t q \quad \text{implies} \quad BSP^{drt*}(A) \vdash p + q = q \tag{9.5.1}$$

and

$$p \leftrightarrow_t p + q \quad \text{implies} \quad BSP^{drt*}(A) \vdash p = p + q. \tag{9.5.2}$$

Property (9.5.1) is proven by induction on the total number of symbols in basic terms p and q. The proof of property (9.5.2) is similar and therefore omitted. Assume $p + q \leftrightarrow_t q$ for some basic terms p and q. The base case of the induction corresponds to the case that the total number of symbols in p and q equals two, namely when p and q are both equal to $\underline{0}$, 0, $\underline{1}$, or 1.

(i) Assume $p \equiv \underline{0}$. Using Axioms A6DR and A1, it trivially follows that $BSP^{drt*}(A) \vdash p + q = \underline{0} + q = q + \underline{0} = q$.

(ii) Assume $p \equiv 0$. By Table 9.4, $p \rightsquigarrow_n$ for all $n \in \mathbf{N}$. By Table 9.2 also $p + q \rightsquigarrow_n$ for all $n \in \mathbf{N}$. Therefore, as $p + q \leftrightarrow_t q$, also $q \rightsquigarrow_n$ for all $n \in \mathbf{N}$. Following Lemma 9.5.6 (ii), $BSP^{drt*}(A) \vdash q = 0 + q$. Then, $BSP^{drt*}(A) \vdash p + q = 0 + q = q$.

(iii) Assume $p \equiv \underline{1}$. Then, $p{\downarrow_0}$ and thus $(p + q){\downarrow_0}$. As $p + q \leftrightarrow_t q$, also $q{\downarrow_0}$. By Lemma 9.5.6 (iii), $BSP^{drt*}(A) \vdash q = \underline{1} + q$. Hence, $BSP^{drt*}(A) \vdash p + q = \underline{1} + q = q$.

(iv) Assume $p \equiv 1$. By Table 9.4, $p{\downarrow_n}$ for all $n \in \mathbf{N}$. By Table 9.2 also $(p + q){\downarrow_n}$ for all $n \in \mathbf{N}$. Therefore, as $p + q \leftrightarrow_t q$, also $q{\downarrow_n}$ for all $n \in \mathbf{N}$. Following Lemma 9.5.6 (iv), $BSP^{drt*}(A) \vdash q = 1 + q$. Then, $BSP^{drt*}(A) \vdash p + q = 1 + q = q$.

The proof of the inductive step consists of a case analysis based on the structure of term p. Using Lemmas 9.5.6 and 9.5.7, this proceeds as in the proof of Theorem 9.4.8 (Ground-completeness $BSP^{drt}(A)$). □

Exercises

9.5.1 Prove the following for all BSP$^{\mathrm{drt}*}(A)$-terms x and y, and all $a \in A$:

(a) $\mathrm{BSP}^{\mathrm{drt}*}(A) \vdash a.x + 0 = a.x$;
(b) $\mathrm{BSP}^{\mathrm{drt}*}(A) \vdash \sigma.x + \sigma^* y = y + \sigma.(x + \sigma^* y)$;
(c) $\mathrm{BSP}^{\mathrm{drt}*}(A) \vdash a.x + \underline{a}.x = a.x$;
(d) $\mathrm{BSP}^{\mathrm{drt}*}(A) \vdash \sigma.x + \sigma^* x = \sigma^* x$.

9.5.2 Prove Proposition 9.5.2 (Reduction to basic terms).

9.5.3 Prove Theorem 9.5.5 (Soundness).

9.5.4 Prove Lemmas 9.5.6 (Towards completeness) and 9.5.7.

9.6 The relation between BSP(A) and BSP$^{\mathrm{drt}*}$(A)

This section discusses the relation between the untimed process theory BSP(A) and the timed theory BSP$^{\mathrm{drt}*}(A)$ in some detail. Usually, when extending a theory, one adds constants and/or operators to the signature, extends the set of axioms, and extends the original deduction system in such a way that with respect to the old signature nothing changes.

Comparing the signatures of BSP(A) and BSP$^{\mathrm{drt}*}(A)$, it can be observed that indeed the latter is an extension of the former. The extension consists of the constants $\underline{0}$ and $\underline{1}$, current-time-slice action-prefix operators $\underline{a}.\_$, the time-prefix operator $\sigma.\_$, and the time-iteration prefix operator $\sigma^*\_$. However, theory BSP$^{\mathrm{drt}*}(A)$ is not an extension of BSP(A) as defined in Definition 2.2.14, because Axiom A6 of BSP(A) is not included in BSP$^{\mathrm{drt}*}(A)$. It can be shown though that theory BSP$^{\mathrm{drt}*}(A)$ is a *ground*-extension, as defined in Definition 2.2.18, see Exercise 9.6.1. Furthermore, as explained below, it turns out that BSP$^{\mathrm{drt}*}(A)$ is a *conservative* ground-extension of BSP(A).

In the operational framework, instead of the transitions and terminations present in the untimed setting, the timed setting has natural numbers indicating the time slice as extra parameters, and the possible delays as extra predicates. Nevertheless, any two closed BSP(A)-terms that are timed bisimilar in the timed setting are also bisimilar in the untimed setting, and vice versa.

Proposition 9.6.1 (Timed vs. strong bisimilarity) For closed BSP(A)-terms p and q, $p \leftrightarrow_{\mathrm{t}} q$ if and only if $p \leftrightarrow q$.

Proof Suppose that $p \leftrightarrow_{\mathrm{t}} q$. Assume that this timed bisimilarity is witnessed by the relation R on closed BSP$^{\mathrm{drt}*}(A)$-terms, i.e., R is a timed bisimulation and $(p, q) \in R$. Notice that if $p \;{}_n\!\xrightarrow{a}\; p'$, then p' is a subterm of p, so if p is a BSP(A)-term, then also p' is a BSP(A)-term. If follows that the transition system of a BSP(A)-term in the timed model has the same states as in the untimed model. Moreover, $p \xrightarrow{a} p'$ holds in the untimed model exactly when $p \;{}_{n}\!\xrightarrow{a} p'$ holds in the timed model (for all $n \in \mathbf{N}$), and, similarly, $p\downarrow$ holds in the untimed model exactly when $p\downarrow_n$ holds in the timed model (for all $n \in \mathbf{N}$). Thus, the relation R is also a bisimulation relation on the term algebra of BSP(A), showing that $p \leftrightarrow q$. The other implication follows from a similar reasoning. □

Using among others this proposition, it can be shown that $\mathrm{BSP}^{\mathrm{drt}*}(A)$ is a conservative ground-extension of BSP(A).

Theorem 9.6.2 (Conservative ground-extension) Theory $\mathrm{BSP}^{\mathrm{drt}*}(A)$ is a conservative ground-extension of theory BSP(A).

Proof According to Definitions 2.2.18 (Ground-extension) and 2.2.19 (Conservative ground-extension), it needs to be shown that, for all closed BSP(A)-terms p and q, $\mathrm{BSP}(A) \vdash p = q$ if and only if $\mathrm{BSP}^{\mathrm{drt}*}(A) \vdash p = q$. The implication from left to right, showing that $\mathrm{BSP}^{\mathrm{drt}*}(A)$ is a ground-extension of BSP(A), follows from the observation that all axioms of BSP(A) with the exception of Axiom A6 are also axioms of $\mathrm{BSP}^{\mathrm{drt}*}(A)$ and the first part of Exercise 9.6.1. The other implication, showing conservativity, can be shown as follows. If $\mathrm{BSP}^{\mathrm{drt}*}(A) \vdash p = q$ for closed BSP(A)-terms p and q, it follows from the soundness of $\mathrm{BSP}^{\mathrm{drt}*}(A)$ that $p \leftrightarrow_{\mathrm{t}} q$. Proposition 9.6.1 (Timed vs. strong bisimilarity) shows that then also $p \leftrightarrow q$. Since BSP(A) is ground-complete, Theorem 4.4.12, it follows that $\mathrm{BSP}(A) \vdash p = q$, completing the proof. As an alternative, it is possible to prove the result via meta-results in the style of Chapter 3. The interested reader is referred to (Baeten *et al.*, 2005). □

The process algebra ACP (Bergstra & Klop, 1984a; Baeten & Weijland, 1990) has action constants instead of action prefixing. At this point, a drawback of the ACP approach can be appreciated. For, an action constant a in ACP satisfies the law $a \cdot 1 = a$, and it has the operational rule $a \xrightarrow{a} 1$. This means, interpreted in a timed theory, that after a number of time steps, a is executed, *necessarily* followed by the option to execute any number of time steps followed by termination. This means that processes like $a.\underline{1}$ or $a.\underline{0}$ cannot be expressed in a conservative timed extension of ACP. If, as is common in ACP process algebra, the process 1 does not exist, this problem nevertheless resurfaces when silent actions are added, for then the law $a \cdot \tau = a$ holds, leading to $a \xrightarrow{a} \tau$, and again in a timed setting necessarily any number of time steps are allowed to be executed after execution of a. For a more elaborate discussion on this issue, the interested reader is referred to (Baeten & Reniers, 2007).

Exercises

9.6.1 Prove that $\mathrm{BSP}^{\mathrm{drt}*}(A) \vdash p + 0 = p$ for closed BSP(A)-terms p. Also, give a counterexample for $\mathrm{BSP}^{\mathrm{drt}*}(A) \vdash p + 0 = p$ for closed $\mathrm{BSP}^{\mathrm{drt}*}(A)$-terms p.

9.7 The process theory $\mathrm{TCP}^{\mathrm{drt}*}(A, \gamma)$

In this section, the process theory $\mathrm{BSP}^{\mathrm{drt}*}(A)$ is extended to the process theory $\mathrm{TCP}^{\mathrm{drt}*}(A, \gamma)$. This extension is obtained by extending the signature of $\mathrm{BSP}^{\mathrm{drt}*}(A)$ with the *sequential-composition* operator $\_ \cdot \_$, the *current-time-slice timeout* operator ν, the *encapsulation* operators ∂_H (for $H \subseteq A$), and the *parallel-composition* operators $\_ \parallel \_$, $\_ \mathbin{⌊\!⌊} \_$, and $\_ \mid \_$.

The axioms of the process theory are given in Table 9.5. Sequential composition is as before, but here the role of identity that was played by 1 in the untimed theory, is taken over by the current-time-slice termination constant $\underline{1}$ (see Axioms A8DR and A9DR). In this setting, it can be derived that $1 \cdot x = \sigma^* x$ instead. The sequential-composition operator has two left-zero elements: both undelayable inaction (see Axiom A7DR) and delayable inaction act as such. The axiom $0 \cdot x = 0$ (A7) has disappeared since it is derivable from the remaining axioms. The axiom $a.x \cdot y = a.(x \cdot y)$ (A10) from the untimed theory is now also derivable. Axioms A10DRb and A10DRc express that the passage of time is measured relative to the previous action and thus has no consequences for the future actions: the timing of y is relative to the last action of x, regardless of the time-prefix or time-iteration operator.

The current-time-slice timeout operator, with Axioms RTO1–5 (from Relative TimeOut), disallows all initial passage of time. It extracts the part of the behavior that executes an action or performs termination in the current time slice. Notice that the equation $\nu(\sigma^* x) = \nu(x)$ can be derived from the axioms given. The encapsulation operator is as defined before: encapsulation disallows the actions that occur in the set H and allows all other behavior including passage of time.

Before continuing with the other operators and axioms in the theory, the following proposition summarizes some simple identities concerning sequential composition, encapsulation, and the current-time-slice timeout operator that can be derived from the theory.

$\mathrm{TCP}^{\mathrm{drt}*}(A,\gamma)$			
$\mathrm{BSP}^{\mathrm{drt}*}(A)$;			
unary: ν, $(\partial_H)_{H\subseteq A}$;	binary: $\_\cdot\_$, $\_\parallel\_$, $\_\lfloor\!\lfloor\_$, $\_\mid\_$;		
x, y, z;			
$(x+y)\cdot z = x\cdot z + y\cdot z$	A4	$\nu(\underline{1}) = \underline{1}$	RTO1
$(x\cdot y)\cdot z = x\cdot(y\cdot z)$	A5	$\nu(\underline{0}) = \underline{0}$	RTO2
$\underline{0}\cdot x = \underline{0}$	A7DR	$\nu(\underline{a}.x) = \underline{a}.x$	RTO3
$x\cdot\underline{1} = x$	A8DR	$\nu(x+y) = \nu(x)+\nu(y)$	RTO4
$\underline{1}\cdot x = x$	A9DR	$\nu(\sigma.x) = \underline{0}$	RTO5
$\underline{a}.x\cdot y = \underline{a}.(x\cdot y)$	A10DRa		
$(\sigma.x)\cdot y = \sigma.(x\cdot y)$	A10DRb		
$\sigma^* x\cdot y = \sigma^*(x\cdot y)$	A10DRc		
$\partial_H(\underline{1}) = \underline{1}$	D1DR	$\partial_H(x+y) = \partial_H(x)+\partial_H(y)$	D5
$\partial_H(\underline{0}) = \underline{0}$	D2DR	$\partial_H(\sigma.x) = \sigma.\partial_H(x)$	D6DR
$\partial_H(\underline{a}.x) = \underline{0}$ if $a\in H$	D3DR	$\partial_H(\sigma^* x) = \sigma^*\partial_H(x)$	D7DR
$\partial_H(\underline{a}.x) = \underline{a}.\partial_H(x)$ otherwise	D4DR		
$x\parallel y = x\lfloor\!\lfloor y + y\lfloor\!\lfloor x + x\mid y$	M		
$\underline{0}\lfloor\!\lfloor x = \underline{0}$	LM1DR		
$\underline{1}\lfloor\!\lfloor x = \underline{0}$	LM2DR		
$\underline{a}.x\lfloor\!\lfloor y = \underline{a}.(x\parallel y)$	LM3DR		
$(x+y)\lfloor\!\lfloor z = x\lfloor\!\lfloor z + y\lfloor\!\lfloor z$	LM4		
$\sigma.x\lfloor\!\lfloor \nu(y) = \underline{0}$	LM5DR		
$\sigma.x\lfloor\!\lfloor(\nu(y)+\sigma.z) = \sigma.(x\lfloor\!\lfloor z)$	LM6DR		
$\sigma^* x\lfloor\!\lfloor\sigma^*\nu(y) = \sigma^*(x\lfloor\!\lfloor\sigma^*\nu(y))$	LM7DR		
$x\mid y = y\mid x$	SC1	$(x\parallel y)\parallel z = x\parallel(y\parallel z)$	SC4
$x\parallel 1 = x$	SC2	$(x\mid y)\mid z = x\mid(y\mid z)$	SC5
$\underline{1}\mid x+\underline{1} = \underline{1}$	SC3DR	$(x\lfloor\!\lfloor y)\lfloor\!\lfloor z = x\lfloor\!\lfloor(y\parallel z)$	SC6
$x\cdot 1\lfloor\!\lfloor 0 = x\cdot 0$	SC8DR	$(x\mid y)\lfloor\!\lfloor z = x\mid(y\lfloor\!\lfloor z)$	SC7
$\underline{0}\mid x = \underline{0}$	CM1DR		
$(x+y)\mid z = x\mid z + y\mid z$	CM2		
$\underline{1}\mid\underline{1} = \underline{1}$	CM3DR		
$\underline{a}.x\mid\underline{1} = \underline{0}$	CM4DR		
$\underline{a}.x\mid\underline{b}.y = \underline{c}.(x\parallel y)$ if $\gamma(a,b)=c$	CM5DR		
$\underline{a}.x\mid\underline{b}.y = \underline{0}$ if $\gamma(a,b)$ not defined	CM6DR		
$\sigma.x\mid\nu(y) = \underline{0}$	CM7DR		
$\sigma.x\mid\sigma.y = \sigma.(x\mid y)$	CM8DR		
$\sigma^* x\mid\sigma^* y = \sigma^*(x\mid\sigma^* y + \sigma^* x\mid y)$	CM9DR		

Table 9.5. The process theory $\mathrm{TCP}^{\mathrm{drt}*}(A,\gamma)$ (with $a,b,c\in A$).

Proposition 9.7.1 (Identities in $\mathrm{TCP}^{\mathrm{drt}*}(A,\gamma)$) For any $\mathrm{TCP}^{\mathrm{drt}*}(A,\gamma)$-terms x, y, action $a\in A$, and $H\subseteq A$,

(i) $\mathrm{TCP}^{\mathrm{drt}*}(A,\gamma)\vdash\nu(0) = \underline{0}$;

(ii) $\mathrm{TCP}^{\mathrm{drt}*}(A, \gamma) \vdash \nu(1) = \underline{1}$;
(iii) $\mathrm{TCP}^{\mathrm{drt}*}(A, \gamma) \vdash \nu(a.x) = \underline{a}.x$;
(iv) $\mathrm{TCP}^{\mathrm{drt}*}(A, \gamma) \vdash \nu(\sigma^* x) = \nu(x)$;
(v) $\mathrm{TCP}^{\mathrm{drt}*}(A, \gamma) \vdash \partial_H(0) = 0$;
(vi) $\mathrm{TCP}^{\mathrm{drt}*}(A, \gamma) \vdash \partial_H(1) = 1$;
(vii) for $a \in H$, $\mathrm{TCP}^{\mathrm{drt}*}(A, \gamma) \vdash \partial_H(a.x) = 0$;
(viii) for $a \notin H$, $\mathrm{TCP}^{\mathrm{drt}*}(A, \gamma) \vdash \partial_H(a.x) = a.\partial_H(x)$;
(ix) $\mathrm{TCP}^{\mathrm{drt}*}(A, \gamma) \vdash 0 \cdot x = 0$;
(x) $\mathrm{TCP}^{\mathrm{drt}*}(A, \gamma) \vdash 1 \cdot x = \sigma^* x$;
(xi) $\mathrm{TCP}^{\mathrm{drt}*}(A, \gamma) \vdash a.x \cdot y = a.(x \cdot y)$;
(xii) $\mathrm{TCP}^{\mathrm{drt}*}(A, \gamma) \vdash \sigma^* x + 0 = \sigma^* x$.

Proof See Exercise 9.7.1. □

The axioms for parallel composition and the auxiliary parallel-composition operators are such that parallel processes can only delay if both components allow this delay. Within each time slice, parallel processes interleave their actions or communicate. To stay as closely as possible to the interpretation of the axioms in the untimed setting, it is necessary for both left merge and communication merge to synchronize passage of time as well (Axioms LM6DR and CM8DR). The empty process 1 is still the identity element of parallel composition (Axiom SC2). Some axioms of the untimed theory are no longer valid in full generality, e.g., $0 \mathbin{⌊\!⌊} x = 0$ (LM1) is not valid for all processes x (take e.g. $\underline{0}$ for x), but only for processes that allow an initial arbitrary delay, i.e., *delayable* processes in the sense of Axioms DD, DT, and DA of Table 9.3. Delayable processes are processes that can be written in the form $\sigma^* \nu(y)$. Axiom ATS implies that the progress of time does not affect a delayable process. The following proposition gives some identities concerning parallel-composition operators that can be derived from $\mathrm{TCP}^{\mathrm{drt}*}(A, \gamma)$. Most of these identities are directly derived from axioms of the untimed theory $\mathrm{TCP}(A, \gamma)$. Some of them are in fact identical to axioms from this theory, whereas others are axioms reformulated for delayable processes only.

Proposition 9.7.2 (Identities in $\mathrm{TCP}^{\mathrm{drt}*}(A, \gamma)$) For arbitrary $\mathrm{TCP}^{\mathrm{drt}*}(A, \gamma)$-terms x, y and actions $a, b, c \in A$,

(i) $\mathrm{TCP}^{\mathrm{drt}*}(A, \gamma) \vdash \sigma.x \parallel \sigma.y = \sigma.(x \parallel y)$;
(ii) $\mathrm{TCP}^{\mathrm{drt}*}(A, \gamma) \vdash 0 \mathbin{⌊\!⌊} \sigma^* \nu(x) = 0$;
(iii) $\mathrm{TCP}^{\mathrm{drt}*}(A, \gamma) \vdash 1 \mathbin{⌊\!⌊} \sigma^* \nu(x) = 0$;
(iv) $\mathrm{TCP}^{\mathrm{drt}*}(A, \gamma) \vdash a.x \mathbin{⌊\!⌊} \sigma^* \nu(y) = a.(x \parallel \sigma^* \nu(y))$;
(v) $\mathrm{TCP}^{\mathrm{drt}*}(A, \gamma) \vdash 0 \mid \sigma^* \nu(x) = 0$;

(vi) $\mathrm{TCP}^{\mathrm{drt}^*}(A, \gamma) \vdash 1 \mid 1 = 1$;
(vii) $\mathrm{TCP}^{\mathrm{drt}^*}(A, \gamma) \vdash 1 \parallel 1 = 1$;
(viii) $\mathrm{TCP}^{\mathrm{drt}^*}(A, \gamma) \vdash a.x \mid 1 = 0$;
(ix) $\mathrm{TCP}^{\mathrm{drt}^*}(A, \gamma) \vdash a.x \mid b.y = c.(x \parallel y)$ if $\gamma(a, b) = c$;
(x) $\mathrm{TCP}^{\mathrm{drt}^*}(A, \gamma) \vdash a.x \mid b.y = 0$ if $\gamma(a, b)$ is not defined;
(xi) $\mathrm{TCP}^{\mathrm{drt}^*}(A, \gamma) \vdash 1 \mid \sigma^*\nu(x) + 1 = 1$.

Proof See Exercise 9.7.2. □

The first property of the next proposition shows that terms over the signature of the untimed process theory $\mathrm{TCP}(A, \gamma)$ of Section 7.7 are delayable. For untimed processes, delayability can be expressed in several different means, as illustrated by this property. The second property in the proposition shows that an untimed process also allows arbitrary passage of time at the end. In combination with the previous two propositions, Proposition 9.7.3 implies that the axioms of the untimed theory are in the timed setting still valid for terms of the untimed theory (Exercise 9.7.4).

Proposition 9.7.3 (Delayability of untimed processes) For any arbitrary closed $\mathrm{TCP}(A, \gamma)$-term p,

$$\mathrm{TCP}^{\mathrm{drt}^*}(A, \gamma) \vdash p = 1 \cdot p = \sigma^* p = \sigma^* \nu(p)$$

and

$$\mathrm{TCP}^{\mathrm{drt}^*}(A, \gamma) \vdash p = p \cdot 1.$$

Proof See Exercise 9.7.3. □

As expected, the operators that are new in $\mathrm{TCP}^{\mathrm{drt}^*}(A, \gamma)$ when compared to $\mathrm{BSP}^{\mathrm{drt}^*}(A)$ can be eliminated.

Theorem 9.7.4 (Elimination) For any closed $\mathrm{TCP}^{\mathrm{drt}^*}(A, \gamma)$-term p, there is a closed $\mathrm{BSP}^{\mathrm{drt}^*}(A)$-term q such that $\mathrm{TCP}^{\mathrm{drt}^*}(A, \gamma) \vdash p = q$.

Proof It suffices to prove that for any closed $\mathrm{TCP}^{\mathrm{drt}^*}(A, \gamma)$-term p, there is a *basic* $\mathrm{BSP}^{\mathrm{drt}^*}(A)$-term q (see Definition 9.5.1) such that $\mathrm{TCP}^{\mathrm{drt}^*}(A, \gamma) \vdash p = q$. The proof does not use rewriting, as the axioms of $\mathrm{TCP}^{\mathrm{drt}^*}(A, \gamma)$ are not in a convenient form for such a proof. Instead, the proof uses induction. (Note that also Exercise 4.5.4 requests an induction-based proof of an elimination theorem.) The following properties are needed:

(i) for any basic $\mathrm{BSP}^{\mathrm{drt}^*}(A)$-term p, there exists a basic $\mathrm{BSP}^{\mathrm{drt}^*}(A)$-term q such that $\mathrm{TCP}^{\mathrm{drt}^*}(A, \gamma) \vdash \nu(p) = q$;

(ii) for any basic $\mathrm{BSP}^{\mathrm{drt}*}(A)$-term p and any $H \subseteq A$, there exists a basic term q such that $\mathrm{TCP}^{\mathrm{drt}*}(A, \gamma) \vdash \partial_H(p) = q$;

(iii) for any basic terms p and p', there exists a basic term q such that $\mathrm{TCP}^{\mathrm{drt}*}(A, \gamma) \vdash p \cdot p' = q$;

(iv) for any basic terms p and p', there exists a basic term q such that $\mathrm{TCP}^{\mathrm{drt}*}(A, \gamma) \vdash p \mathbin{|\!\!\lfloor} p' = q$;

(v) for any basic terms p and p', there exists a basic term q such that $\mathrm{TCP}^{\mathrm{drt}*}(A, \gamma) \vdash p \mid p' = q$;

(vi) for any basic terms p and p', there exists a basic term q such that $\mathrm{TCP}^{\mathrm{drt}*}(A, \gamma) \vdash p \parallel p' = q$.

The first three properties are proven by induction on the structure of basic term p. For the third, it is necessary to consider the form of p' in case p is of the form $\sigma^n 1$, and use the tenth item of Proposition 9.7.1 (Identities in $\mathrm{TCP}^{\mathrm{drt}*}(A, \gamma)$) together with the axioms of time iteration.

The last three properties are proven simultaneously by induction on the number of symbols of p and p'. For the first of these three cases, if p' is an alternative composition, it is necessary to consider several subcases.

The proof can now be completed by applying properties (i)–(vi) to eliminate all the six operators that are new in $\mathrm{TCP}^{\mathrm{drt}*}(A, \gamma)$ when compared to $\mathrm{BSP}^{\mathrm{drt}*}(A)$, starting with the smallest subterm(s) containing any of the new operators and gradually working outwards. The details of the proof are left for Exercise 9.7.13. □

A term model can be constructed along the same lines as before, except that it is necessary to introduce a class of auxiliary operators. It is not known whether a term deduction system for $\mathrm{TCP}^{\mathrm{drt}*}(A, \gamma)$ exists without such auxiliary operators. Although not strictly necessary, the auxiliary operators are introduced in the equational theory first. For each natural number n, the *shift* operator $n \gg \_$ shifts a process in time by n time slices. Applying the $n \gg \_$ operator to a process results in the behavior that remains after n units of time have passed. Table 9.6 presents theory $\mathrm{TCP}^{\mathrm{drt}*}\!\gg\!(A, \gamma)$, $\mathrm{TCP}^{\mathrm{drt}*}(A, \gamma)$ with shift operators.

As an example of a derivation in $\mathrm{TCP}^{\mathrm{drt}*}\!\gg\!(A, \gamma)$, consider the following: $\mathrm{TCP}^{\mathrm{drt}*}\!\gg\!(A, \gamma) \vdash (n+1) \gg \sigma^*(\underline{a}.\underline{1} + \sigma.\underline{0}) = (n+1) \gg \sigma^*\nu(\underline{a}.\underline{1}) + (n+1) \gg \sigma^*\sigma.\underline{0} = \sigma^*\nu(\underline{a}.\underline{1}) + (n+1) \gg \sigma.\sigma^*\underline{0} = \sigma^*\underline{a}.\underline{1} + n \gg \sigma^*\underline{0} = \sigma^*\underline{a}.\underline{1} + \sigma^*\underline{0} = \sigma^*(\underline{a}.\underline{1} + \underline{0}) = \sigma^*\underline{a}.\underline{1} = a.\underline{1}$.

At this point, a term model for the extended theory $\mathrm{TCP}^{\mathrm{drt}*}\!\gg\!(A, \gamma)$ can be constructed in the standard way. The resulting model is also a model for theory $\mathrm{TCP}^{\mathrm{drt}*}(A, \gamma)$. The term deduction system $TDS(\mathrm{TCP}^{\mathrm{drt}*}\!\gg\!(A, \gamma))$ consists of

$\_\mathrm{TCP}^{\mathrm{drt}*} \gg (A, \gamma)$	
$\mathrm{TCP}^{\mathrm{drt}*}(A, \gamma)$;	
unary: $(n \gg \_)_{n \in \mathbf{N}}$;	
x, y;	
$0 \gg x = x$	SH1
$n \gg \underline{0} = \underline{0}$	SH2
$(n + 1) \gg \underline{1} = \underline{0}$	SH3
$(n + 1) \gg \underline{a}.x = \underline{0}$	SH4
$n \gg (x + y) = n \gg x + n \gg y$	SH5
$(n + 1) \gg \sigma.x = n \gg x$	SH6
$n \gg \sigma^* \nu(x) = \sigma^* \nu(x)$	SH7

Table 9.6. Axioms for $\mathrm{TCP}^{\mathrm{drt}*}(A, \gamma)$ shift operators ($a \in A, n \in \mathbf{N}$).

the deduction rules from $TDS(\mathrm{BSP}^{\mathrm{drt}*}(A))$ and additionally the deduction rules given in Table 9.7.

The rules for sequential composition and encapsulation are straightforward. The 'now' operator ν only allows activity in the current time slice, so with time-stamp 0. For parallel composition, in order for termination or communication to occur, both components have to allow this in the same time slice. If a component executes an action itself, the other component must be able to reach the time slice in which the action occurs; after this action, the other component must be updated to that time slice. This is achieved via a shift operator. Operational rules for this operator are straightforward.

The algebra $\mathbb{P}(\mathrm{TCP}^{\mathrm{drt}*} \gg (A, \gamma)) = (\mathcal{C}(\mathrm{TCP}^{\mathrm{drt}*} \gg (A, \gamma)), +, \cdot, \|, \lfloor\!\lfloor, \mid, (n \gg \_)_{n \in \mathbf{N}}, (\underline{a}.\_)_{a \in A}, \sigma.\_, (a.\_)_{a \in A}, \sigma^*, \nu, (\partial_H)_{H \subseteq A}, \underline{0}, \underline{1}, 0, 1)$ is the term algebra for theory $\mathrm{TCP}^{\mathrm{drt}*} \gg (A, \gamma)$.

Proposition 9.7.5 (Congruence) Timed bisimilarity is a congruence on the term algebra $\mathbb{P}(\mathrm{TCP}^{\mathrm{drt}*} \gg (A, \gamma))$.

Proof The term deduction system is in path format, so congruence follows immediately; see the proof of Theorem 9.4.3 for additional explanation. □

Definition 9.7.6 (Term model of $\mathrm{TCP}^{\mathrm{drt}*} \gg (A, \gamma)$**)** The term model of theory $\mathrm{TCP}^{\mathrm{drt}*} \gg (A, \gamma)$ is the quotient algebra $\mathbb{P}(\mathrm{TCP}^{\mathrm{drt}*} \gg (A, \gamma))_{/\leftrightarrow_t}$.

Theorem 9.7.7 (Soundness) Theory $\mathrm{TCP}^{\mathrm{drt}*} \gg (A, \gamma)$ is a sound axiomatization of $\mathbb{P}(\mathrm{TCP}^{\mathrm{drt}*} \gg (A, \gamma))_{/\leftrightarrow_t}$, i.e., $\mathbb{P}(\mathrm{TCP}^{\mathrm{drt}*} \gg (A, \gamma))_{/\leftrightarrow_t} \models \mathrm{TCP}^{\mathrm{drt}*} \gg (A, \gamma)$.

$TDS(\mathrm{TCP}^{\mathrm{drt}*} \gg (A, \gamma))$

$TDS(\mathrm{BSP}^{\mathrm{drt}*}(A))$;

unary: ν, $(\partial_H)_{H \subseteq A}$, $(n \gg \_)_{n \in \mathbf{N}}$; binary: $\_ \cdot \_$, $\_ \parallel \_$, $\_ \mathbin{⌊\!⌊} \_$, $\_ \mid \_$;

x, x', y, y';

$$\frac{x \downarrow_n \quad y \downarrow_m}{x \cdot y \downarrow_{n+m}} \qquad \frac{x \;{}_n\!\xrightarrow{a}\; x'}{x \cdot y \;{}_n\!\xrightarrow{a}\; x' \cdot y} \qquad \frac{x \downarrow_n \quad y \;{}_m\!\xrightarrow{a}\; y'}{x \cdot y \;{}_{n+m}\!\xrightarrow{a}\; y'}$$

$$\frac{x \rightsquigarrow_n}{x \cdot y \rightsquigarrow_n} \qquad \frac{x \downarrow_n \quad y \rightsquigarrow_m}{x \cdot y \rightsquigarrow_{n+m}}$$

$$\frac{x \downarrow_0}{\nu(x) \downarrow_0} \qquad \frac{x \;{}_0\!\xrightarrow{a}\; x'}{\nu(x) \;{}_0\!\xrightarrow{a}\; x'}$$

$$\frac{x \downarrow_n}{\partial_H(x) \downarrow_n} \qquad \frac{x \;{}_n\!\xrightarrow{a}\; x' \quad a \notin H}{\partial_H(x) \;{}_n\!\xrightarrow{a}\; x'} \qquad \frac{x \rightsquigarrow_n}{\partial_H(x) \rightsquigarrow_n}$$

$$\frac{x \downarrow_n \quad y \downarrow_n}{x \parallel y \downarrow_n} \qquad \frac{x \downarrow_n \quad y \downarrow_n}{x \mid y \downarrow_n}$$

$$\frac{x \;{}_n\!\xrightarrow{a}\; x' \quad y \rightsquigarrow_n}{x \parallel y \;{}_n\!\xrightarrow{a}\; x' \parallel (n \gg y)} \qquad \frac{x \rightsquigarrow_n \quad y \;{}_n\!\xrightarrow{a}\; y'}{x \parallel y \;{}_n\!\xrightarrow{a}\; (n \gg x) \parallel y'} \qquad \frac{x \;{}_n\!\xrightarrow{a}\; x' \quad y \rightsquigarrow_n}{x \mathbin{⌊\!⌊} y \xrightarrow{a} x' \parallel (n \gg y)}$$

$$\frac{x \;{}_n\!\xrightarrow{a}\; x' \quad y \;{}_n\!\xrightarrow{b}\; y' \quad \gamma(a,b) = c}{x \parallel y \;{}_n\!\xrightarrow{c}\; x' \parallel y'} \qquad \frac{x \;{}_n\!\xrightarrow{a}\; x' \quad y \;{}_n\!\xrightarrow{b}\; y' \quad \gamma(a,b) = c}{x \mid y \xrightarrow{c} x' \parallel y'}$$

$$\frac{x \rightsquigarrow_n \quad y \rightsquigarrow_n}{x \parallel y \rightsquigarrow_n} \qquad \frac{x \rightsquigarrow_n \quad y \rightsquigarrow_n}{x \mathbin{⌊\!⌊} y \rightsquigarrow_n} \qquad \frac{x \rightsquigarrow_n \quad y \rightsquigarrow_n}{x \mid y \rightsquigarrow_n}$$

$$\frac{x \;{}_{n+m}\!\xrightarrow{a}\; x'}{n \gg x \;{}_m\!\xrightarrow{a}\; x'} \qquad \frac{x \downarrow_{n+m}}{n \gg x \downarrow_m} \qquad \frac{x \rightsquigarrow_{n+m}}{n \gg x \rightsquigarrow_m}$$

Table 9.7. Term deduction system for $\mathrm{TCP}^{\mathrm{drt}*} \gg (A, \gamma)$ (with $a, b, c \in A$, $n, m \in \mathbf{N}$, and $H \subseteq A$).

Proof See Exercise 9.7.14. □

Theorem 9.7.8 (Ground-completeness) Theory $\mathrm{TCP}^{\mathrm{drt}*} \gg (A, \gamma)$ is a complete axiomatization of the term model $\mathbb{P}(\mathrm{TCP}^{\mathrm{drt}*} \gg (A, \gamma))_{/\leftrightarrow_{\mathrm{t}}}$, i.e., for any closed $\mathrm{TCP}^{\mathrm{drt}*} \gg (A, \gamma)$-terms p and q, $\mathbb{P}(\mathrm{TCP}^{\mathrm{drt}*} \gg (A, \gamma))_{/\leftrightarrow_{\mathrm{t}}} \models p = q$ implies $\mathrm{TCP}^{\mathrm{drt}*} \gg (A, \gamma) \vdash p = q$.

Proof The proof goes along the usual lines, see e.g., Theorem 6.3.9 (Ground-completeness of TSP(A)), but using the generalized operational framework with transition systems with multiple types of transitions and/or state predicates of (Baeten & Verhoef, 1995). □

To end this section, it is interesting to observe that the process theory developed in this section is a conservative ground-extension with respect to earlier timed and untimed theories.

Theorem 9.7.9 (Conservative ground-extension) Theory $\text{TCP}^{\text{drt}*} \gg (A, \gamma)$ is a conservative ground-extension of theory $\text{BSP}^{\text{drt}*}(A)$.

Proof The theorem follows from results for the generalized operational framework with transition systems with multiple types of transitions and/or state predicates of (Baeten & Verhoef, 1995). □

Theorem 9.7.10 (Conservative ground-extension) Theory $\text{TCP}^{\text{drt}*} \gg (A, \gamma)$ is a conservative ground-extension of theory $\text{TCP}(A, \gamma)$.

Proof The proof uses a generalization of Proposition 9.6.1 (Timed vs. strong bisimilarity) to closed $\text{TCP}(A, \gamma)$-terms, and then goes along the same lines as Theorem 9.6.2 (Conservative ground-extension). Alternative proofs use the meta-theory of (Baeten *et al.*, 2005) or the result of Exercise 9.7.4. □

Exercises

9.7.1 Prove Proposition 9.7.1 (Identities in $\text{TCP}^{\text{drt}*}(A, \gamma)$).

9.7.2 Prove Proposition 9.7.2 (Identities in $\text{TCP}^{\text{drt}*}(A, \gamma)$).

9.7.3 Prove Proposition 9.7.3 (Delayability of untimed processes).

9.7.4 Prove that, for all closed $\text{TCP}(A, \gamma)$-terms, all axioms of the untimed process theory $\text{TCP}(A, \gamma)$ are derivable from the axioms of $\text{TCP}^{\text{drt}*}(A, \gamma)$.

9.7.5 Prove that

$$\text{TCP}^{\text{drt}*}(A, \gamma) \vdash \nu(\partial_H(p)) = \partial_H(\nu(p)),$$

for all $H \subseteq A$ and all closed $\text{TCP}^{\text{drt}*}(A, \gamma)$-terms p.

9.7.6 Prove that

$$\text{TCP}^{\text{drt}*}(A, \gamma) \vdash \underline{1} \mid p = \nu(\partial_A(p)),$$

for all closed $\text{TCP}^{\text{drt}*}(A, \gamma)$-terms p.

9.7.7 Prove that in the process theory obtained from $TCP^{drt*}(A, \gamma)$ by removing axioms $\underline{1} \mid \underline{1} = \underline{1}$ and $\underline{a}.x \mid \underline{1} = \underline{0}$, and adding axiom $\underline{1} \mid x = \nu(\partial_A(x))$ the removed identities are derivable.

9.7.8 Prove that

$$TCP^{drt*}(A, \gamma) \vdash 1 \mid p = \partial_A(p),$$

for all closed $TCP^{drt*}(A, \gamma)$-terms p.

9.7.9 Prove that the following identities are derivable from $TCP^{drt*}(A, \gamma)$ for all $TCP^{drt*}(A, \gamma)$-terms x, y:

(a) $1 \cdot 1 = 1$;
(b) $1 \cdot \sigma.x = \sigma.1 \cdot x$;
(c) $1 \cdot (x + y) = 1 \cdot x + 1 \cdot y$.

9.7.10 Establish whether the following identities are derivable from theory $TCP^{drt*}(A, \gamma)$; if so, give a derivation, if not, give a counterexample.

(a) $\sigma^* x \mathbin{\|\!\!\lfloor} \sigma^* y = \sigma^*(\sigma^* x \mathbin{\|\!\!\lfloor} \sigma^* y)$;
(b) $\sigma^* x \mid \sigma^* y = \sigma^*(\sigma^* x \mid \sigma^* y)$;
(c) $\sigma^* x \parallel \sigma^* y = \sigma^*(\sigma^* x \parallel \sigma^* y)$.

9.7.11 Establish whether the following identities are derivable from theory $TCP^{drt*}(A, \gamma)$ for closed terms p and q; if so, give a proof, if not, give a counterexample.

(a) $\sigma^* p \mathbin{\|\!\!\lfloor} \nu(q) = \nu(p) \mathbin{\|\!\!\lfloor} \nu(q)$;
(b) $\sigma^* p \mid \nu(q) = \nu(p) \mid \nu(q)$;
(c) $\sigma^* p \mathbin{\|\!\!\lfloor} \sigma^* q = \sigma^*(p \mathbin{\|\!\!\lfloor} \sigma^* q)$;
(d) $\sigma^* \nu(p) \mid \sigma^* \nu(q) = \sigma^*(\nu(p) \mid \nu(q))$.

9.7.12 Prove that the identity

$$\sigma^*(x \mid y) = \sigma^* x \mid \sigma^* y$$

is not derivable from the axioms of $TCP^{drt*}(A, \gamma)$.

9.7.13 Prove Theorem 9.7.4 (Elimination).

9.7.14 Prove Theorem 9.7.7 (Soundness).

9.8 Fischer's protocol

Fischer's protocol (Lamport, 1987) is a well known mutual-exclusion protocol for timed processes. This section describes the protocol using the theory $TCP^{drt*}(A, \gamma)$ extended with recursion. The protocol is linearized, i.e., written in the form of a linear recursive specification, and the timed transition system corresponding to the protocol is given. Recursion has not been introduced formally in the previous sections of this chapter. Recursion can be added similarly as in the untimed theory, be it that the time-prefix operator $\sigma._{-}$ should also be considered as a guard for recursion variables. On the other hand, time iteration cannot be considered a guard.

Mutual exclusion is relevant in a context where processes have so-called critical sections. The goal of a mutual-exclusion protocol is to guarantee that at any time at most one of the processes, called protocol entities from now to distinguish them from other processes, is in a critical section, in combination with the requirement that at least one of the protocol entities is able to proceed at each moment in time.

The protocol entities that use Fischer's protocol to guarantee mutual exclusion make use of a shared variable to exchange information. A protocol entity that wants to enter its critical section, checks if the value of the shared variable is 0, which represents that no entity is trying to enter the critical section. Then, it assigns its unique identifier to the shared variable. In case the variable still has this value after some time, it decides to enter the critical section. Otherwise, it will try again later. The delay that is introduced before an entity enters a critical section causes the protocol entity to wait sufficiently long so that other protocol entities that *concurrently* assigned their unique identifiers have had time enough to do so. This is necessary to guarantee the mutual-exclusion property.

In the variant of Fischer's protocol that is described in this section, only two protocol entities are considered for which the unique identifiers 1 and 2 are used. The protocol entities can perform two actions with respect to the shared variable x. The first action is inspection of the value of the variable; the second is the assignment of a value to the variable. For the description in this section, it is assumed that both the assignment of a value to the shared variable and the testing of the shared variable for a specific value take no time, i.e., occur instantaneously.

In $\mathrm{TCP}^{\mathrm{drt}*}(A, \gamma)$, the shared variable x is modeled by a set of recursion variables X_v, where v denotes the value of x. The actions of the two entities with respect to the shared variable are modeled by communication. The shared-variable process is at all times willing to send its value to the environment with the action $!(x = v)$. Of course this has no effect on the value of the variable. On the other hand, the shared-variable process receives assignments to the variable by means of the action $?(x := w)$, where w is some value. Of course the value of the variable is adapted accordingly. Finally, the variable may terminate at any time. This behavior is described by the following recursive equation:

$$X_v = 1 + !(x = v).X_v + \sum_{w \in \{0,1,2\}} ?(x := w).X_w.$$

An equivalent, but from the viewpoint of manipulation by means of the axioms more convenient specification of the variable is the following, where the any-time-slice termination and the any-time-slice action prefixes are removed and all initial time passage is combined into one summand:

$$X_v = \underline{1} + \underline{!(x = v)}.X_v + \sum_{w \in \{0,1,2\}} \underline{?(x := w)}.X_w + \sigma.X_v .$$

The two protocol entities that play a role in the version of Fischer's protocol that is described in this section have similar behavior. The only difference is that they have different identities, 1 and 2 respectively. The delay period between setting the value of the shared variable and testing the shared variable for this same value, is taken to be one time unit, which is sufficient given the assumption that writing a value to the shared variable is instantaneous. Furthermore, once a protocol entity has entered its critical section, it can stay there for any amount of time. The recursive specifications for the protocol entities are as follows. Recursion variable A describes protocol entity 1 and recursion variable B describes protocol entity 2.

$$\begin{aligned} A = {} & 1 + ?(x = 0).\underline{!(x := 1)}.\sigma. \\ & (\ \ \underline{?(x = 0)}.A \\ & + \underline{?(x = 1)}.\underline{\mathit{enterCS_1}}.\mathit{leaveCS_1}.\underline{!(x := 0)}.A \\ & + \underline{?(x = 2)}.A \\ &) , \end{aligned}$$

$$\begin{aligned} B = {} & 1 + ?(x = 0).\underline{!(x := 2)}.\sigma. \\ & (\ \ \underline{?(x = 0)}.B \\ & + \underline{?(x = 1)}.B \\ & + \underline{?(x = 2)}.\underline{\mathit{enterCS_2}}.\mathit{leaveCS_2}.\underline{!(x := 0)}.B \\ &) . \end{aligned}$$

The whole system is given by the recursion variable FP with the following recursive specification:

$$FP = \partial_H(A \parallel X_0 \parallel B),$$

where for all $\alpha \in \{x = i, x := i \mid i \in \{0, 1, 2\}\}$

$$\gamma(!\alpha, ?\alpha) = \gamma(?\alpha, !\alpha) = ?\alpha$$

and γ is undefined otherwise, and where

$$H = \{!\alpha, ?\alpha \mid \alpha \in \{x = i, x := i \mid i \in \{0, 1, 2\}\}\}.$$

Using the axioms, a linear version of Fischer's protocol is obtained easily. First, linear versions of the protocol entities themselves are presented. The recursion variables A_i describe protocol entity 1 and the recursion variables B_i

describe protocol entity 2. It can be proven that $(\mathrm{TCP}^{\mathrm{drt}^*}_{\mathrm{rec}} + \mathrm{RSP})(A, \gamma) \vdash A = A_0$ and $(\mathrm{TCP}^{\mathrm{drt}^*}_{\mathrm{rec}} + \mathrm{RSP})(A, \gamma) \vdash B = B_0$.

$$
\begin{aligned}
A_0 &= \underline{1} + \underline{?(x = 0)}.A_1 + \sigma.A_0 \\
A_1 &= \underline{!(x := 1)}.A_2 \\
A_2 &= \sigma.A_3 \\
A_3 &= \underline{?(x = 0)}.A_0 + \underline{?(x = 1)}.A_4 + \underline{?(x = 2)}.A_0 \\
A_4 &= \underline{enterCS_1}.A_5 \\
A_5 &= \underline{leaveCS_1}.A_6 + \sigma.A_5 \\
A_6 &= \underline{!(x := 0)}.A_0
\end{aligned}
$$

$$
\begin{aligned}
B_0 &= \underline{1} + \underline{?(x = 0)}.B_1 + \sigma.B_0 \\
B_1 &= \underline{!(x := 2)}.B_2 \\
B_2 &= \sigma.B_3 \\
B_3 &= \underline{?(x = 0)}.B_0 + \underline{?(x = 1)}.B_0 + \underline{?(x = 2)}.B_4 \\
B_4 &= \underline{enterCS_2}.B_5 \\
B_5 &= \underline{leaveCS_2}.B_6 + \sigma.B_5 \\
B_6 &= \underline{!(x := 0)}.B_0
\end{aligned}
$$

Linearizing process *FP*, which is derivably equal to $\partial_H(A_0 \parallel X_0 \parallel B_0)$, results in the following 32 recursive equations. The recursion variable S_{ijk} corresponds to the process term $\partial_H(A_i \parallel X_j \parallel B_k)$, which means that $FP \equiv S_{000}$.

$$
\begin{aligned}
S_{000} &= \partial_H(A_0 \parallel X_0 \parallel B_0) \\
&= \underline{1} + \underline{\mathbf{?}(x = 0)}.\partial_H(A_1 \parallel X_0 \parallel B_0) \\
&\qquad + \underline{\mathbf{?}(x = 0)}.\partial_H(A_0 \parallel X_0 \parallel B_1) + \sigma.\partial_H(A_0 \parallel X_0 \parallel B_0) \\
&= \underline{1} + \underline{\mathbf{?}(x = 0)}.S_{100} + \underline{\mathbf{?}(x = 0)}.S_{001} + \sigma.S_{000}
\end{aligned}
$$

$$
\begin{aligned}
S_{100} &= \partial_H(A_1 \parallel X_0 \parallel B_0) \\
&= \underline{\mathbf{?}(x := 1)}.\partial_H(A_2 \parallel X_1 \parallel B_0) + \underline{\mathbf{?}(x = 0)}.\partial_H(A_1 \parallel X_0 \parallel B_1) \\
&= \underline{\mathbf{?}(x := 1)}.S_{210} + \underline{\mathbf{?}(x = 0)}.S_{101}
\end{aligned}
$$

$$
\begin{aligned}
S_{001} &= \partial_H(A_0 \parallel X_0 \parallel B_1) \\
&= \underline{\mathbf{?}(x = 0)}.\partial_H(A_1 \parallel X_0 \parallel B_1) + \underline{\mathbf{?}(x := 2)}.\partial_H(A_0 \parallel X_2 \parallel B_2) \\
&= \underline{\mathbf{?}(x = 0)}.S_{101} + \underline{\mathbf{?}(x := 2)}.S_{022}
\end{aligned}
$$

$$
\begin{aligned}
S_{210} &= \partial_H(A_2 \parallel X_1 \parallel B_0) \\
&= \sigma.\partial_H(A_3 \parallel X_1 \parallel B_0) \\
&= \sigma.S_{310}
\end{aligned}
$$

$$
\begin{aligned}
S_{101} &= \partial_H(A_1 \parallel X_0 \parallel B_1) \\
&= \underline{\mathbf{?}(x := 1)}.\partial_H(A_2 \parallel X_1 \parallel B_1) + \underline{\mathbf{?}(x := 2)}.\partial_H(A_1 \parallel X_2 \parallel B_2) \\
&= \underline{\mathbf{?}(x := 1)}.S_{211} + \underline{\mathbf{?}(x := 2)}.S_{122}
\end{aligned}
$$

$$\begin{aligned} S_{022} &= \partial_H(A_0 \parallel X_2 \parallel B_2) \\ &= \sigma.\partial_H(A_0 \parallel X_2 \parallel B_3) \\ &= \sigma.S_{023} \end{aligned}$$

$$\begin{aligned} S_{310} &= \partial_H(A_3 \parallel X_1 \parallel B_0) \\ &= \underline{?(x = 1)}.\partial_H(A_4 \parallel X_1 \parallel B_0) \\ &= \underline{?(x = 1)}.S_{410} \end{aligned}$$

$$\begin{aligned} S_{211} &= \partial_H(A_2 \parallel X_1 \parallel B_1) \\ &= \underline{?(x := 2)}.\partial_H(A_2 \parallel X_2 \parallel B_2) \\ &= \underline{?(x := 2)}.S_{222} \end{aligned}$$

$$\begin{aligned} S_{122} &= \partial_H(A_1 \parallel X_2 \parallel B_2) \\ &= \underline{?(x := 1)}.\partial_H(A_2 \parallel X_1 \parallel B_2) \\ &= \underline{?(x := 1)}.S_{212} \end{aligned}$$

$$\begin{aligned} S_{023} &= \partial_H(A_0 \parallel X_2 \parallel B_3) \\ &= \underline{?(x = 2)}.\partial_H(A_0 \parallel X_2 \parallel B_4) \\ &= \underline{?(x = 2)}.S_{024} \end{aligned}$$

$$\begin{aligned} S_{410} &= \partial_H(A_4 \parallel X_1 \parallel B_0) \\ &= \underline{enterCS_1}.\partial_H(A_5 \parallel X_1 \parallel B_0) \\ &= \underline{enterCS_1}.S_{510} \end{aligned}$$

$$\begin{aligned} S_{222} &= \partial_H(A_2 \parallel X_2 \parallel B_2) \\ &= \sigma.\partial_H(A_3 \parallel X_2 \parallel B_3) \\ &= \sigma.S_{323} \end{aligned}$$

$$\begin{aligned} S_{212} &= \partial_H(A_2 \parallel X_1 \parallel B_2) \\ &= \sigma.\partial_H(A_3 \parallel X_1 \parallel B_3) \\ &= \sigma.S_{313} \end{aligned}$$

$$\begin{aligned} S_{024} &= \partial_H(A_0 \parallel X_2 \parallel B_4) \\ &= \underline{enterCS_2}.\partial_H(A_0 \parallel X_2 \parallel B_5) \\ &= \underline{enterCS_2}.S_{025} \end{aligned}$$

$$\begin{aligned} S_{510} &= \partial_H(A_5 \parallel X_1 \parallel B_0) \\ &= \underline{leaveCS_1}.\partial_H(A_6 \parallel X_1 \parallel B_0) + \sigma.\partial_H(A_5 \parallel X_1 \parallel B_0) \\ &= \underline{leaveCS_1}.S_{610} + \sigma.S_{510} \end{aligned}$$

$$\begin{aligned} S_{323} &= \partial_H(A_3 \parallel X_2 \parallel B_3) \\ &= \underline{?(x = 2)}.S_{023} + \underline{?(x = 2)}.S_{324} \end{aligned}$$

$$\begin{aligned} S_{313} &= \partial_H(A_3 \parallel X_1 \parallel B_3) \\ &= \underline{?(x = 1)}.S_{413} + \underline{?(x = 1)}.S_{310} \end{aligned}$$

$$S_{025} = \partial_H(A_0 \parallel X_2 \parallel B_5) = \underline{leaveCS_2}.S_{026} + \sigma.S_{025}$$

$$S_{610} = \partial_H(A_6 \parallel X_1 \parallel B_0) = \underline{?(x := 0)}.S_{000}$$

$$S_{324} = \partial_H(A_3 \parallel X_2 \parallel B_4) = \underline{?(x = 2)}.S_{024} + \underline{enterCS_2}.S_{325}$$

$$S_{413} = \partial_H(A_4 \parallel X_1 \parallel B_3) = \underline{enterCS_1}.S_{513} + \underline{?(x = 1)}.S_{410}$$

$$S_{026} = \partial_H(A_0 \parallel X_2 \parallel B_6) = \underline{?(x := 0)}.S_{000}$$

$$S_{325} = \partial_H(A_3 \parallel X_2 \parallel B_5) = \underline{?(x = 2)}.S_{025} + \underline{leaveCS_2}.S_{326}$$

$$S_{513} = \partial_H(A_5 \parallel X_1 \parallel B_3) = \underline{leaveCS_1}.S_{613} + \underline{?(x = 1)}.S_{510}$$

$$S_{326} = \partial_H(A_3 \parallel X_2 \parallel B_6) = \underline{?(x = 2)}.S_{026} + \underline{?(x := 0)}.S_{300}$$

$$S_{613} = \partial_H(A_6 \parallel X_1 \parallel B_3) = \underline{?(x := 0)}.S_{003} + \underline{?(x = 1)}.S_{610}$$

$$S_{300} = \partial_H(A_3 \parallel X_0 \parallel B_0) = \underline{?(x = 0)}.S_{000} + \underline{?(x = 0)}.S_{301}$$

$$S_{003} = \partial_H(A_0 \parallel X_0 \parallel B_3) = \underline{?(x = 0)}.S_{103} + \underline{?(x = 0)}.S_{000}$$

$$S_{301} = \partial_H(A_3 \parallel X_0 \parallel B_1) = \underline{?(x = 0)}.S_{001} + \underline{?(x := 2)}.S_{322}$$

$$S_{103} = \partial_H(A_1 \parallel X_0 \parallel B_3) = \underline{?(x := 1)}.S_{213} + \underline{?(x = 0)}.S_{100}$$

$$S_{322} = \partial_H(A_3 \parallel X_2 \parallel B_2) = \underline{?(x = 0)}.S_{022}$$

$$S_{213} = \partial_H(A_2 \parallel X_1 \parallel B_3) = \underline{?(x = 1)}.S_{210}$$

Figure 9.3 gives the timed transition system corresponding to the process term *FP*. The ? symbol is omitted from the labels. Also the enter and leave labels are simplified. Whenever a transition has a natural number n as a label, this means that there is a transition for every natural number. By careful inspection of the timed transition system, it can easily be established that indeed there is no possibility to enter a critical section in case the other critical section has already been entered and not yet left.

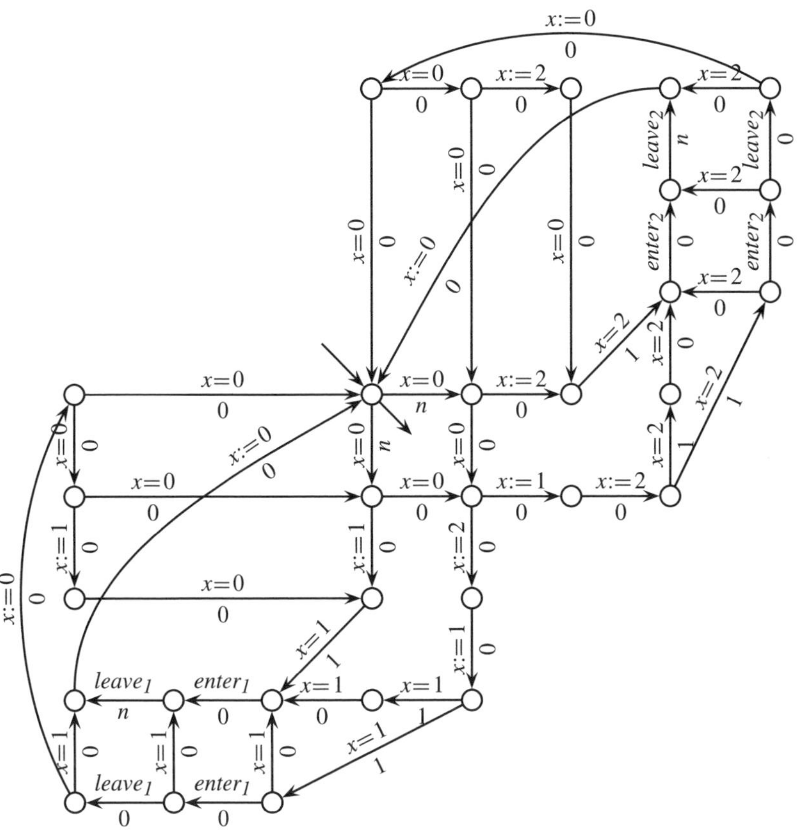

Fig. 9.3. Timed transition system for Fischer's protocol.

9.9 Bibliographical remarks

This chapter finds its origin in (Baeten & Bergstra, 1996). Further development took place in (Baeten, 2003; Baeten & Middelburg, 2002; Baeten & Reniers, 2004; Baeten *et al.*, 2005). Notation follows these references, except that this book uses single underlining instead of double underlining for relative-time theories.

The operational semantics as it is given in this chapter is based on (Baeten

& Reniers, 2004). The treatment of parallel composition is from (Baeten & Reniers, 2007).

The notion of embedding mentioned in Section 9.3 for the relation between the untimed process theory BSP(A)and the timed process theory $\mathrm{BSP}^{\mathrm{drt}}(A)$ is formally defined in (Baeten & Middelburg, 2001).

Essentially, the presentation of Fischer's protocol in Section 9.8 is taken from (Vereijken, 1997). The only difference is that here the protocol entities can stay in their critical sections an arbitrary amount of time, whereas in (Vereijken, 1997) a critical section is left in the same time slice as it was entered.

Closest in syntax elements to the present timed process theory is the work on timed extensions of CSP, see (Reed & Roscoe, 1988; Schneider, 2000). For timed extensions of CCS, see e.g., (Moller & Tofts, 1990; Yi, 1991; Hennessy & Regan, 1995). A comparison is made in (Corradini *et al.*, 1999). Other related timed process theories are ATP, see (Nicollin & Sifakis, 1994), and timed LOTOS, see for example (Quemada *et al.*, 1993).

10

Data and states

10.1 Introduction

In the previous chapters, data types have been handled in an informal way. An alternative composition parameterized by a finite data type D, written as $\sum_{d \in D} t$ with t some process term possibly containing d, was introduced as an abbreviation of a finite expression, and the d occurring in term t was not treated as a (bound) variable. This chapter takes a closer look at data expressions. Such expressions are considered in a more formal way, and the interplay between data and processes is studied. All issues involved can be illustrated by considering just two concrete data types, namely the (finite) data type of the Booleans and the (infinite) data type of the natural numbers. The data type of the natural numbers was also used in the previous chapter to denote time behavior. Considering an uncountable data type as the reals causes additional problems that are avoided in the present text. The use of an uncountable data type in a parameterized alternative composition would, just like the use of an uncountable time domain, provide a means to specify uncountable processes, which is not possible with any of the theories developed in this book.

Notation 10.1.1 (Booleans, propositional logic) Recall from Example 2.3.2 the algebra of the Booleans $\mathbb{B} = (\mathbf{B}, \wedge, \neg, \mathit{true})$. In addition to the constant *true* and the operators $\wedge$ and $\neg$, the binary operators $\vee$ (or) and $\supset$ (implication), and the constant *false* are also used in the remainder. The not so common symbol $\supset$ is used for implication in order to avoid the use of too many arrows in notations.

Let $\mathbf{P} = \{P_1, \ldots, P_n\}$ for some natural number n be a set of so-called propositional variables. Later on, specific instances of these variables are given. Starting from the propositional variables, the Boolean constants and the operators on the Booleans introduced above, it is possible to build terms along the lines of Definition 2.2.3 (Terms). These terms are referred to as propositional terms or propositional logic formulas, and this set of formulas is denoted **FB**. Examples of propositional formulas are $P_1 \wedge true$ and $\neg(P_1 \vee P_2)$. Given specific (Boolean) values for P_1 and P_2, these formulas evaluate either to *true* or to *false*.

Besides a more detailed consideration of data types, this chapter also takes a closer look at the notion of a state. In process algebra, a common assumption is that states are not observable, and the notion of bisimilarity considers unnamed states. Nevertheless, in some cases it is desirable to have certain aspects of a state to be observable. The chapter describes mechanisms in order to realize this. Observable aspects of a state can typically be expressed by means of a propositional logic formula, which links the two main concepts investigated in this chapter, data types and states.

10.2 Guarded commands

The most straightforward connection between data and processes is the use of conditionals. A conditional can be introduced as a constant, or as a unary or binary operator on process terms. In each case, the operator is parameterized by a propositional term. The presentation in this section considers conditionals as unary operators, called the *guarded-command* operators. Given a propositional formula ϕ, the guarded command corresponding to ϕ applied to term x is written as $\phi :\rightarrow x$, with the intuitive meaning '*if* ϕ *then* x'. The extension of basic process theory BSP(A) with guarded commands, called (BSP + GC)(A), is given in Table 10.1. Axioms GC1–6 are mostly self-explanatory.

(BSP + GC)(A)	
BSP(A);	
unary: $(\phi :\rightarrow \_)_{\phi \in \mathbf{FB}}$;	
x, y;	
$true :\rightarrow x = x$	GC1
$false :\rightarrow x = 0$	GC2
$\phi :\rightarrow 0 = 0$	GC3
$\phi :\rightarrow (x + y) = (\phi :\rightarrow x) + (\phi :\rightarrow y)$	GC4
$(\phi \vee \psi) :\rightarrow x = (\phi :\rightarrow x) + (\psi :\rightarrow x)$	GC5
$\phi :\rightarrow (\psi :\rightarrow x) = (\phi \wedge \psi) :\rightarrow x$	GC6

Table 10.1. Process theory (BSP + GC)(A) (with $\phi, \psi \in$ **FB**).

In the remainder, assume, as before, that the unary guarded-command operators bind stronger than binary operators; assume that they bind weaker than other unary operators.

A guarded-command operator blocks further progress if the guard evaluates to false, and does nothing (skips) if the guard evaluates to true. An expression of the form *if* ϕ *then* x *else* y, for propositional formula ϕ and process terms x and y, can be represented by the term $\phi :\rightarrow x + \neg\phi :\rightarrow y$. Guarded commands are similar to encapsulation operators (progress is blocked based on the identity of actions) and projection operators (progress is blocked based on the number of actions that have been executed). However, there are two important differences with these types of operators. First of all, the guarded command applies only to the first action; it disappears as soon as one action is executed. In fact, the absence of an axiom for action-prefix operators in Table 10.1 implies that an action in the context of a guarded command can never be executed without resolving the guard. Second, a guarded command can also block termination ($\mathit{false} :\rightarrow 1 = 0$), whereas encapsulation or projection cannot prevent termination.

An interesting observation is that Axiom GC5, in combination with Axioms GC1 and GC2, causes Axioms A3 and A6 of the basic theory BSP(A) to be derivable (see Exercise 10.2.1).

In line with the above discussion, an expression as $P :\rightarrow a.0$, with P a propositional variable and a an action, cannot be simplified unless the truth value of P is known. As a consequence, there is no elimination theorem as long as there are (unknown) propositional variables.

Related to this last observation is the fact that axioms concerning guarded commands, such as Axioms GC4 and GC5, are in derivations typically used from right to left. In this way, the scope of a conditional is enlarged as much as possible, so that the terms within the scope and/or the signals are amenable to simplification. As a very simple example, consider the following derivation, with x a process term, $a \in A$, and $\phi \in \mathbf{FB}$:

$$
\begin{aligned}
&(\mathrm{BSP} + \mathrm{GC})(A) \vdash \\
&\quad a.(\phi :\rightarrow x + \neg\phi :\rightarrow x) = a.((\phi \vee \neg\phi) :\rightarrow x) = \\
&\qquad a.(\mathit{true} :\rightarrow x) = a.x.
\end{aligned}
$$

In order to give an operational semantics, it is important to note that it is needed to know the values of the propositional variables in order to decide on possible transitions. In realistic processes, furthermore, values of propositional variables can change during the execution of a process. For instance, it can be the case that the value of a propositional variable P is *true* if and only if exactly two actions have been executed. To capture the values of propositional variables in the operational framework of transition-system spaces, it is necessary to associate valuations of the propositional variables, that is, functions v from $\mathbf{P}$ to $\mathbf{B} = \{\mathit{true}, \mathit{false}\}$ to the states of such a space. The set of these valuations is denoted BV. Note that every valuation can easily be extended to a function from propositional formulas in **FB** to **B**. Upon executing an action a in a state with valuation v, a state with a possibly different valuation v' results. The resulting valuation v' is called the *effect* of the execution of action a in a state with valuation v. The effect of action execution can be captured by the following function:

$$\mathit{effect} : A \times BV \to BV.$$

The *effect* function is a parameter of the operational semantics of a process theory with guarded commands. As in the previous chapter, the notion of a transition-system space needs to be redefined. In the current context, it is needed to integrate valuations of propositional variables as explained above. A transition-system space over a set of states is equipped with the following predicates and relations:

- Predicates $\langle \_, v \rangle \downarrow$ for each $v \in BV$;
- Relations $\langle \_, v \rangle \xrightarrow{a} \langle \_, \mathit{effect}(a, v) \rangle$ for each $v \in BV, a \in A$.

The above notation emphasizes that termination predicates and action relations are defined for the combinations of states and valuations. An alternative notation that is in use attaches valuations to the predicate and transition arrows, leading for example to $s \overset{v,a,v'}{\rightarrow} s'$ instead of $\langle s, v \rangle \xrightarrow{a} \langle s', v' \rangle$ (with s and s' states and $v' = \mathit{effect}(a, v)$). This last notation suggests that any valuation-action-effect triple can be seen as a (structured) action itself.

Table 10.2 gives the term deduction system underlying the standard term model for theory $(\mathrm{BSP} + \mathrm{GC})(A)$. Several interesting observations can be made with respect to this term deduction system. First, as already mentioned, the effect function *effect* is a parameter of the term deduction system, which means that the transition systems associated to terms depend on this function. Second, as usual, only $(\mathrm{BSP}+\mathrm{GC})(A)$-terms are considered that do not contain process variables. However, process terms may have propositional variables in guards, because the deduction rules for the guarded-command operators evaluate the guards. $(\mathrm{BSP} + \mathrm{GC})(A)$-terms thus do not need to be closed with respect to propositional variables, but only with respect to process variables. This implies that, for a given *effect* function, the transition system associated to a $(\mathrm{BSP}+\mathrm{GC})(A)$-term that is closed with respect to process variables captures the behavior for *all possible* valuations of the propositional variables *at any point* during the execution of the process.

Example 10.2.1 (Transition systems of $(\mathrm{BSP} + \mathrm{GC})(A)$**-terms)** Let P be a propositional variable, and assume for simplicity that it is the only propositional variable. This means that there are two valuations, v_t with $v_t(P) = \mathit{true}$

$TDS((\mathrm{BSP}+\mathrm{GC})(A), \mathit{effect})$
constant: 0, 1; unary: $(a.\_)_{a \in A}$, $(\phi :\rightarrow \_)_{\phi \in \mathbf{FB}}$; binary: $\_ + \_$;
x, x', y, y';

$$\langle a.x, v\rangle \xrightarrow{a} \langle x, \mathit{effect}(a, v)\rangle \qquad \langle 1, v\rangle\downarrow$$

$$\frac{\langle x, v\rangle \xrightarrow{a} \langle x', v'\rangle}{\langle x+y, v\rangle \xrightarrow{a} \langle x', v'\rangle} \qquad \frac{\langle y, v\rangle \xrightarrow{a} \langle y', v'\rangle}{\langle x+y, v\rangle \xrightarrow{a} \langle y', v'\rangle}$$

$$\frac{\langle x, v\rangle\downarrow}{\langle x+y, v\rangle\downarrow} \qquad \frac{\langle y, v\rangle\downarrow}{\langle x+y, v\rangle\downarrow}$$

$$\frac{\langle x, v\rangle \xrightarrow{a} \langle x', v'\rangle \quad v(\phi) = \mathit{true}}{\langle \phi :\rightarrow x, v\rangle \xrightarrow{a} \langle x', v'\rangle} \qquad \frac{\langle x, v\rangle\downarrow \quad v(\phi) = \mathit{true}}{\langle \phi :\rightarrow x, v\rangle\downarrow}$$

Table 10.2. Term deduction system for $(\mathrm{BSP}+\mathrm{GC})(A)$ (with $\phi \in \mathbf{FB}$, $a \in A$, $v, v' \in BV$).

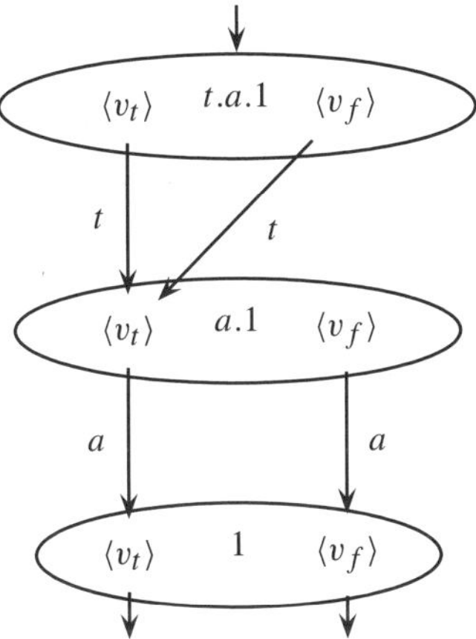

Fig. 10.1. The transition system corresponding to $t.a.1$.

and v_f with $v_f(P) = \mathit{false}$. Thus, $BV = \{v_t, v_f\}$. Let t be an action in A such that for both valuations $v \in BV$, $\mathit{effect}(t, v) = v_t$. Assume that action a does not change a valuation, i.e., $\mathit{effect}(a, v) = v$ for both $v \in BV$.

Consider term $t.a.1$. Figure 10.1 shows the transition system corresponding to this term. The figure visualizes that transitions and termination depend on the valuation of propositional variables.

Figure 10.1 shows that the transition system of a term captures the behavior for all possible valuations for the propositional variables. By assuming an initial valuation, a concrete transition system for that situation can be obtained. For example, when assuming v_t as the initial valuation, term $t.a.1$ results in a transition system of three states with only two transitions. When v_f is the initial valuation, the transition system also has three states and two transitions. The first transition of this transition system changes the valuation from v_f to v_t.

One could wonder whether it is relevant to capture transition $\langle a.1, v_f\rangle \xrightarrow{a} \langle 1, v_f\rangle$ in the transition system. It is clear that this transition can never occur, irrespective of the valuation of the propositional variable P in the initial state. Nevertheless, it is important to capture also this behavior, as becomes clear later on when considering equivalence of processes. As already mentioned, a transition system in the current framework captures the behavior for *all possible* valuations of the propositional variables *in all states* that may occur during the execution of the process.

Another aspect that is worth illustrating is the impact of the *effect* function on state transitions. Assume, for example, that also action t has no effect on the valuation of propositional variable P. This would result in a change of transition $\langle t.a.1, v_f\rangle \xrightarrow{a} \langle a.1, v_t\rangle$ into $\langle t.a.1, v_f\rangle \xrightarrow{a} \langle a.1, v_f\rangle$.

Finally, consider the term $t.(P :\rightarrow a.1)$, assuming the original definition for the *effect* function. Despite the fact that this term has a propositional variable, the term deduction system of Table 10.2 associates a transition system with it. The transition system, shown in Figure 10.2, is very similar to the transition system of Figure 10.1. It has different terms associated with the top two states, and the rightmost transition between the bottom two states does not exist, i.e., $\langle P :\rightarrow a.1, v_f\rangle \stackrel{a}{\not\rightarrow}$. It is interesting to observe that, irrespective of the initial valuation of the propositional variable, the observable transitions of the two transition systems in Figures 10.1 and 10.2 are identical.

The introduction of propositional variables and valuations of those variables has led to an adapted notion of transition-system spaces. It is also necessary to reconsider the notion of bisimilarity. The following example illustrates that it is important to require that two processes can only be bisimilar if they behave the same in all states for all possible valuations of the propositional variables in those states.

Example 10.2.2 (Guarded commands and equivalence of processes)
Consider again terms $t.a.1$ and $t.(P :\rightarrow a.1)$ of Example 10.2.1, and their transition systems given in Figures 10.1 and 10.2. As already explained, when considering any given specific initial valuation of the propositional variable P, these transition systems behave the same. Nevertheless, $t.a.1 = t.(P :\rightarrow a.1)$

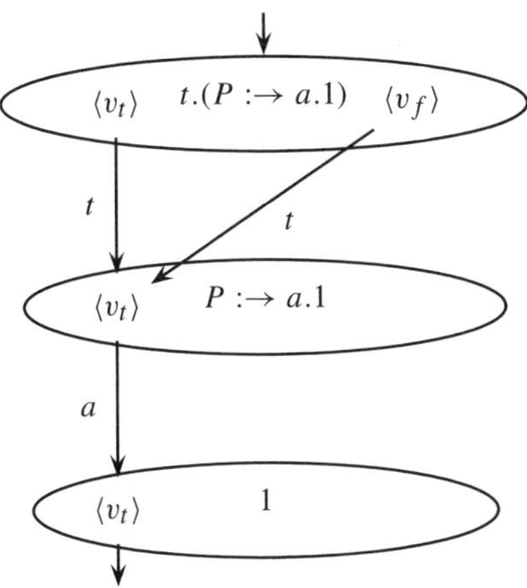

Fig. 10.2. The transition system corresponding to $t.(P :\to a.1)$.

cannot be derived from theory $(\text{BSP} + \text{GC})(A)$, for the simple reason that the theory does not have any axioms to reason in general about processes with propositional variables. As a consequence, the guarded command in the right-hand term cannot be resolved, and it cannot be eliminated.

This apparent mismatch is intentional. The mentioned pair of terms and the processes they define should not be identified. The reason for this becomes clear when considering the extension with parallel composition. Consider again term $t.(P :\to a.1)$. After execution of t, propositional variable P is *true*, but by activity in a parallel component it might be that P has turned *false* again when action a is attempted, effectively blocking the execution of a. The a action cannot be blocked in the process specified by term $t.a.1$. As an example, assume the mentioned processes are running in parallel with the process $f.1$, where f is an action in A such that for all valuations $v \in BV$, $\mathit{effect}(f, v) = v_f$ (with v_f the valuation defined in Example 10.2.1 that sets P to *false*). The resulting processes $t.a.1 \parallel f.1$ and $t.(P :\to a.1) \parallel f.1$ are not equivalent (see Exercise 10.2.3).

By defining an appropriate notion of bisimilarity on the transition systems generated by the operational semantics, it can be ensured that pairs of terms as the one discussed in this example are not bisimilar. The essential point is that all possible valuations of propositional variables should be considered in all states of a process.

Definition 10.2.3 (Bisimilarity) Assume a transition-system space with states S over the set of labels A. A binary relation R on the set of states S is a *bisimulation* relation if and only if the following transfer conditions hold:

(i) for all states $s, t, s' \in S$, whenever $(s, t) \in R$ and $\langle s, v\rangle \xrightarrow{a} \langle s', v'\rangle$ for some $a \in A$ and $v \in BV$ (implying $v' = \mathit{effect}(a, v)$), then there is a state t' such that $\langle t, v\rangle \xrightarrow{a} \langle t', v'\rangle$ and $(s', t') \in R$;

(ii) vice versa, for all states $s, t, t' \in S$, whenever $(s, t) \in R$ and $\langle t, v\rangle \xrightarrow{a} \langle t', v'\rangle$ for some $a \in A$ and $v \in BV$, then there is a state s' such that $\langle s, v\rangle \xrightarrow{a} \langle s', v'\rangle$ and $(s', t') \in R$;

(iii) whenever $(s, t) \in R$ and $\langle s, v\rangle\downarrow$ for some $v \in BV$, then $\langle t, v\rangle\downarrow$;

(iv) whenever $(s, t) \in R$ and $\langle t, v\rangle\downarrow$ for some $v \in BV$, then $\langle s, v\rangle\downarrow$.

Two transition systems $s, t \in S$ are *bisimilar*, denoted by the standard notation as $s \leftrightarrow t$, if and only if there is a bisimulation relation R on S with $(s, t) \in R$.

At this point, it is possible to define a term model for theory $(\text{BSP}+\text{GC})(A)$ along the usual lines. The term algebra consists of the set of $(\text{BSP} + \text{GC})(A)$-terms that are closed with respect to process variables, but not necessarily with respect to propositional variables. The latter is consistent with the fact that the terms define processes whose behavior may depend on the value of propositional variables, of which the value is determined by the initial valuation and the effect of action execution on this valuation. Bisimilarity as defined above is a congruence relation on the resulting algebra of transition systems induced by the term deduction system in Table 10.2. Theory $(\text{BSP} + \text{GC})(A)$ is a sound and ground-complete axiomatization of the term model obtained as the quotient algebra of this algebra of transition systems. Note that this model is parameterized with the *effect* function. The soundness and ground-completeness results hold for *any effect* function and all terms that are closed with respect to process variables. The theory thus allows to prove the equivalence of processes when they behave the same for all possible *effect* functions, all possible initial valuations of propositional variables, and all possible valuations of those variables in any intermediate state. It is not possible to reason about the equivalence of processes for specific *effect* functions and initial valuations. Section 10.5 introduces a family of operators that makes it possible to reason about processes for specific *effect* functions and initial valuations.

Theory $(\text{BSP} + \text{GC})(A)$ is a conservative ground-extension of the basic theory BSP(A). One way to prove this is along the lines of the proof of the conservativity result given in Section 9.6, Theorem 9.6.2. This proof uses the fact that two closed BSP(A)-terms are bisimilar in the current setting if and only if they are strongly bisimilar as defined in the standard framework of Chapter 3. This last result follows from the observations that, in the underlying transition-system space as introduced in this section, successful termination for a closed BSP(A)-term is independent of the particular valuation of the propositional variables and that all transitions with the same action label originating from a given state in the transition-system space end up in the same state.

Extension of theory (BSP + GC)(A) to larger theories, including the extension with recursion, does not present problems. Table 10.3 gives theory (TCP + GC)(A, γ), which extends earlier theories (conservatively with respect to closed terms) with axioms concerning the interplay between guarded commands on the one hand, and sequential composition, encapsulation, or parallel-composition operators on the other hand. In combination with Axiom SC1, Axiom GC9, read from right to left, states that communication can only occur if conditions guarding any of the communicating processes are satisfied.

Consideration should be given to the description of communication. If $\gamma(a, b) = c$, then $\mathit{effect}(c, v)$ should somehow denote the joint effect of the execution of a and b given some valuation v. If the effects of a and b are contradictory, then they should not be able to communicate, and so c cannot be executed. In line with the earlier observation that theory (BSP + GC)(A) can only be used to reason about the equivalence of processes that are equivalent for all valuations of propositional variables in all states of the process, it is necessary to require that a communication between actions a and b can only occur if the effects of these two actions are consistent for all valuations. Formally, for any pair of actions a and b, $\gamma(a, b)$ is defined only if $\mathit{effect}(b, \mathit{effect}(a, v)) = \mathit{effect}(a, \mathit{effect}(b, v)) = \mathit{effect}(\gamma(a, b), v)$ for all valuations $v \in BV$. Table 10.4 shows the deduction rules of the operational semantics of (TCP+GC)(A, γ) that are related to communication. For further details, see Exercise 10.2.5.

(TCP + GC)(A, γ)	
(BSP + GC)(A), TCP(A, γ);	
-	
x, y;	
$\phi :\rightarrow (x \cdot y) = (\phi :\rightarrow x) \cdot y$	GC7
$\phi :\rightarrow (x \mathbin{⌊\!⌊} y) = (\phi :\rightarrow x) \mathbin{⌊\!⌊} y$	GC8
$\phi :\rightarrow (x \mid y) = (\phi :\rightarrow x) \mid y$	GC9
$\phi :\rightarrow \partial_H(x) = \partial_H(\phi :\rightarrow x)$	GC10

Table 10.3. The process theory (TCP + GC)(A, γ) (with $\phi \in \mathbf{FB}$, $H \subseteq A$).

Example 10.2.4 (Guarded commands) Consider a description of the behavior of a spring. There are actions *pull*, *release* and *break*, and propositional variables *extended* and *malfunction*. Action *pull* takes the variable *extended* from *false* to *true*, and action *release* takes this value back from *true* to *false*.

$\underline{\quad TDS((\mathrm{TCP}+\mathrm{GC})(A,\gamma), \mathit{effect}) \qquad\qquad}$
$TDS((\mathrm{BSP}+\mathrm{GC})(A), \mathit{effect})$;

unary: $(\partial_H)_{H \subseteq A}$; binary: $\_\cdot\_, \_\parallel\_, \_\mathbin{⌊\!⌊}\_, \_\mid\_$;

x, x', y, y';

$$\frac{\langle x, v\rangle \xrightarrow{a} \langle x', v'\rangle \quad \langle y, v\rangle \xrightarrow{b} \langle y', v''\rangle \quad \gamma(a,b)=c}{\langle x \parallel y, v\rangle \xrightarrow{c} \langle x' \parallel y', \mathit{effect}(c, v)\rangle}$$

$$\frac{\langle x, v\rangle \xrightarrow{a} \langle x', v'\rangle \quad \langle y, v\rangle \xrightarrow{b} \langle y', v''\rangle \quad \gamma(a,b)=c}{\langle x \mid y, v\rangle \xrightarrow{c} \langle x' \parallel y', \mathit{effect}(c, v)\rangle}$$

...

Table 10.4. Some operational rules from the term deduction system for $(\mathrm{TCP}+\mathrm{GC})(A,\gamma)$ (with $a, b, c \in A$, $v, v', v'' \in BV$).

Action *break* can only occur when the spring is extended, and causes a malfunction, changing the value of *malfunction* from *false* to *true*. The spring can only be pulled again, if it has not yet malfunctioned. The spring process can terminate successfully if the spring is not extended or broken. The following recursive specification defines the process *Spring* with the use of a recursion variable X. There is no communication in this example.

$$\begin{aligned} X &= 1 + \mathit{pull}.\mathit{release}.(\neg \mathit{malfunction} :\rightarrow X) \\ \mathit{Spring} &= X \parallel (1 + \mathit{extended} :\rightarrow \mathit{break}.1). \end{aligned}$$

When assuming the initial valuation that sets propositional variables *extended* and *malfunction* to *false*, process *Spring* has the expected operational behavior (see Exercise 10.2.4).

Exercises

10.2.1 Derive Axioms A3 and A6 from the other axioms of $(\mathrm{BSP}+\mathrm{GC})(A)$.

10.2.2 Draw the transition system for term $t.(P :\rightarrow a.1 + \neg P :\rightarrow b.0)$. Assume that P, t, and a are as defined in Example 10.2.1 (Transition systems of $(\mathrm{BSP}+\mathrm{GC})(A)$-terms), and assume that b has no effect on the value of propositional variable P. Establish, using Definition 10.2.3 (Bisimilarity), that the transition system is not bisimilar to the transition system of term $t.a.1$, illustrated in Figure 10.1.

10.2.3 Consider the terms $t.a.1 \parallel f.1$ and $t.(P :\rightarrow a.1) \parallel f.1$ discussed in Example 10.2.2 (Guarded commands and equivalence of processes), and assume that there is no communication. Draw the transition systems for these two terms, and establish that they are not bisimilar.

10.2.4 Draw the transition system of the spring in Example 10.2.4 (Guarded commands) for the concrete initial valuation that sets both variables *extended* and *malfunction* to *false*. Give for each state the variables that are true in that state.

10.2.5 Complete the term deduction system given in Table 10.4 for theory $(\text{TCP} + \text{GC})(A, \gamma)$. Prove a soundness and ground-completeness result. Prove that all operators new in $(\text{TCP} + \text{GC})(A, \gamma)$ compared to $(\text{BSP} + \text{GC})(A)$ can be eliminated and show that $(\text{TCP} + \text{GC})(A, \gamma)$ is a conservative ground-extension of $(\text{BSP} + \text{GC})(A)$.

10.3 The inaccessible process

In the course of the explorations performed in the remainder of this chapter, inconsistency of a state can be encountered. This section therefore introduces a new constant $\perp$ that denotes an inaccessible state, a state that cannot be entered by the execution of an action. Intuitively, this process denotes a state where *false* holds. As *false* can never hold, this is a state that a process can never get into. Sometimes, this process is called (rather contradictorily) the non-existent process. Here, the name *inaccessible process* is used. The theory $\text{BSP}_\perp(A)$ extends the theory BSP(A) with the extra constant $\perp$ and adds two axioms. Table 10.5 gives theory $\text{BSP}_\perp(A)$, BSP(A) with the inaccessible process. Axiom IP1 explains that in an inaccessible state, it does not matter which extra options are available, as the state will remain inaccessible; Axiom IP2 states that an inaccessible state cannot be entered by executing an action, as the action will be blocked in this case. $\text{BSP}_\perp(A)$ is a conservative ground-extension of BSP(A); the inaccessible process cannot be eliminated.

$\text{BSP}_\perp(A)$	
BSP(A);	
constant: $\perp$;	
x;	
$x + \perp = \perp$	IP1
$a.\perp = 0$	IP2

Table 10.5. The process theory $\text{BSP}_\perp(A)$ (with $a \in A$).

The term model for the basic process theory $\text{BSP}_\perp(A)$ is omitted. Instead, an operational semantics is given for an equational theory combining the inaccessible process and guarded commands.

Theory $(\mathrm{BSP}_\perp + \mathrm{GC})(A)$, the theory of basic sequential processes with the inaccessible process and guarded commands, simply combines the signature and axioms of theories $(\mathrm{BSP} + \mathrm{GC})(A)$ of Table 10.1 and $\mathrm{BSP}_\perp(A)$ given above. To give an operational semantics for $(\mathrm{BSP}_\perp + \mathrm{GC})(A)$, it is not only necessary to consider valuations of propositional variables, as in the previous section, but it is also necessary to take into account the consistency of states. To do so, a transition-system space as introduced in the previous section is equipped with the following additional set of predicates:

- A predicate $\langle \_, v\rangle \searrow$ for each $v \in BV$, denoting the consistency of the operand state for the given valuation.

In the transition-system space that underlies an operational semantics for a process theory with the inaccessible process $\perp$, predicates $\langle \_, v\rangle \searrow$ are needed to distinguish $\perp$ from other processes. In the current context, consistency of states does not depend on the valuation of propositional variables. All these predicates hold for all processes that do not reduce to $\perp$. Later in this chapter, consistency does depend on the valuations.

Table 10.6 gives the term deduction system underlying the standard term model for theory $(\mathrm{BSP}_\perp + \mathrm{GC})(A)$. Compared to the term deduction system given for $(\mathrm{BSP}{+}\mathrm{GC})(A)$ in Table 10.2, Table 10.6 contains extra rules defining the consistency predicates; furthermore, the deduction rules for the termination predicates and the transition relations contain extra consistency requirements in the premises, conforming to the intuition behind the inaccessible process. For example, the rule defining the transition relation for action-prefix operators requires that the process resulting after performing the action should be consistent, in line with Axiom IP2.

Because of the introduction of the consistency predicates, it is necessary to reconsider the notion of bisimilarity.

Definition 10.3.1 (Bisimilarity) Assume a transition-system space with states S over the set of labels A. A binary relation R on the set of states S is a bisimulation relation if and only if it satisfies the transfer conditions of Definition 10.2.3 and the following additional conditions:

(v) whenever $(s, t) \in R$ and $\langle s, v\rangle \searrow$ for some $v \in BV$, then $\langle t, v\rangle \searrow$;
(vi) whenever $(s, t) \in R$ and $\langle t, v\rangle \searrow$ for some $v \in BV$, then $\langle s, v\rangle \searrow$.

As before, two transition systems $s, t \in S$ are *bisimilar*, again denoted $s \leftrightarrow t$, if and only if there is a bisimulation relation R on S with $(s, t) \in R$.

$TDS((\mathrm{BSP}_\perp + \mathrm{GC})(A), \mathit{effect})$
constant: $0, 1, \perp$; unary: $(a.\_)_{a \in A}, (\phi :\rightarrow \_)_{\phi \in \mathbf{FB}}$; binary: $\_ + \_$;
x, x', y, y';

$$\langle 0, v\rangle \searrow \qquad \langle 1, v\rangle \searrow \qquad \langle 1, v\rangle\downarrow$$

$$\frac{\langle x, v'\rangle \searrow \quad v' = \mathit{effect}(a, v)}{\langle a.x, v\rangle \xrightarrow{a} \langle x, v'\rangle} \qquad \langle a.x, v\rangle \searrow$$

$$\frac{\langle x, v\rangle \xrightarrow{a} \langle x', v'\rangle \quad \langle y, v\rangle \searrow}{\langle x + y, v\rangle \xrightarrow{a} \langle x', v'\rangle} \qquad \frac{\langle y, v\rangle \xrightarrow{a} \langle y', v'\rangle \quad \langle x, v\rangle \searrow}{\langle x + y, v\rangle \xrightarrow{a} \langle y', v'\rangle}$$

$$\frac{\langle x, v\rangle\downarrow \quad \langle y, v\rangle \searrow}{\langle x + y, v\rangle\downarrow} \qquad \frac{\langle y, v\rangle\downarrow \quad \langle x, v\rangle \searrow}{\langle x + y, v\rangle\downarrow} \qquad \frac{\langle x, v\rangle \searrow \quad \langle y, v\rangle \searrow}{\langle x + y, v\rangle \searrow}$$

$$\frac{\langle x, v\rangle \searrow \quad v(\phi) = \mathit{true}}{\langle \phi :\rightarrow x, v\rangle \searrow} \qquad \frac{\langle x, v\rangle \downarrow \quad v(\phi) = \mathit{true}}{\langle \phi :\rightarrow x, v\rangle \downarrow}$$

$$\frac{\langle x, v\rangle \xrightarrow{a} \langle x', v'\rangle \quad v(\phi) = \mathit{true}}{\langle \phi :\rightarrow x, v\rangle \xrightarrow{a} \langle x', v'\rangle} \qquad \frac{v(\phi) = \mathit{false}}{\langle \phi :\rightarrow x, v\rangle \searrow}$$

Table 10.6. Term deduction system for $(\mathrm{BSP}_\perp + \mathrm{GC})(A)$ (with $\phi \in \mathbf{FB}$, $a \in A$, $v, v' \in BV$).

At this point, a term model of $(\mathrm{BSP}_\perp + \mathrm{GC})(A)$ can be constructed along the usual lines, for which $(\mathrm{BSP}_\perp + \mathrm{GC})(A)$ is a ground-complete axiomatization. As in the previous section, the *effect* function is a parameter of this model. Theory $(\mathrm{BSP}_\perp + \mathrm{GC})(A)$ does not allow any elimination results, but it is a conservative ground-extension of theories $\mathrm{BSP}_\perp(A)$ and $(\mathrm{BSP} + \mathrm{GC})(A)$.

Theory $(\mathrm{BSP}_\perp + \mathrm{GC})(A)$ can be extended to larger theories as usual. Table 10.7 gives theory $(\mathrm{TCP}_\perp + \mathrm{GC})(A, \gamma)$. As in the previous section, the communication and *effect* functions should be defined in a consistent way. Further details are left to the reader.

Exercises

10.3.1 Give an operational semantics for theory $\mathrm{BSP}_\perp(A)$, based on a transition-system space without valuation predicates but with a (single) consistency predicate.

10.3.2 Recall Proposition 5.5.14 (Guardedness). Consider theory $\mathrm{BSP}_\perp(A)$ with recursion. Prove that the unguarded recursive specification $\{X = \perp + X\}$ has only one solution, for any action set A.

(TCP$_\perp$ + GC)(A, γ)	
(TCP + GC)(A, γ), BSP$_\perp(A)$;	
-	
x;	
$\perp \cdot x = \perp$	IP3
$\perp \mathbin{\|\!\lfloor} x = \perp$	IP4
$x \mathbin{\|\!\lfloor} \perp = \perp$	IP5
$\perp \mid x = \perp$	IP6
$\partial_H(\perp) = \perp$	IP7

Table 10.7. Theory (TCP$_\perp$ + GC)(A, γ) (with $H \subseteq A$).

10.3.3 The inaccessible process $\perp$ resembles to some extent the chaos process τ^*0 discussed in Section 8.7, that led to theory (BSP$^*_\tau$ + CH)(A) of Table 8.11 with a non-standard model developed in Exercise 8.7.6. Compare the inaccessible process and the chaos process, by investigating typical laws satisfied by these two processes.

10.4 Propositional signals

Building upon the concepts of conditionals and the inaccessible process of the previous sections, this section describes a mechanism that allows to observe aspects of the current state of a process in the equational theory. The central assumption is that the visible part of the state of a process is a proposition, an expression in propositional logic as defined in Notation 10.1.1. Such a proposition representing the visible aspects of a process state is called a *signal*. Conditionals are used to observe signals.

The introduction of the *root-signal emission operator* $\wedge\!\!\!\!\!\blacktriangle$ is done in Table 10.8. A term of the form $\phi \wedge\!\!\!\!\!\blacktriangle x$ represents the process x, that shows the signal ϕ in its initial state.

Axiom RSE1 states that any process emits a *true* signal. A process emitting a signal denotes that this signal holds in the initial state of the process. Falsity never holds, so a state emitting *false* cannot occur, is inaccessible. This explains RSE2, and shows the usefulness of the inaccessible process. (Technically, the inclusion of the inaccessible process in the theory is not strictly necessary because its role can be taken over by a term such as *false* $\wedge\!\!\!\!\!\blacktriangle 0$.) Axiom RSE3 states that the inaccessible process does not emit any signals. Note that Axiom RSE3 is derivable from the other axioms of (BSP$_\perp$ + RSE)(A) (see Exercise 10.4.1).

Axiom RSE4 in Table 10.8 shows that the signals of a summand in an

(BSP$_\perp$ + RSE)(A)
(BSP$_\perp$ + GC)(A);
unary: $(\phi \mathbin{{}^{\wedge\!\!\blacktriangle}} \_)_{\phi \in \mathbf{FB}}$;
x, y;
$true \mathbin{{}^{\wedge\!\!\blacktriangle}} x = x$ — RSE1
$false \mathbin{{}^{\wedge\!\!\blacktriangle}} x = \perp$ — RSE2
$\phi \mathbin{{}^{\wedge\!\!\blacktriangle}} \perp = \perp$ — RSE3
$(\phi \mathbin{{}^{\wedge\!\!\blacktriangle}} x) + y = \phi \mathbin{{}^{\wedge\!\!\blacktriangle}} (x + y)$ — RSE4
$\phi \mathbin{{}^{\wedge\!\!\blacktriangle}} (\psi \mathbin{{}^{\wedge\!\!\blacktriangle}} x) = (\phi \wedge \psi) \mathbin{{}^{\wedge\!\!\blacktriangle}} x$ — RSE5
$\phi :\rightarrow (\psi \mathbin{{}^{\wedge\!\!\blacktriangle}} x) = (\phi \supset \psi) \mathbin{{}^{\wedge\!\!\blacktriangle}} (\phi :\rightarrow x)$ — RSE6
$\phi \mathbin{{}^{\wedge\!\!\blacktriangle}} (\phi :\rightarrow x) = \phi \mathbin{{}^{\wedge\!\!\blacktriangle}} x$ — RSE7

Table 10.8. The process theory (BSP$_\perp$ + RSE)(A) (with $\phi, \psi \in \mathbf{FB}$).

alternative composition carry over to the whole process. It can be given in a more symmetric form as follows:

$$(\phi \mathbin{{}^{\wedge\!\!\blacktriangle}} x) + (\psi \mathbin{{}^{\wedge\!\!\blacktriangle}} y) = (\phi \wedge \psi) \mathbin{{}^{\wedge\!\!\blacktriangle}} (x + y) .$$

This identity depends on the fact that the roots of two processes in an alternative composition are identified. Therefore, signals must be combined. Exercise 10.4.2 shows that this generalized version of Axiom RSE4 is derivable from the theory. It is straightforward to show that the general identity implies Axiom RSE4 as given in Table 10.8. Also notice that Axiom IP1, given in Table 10.5, is derivable from RSE4.

Axiom RSE5 expresses the fact that there is no sequential order in the presentation of signals. The combination of the signals is taking both of them.

As an example, consider the following derivation:

$$\begin{aligned}&(\mathrm{BSP}_\perp + \mathrm{RSE})(A) \vdash \\ &\quad a.((\phi \mathbin{{}^{\wedge\!\!\blacktriangle}} x) + (\neg\phi \mathbin{{}^{\wedge\!\!\blacktriangle}} x)) = a.((\phi \wedge \neg\phi) \mathbin{{}^{\wedge\!\!\blacktriangle}} x) = \\ &\qquad a.(false \mathbin{{}^{\wedge\!\!\blacktriangle}} x) = a.\perp = 0.\end{aligned}$$

Axiom RSE6 expresses how to take a signal outside of a conditional: signal ψ is only emitted if condition ϕ is true. The last axiom, RSE7, is the *signal inspection rule*. It says that a conditional can be removed if the state emits a signal that validates the conditional. In other words, if a signal ϕ is emitted, then ϕ holds in the current state and a conditional with guard ϕ can be removed. Note that RSE7 can be generalized as follows:

$$\begin{aligned}&(\mathrm{BSP}_\perp + \mathrm{RSE})(A) \vdash \\ &\quad \phi \mathbin{{}^{\wedge\!\!\blacktriangle}} ((\phi \wedge \psi) :\rightarrow x) = \phi \mathbin{{}^{\wedge\!\!\blacktriangle}} (\phi :\rightarrow (\psi :\rightarrow x)) = \phi \mathbin{{}^{\wedge\!\!\blacktriangle}} (\psi :\rightarrow x) .\end{aligned}$$

An interesting identity that follows from the theory is the following:

Proposition 10.4.1 (Signals) $(\mathrm{BSP}_\perp + \mathrm{RSE})(A) \vdash \phi \mathbin{^\wedge} x = (\phi \mathbin{^\wedge} 0) + x$.

Proof Exercise 10.4.2. □

The equation in Proposition 10.4.1 is very useful for writing process specifications because it allows to a large extent to work with algebraic expressions that are not cluttered with signal emissions. It provides the basis for a notion of basic terms, as introduced before in Chapters 2 and 9. Only the inaction constant emits a signal in basic terms. As conditions, only propositional formulas different from *false* are allowed. This guarantees that all actions and terminations occurring in a term can actually be executed at some point. Signal *false* is allowed as a signal emitted by the 0 constant. By doing so, it is possible to represent $\perp$ as $\mathit{false} \mathbin{^\wedge} 0$.

Definition 10.4.2 (Basic $(\mathrm{BSP}_\perp + \mathrm{RSE})(A)$-terms) The set of basic $(\mathrm{BSP}_\perp + \mathrm{RSE})(A)$-terms is defined inductively:

(i) if $\phi \in \mathbf{FB}$, then $\phi \mathbin{^\wedge} 0$ is a basic term;
(ii) if ϕ is not equivalent to *false*, then $\phi :\rightarrow 1$ is a basic term;
(iii) if ϕ is not equivalent to *false*, if $a \in A$ and if t is a basic $(\mathrm{BSP}_\perp + \mathrm{RSE})(A)$-term, then $\phi :\rightarrow a.t$ is a basic term;
(iv) if s, t are basic terms, then $s + t$ is a basic term.

Each basic term can be written in the form

$$\chi \mathbin{^\wedge} 0 + \sum_{i=1}^{n} \phi_i :\rightarrow a_i.t_i + (\psi :\rightarrow 1),$$

where $n \geq 0$, where $\chi \in \mathbf{FB}$ is an arbitrary propositional formula, conditions ϕ_i and ψ are formulas all different from *false*, where all $a_i \in A$ and all t_i are basic terms, and where the termination term may or may not occur (as denoted via the parentheses).

As before, an elimination result can be proven. The proof uses Proposition 10.4.1 (Signals) and the lemma given below. Note that it is not possible to eliminate signals entirely. Theory $(\mathrm{BSP}_\perp + \mathrm{RSE})(A)$ does in general not have any means to remove signals that do not resolve to *true* or *false*.

Proposition 10.4.3 (Reduction to basic terms) For any closed $(\mathrm{BSP}_\perp + \mathrm{RSE})(A)$-term p, there exists a basic $(\mathrm{BSP}_\perp + \mathrm{RSE})(A)$-term q such that $(\mathrm{BSP}_\perp + \mathrm{RSE})(A) \vdash p = q$.

Proof Exercise 10.4.3. □

Lemma 10.4.4 $(\mathrm{BSP}_\perp + \mathrm{RSE})(A) \vdash \phi :\rightarrow \perp = \neg\phi \,{}^\wedge 0$.

Proof

$$(\mathrm{BSP}_\perp + \mathrm{RSE})(A) \vdash \phi :\rightarrow \perp = \phi :\rightarrow (\mathit{false} \,{}^\wedge 0) = (\phi \supset \mathit{false}) \,{}^\wedge (\phi :\rightarrow 0) = \neg\phi \,{}^\wedge 0 .$$

□

$(\mathrm{BSP}_\perp + \mathrm{RSE})(A)$ is a conservative ground-extension of $(\mathrm{BSP}_\perp + \mathrm{GC})(A)$.

The next step is to look at an operational semantics. Table 10.9 presents the term deduction system for $(\mathrm{BSP}_\perp + \mathrm{RSE})(A)$, which builds upon the term deduction system of $(\mathrm{BSP}_\perp + \mathrm{GC})(A)$ that is given in Table 10.6. It has an *effect* function as a parameter, and besides transition and termination predicates, it contains a consistency predicate, as explained in the previous section. The rules are straightforward: in order to execute an action, terminate or be consistent in a certain state, the signal emitted in that state must evaluate to true. The development of a term model for which $(\mathrm{BSP}_\perp + \mathrm{RSE})(A)$ is a ground-complete axiomatization goes along the usual lines.

$TDS((\mathrm{BSP}_\perp + \mathrm{RSE})(A), \mathit{effect})$
$TDS((\mathrm{BSP}_\perp + \mathrm{GC})(A), \mathit{effect})$;
unary: $(\phi \,{}^\wedge \_)_{\phi \in \mathbf{FB}}$;
x, x';
$\dfrac{\langle x, v\rangle \xrightarrow{a} \langle x', v'\rangle \quad v(\phi) = \mathit{true}}{\langle \phi \,{}^\wedge x, v\rangle \xrightarrow{a} \langle x', v'\rangle}$
$\dfrac{\langle x, v\rangle \downarrow \quad v(\phi) = \mathit{true}}{\langle \phi \,{}^\wedge x, v\rangle \downarrow}$ $\qquad$ $\dfrac{\langle x, v\rangle \searrow \quad v(\phi) = \mathit{true}}{\langle \phi \,{}^\wedge x, v\rangle \searrow}$

Table 10.9. Term deduction system for $(\mathrm{BSP}_\perp + \mathrm{RSE})(A)$ (with $\phi \in \mathbf{FB}$, $a \in A$, $v, v' \in BV$).

Extensions follow the usual pattern. The next example shows a stack specification, using $(\mathrm{BSP}_\perp + \mathrm{RSE})(A)$ extended with recursion.

Example 10.4.5 (Stack) The specification of the stack from Section 5.6 can be modified with signals *empty* and *ontop*(d) for all $d \in D$ that show the top of the stack.

$$\begin{aligned} \mathit{Stack}1 &= S_\epsilon, \\ S_\epsilon &= \mathit{empty} \,{}^\wedge 1 + \sum_{d \in D} \mathit{push}(d).S_d, \text{ and, for all } d \in D, \sigma \in D^*, \\ S_{d\sigma} &= \mathit{ontop}(d) \,{}^\wedge \mathit{pop}(d).S_\sigma + \sum_{e \in D} \mathit{push}(e).S_{ed\sigma}. \end{aligned}$$

The extension of $(\mathrm{BSP}_\perp + \mathrm{RSE})(A)$ with sequential composition also does not present difficulties. Axioms are presented in Table 10.10, and operational rules in Table 10.11. The operational rules reflect that, if x may terminate immediately, also y must be considered in order to establish consistency of $x \cdot y$. The format of the operational deduction rules used in this book up to this point is left in the term deduction system for $(\mathrm{TSP}_\perp + \mathrm{RSE})(A)$: the last rule shows a so-called *negative premise*; the negation of a predicate is used. Nevertheless, by an extension of the theory in Chapter 3, it can be established that these rules determine a unique transition system for each closed term. The details of creating a model for which equational theory $(\mathrm{TSP}_\perp + \mathrm{RSE})(A)$ is ground-complete, are not treated here. The interested reader is referred to (Baeten & Bergstra, 1997), where such a model is developed in a slightly different operational context. For the development of meta-theory in the style of Chapter 3 that allows to establish a standard term model for which the theory is ground-complete, see (Verhoef, 1994).

$(\mathrm{TSP}_\perp + \mathrm{RSE})(A)$	
$(\mathrm{BSP}_\perp + \mathrm{RSE})(A)$, $\mathrm{TSP}(A)$;	
-	
x, y;	
$\perp \cdot x = \perp$	IP3
$\phi :\rightarrow (x \cdot y) = (\phi :\rightarrow x) \cdot y$	GC7
$\phi {}^\wedge\!\!\blacktriangle (x \cdot y) = (\phi {}^\wedge\!\!\blacktriangle x) \cdot y$	RSE8

Table 10.10. The process theory $(\mathrm{TSP}_\perp + \mathrm{RSE})(A)$ (with $\phi \in \mathbf{FB}$).

TDS($(\mathrm{TSP}_\perp + \mathrm{RSE})(A)$, *effect*)

TDS($(\mathrm{BSP}_\perp + \mathrm{RSE})(A)$, *effect*);

binary: $\cdot$;

x, x', y, y' :

$$\frac{\langle x, v\rangle \xrightarrow{a} \langle x', v'\rangle \quad \langle x' \cdot y, v'\rangle \searrow}{\langle x \cdot y, v\rangle \xrightarrow{a} \langle x' \cdot y, v'\rangle} \qquad \frac{\langle x, v\rangle\downarrow \quad \langle y, v\rangle \xrightarrow{a} \langle y', v'\rangle}{\langle x \cdot y, v\rangle \xrightarrow{a} \langle y', v'\rangle}$$

$$\frac{\langle x, v\rangle\downarrow \quad \langle y, v\rangle\downarrow}{\langle x \cdot y, v\rangle\downarrow} \qquad \frac{\langle x, v\rangle\downarrow \quad \langle y, v\rangle \searrow}{\langle x \cdot y, v\rangle \searrow} \qquad \frac{\langle x, v\rangle \searrow \quad \langle x, v\rangle\not\downarrow}{\langle x \cdot y, v\rangle \searrow}$$

Table 10.11. Term deduction system for $(\mathrm{TSP}_\perp + \mathrm{RSE})(A)$ (with $a \in A$, $v, v' \in BV$).

In line with before, occurrences of the sequential-composition operator can be eliminated from closed $(\mathrm{TSP}_\perp + \mathrm{RSE})(A)$-terms, yielding (basic) $(\mathrm{BSP}_\perp + \mathrm{RSE})(A)$-terms. The ground-extension is conservative.

With the addition of parallel composition, the mechanism of signal observation can be discussed. A process can synchronize with a process running in parallel by using conditionals that test signals emitted by the other process. This provides a new synchronization mechanism, besides the already known communication mechanism. Additional axioms are presented in Table 10.12 and explained below. As earlier in this chapter, the communication function γ needs to be defined in a way that is consistent with the *effect* function that is a parameter in the operational semantics.

$(\mathrm{BCP}_\perp + \mathrm{RSE})(A, \gamma)$	
$(\mathrm{BSP}_\perp + \mathrm{RSE})(A)$, $\mathrm{BCP}(A, \gamma)$;	
unary: rs;	
x, y;	
$(\phi :\rightarrow x) \mathbin{\|\!\lfloor} y = \phi :\rightarrow (x \mathbin{\|\!\lfloor} y)$	GC8
$(\phi :\rightarrow x) \mid y = rs(y) + \phi :\rightarrow (x \mid y)$	GC9S
$\partial_H(\phi :\rightarrow x) = \phi :\rightarrow \partial_H(x)$	GC10
$(\phi \wedge\!\!\blacktriangle x) \mathbin{\|\!\lfloor} y = \phi \wedge\!\!\blacktriangle (x \mathbin{\|\!\lfloor} y)$	RSE9
$(\phi \wedge\!\!\blacktriangle x) \mid y = \phi \wedge\!\!\blacktriangle (x \mid y)$	RSE10
$\partial_H(\phi \wedge\!\!\blacktriangle x) = \phi \wedge\!\!\blacktriangle \partial_H(x)$	RSE11
$rs(\perp) = \perp$	RS1
$rs(1) = 0$	RS2
$rs(0) = 0$	RS3
$rs(a.x) = 0$	RS4
$rs(x + y) = rs(x) + rs(y)$	RS5
$rs(\phi :\rightarrow x) = \phi :\rightarrow rs(x)$	RS6
$rs(\phi \wedge\!\!\blacktriangle x) = \phi \wedge\!\!\blacktriangle rs(x)$	RS7

Table 10.12. The process theory $(\mathrm{BCP}_\perp + \mathrm{RSE})(A)$ (with $a \in A$, $H \subseteq A$, $\phi \in \mathbf{FB}$).

Besides the three usual parallel-composition operators and encapsulation operators needed to enforce communication, theory $(\mathrm{BCP}_\perp + \mathrm{RSE})(A)$ has one additional auxiliary operator, the root-signal operator rs, that essentially reduces a term to the signal it emits. It allows to reduce any closed term to a term of the form $\phi \wedge\!\!\blacktriangle 0$ for some propositional formula ϕ.

The additional RSE axioms in $(\mathrm{BCP}_\perp + \mathrm{RSE})(A)$ are self-explanatory. Note that Axiom RSE10 states that a signal emitted by one process of a pair of communicating processes is also emitted by the pair of communicating processes as a whole.

Two of the three guarded-command axioms appear in Table 10.3 in a context without signals as well (although here these axioms are presented with their left- and right-hand sides exchanged when compared to Table 10.3). Axiom GC9S replaces Axiom GC9 from Table 10.3 in a context with signals. Axiom GC9 states that a communication can only occur if conditions guarding any of the communicating processes are satisfied. Axiom GC9S states in addition that the signals emitted by any of the communicating processes remain visible at all times, even when a condition of one of the communicating processes is false (which effectively prevents communication).

Example 10.4.6 (Signal observation) A simple example of signal observation is the following. A process executing an action a that changes the value of a propositional variable P from true to false, and emitting this fact, can be specified as follows:

$$P \mathbin{\hat{\blacktriangle}} a.(\neg P \mathbin{\hat{\blacktriangle}} 1).$$

A process in parallel can observe these signals, and make progress dependent on them. Consider the following process, to be executed in parallel with the above process.

$$P :\rightarrow b.(\neg P :\rightarrow 1).$$

If in the parallel composition a is executed first, then deadlock will ensue. If b is executed first, then termination can be reached. Assume a and b cannot communicate.

$$\begin{aligned}
&(\mathrm{BCP}_{\perp} + \mathrm{RSE})(A) \vdash \\
&\quad P \mathbin{\hat{\blacktriangle}} a.(\neg P \mathbin{\hat{\blacktriangle}} 1) \parallel P :\rightarrow b.(\neg P :\rightarrow 1) \\
&= P \mathbin{\hat{\blacktriangle}} a.(\neg P \mathbin{\hat{\blacktriangle}} 1) \mathbin{|\!\lfloor} P :\rightarrow b.(\neg P :\rightarrow 1) \\
&\quad + P :\rightarrow b.(\neg P :\rightarrow 1) \mathbin{|\!\lfloor} P \mathbin{\hat{\blacktriangle}} a.(\neg P \mathbin{\hat{\blacktriangle}} 1) \\
&\quad + P \mathbin{\hat{\blacktriangle}} a.(\neg P \mathbin{\hat{\blacktriangle}} 1) \mid P :\rightarrow b.(\neg P :\rightarrow 1) \\
&= P \mathbin{\hat{\blacktriangle}} (a.(\neg P \mathbin{\hat{\blacktriangle}} 1) \mathbin{|\!\lfloor} P :\rightarrow b.(\neg P :\rightarrow 1)) \\
&\quad + P :\rightarrow (b.(\neg P :\rightarrow 1) \mathbin{|\!\lfloor} P \mathbin{\hat{\blacktriangle}} a.(\neg P \mathbin{\hat{\blacktriangle}} 1)) \\
&\quad + P \mathbin{\hat{\blacktriangle}} 0 \\
&= P \mathbin{\hat{\blacktriangle}} a.(\neg P \mathbin{\hat{\blacktriangle}} 1 \parallel P :\rightarrow b.(\neg P :\rightarrow 1)) \\
&\quad + P \mathbin{\hat{\blacktriangle}} P :\rightarrow b.(\neg P :\rightarrow 1 \parallel P \mathbin{\hat{\blacktriangle}} a.(\neg P \mathbin{\hat{\blacktriangle}} 1)) \\
&= P \mathbin{\hat{\blacktriangle}} a.(\neg P \mathbin{\hat{\blacktriangle}} 0 + P :\rightarrow b.(\neg P :\rightarrow 1 \parallel \neg P \mathbin{\hat{\blacktriangle}} 1) + \neg P \mathbin{\hat{\blacktriangle}} 0) \\
&\quad + P \mathbin{\hat{\blacktriangle}} b.(\neg P :\rightarrow (1 \mathbin{|\!\lfloor} P \mathbin{\hat{\blacktriangle}} a.(\neg P \mathbin{\hat{\blacktriangle}} 1)) \\
&\qquad\qquad + P \mathbin{\hat{\blacktriangle}} a.(\neg P \mathbin{\hat{\blacktriangle}} 1 \parallel \neg P :\rightarrow 1) + P \mathbin{\hat{\blacktriangle}} 0) \\
&= P \mathbin{\hat{\blacktriangle}} a.(\neg P \mathbin{\hat{\blacktriangle}} P :\rightarrow b.(\neg P :\rightarrow 1 \parallel \neg P \mathbin{\hat{\blacktriangle}} 1)) \\
&\quad + P \mathbin{\hat{\blacktriangle}} b.(\neg P :\rightarrow 0 \\
&\qquad\qquad + P \mathbin{\hat{\blacktriangle}} a.(\neg P \mathbin{\hat{\blacktriangle}} 0 + \neg P :\rightarrow 0 + \neg P \mathbin{\hat{\blacktriangle}} \neg P :\rightarrow 1)) \\
&= P \mathbin{\hat{\blacktriangle}} a.(\neg P \mathbin{\hat{\blacktriangle}} 0) + b.(P \mathbin{\hat{\blacktriangle}} a.(\neg P \mathbin{\hat{\blacktriangle}} 1)).
\end{aligned}$$

Note that this example illustrates that signal observation provides an *asynchronous* communication and synchronization mechanism, as opposed to the *synchronous* mechanism provided via the communication merge and communication function.

Theory $(\mathrm{BCP}_\perp + \mathrm{RSE})(A, \gamma)$ admits an elimination result. Closed terms can be rewritten into (basic) $(\mathrm{BSP}_\perp + \mathrm{RSE})(A)$-terms. The ground-extension is furthermore conservative.

Using the elimination result, it is possible to determine the root signal of arbitrary closed $(\mathrm{BCP}_\perp + \mathrm{RSE})(A, \gamma)$-terms. The root signal of a basic term as defined in Definition 10.4.2 (Basic $(\mathrm{BSP}_\perp + \mathrm{RSE})(A)$-terms) is the signal χ in the format given in that definition. Applying the root-signal operator to such a basic term results in term $\chi \mathbin{{}^{\wedge}\!\!\blacktriangle} 0$. Exercise 10.4.8 illustrates several identities that can be derived for the root-signal operator. As a note aside, it is interesting to observe that there is no such simple identity for sequential composition (when that operator is added to the theory), see Exercise 10.4.10. The root signal emitted by a sequential composition is the signal emitted by the first operand of the composition, unless this term can terminate, in which case the root signal of the composition is the conjunct of the signals emitted by the two operands.

Some of the additional operational rules underlying the term model for process theory $(\mathrm{BCP}_\perp + \mathrm{RSE})(A, \gamma)$ are presented in Table 10.13, namely the rules for the merge and root-signal operators. Note that only one rule is necessary for the root-signal operator, which defines the consistency predicate. The absence of any other rules illustrates that a 'root-signal process' cannot perform any actions nor terminate successfully.

Example 10.4.7 (Signal observation: a traffic light) A more realistic example of signal observation than the example given in Example 10.4.6 is a traffic light, or, more precisely, the interaction between a car driver and a traffic light. Assume a set of propositional variables $\{red, yellow, green\}$. The following specification defines a (Dutch) traffic light, as it is observed by a passing car driver. The latter explains the termination options in the specification, signifying the option to stop observing the traffic light.

$$\begin{aligned}
TL_r &= (red \wedge \neg yellow \wedge \neg green) \mathbin{{}^{\wedge}\!\!\blacktriangle} (1 + change.TL_g),\\
TL_y &= (\neg red \wedge yellow \wedge \neg green) \mathbin{{}^{\wedge}\!\!\blacktriangle} (1 + change.TL_r),\\
TL_g &= (\neg red \wedge \neg yellow \wedge green) \mathbin{{}^{\wedge}\!\!\blacktriangle} (1 + change.TL_y)\ .
\end{aligned}$$

The following specifies a careful car driver that (initially) stops not only at a red light, but also at a yellow light.

—$TDS((\mathrm{BCP}_\perp + \mathrm{RSE})(A, \gamma), \mathit{effect})$—

$TDS((\mathrm{BSP}_\perp + \mathrm{RSE})(A), \mathit{effect})$;

unary: rs, $(\partial_H)_{H \subseteq A}$; binary: $\_ \parallel \_$, $\_ ⌊⌊ \_$, $\_ \mid \_$;

x, x', y, y';

$$\frac{\langle x, v\rangle \xrightarrow{a} \langle x', v'\rangle \quad \langle y, v\rangle \searrow \quad \langle y, v'\rangle \searrow}{\langle x \parallel y, v\rangle \xrightarrow{a} \langle x' \parallel y, v'\rangle}$$

$$\frac{\langle x, v\rangle \xrightarrow{a} \langle x', v'\rangle \quad \langle y, v\rangle \xrightarrow{b} \langle y', v''\rangle \quad \gamma(a, b) = c \quad \langle x' \parallel y', \mathit{effect}(c, v)\rangle \searrow}{\langle x \parallel y, v\rangle \xrightarrow{c} \langle x' \parallel y', \mathit{effect}(c, v)\rangle}$$

$$\frac{\langle x, v\rangle\downarrow \quad \langle y, v\rangle\downarrow}{\langle x \parallel y, v\rangle\downarrow} \qquad \frac{\langle x, v\rangle \searrow \quad \langle y, v\rangle \searrow}{\langle x \parallel y, v\rangle \searrow}$$

...

$$\frac{\langle x, v\rangle \searrow}{\langle rs(x), v\rangle \searrow}$$

...

Table 10.13. Term deduction system for $(\mathrm{BCP}_\perp + \mathrm{RSE})(A, \gamma)$ (with $a, b, c \in A$, $v, v', v'' \in BV$).

$$\begin{aligned} CD = {} & \mathit{approach}.(\mathit{green} :\rightarrow \mathit{drive}.1 \\ & + \neg \mathit{green} :\rightarrow \mathit{stop}.(\mathit{green} :\rightarrow \mathit{start}.(\neg \mathit{red} :\rightarrow \mathit{drive}.1))). \end{aligned}$$

Expression $TL_r \parallel CD$ now describes the expected interaction between an initially red traffic light and an approaching driver. There is no communication. The transition system is shown in Figure 10.3. States are aligned in rows, according to the color of the traffic light. The colors are of course red, yellow, and green, reading from top to bottom. Signals are not shown. Action *change* changes the values of the propositional values as expected. Other actions do not affect these values.

Example 10.4.8 (Communication and signal observation) For a slightly more elaborate example, that illustrates the trade-off between (synchronous) communication and (asynchronous) signal observation, reconsider the communicating buffers of Section 7.6, illustrated in Figure 7.3. The original specification describes two one-place buffers communicating over ports i and l, and l and o, respectively. The parallel composition gives a two-place buffer

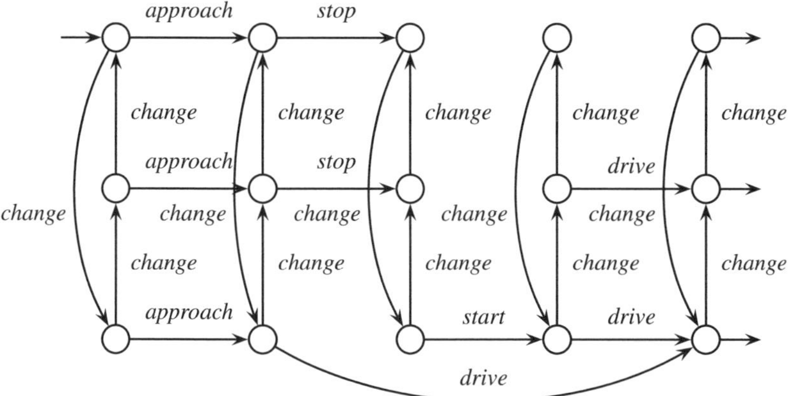

Fig. 10.3. The interaction between a traffic light and a car driver.

with ports i and o, when enforcing communication over the internal port l. The following specification adds signals that show the contents of the two one-place buffers at their respective output ports.

$$
\begin{aligned}
BS_{il} &= show_l\emptyset \,{\wedge}\!\!\!\!{\scriptstyle\blacktriangle}\,(1 + \sum_{d \in D} i?d.(show_l d \,{\wedge}\!\!\!\!{\scriptstyle\blacktriangle}\, l!d.BS_{il})),\\
BS_{lo} &= show_o\emptyset \,{\wedge}\!\!\!\!{\scriptstyle\blacktriangle}\,(1 + \sum_{d \in D} l?d.(show_o d \,{\wedge}\!\!\!\!{\scriptstyle\blacktriangle}\, o!d.BS_{lo}))\,.
\end{aligned}
$$

It is now possible to repeat the derivations for the two-place buffer of Section 7.6, with the only difference that the content of the buffers is visible over ports l and o.

Signals as used in the above specification allow moving the parameter d in the actions and communications to a signal observation. Define the action set as $\{p?, p!, p\boldsymbol{?} \mid p \in \{i, l, o\}\}$. Assume there is only one communication, namely $\gamma(l?, l!) = l\boldsymbol{?}$. Consider the following specification.

$$
\begin{aligned}
BS2_{il} &= show_l\emptyset \,{\wedge}\!\!\!\!{\scriptstyle\blacktriangle}\,(1 + \sum_{d \in D} show_i d :\to i?.(show_l d \,{\wedge}\!\!\!\!{\scriptstyle\blacktriangle}\, l!\,.BS2_{il})),\\
BS2_{lo} &= show_o\emptyset \,{\wedge}\!\!\!\!{\scriptstyle\blacktriangle}\,(1 + \sum_{d \in D} show_l d :\to l?.(show_o d \,{\wedge}\!\!\!\!{\scriptstyle\blacktriangle}\, o!\,.BS2_{lo}))\,.
\end{aligned}
$$

Assume furthermore that all of the basic signals are exclusive, i.e., the following signal is an invariant in the above processes:

$$
\begin{aligned}
\textstyle\bigwedge_{p \in \{i,l,o\}} & ((show_p\emptyset \supset \textstyle\bigwedge_{d \in D} \neg show_p d)\\
& \wedge \textstyle\bigwedge_{d \in D}(show_p d \supset (\neg show_p\emptyset \wedge \textstyle\bigwedge_{e \in D\setminus\{d\}} \neg show_p e))).
\end{aligned}
$$

Note that this can be achieved by adding the signal as a conjunct to all of the signals shown in the specifications. The invariant is omitted from the specifications for readability.

The process $\partial_H(BS2_{il} \,\|\, BS2_{lo})$, with $H = \{l?, l!\}$, now again specifies a two-place buffer. Note that this two-place buffer can only perform input actions under the condition that $show_i d$ is satisfied. This condition makes explicit that the environment is expected to provide data to the buffer.

In order to get rid of the last remaining communication, intuitively two extra signals per port are needed, because the original communication is synchronous, whereas signal observations are asynchronous. The *rdy* (ready) signals in the following specifications indicate that a buffer is ready to receive a value over its input port; the *flg* (flag) signals indicate that a buffer is ready to provide an output over the indicated port. The specifications use actions *in* and *out* for obtaining input and providing output. These actions modify the ready and flag signals as appropriate. Reset actions are included in the specifications to reset signals to their original settings after an output has been acknowledged by the environment. None of the actions can communicate. Observe that the specifications do not allow simultaneous inputs and outputs. Specification $BS3_{lo}$, for example, requires $\neg flg_l$ to hold before it can perform an out_o.

$$
\begin{aligned}
BS3_{il} = {} & (rdy_i \wedge show_l\emptyset \wedge \neg flg_l) \,\hat{}\, (\\
& 1 + \textstyle\sum_{d \in D} (flg_i \wedge show_i d) :\to in_i \,. \\
& \qquad (\neg rdy_i \wedge show_l d \wedge flg_l) \,\hat{}\, (rdy_l \wedge \neg flg_i) :\to out_l \,. \\
& \qquad (\neg rdy_i \wedge show_l d \wedge flg_l) \,\hat{}\, (\neg rdy_l :\to reset_l . BS3_{il})), \\
BS3_{lo} = {} & (rdy_l \wedge show_o\emptyset \wedge \neg flg_o) \,\hat{}\, (\\
& 1 + \textstyle\sum_{d \in D} (flg_l \wedge show_l d) :\to in_l \,. \\
& \qquad (\neg rdy_l \wedge show_o d \wedge flg_o) \,\hat{}\, (rdy_o \wedge \neg flg_l) :\to out_o \,. \\
& \qquad (\neg rdy_l \wedge show_o d \wedge flg_o) \,\hat{}\, (\neg rdy_o :\to reset_o . BS3_{lo})).
\end{aligned}
$$

Assuming as before the invariant mentioned above, it can again be shown that the parallel composition behaves as a two-place buffer.

As a final observation, note that the flag and ready signals in the above specifications are technically redundant. It is possible to encode the synchronization behavior with the existing *show* signals; see Exercise 10.4.14.

Observe from the various examples given so far that synchronization between signals is enforced via the signal names. In a more general setting, one could consider a signal communication function that relates signals that are expected to match. In the buffers example, for example, it would then be possible to connect buffers with arbitrary ports, stating that port p is connected to port q for arbitrary p and q. Furthermore, note that in the above buffers example, communications over internal ports are visible. To abstract from those internal actions, the present theory needs to be extended with abstraction as considered in Chapter 8. Both extensions do not present problems, and are not treated here.

It is also desirable to have a means to abstract from signals at internal ports, to hide those typically meaningless signals from an external observer. This section is concluded by describing a mechanism for signal hiding. Notation $P \Delta x$ denotes that propositional variable P is hidden in process expression x.

Table 10.14 gives axioms for signal hiding, leading to theory $(\mathrm{BSP}_\perp + \mathrm{SHD})(A)$. The essential idea is that a propositional variable that is hidden is replaced by both true and false, which are the two values that it can possibly take. Axioms SHD2–5 follow the structure of basic terms (see Definition 10.4.2), with additional signal emissions in Axioms SHD2–4, for which the reason is explained below. Axiom SHD1 states the effect of signal hiding on the inaccessible process. Since $\perp$ is derivably equal to $\mathit{false} \,\hat{\wedge}\, 0$, Axiom SHD1 is derivable from the other axioms of the theory using Axiom SHD2.

The crucial axiom in theory $(\mathrm{BSP}_\perp + \mathrm{SHD})(A)$ is Axiom SHD5. It states that signal hiding distributes over choice when preserving the root signal of the two alternatives. This is in line with the fact that signals emitted by alternatives of a process carry over to the process as a whole. Axiom SHD5 is the reason that it is necessary to include the root-signal operator of the theory $(\mathrm{BCP}_\perp + \mathrm{RSE})(A, \gamma)$ in the current theory, with the same axioms. The presence of the root-signal terms in Axiom SHD5 is also the reason why it is necessary to explicitly add signals in the left-hand sides of Axioms SHD2–4. Without those signals, it would not be possible to eliminate signal-hiding operators from (closed) terms involving choices.

As a final remark, note that after an action is executed, both options to replace a propositional variable by true or false must be included again, as signals are not persistent.

The following is a simple example of a calculation.

$$
\begin{aligned}
&(\mathrm{BSP}_\perp + \mathrm{SHD})(A) \vdash P \Delta (a.(P \,\hat{\wedge}\, 1) + a.(\neg P \,\hat{\wedge}\, 1)) \\
&\qquad = a.(\mathit{true} \,\hat{\wedge}\, \mathit{true} :\rightarrow 1) + a.(\mathit{true} \,\hat{\wedge}\, \mathit{true} :\rightarrow 1) = a.1.
\end{aligned}
$$

The term deduction system in Table 10.15 reflects that the value of a propositional variable in a state does not matter when it is hidden.

Exercises

10.4.1 Show that Axioms IP1, $x + \perp = \perp$, and RSE3, $\phi \,\hat{\wedge}\, \perp = \perp$, are derivable from the other axioms of theory $(\mathrm{BSP}_\perp + \mathrm{RSE})(A)$.

10.4.2 Show that the following identities are derivable from theory $(\mathrm{BSP}_\perp + \mathrm{RSE})(A)$:

(BSP$_\perp$ + SHD)(A)	
(BSP$_\perp$ + RSE)(A);	
unary: rs, $(P\Delta\_)_{P\in\mathbf{P}}$;	
x, y;	
$P\Delta\perp = \perp$	SHD1
$P\Delta(\phi :\!\!\blacktriangle 0) = (\phi[true/P] \vee \phi[false/P]) :\!\!\blacktriangle 0$	SHD2
$P\Delta(\phi :\!\!\blacktriangle \psi :\rightarrow 1) = (\phi[true/P] \vee \phi[false/P]) :\!\!\blacktriangle$ $((\phi \wedge \psi)[true/P] :\rightarrow 1 + (\phi \wedge \psi)[false/P] :\rightarrow 1)$	SHD3
$P\Delta(\phi :\!\!\blacktriangle \psi :\rightarrow a.x) = (\phi[true/P] \vee \phi[false/P]) :\!\!\blacktriangle$ $((\phi \wedge \psi)[true/P] :\rightarrow a.(P\Delta x)$ $+(\phi \wedge \psi)[false/P] :\rightarrow a.(P\Delta x))$	SHD4
$P\Delta(x + y) = P\Delta(rs(y) + x) + P\Delta(rs(x) + y)$	SHD5
$rs(\perp) = \perp$	RS1
$rs(1) = 0$	RS2
$rs(0) = 0$	RS3
$rs(a.x) = 0$	RS4
$rs(x + y) = rs(x) + rs(y)$	RS5
$rs(\phi :\rightarrow x) = \phi :\rightarrow rs(x)$	RS6
$rs(\phi :\!\!\blacktriangle x) = \phi :\!\!\blacktriangle rs(x)$	RS7

Table 10.14. The process theory BSP(A) with signal hiding (with $\phi, \psi \in$ **FB** and $P \in$ **P** a propositional variable).

(a) $\phi :\!\!\blacktriangle x = (\phi :\!\!\blacktriangle 0) + x$;

(b) $(\phi :\!\!\blacktriangle x) + (\psi :\!\!\blacktriangle y) = (\phi \wedge \psi) :\!\!\blacktriangle (x + y)$.

10.4.3 Prove Proposition 10.4.3 (Reduction to basic terms).

10.4.4 Prove that theory (BSP$_\perp$ + RSE)(A) is a conservative ground-extension of theory (BSP$_\perp$ + GC)(A).

10.4.5 Modify the specification of the stack in Example 10.4.5 (Stack) so that the top element is only shown when an action *top* is executed. Executing actions *top* and *pop*(d) on an empty stack will cause an *error* signal to be emitted. Give different variants of the stack, where an error leads to deadlock, or to a state of underflow from which recovery is possible by execution of a push action.

10.4.6 Show that equation $\perp \parallel x = \perp$ is derivable from theory (BCP$_\perp$ + RSE)(A, γ).

10.4.7 Show that equation $\phi :\!\!\blacktriangle x \parallel y = \phi :\!\!\blacktriangle (x \parallel y)$ is *not* derivable from theory (BCP$_\perp$ + RSE)(A, γ).

10.4.8 Prove that, for any closed (BCP$_\perp$ + RSE)(A, γ)-terms p and q and any $H \subseteq A$, the following identities for the root-signal operator are derivable from theory (BCP$_\perp$ + RSE)(A, γ):

— $TDS((\mathrm{BSP}_\perp + \mathrm{SHD})(A), \mathit{effect})$ —
$TDS((\mathrm{BSP}_\perp + \mathrm{RSE})(A), \mathit{effect})$;

unary: rs, $(P\Delta\_)_{P\in\mathbf{P}}$;

x, x';

$$\frac{\langle x, v[true/P]\rangle \xrightarrow{a} \langle x', v'\rangle}{\langle P\Delta x, v\rangle \xrightarrow{a} \langle P\Delta x', \mathit{effect}(a, v)\rangle} \qquad \frac{\langle x, v[false/P]\rangle \xrightarrow{a} \langle x', v'\rangle}{\langle P\Delta x, v\rangle \xrightarrow{a} \langle P\Delta x', \mathit{effect}(a, v)\rangle}$$

$$\frac{\langle x, v[true/P]\rangle\downarrow}{\langle P\Delta x, v\rangle\downarrow} \qquad \frac{\langle x, v[false/P]\rangle\downarrow}{\langle P\Delta x, v\rangle\downarrow}$$

$$\frac{\langle x, v[true/P]\rangle \searrow}{\langle P\Delta x, v\rangle \searrow} \qquad \frac{\langle x, v[false/P]\rangle \searrow}{\langle P\Delta x, v\rangle \searrow}$$

$$\frac{\langle x, v\rangle \searrow}{\langle rs(x), v\rangle \searrow}$$

Table 10.15. Term deduction system for $(\mathrm{BSP}_\perp + \mathrm{SHD})(A)$ (with $a \in A$, $v, v' \in BV$, and $P \in \mathbf{P}$).

(a) $rs(p \mid q) = rs(q) + rs(q)$;
(b) $rs(p \mathbin{\lfloor\!\lfloor} q) = rs(p)$;
(c) $rs(p \parallel q) = rs(p) + rs(q)$;
(d) $rs(\partial_H(p)) = rs(p)$.

10.4.9 Prove that, for any closed $(\mathrm{BCP}_\perp + \mathrm{RSE})(A, \gamma)$-term p, $(\mathrm{BCP}_\perp + \mathrm{RSE})(A, \gamma) \vdash rs(p) = \phi :\rightarrow 0$, for some $\phi \in \mathbf{FB}$.

10.4.10 Show that both $rs(x \cdot y) = rs(x) + rs(y)$ and $rs(x \cdot y) = rs(x)$ are not derivable from theory $(\mathrm{TCP}_\perp + \mathrm{RSE})(A, \gamma)$ (i.e., $(\mathrm{BCP}_\perp + \mathrm{RSE})(A, \gamma)$ extended with sequential composition), not even for closed terms.

10.4.11 Give details for the construction of term models for the various equational theories introduced in this section. Investigate elimination, soundness, ground-completeness, and conservativity.

10.4.12 Derive a recursive specification in $(\mathrm{BCP}_\perp + \mathrm{RSE})(A, \gamma)$ for the process $TL_r \parallel CD$ of Example 10.4.7 (Signal observation: traffic light). Also make the *effect* function specifying the effect of actions on valuations of propositional variables explicit.

10.4.13 Derive recursive specifications in $(\mathrm{BCP}_\perp + \mathrm{RSE})(A, \gamma)$ for the three buffer processes $\partial_H(BS_{il} \parallel BS_{lo})$ (with $H = \{l?d, l!d \mid d \in D\}$), $\partial_H(BS2_{il} \parallel BS2_{lo})$ (with $H = \{l?, l!\}$) and $BS3_{il} \parallel BS3_{lo}$ of Example 10.4.8 (Communication and signal observation). Make the *effect* function specifying the effect of actions on valuations of propositional variables explicit, and draw a transition system for each of the three processes. Finally, apply signal hiding, to hide all signals in the resulting specifications.

10.4.14 Give an alternative specification for the buffer processes $BS3_{il}$ and $BS3_{lo}$ of Example 10.4.8 (Communication and signal observation) that does not use communication or any of the flag or ready signals. That is, encode all the required synchronization in the *show* signals. Show that the alternative specifications when put in parallel yield the same result as $BS3_{il} \parallel BS3_{lo}$.

10.5 State operators

So far in this chapter, the state a process is in is not visible completely, is not directly accessible in the equational theory. The state is only visible through validity of propositional formulas, the emitted signals. In the operational semantics, the state is modeled by means of a valuation, that gives the value of all data variables. In this section, process states are modeled more explicitly in the equational theory, by means of a parameter attached to a unary operator, resulting in the class of so-called *state operators*.

First of all, suppose that a state space S is given. This set is left unspecified, but could consist of valuations of variables. Let us assume there is a special state $\perp \in S$ that denotes the inaccessible state. Further, there are three functions:

(i) A signal function $sig : S \to \mathbf{FB}$, that denotes the signal that is emitted in the state. Always, it is required that $sig(\perp) = false$. If it is not necessary to use signals in a particular setting, $sig(s) = true$ can be stipulated for all $s \in S \setminus \{\perp\}$.

(ii) A function $effect : A \times S \to S$, that denotes the resulting state if $a \in A$ is executed in state $s \in S$. If $effect(a, s) = \perp$, then a is blocked, cannot be executed in state s; $effect(a, \perp) = \perp$, for all $a \in A$.

(iii) A function $action : A \times S \to A$, which is a generalization of a renaming function. It denotes the action that can be observed if $a \in A$ is executed in state $s \in S$. Usually, this function can be taken to be trivial, i.e., $action(a, s) = a$ can be defined for all $a \in A, s \in S$.

In some applications, it is useful to use more than one state operator in a specification. For this reason, a state operator takes a second parameter. Process $\lambda_s^m(x)$ denotes that *machine* m executes program x and is currently in state s, where the machine m is a 4-tuple of the state set and the functions introduced above. That is, $m = (S, sig, effect, action)$. Let M be the set of all machines (for the given action set A). The equational theory for state operators is presented in Table 10.16.

$\_\_\,(\mathrm{BSP} + \mathrm{SO})(A)$ ____________________

$(\mathrm{BSP}_\perp + \mathrm{RSE})(A)$;

---

unary: $(\lambda_s^m)_{m=(S,sig,\mathit{effect},action)\in M, s\in S}$;

---

x, y;

$\lambda_s^m(\perp) = \perp$	SO1
$\lambda_\perp^m(x) = \perp$	SO2
$\lambda_s^m(0) = sig(s) {}^{\wedge}\!\!\blacktriangle 0$	SO3
$\lambda_s^m(1) = sig(s) {}^{\wedge}\!\!\blacktriangle 1$	SO4
$\lambda_s^m(a.x) = sig(s) {}^{\wedge}\!\!\blacktriangle action(a,s) . \lambda_{\mathit{effect}(a,s)}^m(x)$	SO5
$\lambda_s^m(x + y) = \lambda_s^m(x) + \lambda_s^m(y)$	SO6
$\lambda_s^m(\phi :\rightarrow x) = sig(s) {}^{\wedge}\!\!\blacktriangle \phi :\rightarrow \lambda_s^m(x)$	SO7
$\lambda_s^m(\phi {}^{\wedge}\!\!\blacktriangle x) = \phi {}^{\wedge}\!\!\blacktriangle \lambda_s^m(x)$	SO8

Table 10.16. The process theory $(\mathrm{BSP} + \mathrm{SO})(A)$ (with $a \in A, \phi \in \mathbf{FB}$ and $s \in S \setminus \{\perp\}$).

Operational rules are presented in Table 10.17. Observe that the *effect* function is no longer a parameter of the operational semantics, because it is part of the equational theory. The development of a term model for which the equational theory is sound and ground-complete goes as before. Also extensions go along the usual lines. The machine superscript is omitted when it is clear from the context.

$\_\_\,TDS((\mathrm{BSP} + \mathrm{SO})(A))$ ____________________

$TDS((\mathrm{BSP}_\perp + \mathrm{RSE})(A), \mathit{effect})$;

---

unary: $(\lambda_s^m)_{m=(S,sig,\mathit{effect},action)\in M, s\in S}$;

---

x, x';

$$\frac{\langle sig(s) {}^{\wedge}\!\!\blacktriangle x, v\rangle \xrightarrow{a} \langle x', v'\rangle \qquad b = action(a,s) \quad s' = \mathit{effect}(a,s) \quad v'(sig(s')) = true}{\langle \lambda_s^m(x), v\rangle \xrightarrow{b} \langle \lambda_{s'}^m(x'), v'\rangle}$$

$$\frac{\langle sig(s) {}^{\wedge}\!\!\blacktriangle x, v\rangle \downarrow}{\langle \lambda_s^m(x), v\rangle \downarrow} \qquad \frac{\langle sig(x) {}^{\wedge}\!\!\blacktriangle x, v\rangle \searrow}{\langle \lambda_s^m(x), v\rangle \searrow}$$

Table 10.17. Term deduction system for $(\mathrm{BSP} + \mathrm{SO})(A)$ (with $a, b \in A$, $s' \in S, v, v' \in BV$).

Example 10.5.1 (Stack) As an example, another specification is presented of the stack of Section 5.6. The state space consists of the possible contents of the stack, so sequences in D^*, with D the set of data elements. The signal function *sig* should at least show whether or not the stack is empty, but can also show the top element of the stack (as in Example 10.4.5 (Stack)); the *action* function is trivial and does not rename any actions, and the *effect* function is given by:

$$\begin{aligned}&\mathit{effect}(\mathit{push}(d), \sigma) = \sigma d, \text{ for all } \sigma \in D^*, d \in D;\\&\mathit{effect}(\mathit{pop}, \epsilon) = \bot;\\&\mathit{effect}(\mathit{pop}, \sigma d) = \sigma, \text{ for all } \sigma \in D^*, d \in D.\end{aligned}$$

The specification of the stack is now given by:

$$\begin{aligned}\mathit{Stack} &= \lambda_\epsilon(X),\\X &= \mathit{empty} :\to 1 + \mathit{pop}.X + \sum_{d \in D} \mathit{push}(d).X.\end{aligned}$$

This section is concluded with a more involved example, that is difficult to describe without the use of state operators.

Example 10.5.2 (Buffers) In this example, two buffers A and B with data from the finite set D are maintained. Both buffers have capacity $k > 1$. The process to be defined allows to read data into both buffers in a concurrent mode. For both buffers A and B, there are two propositional variables: empty_A indicates that A is empty (likewise for B), and open_A indicates that there is still room in A (likewise for B). When both buffers have been loaded, the process C compares the contents of the buffers. The comparison will output value *true* if the buffers were equal and *false* otherwise. Thereafter, the buffers are made empty again and the process restarts. The system is described in a top-down fashion, first explaining the overall architecture and then completing the details.

$$\mathit{SYS} = \lambda_{\langle \epsilon, \epsilon \rangle}(A \parallel B \parallel C).$$

The state consists of the contents of the pair of buffers A and B. Initially, both are empty. The signals produced by a state $\langle \alpha, \beta \rangle$ are given by the following signal function. Let $|\sigma|$ denote the length of a sequence σ.

$$\begin{aligned}&\mathit{sig}(\langle \alpha, \beta \rangle) = \mathit{empty}_A \wedge \mathit{open}_A \wedge \mathit{empty}_B \wedge \mathit{open}_B,\\&\qquad\qquad\qquad\qquad\text{if } |\alpha| = 0 = |\beta|;\\&\mathit{sig}(\langle \alpha, \beta \rangle) = \mathit{empty}_A \wedge \mathit{open}_A \wedge \neg\mathit{empty}_B \wedge \mathit{open}_B,\\&\qquad\qquad\qquad\qquad\text{if } |\alpha| = 0 \text{ and } 0 < |\beta| < k;\\&\mathit{sig}(\langle \alpha, \beta \rangle) = \neg\mathit{empty}_A \wedge \mathit{open}_A \wedge \mathit{empty}_B \wedge \mathit{open}_B,\\&\qquad\qquad\qquad\qquad\text{if } 0 < |\alpha| < k \text{ and } |\beta| = 0;\end{aligned}$$

$$sig(\langle\alpha, \beta\rangle) = \neg empty_A \wedge open_A \wedge \neg empty_B \wedge open_B, \quad \text{if } 0 < |\alpha| < k \text{ and } 0 < |\beta| < k;$$
$$sig(\langle\alpha, \beta\rangle) = empty_A \wedge open_A \wedge \neg empty_B \wedge \neg open_B, \quad \text{if } |\alpha| = 0 \text{ and } |\beta| = k;$$
$$sig(\langle\alpha, \beta\rangle) = \neg empty_A \wedge \neg open_A \wedge empty_B \wedge open_B, \quad \text{if } |\alpha| = k \text{ and } |\beta| = 0;$$
$$sig(\langle\alpha, \beta\rangle) = \neg empty_A \wedge open_A \wedge \neg empty_B \wedge \neg open_B, \quad \text{if } 0 < |\alpha| < k \text{ and } |\beta| = k;$$
$$sig(\langle\alpha, \beta\rangle) = \neg empty_A \wedge \neg open_A \wedge \neg empty_B \wedge open_B, \quad \text{if } |\alpha| = k \text{ and } 0 < |\beta| < k;$$
$$sig(\langle\alpha, \beta\rangle) = \neg empty_A \wedge \neg open_A \wedge \neg empty_B \wedge \neg open_B, \quad \text{if } |\alpha| = k \text{ and } |\beta| = k.$$

The processes A, B, and C are defined as follows. Processes A and B use receive actions over ports a and b, and C uses a *compare* action, as expected.

$$A = empty_A :\rightarrow 1 + open_A :\rightarrow \sum_{d \in D} a?d.A,$$
$$B = empty_B :\rightarrow 1 + open_B :\rightarrow \sum_{d \in D} b?d.B,$$
$$C = 1 + \neg open_A \wedge \neg open_B :\rightarrow compare.C.$$

The *action* function is trivial except in the following cases, where !*true* and !*false* are actions to communicate the result of a *compare* action.

$$action(compare, \langle\alpha, \beta\rangle) = !true, \text{ if } \alpha = \beta;$$
$$action(compare, \langle\alpha, \beta\rangle) = !false, \text{ otherwise.}$$

Finally, the last step is to explain the *effect* function:

$$effect(a?d, \langle\alpha, \beta\rangle) = \langle\alpha d, \beta\rangle;$$
$$effect(b?d, \langle\alpha, \beta\rangle) = \langle\alpha, \beta d\rangle;$$
$$effect(compare, \langle\alpha, \beta\rangle) = \langle\epsilon, \epsilon\rangle.$$

The use of the state operator in this example is hard to avoid because of the parallel reading of data that must be used simultaneously later on. It is left as an exercise to compute a (linear) recursive specification of the system that does not use state operators.

Exercises

10.5.1 Derive a recursive specification over the signature of theory $(\mathrm{BSP}_\perp + \mathrm{RSE})(A)$ for the stack given in Example 10.5.1 (Stack). In other words, eliminate the state operator from the given specification.

10.5.2 Derive a recursive specification without state operators for the process *SYS* of Example 10.5.2 (Buffers).

10.5.3 Consider a pair of serial switches controlling a lamp. Each switch has just one action, *switch*, and the parallel composition of the two switches should show the signal *on* only when the lamp is on. Give a specification for this system.

10.5.4 Recall Exercise 8.8.7. In this exercise, consider two processes doing a random walk on a three by three grid. Each process has actions *begin*, *north*, *west*, *south*, *east*, *end*. The processes start in the lower left and upper right corners, respectively. The processes may not occupy the same square. Specify these two processes. What are the possible states after two moves?

10.5.5 Consider a simple sequential programming language. Can state operators be used to give a semantics of this programming language?

10.5.6 As an illustration of the defining power of state operators, consider the following guarded finite recursive specification of the queue over BSP(A) extended with state operators. Only an empty signal is used. The state space is $S = D \cup \{0, 1, \bot\}$, with D a set of data items. The *action* and *effect* functions are trivial except in the following cases, with $d, e \in D$:

$$\begin{aligned}
&\mathit{effect}(\mathit{out}, 0) = \bot;\\
&\mathit{action}(\mathit{out}, d) = o!d,\ \mathit{effect}(\mathit{out}, d) = 1;\\
&\mathit{action}(o!d, e) = o!e,\ \mathit{effect}(o!d, e) = d.
\end{aligned}$$

Now define the process *Queue*4 as follows:

$$\begin{aligned}
\mathit{Queue}4 &= \lambda_0(X),\\
X &= \mathit{empty} :\rightarrow 1 + \sum_{d \in D} i?d.\lambda_d(X) + \mathit{out}.X.
\end{aligned}$$

Define the *sig* function explicitly. Prove that *Queue*4, after signal hiding (see Table 10.14), is equal to process *Queue*1 of Section 7.7.

10.6 Choice quantification

The previous sections introduced the data type of the Booleans in a process-algebraic setting, ultimately leading to signals and the ability to reason about process states in an equational setting. This section adds a second data type. For simplicity, a single, well-known, data type is selected, the data type of the natural numbers. It is stressed, however, that also other data types could be used, including user-defined ones.

Notation 10.6.1 (Naturals) Recall the algebra of the natural numbers $\mathbb{N} = (\mathbf{N}, +, \times, \mathit{succ}, 0)$ of Example 2.3.3 (Algebra $\mathbb{N}$), that defines the following signature on the naturals: the binary operators $+$ and $\times$, a unary operator *succ*, and a constant 0; variables are in the remainder typically denoted n, m, n', $n'', n_i, \ldots$. This gives a set of terms over natural numbers denoted **FN**. Characters ν, μ are used to range over **FN**. Valuations for the natural-number variables are functions mapping each variable to a natural number. The set of these valuations is denoted *NV*. Obviously, such a valuation can be extended to a function from **FN** to **N**.

In the introduction, a set of Boolean formulas, the set of propositional logic formulas, was introduced starting from a set of propositional variables. In this section, a specific instantiation of this set with atomic propositions is given, as a basis for a specific instance of the set of Boolean formulas.

Notation 10.6.2 (Booleans) Recall Notation 10.1.1 (Booleans). An instance of the set **P** of propositional variables is constructed from **FN** by means of the operators $=, <, \leq, >$, and $\geq$. For each $\nu, \mu \in$ **FN**, the following are atomic propositions in **P**: $\nu = \mu, \nu < \mu, \nu \leq \mu, \nu > \mu$, and $\nu \geq \mu$. Given a valuation of the natural-number variables occurring in these expressions, their truth value can be determined. As such, expressions of this form are Boolean formulas in **FB**, that can for example occur in conditionals as described in the previous section.

The set of Boolean formulas **FB** is, as in Notation 10.1.1 (Booleans), built from the propositional variables, the Boolean constants, and the Boolean operators. However, in this section, also quantification over natural-number variables is allowed. For any Boolean formula $\phi \in$ **FB**,

- $\exists n \phi$ is a Boolean formula in **FB**, stating that there is a natural number $n \in$ **N** such that ϕ holds;
- $\forall n \phi$ is a Boolean formula in **FB**, stating that for all $n \in$ **N**, ϕ holds.

Note that the addition of quantification turns **FB** into a predicate calculus.

The Boolean and natural-number data types introduced in the above two notations are used in this section both in the considered equational theory and in the standard term model. It is assumed that all Boolean formulas that are encountered can be decided to be *true* or *false*, given some natural-number valuation in *NV*. The equational theory of the data types is left implicit. An alternative approach, taken for example in the language μCRL (Groote & Ponse, 1995), would be to make the equational theory of data types explicit, and require that both processes and the data types used by these processes are defined explicitly in the equational framework.

In the equational theory developed in this section, natural-number expressions from **FN** are used to parameterize actions and recursion variables. For any $\nu \in \mathbf{FN}$,

- $a(\nu)$ is an action in A, for any action name a, and
- recursion variable $X(\nu)$ defines a process parameterized with ν, for any X.

For simplicity, the theory $(\text{BSP}+\text{GC})(A)$ of Section 10.2 is taken as a starting point in this section. The concepts developed in this section can however also be combined with any of the other theories presented in this chapter.

The basic idea of parameterized actions is that expressions occurring in an atomic action should in the term model be evaluated by the valuation of the natural-number variables in the current state of a process. This means that the deduction rule for action prefix in Table 10.2 is replaced by the rule given in Table 10.18. Note that the valuations in a process state are now natural-number valuations, as opposed to the Boolean valuations used earlier. The *effect* function takes a natural-number valuation as its second argument, and results in a natural-number valuation. A parameter ν in an action can be seen as a function that, given values for the variables occurring in ν, results in the value for ν. Executed actions in the term model always have a concrete value as a parameter.

$x;$

$$\frac{v(\nu) = p}{\langle a(\nu).x, v\rangle \overset{a(p)}{\to} \langle x, \mathit{effect}(a(p), v)\rangle}$$

Table 10.18. Term deduction rule for action-prefix operators with parameterized actions (with $a(\nu) \in A$, $v \in NV$, $p \in \mathbf{N}$).

The parameterization of recursion variables has a different intention. A recursive specification may contain equations of the form $X(n) = t$, where n is a variable ranging over natural numbers and t some process term typically containing n. Such an equation is interpreted as the specification of infinitely many processes $X(0), X(1), \ldots$, one for each natural number. If $p \in \mathbf{N}$, then the defining equation of process $X(p)$ is obtained by substituting p for n everywhere in the right-hand side t. A parameterized recursion variable can thus be seen as a function from natural numbers to recursion variables. By substituting arbitrary natural-number expressions $\nu \in \mathbf{FN}$ for n, it is possible to obtain defining equations for any recursion variable $X(\nu)$. This allows equational reasoning for recursion variables $X(\nu)$ for general expressions ν in **FN**. The parameterization of recursion variables requires two extra deduction rules for recursion underlying the standard term model, in addition to the rules given in Table 5.2. Table 10.19 gives the additional rules, that state that a recursion variable parameterized with an expression inherits actions and termination options from the concrete process instance corresponding to the current valuation.

$y;$

$$\frac{\langle \mu X(p).E, v\rangle\downarrow \quad v(\nu)=p}{\langle \mu X(\nu).E, v\rangle\downarrow} \qquad \frac{\langle \mu X(p).E, v\rangle \overset{a(q)}{\to} \langle y, v'\rangle \quad v(\nu)=p}{\langle \mu X(\nu).E, v\rangle \overset{a(q)}{\to} \langle y, v'\rangle}$$

Table 10.19. Extra term deduction rules for parameterized recursion variables (with $\nu \in \mathbf{FN}$, $p, q \in \mathbf{N}$, $a(q) \in A$, $v, v' \in NV$, $X(n) = t \in E$).

The following examples illustrate the use of parameterized actions and recursion.

Example 10.6.3 (Parameterized actions and recursion variables) Assume that $a(\nu) \in A$ for any $\nu \in \mathbf{FN}$, and let X and Y be the names of parameterized recursion variables; assume n is a variable ranging over the natural numbers.

(i) Define a guarded recursive specification consisting of the parameterized equation $X(n) = a(n+n).X(succ(n))$. The process $X(0)$ is found by substituting 0 for n. Thus, $X(0) = a(0).X(1)$. Continuing in this way, a possible derivation is $X(0) = a(0).a(2).a(4).X(3)$.
(ii) Define a guarded recursive specification by $Y(n) = n < 2 :\to (a(n).Y(n+1))$. It is possible to derive $Y(0) = a(0).a(1).0$.

The crucial step in developing an equational theory to exploit and reason about parameterized actions and parameterized recursive processes is now to allow choices over natural numbers. This is a generalization of alternative composition, that goes beyond a purely algebraic approach to process theory, as this involves binding of variables. A family of unary operators $\sum_n$, for each natural-number variable n, is introduced. These operators are called *choice quantifiers*.

Among others for providing an axiomatization of choice quantifiers, it is important to know when a variable is free or bound in a term.

Definition 10.6.4 (Free variables) The free occurrence of natural-number variables in process terms is defined by structural induction. Variable n

- is free in any natural-number expression $\nu \in$ **FN** if and only if it occurs in ν;
- is not free in Boolean formulas *true* and *false*;
- is free in proposition $\nu \sim \mu$ for any natural-number formulas $\nu, \mu \in$ **FN** and any $\sim \in \{=, <, \leq, >, \geq\}$ if and only if it is free in ν or μ;
- is free in $\neg\phi$ for any Boolean formula $\phi \in$ **FB** if and only if it is free in ϕ;
- is free in $\phi \otimes \psi$ for any Boolean formulas $\phi, \psi \in$ **FB** and any $\otimes \in \{\vee, \wedge, \supset\}$ if and only if it is free in ϕ or ψ;
- is free in $\exists m\phi$ or $\forall m\phi$, for any Boolean formula $\phi \in$ **FB**, if and only if it is free in ϕ and $n \neq m$;
- is not free in the constant process terms $1, 0$;
- is free in action prefix $a(\nu).x$ if and only if it is free in process term x or in natural-number formula ν;
- is free in choice $x + y$ if and only if it is free in x or free in y;
- is free in guarded command $\phi :\rightarrow x$ if and only if it is free in process term x or in Boolean formula ϕ;
- is free in choice quantification $\sum_m x$ if and only if it is free in x and $n \neq m$.

With the addition of a class of binding operators, the notion of derivability of Definition 2.2.8 (Derivability) has to be adapted. In line with earlier, for any natural-number formula $\nu \in$ **FN**, ν/n is the substitution that replaces n with ν and leaves all other variables unaffected.

Definition 10.6.5 (Derivability) Let T be an equational theory extending theory $(\mathrm{BSP} + \mathrm{CQ})(A)$ of Table 10.20; let s and t be T-terms. Equation $s = t$ is derivable from theory T, as before denoted $T \vdash s = t$, if and only if it follows from the following rules:

(Axiom rule) as before in Definition 2.2.8 (Derivability);

(Substitution) for any T-terms s, t and any substitution σ of process variables and *free* natural-number variables, $T \vdash s = t$ implies that
$$T \vdash s[\sigma] = t[\sigma];$$

(Equivalence) i.e., reflexivity, symmetry, and transitivity, as before;

(Context rule) as before; note that the context rule also covers the newly introduced choice quantifiers;

(Tautology) if for all natural-number variable valuations ϕ is true if and only if ψ is true, then
$$T \vdash \phi :\rightarrow x = \psi :\rightarrow x;$$

(Alpha conversion) for any T-term t in which m does not occur free,
$T \vdash \sum_n t = \sum_m t[m/n]$.

(BSP + CQ)(A)		
(BSP + GC)(A);		
unary: $(\sum_n \text{-})_{n \in \mathbf{N}}$;		
x, y;		
$\sum_n x = x$	if n not free in x	CQ1
$\sum_n x = x + \sum_n x$		CQ2
$\sum_n (x + y) = \sum_n x + \sum_n y$		CQ3
$\sum_n \phi :\rightarrow x = \phi :\rightarrow \sum_n x$	if n not free in ϕ	CQ4
$\sum_n \phi :\rightarrow x = \exists n \phi :\rightarrow x$	if n not free in x	CQ5
$\sum_n (n = \nu) :\rightarrow x = \sum_n (n = \nu) :\rightarrow x[\nu/n]$		CQ6

Table 10.20. The process theory (BSP + CQ)(A) (with $\nu \in \mathbf{FN}$, $\phi \in \mathbf{FB}$).

The axioms for choice quantification are given in Table 10.20. This table presents the theory of basic sequential processes with choice quantification, that extends BSP(A) with guarded commands. Choice quantification binds weaker than other unary operators and stronger than binary operators. The first axiom, CQ1, considers the case where the variable does not occur free in the term x. In that case, all summands are equal and by idempotency, the sum is equal to one term. The second axiom, CQ2, deals with separating out one summand. Given Axiom CQ1, the interesting case is when n occurs free in x. Then, considering the (adapted) substitution rule in the definition of derivability above, any expression over natural numbers (also containing bound or free variables) can be substituted for n in the x summand of the right-hand side of CQ2. Axiom CQ3 states that choice quantification distributes over alternative composition. Axiom CQ4 gives distribution over guarded commands, under the condition that the bound variable does not occur free in the guarded command. The other law concerning the interplay with guarded commands, CQ5, necessitates the extension of the set of expressions of our Boolean algebra **FB** to allow quantification over natural-number variables, as done in Notation 10.6.2 (Booleans). Axiom CQ5 states that a choice quantification over a conditional reduces to a Boolean existential quantification in the conditional if the bound variable does not occur in the guarded term. Finally, CQ6 allows to substitute for a variable any expression it is equal to.

Example 10.6.6 (Derivations with choice quantifiers) An example shows the kind of calculations that can be done with the theory of Table 10.20.

$$
\begin{aligned}
&(\mathrm{BSP}+\mathrm{CQ})(A) \vdash \\
&\quad \textstyle\sum_n n < 2 :\rightarrow a(n).0 \\
&= \textstyle\sum_n (n = 0 \vee n = 1) :\rightarrow a(n).0 \\
&= \textstyle\sum_n (n = 0 :\rightarrow a(n).0 + n = 1 :\rightarrow a(n).0) \\
&= \textstyle\sum_n n = 0 :\rightarrow a(n).0 + \sum_n n = 1 :\rightarrow a(n).0 \\
&= \textstyle\sum_n n = 0 :\rightarrow a(0).0 + \sum_n n = 1 :\rightarrow a(1).0 \\
&= \exists n(n = 0) :\rightarrow a(0).0 + \exists n(n = 1) :\rightarrow a(1).0 \\
&= \mathit{true} :\rightarrow a(0).0 + \mathit{true} :\rightarrow a(1).0 \\
&= a(0).0 + a(1).0.
\end{aligned}
$$

Giving operational rules for choice quantification and a term model for theory $(\mathrm{BSP}+\mathrm{CQ})(A)$ actually turns out to be pretty straightforward. The term deduction system for theory $(\mathrm{BSP}+\mathrm{CQ})(A)$ is presented in Table 10.21. Assume that $\mathit{TDS}((\mathrm{BSP}+\mathrm{GC})(A), \mathit{effect})_{\mathrm{par}}$ is the term deduction system for theory $(\mathrm{BSP}+\mathrm{GC})(A)$ with parameterized actions, i.e., the term deduction system obtained from $\mathit{TDS}((\mathrm{BSP}+\mathrm{GC})(A), \mathit{effect})$ of Table 10.2 with the deduction rule for action prefix replaced by the rule in Table 10.18.

$\mathit{TDS}((\mathrm{BSP}+\mathrm{CQ})(A), \mathit{effect})$	
$\mathit{TDS}((\mathrm{BSP}+\mathrm{GC})(A), \mathit{effect})_{\mathrm{par}}$;	
unary: $(\sum_n \text{-})_{n \in \mathbf{N}}$;	
x, x';	
$\dfrac{\langle x[p/n], v\rangle \overset{a(q)}{\rightarrow} \langle x', v'\rangle}{\langle \sum_n x, v\rangle \overset{a(q)}{\rightarrow} \langle x', v'\rangle}$	$\dfrac{\langle x[p/n], v\rangle \downarrow}{\langle \sum_n x, v\rangle \downarrow}$

Table 10.21. Term deduction system for $(\mathrm{BSP}+\mathrm{CQ})(A)$ (with $p, q \in \mathbf{N}$, $a(q) \in A$, $v, v' \in \mathit{NV}$).

The term deduction system of Table 10.21 can be turned into a term model in the usual way. It is not too difficult to prove soundness. Ground-completeness however is more involved, because one has to account for decidability and/or completeness of the theory for reasoning about data types. Details are beyond the scope of this book. The interested reader is referred to (Luttik, 2002). Choice quantifiers cannot be eliminated, but $(\mathrm{BSP}+\mathrm{CQ})(A)$ is a conservative ground-extension of $(\mathrm{BSP}+\mathrm{GC})(A)$ (when assuming the set of Boolean formulas of the present section).

Example 10.6.7 (Program semantics) The process theory of this section, with the usual extensions such as sequential composition, can be used to capture the semantics of imperative programs. This is illustrated by means of an example. Consider the following simple program for computing the factorial of a value provided by the user of the program.

```
program factorial;

var n : Nat;
    fac : Nat;

begin
    read(n);
    fac := 1;
    while n <> 1 do fac := fac * n; n := n-1 od;
    print(fac);
end.
```

The program is composed of some typical constructs offered by imperative programming languages.

The statement `read(n)` assigns a value provided by the user of the program to the variable `n`. To capture this in the process-algebraic semantics of the program, a choice quantification and a parameterized read action are needed to describe all possibilities of receiving an input value. The *effect* function codes that the received value is assigned to the program variable `n`. The assignments in the program are captured in the semantics by actions. The effect on the value of program variables is again described in the *effect* function. For the while-loop, a recursion variable is used in combination with a conditional that decides whether the recursion should stop. This yields the following recursive specification:

$$
\begin{array}{lcl}
\mathit{Factorial} & = & \sum_n \mathit{read}(n).\mathit{init}.1 \cdot \mathit{Loop} \cdot \mathit{print}(\mathit{fac}).1 \\
\mathit{Loop} & = & \quad n > 1 :\rightarrow \mathit{multiply}(n).\mathit{decrease}.\mathit{Loop} \\
 & & + \; n = 1 :\rightarrow 1.
\end{array}
$$

The *effect* function defines the effect of actions on the valuations of variables n and fac and is given as follows. For any $d \in \mathbf{N}$ and valuation $v \in NV$,

$$
\begin{array}{ll}
\mathit{effect}(\mathit{read}(d), v)(n) & = d, \\
\mathit{effect}(\mathit{read}(d), v)(\mathit{fac}) & = v(\mathit{fac}), \\
\mathit{effect}(\mathit{init}, v)(n) & = v(n), \\
\mathit{effect}(\mathit{init}, v)(\mathit{fac}) & = 1, \\
\mathit{effect}(\mathit{print}(d), v)(n) & = v(n), \\
\mathit{effect}(\mathit{print}(d), v)(\mathit{fac}) & = v(\mathit{fac}), \\
\mathit{effect}(\mathit{multiply}(d), v)(n) & = v(n), \\
\mathit{effect}(\mathit{multiply}(d), v)(\mathit{fac}) & = v(\mathit{fac}) \times d, \\
\mathit{effect}(\mathit{decrease}, v)(n) & = v(n) - 1, \\
\mathit{effect}(\mathit{decrease}, v)(\mathit{fac}) & = v(\mathit{fac}).
\end{array}
$$

Exercises

10.6.1 Extend the process theory presented in this section with sequential composition and with parallel composition. Provide term models.

10.6.2 Consider the calculations for the Alternating-Bit Protocol in Section 7.8. Replace the data set D employed in that section by the set of natural numbers $\mathbf{N}$, and redo the calculations, using the axioms introduced in the present section.

10.6.3 Consider the Fibonacci sequence defined by $F(0) = 0$, $F(1) = 1$, and for all $n \in \mathbf{N}$, $F(n + 2) = F(n + 1) + F(n)$. Give a simple imperative program to compute the n-th Fibonacci number $F(n)$, for $n \in \mathbf{N}$, and provide it with a semantics in line with Example 10.6.7 (Program semantics).

10.7 Bibliographical remarks

Most of this chapter is based on (Baeten & Bergstra, 1997). Guarded commands originate from (Dijkstra, 1976). They were first treated in a process-algebraic context in (Ponse, 1992). The treatment of choice quantification in this chapter is based on (Luttik, 2002). State operators were first introduced in (Baeten & Bergstra, 1988).

Parameterizing processes and actions with data is an essential feature of specification languages. Many process specifications are written in the language PSF, see (Mauw & Veltink, 1993). The language μCRL (Groote & Ponse, 1995) with its accompanying toolkit has been used extensively in the specification and verification of systems by means of process algebra. Recently, the language and toolkit are superseded by mCRL2, see (Groote *et al.*, 2006). This chapter also provides the basis for the hybrid process algebra of (Bergstra & Middelburg, 2005), and further work in (Khadim, 2008).

11

Features

The various chapters so far have introduced the basics of process-algebraic reasoning, including essential concepts such as recursion, parallel composition, and abstraction, and several extensions of this basic framework with time, data, and state. This one-but-last chapter introduces two more extensions, to reason about priorities and probabilities, and elaborates briefly on mobility and variants of parallel composition in Sections 11.3 and 11.4.

11.1 Priorities

In order to specify certain applications, it is useful to be able to restrict the non-determinism in process descriptions, by allowing certain actions to have priority over others in a choice context. A priority mechanism has proved itself useful in the following circumstances:

(i) when describing interrupts and disrupts, where the normal execution of a system is pre-empted by an event that has priority;
(ii) when giving semantics to certain features of programming languages such as interrupt or error handling mechanisms;
(iii) when timing is involved, when some events may not happen prematurely and other events may need to happen as soon as possible (maximal progress);
(iv) when describing scheduling algorithms.

This section introduces a priority mechanism in the equational and operational frameworks introduced in earlier chapters. Assume that certain actions have priority over other actions. This is expressed by assuming there is some (irreflexive) partial ordering $\prec$ on the set of actions A. For simplicity, consider this partial ordering to be fixed. This means the priority is *static*. Alternatively, it is possible to specify that, given a certain partial ordering, executing a certain action leads to another partial ordering (*dynamic priority*). This possibility is not considered here, but can be developed using concepts such as the *effect* function from the previous chapter.

Thus, assume a partial ordering $\prec$ on the set of actions A. This means the following properties are satisfied:

(i) for all $a, b \in A$, *at most one* of $a \prec b, b \prec a, a = b$ is the case;

(ii) relation $\prec$ is transitive, i.e., for all $a, b, c \in A$, $a \prec b$ and $b \prec c$ implies $a \prec c$.

When $a \prec b$, then b has *priority* over a. Priority relation $\prec$ is a parameter of the process theory to be defined, BSP$\theta(A, \prec)$, BSP(A) with priorities.

The idea is to define an operator θ that enforces priorities, i.e., if $a \prec b$ and $a \prec c$ and b and c are not related by the priority relation, then the following identities are expected to hold, for any processes x and y, $\theta(a.x + b.y) = b.\theta(y)$, $\theta(a.x + c.y) = c.\theta(y)$ but $\theta(b.x + c.y) = b.\theta(x) + c.\theta(y)$. When the priority operator is applied to a system of communicating processes, it can be assumed to describe *global* priorities; when it is applied to separate components of a communication network, it describes *local* priorities.

It is not straightforward to come up with an axiomatization of the priority operator θ. As in the case of the parallel-composition operator, there is a need for an auxiliary operator. This auxiliary operator is obtained by turning the priority operator into a *binary* operator. To understand the intuition behind the binary priority operator, observe the two roles of x in a term $\theta(x)$. Term x specifies both the high-priority behavior and the low-priority behavior pre-empted by the high-priority behavior. The binary priority operator, $\_\vartheta\_$, separates these two roles. Intuitively, in $x \vartheta y$, term y specifies which behaviors have high priority, filtering all summands of x that are prioritized by a summand of y, turning those low-priority summands of x into 0. The axiomatization of the binary priority operator is straightforward. Table 11.1 presents theory BSP$\theta(A, \prec)$.

The term deduction system for theory BSP$\theta(A, \prec)$ is given in Table 11.2. The operational rules in Table 11.2 capture the intuitive behavior of priorities and are not difficult to understand: an action a can be executed when no action with priority can be executed. Notice that this term deduction system contains negative premises.

The equational theory given in Table 11.1 is sound and ground-complete for the term model induced by the term deduction system of Table 11.2. Metatheory in the style of Chapter 3 that can cope with negative premises and that allows to establish the ground-completeness result is developed in (Verhoef,

BSP$\theta(A, \prec)$

BSP(A)

unary: θ; binary: $\_\vartheta\_$;

x, y, z;

$\theta(x) = x\vartheta x$	PRI0	$a.x\vartheta 1 = a.\theta(x)$		PRI4
		$a.x\vartheta b.y = 0$	if $a \prec b$	PRI5
$0\vartheta x = 0$	PRI1	$a.x\vartheta b.y = a.\theta(x)$	if $a \not\prec b$	PRI6
$1\vartheta x = 1$	PRI2	$(x + y)\vartheta z = x\vartheta z + y\vartheta z$		PRI7
$a.x\vartheta 0 = a.\theta(x)$	PRI3	$x\vartheta(y + z) = (x\vartheta y)\vartheta z$		PRI8

Table 11.1. The process theory BSP$\theta(A, \prec)$ (with $a, b \in A$).

TDS(BSP$\theta(A, \prec)$)

TDS(BSP(A));

unary: θ; binary: $\_\vartheta\_$;

x, x', y;

$$\frac{x\downarrow}{\theta(x)\downarrow} \qquad \frac{x \xrightarrow{a} x' \quad \text{for all } b \in A \text{ with } a \prec b,\ x \not\xrightarrow{b}}{\theta(x) \xrightarrow{a} \theta(x')}$$

$$\frac{x\downarrow}{x\vartheta y\downarrow} \qquad \frac{x \xrightarrow{a} x' \quad \text{for all } b \in A \text{ with } a \prec b,\ y \not\xrightarrow{b}}{x\vartheta y \xrightarrow{a} \theta(x')}$$

Table 11.2. Term deduction system for BSP$\theta(A, \prec)$ (with $a \in A$).

1994). A ground-completeness proof in a slightly different setting can be found in (Baeten *et al.*, 1986).

Occurrences of the two priority operators can be eliminated from closed BSP$\theta(A, \prec)$-terms, resulting in closed BSP(A)-terms. BSP$\theta(A, \prec)$ is a conservative ground-extension of BSP(A).

The following two propositions list some expected identities for the unary priority operator θ that are derivable from the defining axiom for θ and the axioms for the binary priority operator of theory BSP$\theta(A, \prec)$, either for arbitrary terms or for closed terms.

Proposition 11.1.1 (Identities) The following equations are derivable from BSP$\theta(A, \prec)$:

(i) $\theta(0) = 0$;
(ii) $\theta(1) = 1$;
(iii) $\theta(a.x) = a.\theta(x)$;
(iv) $\theta(x + y) = \theta(x)\vartheta y + \theta(y)\vartheta x$;

(v) $\theta(x + y)\vartheta x = \theta(x + y)$.

Proof See exercises. □

Proposition 11.1.2 (Closed-term identities) The following two identities are derivable from BSP$\theta(A, \prec)$, for all closed terms p, q:

(i) $\theta(\theta(p)) = \theta(p)$;
(ii) $p + p\vartheta q = p$.

Proof See exercises. □

The standard extension of the basic theory with communication and recursion turns out to cause a problem in the development of a standard term model.

Example 11.1.3 (Priority anomaly) Suppose the term deduction system for BSP$\theta(A, \prec)$ of Table 11.2 is extended with the usual rules for parallel composition, encapsulation, and recursion. Assume actions $a, b, c \in A$ with priority ordering $b \prec c$ and communication function $\gamma(a, b) = c$. Consider the following (unguarded) recursive equation:

$$X = a.1 \parallel \partial_{\{c\}}(\theta(b.1 + X)).$$

Then, it can be inferred that $X \xrightarrow{c} 1 \parallel 1$ if and only if $X \stackrel{c}{\nrightarrow}$. This is a contradiction.

The contradiction illustrated in the above example ensues from the combination of communication, priorities, and unguarded recursion. It shows that the standard term deduction system for theory TCP$\theta_{\text{rec}}(A, \prec, \gamma)$, TCP with priorities and recursion, does not define a transition system for all the closed terms in the theory. The problem can be avoided by restricting the set of recursive equations to guarded recursive equations, or in other words, by considering only processes that are definable over theory TCP$\theta(A, \prec, \gamma)$, TCP with priorities, as defined in Definition 5.7.5 (Definability). TCP$\theta_{\text{grec}}(A, \prec, \gamma)$ denotes theory TCP with priorities and guarded recursion. The standard term model for this theory based on the usual deduction rules for communication and recursion is well-defined (in the sense that a proof of the existence of a transition in the transition-system space, based on Definition 3.2.3 (Transition-system space induced by a deduction system), is finite; in terms of the meta-theoretical framework of (Verhoef, 1994), it can be shown that a stratification for the deduction rules exists). The following two examples are formulated in theory TCP$\theta_{\text{grec}}(A, \prec, \gamma)$.

Example 11.1.4 (Interrupts) A printer P has to print a sequence of data $\langle d_0, d_1, \ldots\rangle$, where $d_i \in D$ (for some given finite data set D), but can be interrupted by a keyboard K. There is a (nameless) communication port between P and K. The standard communication function is used. Assume the following atomic actions:

(i) $key(break)$, $!break$, $key(start)$, $!start$ (actions of K);
(ii) $?break$, $?start$, and $print(d)$ for $d \in D$ (actions of P).

Consider the following guarded recursive specification.

$$\begin{aligned} K &= 1 + key(break).!break.K + key(start).!start.K \\ P &= W_0 \\ W_i &= 1 + ?start.P_i + ?break.W_i && (i \in \mathbf{N}) \\ P_i &= print(d_i).P_{i+1} + ?start.P_i + ?break.W_i && (i \in \mathbf{N}). \end{aligned}$$

In this specification, P_i is the state of the printer after $d_0, \ldots, d_{i-1}$ have been printed and it is ready to print d_i, and W_i is the state of the printer after $d_0, \ldots, d_{i-1}$ have been printed and it is waiting for a start signal. The encapsulation set is

$$H = \{?break, !break, ?start, !start\}.$$

Now it has to be enforced that commands from the keyboard are accepted by the printer right away, and that no further print actions take place. Priorities are used to enforce this. The priority partial ordering on the set of action is given by

$$print(d) \prec ¿break, print(d) \prec ¿start,$$

for each $d \in D$.

For the composed system $\theta(\partial_H(K \parallel P))$, the following recursive specification can be derived:

$$\begin{aligned} X_i &= 1 + key(break).¿break.X_i + key(start).¿start.Y_i \\ Y_i &= print(d_i).Y_{i+1} + key(break).¿break.X_i + key(start).¿start.Y_i, \end{aligned}$$

for each $i \in \mathbf{N}$. Expressions $\theta(\partial_H(K \parallel W_i))$ are a solution for the X_i, and expressions $\theta(\partial_H(K \parallel P_i))$ are a solution for the Y_i.

Example 11.1.5 (Error handling) A file F contains a sequence of data $\langle d_0, d_1, \ldots\rangle$, with $d_i \in D$ for some given finite data set D, that has to be printed out by printer P, unless a file crash occurs. If a file crash occurs, an error message should be printed. There is a communication port between processes F and P. Standard communication is used. Consider the following actions:

(i) $get(d)$, $!d$ (for $d \in D$), and $crash$ (actions of F);

(ii) $?d, print(d)$ (for $d \in D$), $observe(crash)$, and $print(crash)$ (actions of P).

Consider the following guarded recursive specifications.

$$\begin{aligned} F &= F_0 \\ F_i &= 1 + get(d_i).!d_i.F_{i+1} + crash.1 \qquad (i \in \mathbf{N}) \\ P &= 1 + \sum_{d \in D} ?d.print(d).P + observe(crash).print(crash).1. \end{aligned}$$

In this specification, F_i is the state of the file after $d_0, \ldots, d_{i-1}$ have been sent. The encapsulation set is

$$H = \{?d, !d \mid d \in D\}.$$

To enforce that the observation of the file crash only occurs when the file has actually crashed, priorities are used. The priority partial ordering is given by

$$observe(crash) \prec get(d), observe(crash) \prec \text{?`}d,$$

for each $d \in D$.

For the composed system $\theta(\partial_H(F \parallel P))$, the following recursive specification can be derived,

$$\begin{aligned} X_i &= 1 + get(d_i).\text{?`}d_i.Y_i + crash.observe(crash).print(crash).1 \\ Y_i &= print(d_i).X_{i+1} + get(d_{i+1}).print(d_i).\text{?`}d_{i+1}.Y_{i+1} \\ &\quad + crash.print(d_i).observe(crash).print(crash).1, \end{aligned}$$

for each $i \in \mathbf{N}$. Expressions $\theta(\partial_H(F_i \parallel P))$ are a solution for the X_i, and expressions $\theta(\partial_H(F_{i+1} \parallel print(d_i).P))$ are a solution for the Y_i.

This specification can be simplified further by assuming extra priorities: define

$$print(e) \prec get(d), print(e) \prec \text{?`}d,$$

for each $d, e \in D$. This expresses somehow that the 'internal' actions $get(d)$ and $\text{?`}d$ are executed much faster than the external actions $print(e)$, and therefore have priority. The specification becomes:

$$\begin{aligned} X &= 1 + get(d_0).\text{?`}d_0.Y_0 + crash.observe(crash).print(crash).1 \\ Y_i &= get(d_{i+1}).print(d_i).\text{?`}d_{i+1}.Y_{i+1} \\ &\quad + crash.print(d_i).observe(crash).print(crash).1, \end{aligned}$$

for each $i \in \mathbf{N}$.

An extension of the current theory with the silent action and abstraction is not straightforward. Consider the following example. Suppose there are atomic actions a, b, c with priority relation $\tau \prec c$ and $c \prec b$. By the branching law, Axiom B from Table 8.1, it holds that $a.(\tau.(b.1 + c.1) + c.1) = a.(b.1 + c.1)$. But then

$$a.c.1 = \theta(a.(\tau.(b.1 + c.1) + c.1)) = \theta(a.(b.1 + c.1)) = a.b.1,$$

which is an unwanted equality. It is necessary either to require that τ always has maximal priority, or to use an even finer equivalence notion than branching bisimilarity, so-called *orthogonal* bisimilarity (Bergstra *et al.*, 2003).

Exercises

11.1.1 Prove Proposition 11.1.1 (Identities).

11.1.2 Prove Proposition 11.1.2 (Closed-term identities).

11.1.3 Consider the following generalization of Proposition 11.1.1(iv):
$\theta(x + y + z) = \theta(x)\vartheta(y + z) + \theta(y)\vartheta(x + z) + \theta(z)\vartheta(x + y)$.
Prove that this identity is derivable from BSP$\theta(A, \prec)$.

11.1.4 Verify the problem with the operational semantics of priorities that is mentioned in Example 11.1.3 (Priority anomaly).

11.1.5 Give the derivation of the recursive specification in Example 11.1.4 (Interrupts) and draw the transition system of the printer process X_0. Since the specification of X_0 is a specification over the signature of theory BSP(A), abstraction can be applied. Consider $\tau_I(X_0)$, with $I = \{$*key*(*break*), ‽*break*, *key*(*start*), ‽*start*$\}$. Derive a specification for $\tau_I(X_0)$ using KFAR^{b}, and interpret your answer.

11.1.6 Give the derivation concerning the first recursive specification given in Example 11.1.5 (Error handling) and draw the transition system of X_0. Consider process $\tau_I(X_0)$, with $I = \{‽d, get(d) \mid d \in D\} \cup \{$*crash*, *observe*(*crash*)$\}$. Derive a specification for $\tau_I(X_0)$, and interpret your answer. Do the same for the final recursive specification in Example 11.1.5, considering $\tau_I(X)$.

11.2 Probabilities

In Section 7.8, an unreliable communication channel was specified as follows. Recall that F is the set of frames possibly carried by the channel.

$$K = 1 + \sum_{x \in F} sk?x.(t.kr!x.K + t.kr!\bot.K).$$

The specification uses a special internal action t and a non-deterministic choice in order to model the uncertainty, whether or not the frame will be forwarded correctly (denoting a corrupted frame as $\bot$). In the verification of Section 8.9, a notion of fairness was needed in order to conclude that, eventually, a message will be forwarded correctly.

In practice, there is often a bound on the occurrence of failure, e.g., it is known that the channel fails at most 10 % of the time. Based on such a bound, it becomes possible to address the performance of an unreliable channel or the performance of a protocol. In such cases, it is advantageous to replace the non-deterministic choice by a *probabilistic choice*. The present section gives a brief introduction to some of the issues involved when probabilistic choice is added to a process algebraic theory.

Assume a class of binary operators $\boxplus_p$, called probabilistic choice operators, where parameter p is a number between 0 and 1, i.e., $p \in (0, 1)$. Process $x \boxplus_p y$ is either x or it is y: it is x with probability p and it is y with probability $1 - p$. Notice that, different from the choice in $x + y$, a probabilistic choice is a choice that cannot be influenced by the environment. A process $x \boxplus_{.9} y$ can be determined by an experiment: if it is executed a large number of times, say 1000, x will be found in some 900 cases, and y in some 100 cases. Using a probabilistic choice operator, the specification of an unreliable channel with a failure rate of 10 % can be given as follows:

$$K = 1 + \sum_{x \in F} sk?x.(kr!x.K \boxplus_{.9} kr!\bot.K).$$

Note that probabilistic choice can be used to replace the non-deterministic choice in the forwarding of a frame in the channel, but not the choice in the message to be received at port *sk*, leading to the choice quantification over the set of frames F. So, probabilistic choice can be used to replace some uses of alternative composition, but not all. In particular, use of alternative composition in receipt of data, but also alternative composition used in the expansion of parallel composition (denoting interleaving) cannot be replaced. Thus, in this section an existing process theory with the choice operator, BSP(A) of Section 4.4, is extended with probabilistic choice.

It turns out that the axioms of BSP(A) cannot be maintained in full in the presence of probabilistic choice. This is because, in $x+x$, when x has the form of a probabilistic choice, in fact two separate experiments are going on at the same time, and the outcome on the left may be different from the outcome on the right. This point is further elaborated below.

Table 11.3 presents theory BSPprb(A), BSP(A) with probabilistic choice. Axiom A3 of BSP(A) is replaced by two new axioms, Axioms AA3 and EA3. Since Axiom A6 implies that $0 + 0 = 0$, it is possible to prove idempotency of alternative composition for all closed BSP(A)-terms (see the exercises).

Since not all axioms of BSP(A) are maintained in BSPprb(A), the latter is, technically, not an extension of the former, as defined in Definition 2.2.14. However, it is a conservative ground-extension (see Definition 2.2.19).

Consider the new axioms, PRB1–4. PRB1 is a kind of commutativity for probabilistic choice: when the positions of x and y are switched, the complement of the probability is taken. PRB3, the idempotency of probabilistic

BSPprb(A)		
constant: 0, 1;	unary: $(a.\_)_{a \in A}$;	binary: $\_ + \_$, $(\_ \boxplus_p \_)_{p \in \langle 0,1 \rangle}$;
x, y, z;		
$x + y = y + x$		A1
$(x + y) + z = x + (y + z)$		A2
$a.x + a.x = a.x$		AA3
$1 + 1 = 1$		EA3
$x + 0 = x$		A6
$x \boxplus_p y = y \boxplus_{1-p} x$		PRB1
$x \boxplus_p (y \boxplus_r z) = (x \boxplus_{p/(p+r-pr)} y) \boxplus_{p+r-pr} z$		PRB2
$x \boxplus_p x = x$		PRB3
$(x \boxplus_p y) + z = (x + z) \boxplus_p (y + z)$		PRB4

Table 11.3. The process theory BSPprb(A).

choice, is obvious as the outcome of the experiment is x in every case, and PRB4 serves to distribute alternative composition over probabilistic choice. Finally, consider the associativity law PRB2, which requires some explanation. In $x \boxplus_p (y \boxplus_r z)$, the probability of x is p, the probability of y is $(1 - p)r$ and the probability of z is $(1 - p)(1 - r)$. Taking the complement of the last probability gives $p + r - pr$, which explains the second number on the right-hand side of PRB2. Of this last probability $p + r - pr$, x should get a fraction equal to p and y the rest, which is obtained by the choice for the first probability in the right-hand side of PRB2, because $p = (p/(p + r - pr))(p + r - pr)$.

Example 11.2.1 (Probabilistic choice) Using Axiom PRB4 of BSPprb(A), the following derivation can be made:

$$
\begin{aligned}
\mathrm{BSPprb}(A) \vdash \\
& (1 \boxplus_{1/2} 0) + (1 \boxplus_{1/2} 0) \\
= {} & (1 + (1 \boxplus_{1/2} 0)) \boxplus_{1/2} (0 + (1 \boxplus_{1/2} 0)) \\
= {} & ((1 + 1) \boxplus_{1/2} (1 + 0)) \boxplus_{1/2} (1 \boxplus_{1/2} 0) \\
= {} & (1 \boxplus_{1/2} 1) \boxplus_{1/2} (1 \boxplus_{1/2} 0) \\
= {} & 1 \boxplus_{1/2} (1 \boxplus_{1/2} 0) \\
= {} & (1 \boxplus_{2/3} 1) \boxplus_{3/4} 0 \\
= {} & 1 \boxplus_{3/4} 0.
\end{aligned}
$$

This example shows that idempotency of alternative composition does not hold for processes with probabilistic choice as the main operator.

In order to give transition systems for the closed terms of theory BSPprb(A), it is needed to consider two kinds of transitions: besides the action transitions as usual, there is a need for probabilistic transitions. In the operational rules of the term deduction system, just the existence of a probabilistic transition is determined; the actual value of the probability will be determined separately. This is because, in a term $a.1 \boxplus_{1/2} b.1$, the probabilistic transition to $a.1$ has probability $1/2$, but in term $a.1 \boxplus_{1/2} a.1$, the probability is 1, and this is difficult to achieve in operational rules.

The set of closed BSPprb(A)-terms can be divided into two parts: the *probabilistic* terms and the *dynamic* terms. The probabilistic terms are the terms that have a probabilistic choice as the main operator, or they are an alternative composition of subterms of which at least one has a probabilistic choice as the main operator. These terms will have only outgoing probabilistic transitions to dynamic terms. All closed terms that are not probabilistic are called dynamic: they can be written in the form $\sum_{i<n} a_i.q_i (+1)$ for some natural number n, atomic actions a_i, subterms q_i and possibly occurring termination constant. Dynamic terms do not have any outgoing probabilistic transitions, but only action transitions and a termination predicate. The dynamic terms are the terms satisfying idempotence of alternative composition ($x + x = x$).

Thus, in the operational rules in Table 11.4, an extra binary relation $\rightsquigarrow$ is defined denoting a probabilistic transition, such that,

- if $x \rightsquigarrow x'$, then x is a probabilistic term and x' is a dynamic term;
- if x is a dynamic term, then $x \not\rightsquigarrow$, i.e., it does not have a probabilistic transition.

A *probability distribution function* μ is defined in order to assign probabilities to the probabilistic transitions.

Definition 11.2.2 (Probability distribution function) The probability distribution function μ gives the probability of a transition between any two closed BSPprb(A)-terms. For each pair of closed BSPprb(A)-terms, it has a value in the closed interval $[0, 1]$, and it is defined structurally by the following clauses. Let $p \in (0, 1)$ and let q, r, q', r', and s be closed BSPprb(A)-terms.

- $\mu(a.q, a.q) = 1$,
- $\mu(0, 0) = 1$,
- $\mu(1, 1) = 1$,
- $\mu(q + r, q' + r') = \mu(q, q') \cdot \mu(r, r')$,
- $\mu(q \boxplus_p r, s) = p \cdot \mu(q, s) + (1 - p) \cdot \mu(r, s)$, and
- $\mu(q, r) = 0$, in all other cases.

$TDS(\mathrm{BSPprb}(A))$		
constant: 0; 1;	unary: $(a.\_)_{a \in A}$;	binary: $\_ + \_$; $(\_ \boxplus_p \_)_{p \in (0,1)}$;
x, x', y, y';		

$$a.x \xrightarrow{a} x \qquad 1\downarrow$$

$$\frac{x \rightsquigarrow x' \quad y \rightsquigarrow y'}{x + y \rightsquigarrow x' + y'} \quad \frac{x \rightsquigarrow x' \quad y \not\rightsquigarrow}{x + y \rightsquigarrow x' + y} \quad \frac{y \rightsquigarrow y' \quad x \not\rightsquigarrow}{x + y \rightsquigarrow x + y'}$$

$$\frac{x \xrightarrow{a} x' \quad y \not\rightsquigarrow}{x + y \xrightarrow{a} x'} \quad \frac{y \xrightarrow{a} y' \quad x \not\rightsquigarrow}{x + y \xrightarrow{a} y'}$$

$$\frac{x\downarrow \quad y \not\rightsquigarrow}{(x + y)\downarrow} \quad \frac{y\downarrow \quad x \not\rightsquigarrow}{(x + y)\downarrow}$$

$$\frac{x \rightsquigarrow x'}{x \boxplus_p y \rightsquigarrow x'} \quad \frac{y \rightsquigarrow y'}{x \boxplus_p y \rightsquigarrow y'} \quad \frac{x \not\rightsquigarrow}{x \boxplus_p y \rightsquigarrow x} \quad \frac{y \not\rightsquigarrow}{x \boxplus_p y \rightsquigarrow y}$$

Table 11.4. Term deduction system for BSPprb(A) (with $a \in A$).

This function can be generalized to give the total probability to pass to a *set* M of closed BSPprb(A)-terms, by the following clause:

$$\mu(q, M) = \sum_{q' \in M} \mu(q, q').$$

Observe that it can be derived from the operational rules that, for any pair p, q of closed BSPprb(A)-terms, $p \rightsquigarrow q$ exactly when $\mu(p, q) > 0$.

Next, the notion of (strong) bisimilarity is adapted as follows.

Definition 11.2.3 (Probabilistic bisimilarity) Let B be an equivalence relation on closed BSPprb(A)-terms. Denote the equivalence class of a term p by $[p]_B$. Then B is a *(probabilistic) bisimulation* if and only if for all closed BSPprb(A)-terms p, p', q, q',

- if $B(p, q)$ and $p \rightsquigarrow p'$, then either
  - there is a closed BSPprb(A)-term q' such that $q \rightsquigarrow q'$ and $B(p', q')$ and $\mu(p, [p']_B) = \mu(q, [q']_B)$ or
  - $B(p', q)$ and $\mu(p, [p']_B) = 1$;
- if $B(p, q)$ and $p \xrightarrow{a} p'$ for some action a, then there is a closed BSPprb(A)-term q' such that $q \xrightarrow{a} q'$ and $B(p', q')$;
- if $B(p, q)$ and $p\downarrow$, then $q\downarrow$.

If there is a probabilistic bisimulation relating closed BSPprb(A)-terms p, q, then p, q are probabilistically bisimilar, notation $p \leftrightarrow q$.

The first clause in the previous definition necessitates to presuppose that any probabilistic bisimulation is an equivalence relation. The resulting symmetry implies that symmetric clauses as in earlier bisimilarity definitions are not necessary here. To see why it is needed to formulate the definition of a probabilistic bisimulation in this way, consider the transition systems generated by the rules of Table 4.6 for terms $1 \boxplus_{1/2} 0$ and $(1 \boxplus_{1/3} (1+1)) \boxplus_{1/2} 0$ (Exercise 11.2.4).

Now it can be established that probabilistic bisimilarity is a congruence relation on the term algebra of BSPprb(A), and that the axioms of BSPprb(A) are sound and ground-complete for the term model.

Exercises

11.2.1 Prove that, for all closed BSP(A)-terms p, BSPprb(A) $\vdash p + p = p$.

11.2.2 Prove that BSPprb(A) is a conservative ground-extension of BSP(A).

11.2.3 Argue that the toss of a fair coin can be modeled by the process $\mathit{flip}.(\mathit{heads}.1 \boxplus_{1/2} \mathit{tails}.1)$. Draw the transition system generated by the operational rules of Table 4.6, and put in the values of the probabilities involved.

11.2.4 Draw the transition systems generated by the operational rules of Table 4.6 for terms $1 \boxplus_{1/2} 0$ and $(1 \boxplus_{1/3} (1+1)) \boxplus_{1/2} 0$, and put in the values of the probabilities involved. Argue why a probabilistic bisimulation needs to be an equivalence relation.

11.2.5 Prove for all closed BSPprb(A)-terms p and q that $p \rightsquigarrow q$ if and only if $\mu(p, q) > 0$.

11.2.6 Consider the recursive equation $X = 1 \boxplus_{1/2} X$. Now $X = 1$ cannot be derived, but argue that the probability that X equals 1 is 1.

11.2.7 Consider the extension of the present theory with sequential composition. Give an example to show that the distributive law A4 ($(x + y) \cdot z = x \cdot z + y \cdot z$) is not valid in general. Argue that the law $(a.x + y) \cdot z = a.x \cdot z + y \cdot z$ is valid, and show that, using this law, it can be derived that the distributive law holds for all closed BSPprb(A)-terms p, q that do not contain a 1 summand.

11.2.8 Consider the extension of the present theory with parallel composition. The duplication of variables in the merge axiom M leads to difficulties. The identity can only be maintained for dynamic processes; probabilities have to be resolved before interleaving can be enacted. Develop operational rules and an axiomatization for parallel composition.

11.3 Mobility

Mobile processes are processes that move around in space, and that can change their communication links when doing so. Also, names of communication ports can be communicated. Some simple examples of process mobility are presented next.

Example 11.3.1 (Mobile buffers) Recall the definition of a one-place buffer with input port i and output port o from Section 7.6:

$$Buf1_{io} = 1 + \sum_{d \in D} i?d.o!d.Buf1_{io}.$$

If there is a set of communication ports P (with $P \cap D = \emptyset$), and a number of these one-place buffers are connected in sequence, then termination of the whole system can only take place when all the buffers are empty.

Consider instead a situation, where a buffer that is empty and that has a left neighbor that is full, can cut itself out of the sequence, passing its output port to its left neighbor, and die. This can be described by the following equations.

$$Buf1mob_{io} = i!o.1 + \sum_{d \in D} i?d.Buf1mob^d_{io} \quad \text{and, for all } d \in D,$$
$$Buf1mob^d_{io} = o!d.Buf1mob_{io} + \sum_{p \in P} o?p.Buf1mob^d_{ip}.$$

The mobile buffer $Buf1mob_{io}$ can, when it is empty, send its output port o to the left via its input port i and terminate, or it can receive an input from the left via its input port i, and become full. When it is full, containing data d, it can either send its contents to the right via port o in the normal way, or receive a new output port p from the right via its original output port o; it then changes its output port to p, while remaining full and maintaining the original data d. Exercise 11.3.1 asks for some calculations.

Example 11.3.2 (A car in a communication network) Consider a car that is moving in a communication network, consisting of a number of base stations $Station_n$ (with $n \in N$). Each base station has a port no that can be connected to a car and a port ni that is connected to a control process. The car receives messages $m \in M$ from base stations, and sends back messages with its location $\ell \in L$. The base station forwards this information to the control process that takes the location information, and based on it determines whether or not a handover should take place. Assume that $\overline{\ell}$ denotes the base station that is closest to a given location ℓ.

Figure 11.1 visualizes the situation with two base stations, $n = 1, 2$. Initially, the car is connected to base station $Station_1$, and its location ℓ has this base station as the closest station, $\overline{\ell} = 1$. The car process is denoted $Car_{\ell,1}$,

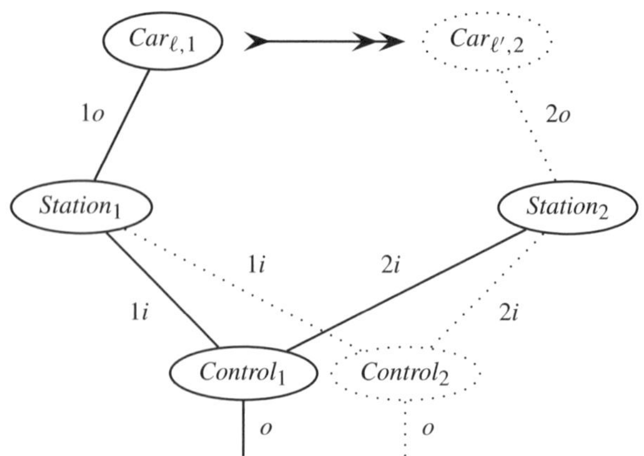

Fig. 11.1. A car in a communication network.

the indices denoting the location and the base station id the car is connected to. The process describing the movement of the car and the accompanying network management starts by the control process inputting a message at a port o that synchronizes the control process with the environment. The control process is denoted by $Control_1$, the index representing the base station to which the car is currently connected. The message received over o is forwarded to the car via base station 1, and the car sends back a reply and its current location ℓ'. If the location matches the current connection, this is maintained; otherwise the control will switch by sending the number of the new base station along base station 1. The total system is given by term

$$\partial_H(Car_{\ell,1} \parallel Station_1 \parallel Station_2 \parallel Control_1),$$

where $\overline{\ell} = 1$ and all sends and receives at ports $1o, 2o, 1i, 2i$ are encapsulated via H. The processes in the parallel composition are specified as follows, where it is not specified how a response is generated and a new location is determined when the car receives a message. Let $m' \in M, n' \in N$. For all $n \in N$,

$$\begin{aligned}
Control_n &= \sum_{m\in M} o?m.ni!m. \sum_{m\in M,\ell\in L} ni?(m,\ell).o!(m,\overline{\ell}). \\
&\qquad\qquad\qquad\qquad ((\overline{\ell} = n) :\rightarrow Control_n \\
&\qquad\qquad\qquad\qquad +(\overline{\ell} \neq n) :\rightarrow ni!\overline{\ell}.Control_{\overline{\ell}} \\
&\qquad\qquad\qquad\qquad), \\
Car_{\ell,n} &= \sum_{m\in M} no?m.no!(m',\ell').Car_{\ell',n} + \sum_{n'\in N} no?n'.Car_{\ell',n'}, \\
Station_n &= \sum_{m\in M} ni?m.no!m. \sum_{m'\in M,\ell'\in L} no?(m',\ell').ni!(m',\ell').Station_n \\
&\qquad\qquad\qquad\qquad + \sum_{n'\in N} ni?n'.no!n'.Station_n.
\end{aligned}$$

The equations use the guarded command of Section 10.2. When some of the sum operators are not considered as abbreviations, the theory of Section 10.6 must be used, involving the choice-quantification operator that binds variables. The π-calculus of (Milner, 1999; Sangiorgi & Walker, 2001) that treats mobility in depth has even more variable binding operators. The interested reader is referred to these publications.

Exercise 11.3.2 below asks for the calculations that show a handover.

Exercises

11.3.1 Consider the buffers of Example 11.3.1 (Mobile buffers). Calculate the behavior of the system

$$\partial_H(Buf1mob_{il} \parallel Buf1mob_{lo}),$$

where H is such that all sends and receives on port l are encapsulated.

11.3.2 Consider the car of Example 11.3.2 (A car in a communication network). In the system

$$\partial_H(Car_{\ell,1} \parallel Station_1 \parallel Station_2 \parallel Control_1),$$

all sends and receives at ports $1o, 2o, 1i, 2i$ are encapsulated via H. Assume $\overline{\ell} = 1$ and $\overline{\ell'} = 2$. Calculate a number of steps until the handover is achieved.

11.4 Parallel composition revisited

This section takes a closer look at parallel composition and some of its variations. Parallel composition as it has been considered up to this point has *asynchronous cooperation* (processes can proceed to execute actions independently) and *synchronous communication* (interaction between processes occurs by means of synchronization). Moreover, communication is *symmetric*: there is no basic difference between sender and receiver. (Only in modeling value passing, see for example the communicating buffers of Section 7.6, Figure 7.3, asymmetry is involved.) This section briefly considers other mechanisms.

First of all, consider *asynchronous communication*. This form of communication occurs when a process can output a message without waiting for a synchronization with a receiving process. This can be modeled by putting a channel process in the middle (like in the description of the Alternating-Bit Protocol in Section 7.8), but can also be done directly by using the state operators of Section 10.5. In the latter case, the set or the sequence of messages that are sent but not yet received, is kept in the state of the state operators. Note that a difference can be made by treating outstanding messages as a sequence (the channel is queue-like) or as a set (the channel is bag-like). For each communication channel c, a separate set of state operators λ^c can be used.

Another option is to consider synchronous cooperation. In this case, parallel components proceed in lock-step, as for instance in an integrated circuit. It can be said that parallel composition reduces to the communication merge in this case, and all left-merge terms reduce to 0. But then, communication, or in fact synchronization, should be defined for all pairs of atomic actions, preserving their identity. Thus, these are a kind of *multi-actions*, bags of atomic actions.

Next, consider asymmetric variants of communication. The standard communication function γ_S is symmetric, where both send and receive actions are encapsulated if communication is to be enforced. The send actions can be replaced by a *put* action, when the sender process outputs a message at a port, no matter whether the receiver is able to receive or not. Still, put actions synchronize with receive actions to yield communication actions, but only receive actions are encapsulated, and put actions are given lower priority than communication actions. Thus, the priority operator of Section 11.1 is used.

The reverse case, where the receive action is replaced by a *get* action, is somewhat similar. In addition to get actions along a port parameterized by a data element, also a get action with an error parameter is needed, in case no send action is offered. Get actions synchronize with send actions to yield communication actions, and all regular get actions and all send actions are encapsulated. The error get action is given lower priority than communication actions.

Exercises

11.4.1 Work out the case of asynchronous communication via state operators, by giving atomic actions involved, and specifying *action* and *effect* functions of the state operators.

11.4.2 Define a parallel composition operator that is based on synchronous cooperation on top of the theory BSP(A). It may be useful to consider vector notation for multi-actions. Elaborate an axiomatization and operational rules.

11.4.3 Work out the case of asymmetric communication. Is it possible to generalize the put mechanism to a broadcast mechanism, involving multiple receivers?

11.5 Bibliographical remarks

Section 11.1 is based on (Baeten *et al.*, 1986), but the axiomatization comes from (Aceto *et al.*, 1994). For more on priorities, see (Cleaveland *et al.*, 2001). For orthogonal bisimilarity, see (Bergstra *et al.*, 2003). Section 11.2 is based on (Andova, 2002). The operational semantics presented is new here, and does not yield a strictly alternating model in which probabilistic and action transitions always alternate. The first definition of a notion of bisimulation for probabilistic processes can be found in (Larsen & Skou, 1991), which shows the need for the requirement that a probabilistic bisimulation relation is an equivalence relation. For more on probabilities, see (Jonsson *et al.*, 2001) and (Markovski, 2008).

The section on mobility uses two examples taken from (Milner, 1999). This section briefly describes a mechanism of mobility. Much more about mobility can be found in the π-calculus, see e.g. (Milner, 1999; Sangiorgi & Walker, 2001).

Background material on asynchronous communication can be found in (Baeten & Weijland, 1990), which in turn is based on (Bergstra *et al.*, 1985). For synchronous cooperation, see (Weijland, 1989), partly based on (Bergstra & Klop, 1984a). For a version of CCS with synchronous cooperation, see (Milner, 1983). Finally, for asymmetric communication, the best reference is (Baeten & Weijland, 1990).

12
Semantics

So far, strong bisimilarity and several of its variants have been chosen as the semantic equivalence for processes. This chapter takes another look at the semantic domain. In Chapter 3, the domain of a transition-system space was introduced, and the equivalence relations language equivalence and strong bisimilarity were introduced. Bisimilarity was chosen as the preferred notion of equivalence, because it allows to distinguish between processes with different moments of choice, different branching structures. This chapter discusses other equivalences, and axiom systems that are ground-complete with respect to these other equivalences. For the most part, discussion is restricted to the process theory BSP(A). The addition of the silent action τ leads to many interesting observations, and a vastly increased complexity. In order to focus on a few key issues, this extension is not considered here.

12.1 Bisimilarity and trace semantics

Theorems 4.4.7 (Soundness of BSP(A)) and 4.4.12 (Ground-completeness of BSP(A)) from Section 4.4 are repeated here, to start off the discussion.

Theorem 12.1.1 (Soundness and ground-completeness) Theory BSP(A) is a sound and ground-complete axiomatization of the standard term model $\mathbb{P}(\mathrm{BSP}(A))_{/\leftrightarrow}$, i.e., for any closed BSP(A)-terms p and q, $\mathrm{BSP}(A) \vdash p = q$ if and only if $\mathbb{P}(\mathrm{BSP}(A))_{/\leftrightarrow} \models p = q$.

It is the intention to also state and prove similar results for other notions of semantic equivalence in this chapter. First of all, consider the notion of language equivalence introduced in Definition 3.1.7 (Run, language equivalence). This equivalence identifies two transition systems if and only if they have the same set of complete executions, called runs in the referred definition. Thus, any executions that terminate unsuccessfully are ignored; in particular, processes $a.0$ and $b.0$ are identified, because both have an empty set of runs. This chapter considers only process equivalences that distinguish a process that is able to do an a-step from a process that is able to do a b-step. Language equivalence does not satisfy this restriction. However, the notion can be adapted so that also unsuccessfully terminating runs are taken into account.

Definition 12.1.2 (Traces and trace equivalence) Let s be a state in the set of states S of a transition-system space over the set of labels L. A sequence $\sigma \in L^*$ is a *trace* of s if and only if there is a state $t \in S$ with $s \stackrel{\sigma}{\rightarrow}^* t$ (as defined in Definition 3.1.3 (Reachability)). A sequence $\sigma\downarrow$ (with $\sigma \in L^*$) is an *accepting trace* of s if and only if there is a state $t \in S$ with $s \stackrel{\sigma}{\rightarrow}^* t$ and $t\downarrow$.

The *trace set* of a state s is its set of traces and accepting traces. The trace set of a transition system is the trace set of its initial state. Two transition systems are *trace equivalent* if and only if they have the same trace sets.

Note that the trace set Z of a transition system has the following property. For all sequences $\sigma, \rho \in L^*$,

$$\sigma\rho \in Z \quad \Rightarrow \quad \sigma \in Z.$$

It is said that the set Z is *prefix closed*. Moreover, observe that a trace set of a transition system is non-empty (because it always has at least the empty sequence as an element).

It can be shown, see Exercise 12.1.7, that BSP(A) is a sound axiomatization of the term model obtained from the algebra of transition systems $\mathbb{P}$(BSP(A)) of Definition 4.4.2 (Term algebra) modulo trace equivalence. Interestingly, it is also possible to consider the set of non-empty prefix-closed trace sets, independently of any specific transition-system space. If $\mathbb{T}(A)$ is the set of non-empty prefix-closed trace sets given some set of actions A that serve as the labels, then $Z \in \mathbb{T}(A)$ consists of sequences of actions, perhaps ending in $\downarrow$, such that each prefix of a sequence in Z is also in Z. In line with before, ϵ denotes the empty trace. As each trace set is non-empty and prefix closed, $\epsilon \in Z$ always holds. $\mathbb{T}(A)$ can be turned into a model of BSP(A) by defining an interpretation *tr* from the signature of BSP(A) into $\mathbb{T}(A)$.

Definition 12.1.3 (Trace set of a closed BSP(A)**-term)** The function *tr* provides an interpretation of closed terms over the signature of BSP(A) into the set of non-empty prefix-closed trace sets $\mathbb{T}(A)$.

(i) $tr(0) = \{\epsilon\}$;
(ii) $tr(1) = \{\epsilon, \downarrow\}$;

(iii) $tr(a.p) = \{\epsilon\} \cup \{a\sigma \mid \sigma \in tr(p)\}$, for all actions $a \in A$ and closed BSP(A)-terms p;
(iv) $tr(p + q) = tr(p) \cup tr(q)$, for all closed BSP($A$)-terms p, q.

With this interpretation, the non-empty prefix-closed trace sets $\mathbb{T}(A)$ form a model of BSP(A), i.e., for any closed BSP(A)-terms p and q, BSP(A)$\vdash p = q$ implies $tr(p) = tr(q)$.

However, theory BSP(A) is not a ground-complete axiomatization of the model. Consider the extra axiom in Table 12.1. This axiom is called the *Trace Axiom*. Theory $\mathrm{BSP}_{\mathrm{tr}}(A)$ is also referred to as the basic equational theory of traces, or simply *trace theory*.

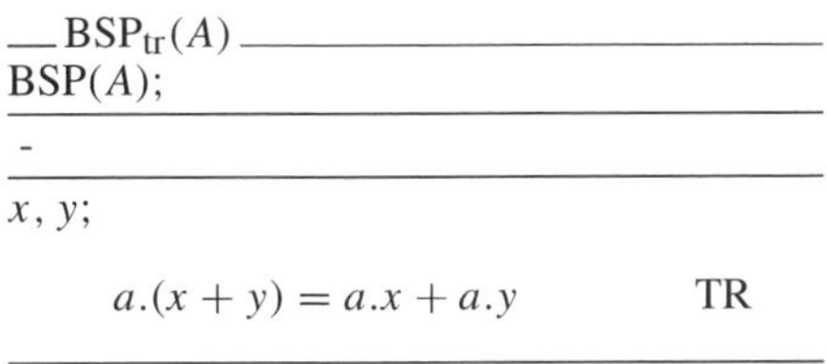

Table 12.1. The process theory $\mathrm{BSP}_{\mathrm{tr}}(A)$ (with $a \in A$).

Theorem 12.1.4 (Soundness, ground-completeness of trace theory) Equational theory $\mathrm{BSP}_{\mathrm{tr}}(A)$ is a sound and ground-complete axiomatization of the model $\mathbb{T}(A)$, i.e., for any closed BSP(A)-terms p and q, $\mathrm{BSP}_{\mathrm{tr}}(A) \vdash p = q$ if and only if $tr(p) = tr(q)$.

Proof First, consider soundness. Validity of Axioms A1–3 of Table 4.1 follows directly from the interpretation of alternative composition as set union in Definition 12.1.3 above. Axiom A6 follows as each non-empty prefix closed-trace set contains the empty trace. Finally, consider Axiom TR. Then, for all actions $a \in A$ and closed BSP(A)-terms p and q, $tr(a.(p + q)) = \{\epsilon\} \cup \{a\sigma \mid \sigma \in tr(p + q)\} = \{\epsilon\} \cup \{a\sigma \mid \sigma \in tr(p) \cup tr(q)\} = \{\epsilon\} \cup \{a\sigma \mid \sigma \in tr(p)\} \cup \{a\sigma \mid \sigma \in tr(q)\} = tr(a.p + a.q)$. This proves soundness.
Second, the outline of the ground-completeness proof is as follows. Consider two closed BSP(A)-terms p, q with the same trace set. Using Axioms TR and A2, all parentheses in p and q can be removed. Next, by A3, all duplicate occurrences of summands can be removed. In this way, normal forms p' and q' are obtained from which the trace sets can be immediately read off. Thus, p' and q' are identical except for the order of the summands. This means that they can be proved equal by use of Axiom A1. □

Thus, a very simple model of BSP(A) is obtained. However, this model is not suitable to describe deadlock behavior, since terms with a deadlock are always identified with terms that have no deadlock possibility: in $\mathrm{BSP}_{\mathrm{tr}}(A)$, the following derivation can be made:

$$a.1 = a.(1 + 0) = a.1 + a.0.$$

To put this differently, trace semantics does not preserve deadlock behavior, and so trace semantics cannot be used in applications in which deadlock behavior of processes is relevant. For this reason, other semantics were suggested, identifying more processes than bisimulation semantics, but fewer than trace semantics, so that deadlock behavior can be modeled. In the next section, some of these semantics are considered.

For now, note that also deadlock information can be added explicitly to traces, e.g., by marking which traces are *deadlock traces*. In a transition-system space, this notion can be defined as follows: if s is a state in the set of states S of a transition-system space over the set of labels L, then $\sigma \in L^*$ is a *deadlock trace* of s if and only if there is a state $t \in S$ with $s \xrightarrow{\sigma}{}^{*} t$ and t is a deadlock state (i.e., a state without outgoing transitions and without successful-termination option, as defined in Definition 3.1.14 (Deadlock)). The *completed-trace set* of s is its set of traces, accepting traces, and deadlock traces. The completed trace set allows a finer notion of equivalence than trace semantics, the so-called *completed-trace semantics*: two transition systems are equivalent if and only if they have the same traces, the same accepting traces, and the same deadlock traces. Section 12.3 considers completed-trace equivalence in a bit more detail.

Exercises

12.1.1 Consider an extension of trace theory with recursion. Give the trace sets of the following recursively defined processes:

(a) the solution of $X = a.X$;
(b) the solution of $X = a.X + 1$.

12.1.2 The process defined by a closed BSP(A)-term p is *deterministic* if and only if for all the states q of the transition system of p generated by the operational rules of the standard term model, it holds that, for any action a and states s and t, $q \xrightarrow{a} s$ and $q \xrightarrow{a} t$ implies $s = t$. Show that for deterministic processes the deadlock behavior, as defined in Definition 3.1.14, can be derived from the trace set.

12.1.3 Prove that completed-trace equivalence preserves deadlock behavior of transition systems, as defined in Definition 3.1.14 (Deadlock).

12.1.4 Prove that completed-trace equivalence is a congruence relation on closed BSP(A)-terms. Investigate a sound and ground-complete axiomatization.

12.1.5 Extend the interpretation *tr* of closed BSP(A)-terms of Definition 12.1.3 into trace sets to sequential composition. Consider the extra axiom $x \cdot (y + z) = x \cdot y + x \cdot z$. Show that the extension of theory TSP(A) of Table 6.1 with this extra axiom and Trace Axiom TR leads to a sound and ground-complete axiomatization of the model of trace sets $\mathbb{T}(A)$.

12.1.6 Extend the interpretation of closed BSP(A)-terms of Definition 12.1.3 into trace sets to parallel composition. Develop a sound and ground-complete axiomatization of $\mathbb{T}(A)$ based on process theory BCP(A, γ) of Table 7.1. Note that, for trace sets, equality $(x+y) \parallel z = x \parallel z + y \parallel z$ holds. Can you develop an alternative sound and ground-complete axiomatization that does not use the auxiliary left-merge and communication-merge operators?

12.1.7 Show that trace theory, BSP$_{tr}$(A), is a sound and ground-complete axiomatization of the term algebra $\mathbb{P}$(BSP(A)) modulo trace equivalence, i.e., for any closed BSP(A)-terms p and q, BSP$_{tr}(A) \vdash p = q$ if and only if their trace sets are equal.

12.1.8 Consider the silent action τ in trace semantics. Should it be possible to distinguish $\tau.1$ from 1?

12.2 Failures and readiness semantics

It turned out that deadlock behavior is not preserved in standard trace semantics. It is preserved by completed-trace equivalence that adds deadlock information to traces. This section defines another semantics, *failures semantics*, that also adds extra information about deadlock behavior to the trace set of a process, and that therefore also preserves deadlock behavior. In the course of defining failures semantics, also a variant is considered, called *readiness semantics*. Both readiness semantics and failures semantics are used in concurrency theory. Again, the point of departure is a transition-system space, but also a more direct representation is considered.

Definition 12.2.1 (Ready pair, failure pair) Let s be a state in the set of states S of a transition-system space over the set of labels L. Let $\sigma \in L^*$ be a trace from s to a state $t \in S$. Let *menu*(t) $\subseteq L \cup \{\downarrow\}$ be the *menu* of t, i.e., its set of outgoing transitions, including $\downarrow$ if t has a termination option. The pair $(\sigma, menu(t))$ is called a *ready pair* of s, and for each $X \subseteq (L \cup \{\downarrow\}) \setminus menu(t)$, pair $[\sigma, X]$ is called a *failure pair* of s. Thus, there is a failure pair for each subset of the complement of the second argument of a ready pair.

The *ready set* of s is the set of all ready pairs of s; the *failure set* of s is the set of all failure pairs of s. Two transition systems s and t are *ready equivalent* if and only if they have the same ready set, and *failures equivalent* if and only if they have the same failure set.

Example 12.2.2 (Readiness and failures equivalence) Consider the transition-system space generated by the term deduction system for BSP(A). The ready set of 1 is $\{(\epsilon, \{\downarrow\})\}$ and its failure set $\{[\epsilon, X] \mid X \subseteq A\}$. The ready set of 0 is $\{(\epsilon, \emptyset)\}$ and its failure set $\{[\epsilon, X] \mid X \subseteq A \cup \{\downarrow\}\}$. The two terms $a.1$ and $a.1 + a.0$ are distinguished by the ready pair $(a, \emptyset)$ and the failure pairs $[a, X]$ with $\downarrow \in X$. Thus, it can be seen that in readiness and failures semantics, deadlock behavior is recorded.

Proposition 12.2.3 (Congruence) Readiness equivalence and failures equivalence are congruence relations on the algebra of transition systems for BSP(A) (Definition 4.4.2 (Term algebra)).

Proof See Exercise 12.2.3. □

Theorem 12.2.4 (Semantic relationships) Let s, t be two transition systems in some given transition-system space that contains at least all the transition systems induced by closed BSP(A)-terms in the standard term model, with A containing at least two actions.

(i) If $s \leftrightarrow t$, then s and t are ready equivalent, but not conversely;
(ii) if s and t are ready equivalent, then they are failures equivalent, but not conversely;
(iii) if s and t are failures equivalent, then they are (completed-)trace equivalent, but not conversely.

Proof See Exercise 12.2.4. The following are counterexamples showing that the converse properties are not true:

(i) $a.b.1 + a.(b.0 + 1)$ and $a.b.0 + a.(b.1 + 1)$;
(ii) $a.b.0 + a.1$ and $a.b.0 + a.1 + a.(b.0 + 1)$;
(iii) $a.b.0 + a.a.0$ and $a.(b.0 + a.0)$.

□

By the first part of Theorem 12.2.4, the term model generated by the algebra of transition systems for BSP(A) modulo ready equivalence becomes a model of BSP(A). But, more can be proved. Consider the theory in Table 12.2, which extends BSP(A) with an extra axiom, called the *Ready Axiom*.

$\mathrm{BSP_{re}}(A)$	
BSP(A);	
-	
x, y, u, v;	
$a.(b.x + u) + a.(b.y + v) = a.(b.x + b.y + u) + a.(b.x + b.y + v)$	RE

Table 12.2. The process theory $\mathrm{BSP_{re}}(A)$ (with $a, b \in A$).

Theorem 12.2.5 (Soundness, ground-completeness of readiness theory) Theory $\mathrm{BSP_{re}}(A)$ is a sound and ground-complete axiomatization of the term algebra $\mathbb{P}(\mathrm{BSP}(A))$ modulo ready equivalence, i.e., for any closed BSP(A)-terms p and q, $\mathrm{BSP_{re}}(A) \vdash p = q$ if and only if their ready sets are equal.

Proof See Exercise 12.2.5. □

Also the term model generated by the term deduction system for BSP(A) modulo failures equivalence is a model of BSP(A). But again, more can be proved. Consider the extra axiom in Table 12.3, called the *Failures Axiom*. Adding this axiom to the readiness theory $\mathrm{BSP_{re}}(A)$ yields a sound and ground-complete axiomatization of failures equivalence.

$\mathrm{BSP_{fa}}(A)$	
$\mathrm{BSP_{re}}(A)$;	
-	
x, y, z;	
$a.x + a.(y + z) = a.x + a.(x + y) + a.(y + z)$	FA

Table 12.3. The process theory $\mathrm{BSP_{fa}}(A)$ (with $a \in A$).

Theorem 12.2.6 (Soundness, ground-completeness of failures theory) Theory $\mathrm{BSP_{fa}}(A)$ is a sound and ground-complete axiomatization of the term algebra $\mathbb{P}(\mathrm{BSP}(A))$ modulo failures equivalence, i.e., for any closed BSP(A)-terms p and q, $\mathrm{BSP_{fa}}(A) \vdash p = q$ if and only if their failure sets are equal.

Proof See Exercise 12.2.6. □

So far, ready equivalence and failures equivalence have been considered on a transition-system space. However, it is also possible to consider these notions directly, independent of transition systems. The definitions necessary in the case of ready equivalence are presented to conclude this section.

Definition 12.2.7 (Readiness semantics) A *ready set* R is a set of pairs (σ, X) with $\sigma \in A^*$ and $X \subseteq A \cup \{\downarrow\}$, satisfying the following conditions.

(i) Set R has exactly one ready pair (ϵ, X) with as first component the empty sequence. The set X is the menu of R, denoted $menu(R)$ in the remainder.
(ii) For each $a \in A$, there is a set X with $(\sigma a, X) \in R$ if and only if there is a set Y with $(\sigma, Y \cup \{a\}) \in R$.

The set of ready sets can be turned into a model for $\mathrm{BSP}_{\mathrm{re}}(A)$, see Exercise 12.2.7, by providing the following interpretation:

(i) the ready set of 0 is $\{(\epsilon, \emptyset)\}$;
(ii) the ready set of 1 is $\{(\epsilon, \{\downarrow\})\}$;
(iii) if R is a ready set, then, for any $a \in A$, $a.R$ is the ready set $\{(\epsilon, \{a\})\} \cup \{(a\sigma, X) \mid (\sigma, X) \in R\}$;
(iv) if R, S are ready sets, then $R + S$ is the ready set $\{(\epsilon, menu(R) \cup menu(S))\} \cup (R \setminus \{(\epsilon, menu(R))\}) \cup (S \setminus \{(\epsilon, menu(S))\})$.

Failures semantics has a special place among the different notions of equivalence that are considered in this chapter. It is the semantics that identifies the most processes while still preserving deadlock behavior, and that allows the definition of a parallel-composition operator (as used in the process algebra CSP) (Bergstra *et al.*, 1987). However, as shown in the next section, the priority operator (see Section 11.1) cannot be defined in failures semantics.

Exercises

12.2.1 Determine the failure sets and the ready sets of the transition systems of the following terms:

(a) $a.1 + a.0$;
(b) $a.b.1 + a.1$;
(c) $a.(b.0 + c.0)$;
(d) $a.(b.1 + c.1)$;
(e) $a.b.0 + a.b.0$;
(f) $a.b.0 + a.b.0 + a.(b.0 + c.0)$.

12.2.2 Prove that the Ready Axiom of Table 12.2 implies that the identity $a.b.x + a.b.y = a.(b.x + b.y)$, for arbitrary terms x and y and actions a and b, is derivable. Thus, failures and readiness semantics allow to reduce non-determinism.

12.2.3 Prove Proposition 12.2.3 (Congruence).

12.2.4 Complete the proof of Theorem 12.2.4 (Semantic relationships). Show that Properties (i) and (ii) are still valid if A contains only one action, but that (iii) is then no longer valid.

12.2.5 Prove Theorem 12.2.5 (Soundness, ground-completeness of readiness theory).

12.2.6 Prove Theorem 12.2.6 (Soundness, ground-completeness of failures theory).

12.2.7 Show that the set of ready sets as defined in Definition 12.2.7 (Readiness semantics) is a model of theory $\mathrm{BSP}_{\mathrm{re}}(A)$.

12.2.8 Give an explicit presentation of a failures model for the theory $\mathrm{BSP}_{\mathrm{fa}}(A)$, similar to the presentation in Definition 12.2.7 (Readiness semantics).

12.2.9 Prove that failures semantics preserves deadlock behavior of transition systems, as defined in Definition 3.1.14 (Deadlock).

12.2.10 Recall Definition 12.2.1 (Ready pair, failure pair). Define, for any state s in a transition-system space over labels L, trace $\sigma \in L^*$, and set $X \subseteq (L \cup \{\downarrow\})$, $s\ \mathit{after}\ \sigma\ \mathit{MUST}\ X$ if and only if whenever $s \stackrel{\sigma}{\rightarrow}^* t$ then $\mathit{menu}(t) \cap X \neq \emptyset$. Show that state s is failures equivalent with state t if and only if for all σ, X it holds that $s\ \mathit{after}\ \sigma\ \mathit{MUST}\ X \Leftrightarrow t\ \mathit{after}\ \sigma\ \mathit{MUST}\ X$.

12.2.11 A pair $[\sigma, X]$ is called a *singleton-failure pair* of state s in a transition-system space if and only if it is a failure pair of s and set X is a singleton. Two states are *singleton-failures equivalent* if and only if they have the same set of singleton-failure pairs. Find two processes that are singleton-failures equivalent, but not failures equivalent. Find two processes that are singleton-failures equivalent but not completed-trace equivalent, and two processes that are completed-trace equivalent but not singleton-failures equivalent. Show also that sequential composition of processes cannot be defined in a meaningful way in singleton-failures semantics.

12.3 The linear time – branching time lattice

Trace semantics abstracts from all information concerning the branching structure of processes, all moments of choice are hidden. On the other hand, bisimulation semantics keeps all information about the branching structure. For this reason, trace semantics is said to be a *linear time* semantics, and bisimulation semantics a *branching time* semantics. These semantics are at the opposite ends of the so-called *linear time – branching time spectrum*. This section gives an overview of other semantics that can be defined on the basis of a transition-system space. When considering the number of processes differentiated by a semantics, the semantics discussed in this section are all in between trace semantics, that identifies the largest number of transition systems thus distinguishing the smallest number of processes, and bisimulation semantics, that distinguishes the largest number of processes. All discussed semantics abstract from branching structure to a certain degree. To conclude the section, the so-called *semantic lattice* is presented, giving an overview of the relationship between the different semantics.

As a first observation, it is noted that readiness and failures semantics, introduced in the previous section, do not allow the definition of the priority operator of Section 11.1.

Proposition 12.3.1 (Priorities in failures and readiness semantics) The priority operator θ cannot be added in a meaningful way to failures or readiness semantics.

Proof Suppose A contains atomic actions a, b, c, d, e, f with priorities $f \prec b \prec d$. Consider the process expressions $p = a.(b.c.0 + d.0) + a.(b.e.0 + f.0)$ and $q = a.(b.e.0 + d.0) + a.(b.c.0 + f.0)$. Then, the transition systems induced by p and q are ready equivalent; so, by Theorem 12.2.4 (Semantic relationships), they are also failures equivalent. However, theory $\text{BSP}\theta(A, \prec)$ of Section 11.1 allows to derive the intuitively expected result that $\theta(p) = a.d.0 + a.b.e.0$ and $\theta(q) = a.d.0 + a.b.c.0$. Since the axioms of $\text{BSP}\theta(A, \prec)$ are sound with respect to bisimilarity, by again Theorem 12.2.4 (Semantic relationships), it is expected that $\theta(p)$ and $\theta(q)$ are ready and failures equivalent. However, $\theta(p)$ and $\theta(q)$ do not even have the same trace sets, which by Theorem 12.2.4 shows that $\theta(p)$ and $\theta(q)$ cannot be ready or failures equivalent. □

The semantic notions of *ready-trace* and *failure-trace* equivalence, to be defined next, do allow the definition of the priority operator, as shown in Exercise 12.3.1.

Definition 12.3.2 (Ready-trace and failure-trace equivalence) Let s be a state in the set of states S of a transition-system space over the set of labels L. A *ready trace* of s is a trace $\sigma \in L^*$ of s, together with, for every state t that

σ passes through, the menu $menu(t) \subseteq L \cup \{\downarrow\}$, as defined in Definition 12.2.1 (Ready pair, failure pair). A *failure trace* is a trace $\sigma \in L^*$ of s, together with, for every state t that σ passes through, a set $X \subseteq L \cup \{\downarrow\}$ disjoint from the menu, i.e., $X \cap menu(t) = \emptyset$. Thus, the menu, respectively a failure, is given for every state that is traversed in the trace.

The *ready-trace set* of s is the set of all ready traces of s; the *failure-trace set* of s is the set of all failure traces of s. Two transition systems s and t are *ready-trace equivalent* if and only if they have the same ready-trace set, and *failure-trace equivalent* if and only if they have the same failure-trace set.

Next, consideration is given to notions that are based on the notion of a *simulation*: a simulation is a one-way bisimulation, and processes are simulation equivalent if and only if there are two simulations, back and forth between the two processes.

Definition 12.3.3 (Simulation) Consider a transition-system space with set of states S. A binary relation R on S is a *simulation* relation if and only if, whenever $(s, t) \in R$ for two states $s, t \in S$, the following transfer conditions hold:

(i) whenever $s \xrightarrow{a} s'$ for some label a and state s', there is a state t' such that $t \xrightarrow{a} t'$ and $(s', t') \in R$;
(ii) whenever $s\downarrow$, then $t\downarrow$.

Two transition systems $s, t \in S$ are *simulation equivalent* if and only if there is a simulation relation R with $(s, t) \in R$ and there is also a simulation relation R' with $(t, s) \in R'$.

The important difference with bisimilarity is that different simulation relations can be used in the two directions. To give an example, the processes $a.(b.1 + 1)$ and $a.(b.1 + 1) + a.1$ are simulation equivalent but not bisimilar.

Finally, consider two extra additions to simulation equivalence.

Definition 12.3.4 (Completed simulation, ready simulation) Consider a transition-system space over labels L with set of states S. A binary relation R on S is a *completed-simulation* relation if and only if it is a simulation relation and, moreover, whenever $(s, t) \in R$ for two states $s, t \in S$, then s is a deadlock state if and only if t is a deadlock state. A binary relation R on S is a *ready-simulation* relation if and only if it is a simulation relation and, moreover, whenever $(s, t) \in R$ for two states $s, t \in S$, then $menu(s) = menu(t)$.

Two transition systems $s, t \in S$ are *completed-simulation equivalent* if and only if there is a completed-simulation relation R with $(s, t) \in R$ and there is also a completed-simulation relation R' with $(t, s) \in R'$. Transition systems $s, t \in S$ are *ready-simulation equivalent* if and only if there is a ready-simulation relation R with $(s, t) \in R$ and there is also a ready-simulation relation R' with $(t, s) \in R'$.

In all, ten semantic notions have been defined. All notions define different semantic equivalence relations on the transition-system space induced by the term algebra of BSP(A). They are related as shown in Figure 12.1.

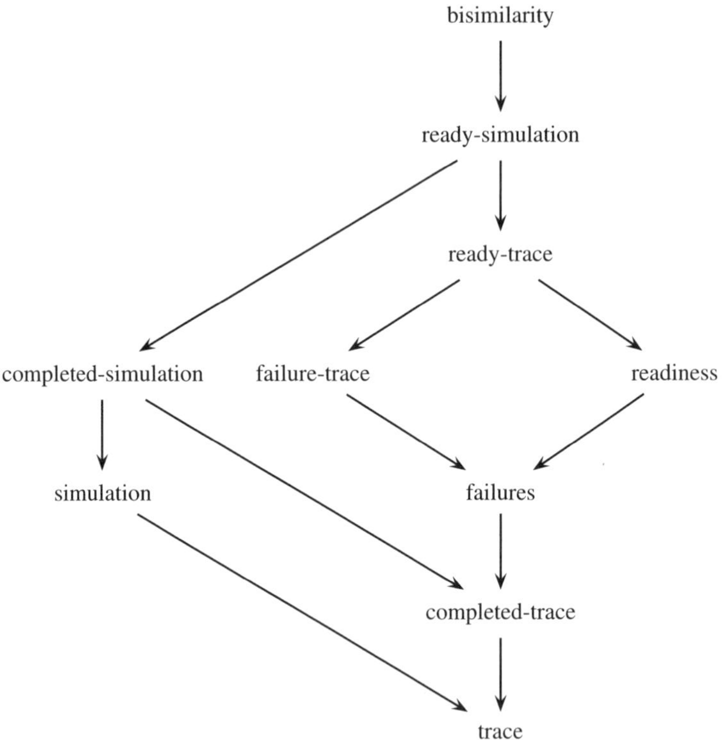

Fig. 12.1. Semantic lattice.

Whenever there is a sequence of arrows in Figure 12.1 from one semantic notion to another semantic notion, that means that any pair of transition systems equivalent in the former notion is also equivalent in the latter notion (but not conversely). When such a path of arrows does not exist, the notions are independent: there is a pair of transition systems related under one notion but not the other, and conversely.

The axioms needed for ground-complete axiomatizations of the new semantic notions not axiomatized so far are presented in Table 12.4. The last two axioms are conditional axioms with a condition expressing that the menu of two processes is the same. The first projection π_1 from the signature of theory (BSP + PR)(A) is used for this; that is, $\pi_1(x) = \pi_1(y)$ is used to express that the menu of x (the set of initial steps of x) is equal to the menu of y.

$x, y, z, u, v;$	
$a.(x + y) = a.(x + y) + a.y$	S
$a.(b.x + u) + a.(c.y + v) = a.(b.x + c.y + u + v)$	CT1
$a.(b.x + u) + a.1 = a.(b.x + u + 1)$	CT2
$a.(x + b.y + z) = a.(x + b.y + z) + a.(b.y + z)$	CS1
$a.(x + 1) = a.(x + 1) + a.1$	CS2
$a.x + a.y = a.x + a.(x + y) + a.y$	FT
$\pi_1(x) = \pi_1(y) \Rightarrow a.x + a.y = a.(x + y)$	RT
$\pi_1(x) = \pi_1(y) \Rightarrow a.(x + y) = a.(x + y) + a.y$	RS

Table 12.4. Axioms needed for the axiomatization of the equivalences in the semantic lattice (assuming the signature of (BSP+PR)(A), with $a, b, c \in A$).

Theorem 12.3.5 (Soundness, ground-completeness)

(i) Theory (BSP+S)(A) is a sound and ground-complete axiomatization of the term algebra of BSP(A) modulo simulation equivalence, i.e., for any closed BSP(A)-terms p and q, (BSP + S)(A) $\vdash p = q$ if and only if p and q are simulation equivalent.

(ii) Theory (BSP+CT1,2)(A) is a sound and ground-complete axiomatization of the term algebra of BSP(A) modulo completed-trace equivalence, i.e., for any closed BSP(A)-terms p and q, (BSP+CT1,2)(A)$\vdash$ $p = q$ if and only if p and q have the same completed-trace sets.

(iii) Theory (BSP + CS1,2)(A) is a sound and ground-complete axiomatization of the term algebra of BSP(A) modulo completed-simulation equivalence, i.e., for any closed BSP(A)-terms p and q, (BSP + CS1,2)(A) $\vdash p = q$ if and only if p and q are completed-simulation equivalent.

(iv) Theory (BSP + PR + RT + FT)(A) is a sound and ground-complete axiomatization of the term algebra of (BSP + PR)(A) modulo failure-trace equivalence, i.e., for any closed (BSP + PR)(A)-terms p and q, (BSP + PR + RT + FT)(A) $\vdash p = q$ if and only if p and q have the same failure-trace sets.

(v) Theory (BSP + PR + RT)(A) is a sound and ground-complete axiomatization of the term algebra of (BSP + PR)(A) modulo ready-trace equivalence, i.e., for any closed $(\mathrm{BSP} + \mathrm{PR})(A)$-terms p and q, $(\mathrm{BSP} + \mathrm{PR} + \mathrm{RT})(A) \vdash p = q$ if and only if p and q have the same ready-trace set.

(vi) Theory $(\mathrm{BSP} + \mathrm{PR} + \mathrm{RS})(A)$ is a sound and ground-complete axiomatization of the term algebra of $(\mathrm{BSP} + \mathrm{PR})(A)$ modulo ready-simulation equivalence, i.e., for any closed $(\mathrm{BSP} + \mathrm{PR})(A)$-terms p and q, $(\mathrm{BSP} + \mathrm{PR} + \mathrm{RS})(A) \vdash p = q$ if and only if p and q are ready-simulation equivalent.

Exercises

12.3.1 Show that the priority operator can be defined in a meaningful way in failure-trace semantics.

12.3.2 Show that, if two transition systems are failure-trace equivalent, then they are also failures equivalent, but not conversely. For the counterexample, use the processes in the proof of Proposition 12.3.1 (Priorities in failures and readiness semantics).

12.3.3 Show that, if two transition systems are ready-trace equivalent, then they are also failure-trace equivalent, but not conversely. For the counterexample, use the same pair of processes as in the second part of the proof of Theorem 12.2.4 (Semantic relationships).

12.3.4 Show that readiness semantics and failure-trace semantics are independent: there is a pair of processes that is ready equivalent but not failure-trace equivalent, and vice versa. Use the examples of the previous two exercises.

12.3.5 Show that, if two transition systems are simulation equivalent, then they are also trace equivalent, but not conversely. On the other hand, show that simulation equivalence and completed-trace equivalence are independent, and that simulation equivalence and ready-trace equivalence are independent.

12.3.6 Show that, if two transition systems are ready-simulation equivalent, then they are also ready-trace equivalent, but not conversely.

12.3.7 Show that completed-simulation equivalence is independent of ready-trace equivalence and independent of failures equivalence.

12.3.8 Prove Theorem 12.3.5 (Soundness, ground-completeness).

12.3.9 Consider a transition-system space with set of states S. A pair $\langle \sigma, X \rangle$ is called a *possible future* of state $s \in S$ if and only if there is a state $t \in S$ with $s \xrightarrow{\sigma}{}^{*} t$ and trace set X. Two transition systems are possible-futures equivalent if and only if their initial states have the same set of possible futures. Show that if two transition systems are possible-futures equivalent, then they are ready equivalent. On the other hand, show that possible-futures equivalence and ready-simulation equivalence are independent, and that possible-futures equivalence and failure-trace equivalence are independent.

12.3.10 A relation on the set of states S of a transition-system space is a *2-nested-simulation* relation if and only if it is a simulation relation that only relates states that are simulation equivalent. Two transition systems $s, t \in S$ are *2-nested-simulation equivalent* if and only if there is a 2-nested simulation relating s to t and a 2-nested simulation relating t to s. Show that if two states are 2-nested-simulation equivalent, then they are ready-simulation equivalent and also possible-futures equivalent, but not conversely. Show that if two states are bisimilar, then they are also 2-nested-simulation equivalent, but not conversely.

12.3.11 State s in a transition-system space is a *possible world* of state t if s is deterministic (as defined in Exercise 12.1.2) and there is a ready simulation relating s to t. Two transition systems are *possible-worlds equivalent* if and only if their initial states have the same set of possible worlds. Show that if two transition systems are ready-simulation equivalent, then they are possible worlds equivalent, but not conversely. Show that if two states are possible worlds equivalent, then they are ready-trace equivalent, but not conversely. Show that a ground-complete axiomatization of possible worlds equivalence is achieved by adding axiom $a.(b.x+b.y+z) = a.(b.x+z)+a.(b.y+z)$, for actions a and b and process terms x, y, and z, to BSP(A).

12.3.12 Investigate which semantics presented in this chapter allows a consistent definition of the renaming operator.

12.3.13 Investigate which semantics presented in this chapter allows a consistent definition of the priority operator.

12.4 Partial-order semantics

So far in this chapter, the discussion centered on the linear time – branching time spectrum. Other dimensions can be considered. One such dimension is the treatment of the silent step τ. Another is the treatment of infinity. Both of these are not considered here. This section contains just a brief discussion on another dichotomy: the distinction between total-order and partial-order process theories. So far in this book, only total-order theories have been considered. This means that every execution of a process is the execution of a number of actions that are totally ordered in time. At each moment of time, at most one action is executed. This is a simplifying assumption that eases calculations considerably, and is also appropriate in the applications that have been considered. Partial-order semantics allows that action executions are only partially ordered in time.

The issue can be illustrated by considering the process $a.1 \parallel b.1$, assuming no communication. In process algebra as considered up to this point, this term equals $a.b.1 + b.a.1$. This depends on the total-order assumption. Rejecting this assumption, it can be argued that in $a.1 \parallel b.1$, actions a and b can happen concurrently, can have overlapping executions, whereas in $a.b.1 + b.a.1$, the second action can only start if the first has finished.

One approach to obtain a partial-order theory is to extend the communication function γ to include *multi-actions*, bags of concurrently executing actions. Suppose the existence of a set $CA \subset A$ of core atomic actions. From this set, the set A can be generated as the set consisting of all bags (or multisets) of elements of CA. This turns an action-prefix operation $a.x$ into an operation that executes a bag of elements a, and then proceeds as x. Two binary relations are considered on the set CA. First, there is the *conflict* relation. If two core actions are in conflict, then they cannot be executed at the same time, and this is enforced by keeping $\gamma(a, b)$ undefined when the bag a contains a core action that is in conflict with a core action of b. Second, there is the *communication* relation. When an element of a communicates with an element of b, then in $\gamma(a, b)$ they are both taken out, and replaced by their communication. Apart from this, γ behaves as multi-set union.

When this approach is applied to theory BCP(A, γ) as introduced in Section 7.4, the resulting theory is a partial-order theory that axiomatizes a semantics called *step bisimulation*. In each step, a multi-set of core actions is executed.

The advantage of the approach that extends the communication function is that the expansion theorem, Theorem 7.4.7, still holds. A process theory that admits an expansion theorem, i.e., that allows to reduce a parallel composition to a set of alternatives, is called an *interleaving theory*. Thus, this first approach to develop an equational theory for a partial-order semantics results in a theory that still is an interleaving theory. Other approaches to build partial-order theories do not have this advantage.

Another approach to develop a partial-order theory is to consider actions that have duration. Each action is split into two core actions: its beginning and its ending. Denoting the beginning of a as a^+, the ending as a^-, the deduction rule $a.x \xrightarrow{a} x$ in the term deduction system of MPT(A) underlying all theories developed in this book, is replaced by the two rules

$$a.x \xrightarrow{a^+} a^-.x \text{ and } a^-.x \xrightarrow{a^-} x.$$

Define that two standard terms (i.e., those not including any occurrences of beginnings a^+ or endings a^-, for example, BSP(A)-terms) are *split-bisimulation* equivalent if and only if they are bisimilar in the term model generated by this modified set of operational rules. Different from the first approach, the standard axioms for, for example, parallel composition are no longer valid in split-bisimulation semantics. Exercise 12.4.1 asks to develop a sound and ground-complete axiomatization for split-bisimulation semantics. As a remark, note that it is also possible to consider some actions as durational, but others not.

If this second approach is applied to a theory with communication, the communication function needs to be extended. If two actions communicate, then also their beginnings and endings should communicate. For example, consider standard communication, given by $\gamma(?, !) = \gamma(!, ?) = \text{‽}$. Then, it should be also defined that

$$\gamma(?^+, !^+) = \gamma(!^+, ?^+) = \text{‽}^+ \text{ and } \gamma(?^-, !^-) = \gamma(!^-, ?^-) = \text{‽}^-.$$

A drawback of split semantics is that it is not always clear which ending matches a certain beginning. The problem can be illustrated with the following example, which uses the aforementioned standard communication. Consider the term

$$!.1 \parallel !.!.1 \parallel ?.?.1 \parallel ?.1.$$

The following execution can be started, first starting a communication between the first and third component, and then starting a communication between the second and fourth component:

$$\begin{aligned} !.1 \parallel !.!.1 \parallel ?.?.1 \parallel ?.1 &\xrightarrow{\text{‽}^+} !^-.1 \parallel !.!.1 \parallel ?^-.?.1 \parallel ?.1 \\ &\xrightarrow{\text{‽}^+} !^-.1 \parallel !^-.!.1 \parallel ?^-.?.1 \parallel ?^-.1. \end{aligned}$$

Now, another ‽^+ should only occur after two ‽^- have occurred, but this is not the case: the communications can be 'criss-crossed' as follows:

$$\begin{aligned} !^-.1 \parallel !^-.!.1 \parallel ?^-.?.1 \parallel ?^-.1 &\xrightarrow{\text{‽}^-} !^-.1 \parallel !.1 \parallel ?.1 \parallel ?^-.1 \\ &\xrightarrow{\text{‽}^+} !^-.1 \parallel !^-.1 \parallel ?^-.1 \parallel ?^-.1. \end{aligned}$$

For this reason, a mechanism should be provided that matches an ending to the correct beginning. A so-called *history pointer* can be used, a counter that tells how many actions back of the current one the corresponding beginning took place. In each step of a component in a parallel composition, the history pointers in the other components should be increased by one. If this is done, the resulting equivalence relation is called *ST bisimulation* equivalence. The notion of history counters also allows the development of an equational theory for ST bisimulation semantics.

Exercises

12.4.1 Develop an equational theory that is a sound and ground-complete axiomatization for a standard term model based on split bisimulation equivalence.

12.4.2 Extend the basic theory BSP(A) with the history-pointer operator. Use this operator to develop an equational theory that provides a sound and ground-complete axiomatization for a standard term model based on ST bisimulation equivalence.

12.5 Bibliographical remarks

Sections 12.1 and 12.2 are adapted from (Baeten & Weijland, 1990). The material in Section 12.3 is from (Van Glabbeek, 2001). Concerning Section 12.4, background material for step semantics can be found in (Baeten & Basten, 2001). For split and ST bisimulation, references are (Van Glabbeek & Vaandrager, 1987; Hennessy, 1988b; Gorrieri & Laneve, 1995). The example of the drawback of split semantics is taken from (Baeten & Bergstra, 1998).

Bibliography

Aceto, L., Bloom, B., & Vaandrager, F.W. (1994). Turning SOS Rules into Equations. *Information and Computation*, **111**(1), 1–52.

Aceto, L., & Fokkink, W.J. (2004). Guest Editors' Introduction: Special Issue on Structural Operational Semantics. *Journal of Logic and Algebraic Programming*, **60–61**, 1–2.

Aceto, L., Fokkink, W.J., & Ingólfsdóttir, A. (1998). A Cook's Tour of Equational Axiomatization for Prefix Iteration. Pages 20–34 of: Nivat, M. (ed), *Foundations of Software Science and Computation Structures, FoSSaCS 1998, Proceedings*. Lecture Notes in Computer Science, no. 1387. Springer, Berlin, Germany.

Aceto, L., Fokkink, W.J., & Verhoef, C. (2001). Structural Operational Semantics. Pages 197–292 of: Bergstra, J.A., Ponse, A., & Smolka, S.A. (eds), *Handbook of Process Algebra*. Elsevier Science, Amsterdam, the Netherlands.

Aceto, L., & Hennessy, M. (1992). Termination, Deadlock, and Divergence. *Journal of the ACM*, **39**(1), 147–187.

Andova, S. (2002). *Probabilistic Process Algebra*. Ph.D. thesis, Eindhoven University of Technology, Department of Mathematics and Computer Science, Eindhoven, the Netherlands.

Austry, D., & Boudol, G. (1984). Algèbre de Processus et Synchronisation. *Theoretical Computer Science*, **30**(1), 91–131. In French.

Baeten, J.C.M. (1986). *Procesalgebra*. Programmatuurkunde. Kluwer, Deventer, the Netherlands. In Dutch.

Baeten, J.C.M. (2003). Embedding Untimed into Timed Process Algebra: The Case for Explicit Termination. *Mathematical Structures in Computer Science*, **13**(4), 589–618.

Baeten, J.C.M. (2005). A Brief History of Process Algebra. *Theoretical Computer Science*, **335**(2/3), 131–146.

Baeten, J.C.M., & Basten, T. (2001). Partial-Order Process Algebra (and its Relation to Petri Nets). Pages 769–872 of: Bergstra, J.A., Ponse, A., & Smolka, S.A. (eds), *Handbook of Process Algebra*. Elsevier Science, Amsterdam, the Netherlands.

Baeten, J.C.M., & Bergstra, J.A. (1988). Global Renaming Operators in Concrete Process Algebra. *Information and Computation*, **78**(3), 205–245.

Baeten, J.C.M., & Bergstra, J.A. (1996). Discrete Time Process Algebra. *Formal Aspects of Computing*, **8**(2), 188–208.

Baeten, J.C.M., & Bergstra, J.A. (1997). Process Algebra with Propositional Signals. *Theoretical Computer Science*, **177**(2), 381–406.

Baeten, J.C.M., & Bergstra, J.A. (1998). Deadlock Behaviour in Split and ST Bisimulation Semantics. *Electronic Notes in Theoretical Computer Science*, **16**(2), 101–114. Proceedings Expressiveness in Concurrency, 5th International Workshop, EXPRESS 1998.

Baeten, J.C.M., Bergstra, J.A., Hoare, C.A.R., Milner, R., Parrow, J., & de Simone, R. (1991). *The Variety of Process Algebra*. Deliverable ESPRIT Basic Research Action 3006, CONCUR. University of Edinburgh, Edinburgh, UK.

Baeten, J.C.M., Bergstra, J.A., & Klop, J.W. (1986). Syntax and Defining Equations for an Interrupt Mechanism in Process Algebra. *Fundamenta Informaticae*, **IX**(2), 127–168.

Baeten, J.C.M., Bergstra, J.A., & Klop, J.W. (1987a). Conditional Axioms and α/β-Calculus in Process Algebra. Pages 77–103 of: Wirsing, M. (ed), *Formal Description of Programming Concepts - III, IFIP Conference, Proceedings*. Elsevier Science, Amsterdam, the Netherlands.

Baeten, J.C.M., Bergstra, J.A., & Klop, J.W. (1987b). On the Consistency of Koomen's Fair Abstraction Rule. *Theoretical Computer Science*, **51**(1/2), 129–176.

Baeten, J.C.M., & Bravetti, M. (2005). A Ground-Complete Axiomatization of Finite State Processes in Process Algebra. Pages 248–262 of: Abadi, M., & de Alfaro, L. (eds), *CONCUR 2005 - Concurrency Theory, 16th International Conference, Proceedings*. Lecture Notes in Computer Science, no. 3653. Springer, Berlin, Germany.

Baeten, J.C.M., & Bravetti, M. (2006). A Generic Process Algebra. *Electronic Notes in Theoretical Computer Science*, **162**, 65–71. Proceedings Essays on Algebraic Process Calculi, Workshop, APC 25.

Baeten, J.C.M., Corradini, F., & Grabmayer, C.A. (2007). A Characterization of Regular Expressions under Bisimulation. *Journal of the ACM*, **54**(2), 6.1–28.

Baeten, J.C.M., & Glabbeek, R.J. van. (1987). Merge and Termination in Process Algebra. Pages 153–172 of: Nori, K.V. (ed), *Foundations of Software Technology and Theoretical Computer Science, 7th Conference, FST&TCS 1987, Proceedings*. Lecture Notes in Computer Science, no. 287. Springer, Berlin, Germany.

Baeten, J.C.M., & Middelburg, C.A. (2001). Process Algebra with Timing: Real Time and Discrete Time. Pages 627–684 of: Bergstra, J.A., Ponse, A., & Smolka, S.A. (eds), *Handbook of Process Algebra*. Elsevier Science, Amsterdam, the Netherlands.

Baeten, J.C.M., & Middelburg, C.A. (2002). *Process Algebra with Timing*. Monographs in Theoretical Computer Science. An EATCS Series. Springer, Berlin, Germany.

Baeten, J.C.M., Mousavi, M.R., & Reniers, M.A. (2005). Timing the Untimed: Terminating Successfully while Being Conservative. Pages 251–279 of: Middeldorp, A., Oostrom, V. van, Raamsdonk, F. van, & Vrijer, R. de (eds), *Processes, Terms and Cycles: Steps on the Road to Infinity, Essays Dedicated to Jan Willem Klop on the Occasion of his 60th Birthday*. Lecture Notes in Computer Science, no. 3838. Springer, Berlin, Germany.

Baeten, J.C.M., & Reniers, M.A. (2004). Timed Process Algebra (With a Focus on Explicit Termination and Relative-Timing). Pages 59–97 of: Bernardo, M., & Corradini, F. (eds), *Formal Methods for the Design of Real-Time Systems*. Lecture Notes in Computer Science, no. 3185. Springer, Berlin, Germany.

Baeten, J.C.M., & Reniers, M.A. (2007). Duplication of Constants in Process Algebra. *Journal of Logic and Algebraic Programming*, **70**(2), 151–171.

Baeten, J.C.M., & Verhoef, C. (1993). A Congruence Theorem for Structured Operational Semantics with Predicates. Pages 477–492 of: Best, E. (ed), *Concurrency Theory, 4th International Conference, CONCUR 1993, Proceedings*. Lecture Notes in Computer Science, no. 715. Springer, Berlin, Germany.

Baeten, J.C.M., & Verhoef, C. (1995). Concrete Process Algebra. Pages 149–269 of: Abramsky, S., Gabbay, D.M., & Maibaum, T.S.E. (eds), *Handbook of Logic in Computer Science*, vol. 4. Oxford University Press, Oxford, UK.

Baeten, J.C.M., & Weijland, W.P. (1990). *Process Algebra*. Cambridge Tracts in Theoretical Computer Science, no. 18. Cambridge University Press, Cambridge, UK.

Bakker, J.W. de, & Zucker, J.I. (1982a). Denotational Semantics of Concurrency. Pages 153–158 of: *Theory of Computing, 14th Annual ACM Symposium, Proceedings*. ACM, New York, NY, USA.

Bakker, J.W. de, & Zucker, J.I. (1982b). Processes and the Denotational Semantics of Concurrency. *Information and Control*, **54**(1/2), 70–120.

Bartlett, K.A., Scantlebury, R.A., & Wilkinson, P.T. (1969). A Note on Reliable Full-Duplex Transmission over Half-Duplex Lines. *Communications of the ACM*, **12**(5), 260–261.

Basten, T. (1996). Branching Bisimilarity is an Equivalence Indeed! *Information Processing Letters*, **58**(3), 141–147.

Basten, T. (1998). *In Terms of Nets: System Design with Petri Nets and Process Algebra*. Ph.D. thesis, Eindhoven University of Technology, Department of Mathematics and Computing Science, Eindhoven, the Netherlands.

Bekič, H. (1971). *Towards a Mathematical Theory of Processes*. Tech. rept. TR 25.125. IBM Laboratory Vienna, Vienna, Austria.

Bekič, H. (1984). *Programming Languages and Their Definition*, H. Bekič (1936-1982), Selected Papers edited by C.B. Jones. Lecture Notes in Computer Science, no. 177. Springer, Berlin, Germany.

Bergstra, J.A., Bethke, I., & Ponse, A. (1994). Process Algebra with Iteration and Nesting. *The Computer Journal*, **37**(4), 243–258.

Bergstra, J.A., Fokkink, W.J., & Ponse, A. (2001). Process Algebra with Recursive Operations. Pages 333–389 of: Bergstra, J.A., Ponse, A., & Smolka, S.A. (eds), *Handbook of Process Algebra*. Elsevier Science, Amsterdam, the Netherlands.

Bergstra, J.A., & Klop, J.W. (1982). *Fixed Point Semantics in Process Algebra*. Tech. rept. IW 208. Mathematical Centre, Amsterdam, the Netherlands.

Bergstra, J.A., & Klop, J.W. (1984a). Process Algebra for Synchronous Communication. *Information and Control*, **60**(1/3), 109–137.

Bergstra, J.A., & Klop, J.W. (1984b). The Algebra of Recursively Defined Processes and the Algebra of Regular Processes. Pages 82–95 of: Paredaens, J. (ed), *Automata, Languages and Programming, 11th Colloquium, ICALP 1984, Proceedings*. Lecture Notes in Computer Science, no. 172. Springer, Berlin, Germany.

Bergstra, J.A., & Klop, J.W. (1985). Algebra of Communicating Processes with Abstraction. *Theoretical Computer Science*, **37**(1), 77–121.

Bergstra, J.A., & Klop, J.W. (1986a). Algebra of Communicating Processes. Pages 89–138 of: Bakker, J.W. de, Hazewinkel, M., & Lenstra, J.K. (eds), *Mathematics and Computer Science I, CWI Symposium, Proceedings*. CWI Monographs, no. 1. Elsevier Science, Amsterdam, the Netherlands.

Bergstra, J.A., & Klop, J.W. (1986b). Process Algebra: Specification and Verification in Bisimulation Semantics. Pages 61–94 of: Hazewinkel, M., Lenstra, J.K., &

Meertens, L.G.L.T. (eds), *Mathematics and Computer Science II, CWI Symposium, Proceedings.* CWI Monographs, no. 4. Elsevier Science, Amsterdam, the Netherlands.

Bergstra, J.A., & Klop, J.W. (1986c). Verification of an Alternating Bit Protocol by Means of Process Algebra. Pages 9–23 of: Bibel, W., & Jantke, K.P. (eds), *Mathematical Methods of Specification and Synthesis of Software Systems 1985, International Spring School, Proceedings.* Lecture Notes in Computer Science, no. 215. Springer, Berlin, Germany.

Bergstra, J.A., & Klop, J.W. (1988). A Complete Inference System for Regular Processes with Silent Moves. Pages 21–81 of: Drake, F.R., & Truss, J.K. (eds), *Logic Colloquium, Proceedings.* Elsevier Science, Amsterdam, the Netherlands.

Bergstra, J.A., & Klop, J.W. (1992). A Convergence Theorem in Process Algebra. Pages 164–195 of: Bakker, J.W. de, & Rutten, J.J.M.M. (eds), *Ten Years of Concurrency Semantics.* World Scientific, Singapore.

Bergstra, J.A., Klop, J.W., & Olderog, E.-R. (1987). Failures without Chaos: A new Process Semantics for Fair Abstraction. Pages 77–103 of: Wirsing, M. (ed), *Formal Description of Programming Concepts - III, IFIP Conference, Proceedings.* Elsevier Science, Amsterdam, the Netherlands.

Bergstra, J.A., Klop, J.W., & Tucker, J.V. (1985). Process Algebra with Asynchronous Communication Mechanisms. Pages 76–95 of: Brookes, S.D., Roscoe, A.W., & Winskel, G. (eds), *Seminar on Concurrency, Proceedings.* Lecture Notes in Computer Science, no. 197. Springer, Berlin, Germany.

Bergstra, J.A., & Middelburg, C.A. (2005). Process Algebra for Hybrid Systems. *Theoretical Computer Science*, **335**(2/3), 215–280.

Bergstra, J.A., Ponse, A., & Zwaag, M.B. van der (2003). Branching Time and Orthogonal Bisimulation Equivalence. *Theoretical Computer Science*, **309**(1–3), 313–355.

Bergstra, J.A., & Tiuryn, J. (1987). Process Algebra Semantics for Queues. *Fundamenta Informaticae*, **X**, 213–224.

Bergstra, J.A., & Tucker, J.V. (1984). Top Down Design and the Algebra of Communicating Processes. *Science of Computer Programming*, **5**(2), 171–199.

Bosscher, D.J.B. (1997). *Grammars Modulo Bisimulation.* Ph.D. thesis, University of Amsterdam, Amsterdam, the Netherlands.

Bradfield, J.C., & Stirling, C. (2001). Modal Logics and Mu-Calculi: An Introduction. Pages 293–330 of: Bergstra, J.A., Ponse, A., & Smolka, S.A. (eds), *Handbook of Process Algebra.* Elsevier Science, Amsterdam, the Netherlands.

Brookes, S.D. (1983). On the Relationship of CCS and CSP. Pages 83–96 of: Diaz, J. (ed), *Automata, Languages and Programming, 10th Colloquium, ICALP 1983, Proceedings.* Lecture Notes in Computer Science, no. 154. Springer, Berlin, Germany.

Brookes, S.D., Hoare, C.A.R., & Roscoe, A.W. (1984). A Theory of Communicating Sequential Processes. *Journal of the ACM*, **31**(3), 560–599.

Broy, M. (1987). Views on Queues. *Science of Computer Programming*, **11**(1), 65–86.

Bundy, A. (1999). A Survey of Automated Deduction. Pages 153–174 of: Wooldridge, M.J., & Veloso, M. (eds), *Artificial Intelligence Today: Recent Trends and Developments.* Lecture Notes in Computer Science, vol. 1600. Springer, Berlin, Germany.

Burris, S., & Sankappanavar, H.P. (1981). *A Course in Universal Algebra.* Graduate Texts in Mathematics. Springer, Berlin, Germany.

Christensen, S. (1993). *Decidability and Decomposition in Process Algebras.* Ph.D. thesis, University of Edinburgh, Department of Computer Science, Edinburgh, UK.

Clarke, E.M., Grumberg, O., & Peled, D.A. (2000). *Model Checking*. The MIT Press, Cambridge, MA, USA.

Cleaveland, R., Lüttgen, G., & Natarajan, V. (2001). Priority in Process Algebra. Pages 711–765 of: Bergstra, J.A., Ponse, A., & Smolka, S.A. (eds), *Handbook of Process Algebra*. Elsevier Science, Amsterdam, the Netherlands.

Copi, I.M., Elgot, C.C., & Wright, J.B. (1958). Realization of Events by Logical Nets. *Journal of the ACM*, **5**(2), 181–196.

Corradini, F., D'Ortenzio, D., & Inverardi, P. (1999). On the Relationships among Four Timed Process Algebras. *Fundamenta Informaticae*, **38**(4), 377–395.

D'Argenio, P.R. (1995). *τ-Angelic Choice for Process Algebras (Revised Edition)*. Tech. rept., Universidad Nacional de La Plata, LIFIA, Depto. de Informática, Fac. de Cs. Exactas, La Plata, Buenos Aires, Argentina.

Denvir, B.T., Harwood, W.T., Jackson, M.I., & Ray, M.J. (eds). (1985). *The Analysis of Concurrent Systems, Proceedings*. Lecture Notes in Computer Science, no. 207. Springer, Berlin, Germany.

Dershowitz, N., & Jouannaud, J.-P. (1990). Rewrite Systems. Pages 243–320 of: Leeuwen, J. van (ed), *Handbook of Theoretical Computer Science*, vol. B: Formal Models and Semantics. Elsevier Science, Amsterdam, the Netherlands.

Dijkstra, E.W. (1975). Guarded Commands, Nondeterminacy, and Formal Derivation of Programs. *Communications of the ACM*, **18**(8), 453–457.

Dijkstra, E.W. (1976). *A Discipline of Programming*. Prentice Hall, Englewood Cliffs, NJ, USA.

Floyd, R.W. (1967). Assigning Meanings to Programs. Pages 19–32 of: Schwartz, J.T. (ed), *Symposium in Applied Mathematics, XIX, Proceedings*. Mathematical Aspects of Computer Science. American Mathematical Society, Providence, RI, USA.

Fokkink, W.J. (1994). A Complete Equational Axiomatisation for Prefix Iteration. *Information Processing Letters*, **52**(6), 333–337.

Fokkink, W.J. (2000). *Introduction to Process Algebra*. Texts in Theoretical Computer Science. An EATCS Series. Springer, Berlin, Germany.

Francez, N. (1986). *Fairness*. Springer, Berlin, Germany.

Glabbeek, R.J. van. (1987). Bounded Nondeterminism and the Approximation Induction Principle in Process Algebra. Pages 336–247 of: Brandenburg, F.J., Vidal-Naquet, G., & Wirsing, M. (eds), *Theoretical Aspects of Computer Science, 4th Annual Symposium, STACS 1987, Proceedings*. Lecture Notes in Computer Science, no. 247. Springer, Berlin, Germany.

Glabbeek, R.J. van. (1990). *Comparative Concurrency Semantics, with Refinement of Actions*. Ph.D. thesis, Vrije Universiteit, Amsterdam, the Netherlands.

Glabbeek, R.J. van. (1993). The Linear Time – Branching Time Spectrum II: The Semantics of Sequential Systems with Silent Moves (Extended Abstract). Pages 66–81 of: Best, E. (ed), *Concurrency Theory, 4th International Conference, CONCUR 1993, Proceedings*. Lecture Notes in Computer Science, vol. 715. Springer, Berlin, Germany.

Glabbeek, R.J. van. (1994). What is Branching Time Semantics and Why to Use it? *Bulletin of the EATCS*, **53**, 190–198.

Glabbeek, R.J. van. (1997). Notes on the Methodology of CCS and CSP. *Theoretical Computer Science*, **177**(2), 329–350.

Glabbeek, R.J. van. (2001). The Linear Time – Branching Time Spectrum I: The Semantics of Concrete, Sequential Processes. Pages 3–100 of: Bergstra, J.A., Ponse, A., & Smolka, S.A. (eds), *Handbook of Process Algebra*. Elsevier Science, Amsterdam, the Netherlands.

Glabbeek, R.J. van, Luttik, S.P., & Trčka, N. (2008). *Branching Bisimilarity with Explicit Divergence*. Tech. rept. CS-R-08-25. Eindhoven University of Technology, Department of Mathematics and Computer Science, Eindhoven, the Netherlands.

Glabbeek, R.J. van, & Vaandrager, F.W. (1987). Petri Net Models for Algebraic Theories of Concurrency. Pages 224–242 of: Bakker, J.W. de, Nijman, A.J., & Treleaven, P.C. (eds), *Parallel Architectures and Languages Europe, PARLE 1987, Proceedings, Volume II*. Lecture Notes in Computer Science, no. 259. Springer, Berlin, Germany.

Glabbeek, R.J. van, & Vaandrager, F.W. (1989). Modular Specifications in Process Algebra — With Curious Queues. Pages 465–506 of: Wirsing, M., & Bergstra, J.A. (eds), *Algebraic Methods: Theory, Tools and Applications*. Lecture Notes in Computer Science, no. 394. Springer, Berlin, Germany.

Glabbeek, R.J. van, & Vaandrager, F.W. (1993). Modular Specification of Process Algebras. *Theoretical Computer Science*, **113**(2), 293–348.

Glabbeek, R.J. van, & Weijland, W.P. (1989). Branching Time and Abstraction in Bisimulation Semantics (extended abstract). Pages 613–618 of: Ritter, G.X. (ed), *Information Processing 89, 11th IFIP World Computer Congress, Proceedings*. Elsevier Science Publishers B.V., North-Holland, Amsterdam, the Netherlands. Full version appeared as (Van Glabbeek & Weijland, 1996).

Glabbeek, R.J. van, & Weijland, W.P. (1996). Branching Time and Abstraction in Bisimulation Semantics. *Journal of the ACM*, **43**(3), 555–600.

Gorrieri, R., & Laneve, C. (1995). Split and ST Bisimulation Semantics. *Information and Computation*, **118**(2), 272–288.

Groote, J.F., Matthijssen, A., Weerdenburg, M. van, & Usenko, Y.S. (2006). From μCRL to mCRL2: Motivation and Outline. *Electronic Notes in Theoretical Computer Science*, **162**, 191–196. Proceedings Essays on Algebraic Process Calculi, Workshop, APC 25.

Groote, J.F., & Ponse, A. (1995). The Syntax and Semantics of μCRL. Pages 26–62 of: Ponse, A., Verhoef, C., & Vlijmen, S.F.M. van (eds), *Algebra of Communicating Processes, ACP 1994, Proceedings*. Workshops in Computing Series. Springer, Berlin, Germany.

Groote, J.F., & Reniers, M.A. (2001). Algebraic Process Verification. Pages 1151–1208 of: Bergstra, J.A., Ponse, A., & Smolka, S.A. (eds), *Handbook of Process Algebra*. Elsevier Science, Amsterdam, the Netherlands.

Halpern, J.Y., & Zuck, L.D. (1987). A Little Knowledge Goes a Long Way: Simple Knowledge-Based Derivations and Correctness Proofs for a Family of Protocols (Extended Abstract). Pages 269–280 of: *Principles of Distributed Computing, 6th Annual ACM Symposium, PODC 1987, Proc.* ACM, New York, NY, USA.

Heijenoort, J. van. (1967). *From Frege to Gödel: A Sourcebook in Mathematical Logic, 1879-1931*. Harvard University Press, Cambridge, MA, USA.

Hennessy, M. (1981). A Term Model for Synchronous Processes. *Information and Control*, **51**(1), 58–75.

Hennessy, M. (1988a). *Algebraic Theory of Processes*. MIT Press, Cambridge, MA, USA.

Hennessy, M. (1988b). Axiomatising Finite Concurrent Processes. *SIAM Journal on Computing*, **17**(5), 997–1017.

Hennessy, M., & Milner, R. (1980). On Observing Nondeterminism and Concurrency. Pages 299–309 of: Bakker, J.W. de, & Leeuwen, J. van (eds), *Automata, Languages and Programming, 7th Colloquium, ICALP 1980, Proceedings*. Lecture Notes in Computer Science, no. 85. Springer, Berlin, Germany.

Hennessy, M., & Regan, T. (1995). A Process Algebra for Timed Systems. *Information and Computation*, **117**(2), 221–239.

Hoare, C.A.R. (1969). An Axiomatic Basis for Computer Programming. *Communications of the ACM*, **12**(10), 576–580.

Hoare, C.A.R. (1978). Communicating Sequential Processes. *Communications of the ACM*, **21**(8), 666–677.

Hoare, C.A.R. (1980). A Model for Communicating Sequential Processes. Pages 229–254 of: McKeag, R.M., & Macnaghten, A.M. (eds), *On the Construction of Programs*. Cambridge University Press, Cambridge, UK.

Hoare, C.A.R. (1985). *Communicating Sequential Processes*. Prentice Hall, Englewood Cliffs, NJ, USA.

Hussman, H. (1985). Unification in Conditional-Equational Theories. Pages 543–553 of: Caviness, B.F. (ed), *European Conference on Computer Algebra, 10th International Conference, EUROCAL 1985, Proceedings Vol. 2: Research Contributions*. Lecture Notes in Computer Science, no. 204. Springer, Berlin, Germany.

Jonsson, B., Yi, Wang, & Larsen, K.G. (2001). Probabilistic Extensions of Process Algebras. Pages 685–710 of: Bergstra, J.A., Ponse, A., & Smolka, S.A. (eds), *Handbook of Process Algebra*. Elsevier Science, Amsterdam, the Netherlands.

Jouannaud, J.-P., & Muñoz, M. (1984). Termination of a Set of Rules Modulo a Set of Equations. Pages 175–193 of: Shostak, R.E. (ed), *Automated Deduction, 7th International Conference, Proceedings*. Lecture Notes in Computer Science, no. 170. Springer, Berlin, Germany.

Khadim, U. (2008). *Process Algebra for Hybrid Systems: Comparison and Development*. Ph.D. thesis, Eindhoven University of Technology, Department of Mathematics and Computer Science, Eindhoven, the Netherlands.

Kleene, S.C. (1956). Representation of Events in Nerve Nets and Finite Automata. Pages 3–41 of: Shannon, C.E., & McCarthy, J. (eds), *Automata Studies*. Princeton University Press, Princeton, NJ, USA.

Klop, J.W. (1987). Term Rewriting Systems: A Tutorial. *Bulletin of the EATCS*, **32**, 143–182.

Koomen, C.J. (1985). Algebraic Specification and Verification of Communication Protocols. *Science of Computer Programming*, **5**(1), 1–36.

Koymans, C.P.J., & Mulder, J.C. (1990). A Modular Approach to Protocol Verification Using Process Algebra. Pages 261–306 of: Baeten, J.C.M. (ed), *Applications of Process Algebra*. Cambridge University Press, Cambridge, UK.

Koymans, C.P.J., & Vrancken, J.L.M. (1985). *Extending Process Algebra with the Empty Process* ϵ. Logic Group Preprint Series 1. Utrecht University, Philosophy Department, Utrecht, the Netherlands.

Kranakis, E. (1987). Fixed Point Equations with Parameters in the Projective Model. *Information and Computation*, **75**(3), 264–288.

Lamport, L. (1987). A Fast Mutual Exclusion Algorithm. *ACM Transactions on Computer Systems*, **5**(1), 1–11.

Larsen, K.G., & Milner, R. (1987). Verifying a Protocol Using Relativized Bisimulation. Pages 126–135 of: Ottmann, Th. (ed), *Automata, Languages and Programming, 14th International Colloquium, ICALP 1987, Proceedings*. Lecture Notes in Computer Science, no. 267. Springer, Berlin, Germany.

Larsen, K.G., & Skou, A. (1991). Bisimulation through Probabilistic Testing. *Information and Computation*, **94**(1), 1–28.

Linz, P. (2001). *An Introduction to Formal Languages and Automata*. Jones and Bartlett, Sudbury, MA, USA.

Luttik, S.P. (2002). *Choice Quantification in Process Algebra*. Ph.D. thesis, University of Amsterdam, Department of Computer Science, Amsterdam, the Netherlands.

MacLane, S., & Birkhoff, G. (1967). *Algebra*. Macmillan, London, UK.

Markovski, J. (2008). *Real and Stochastic Time in Process Algebras for Performance Evaluation*. Ph.D. thesis, Eindhoven University of Technology, Department of Mathematics and Computer Science, Eindhoven, the Netherlands.

Mauw, S., & Mulder, J.C. (1994). Regularity of BPA-Systems is Decidable. Pages 34–47 of: Jonsson, B., & Parrow, J. (eds), *Concurrency Theory, 5th International Conference, CONCUR 1994, Proceedings*. Lecture Notes in Computer Science, no. 836. Springer, Berlin, Germany.

Mauw, S., & Veltink, G.J. (eds). (1993). *Algebraic Specification of Communication Protocols*. Cambridge Tracts in Theoretical Computer Science, no. 36. Cambridge University Press, Cambridge, UK.

McCarthy, J. (1963). A Basis for a Mathematical Theory of Computation. Pages 33–70 of: Braffort, P., & Hirshberg, D. (eds), *Computer Programming and Formal Systems*. North-Holland, Amsterdam, the Netherlands.

Milne, G.J. (1982). Abstraction and Nondeterminism in Concurrent Systems. Pages 358–364 of: *Distributed Computing Systems, 3rd International Conference, ICDCS 1982, Proceedings*. IEEE Computer Society Press, Los Alamitos, CA, USA.

Milne, G.J. (1983). CIRCAL: A Calculus for Circuit Description. *Integration, the VLSI Journal*, **1**(2–3), 121–160.

Milne, G.J., & Milner, R. (1979). Concurrent Processes and Their Syntax. *Journal of the ACM*, **26**(2), 302–321.

Milner, R. (1973). An Approach to the Semantics of Parallel Programs. Pages 285–301 of: *Convegno di Informatica Teoretica, Proceedings*. Instituto di Elaborazione della Informazione, Pisa, Italy.

Milner, R. (1975). Processes: A Mathematical Model of Computing Agents. Pages 157–174 of: Rose, H.E., & Shepherdson, J.C. (eds), *Logic Colloquium, Proceedings*. North-Holland, Amsterdam, the Netherlands.

Milner, R. (1978a). Algebras for Communicating Systems. In *AFCET/SMF Joint Colloquium in Applied Mathematics, Proceedings*. Paris, France. Also available as Tech. rept. CSR-25-78, University of Edinburgh, Computer Science Department, Edinburgh, UK, 1978.

Milner, R. (1978b). Synthesis of Communicating Behaviour. Pages 71–83 of: Winkowski, J. (ed), *Mathematical Foundations of Computer Science, 7th Symposium, MFCS 1978, Proceedings*. Lecture Notes in Computer Science, no. 64. Springer, Berlin, Germany.

Milner, R. (1979). Flowgraphs and Flow Algebras. *Journal of the ACM*, **26**(4), 794–818.

Milner, R. (1980). *A Calculus of Communicating Systems*. Lecture Notes in Computer Science, no. 92. Springer, Berlin, Germany.

Milner, R. (1983). Calculi for Synchrony and Asynchrony. *Theoretical Computer Science*, **25**(3), 267–310.

Milner, R. (1989). *Communication and Concurrency*. Prentice Hall, Englewood Cliffs, NJ, USA.

Milner, R. (1999). *Communicating and Mobile Systems: the Pi-Calculus*. Cambridge University Press, Cambridge, UK.

Moller, F. (1989). *Axioms for Concurrency*. Ph.D. thesis, University of Edinburgh, Computer Science Department, Edinburgh, UK.

Moller, F., & Tofts, C. (1990). A Temporal Calculus of Communicating Systems.

Pages 401–415 of: Baeten, J.C.M., & Klop, J.W. (eds), *Theories of Concurrency: Unification and Extension, CONCUR 1990, Proceedings*. Lecture Notes in Computer Science, no. 458. Springer, Berlin, Germany.

Mousavi, M.R., & Reniers, M.A. (2005). Orthogonal Extensions in Structural Operational Semantics. Pages 1214–1225 of: *Automata, Languages and Programming, 32nd International Colloquium, ICALP 2005, Proceedings*. Lecture Notes in Computer Science, no. 3580. Springer, Berlin, Germany.

Mousavi, M.R., Reniers, M.A., & Groote, J.F. (2007). SOS Formats and Meta-Theory: 20 Years After. *Theoretical Computer Science*, **373**(3), 238–272.

Nicollin, X., & Sifakis, J. (1994). The Algebra of Timed Processes ATP: Theory and Application. *Information and Computation*, **114**(1), 131–178.

Oguztuzun, H.M. (1989). A Game Characterization of the Observational Equivalence of Processes. Pages 195–196 of: *Algebraic Methodology and Software Technology, 1st Conference, AMAST 1989, Proceedings*. Iowa City, IA, USA.

Osborne, M., & Rubinstein, A. (1994). *A Course in Game Theory*. MIT Press, Cambridge, MA, USA.

Owicki, S., & Gries, D. (1976). Verifying Properties of Parallel Programs: An Axiomatic Approach. *Communications of the ACM*, **19**(5), 279–285.

Park, D.M.R. (1981). Concurrency and Automata on Infinite Sequences. Pages 167–183 of: Deussen, P. (ed), *Theoretical Computer Science, 5th GI Conference, Proc*. Lecture Notes in Computer Science, no. 104. Springer, Berlin, Germany.

Parrow, J. (1985). *Fairness Properties in Process Algebra — With Applications in Communication Protocol Verification*. Ph.D. thesis, Uppsala University, Department of Computer Systems, Uppsala, Sweden.

Petri, C.A. (1962). *Kommunikation mit Automaten*. Ph.D. thesis, Institut fuer Instrumentelle Mathematik, Bonn, Germany. In German.

Plotkin, G.D. (1976). A Powerdomain Construction. *SIAM Journal of Computing*, **5**(3), 452–487.

Plotkin, G.D. (1981). *A Structural Approach to Operational Semantics*. Tech. rept. DAIMI FN-19. Aarhus University, Aarhus, Denmark.

Ponse, A. (1992). *Process Algebras with Data*. Ph.D. thesis, University of Amsterdam, Department of Computer Science, Amsterdam, the Netherlands.

Pratt, V.R. (1982). On the Composition of Processes. Pages 213–223 of: *Principles of Programming Languages, 9th ACM SIGPLAN-SIGACT Symposium, POPL 1982, Proceedings*. ACM, New York, NY, USA.

Quemada, J., de Frutos, D., & Azcorra, A. (1993). TIC: A Timed Calculus. *Formal Aspects of Computing*, **5**(3), 224–252.

Reed, G.M., & Roscoe, A.W. (1988). A Timed Model for Communicating Sequential Processes. *Theoretical Computer Science*, **58**(1–3), 249–261.

Sangiorgi, D., & Walker, D.J. (2001). *The Pi-Calculus: A Theory of Mobile Processes*. Cambridge University Press, Cambridge, UK.

Schneider, S.A. (2000). *Concurrent and Real-Time Systems (the CSP Approach)*. John Wiley & Sons, Chichester, UK.

Scott, D.S., & Strachey, C. (1971). Towards a Mathematical Semantics for Computer Languages. Pages 19–46 of: Fox, J. (ed), *Computers and Automata, Symposium, Proceedings*. Polytechnic Institute of Brooklyn Press, New York, NY, USA.

Sewell, P. (1997). Nonaxiomatisability of Equivalences over Finite State Processes. *Annals of Pure and Applied Logic*, **90**(1–3), 163–191.

Smullyan, R. (1982). *The Lady or the Tiger? And Other Logic Puzzles Including a Mathematical Novel that Features Gödel's Great Discovery*. Alfred A. Knopf, Inc., New York, NY, USA.

Troeger, D.R. (1993). Step Bisimulation is Pomset Equivalence on a Parallel Language Without Explicit Internal Choice. *Mathematical Structures in Computer Science*, **3**(1), 25–62.

Usenko, Y.S. (2002). *Linearization in muCRL*. Ph.D. thesis, Eindhoven University of Technology, Department of Mathematics and Computer Science, Eindhoven, the Netherlands.

Vaandrager, F.W. (1986). *Verification of Two Communication Protocols by Means of Process Algebra*. Tech. rept. CS-R8608. CWI, Amsterdam, the Netherlands.

Vereijken, J.J. (1997). *Discrete-Time Process Algebra*. Ph.D. thesis, Eindhoven University of Technology, Department of Mathematics and Computer Science, Eindhoven, the Netherlands.

Verhoef, C. (1994). A General Conservative Extension Theorem in Process Algebra. Pages 149–168 of: Olderog, E.-R. (ed), *Programming Concepts, Methods and Calculi, IFIP TC2/WG2.1/WG2.2/WG2.3 Working Conference, PROCOMET 1994, Proceedings*. IFIP Transactions, vol. A-56. North-Holland, Amsterdam, the Netherlands.

Vrancken, J.L.M. (1997). The Algebra of Communicating Processes with Empty Process. *Theoretical Computer Science*, **177**(2), 287–328.

Walker, D.J. (1990). Bisimulation and Divergence. *Information and Computation*, **85**(2), 202–241.

Weijland, W.P. (1989). The Algebra of Synchronous Processes. *Fundamenta Informaticae*, **XII**, 139–162.

Winskel, G. (1982). Event Structure Semantics for CCS and Related Languages. Pages 561–576 of: Nielsen, M., & Schmidt, E.M. (eds), *Automata, Languages and Programming, 9th Colloquium, ICALP 1982, Proceedings*. Lecture Notes in Computer Science, no. 140. Springer, Berlin, Germany.

Yi, Wang (1991). CCS + Time = An Interleaving Model for Real Time Systems. Pages 217–228 of: Leach Albert, J., Monien, B., & Rodríguez Artalejo, M. (eds), *Automata, Languages and Programming, 18th International Colloquium, ICALP 1991, Proceedings*. Lecture Notes in Computer Science, no. 510. Springer, Berlin, Germany.

Index of Symbols and Notations

This index is subdivided into several, mostly self-explanatory, categories. Acronyms of process theories covered in this book are classified under *Acronyms*. Category *Process theories* contains other entries related to the theories of this book; general process-algebraic notations and acronyms are indexed under *Process algebra*. Page numbers in italics refer to defining entries.

General notations

Acronyms

Algebras

Axioms

Equational theories

Constants

Index of Authors

Index of Subjects

Page numbers in italics refer to defining entries.

E

F

T

U